despoil — to plunder, pillage
aegis — shield — Athena
succor — aid

Margery Bailey
1944

THE ILIAD OF HOMER

THE ILIAD OF HOMER

A LINE FOR LINE TRANSLATION IN DACTYLIC HEXAMETERS

BY WILLIAM BENJAMIN SMITH AND WALTER MILLER

Illustrated with the Classical Designs of John Flaxman

NEW YORK:

THE MACMILLAN COMPANY

1944

Composition, Printing & Binding by the Kingsport Press, Inc.
Kingsport, Tennessee, United States of America
Format planned by Richard Ellis

TO

The Honorable Charles Baird

PREFACE

THE present translation of the *Iliad* is, as far as I can discover, the first attempt to reproduce in English Homer's great epic line for line in the metre of the original. Other translations of the *Iliad* have been made into English dactylic hexameters but neither complete nor line for line. It was the German line-for-line translation by Johann Heinrich Voss, published first in 1793, that suggested to the famous philosopher, biblical critic, and universal scholar, William Benjamin Smith, the much more difficult task of doing the same in English. After much happy labor on his part, his renderings were submitted to various classical scholars for criticisms and suggestions. These were so frankly and so generously offered that he was unwilling to seek a publisher until a complete revision of the work could be effected. But his later years were so fully occupied with his philosophical and scientific researches that he never found time to resume his studies of Homer. He frequently talked with me about it and finally, at his death, he left with me, his life-long friend, his manuscript of the *Iliad*, with the request that I do the revising and prepare it for publication. The criticisms submitted were in many ways so radical, and the revision has had to be so drastic that scarcely a line of Dr. Smith's original manuscript has been left without some change; several thousand lines have been entirely rewritten. And yet, whatever merit this translation may have, it could never have been attained without the splendid basis laid by Dr. Smith himself.

I am happy to express our indebtedness to the eminent Homer scholars, John A. Scott and Samuel E. Bassett (now deceased), for their goodness in reading the earlier version and to Edward K. Rand for reading the latest, and for the helpfulness of their suggestions and criticisms. The distich at the head of each book is, in each case, "Another Argument" taken from the famous *Homer's Iliad* of George Chapman that inspired Keats' well-known sonnet.

I alone am responsible for the Introduction and the Index. The latter I have added with a threefold purpose in view: 1, to enable

vii

PREFACE

Students of Homer to turn readily to outstanding topics in the *Iliad*; 2, to distinguish where different heroes have the same name; and 3, to afford a key to the difficult matter of the pronunciation of the proper names. The names have been Latinized, the syllables have been divided, and the accents indicated in accordance with the rules for the pronunciation of Greek and Latin proper names in English, as long established in the Webster dictionaries.

I am grateful to my former pupils, Dr. Frances Emberson and to Dr. Maude Beamer, for their generous help in the reading of the proofs.

WALTER MILLER

University of Missouri
Columbia, Missouri
1944

viii

INTRODUCTION

HOMER AND THE ILIAD

The Poet

OF the poet himself we know next to nothing. He never mentions
himself. We do not know when he was born or where, or where he
spent his life. Dates assigned to him range all the way from the early
tenth to the eighth century B.C. The earlier dates are probably
more nearly correct.

> Seven cities claimed great Homer dead,
> Through which the living Homer begged his bread.

Among the claimants for his birthplace were Athens, Smyrna, and
Chios. He spent his life, apparently, as a wandering minstrel, singing
songs of chivalry at the courts of kings and princes.

Homer is said to have been poor and blind. We have no au-
thentic portrait of him; but some great sculptor in the fourth century
B.C. had a conception of what the poor, blind bard should have
looked like and expressed that conception in a bronze bust of which
we have various marble copies. The finest of these is the well-known
bust in the National Museum in Naples. The furrows upon this
wonderful face suggest the man who had to "beg his bread"; one
feels that those eyes are eyes that never saw the light of the sun;
the spiritual majesty of the countenance bespeaks the inspiration
that gave us the *Iliad* and the *Odyssey*.

The Iliad

The story that lies back of the *Iliad* begins with the marriage of
Peleus and Thetis, the parents of Achilles, the chief hero of the
poem. Zeus had been warned by an oracle that the son of a goddess
whom he desired as a wife would be greater than the sire, and,
suspecting that that goddess might be "silver-footed" Thetis of the

ix

sea, he wedded her, though sore against her will, to Peleus, king of Phthia. To the marriage feast all the gods were invited save Eris ("Strife"). In retaliation for the slight, Eris tossed into the company a golden apple inscribed "for the fairest." The prize of beauty was at once claimed by Hera, Athena, and Aphrodite. The decision was referred to Paris, son of Priam and Hecabe of Troy. He awarded the apple to Aphrodite, and, while he won her favor, he won for himself and for his country the implacable hatred of the other two goddesses.

Aphrodite's reward to Paris was the wife of Menelaüs, whom he visited at Sparta. The result of her abduction was the marshaling of the Greek hosts with their thousand ships for the war against Troy and the recovery of Helen. The siege lasted ten years. The *Iliad* deals with only fifty-one days of action in the tenth year of the war. The subject given by the poet to his great epic is "The Wrath of Achilles," that is, his quarrel with his commander in chief, the occasion for which is presented at the very beginning; and the note of the wrath, like a Wagnerian motif, rings out again and again until the wrath is finally renounced.

Apart from the most ancient books of the Bible the oldest piece of literature of general interest to us and our civilization is the *Iliad* of Homer. It is one of the most extraordinary things about that wonderful people whom we call the Greeks that Greek literature opens with what is still the world's transcendent single piece of literature; and whoever or whatever Homer may have been, his narratives in the *Iliad* and the *Odyssey* have given his name the very first place among the world's poets.

The *Iliad* is not a short poem. The "wrath," with its various episodes and the warring of heroes, requires 15,693 hexameter verses. But it is not the bulk of the *Iliad* that makes it immortal but the majesty and beauty of the poetry, the melody of the metre, the simplicity of the language, the dramatic power of its structure, and the profoundness of the thought. Homer knew how to sound the heights and depths of every human experience, and his poem abounds in passages of exquisite beauty, vivid description, touching pathos, eloquent speeches, the words and deeds of knightly heroes whose whole ambition was "ever to be the best." It presents a vivid picture of a time of war when knighthood was in flower, when men were heroes surpassing in strength the strength of twenty men of the poet's own days, and when women were gifted with the beauty and grace of the immortals. It was a time, too, when the gods were not remote from mortal men. Indeed, Homer's gods are not different from men, except that they are more powerful and not limited by time or space, and they never die. They are not pure spirit, and yet they are omnipresent. They are superhuman but not almighty, though Zeus is often called "the all mighty." They are subject to the same passions of love and hate as are mortals. Morally they may be better, or they may be worse than men and women. They take an active interest in the affairs of mortal men and are never far-distant from them. They appear sometimes openly, sometimes in disguise. They mingle in the assemblies of soldiers or councilors; they join in their battles; they accompany their protegés on their journeys and sit with them at their feasts; they rescue their favorites from disaster or death; they wed their sons and daughters (and even their wives); they comfort them in their sorrows, and they punish them for their sins.

Much of the power of the *Iliad* lies in the vivid character drawing and graphic portrayal of human nature in its many guises, its strength and its weakness, the human heart with all "its tenderness, its joys and fears," its softer sentiments and its wildest passions. Agamemnon is "monarch of men," but he is irritable and moody, selfishly setting his personal desires above the common good; Achilles is passionate, impetuous, in his conscious might appealing everything to the decision of arms. He is relentless in his wrath against Agamemnon and savage in his treatment of dead Hector's body, but he cries like a child at his mother's side and kindly entertains aged Priam, the father of his mortal enemy. Though the son of a goddess, he voluntarily resigns his young life at the call of friendship. Then there is Nestor, the wise old man, loquacious in proportion to his years; Hector, "man-slaying" on the field of battle but showing a heart tender as a woman's in his chivalrous bearing toward his gracious mother Hecabe, toward his lovely wife and child, and even toward his sister-in-law Helen, the guiltless cause

xi

of all the war and woe; Odysseus, quick-witted, resourceful, energetic, wise in counsel but crafty in danger, valiant in war, ruthless in hatred, eloquent in speech, pitiless toward an enemy; "fair-haired" Menelaüs, the wronged and vengeful husband of the beautiful Helen, a valiant soldier, a faithful brother in arms; and so on down through Diomedes, the two Ajaxes, Sarpedon, and the rest, to the ugly, misshapen Thersites, the spokesman of the lower ſtrata of the soldiery, whose mind was as warped and misshapen as his poor body. Each individual's chara∂ter ſtands out in his own words and a∂tions as well as in the artiſt's pi∂tures of him. Homer, like Matthew Arnold's Sophocles, "saw life ſteadily and saw it whole."

In Greece we cannot go back farther than Homer's heroes, except hypothetically. Before him was a dark age; before that a mythological age; after him came the times hiſtorical. With him begins a recital of events and chara∂ters that has in it a large element of hiſtorical reality. People used to talk of the Homeric poems as "mythology" — all fantasy. But it is not an imaginary world that Homer paints for us but the real, feudal world of the Mycenaean period, which came to an end with the Dorian invasion, about 1000 B.C. Of this we have abundant proof in the remains of that civilization which has been brought before us in the excavated ruins of Troy, Mycenae, Tiryns, Pylus, and other cities of the Achaean heroes. From these recovered remains of that earlier day we are forced to the conclusion that Homer wrote poems that might serve not merely as a textbook of mythology but almost as a textbook of geography and a textbook of hiſtory. The discoveries made at those old Homeric sites have brought Homer's heroes back in bodily presence before our eyes. Today Odysseus "of many devices" and Achilles "swift of foot," beauteous Helen and "white-armed" Andromache, wise old Neſtor and Agamemnon, "monarch of men," are quite as near to us and quite as real to us as are King Arthur or Charlemagne or Roland. We may see them in their own peculiar dress and in their armor, in the duties and pleasures of their palace homes or in the moil of war upon the field of battle.

Accepting the traditional date of 1184 B.C. for the fall of Troy and an early date for Homer himself, we see that the poet must have lived long enough after the events he describes for the old traditions to become clothed in clouds of glory and yet not so long after them that they lose their reality, even though he deals with the doings of gods and heroes. Troy and Mycenae, as we see from their excavated sites, were real cities; the Trojan War was a real war; and the poet who idealizes and immortalizes them was a real Homer.

———

For easy identification of the heroes and their allegiance the following key is submitted:

Greeks. The besiegers are never called Greeks by Homer, but interchangeably Argives, Achaeans, and Danaans. Their homeland is Achaia or Argos. Hellas and Hellenes do occur — rarely and only in connection with a small district in Thessaly.

Troy. The city besieged is in the extreme northwest corner of Asia Minor, located at the confluence of the Scamander and the Simois and commanding the Hellespont (the Dardanelles of today). In Homer it is variously called Troy or Troia or Ilium or Dardania or Pergamus — all names derived from the names of ancient kings: Tros, Ilus, Dardanus, Priam.

Outstanding Greek Heroes

Agamemnon, "the monarch of men," commander in chief of the invading Greeks; often called "son of Atreus," or, in one word, "Atrides" or "the Atreid." He came from Mycenae in northeastern Peloponnesus.

Menelaüs, his brother, also called "son of Atreus," or, in one word, "Atrides" or "the Atreid." The brothers are "Atridae." Menelaüs hailed from Sparta in southeastern Peloponnesus.

Achilles, the mightiest of all the warriors, often called "son of Peleus," or, in one word, "Pelides." He came from Phthia in northeastern Greece. He was slain by Paris at a time subsequent to the story of the *Iliad.*

Patroclus, the most intimate friend of Achilles; often called "son of Menoetius"; he was slain, after heroic deeds of valor and wholesale slaughter of the enemy, by Hector in Book XVI.

Diomedes, often called also "son of Tydeus," or, in one word, "Tydides." He came from Argos in northeastern Peloponnesus.

Nestor, the old man eloquent, often called "son of Neleus," or, in one word, "Nelides." He came from Pylus in western Peloponnesus.

Antilochus, son of Nestor and close friend of Achilles. He was slain, after events described in the *Iliad*, by Memnon of Aethiopia.

Odysseus, often called "son of Laertes," wise in counsel, mighty in battle. He hails from the island of Ithaca off the western coast of Greece. He is the hero of the *Odyssey*.

Ajax, son of Telamon, first cousin to Achilles and second to him alone in might and valor. He comes from the island of Salamis near Athens.

Ajax, son of Oïleus, from Locris. He fights equally well with spear or bow and arrows. These two are of no kin but are often grouped together as the "Ajaxes" or "Aeantes."

Outstanding Trojan Heroes

Priam, the king, father of fifty famous sons and twelve daughters.

Hector, his oldest son and mightiest warrior among the Trojans.

Paris, often called "Alexander," son of Priam and abductor of Helen.

Helenus, son of Priam; prophet, seer, and soldier.

Deïphobus, son of Priam; Hector's favorite brother. He wedded Helen after the death of Paris, in times later than the action of the *Iliad*.

Aeneas, son-in-law of Priam; son of Anchises and the goddess Aphrodite; second only to Hector in prowess and valor. He is the hero of Vergil's epic.

Pandarus, son of Lycaon; famous bowman; an ally from Zeleia in Lycia.

Antenor, son-in-law of Priam; sage; counsellor.

Sarpedon, son of Zeus; an ally from Lycia; slain by Patroclus in Book XVI.

Gods Favorable to the Greeks

Hera, daughter of Cronus; sister and wife of Zeus.

Athena, goddess of war, often called "Pallas" or "Pallas Athena" or (rarely) the "Trito-born."

Hephaestus, the god of fire; the master craftsman of Olympus.

Poseidon, ruler of the sea.

Gods Favorable to the Trojans

Zeus, king and father of gods and men; also called the "son of Cronus," or, in one word, "Cronion" or "Cronides" or "the Olympian."

Ares, son of Zeus and Hera, the "blood-stained" god of brutal warfare. Sometimes also inclined to favor the Greeks and therefore called a "renegade."

Apollo, god of light and intelligence; called also "Phoebus" or "Phoebus Apollo" or "god of the silver bow."

Artemis, twin sister of Apollo; the archer goddess, "rainer of arrows."

Aphrodite, the "laughter-loving," "lover of smiles," also called "Cypris" from the chief seat of her worship. She is the mother of Aeneas.

A Note on the Flaxman Drawings

FOR the illustrations of this book we have chosen the famous designs of John Flaxman (1755-1826). Flaxman was one of the greatest sculptors in the history of English art; but, whatever his merits as a sculptor, he was supremely great as a draftsman and a designer of sculpture. He grew up in the midst of his father's stock of casts of ancient sculpture and early attracted the attention of artists like Romney and Blake and Stothard by his masterful drawings, designs, and modelings.

Another famous man attracted by young Flaxman's designs was Josiah Wedgwood, who engaged him as modeler of those classic and domestic friezes, plaques, and ornamental vessels which earned for the manufacturer his great reputation as a producer of elegant objets d' art.

At the age of thirty-two John Flaxman went to Rome, where the whole atmosphere at that time was permeated with the spirit of Greek art and the enthusiasm of the great Winckelmann. And as the representative of that spirit, Flaxman is supreme among the artists of the world. The list of his works is a very long one. At the head of the list, the best known and the most interesting are the superb illustrations to Homer's ILIAD and ODYSSEY. In these we see embodied, at their best, his unrivaled gifts of rhythmical design and penetrating feeling. Of the emotions of love and pity he was the consummate master, and he gives them expression with the utmost simplicity and grace, both of form and of action.

A few detractors of Flaxman as illustrator of Homer have said his designs are lacking in the full-blooded, heroic quality the reader always associates with the Homeric warriors. One critic has remarked that even as Pope in his famous translation put Homer in a periwig, Flaxman has clothed his figures in muslin. But whatever their deficiencies, they remain without question the greatest and most satisfying of the illustrations of the ILIAD.

THE ILLUSTRATIONS OF THE ILIAD
BY JOHN FLAXMAN

THE ILIAD OF HOMER

ILIAD · I (A)

Alpha the prayer of Chryses sings;
The army's plague; the strife of kings.

SING, O Goddess, the wrath of Achilles, scion of Peleus,
Ruinous wrath, that afflicted with numberless woes the Achaeans,
Hurling headlong to Hades souls many and brave ones — of heroes
Slain — ay, gave unto dogs, unto all birds lonelily flying
Them as a prey; and the counsel of Zeus moved aye to fulfilment
E'en from the time when first stood parted in quarrel asunder
Atreus' son, the monarch of men, and godlike Achilles.

Who of the gods, then, joined these twain in strife and contention?
Phoebus, scion of Leto and Zeus, who, wroth with the monarch,
Stirred up a noisome plague in the camp, and the people were dying,
All on account of his priest — whom Atreus' son had dishonored —
Chryses. He it was came to the swift-keeled galleys Achaean
Eager to rescue his daughter, with ransom beyond all telling,
Holding aloft wool-wreaths of his god, far-darting Apollo,
Wreaths on a staff of gold, and he made his prayer to the Argives
All, yet chiefly the twain who marshaled the host, the Atridae.
"Atreus' sons and the rest, all ye well-greavèd Achaeans,
Now may the gods, who dwell in the halls of Olympus, accord you
Sack of the city of Priam with happy return to the homeland!
Only release my child unto me, and, accepting a ransom,
Thus will ye honor Zeus's son, far-darting Apollo."

So he spake; forthwith all the other Argives applauded,
Bidding to rev'rence the priest and accept such glorious ransom.
Only it pleased not the heart of Atrides, king Agamemnon,
Who full rudely dismissed him and laid stern orders upon him:
"Never let me, old man, by the hollow ships again find thee,
Be it or tarrying now or again hereafter returning,
Lest then naught may avail thee the staff of thy god and his fillets!

1

Her I will never release; nay, sooner shall age come upon her
There in my Argive halls, far off from the land of her fathers,
Moving before her loom and serving the couch of her master.
Off, then! Do not provoke me; for so thy departing were safer."

Thus spake he. And in terror the old man, heeding the mandate,
Fared forth, silent, alone, by the sea-marge billow-resounding;
There, as he wandered apart, in a fervent petition the old man
Prayed to Apollo, the king, whose fair-haired mother was Leto:

"Hear me, god of the silver bow, thou warden of Chrysa,
Warden of Cilla divine, who in might over Tenedos reignest,
Sminthian god! If I ever have builded a temple to please thee,
Or if I ever have burned fat cuts from the thighs of a victim,
Whether a bull or a goat, fulfil me this my desire:
Speed those arrows of thine! Make the Danaans pay for my weeping!"

Such was the prayer of the priest, old Chryses. Phoebus Apollo
Hearkening, wroth in his heart, from the heights of Olympus descended
Bearing his bow on his shoulder, a close-shut quiver beside it.
Clanging, rattled and rang on his shoulder the shafts of the godhead,
Striding along in his wrath, like nightfall fearful advancing.
Off from the galleys he sat; then loosed an arrow amid them.
Fearfully came the clang of the bent bow's shivering silver.
First at the mules, at the swift-footed dogs, he directed his onset,
But thereafter, discharging his biting missiles against them,
Men, too, smote he; and aye burned pyres close-crowded of corpses.

Nine days all through the camp kept ranging the bolts of the god-
Till on the tenth Achilles summoned the host to assemble — [head,
Hera, the white-armed goddess, had moved him in spirit to call them,
She whom sorely it grieved thus seeing her Danai dying.

Soon as the folk had assembled, from all sides gathered together,
Full in the midst uprising, fleet-footed Achilles addressed them:

"Atreus' son, methinketh that we, driven back, disappointed,
Homeward again shall be sailing — if any escape death haply —
Since the foul plague and war combine to destroy the Achaeans.
Come, then, let us consult some priest or perchance a diviner
Or some monger of dreams — for a dream, too, cometh from heaven —
Who might haply declare why Phoebus Apollo is raging —

2

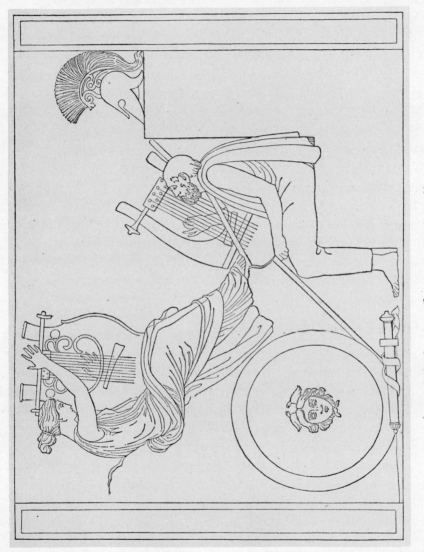

Homer Invoking the Muse

Whether a due hecatomb or a vow unpaid may incense him —
If peradventure the savor of lambs or of goats unblemished
He were disposed to accept, then ward off death from the people."

　　Such words spoken, he sat him down; then rose up among them
Calchas, scion of Thestor, by far the wisest of augurs,
Who knew all that has been, now is, or shall be in the future.
He it was likewise that guided the Argive galleys to Troyland,
All by the saying of sooth, vouchsafed him of Phoebus Apollo.
Kindliest-minded, the seer broke silence and spoke thus among them:
　"Thou, the belovèd of Zeus, thou bidst me tell thee, Achilles,
Whence this wrath of the lord, far-smiting Phoebus Apollo.
Well, then, I will proclaim it, but thou make promise and swear it,
Stoutly with all thy soul, by word, by deed to defend me,
Seeing, methinks, my word may arouse to anger a hero
Who with might sways the Argives all, and Achaeans obey him.
Stronger, in sooth, is a monarch in wrath with a man that is meaner,
Since, though haply for that same day he may swallow his anger,
Yet will he cherish a grudge long after — until he fulfil it —
Deep in his breast; so whether thou wilt protect me, consider."
　　Answered him then and addressed him in turn fleet-footed Achilles:
"Boldly by all means publish the god-sent sign, if thou know it.
For by Apollo, belovèd of Zeus, whom worshiping, Calchas,
Thou to the people revealest a portent sent of the godhead,
None, while I upon earth with my eyes wide open am living,
Here by the hollow ships shall lay a hard hand upon thee —
None of the Argives all, nor e'en if thou name Agamemnon,
Who now deemeth himself foremost by far of Achaeans."
　　Then the unblamable seer took heart and uttered his saying:
　"Well then, not for a vow or a due hecatomb is he raging,
Rather because of his priest whom erst Agamemnon dishonored,
Neither releasing his daughter nor even accepting a ransom.
Therefore sendeth the god, the far-darter — and ever will send us —
Woes, nor ever remove this noisome plague from the Argives,
Ere we deliver the bright-eyed maiden back to her father,
Free, unbought, unransomed, and carry a holy oblation 　　[mercy."
Hence unto Chrysa; we might then appease him and move him to

5

These words spoken, he sat him down. Then rose up among them
Atreus' hero son, wide-ruling king Agamemnon,
Verily sore displeased; and his heart, all darkened within him,
Swelled with wrath, and his eyes flashed out bright-blazing as fire.
Calchas first he accosted, with grim look menacing evil:

"Prophet of ills, who ne'er unto me yet spakest with favor!
Ever the evil it is thy heart finds joy in divining;
Never a word thou'st spoken of cheer, ne'er brought to fulfilment.
Now, too, with words of sooth thou harang'st the Achaeans,
Saying the king far-darter hath sent these evils upon them
Only because I rejected the glorious ransom that Chryses
Offered us all for his child—nay, rather I chose to retain her
There in my home; for I hold her above Clytaemnestra,
Lawfully mate of my couch, to whom *she* is noway inferior,
Neither in favor nor figure, in works nowise nor in wisdom.
Nevertheless even so I will yield her, if so it be better;
I wish rather my folk to be saved than for any to perish.
Only prepare forthwith unto *me* some portion of honor,
Lest I alone of the folk be prizeless; *that* were unseemly.
All ye witness, insooth, what prize of my own is departing."

Answered him then in his turn the divine, swift-footed Achilles:
"Atreus' son, most noble, of all most fond of possessions,
How shall the greathearts now, the Achaeans, give thee a guerdon?
We know naught of a treasure that somewhere lieth in common;
All is apportioned instead, whate'er our plunder from cities,
Neither beseems to collect it again now back from the people.
Come, then, yield this maid for the sake of her god; and the Argives
Threefold, fourfold e'en will repay, if Zeus ever grant us
Wholly to level in ashes yon well-walled city of Troia."

Straightway then unto him made answer the lord Agamemnon:
"Nay, not so—though hardy thou art—O godlike Achilles,
Craftily think to beguile; thou'lt not outwit nor persuade me.
Would'st thou have me insooth, while thou art retaining a guerdon,
Sit here alone in bereavement? and bid me surrender the maiden?
Nay! but if now the Achaeans, the greathearts, give me reguerdon,
Suiting it unto my soul, as an offset due and deservèd,

Well! If they *will not* give it, myself then truly will take it —
Thine, or the prize of an Ajax, or haply that of Odysseus,
Seize and bring home, though likely it anger the hero I visit.
This it were well, however, hereafter again to consider.
Meantime, come, let us launch on the bright sea-waters a sable
Warship, stow inside it a rich hecatomb, then man it
Well at the oars, then also embark Chryseïs the fair-faced
Maiden herself, and appoint some prudent adviser as captain,
Whether Idomeneus haply, or Ajax, noble Odysseus,
Or thyself, most dreaded of all men, scion of Peleus —
So with a rich hecatomb to appease the ruin-averter."
　　Scowlfully eyeing, addressed him at once fleet-footed Achilles:
　"Ah me, clothèd in impudence, thou, upon gain ever heart-set,
How shall an Argive, pray, thy words e'er zealously follow,
Whether fulfilling a journey or fighting amain with a foeman?
Not for a quarrel with Troy's spear-wielders am I come hither
Ready for warfare; nay, for never in aught have they wronged me.
My kine never in truth have they harried nor ever my horses,
Neither have ever in Phthia, the deep-loamed breeder of heroes,
Ravaged a field grain-laden; for much lies truly between us —
Many a shadowy mountain, a sea-plain sounding with surges.
Thou it is, utterly shameless, we follow to win *thee* pleasure,
Seeking revenge for a cur like thee and for Menelaüs —
Here on the Trojans. This thou never regardest or countest,
Nay, dost threaten thyself to despoil me thus of my guerdon,
Guerdon my sore toil won and the sons of Achaeans awarded!
Never for me is a meed co-equal with thine, if the Argives
Utterly ravage and raze some populous keep of the Trojans.
Natheless ever it happens that mine are the hands to uphold it,
Warfare's harassing burden; and yet, when portioning cometh,
Thine is a prize far greater, but I bear back to the galleys
Only a trifle as mine, though battle have wearied and worn me.
Well then! hence unto Phthia I go — since far it were better
Homeward to fare in my curved-beaked galleys — nor am I minded
Here, in dishonor myself, to amass for *thee* wealth and abundance."
　　Then unto him thus replied that monarch of men, Agamemnon:

7

"Flee and begone, if thy heart be set upon going; not *I* will
Beg thee for *my* sake to linger; at *my* side others will gain me
Honor and glory — Zeus above all, who giveth good counsel.
Thou art to me most hateful of all kings Zeus ever nurtured,
Since it is ſtrife thou lovest and always battle and warfare.
Yea, if exceedingly ſtrong, some god so made thee, methinketh.
Hie then home in thy galleys; desert with thy company also;
Over thy Myrmidons lord it; of thee *I* surely shall reck not
Nor shall regard thy anger. But hearken this threat that I make thee:
Since then Phoebus Apollo bereaves me of Chryses' daughter,
Her will I send with a galley of mine and a company likewise
Back to her father; but thine own meed, the fair-faced Briseïs,
I will myself lead home from thy tent; thus haply to show thee
How much mightier I am than thou; so others may shudder
Either to match me in words or in rivalry openly face me."

Thus he. And fury seized on Pelides. Then, as he pondered,
Deep in his shaggy breast, his heart was divided in counsel
Whether to draw from his thigh that keen-edged falchion he wore there,
Scatter the princes assembled, and slaughter the king, Agamemnon,
Or ſtay rather his fury and bridle his fierce indignation.
While in his heart and soul yet pondered Pelides in such wise —
Even in act of unsheathing his broad blade — inſtant Athena
Came at the bidding of Hera, the white-armed goddess, from heaven,
Goddess impartial of heart in her love and concern for both heroes.
Standing behind him, she seized on the gold-red locks of Pelides,
Visible only to him; not one of the others espied her.
Thereat marveled Achilles and turned him about; and he knew her,
Pallas Athena; and fearful her eyes shone gleaming upon him!
Then he uplifted his voice and in accents wingèd addressed her:

"Why art thou come, O daughter of Zeus who wieldeth the aegis?
Haply to view this bluſter of Atreus' son, Agamemnon?
Well, I will speak right out what's certain, I ween, of fulfilment:
Full soon he of his own overbearance likely will perish."

Then unto him in her turn spake the bright-eyed goddess Athena:
"Hither — if haply thou heed me — I come, thine anger to bridle,
Speeding at hest of a goddess, of white-armed Hera, from heaven,

8

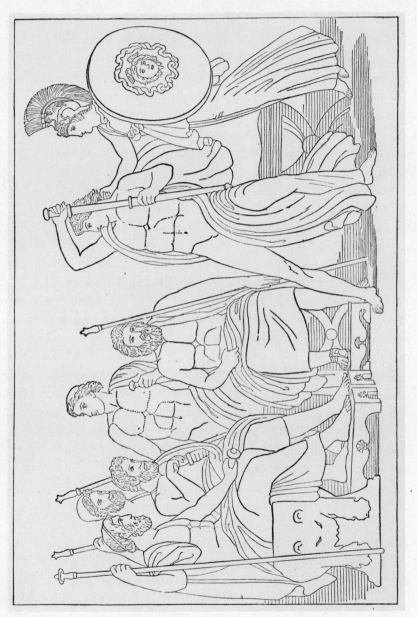

Athena Repressing the Fury of Achilles

(Goddess impartial of heart in her love and concern for both heroes).
Come now, cease this quarrel; the broadsword—leave it unhanded.
Natheless, revile him in words, as occasion hereafter may offer,
Seeing I openly tell thee what surely shall find a fulfilment:
Threefold measure and goodly the gifts that shall come to thee some
All for this insult's sake. Yet bridle thyself and obey us."   [time,
     Answering her, in his turn spake forth fleet-footed Achilles:
  "Needs must man, O Goddess, of you twain keep a commandment,
Howe'er sorely incensed in his heart, since so it is better.
Whoe'er heedeth the gods, unto him most gladly they hearken."
     Saying, he stayed on the hilt's rich silver the weight of his strong
Back then into its scabbard the broadsword thrust he, obedient   [hand,
Unto the word of Athena. But she was away to Olympus,
Unto the gods and the palace of Zeus who wieldeth the aegis.
     Yet again Peleus' son, with harsh words bitterness-laden,
Spake to Atreus' son and in no wise ceased from his anger:
  "Thou, with the face of a hound and the heart of a hind, wine-laden,
Ne'er yet once unto battle to arm thee along with the people
Or with the doughtiest chiefs of Achaia to enter an ambush,
Hast thou had courage to venture—'twould look like death to Atrides!
Safer insooth thus ranging the broad-pitched camp of Achaeans,
Plund'ring him of his meed whoever has spoken against thee,
People-devouring king, who rulest a nation of do-naughts!
Else were an outrage like unto this thy last, Agamemnon.
Now, though, boldly I tell thee, and mighty my oath to confirm it:
By this staff that never with twigs or with leafage shall burgeon,
Since once it left its parent stem there, high on the mountains,
Never to blossom anew—for the bronze completely has shorn it
Both of its leafage and bark; and the sons meanwhile of Achaeans
Wardens of Zeus, to defend his canons and deal out judgment,
Bear it in hand—and the oath thereby unto thee shall be mighty—
One day truly desire of Achilles shall visit the Argives,
All of them. Naught shall avail thee then, for the people's salvation,
Keenest remorse, when many before the man-slaying Hector
Fall down dying; in vain then tear thy spirit within thee,
Wroth that the bravest Achaean of thee found honor in no way."

Thus spake Peleus' son and dashed down before him the sceptre,
Richly bestudded with pure gold nails, then sate him in silence.
Over against him Atrides raged, when up rose among them
Nestor, pleasant of speech, that clear-toned speaker of Pylus,
He whose utterance flowed from his smooth tongue sweeter than honey.
Two generations of mortal men had perished before him—
All that *had* been born of old time and nurtured beside him,
There in his hallowèd Pylus—a third brood now he was ruling.
He then, kindliest-minded, harangued them and spake out among them:
　"Ah me! Great grief truly is come on the land of Achaia!
Truly would Priam exult, yea, all those children of Priam;
Likewise, too, it would greatly rejoice all hearts of the Trojans,
Once all this were declared, how ye twain struggle together,
Ye that are Danaan leaders, in counsel as well as in battle.
Come now, hearken—ye both are warriors younger than I am—
Seeing that I have had dealings with heroes braver than ye are,
Dealt with them oft ere now nor ever was held of them lightly.
Warriors such I have never beheld, nor shall I behold them,
Such as Pirithoüs was, yea, Dryas, shepherd of peoples,
Caeneus, too, and Exadius, and peer of the gods, Polyphemus,
Theseus also, scion of Aegeus, match for immortals.
Mightiest they in their stature of all earth-habiting heroes,
Mightiest surely were they, who still with the mightiest battled—
Half-brutes, homed in the hills, whom *they* made utterly perish—
Even with these it was *I* held converse, haling from Pylus,
Come from a far-off land, for they themselves had invoked me.
Singly I combated also with such foes haply as no one
Now, of the mortals that habit the broad earth, ever would combat.
They it was heeded my words, it was they that regarded my counsel.
Ye, then, hearken as well, since surely to hearken is better.
Strong as thou art, Agamemnon, despoil not *him* of his damsel,
Nay now, leave him the guerdon the sons of Achaeans awarded.
Neither bethink thee, Pelides, to strive with a sovereign, opposing
Might unto might, since none hath an equal allotment of honor
Like as a sceptred king, to whom Zeus apportioneth glory.
Doughty indeed as thou art, yea, child of a mother immortal,

12

Yet is the other a greater, he rules more numerous peoples.
Curb thine anger, Atrides; for lo! it is I importune thee
Now to relent in thy wrath with Achilles, powerful bulwark
Unto the Argives all 'gainst the woes of slaughterous warfare."

　　Answering him, in his turn spake Lord Agamemnon Atrides:
"Yea now, all these things, old man, thou hast fittingly spoken.
There is the man, however, that fain were above all others,
Fain would be master of all, domineer over all men gladly,
Fain give orders to all; but methinks some hardly will hearken.
Though it be haply the gods everlasting crowned him a spearman,
Therefore do they ordain him to utter revilings at pleasure?"

　　Brake in upon him with answer, at that word, goodly Achilles:
"Yea, for a coward in truth I were called, a contemptible craven,
Were I submissive in ev'ry affair unto thee as thou sayest.
Give unto others indeed thine orders — not to Achilles.
Play thou captain; methinks it is I no longer obey thee.
This, moreover, I tell thee, and ponder it well in thy spirit:
My hands ne'er do battle with thee on account of a damsel,
Neither with thee nor another; ye take back what ye have given.
But all else that is mine, beside yon swift sable galley,
Take thou nothing of that, nor bear off, unless at my bidding.
Come on now, make trial, that all these warriors may witness;
Speedily all shall behold thy dark blood gush round my spearhead."

　　Thereat both, as the battle of violent words they had ended,
Rose and dissolved the assembly beside the galleys Achaean.
Peleus' son fared forth to his tents and his trim-rigged vessels;
With him Menoetius' son went, too, and his friends and companions,
While Agamemnon, dragging a swift ship down to the sea beach,
Chose him twenty good oarsmen — embarked rich offerings also,
Meet for a god — then led and seated the fair-faced Chryseïs
Therein. Odysseus of many devices went as the captain.

　　Gathered aboard, then, sailing they went on the ways of the waters,
While Atrides summoned his people to purification.
They, having thoroughly cleansed them and cast in the sea the ablutions,
Offered the far-darting god hecatombs full perfect in number,
Holy, of bulls and of goats, by the shore of the weariless waters.

Eddying round in the smoke, sweet savor ascended to heaven.   [non

    All through the camp they were busied in such wise. Yet Agamem-

Ceased not at all from the ſtrife wherewith he had menaced Achilles;

Rather he summoned Talthybius and also Eurybates to him,

Twain in his waiting as heralds alert, yea, busy attendants:

    "Go, ye twain, to the tent of Achilles, the scion of Peleus;

Thence then, taking her hand, lead forth Briseïs, the fair-faced.

But, an he will not resign her, myself will assuredly seize her;   [ous."

More men will come with me then; and that he will find still more griev-

    Saying, he sent them away, and he laid ſtern mandate upon them.

Though with relu&ctilde;tance, the twain by the shore of the weariless waters

Fared and arrived at the ships of the Myrmidon folk and the barracks.

Seated beside his tent and his black war-galley they found him;

Nor, of a truth, in his heart was Achilles glad to behold them.

Awed and revering the prince, yea, lost in confusion, the heralds

Stood ſtill, never addressing him either a word or a queſtion.

He in his heart underſtood full well; thus then he bespake them:

    "Hail, ye heralds! ye messengers both of Zeus and of mortals,

Draw near. Nowise ye are to blame, but alone Agamemnon,

Who hath despatched you twain on account of the damsel Briseïs.

Haſten, Patroclus, scion of Zeus, go bring them the damsel,

So they may lead her away. But I call themselves unto witness

Here in the presence of mortal men and of blessèd immortals,

Also before that king — that cruel king — should there ever

Need be hereafter of me to defend from scandalous wreckage

Him and the rest — for he rages in ruinous temper; he knows not

Verily how to consider at once both forward and backward,

So that his Argives may battle beside their galleys in safety."

    So spake Pelides. Patroclus, his comrade dear, heeded and quickly

Brought from the tent Briseis, the fair-faced damsel, and gave her

Unto the heralds, to lead her away by the galleys Achaean.

Willingly went not the woman along. But alone then Achilles

Tearfully turned him aside, and aloof from his comrades he sat him

Down on the grey sea's beach, far-viewing the limitless waters.

There in a passion he prayed, with his hands outſtretched, to his mother:

    "Since, O Mother, indeed thou barest me verily short-lived,

The Departure of Briseïs from the Tent of Achilles

Honor at least he was bounden to grant, the Olympian monarch,
Zeus, who thunders in heaven; but me not a little he honors,
Seeing that Atreus' son, wide-regnant king Agamemnon,
Does me dishonor in taking my prize, himself the despoiler."

    Praying amidst his tears, she heard him, his worshipful mother,
Down in the sea-depth seated beside her father, the ancient.
Quickly the goddess arose like mist from the hoary sea-surface,
Came then, seated herself at her son's side, where he was weeping,
Stroked him with gentle caress, then spake a word and addressed him:

    "Why this weeping, my child? What sorrow of soul is upon thee?
Utter it forth! Hide it not in thy heart! Let both of us know it!"

    Heavily moaning, addressed her in turn fleet-footed Achilles:

    "Thou understandest insooth all *these* things — why should I tell
Forth had we fared unto Thèbè, the hallowèd town of Eëtion,   [them?
Utterly sacked it, and thence brought all things hither as booty.
Also the sons of Achaia divided it duly among them,
Choosing a prize for Atrides, a fair-faced maiden, Chryseïs.
Chryses though, that was priest of the god, far-darting Apollo,
Came to the swift war-craft of the bronze-clad sons of Achaia,
Seeking release for his child, with a ransom beyond all telling,
Holding aloft wool-wreaths of his god, far-darting Apollo,
Wreaths on a staff of gold, and he made his prayer to the Argives
All, yet chiefly the twain who marshaled the host, the Atridae.
Thereto shouted a ready assent all other Achaeans,
Bidding to rev'rence the priest and receive such glorious ransom.
Only it pleased not the heart of Atrides, king Agamemnon,
Nay! but he rudely dismissed him and laid stern orders upon him.
Wrathful the seer turned back to his homeland. Wrathful the godhead
Heard, as he prayed, for the priest was exceedingly dear to Apollo.
So on the Argives he sent a death-winged dart, and they perished
One on another, the folk, while speeded the bolts of the godhead,
Ranging the wide-camped host of the Argives all. Unto us then
Uttered a seer, well-knowing, the heavenly sign of the Archer.
I was the first one bade them propitiate angered Apollo.
Therewith choler invaded Atrides' soul; and he rose up
Filling his words with a menace, which now full soon is accomplished.

17

For in a swift ship now the fire-eyed Achaeans are sending
Home fair Chryseïs, and gifts for the god-king burden the galley.
Her, however, the daughter of Briseus, meed the Achaeans
Gave me, Atrides' heralds have taken e'en now from my barrack.
Thou, though, if able at all, bring aid to thy valorous offspring.
Hie thee away to Olympus with prayer unto Zeus, if aforetime
Thou by word or by deed didst gladden the heart of the godhead.
Seeing that many a time in the Pelian halls I have heard thee
Telling in boast how once from the stormcloud-mantled Cronion
Thou of immortals alone didst parry unseemly destruction,
When they had minded to bind him, the other Olympian powers,
Hera and with her Poseidon and likewise Pallas Athena!
Thou then camest betimes, O Goddess, to save him from fetters,
Calling at once unto vasty Olympus the century-handed
(Godheads call him Briareos; all men though call him Aegaeon),
For in his might he exceeded the sea-god even, his father.
There by Cronus' son then he seated him, gleaming in glory.
Fear of him crept over all those blessed gods, and they bound not.
Sit then by Zeus and, clasping his knees, call this to his mem'ry,
If he will render belike a support even now to the Trojans,
Hemming the bay all round, 'mid the sterns of the galleys, the Argives
Falling in slaughter, that all may thus have taste of their ruler,
Yea, and Atrides' self, wide-realmed Agamemnon, may know it,
What was his blindness to honor the bravest Achaean in no way."

Thereupon, dropping a tear, made answer Thetis, his mother:
"Ah me, cursèd in bearing! My child, oh why did I rear thee?
Would thou satest beside yon galleys, with tears and with sorrow
All unacquainted! Since truly thy season is brief, unenduring!
Woe! that at once swift-fated and past all men to be pitied,
Unto an evil lot in the Pelian palace I bore thee!
Yet will I speak this word unto Zeus, the hurler of lightning,
Going myself to Olympus, the snow-clad, there to persuade him.
Meantime, seated beside the swift sea-furrowing galleys,
Rage at the men of Achaia, but take no part in the warfare.
Yesterday Zeus, for a feast with the blameless Aethiopeans,
Went unto Ocean afar — and the gods all followed together —

18

Thetis Calling Briareos to the Assistance of Zeus

Yet on the twelfth day surely returns once more to Olympus.
Then to the palace of Zeus with its threshold of bronze will I haſten,
There on my knees to implore, yea, haply methinketh, persuade him."

   These words spoken, the goddess was gone, there leaving Achilles,
Deep in his soul ſtill wroth on account of the fair-girdled woman,
Whom they had taken by force and defying his will. — But Odysseus
Meanwhile came unto Chrysa, conveying a hecatomb holy.
Soon as they entered the haven, with shores deep-dented, the rowers
Furled the sail and laid it down in the hull of the darksome
Ship; then lowered the mast with the foreſtays into the maſthold
Speedily; laſtly with oars rowed onward the galley to moorage.
Forth then caſting the anchors, they fixed down firmly the cables;
Forth then issued themselves, on the ſtrand of the sea disembarking;
Forth then drave th' hecatomb for the god, far-darting Apollo;
Forth then out from the sea-borne ship came laſtly Chryseïs.
Leading her ſtraight to the altar, Odysseus of many devices
Yielded her into the arms of her father dear and addressed him:

   "Chryses, hither the king of men, Agamemnon, hath sent me
Bringing to thee thy daughter, to Phoebus a holy oblation,
Off'ring it here for the Danaans' sake, to appease us the Sovereign
Who now loads on the Argives a burden of groanful afflicti̇on."

   Thus he spake and reſtored the dear maid to the arms of her father,
Glad to receive her. The rich hecatomb for the deity quickly
Set they in regular order surrounding the well-built altar;
Laſtly they washed their hands and took up the grains of the barley.
Chryses then, with his palms upraised, prayed fervently for them:

   "Hear me, thou of the silver bow, thou warden of Chrysa,
Warden of Cilla divine, who in might over Tenedos reignest,
E'en as aforetime once thou heardest, when I besought thee,
Also, to honor me then, afflicti̇edst the host of Achaeans,
Likewise now again also my heart's wish bring to fulfilment:
Straightway bid it depart, this loathsome plague, from the Argives."

   Chryses thus in petition; and Phoebus Apollo attended.
Now having prayed, they sprinkled the unground grains of the barley
First, then drew back the victims' heads, then slaughtered and flayed
Out of the thighs cut slices, in caul-fat folded the pieces,   [them,

21

Making the slices two-folded, and laid raw collops upon them.
These upon billets the old man burned, then poured in libation
Bright wine; youths at his side held five-pronged forks, in attendance.
Now, as the thighs were consumed, and they of the vitals had tasted,
All of the rest they divided; with spits then piercing the pieces,
Roasted them carefully each, then drew off all of the slices.
Now as the task was accomplished and so made ready the feasting,
Feasted they all—no heart felt stint of a well-balanced banquet.
Now when desire for meat and for drink together was banished,
Young men, thereupon crowning the wine-bowls brimful, apportioned
Rightly for all into goblets, the mean time pouring libation.
Duly the whole day long with song then they worshiped the godhead,
Chanting a beautiful paean, the young men, sons of Achaeans,
Hymning the Sovereign; and he was delighted in heart as he heard them.

Soon as the sun went down and darkness settled upon them,
All at the moorings, along by the stern, they laid them to slumber.
Soon as the dawn appeared, rosy-fingered daughter of morning,
All for the high seas launched and the wide war-camp of the Argives
Under a favoring breeze far-working Apollo had sent them.
Quickly they hoisted the mast and unfurled to the wind the white canvas;
Mid on the sail wide-swelling the wind blew; foaming, a billow
Loudly plashed all along the keel; and the ship of Odysseus
Scudded along on the surge; and her sea-course soon was accomplished.
Now as at length they arrived at the wide war-camp of the Argives,
Straight from the waters they haled the swart ship up to the mainland
High on the sands, and, alining the long props fitly beneath it,
Scattered themselves then quickly amid the galleys and barracks.

Meanwhile tarried in wrath at his swift sea-furrowing galleys
Peleus' son, descendant of Zeus, fleet-footed Achilles,
Never repairing at all to the conclave, bestower of glory,
Never at all to the war, but, his own heart wasting in fury,
There to the spot sat rooted, though yearning for war-cry and battle.

But when the morning, the twelfth thereafter, had risen upon them,
Unto the halls of Olympus the gods everlasting assembled,
All in a company headed by Zeus, while Thetis, forgetting
Never the charge of her son, to the sea-wave surface arising,

Mounted with earliest dawn unto heaven's immense and Olympus.
Far from the others she found wide-thundering Cronides, sitting
'Lone on the topmost summit of many-ridgèd Olympus.
There then, seated before him, his knee with her left hand clasping,
While with her right hand touching his chin underneath, in entreaty,
Uttered the goddess her prayer unto Zeus, sole Sovereign Cronion:

"Zeus, O Father, if ever I aided thee 'mid the immortals
Whether in word or in deed, my heart's wish bring to fulfilment.
Honor my son whose doom is, of all men's, quickest in coming!
Since it is he that truly the monarch of men, Agamemnon,
Deeply dishonors in taking his prize, himself the despoiler.
Thou, O Zeus, however, Olympian master of counsel,
Honor him! Grant a victorious might unto Troy, till the Argives
Render my son due honor and multiply honor upon him."

Thus far Thetis. But Zeus, cloud-gatherer, answered her nothing.
Long time silent he sat. But she with a clasp unrelaxing
Clung close, even as grown to his knees, and her pleading repeated:

"Yea now, promise me sure and with nod of assurance affirm it,
Or as naught thou fearest, refuse; so well shall I know then
How far *I* am accounted of all gods lowest in honor."

Thereupon, sorely perturbed, cloud-gathering Zeus made answer:
"Surely a mischievous matter; for so thou'lt spur me to quarrel
Haply with Hera, when she with her taunting words shall provoke me.
E'en as it is, she upbraids me at all times 'mid the immortals,
Saying, insooth, *I* come to the Trojans' succor in battle.
Now it were well to depart once more, lest Hera observe thee.
Meanwhile all these things shall be my care to fulfil them.
Come, let a nod of my head now lend thee convincing assurance;
Such is the surest token with me unto all the immortals.
Never a promise of mine is recallable, never deceptive,
Never fulfilment can fail, once this my head I have nodded."   [nodded.

Thus spake the son of Cronus, and with darkling eyebrows he
Then the ambrosial locks of the King flowed waving about him,
Down from his head immortal; and thereat trembled Olympus.

Therewith parted the twain, their counsel completed. The goddess
Leaped to the cavernous deeps of the sea from the gleaming Olympus.

23

Zeus to his palace returning, the gods all rose up before him,
Leaving their seats to meet their father; neither would any
Dare to await his approach—nay, all stepped forward to meet him.
So on his throne Zeus sate him down. Yet Hera had no way
Failed to observe, nay, soothly had seen him in council with Thetis—
Thetis the silver-footed, the child of the Ancient of Ocean.
Biting the taunts she straightway hurled at Zeus, son of Cronus:

   "Who of the gods concocted with thee, Sir Craftful, a counsel?
Aye is it pleasing to thee, in aloofness from me, in seclusion
Secret plans to consider and reach thy decisions; nor ever
Hast thou freely consented to tell me a word of thy purpose."

   Therewith spake in answer the father of men and immortals:
"Hera, hoping were idle that even thou ever shouldst fathom
All my plans, too deep for a couch-mate even to know them.
What may insooth be seemly for thine ear, none ever surely—
Whether a god he be or a man—knows sooner than Hera.
But whatsoever apart from the gods I will to consider,
These things do not, I pray thee, inquire or pry into closely."

   Thereupon ox-eyed Hera, the worshipful, made him an answer:
"Most dread scion of Cronus, a word like this to have spoken!
Hitherto never from me a query or word or inquiry—
Nay, but in peace thou bethinkst thee whatever fulfilment thou wishest.
Yet is my heart now sorely a-dread, lest *she* have beguiled thee,
Thetis, the silver-footed, the child of the Ancient of Ocean,
Seeing she clung to thy knees at the earliest dawning, beside thee
Seated. I ween with a nod thou gavest inviolate promise:
Honor to Peleus' son—to Achaeans death at the galleys!"

   Zeus, the compeller of clouds, made answer at once and addressed
   "Spirit of mischief, forever a-weening; nor can I escape thee! [her:
Natheless not one purpose canst thou accomplish but farther
Still be weaned from my heart, thy plight still worsening ever.
Now if the matter be such, however I will it, it will be.
Sit thou silent the while, unto *my* word yielding obedience,
Lest even gods may avail thee—as many as dwell in Olympus—
Naught, when nearing I lay these hands unapproachable on thee."

   Thus he; and Hera was frightened, the ox-eyed worshipful goddess;

Thetis Entreating Zeus to Honor Achilles

Motionless sitting in silence, she bridled her spirit within her,
While through the palace of Zeus the gods of heaven were troubled.
Thereat the far-famed artist, Hephaestus, began to harangue them,
Wishing to comfort his mother, the white-armed worshipful Hera:

"Surely a mischievous matter will this be, bearable noway,
Should such a quarrel divide you twain on account of a mortal
Thus, and a wrangling arise here among us gods. At the goodly
Banquet naught of delight will be left us, evil triumphant.
I recommend unto mother—herself well tutored in wisdom—
Gratify Zeus, dear Father, in all things; then will the Father
Not upbraid us again nor end our feast in confusion.
What! the Olympian hurler of lightnings could, if he willed it,
Dash *us* out of our places!—in might so far he excelleth.
Come now, draw thee anigh him with accents gentle, persuasive.
Straightway then the Olympian will be all kindness toward us."

Thus far he; then arose with a twin-bowled goblet; he gave it
Into the hand of his mother and therewith also addressed her:

"Patience, mother of mine, and endure, though deeply aggrievèd,
Lest I behold thee, dear as thou art, right under my eyes here
Beaten; and sorrowing sorely, in that case I could avail thee
Naught in defense; the Olympian is hard to face as a foeman.
Verily *me* ere this, when eager indeed to defend thee,
Seizing my foot did he fling from the threshold sacred of heaven.
All day long I plunged and at last, as the sun was descending,
Lit on the Lemnian isle, and but little of life was left in me.
There did the Sintian folk right zealously care for me fallen."

Thus he spake; and she smiled—the goddess—the white-armed
Smiling, she also received at the hand of Hephaestus the goblet. [Hera.
He unto all the immortals in order, from right to the leftward,
Poured out nectar as wine, yea, ladled it sweet from the mixer.
Laughter among the immortals, the blest, unquenchable laughter
Rose at beholding Hephaestus a-bustling, a-puffing in heaven.

So for the livelong day, till sunset's coming upon them,
All held feast; not a heart felt stint of a well-balanced banquet,
Nor of the beauteous lyre held aye in the hand of Apollo,
Nor of the sweet-voiced Muses in song, one after another.

27

But as the radiant light of the sun went down to its setting,
Yielding to slumber, they fared, each godhead home to his dwelling,
Where the renownèd Hephaestus, in both hands equally clever,
Had, with a cunning conception, for each god builded a palace.
Zeus, too, went to his couch, the Olympian lord of the lightnings,
As he was wont, unto slumber, whene'er sweet sleep overtook him.
There he went up and reposed, with the gold-throned Hera beside him.

ILIAD · II · (B)

Beta the dream and synod cites
And catalogues the naval knights.

THUS all others, both gods and heroes, drivers of war-cars,
All night long lay sleeping, but no sweet slumber enfettered
Zeus, deep down in his heart still pondering how he could honor
Peleus' son and destroy men in throngs at the galleys Achaean.
Unto his heart at length *this* counsel appeared to be wisest:
Ruinous Dream he would send unto Atreus' son, Agamemnon.
Forthwith, when he had summoned, in accents winged he addressed it:
"Hie thee, Ruinous Dream, to the swift-keeled ships of Achaia!
Go to the tent of the king of men, Agamemnon Atrides;
All my bidding straightly deliver to him, as I charge thee.
Bid him with all speed call to arms the long-haired Achaeans,
Now he may capture perchance the wide-wayed city of Troia,
Since the immortals that dwell in the halls of Olympus have ended
Strife and contention among them, for Hera's entreaties have bent them
All to her will, and disaster impends now over the Trojans."
        Spake he. Obedient Dream, receiving the mission, departed,
Speedily also arrived at the swift war-galleys Achaean,
Straight to Atrides then, unto king Agamemnon; it found him
Sunken in sleep in his barrack, enswathed in ambrosial slumber.
There at the head of the king, in seeming the scion of Neleus,
Nestor, whom of the elders Atrides specially honored,
Stood, in the old man's likeness, the god-sent Dream and addressed him:
"Sleepeth the scion of Atreus, the wise-heart, master of horses?
All-night slumber behooveth a king and counselor noway,
Whose are the weightiest cares, unto whom much folk are entrusted.
Now then quickly give ear; for Zeus's messenger am I,
Who, though far off, careth for thee with exceeding compassion.
Summon to arms with all speed, he bids thee, the long-haired Achaeans!

Now were the season to capture the wide-wayed city of Troia,
Since the immortals that dwell in the halls of Olympus have ended
Strife and contention among them, for Hera's entreaties have bent them
All to her will, and disaster impends now over the Trojans,
Sent them of Zeus! Hold it fast and let no forgetfulness seize thee
Haply, as soon as sleep, honey-hearted sleep, shall release thee!''

    These words uttered, the figure of Dream fled, leaving the hero
Casting about in his mind hopes doomed not then to fulfilment,
Seeing he vowed he would take that same day Ilium-city!
Fool! For he knew not the deeds that Zeus even then was designing,
He that was yet to inflict on the Argive host and the Trojans
Groanings, keen-felt pangs, by reason of hard-fought battles.
Quick he awoke from his sleep — the divine voice echoing round him.
Upright sitting he gathered his soft-wove tunic about him,
Beautiful, bright; and he flung, deep-draped, o'er his shoulders his
Under his shining feet then he bound on his beautiful sandals; [mantle;
Thereupon swung from his shoulder a broadsword studded with silver;
Last laid hold of his sceptre, inherited, ever-enduring. [Achaeans.
Therewith he made his way 'mid the ships of the bronze-mailed

    Meanwhile Morning divine had ascended the vasty Olympus,
Heralding light unto Zeus, nor less unto other immortals.
Then Agamemnon, commander in chief, bade the clear-voiced heralds
Summon forthwith the long-haired Achaeans to meet in assembly.
They then made proclamation. The folk full swiftly assembled.

    First, however, he gathered a council of great-souled elders
There at the galley of Nestor, the Pylian-born king of Pylus,
Called them in session and opened a counsel of cunning before them:

    "Hearken, my friends; for to me in my sleep came a vision from
All in the night ambrosial, and most like Nestor, the godlike, [heaven,
Ay, in its shape, in its size, in its features specially like him;
Over my head it was standing; with utterance thus it addressed me:

    " 'Sleepeth the scion of Atreus, the wise-heart, master of horses?
All-night slumber behooveth a king and a counselor noway,
Whose are the weightiest cares, unto whom much folk are entrusted.
Now then quickly give ear; for Zeus's messenger am I,
Who, though far off, careth for thee with exceeding compassion.

Zeus Sending the Evil Dream to Agamemnon

Summon to arms with all speed, he bids thee, the long-haired Achaeans!
Now were the season to capture the wide-wayed city of Tróia,
Since the immortals that dwell in the halls of Olympus have ended
Strife and contention among them, for Hera's entreaties have bent them
All to her will, and disaſter impends now over the Trojans,
Sent them of Zeus! Hold it fast in thy heart!' And so having spoken,
Flown was the vision and vanished — at once sweet slumber released me.
Come, let us call, as we may, to arms these sons of Achaeans!
I, however, with words will test them first, as is fitting,
Bidding them flee in their many- and well-oared ships to the homeland —
Ye take care in your places with words meanwhile to reſtrain them."

     These words spoken, Atrides returned to his seat; and among them
Up rose Neſtor, a prince that was ruler of Pylus, the sandy.
He then, kindliest-minded of men, harangued and addressed them:

     "Friends of mine, ye commanders and counseling chiefs of the
This dream, were it in truth any other Achaean that told it,   [Argives,
Falsehood we should pronounce it, insooth, and would turn from it rather.
Now though, he that beheld it avows himself best of the Argives.
Come, let us call, as we may, to arms these sons of Achaeans."

     These words spoken, the hero departed the first from the council.
Rose up the rest thereafter, obeying the shepherd of peoples,
All of them sceptred kings; and the people came speeding to join them.
Even as hoſts of bees buzz swarming, thronging together,
Out from a rocky recess, aye ſtreaming in endless succession,
Flying in grapelike cluſters to light on the blossoms of springtime —
Some wing hither in crowds, and the rest fare thither and yonder:
So from the barracks and galleys the tribes, full many in number,
Still kept marching in squadrons along the sinuous seashore,
Headed toward the assembly. And Rumor, a-blazing among them,
Zeus' own messenger, ſtill kept spurring them; so they assembled.
Uproar ruled the assembly. The earth underneath them was groaning,
Under the folk down-sitting in thunderous din; and the heralds —
Nine — kept calling aloud to reſtrain them, if ever from clamor
They would desist, from tumult, and hark to the Zeus-nurtured princes.
Hardly the people were seated and held in their places in order,
Now that the clamor had ceased, when Lord Agamemnon arising

Stood with the staff in his hand, that Hephaestus' cunning had fashioned.
First upon Zeus, upon sovereign Cronion, Hephaestus bestowed it;
Zeus then gave it to Hermes, the messenger, slayer of Argus;
Hermes king then gave it to Pelops, smiter of horses.
Pelops gave it in turn unto Atreus, shepherd of peoples;
Atreus then to Thyestes, of many flocks the possessor;
Lastly Thyestes had left it to Agamemnon to wield it,
Full many islands to govern and bear sway over all Argos.
Leaning upon it, the king now delivered a speech to the Argives:
    "Friends, ye men of Ares' company, Danaans, heroes,
Zeus it is, Cronus' son, that confuses me sorely with blindness.
Hard of heart is he, who once promised me, nodding in sanction,
Sack of the well-walled city of Troy ere sailing for homeland.
Now, it appears, he was planning an evil deceit; for he bids me
Fare unto Argos, disgraced for the ruin I've wrought on the people.
(Such, it appears, is the pleasure of Zeus, the o'erpow'ringly mighty,
Zeus, who hath toppled the turrets of many a city aforetime,
Ay, and will topple again, since his is the mightiest power.)
For it is this that is shameful, that even posterity learn it,
Argive folk so many and goodly thus to be waging
Vainly a war unavailing and thus to be battling with foemen
Fewer in number than we, while still no issue appeareth.
If now we should be minded, th' Achaeans and Trojans together,
Making a binding truce to number both peoples; if then the
Trojans would gather as many as have their homes in the city,
While, in turn, we Achaeans were drawn up and marshaled in decades —
Then should choose from the Trojans cupbearers, one for a decade,
Surely for many a decade a Trojan cupbearer were wanting.
Even so many, I say, are we now, we sons of Achaeans,
More than the Trojans dwelling in town; but allies are enlisted.
Many a city hath sent to their aid spear-brandishing heroes,
Men that repel me afar from my goal, yea, baffle my yearning,
Though I be eager, to ravage the folk-thronged castle of Troyland.
Nine already the years that have passed, of Cronion the mighty,
Long since rotted the timbers of ships, untwisted the cordage.
They meanwhile, as I ween, our wives, our innocent children,

Sit in their mansions at home, still waiting for us. But a labor
All uneffected remaineth, the task we came to accomplish.
Come then, even as *I* may declare, let all be persuaded:
Hence and away in the ships to the well-loved lands of your fathers,
Seeing that never shall *we* take the wide-wayed city of Troia.''

　　Thus he spake and aroused the hearts in the breasts of the soldiers,
Even as many as had not heard the plan of the council.
Then as the multitude moved like long sea-furrowing surges —
Such from th' Icarian main are the winds, both Eurus and Notus,
Wont to upheave, when bursting from clouds of the Father Cronion.
Even as Zephyr, in coming, the deep corn setteth in motion,
Rushing impetuous on it, the heads all bowing before it:
Likewise moved were the folk through all the assembly. With shouting
Off to the galleys they rushed precipitate. Under their footsteps
Rose up the dust in the clouds, while orders they gave one another:
''Lay hold straight on the galleys and hale to the sun-bright waters!''
Yearning for homeland, they hurried to clear the launch-trenches and draw
Props placed under the ships, while the clamor ascended to heaven.　[out
　　Then 'gainst the orders of Fate return had been found for the
Had not Hera addressed this word unto Pallas Athena:　　　　[Argives,
　　''Ay me, daughter of Zeus, the aegis-bearer, thou tireless!
So shall the Argives flee o'er the broad-backed billowy waters
Once more homeward again, to the well loved lands of their fathers,
Leaving behind as a boast unto Priam and Trojans the woman,
Helen of Argos — Helen, for whose sake many Achaeans
Perished in Troyland, far from the dear homeland of their fathers?
Come now, go 'mid the folk of the bronze-mailed, martial Achaeans
(There to restrain each hero with thy soft words of persuasion);
Do not allow them to drag their gallant ships to the salt sea.''
　　So spake Hera; and heedful the bright-eyed goddess Athena
Dropped like a flash at once from the pinnacle peaks of Olympus;
Speedily, too, she arrived at the galleys swift of the Argives.
Quickly she found that peer of Cronion in counsel, Odysseus,
Standing; but never a hand did he lay on his sable and well-benched
Galley, for anguish had entered the mind and the heart of the hero.
Standing near to Odysseus, the bright-eyed Pallas addressed him:

"Zeus-born son of Laërtes, Odysseus of many devices,
So will ye tumble aboard and flee in your many-benched galleys
Homeward away, each man to the dear-loved land of his fathers?
Leaving behind for a boast unto Priam and Trojans the woman,
Helen of Argos — Helen, for whose sake many Achaeans
Perished in Troyland, afar from the dear homeland of their fathers?
Tarry no longer; away! Hie hence to the folk of Achaia,
There to restrain each hero with thy soft words of persuasion;
Do not allow them to drag down their gallant ships to the salt sea."

Thus far Pallas. He knew by her voice what goddess had spoken,
Started to run, flung off him his cloak — Eurybates took it,
Herald from Ithaca's shore, who always waited upon him.
When he had come unto Atreus's son, Agamemnon, the hero
Took at his hands that sceptre, inherited, ever-enduring,
Sped therewith to the ships of the bronze-mailed heroes Achaean.

Whomsoe'er he encountered — a prince or a man of distinction —
Drawing anigh he would check any such with a word of persuasion:
"Good sir, thee it becomes not to fall into cowardly terror.
Rather be seated thyself and induce other folks to be seated.
Not yet clearly thou knowest what may be the mind of Atrides.
Now he is making a test but will soon press hard on the Argives —
We have not all understood what rede he hath spoken in council.
Take heed, lest in his anger he evil-entreat the Achaeans.
Terrible may be the wrath of a king, a ruler Zeus-nurtured;
Honor is his from Zeus, the master of counsel, that loves him." [ing,

Whom of the people, however, he saw, and discovered him shout-
Him with the sceptre he smote and with words, too, roundly upbraided:
"Sit down still, good fellow, and hark to the bidding of others,
Men thy betters; for thou art unwarlike, only a weakling,
Never accounted in battle, nor yet again ever in council.
No way all of us here can be kings, us many Achaeans;
Neither is ruling by many a good; let one be the ruler,
One king, to whom the son of Cronus, the crooked-in-counsel, [you."
Sceptre and judgments hath given, that he may be sovereign among

Thus he, masterful, strode through the host; while they in a tumult
Back to the conclave sped in a throng from the galleys and barracks,

36

Clamorous, like as the voice of the sea's loud-thundering billow
Roars on a rock-bound coast, and the deep-sea welter resoundeth.
Now were the rest all seated and silently held in their places;
Only Thersites still kept up an immoderate chatter,
Who well knew in his heart words many, disordered, unseemly,
Fitted for quarreling vainly with kings — though never in order —
Only whatever he thought most likely to prove for the Argives
Laughable. Most ill-favored of all that had come unto Troyland,
Bow-legged, lame in one foot also — both of his shoulders
Crooked and bent round down on his breast, while, over above them,
Twisted, his pate shot up, and sparse was the stubble upon it.
Unto Achilles he was and Odysseus signally hateful;
Both he was wont to revile. This time on divine Agamemnon
Heaping abuses, he shrieked with a shrill voice. Him the Achaeans,
Grievously vexed in soul, now viewed with deep indignation.
He now kept on bawling and railing against Agamemnon:

"Atreïd, what new complaint hast thou? What findest thou lacking?
Filled are thy tents already with bronze, and many a woman
Serves thy barrack besides, prime choice, whom we, the Achaeans,
Give unto thee first of all, whenever we capture a city.
Gold peradventure thou lackest, which one of the horse-taming Trojans
Bringeth from Troy to ransom a son, whom I or some other
Hero Achaean has taken and brought in captive in fetters?
Or is it haply a maid's full bloom, thy dalliance to pleasure,
Whom thou wouldst keep for thyself apart from the others? Unseemly
Thus for a ruler to bring unto ruin the sons of Achaia!
Faint hearts! Bywords! No more men; mere women of Argos!
Homeward! Home let us fare in our ships, abandoning yon man
Here to digest his prizes in Troyland! So may he find out
Whether insooth we commoners also afford him assistance,
Him who browbeat lately a man far better than he is,
Taking Achilles' prize for himself (the despoiler!) — and keeps it!
Yet no wrath in the mind of Achilles, spiritless fellow!
Else this insult of thine were the last for thee, Agamemnon."

Railing with words like these at Atrides, shepherd of peoples,
Ranted Thersites. Quickly beside him noble Odysseus

Stood. With a scowl he looked and rebuked him in terrible accents:

"Endless babbler, Thersites, a clear-voiced speaker, I grant thee!
Hold thy peace. Think not to be striving singly with princes.
No other one, I maintain, is baser than thou of all mortals
Who with the sons of Atreus came under Ilium's towers.
Dare not with kings' names, then, on thy lips go prating about here,
Heaping reproaches upon them and looking for homeward returning.
We are by no means yet full ware how standeth the matter,
Whether for weal or for woe her sons would return to Achaia.
Therefore now thou sittest reviling the shepherd of peoples,
Atreus' son, Agamemnon, because these Danaan heroes
Load him with gifts in plenty; and tauntingly thou dost address him.
Now will I tell thee a word most sure of fulfilment:
If I again ever catch thee playing the fool as at present,
No more then may the head of Odysseus sit on his shoulders
Safe; nor again let me ever be called Telemachus' father,
If I shall fail to take thee and strip thee of thy precious raiment,
Mantle and tunic and all that thy nakedness hides, and in such wise
Back to the swift-keeled galleys in loud lamentation expel thee,
Beaten and driven with blows of dishonor from out the assembly."

Thus far Ithaca's prince; then both on his back and his shoulders
Smote with the staff. He cringed; big tears slipped out from his eyelids,
Whileas a weal all crimson and bloody arose on the hunchback
Under the staff of gold; and he sat down dumb and affrighted,
Smarting with pain, looked foolish, and brushed off tears from his visage.
Grieved as they were, however, the rest laughed merrily at him,
Whispering also a word, one man, as he glanced at another:

"Well! good works ten thousand, I ween, hath Odysseus accom-
Leading in excellent counsel, as well as arraying for battle.   [plished,
Natheless the best by far he hath wrought e'en now for the Argives,
Since it is he hath estopped this vile word-slinger from speaking.
Hardly again will his insolent heart stir *him*, as I fancy,
Reverend kings to revile with his sland'rous reproaches."

So, as the crowd made murmur, Odysseus, sacker of cities,
Stood up, sceptre in hand, while bright-eyed Pallas beside him,
Guising herself as a herald, commanded the folk to be silent,

So that the sons of Achaeans all, both nearest and farthest,
Hearing alike what he said, might equally ponder his counsel.
He then, friendliest-minded, haranguing addressed the assembly:
    "Atreus' son, the Achaeans are right now minded to make thee
Henceforth chief in dishonor of all men fated to perish,
Nor would accomplish a promise they surely pledged thee aforetime —
While on the way still marching from Argos, pasture of horses —
Ilium's well-walled city to sack ere sailing for homeland,
Seeing that even like children, like babes or widowèd women
Each unto each they are wailing for speedy return to Achaia!
Truly, the toil is well fitted to send one home in vexation;
For whoever afar from his wife even *one month* tarries
Frets in his full-benched ship, when boisterous blasts of the winter
Hem him about and the sea, by storm winds roused to a fury.
Yet is for us now even the *ninth year* slowly revolving,
That we are tarrying here. So I do not blame the Achaeans
Howe'er fretting beside their beakèd galleys. But wholly
Shameful it were to remain so long and return empty-handed.
Nay, dear friends, let us stay and endure for a while. Peradventure
Thus we may learn about Calchas, if truly or no he divineth.
For in our hearts we remember full well — all ye will attest it,
All that the fates of death have not taken. Yesterday only
Or but the day before, the Argive galleys were gath'ring,
Meeting at Aulis, freighted with woes for Priam and Troia.
We, at the hallowèd altars, about a fair-flowing fountain,
Hecatombs perfect, as gifts to the gods immortal, were off'ring
Under a plane tree fair, whence clear, bright water was flowing.
Wondrous, a portent appeared! With back all crimson, a serpent,
Fearful to see — which truly th' Olympian's self unto daylight
Sent forth — darted from under the altar and sped to the plane tree.
There in the tree were sparrows, tender little ones, fledglings,
Nestling under the leaves of the plane tree's uppermost branches,
Eight, and the mother the ninth, who herself had brooded the young
All of the eight the serpent devour'd, as they piteous twittered. [ones.
Then while the mother, bewailing her offspring, fluttered about him,
Coiling himself, the snake caught *her* by a wing, as she circled

Crying. And then, having swallowed alike both brood and the mother,
Lo! he was made a conspicuous sign by the god that revealed him—
Turned into stone by the scion of Cronus crooked-in-counsel.
We, as we stood there, marveled and murmured: 'Miraculous wonder!'
Seeing a direful portent thus interrupted the service.
Calchas prophesied straightway, declaring the purpose of heaven:
   " 'Why are ye thus struck dumb, ye long-haired heroes Achaean?
Zeus it is, master of counsel, hath shown us a marvelous omen,
Late come, late of fulfilment; the fame of it never shall perish.
E'en as the snake devoured these nestlings and with them the mother,
Eight, and the mother the ninth, who herself had brooded the young
Likewise we shall be warring for nine long years over yonder, [ones,
Then in the tenth year capture the wide-wayed city of Troia.'
Such the address of the augur, and all moves sure to fulfilment.
Come then, here let us stay, all ye well-greavèd Achaeans,
Stay right here till we capture the strong-built fortress of Priam."
   Thus far he; and the Argives lustily shouted. The war-ships
All round terribly echoed the loud applause of the Argives,
Voicing acclaim to the word of the godlike Ithacan hero.
Thereupon also addressed them Gerenian Nestor, the horseman:
   "Fie on it! Now of a truth ye speak like children in council,
Babes, indeed, whom noway the business of battle concerneth.
What then shall come of our compacts, and what of the oaths we have
Cast to the flames all counsels and skilful devices of heroes, [given?
Yea, our unmixed libations and pledges of faith that we trusted!
Vainly we wrangle in words, mere words, nor can we discover
Any way out, although for a long time here we have tarried.
Atreus' son, with resolve unshakable now as aforetime
March at the head of the Argives and lead into strenuous battle!
Suffer them merely to perish, if one or two of the Argives
Privately plan—though naught of their plans ever comes to a finish—
Homeward to sail unto Argos, or ever we know if the promise
Zeus who wieldeth the aegis hath made be true or a falsehood.
For I declare that Cronus' son, most mighty, erst nodded—
Even the day we embarked, we Achaean chiefs on our Argive
Ships, full laden with slaughter and doom for the people of Troia—

Lightning gleams on our right proclaiming his omen of favor.
Therefore, none of you hasten to turn back cravenly homeward,
Ere with a captive he couches, a war-won wife of a Trojan,
So to avenge the longings and deep groans uttered by Helen.
Let him — if any desire past measure to sail to the homeland —
Let him forsooth put his hand to his well-decked, dark-colored galley,
So to encounter his death and his doom, and ahead of his comrades!
Sage, O king, thy counsel, thy own; heed also another's.
Not to be slighted, insooth, this saying that now I shall utter:
Muster the men by tribes, likewise by clans, Agamemnon —
Tribe unto tribe, yea, clan unto clan, will thus lend assistance.
Haply if thou *do* so, and if the Achaeans obey thee,
Then thou'lt know what captains are base, what commoners also,
Ay, who also are valiant — for then groupwise they will battle —
Know, too, whether 'tis heaven forbiddeth the sack of the city
Or men's cowardice only and ignorance utter of warfare."

   Thereto in answer addressed him in this wise Lord Agamemnon:
   "Yea, sire, again in the council thou hast outdone the Achaeans.
Would that, O Father Zeus and Athena and Phoebus Apollo,
Ten such Achaeans were mine, like thee, such fellows in counsel!
Then would the city of Priam, the king, right speedily topple,
Haply of our own hands both taken and utterly wasted.
But it is aegis-bearing Zeus that appointeth me sorrows,
Cronus' son — *he* hath involved me in wrangles unending and quarrels,
Seeing that we two strove for a damsel, I and Achilles,
Both of us violent-tongued, though I was the first to be angered.
But if in counsel we ever agree, no longer will thenceforth
Respite from evil remain for the Trojans — not even a little.
Now then each to his dinner, that all may join battle together!
Well let him sharpen his spear, each man set firmly his buckler;
Well let him also provide for his fleet-foot horses their fodder;
Well let him test in all points his car, made ready for combat!
So that the whole day long we may measure our strength in dread
Never a pause interrupting the strife for even a moment —   [battle —
Or ever night oncoming shall stop the fury of warriors.
Sweat upon breast, upon shoulder, shall stream forth under the baldric

Bearing the shield, man's warder, and hands grow weary of javelins —
Sweat gush forth on the courser that tugs at the well-polished war-car.
Whomso haply aloof from the fight I discover, desiring
Here at the curved-beaked galleys to loiter in safety, by no means
He shall escape: thereafter the dogs and the birds shall devour him."

    Thus spake he; and the Argives shouted aloud, as a billow
Roars on a headland high, when the south wind's impetus drives it
Full on a cliff far-jutting and never forsaken of surges
Driven by contrary blasts, now here now yonder arising.
Then they arose. Dispersing, they hastened away to the galleys,
Lit up fires in the barracks, made ready, and there had their dinner,
Offering sacrifice each to one of the gods everlasting,
Praying deliv'rance from death in the war and the tumult of Ares.
Now as the monarch of men, Agamemnon, offered a bullock,
Fatted and five years old, to Zeus supreme in his power,
Elders he also invited, the princes of all the Achaeans,
Nestor foremost in line and Idomeneus, sovereign of Creta,
Next the Ajaxes twain, then Tydeus' son, Diomedes;
Sixth in turn was Odysseus, in counsel the peer of Cronion;
Came of his own will, too, Menelaüs, good at the war-cry,
Knowing in heart full well how heavy the toil of his brother.
Then as they gathered about the ox and uplifted the barley,
King Agamemnon lifted his voice in prayer 'mid the people:
    "Zeus, most glorious, greatest, in cloud wrapt, dwelling in heaven,
Let not the sun go down, nor the night-gloom settle upon us,
Till unto earth I shall cast in ruins the palace of Priam,
Blackened with smoke, consumed with a ravaging fire the doorways;
Let me, too, with my sword from Hector's breast rend the tunic,
Cleft with my weapon of bronze. Let many brave comrades about him,
Falling prone in the dust, with their teeth bite the earth in their death-

    Thus spake he; but Cronion would not yet grant him   [throes."
True, he accepted the victim but multiplied toils unabating. [fulfilment.
When they had prayed, they sprinkled the unground grains of the barley
First, then drew back the victim's head, then slaughtered and flayed it,
Out of the thighs cut slices, in caul-fat folded the pieces,
Making the slices two-folded and laid raw collops upon them.

These they consumed on billets of cleft-wood, leafless, with fire,
Spitting the vitals and holding them over the flame of Hephaestus.
Now, as the thighs were consumed, and they of the vitals had tasted,
All of the rest they divided; with spits then piercing the pieces,
Roasted them carefully each, then drew off all of the slices.
Now as the task was accomplished and so made ready the feasting,
Feasted they all—no heart felt stint of a well-balanced banquet.
Then when desire for meat and for drink together was banished,
Straight did Nestor begin to speak, the Gerenian horseman:

"Atreus' son, most glorious, thou monarch of men, Agamemnon,
Here let us end these parleys and now, no longer delaying,
Speed with the work that God to our hands is clearly committing.
Come then, order the heralds to make proclamation and gather
All the host of the bronze-mailed Achaeans in front of the galleys.
Let us commanders review this wide war-host of the Argives
Groupwise, thus to arouse keen Ares haply the sooner."

Thus he spake. The monarch of men, Agamemnon, obeyed him.
Straight he commanded the clear-voiced heralds to make proclamation,
Summoning them forthwith to the war, those long-haired Achaeans.
Those then shouted the summons, and these full quickly assembled.
Also the princes, nurslings of Zeus, that surrounded Atrides,
Eagerly worked as they marshaled, and bright-eyed Pallas amid them,
Wearing the reverend aegis, unaging for aye and immortal,
Whereon tassels a hundred of pure gold, cunningly woven,
Wave in the air—of each a hundred oxen the value.
Therewith dazzling the sight, as she sped through the host of Achaeans,
Spurring them forward, Athena aroused in the bosom of each one
Might past bounds unto battle and warfare long and unceasing.
Forthwith war became sweeter by far unto them than returning
Home in the hollow ships to the dear-loved land of their fathers.

Like as a ravaging fire inflameth a limitless forest
High on a mountain's top, and the gleam appeareth afar off:
So, as they marched, from the bronze of weapons uncounted the fulgence,
Flashing its sheen all round, through ether ascended to heaven.

Even as tribes full many of feathered fowl of the heavens
(Cranes it may be, or of long-necked swans, or of wild geese haply)

There on the Asian mead, by the stream of Caÿstrus river,
Hither and thither are flutt'ring with pinions joyously flapping,
Settling with loud cries ever afore, and the meadow resoundeth:
So from the barracks and galleys the tribes, full many in number,
Poured forth over the plain of Scamander; the earth underneath them
Terribly echoed beneath their feet and the feet of the horses.
Now in the mead of Scamander, a-blooming with flowers, they halted
Numberless, many as blossoms and leaves that come forth in the spring-

Likewise, too, as the bevies of flies thick-swarming are many, [time.
What time, buzzing about, at a herdsman's steading they hover,
When, in the spring-tide season, the bright milk drenches the vessels:
So many, facing the Trojans, the long-haired heroes Achaean
Stood in the plain, all eager to rend them asunder in battle.

Even as goatherds divide the wide-ranging goats in a pasture
Easily, when by chance the flocks have mingled together:
So the commanders arrayed them to one and another position,
Ready to enter the conflict; among them the Lord Agamemnon,
Like in his eyes, in his head, unto Zeus, the hurler of thunder,
Girth of an Ares his, with a breast like unto Poseidon's —
E'en as a bull in a herd over all preëminent tow'reth
High in the midst of the kine, conspicuous far in the pasture;
So it was Zeus made there, upon *that* day, King Agamemnon
Eminent, high amid many, and foremost far of the heroes.

Tell me now, ye Muses, who dwell in the halls of Olympus,
Since ye are goddesses, ever at hand, with a knowledge of all things —
We hear only report, we know for a certainty nothing —
Who were the chieftains leading the Danaans, who their commanders.
But of the privates I could not give the numbers or name them,
E'en though ten were my tongues, my mouths so many in number,
Voice unwearied mine, and my heart, too, bronzen within me,
Did not the daughters of Zeus who wieldeth the aegis, Olympian
Muses, call to my mind how many there came against Troia.
Yet the commanders at least and their war-ships all I will mention.

·   Now of Boeotians, first, were Peneleos, Leïtus leaders,
Clonius, too, Prothoënor, and also Arcesilaüs;
Whoso inhabited Hyria and likewise Aulis the rocky,

Schoenus and Scolus as well and the myriad-ridged Eteonus,
Graia, too, Mycalessus of wide lawns, also Thespeia;
They who dwelt about Harma, Ilesium, yea, and Erythrae,
Dwellers in Eleon too, and in Hyle and Peteon likewise,
Ay, of Ocalea too, and Medeon's well-builded city,
Copae as well, Eutresis, and Thisbe haunted of pigeons;
All they who Coroneia, and who Haliartus the grassy,
All that Plataea possessed, ay, they who inhabited Glisas,
They that dwelt in the well-built city of Thebae the Lower,
Holy Onchestus as well, that glorious grove of Poseidon;
They that the vine-rich Arne possessed, yea, those that Mideia,
Nisa the sacred as well, ay, uttermost-lying Anthedon.
Two score galleys and ten bore Troyward these — upon each one
Youths Boeotian embarked, in number a hundred and twenty.

All that were homed in Aspledon, Orchomenus too, of the Minyae,
Them did Ascalaphus lead and Ialmenus, children of Ares,
Whom to the powerful god, in the palace of Azeïd Actor,
August maiden Astyoche bore erewhile; for she entered
Lonely her chamber above, and the god lay privily with her.
Thirty the hollow ships that bore these heroes to Troia.

Schedius led — and with him Epistrophus — Phocian warriors,
Both of them sons of Iphitus, the great-souled, of Naubolus scion —
Those who possessed Cyparissus and likewise Pytho the rocky,
Panopeus also and Crisa, the favored of heaven, and Daulis;
Those who dwelt in the round of Hyampolis, Anemoreia
Also, and lived on the banks of the sun-bright river Cephissus,
Who at Cephissus' springs were owners as well of Lilaia.
Black ships forty in number with these clans followed to Troia.
Busy were both as they marshaled in files that Phocian people,
Stationed there on the left, hard by the lines of Boeotians.

Captain of Locris' men was swift Ajax, son of Oïleus
(Ajax the less, not at all like great Telamonian Ajax;
Nay, he was less by far, small even, with corselet of linen,
Yet with the lance surpassing Hellenes all and Achaeans),
Such as inhabited Cynus, Calliarus also, and Opus,
Bessa and Scarphe as well, and Augeiae's loveliness also,

45

Tarphe and Thronium too, by the streams of Boagrius river.
Forty the black ships numbered that followed Oïlean Ajax,
Galleys of Locrians dwelling across from Euboea the holy.

Such as Euboea possessed — the Abantes, breathers of fury —
Chalcis, Eretria too, and the vine-clad town Histiaea,
Seaside keep of Cerinthus, the lofty fortress of Dium,
Such as Carystus possessed, yea, men that inhabited Styra —
Leader of all these clans, Elephenor, scion of Ares,
Son of Chalcodon, commander of all great-hearted Abantes.
Him the Abantes fleet, with their back hair long, swiftly followed —
Followed as spearmen and eager, with spear-shafts ashen extended
Forward, to shatter the corselets of bronze on the breasts of their foe-
Black ships forty in number with this chief followed to Troia.   [men.

Then, too, they that possessed the well-built city of Athens,
Realm of Erechtheus, mighty of soul, whom one time Athena,
Daughter of Zeus, had fostered, when Earth, grain-giver, had borne
Also in Athens she gave him her own rich shrine for a dwelling.   [him;
Still are Athenian youths, as the years roll round in their courses,
Ever accustomed with bulls and with young rams slain to appease him.
All these levies were led by Peteos' son, brave Menestheus.
Nowhere like unto him was there any of earth-born mortals
Skilful to marshal both cars and warriors, bearers of bucklers;
Nestor alone was a rival, for he by birth was the elder.
Black ships fifty in number with this chief followed to Troia.

Ajax from Salamis led his warships; twelve was the number
(Led them and stationed them where the Athenians stood in battalions).

They who dwelt in Argos and Tiryns, mighty of ramparts,
Asine too, and Hermione, deep gulf-waters enfolding,
Troezen, Eïonae too, and the vine-rich deme Epidaurus;
They that possessed Aegina and Mases, youths of Achaeans —
All these followed as chief Diomedes, good at the war-cry,
Sthenelus too (and of him was the far-famed Capaneus father).
Third in the company came Euryalus, godlike warrior,
Son of Mecisteus, him that was Talaüs' son and a sovereign.
Diomed over them all with his loud war-cry, was commander.
Black ships followed along with these war-chiefs — eighty in number.

They too who dwelt in Mycenae, that well-built city and fortress,
Corinth the wealthy as well, and the well-built town of Cleonae;
Who Araethyrea, the lovely, inhabited, also Orneiae,
Sicyon too, wherein at the first was Adrestus the monarch;
They that the high-built town Hyperesia, steep Gonoëssa,
Yea, and Pellene possessed, all round about Aegium dwelling,
Habiting all that coast, all Helice's wide-drawn circuit —
All in their galleys a hundred were led of the Lord Agamemnon,
Atreus' son. The most, yea, the goodliest far of the peoples
Followed with him. Himself in his armor of bronze all refulgent
Gloried among them and shone preëminent 'mid all the heroes,
Seeing that he was the best and led the goodliest numbers.

Those who dwelt 'neath the steep ravines of stern Lacedaemon,
Cities of Pharis and Sparta, with Messa abounding in pigeons;
Such as Briseia inhabited, too, and Augeiae the lovely;
Such as Amyclae possessed and the seaside castle of Helos;
Dwellers of Laas, and all in the district of Oetylus dwelling —
These his brother led, Menelaüs, good at the war-cry.
Sixty the ships he commanded, apart in array from his brother's;
'Mongst his people he moved, on his own zeal proudly reliant,
Urging them onward to war, outdoing the others in ardor,
Set to avenge the longings and deep groans uttered by Helen.

Such as inhabited Pylus afar and lovely Arene,
Thryum, ford of Alpheüs, a well-built borough of Aepy;
Such as in Cyparisseïs and Amphigeneia were dwellers,
Pteleüs also, and Helos, and Dorium — where had the Muses
Lighted on Thamyris, Thracian, and ended his singing forever,
Whileas he fared from Oechalia, from Eurytus' home, in Oechalia —
He that averred with a vaunt he would conquer, with even the Muses,
Daughters of Zeus who wieldeth the aegis, singing against him.
Dumb then smote him in anger the Maidens, reft him of singing,
Gift of the gods, and they made him forget his skill as a harper —
All these forces the knightly Gerenian Nestor commanded.
Ninety the hollow ships that sailed in array with this hero.

Under the mountainous steep of Cyllene, such as Arcadia
Held near Aepytus' tomb, where men join close in the battle;

47

Men of Orchomenus, rich in flocks, and in Pheneüs dwelling,
Rhipe, Stratia too, and the bald, wind-beaten Enispe;
Tegea also was theirs and withal Mantinea the lovely;
Such as possessed Stymphalus and dwelt in Parrhasia city —
These it was Lord Agapenor, Ancaeus' son, that commanded.
Sixty in number his galleys; and on each ship there were many
Heroes embarked — Arcadian men who were skilful in warfare.
King of men, Agamemnon himself, for them had provided
Well-benched vessels for crossing the wine-dark face of the waters;
Ships of their own had they none, for them sea-faring concerned not.

They that dwelt in Buprasium and also in Elis the goodly —
Even as far as Hyrmine and Myrsinus, built on the borders,
Bound with Olenian Rock and Alesium-city between them —
Four were leaders of these, and ten ships followed with each one,
Galleys gallant and swift, with many Epeians aboard them.
Thalpius led one part, Amphimachus jointly commanding,
Actorids — this one of Cteatus, th' other of Eurytus, scion.
Doughty Diores headed a troop, Amarynceus' offspring;
Fourth was a company led by a godlike chief, Polyxinus,
Son of Agasthenes, sovereign himself and a son of Augeas.

Those of Dulichium, too, and the hallowed Isles Echineän,
Situate far off over the salt sea, opposite Elis.
Meges Phylides, of Ares the peer, of these was the leader —
He whom Phyleus, horseman beloved of Zeus, had begotten.
Wroth with his father this Phyleus had moved to Dulichium erstwhile.
With him followed along black ships some forty in number.

All Cephallenian folk, stanch yeomen, were led of Odysseus:
Holders of Ithaca's isle and of Neritum waving its leafage;
Dwellers in far Crocyleia and Aegilips island, the rugged;
They that woody Zacynthus possessed and inhabited Samos;
Such as the mainland owned and dwelt in, skirting the waters;
These Odysseus, the peer of Zeus in counsel, commanded.
Twelve ships followed with him, their prow-cheeks painted vermilion.

Now of Aetolians Thoas, the son of Andraemon, was leader —
Such as inhabited Pleuron and Olenus, also Pylene,
Chalcis that lay on the shore of Aetolia, Calydon rocky —

Seeing the children of Oeneus, the mighty of spirit, had perished,
Neither himself lived longer — and dead was the fair Meleäger.
So was committed to Thoas alone to rule the Aetolians.
Black ships forty in number with him sailed on to the muster.

Spear-famed wielder of lances Idomeneus marshaled the Cretans,
Them the possessors of Cnossus and Gortyn, mighty of ramparts,
Lyctus, Miletus as well, and the chalk-cliffed, gleamy Lycastus,
Phaestus and Rhytium too — all towns well-peopled with dwellers.
All of the rest that were dwelling in Creta, century-citied,
Unto the muster were led of Idomeneus, spearman renownèd,
Him and Meriones, match for the war-god, slayer of heroes.
Black war-galleys, in number some four score, followed these leaders.

Next came Heracles' son, Tlepolemus, goodly and mighty.
Nine were the galleys from Rhodes that he led, of impetuous Rhodians,
Such as inhabited Rhodes in a threefold order established,
Both Ialysus and Lindus and chalk-cliffed, gleamy Camirus —
All these spearman renowned, Tlepolemus, led to the muster,
He that was born unto Heracles mighty by Astyocheia,
Maiden he led from Ephyra-town on the river Selleïs,
After sacking many a city of Zeus-nurtured valiants.
Now had Tlepolemus, reared in the well-walled palace to manhood,
Slain, soon after, his father's maternal uncle belovèd,
Even Licymnius, scion of Arcs, aging already.
Thereat quickly he builded him ships, then gath'ring a cohort
Round him he fled far over the sea, for they threatened to kill him,
Even the rest of the mighty Heracles' sons and his grandsons.
So had he come unto Rhodes in his wand'ring, suffering hardships.
Tripart there they are settled, his people, in clans; and Cronion
Loved them, Zeus that is lord in sway over men and immortals
All, and he poured out upon them abundance of riches from heaven.

Nireus led three only of trim-rigged galleys from Syme,
Nireus, son of Aglaia (his father was Charopus mighty) —
Nireus, fairest of men in the muster at Ilium city,
Fairest of Danaans all, save only the faultless Pelides;
Howbeit *he* was a weakling, and scanty his forces that followed.

Such as Nisyros possessed and the Carpathos island and Casos,

Cos that was town of Eurypylus, too, and the isles of Calydnae —
All these Antiphus headed along with Phidippus, his brother.
These were sons of Heracles' son, King Thessalus, mighty.
Thirty in all were the hollow ships that bore them to Troyland.

Now, moreover, as many as dwelt in Pelasgian Argos,
All that inhabited Alus and Alope also and Trachis,
All the possessors of Phthia and Hellas of beautiful women,
Such as were Myrmidons called and Hellenes, also Achaeans —
These men's galleys, fifty in number, were led by Achilles.
None of them gave any thought, howbeit, to dissonant warfare,
Seeing that no one remained to array them in line for the battle.
Idle among the ships lay the fleet-footed, godlike Achilles,
Wroth for the sake of the fair-haired maiden, Briseïs, his captive,
Whom erewhile he had won at Lyrnessus in arduous travail,　　　[sus,
What time once he had razed to the ground Thebè's walls and Lyrnes-
Laid low Mynes and with him Epiſtrophus, famous as spearmen —
Both of them sons of Selepius' son, the royal Evenus.
Lying in sorrow for her sake now, he was soon to be rising!

Dwellers in Phylace, also in Pyrasus blooming with flowers,
Close of Demeter; and Iton, of flocks a mother prolific;
Antron splashed by the sea and Pteleüs bedded in grasses —
All these Protesilaüs in turn, the martial, commanded
While yet alive; already the black earth held him a captive;
Lone in Phylace-city his wife wept, marring her visage,
There in his house half-built. For him a Dardanian warrior
Slew, as he leaped from his galley, by far the first of Achaeans.
Yet were his men not leaderless left, sore-grieved for their leader:
Quickly a marshal was found, Podarces, scion of Ares,
Son of Iphiclus, Phylacus' son, the owner of many
Flocks, own brother himself of the great-souled Protesilaüs.
Younger was he by birth; the other was older and braver,
Protesilaüs, the hero, the warlike. Natheless the people
Lacked not a leader at all, though mourning a noble one fallen.
Black ships forty in number followed along with the hero.

They that along the lake Boebeian were dwelling in Pherae,
Boebe, Glaphyrae too, and the well-built town of Iolcus —

They in eleven ships were led by the son of Admetus,
Loved Eumelus — Alcestis had borne him, fair among women,
She that was held most goodly in form of Pelias' daughters.

They that were wont to dwell in Thaumacia-town and Methone,
Such as possessed Meliboea and dwelt in rugged Olizon —
Their ships, seven in number, were led by the great Philoctetes,
Cunning in archery. Rowers embarked on each of the galleys,
Fifty, to battle amain, well knowing the art of the bowman.
He lay lone on an island, in anguish, sorely afflicted;
Lone upon Lemnos goodly the sons of Achaia had left him
Wofully vexed with a wound from a water-snake, venemous viper.
There he was pining in pain. Meanwhile the Argives were destined
Soon beside their ships to bethink them of king Philoctetes.
Yet were his men not left unled, sore-grieved for their leader:
Medon was marshal for them, a bastard son of Oïleus,
He whom Rhene had borne to Oïleus, sacker of cities.

Who were of Tricca possessed and Ithome, rocky and terraced,
Who of Oechalia, city of Eurytus, famous Oechalian —
Twain were the leaders that led them. Both were Asclepius' children,
Excellent leeches, the one Podalirius, the other Machaon.
Thirty the hollow ships that moved with these warriors to Troyland.

They that possessed Ormenium or drank from the fount Hypereia,
They that Asterium owned and Titanus' battlements gleaming —
These did Eurypylus captain, the valiant son of Euaemon.
Forty black ships followed him on the expedition to Troyland.

They that Argissa possessed and all that dwelt in Gyrtona,
Orthe, Elone as well, and the chalk-white town Oloösson —
Leader of these was a chief unflinching in fight, Polypoetes,
Son of Pirithoüs, hero begotten of Zeus the immortal.
Far-famed Hippodamia, Pirithoüs' bride, had conceived him,
What time the sire had punished those wild folk, shaggy and monstrous,
Drave them from Pelion, chased to the far-west tribes of Aethices.
Not sole leader, but with him Leonteus, scion of Ares,
He that was son of Coronus, the great-souled offspring of Caeneus.
Forty black ships followed them on the voyage to Troyland. ⌈Cyphus.

Twenty and two were the galleys that Guneus headed from

Him Enienes followed and, steadfast in war, the Peraebians.
These were a folk that had founded them homes round wintry Dodona;
They who were busied on farms on the banks of the bright Titaresius,
Emptying into Peneüs his fair-flowing torrent of water—
Yet he commingles it not with the silvery eddies Peneian;
Like unto smooth oil rather in broad flow on and above them
Glides; since he is a branch of the dread oath-river, the Stygian.

  Prothoüs, fleet-footed son of Tenthredon, led the Magnetes,
Dwellers about the Peneüs and Pelion's foliage-waving
Mount; it was they that then the fleet-footed Prothoüs marshaled.
Black ships forty in number came following him unto Troyland.

  So then these were the Danaan leaders, these the commanders.
Tell now, I pray, O Muse, who foremost far was among them,
Whether of men or of horses, that followed the Atreïd brothers.
Goodliest far of the horses were those of the scion of Pheres,
Mares that Eumelus drove, like birds of the heavens in fleetness,
Coated and agèd alike, their backs, too, straight as an arrow.
These the god of the silver bow had bred in Pereia—
Both fleet mares that carried right onward the terror from Ares.
But of the men, by far, Telamonian Ajax was strongest,
Pending the wrath of Achilles; for *he* transcended the others
Greatly—he and the steeds of his war-car—blameless Pelides.
He, however, in wrath with the shepherd of hosts, Agamemnon,
Atreus' son, at his ships whose curved beaks furrowed the waters
Now lay idle. His folk, on the seashore sounding with surges,
Found their pleasure in throwing the disk and casting the javelin,
Shooting the bow; the while at the war-wains waited the horses,
Each at his own car champing the marsh-grown parsley and clover.
Idle they stood; and the war-chiefs' cars, all carefully covered,
Lay in the huts. Men yearned for their leader, belovèd of Ares,
Wand'ring hither and thither in camp and aloof from the battle.

                [ing.
  So were they marching along, as if fire the whole earth were wast-
Earth groaned under their tread as at Zeus, dread launcher of lightnings,
When in his wrath he lashes the region that girdles Typhoeus,

Land of the Arimi, where (men say) is the giant embedded.
Thus then under their feet did the earth groan under their marching —
Mightily groan; and over the plain they were swiftly advancing.

　　Wind-footed Iris anon, fleet messenger, came to the Trojans,
Bringing from aegis-bearing Zeus a dolorous message.
They at the doors of Priam had been debating in council,
All, both the young and the old, in council assembled together.
Taking her stand hard by them, the fleet-footed Iris addressed them,
Lik'ning her voice unto that of Polites, scion of Priam.
He did sentinel duty for Troy, on his fleetness reliant,
Wont to sit on the top of the barrow of old Aesyëtes,
Watching if e'er the Achaeans should issue in force from the galleys.
So in Polites' semblance the fleet-footed Iris addressed him:
　　"Old man, ever to thee words endless in number are pleasant
Just as in days of peace; but a war unabating is risen.
Verily, oft I have entered the battles of heroes, exceeding
Oft, but have never beheld so goodly a host and so many.
Like to the leaves of the forest are they or sands of the seaside,
Over the champaign marching, to bring war nigh to the city.
Hector, especially thee do I charge to accomplish my saying.
Seeing how many allies now throng the great city of Priam,
Yea, and the tongues are diverse of diverse and far-scattered peoples,
Let now the order be given by each unto whom he commandeth;
Them let him lead forth now, each chieftain his countrymen marshal."
　　Thus she. And Hector failed not to know the voice of the goddess.
Straight he adjourned the assembly. To arms rushed all in a moment.
Then, as the gates all swung wide open, out poured the people,
Footmen and horsemen together; and mighty the din they awakened.
　　There is an eminence steep, and it lieth in front of the city
Out on the plain, apart; and clear space spreads all about it.
Mortal men are accustomed to call this mound "Batieia";
Gods, however, immortal, "the Barrow of lissome Myrine."
There then allies and Trojans divided their several armies.
　　Chief of the Trojans *he*, great shimmering-helmeted Hector,
Priam's son; and with him the goodliest far of the people,

Bravest and most, were arrayed, all eager for battle with lances.

Next the Dardanians followed the stalwart son of Anchises,
Even Aeneas, borne unto him of the bright Aphrodite
Deep in Idaean recesses—a goddess that couched with a mortal.
Yet not alone went he; two sons of Antenor were with him,
Acamas ("Tireless") *and* Archelochus, masters of warfare.

Trojans that dwelt in Zeleia at Ida's nethermost bases,
Rich in possessions, who drink of the dark-hued flood of Aesepus—
These men followed the lead of the glorious son of Lycaon,
Pandarus, armed with a bow that Apollo himself had presented.

Those who possessed Adresteia and held the land of Apaesus;
Those who possessed Pityeia and held the steep mount of Tereia;
All of Adrestus were led and Amphius with corselet of linen:
Children of Merops these, the Percosian, one that exceeded
All in the gifts of divining. He tried to hinder his children's
Marching to murderous war; but the father availed to persuade them
Noway, seeing the fates of black death guided them onward.

Such as abroad in the region of Practius dwelt and Percote;
Such as Abydus possessed, yea, goodly Arisbe and Sestus—
All such Asius led, a commander of men and a hero,
Asius, Hyrtacus' son, far-borne in his car from Arisbe,
Borne by his tall roan steeds from the bank of the river Selleïs.

All the Pelasgian tribes, spear-wielders, Hippothoüs followed,
Such as were wont to inhabit the deep-soiled land of Larissa.
These did Hippothoüs lead and Pylaeus, scion of Ares,
Both brave sons of Pelasgian Lethus, Teutamus' grandson.

Acamas headed the Thracians—and *with* him Piroüs, hero—
All whose land is engirt of the powerful flood Hellespontine.
All the Ciconian lancers were led of heroic Euphemus,
Son of Troezenus, a prince Zeus-fostered, scion of Ceas.

Next, with their curved bows, came the Paeonians, led of Pyraech-
Even from Amydon far and the wide-flowing Axius river—   [mes
Axius, whose waters of all that spread o'er the earth are the fairest.

Rugged heart of Pylaemenes led Paphlagonian levies
Out from the Eneti-land, wide-known as a breeder of wild mules.
These men dwelt in the district of Sesamus, owning Cytorus,

Habiting far-famed houses about Parthenius river,
Cromna, Aegialus, too, and the lofty town Erythini.

Odius led th' Halizones — Epistrophus too was their leader —
Led them from Alybe far, that land, the birthplace of silver.

Chromis was leader of Mysians, with Ennomus, skilful as augur,
Yet were his auguries all unavailing to ward off the augur's
Black fate — — slain by the hand of Aeacus' fleet-footed grandson,
There in the river, when *he* made havoc of Trojans and others.

Phorcys and godlike hero Ascanius headed the Phrygians
Out from Ascania far, all fierce for the tumult of battle.

Mesthles and Antiphus, too, commanded Maeonian levies —
Brothers, Talaemenes' sons, their mother the mere of Gygaea —
All the Maeonians, born at the foot of Tmolus, they headed.

Next came Nastes, leader of Carians, rough-voiced speakers,
Owning Miletus and Phthires, a mountain of limitless leafage,
Mycale's toppling steeps and the far-famed floods of Maeander.
All these Nastes commanded, his brother Amphimachus with him.
Nastes, now, and his brother were glorious sons of Nomion.
Golden of garment he came like a girl to the field of the battle.
Fond man! sure it availed him to ward off grievous destruction
Noway, seeing the hands of the fleet-footed Aeacid quelled him
There in the river; his gold was the spoil of wise-hearted Achilles.

Last were the Lycians, led of Sarpedon and Glaucus the blameless,
Levies from Lycia far, from Xanthus' eddying river.

ILIAD · III · (Γ)

Gamma the single fight doth sing
'Twixt Paris and the Spartan king.

WHEN now these were arrayed, each company thus with its captain,
    All with tumult and cry, like birds, the Trojans went onward:
E'en as a clamor of cranes in the face of the heavens ariseth,
When they would flee unspeakable rains and storms of the winter,
Clamorous thus while flying afar to the currents of Ocean,
Bearing destruction and doom unto men — to the race of the Pygmies;
Battle and ruinous strife they offer to them at the dawning.
Not so, bravery-breathing, in silence the sons of Achaeans
Marched, all eager in spirit to lend aid each to his fellow.
Even as mist that is shed by the southwind high in the mountains,
Mist unfriendly to herdsmen, to thieves, though, kinder than nightfall,
When one seeth as far as a stone's throw only before one:
Even so under their feet rose eddying dust and beclouded
Rank upon rank, as over the plain they speedily covered the distance.
    Now they had come close up in the onrush 'gainst one another —
Lo! Alexander, the godlike, advanced to the fore of the Trojans,
Wearing a panther's pelt, with a bent bow hung on his shoulders,
Also a sword; two lances, with bronze bright-shodden, he brandished.
Any and all of the Argive chieftains, the bravest, he challenged,
Man against man, in a single, deadly encounter to fight him.
    Forthwith, when Menelaüs, belovèd of Ares, espied him
Marching with long strides, proudly parading in front of the army,
Like as a lion is glad when he lights by chance on a carcass
Huge of a branch-horned stag or a horned wild goat in a forest —
He in his ravenous hunger devoureth amain, no matter
Even though many fleet hounds and young men lusty beset him:
Thus Menelaüs rejoiced, when before him he saw Alexander
Godlike under his eyes; for he vowed in his heart to avenge him

57

There on the sinner, and leaped full-armored down from his chariot.

When Alexander, the godlike, saw Menelaüs approaching,
Eminent there in the van of the war-host — smitten with terror
Back to the throng of his fellows, evading his doom, he retreated.
Like as a man starts back, if he suddenly seeth a serpent
Deep in a mountain ravine, while shuddering seizes his members,
Backward he also recedeth, his cheeks all covered with pallor:
So, when he saw Menelaüs, the godlike prince Alexander
Quailed, and he shrank back into the throng of impetuous Trojans.

Hector, beholding, upbraided in accents scornful his brother:

"Shame-Paris! fairest in form, thou woman-demented seducer!
Would thou wert yet unborn or else had perished unwedded!
That I could haply desire, and even so, sure it were better
Far than to be a reproach, unto all men naught but a byword.
Doubtless the long-haired Achaeans are laughing now in derision,
Deeming a prince is our captain, only because he is handsome,
Goodly in form — but his heart sore lacketh in courage and prowess.
Being then such as thou art, didst thou in sea-faring galleys
Dare sail over the deep, with a band of trusty companions,
Mingle with foreigners there, and return with a beauteous woman
Out from a far-off region, a sister-in-law unto spearmen,
Sore bane unto thy father, the city, and all of our people,
Joy to our foemen, forsooth, to thyself but humiliation?
Darest thou not then await Menelaüs, belovèd of Ares?   [helpmeet.
Then thou wouldst learn from what manner of man thou hast taken his
Naught will the lyre avail, naught gifts of the Queen Aphrodite,
Lovelocks nothing, and beauty, when once with the dust thou art min-
Ay, but the Trojans are craven insooth; else surely had Paris   [gled.
Long since donned him a tunic of stone for the ills he hath wrought them!"

Then in his turn to his brother replied Alexander, the godlike:

"Seeing thou chidest me, Hector, in measure and not over measure —
Alway, like as an ax, thy heart is unwearied within thee,
Ax that a mast-beam cleaves; in the hand of a carpenter, shaping
Cunningly timber for ships, it enforces the blow of the wielder:
Alway so is the heart in thy breast undaunted within thee.
Natheless decry not, I pray, the love-gifts of gold Aphrodite,

58

Seeing the glorious gifts of the gods may never be slighted,
Gifts of their good will given, that no man winneth by willing.
If, however, thou'dst have me engage in battle and warfare,
Bid that the rest be seated, the Trojans and all the Achaeans,
Straight. Then let in the midst me only and prince Menelaüs,
Ares-beloved, do combat for Helen and all her possessions.
Which of us twain then is victor and proves himself to be stronger,
His be the treasure entire; let him lead home with him the woman.
All ye others shall pledge sure oaths with a treaty of friendship:
Ye to inhabit the deep-loamed Troyland; they unto Argos,
Pasture of steeds, to return, to Achaia of beautiful women."

    Thus spake he; and Hector was greatly rejoiced as he heard him.
Into the mid-space faring, he held back Troia's battalions,
Grasping his spear in the middle; and all were brought to a stand-still.
'Gainst him, however, the long-haired Achaeans kept bending their long-
Aiming their death-dealing arrows, and hurling stones as their   [bows,
Loud then shouted amid them the king of men, Agamemnon: [missiles.

    "Hold, ye Argives! Hurl not a spear, ye sons of Achaeans!
Fain would he speak us a word, yon shimmering-helmeted Hector."

    So he spake. They refrained from battle and dropped into silence
Suddenly. Midway 'twixt the two hosts then Hector harangued them:

    "Hearken to me, ye Trojans, and ye, well-greavèd Achaeans.
Hear Alexander's proposal, for whose sake strife hath arisen.
All other Trojans he biddeth, and likewise all the Achaeans,
Here on the bounteous earth to doff their beauteous armor,
While in the midst Menelaüs, beloved of Ares, shall battle
Singly, and with him only, for Helen and all her possessions.
Which of the twain then is victor and proves himself to be stronger,
His be the treasure at stake; let him to his home lead the woman.
All we others will pledge sure oaths with a treaty of friendship."

    So spake Hector. The others all mutely attended in silence.
Then in the midst spoke out Menelaüs, good at the war-cry:

    "Hearken now also to me; for above all, sorrow assaileth
My heart. *I* too am minded that now these foemen be parted,
Argive heroes and Trojan; for many the ills ye have suffered
All for a quarrel of mine, first started of him, Alexander.

Well, whiche'er of us twain unto death's dark doom is appointed,
Dead let him lie, and the rest be straightway parted asunder.
Bring ye hither two lambs, a white-fleeced ram and a black ewe,
Meet for the Earth and the Sun; we to Zeus will offer another.
Bring ye also the mighty Priam, that oaths he may pledge us,
Priam himself (for his children are too overweening and faithless),
Lest, through some transgression, the Zeus-oath fail of its purpose.
Always the minds of the younger are wilful and tend to be flighty;
But when an old man enters, he looks both backward and forward
Steadily, so may result unto both sides far the best issue."

Spake he; thereat were gladdened alike both Trojan and Argive,
Hoping thus for release from the warfare's woful affliction.   [chariots,
Then through the ranks they curbed their steeds; they alit from the
Doffing their armor; they laid their suits on the ground beside them—
One suit close to another, with right small spaces around them.

Two were the envoys Hector despatched forthwith to the city,
Quickly to bring him the lambs and bear the summons to Priam.
Also Lord Agamemnon despatched Talthybius, bade him
Haste to the hollow ships and bring back with him a victim,
Even the ram. He promptly obeyed the divine Agamemnon.

Now came, bearing a message to white-armed Helen, the goddess
Iris in guise of her husband's sister, th' Antenorid's consort.
Lord Helicaon, the son of Antenor, had wedded the maiden,
Even Laodice, fairest in form of the daughters of Priam.
Helen she found in her chamber, weaving a web full ample,
Twofold, purple; and into it many a battle she'd woven,
Battles of Troy's steed-tamers and bronze-mailed sons of Achaeans,
That for her own sake, under the war-god's hands, they had suffered.
Close to her side came Iris, the fleet-foot, now and addressed her:

"Come, dear lady, and see what wonderful things they are doing,
Trojans, tamers of steeds, and the bronze-mailed warrior Achaeans,
They that against one another were waging a tear-fraught warfare
There on the plain and longing erewhile for the deadliest battle.
Now they are seated in silence — the while all combat is ended —
See! on their bucklers leaning, their long spears planted beside them.
Meanwhile Paris and prince Menelaüs, dear unto Ares,

Aphrodite Disguised, Inviting Helen to the Chamber of Paris

All in a duel for thee long lances will presently level.
Thou shalt be called dear wife of him to whom victory falleth."

    These words uttered, the goddess put into her bosom a yearning
Sweet for her husband of old, her city, and also her parents.
Straightway, hiding her face in a veil of glistening linen,
Forth from her chamber she hastened, with tear drops copious falling—
Not unaccompanied; two were the handmaids following after
(Aethra, Pittheus' daughter, and ox-eyed Clymene with her).
Soon they arrived at the point where the Scaean Gate was erected.
There the attendants of Priam—Thymoetes and Lampus were sitting,
Panthoüs, Clytius, too, Hicetaon, scion of Ares,
Two other sages, Antenor and agèd Ucalegon—these men,
Elders revered of the people, were seated aloft at the gateway
Scaean, retired from the battle for age, but as orators gifted,
Brilliant, like the cicadas accustomed to chirp in a forest,
High up-perched on a tree, and to send forth voice of the lily:
Such were the men that sat on the tower, the leaders of Troia.

    Now, as the elders beheld fair Helen approaching the tower,
Low-toned one to another in accents wingèd they murmured: [Achaeans
    "Blame is there none that the Trojans and well-greaved sons of
Long years suffer in travail, when such is the woman they fight for,
Marvelous, like in her figure and face to a goddess immortal.
Yet, although she is such, now let her depart in the galleys,
Neither be left as a bane unto us and our children hereafter."

    Thus they murmured; but Priam aloud called Helena to him:
    "Hither, my child, come hither; be seated, I pray thee, before me,
Would'st thou see thy friends of aforetime, husband, and kindred.
Nowise thee do I blame; for to blame are the deities only.
They it is stirred up against me the tear-fraught war of the Argives.
Come now hither and tell me his name, that wonderful hero's,
Whoe'er now he may be, that goodly, majestic Achaean.
Others, indeed, I discern who e'en by a head may be taller,
Yet have my eyes—no, never—beheld so handsome a hero,
Nor so stately as he; like a man that is king he appeareth."

    Answering him with her words, spake Helen, divinest of women:
    "Reverend art thou to me, my lord's dear father, and awful.

Would I had chosen indeed grim death ere hither I followed
Him, thy son, and deserted my nuptial chamber and kindred,
Daughter tenderly loved, and the cherished friends of my girlhood.
Not so it happened, alas! and my heart now melteth with weeping.
Yet I will tell thee whereof thou askest and makest inquiry:
Atreus' son is the man, wide-ruling king Agamemnon,
Goodly, insooth, as a king and as powerful, too, as a spearman,
Likewise brother-in-law to a cur like me — if he e'er was."

Thus spake she. At him the old man marveled and answered:
"Ah! Blest Atrides, fortune's child, thou favored of heaven!
Many they be that are subject to thee, of the sons of Achaia.
Long time ago I fared unto Phrygia, land of the vineyard.
There I beheld those drivers of fleet steeds, Phrygians many,
People of Otreus they, and of Mygdon, match for immortals,
Who even then were encamping along the Sangarius river.
I, too, among them (as being allied with their people) was numbered,
What time the Amazons, equals of men, came warring upon them.
Still not so many were they as the flashing-eyed sons of Achaia."

Next after him the old man caught sight of Odysseus and asked her:
"Come, dear child, and tell me of this man — who is he, yonder?
Shorter, indeed, by a head than is Atreus' son, Agamemnon;
Yet, to behold, he is broader of chest and broader of shoulders.
There on the bounteous earth, thou seest, his armor is lying,
While, like a ram, he ranges along the ranks of the heroes;
Unto a thick-fleeced ram most aptly indeed I compare him,
Head of a numerous flock white-gleaming — that ranges amid them."

Thereupon Helen, begotten of Zeus, made answer to Priam:
"That is Laërtes' son, Odysseus of many devices,
One that was reared in Ithaca-land — be it never so rugged —
Skilful in varied contrivance is he and in counsels of cunning."

Sage Antenor in turn then answered and spake unto Helen:
"Lady, indeed it is true, this word thou even hast spoken.
Once came hither the goodly Odysseus, sent on a mission
With Menelaüs, belovèd of Ares, for thy sake commissioned.
I was host to the twain and in my halls entertained them,
Came to know well the natures of both and their counsels of wisdom.

Then when the heroes appeared amid the Trojans assembled,
Shoulders broad and high above all, when they stood, Menelaüs
Towered; but when they sat down, Odysseus was the more stately.
There, in weaving for all the web of words and of counsels,
Fluently then spake King Menelaüs words few (like a Spartan),
Clearly, however (for he was a man not given to talking),
Always hitting the mark with his words, though in years he was
But when Odysseus rose up—Odysseus of many devices—   [younger.
Fixing his eyes on the ground he stood there, downwardly gazing,
Not once waving his staff, not backward nor yet again forward,
Holding it motionless, all as a wight untutored in knowledge.
Thou would'st say he was churlish, perchance, or a simpleton merely.
But when he uttered his voice from his breast with a mighty deliv'rance,
Moulded in words that were like unto snowflakes falling in winter,
Then it appeared no other of mortals could vie with Odysseus;
Then we did not so much wonder, beholding the looks of Odysseus."

    Third now, when he espied him, the old man asked about Ajax:
"Who is the other Achaean, a man both goodly and stalwart,
Rising head and shoulders above the rest of the Argives?"

    Long-robed Helen, fairest of women, to him then made answer:
"Ajax is he, the colossal, the bulwark strong of Achaia.
Look! over there in the midst of his Cretans Idomeneus standeth,
Like to a god; and about him are gathered the Cretan commanders.
Often indeed Menelaüs, of Ares beloved, entertained him
There in our home as a guest, when thither from Creta he journeyed.
Yea, and the rest I behold of the glancing-eyed sons of Achaia,
All I could clearly distinguish and even by name could recall them.
Two, though, I cannot descry, two marshaling chiefs of the peoples,
Castor, tamer of steeds, Polydeuces, valorous boxer,
Both full brothers of mine, one only the mother that bare us.
Either they came not along with the others from fair Lacedaemon,
Or, though hither they followed in black sea-furrowing galleys,
Now are unwilling to plunge in the battle of militant heroes,
Dreading the insults heaped upon me and the many reproaches."

    Thus she spake. But the life-giving Earth already confined them
There in the land of their fathers, in far-off, loved Lacedaemon.

Up through the city the heralds the gods' oath-off'rings were bring-
Now, two lambs and the wine, heart-gladd'ning fruit of the vineland, 　[ing
Held in a goat-skin flask; and the herald Idaeus was bearing
Cups fair-fashioned of gold, and a shimm'ring bowl for a mixer.
Close by Priam the herald stopped and exhorted him, saying:

　　"Son of Laomedon, rouse thee and hearken, the captains are calling —
Trojans, tamers of steeds, and the bronze-clad sons of Achaia —
Thee to descend to the plain, that oaths trustworthy be given,
Since Alexander will meet Menelaüs, dear unto Ares,
Now in a duel with long ash spears, for the sake of the woman.
His be the wife and the wealth, whiche'er of the heroes is victor.
All we others will pledge sure oaths with a treaty of friendship:
We to inhabit the deep-loamed Troyland, they unto Argos,
Pasture of steeds, to return, to Achaia of beautiful women."

　　Thus spake he. With a shudder the old man bade his companions
Straightway yoke up the horses; right prompt they were in obeying.
Priam mounted and grasped the reins, then tightened them backward,
While on the beauteous wain to his side ascended Antenor.
Out through the Scaean Gate to the plain they drove the fleet horses.

　　Now, on arriving among the war-host, Trojan-Achaean,
Out from the car they descended to Earth, all-nurturing mother,
Marched then into the space midway of the opposite armies.
Forthwith rose up the king of men, Agamemnon Atrides;
Rose up Odysseus of many devices. And high-born heralds
Brought up the gods' oath-off'rings, the lambs and the wine in a mixer
Mingled, and poured out water anon on the hands of the princes.
Thereupon Atreus' son with his hand unsheathing his dagger —
Alway there at the side of his sword's great scabbard suspended —
Cut from the heads of the victims the foretop lock; and the heralds
Duly apportioned it all to the princes, Achaean and Trojan.
Then in the midst, uplifting his hands, prayed loud the Atrides:

　　"Zeus, thou Father that rulest from Ida, most glorious, greatest,
Thou, Sun, thou beholder of all things, hearer of all things,
Ye, too, Rivers and Earth, ye Powers whoever thereunder
Punish the man outworn, whoever hath sworn to a falsehood,
Be ye witnesses now of the oaths, inviolate guard them.

If in the duel, perchance, Alexander shall slay Menelaüs,
Henceforth he shall have Helen, his own, and all her possessions;
We will return to our homes in our galleys crossing the waters.
But if, perchance, fair-haired Menelaüs shall slay Alexander,
Then shall the Trojans surrender us Helen and all her possessions,
Pay an indemnity, too, to the Argives, such as is fitting,
Such as in ages to come may serve to men as example.
But if it happen that Priam refuse, and the children of Priam,
Full compensation to pay me, in case Alexander hath fallen,
I shall abide right here and fight for the recompense due us,
Steadfast, till I attain to the goal of the war we are waging." [victims,

Thus he spake and with pitiless bronze cut the throats of the
Down on the ground then laid them, the while still gasping convulsive,
Failing of life, of breath, for of strength the weapon had reft them.
Next from the bowl they drew into cups the wine for libation,
Then on the ground outpoured it with prayer to the gods ever-living,
Many a one thus saying, alike the Achaeans and Trojans:

"Zeus, most glorious, greatest, and all ye other immortals,
Whiche'er first of the folks doth violence unto the pledges,
So may their brains be poured out here on the earth, as the wine is,
Theirs and their children's as well—their wives be slaves unto others."

Such the petition. Cronion would nowise grant it fulfilment.
Therewith spake out amid them the scion of Dardanus, Priam:

"Hearken to me, ye Trojans and well-greaved sons of Achaeans.
Verily I must again to wind-swept Ilium hie me,
Seeing that I could endure noway with my eyes to behold him,
My son, battling against Menelaüs, belovèd of Ares.
Zeus it is knoweth, methinks, and the rest of the gods everlasting
Unto which of the twain the end of death is appointed."

Thus spake the godlike man and lifted the lambs to his chariot,
Mounted the car himself and tightened the reins drawn backward,
While to his side on the beauteous car ascended Antenor.
Back again those twain to Ilium city departed.

Hector, Priam's son, and with him the goodly Odysseus
Then, in the first place, measured the space; and then, in the second,
Lots that were taken they cast in a bronze-bound helm, to determine

Which of the twain should be first to let fly his bronze-pointed javelin.
Meantime the hosts to the gods, with hands uplifted to heaven,
Prayed; and thus spake many a one, Achaean and Trojan:
 "Zeus, thou Father that rulest from Ida, most glorious, greatest,
Which of the twain on both peoples hath brought these woful afflictions,
Yield thou him unto death! Let him enter the mansion of Hades!
Ours henceforth be the portion of friendship's pledges unbroken." [him,
 Thus they spake. Great Hector, with glancing helm, looking behind
Shook up the casque. Full quickly the lot leaped forth, Alexander's!
All now rested around in ranks, wherever awaited
Steeds, high-stepping, for each, and his rich-wrought armor was lying.
 Now Alexander, the goodly, the husband of fair-haired Helen,
Hastened to arm him for battle with bright war-gear on his shoulders.
First on his legs he fastened his greaves, all round about deftly,
Beautiful, fitted with buckles of silver and firm at the ankles;
Secondly, donned him a corselet engirdling his breast all about him—
Erewhile worn of his brother Lycaon—fitting it on him.
Over his shoulders he slung his sword, all studded with silver—
Bronze was the blade. Then he took up his shield, formed ponderous,
Then on his valorous temples a well-wrought helmet he fitted, [ample.
Horse-hair crested; the plume all fearfully nodded above it.
Lastly he grasped his doughty spear, to his hand nicely fitted.
Likewise, too, Menelaüs, the martial, clothed him in harness.
 Now as the heroes were armed on either side of the war-throng,
Forth they strode to the middle, between the Achaeans and Trojans,
Terribly glaring; and wonder alit upon all that beheld them,
Trojans, tamers of horse, and well-greaved sons of Achaeans.
Nigh together they took their stand in the space that was marked off,
Brandishing lances in rancor, in fury each against other.
First Alexander, uplifting his spear far-shadowing, hurled it
Driving it full on the shield, all evenly round, of Atrides.
Through it the bronze brake not, for the spear-point backward was
Deep in the stalwart shield. Then spake Menelaüs Atrides— [bended
Poising his bronze-pointed spear—in prayer to Cronion, the Father:
 "Grant me revenge, O Sovereign Zeus, upon him that hath wronged
First, Alexander, the goodly, that under my hands I subdue him. [me

So, of the men that are born hereafter many may shudder,
Fearful an outrage to wreak on a host that treateth them kindly.''

    Thus he spake. Then, poising his spear far-shadowing, hurled it,
Smiting directly the shield all evenly rounded of Paris.
Through the shimmering shield went driving the ponderous missile;
On still it went and traversed the breastplate cunningly moulded,
Clear on down past his flank it mowed its way through his tunic—
Powerful spear! but he swerved and avoided the black death's onset.
Quick then, drawing his blade, all studded with silver, Atrides
Smote, with an uplift, high on the ridge of the helmet; around it,
Shattered in fragments three, ay four, from his hand fell his weapon.
Then, as he lifted his eyes to the broad sky, groaned Menelaüs:

    "Zeus, O Father, in truth no god is more cruel than thou art!
Surely I thought to avenge Alexander's iniquity on him;
Nay! but the sword broke now in my hand, and the javelin darted
Out of my grasp unavailing; and thus did I fail to subdue him.''

    Thus he; and, leaping upon him, he seized on his plumèd helmet,
Wheeled him round, and strove to the well-greaved Achaeans to hale him.
Richly embroidered, the strap was strangling the soft-throated Trojan,
Made tight under his chin, as it was, for securing his helmet.
So Menelaüs had dragged him and won ineffable glory,
Had not the daughter of Zeus, Aphrodite, swift to observe it,
Severed the strap of hide, from the ox once forcefully slaughtered.
Empty the casque came off in the stalwart hand of Atrides.
Then, with a swing in a circle, away the great hero whirled it
Unto his well-greaved host, and his trusty companions received it:
On then he charged yet again, all eagerly yearning to slay him
There with his spear of bronze; but away Aphrodite had caught him
Lightly—for she was divine. In a thick cloud veiling him, she then
Set him down in his fresh and perfume-breathing apartment.
She then went with the purpose of summoning Helen and found her
High on a tower, with women of Troy close-thronging about her.
She laid hold with her hand on the heavenly raiment of Helen,
Drawing upon it. In guise of an old-time matron—a one-time
Comber of comeliest wools, both skilful and wont to prepare them,
Ere she had left Lacedaemon, and Helen especially loved her—

All in the old dame's likeness, divine Aphrodite addressed her:

"Hither come; lo! Alexander is calling thee homeward to hasten.
There in his chamber is he, on the rich-wrought couches reclining,
All in his beauty and vesture agleam; none ever would deem him
Just to have issued from fight with a foeman; rather he seemeth
Ready to enter the dance or just seated, the dance having ended."·

Thus she spake. Her words stirred the heart in the bosom of Helen.
So then, when *she* caught sight of the beauteous neck of the goddess,
Seeing as well the lovely breast and eyes brightly sparkling,
Helen marveled at first, then uttered a word and addressed her:

"Strange Queen, why dost thou wish in this wise now to delude me?
Doubtless to lead me away to a populous city, remoter
Still—some Phrygian city or lovely Maeonian haply,
If there also perchance is some darling of thine among mortals?
Since even now Menelaüs has vanquished divine Alexander,
Fully determined to lead home now even me, the abhorrèd,
Therefore art thou come hither and standest by me to beguile me.
Go, sit by him thyself and abandon the paths of immortals,
Never again, nay, never to turn thy feet to Olympus.
·Nay, fret ever for *him* and a watch hold over him ever,
Till, condescending, he make thee his wife or haply his slave-girl!
Thither I will not go—for that would only be sinful—
That man's couch to share; hereafter the women of Troia
All will denounce me; and now—unending the woes of my spirit!"

Roused unto wrath, the divine Aphrodite in answer addressed her:

"Nettle me not, malapert, lest I in my anger desert thee,
Hating thee even as fiercely as now past measure I've loved thee,
Lest I devise new enmities, hatreds grievous, among them,
Trojans and Danaans too; by an evil fate wouldst thou perish."

So said she; and Helen, daughter of Zeus, sore affrighted,
Went without words, closely wrapping herself in her shining apparel,
Passing unseen of the women of Troy. The goddess preceded.

Soon as the twain had arrived at the beautiful palace of Paris,
Quickly the women in waiting returned to their labors appointed.
She to her high-roofed chamber, divinest of women, betook her,
While Aphrodite, lover of smiles, herself as attendant,

70

Aphrodite Presenting Helen to Paris

Brought her a settle—the goddess—and placed it before Alexander.
There then Helen, the daughter of Zeus who wieldeth the aegis,
Sat and averted her eyes and with sharp words chided her husband:

"Well then! Back from the fight! If only thou rather hadst perished,
Vanquished by that great warrior, who *was my* husband aforetime!
Verily often above Menelaüs, belovèd of Ares,
Thou wouldst boast thyself for the might of thine arm and thy javelin.
Go now, challenge again Menelaüs, belovèd of Ares,
That he may fight thee aface—nay now! I rather enjoin thee,
Henceforth wisely refrain nor against fair-haired Menelaüs
Fight again, man to man, nor recklessly ever attack him,
Lest perchance in the conflict his spear shall bring thee destruction."

Paris to her made answer with words, and thus he addressed her:
"Do not rebuke, dear wife, my soul with cruel upbraidings.
Now Menelaüs hath won over me—with the aid of Athena!
Next time, I over him! gods also, methinks, are on our side.
Come then; lulled in repose, let us turn unto pleasure in loving.
Never till now hath a hunger for thee so shrouded my senses—
Not even when, at the first, from fair Lacedaemon I caught thee,
Bore thee sailing away in galleys that fare o'er the waters,
There in Cranaë island in converse sweet to commingle—
Even as now I desire, now tenderest yearning invades me."

This said, he led the way to the couch; his wife followed with him.
There on the inlaid couch the twain then laid them to slumber.

Like as a wild beast, ranging the host meanwhile, Menelaüs
Strode, if haply he might spy somewhere Alexander, the godlike,
But not one of the Trojans or famous allies could discover
Prince Alexander to *him*, Menelaüs, belovèd of Ares.
Nor did they hide him from kindness, if anyone saw him—by no means.
Seeing that he of them all like black death even was hated.
So Agamemnon, the king of men, then shouted amid them:

"Hear me, Trojans and Dardans and ye allies of the city!
Now, it appears, Menelaüs, belovèd of Ares, is victor.
Give back Helen of Argos and with her all her possessions.
Pay an indemnity, too, whatever may seem to be fitting,
Such as in ages to come may serve unto men as example."

Thus Atrides spake, and the other Achaeans applauded.

ILIAD · IV · (Δ)

In Delta is the gods' assize;
The truce is broke; wars freshly rise.

NOW were the gods all seated with Zeus while holding assembly
There on the pavement of gold; and worshipful Hebe amid them
Poured out nectar as wine, while they with their chalices golden
Pledged one another and gazed meantime at the city of Troia.
  Then the Cronion essayed with a word of derision to stir up
Hera to strife and harangued with a taunting allusion his hearers:
  "There be goddesses twain who are wont to assist Menelaüs,
Argive Hera and also Alalcomenean Athena.
These find pleasure, it seemeth, in merely beholding afar off,
Sitting apart; but the lover of laughter and smiles, Aphrodite,
Stands aye close to her own and wards off fate from the Trojan.
Lo! even now she hath saved him, although he was thinking to perish.
Yet is the victor, insooth, Menelaüs, belovèd of Ares.
Now, as for us, let *us* take thought what were best to be doing:
Whether again to arouse grim war and the din of the awful
Combat or to establish between the two parties a friendship.
Now, could all of us find this second alternative pleasing,
Then may men continue to dwell in the city of Priam,
While Menelaüs leads back to his home fair Helen of Argos."
  Thus he spake; but thereat low muttered Athena and Hera,
Seated close to each other, devising ills for the Trojans.
Pallas, in truth, kept still, and not a word did she utter —
Wrathful at Father Zeus — and fierce was the fury that seized her.
Hera, unable to stifle the rage in her bosom, addressed him:
  "Most dread scion of Cronus, what word is this thou hast spoken!
How? Hast thou then the will to make vain and idle my labor,
All that sweat I sweated with toil, and I wearied my horses,
Rousing the host, unto Priam a bane and a bane to his children?

75

Do it! However, not all of us other gods will approve it."

   Sorely incensed, cloud-gathering Zeus in answer addressed her:
"Tell me, infatuate woman, what wrong so monstrous hath Priam
Wrought thee; what have his children, that thou so relentlessly ragest
Ilium's well-built city to sack, yea, level in ashes?
Well now, enter the gates and the long-drawn wall of the fortress;
Seize old Priam himself and the children of Priam; devour them
Raw, and the Trojans all—thy wrath then haply were sated!
Do now e'en as thou wilt! And let hereafter the quarrel
Be unto me and to thee no breeder of bitter contention.
This, however, I tell thee, and deep in thy heart do thou lay it:
Whensoever belike I, too, shall be eager to pillage
Wholly a town where mortals are born whom dearly thou lovest,
Think not to thwart that wrath of mine; nay, rather allow me
Even as I yield freely to thee, yet unwilling of spirit,
Seeing of all proud cities inhabited under the starry
Heaven, yea, under the sun, by earth-born races of mortals,
Ever in my heart surely most honored was Ilium holy,
Priam, lord of the ashen spear, and the people of Priam.
Never an altar of mine there wanted a well-balanced banquet,
Off'ring of drink or of meat, whatever in worship is due us."

   Ox-eyed, worshipful Hera in turn then readily answered:
"Verily, three are the ones far dearest to me of all cities:
Argos and Sparta and wide-wayed Mycenae—three cities Achaean.
These thou mayest lay waste, whensoe'er thy heart finds them hateful.
Them will I never protect; unto thee will I never refuse them
[Nay, e'en though I be jealous and even would save them from ruin,
Jealousy naught will avail, since thou art greatly the stronger].
Even my toil, however, must not be rendered all useless,
Since *I*, too, am divine; my lineage even as thine is.
Cronus, the crooked-in-counsel, begat *me*, too, unto chiefest
Honor, and doubly: in race and because I am counted the consort
Even of thee, who reignest as lord o'er all the immortals.
Wherefore let us submit us in these things, one to the other,
I unto thee, unto me thou too, and the others will follow,
All these gods everlasting. But bid thou Pallas Athena

76

The Council of the Gods

Speedily hie to the dread war-din of Achaeans and Trojans,
There to contrive that the Trojans—in first violating the compact—
Wreak some treacherous wrong on the over-exultant Achaeans."

Thus spake she; and he heeded, the father of men and immortals.
Forthwith then he addressed, in accents wingèd, Athena:

"Speed to the war-host quickly, amid the Achaeans and Trojans,
There to contrive that the Trojans—in first violating the compact—
Wreak some treacherous wrong on the over-exultant Achaeans."

These words roused up Athena, in heart all eager and waiting,
Who with a flash went down from the pinnacled heights of Olympus.
Even as haply the son of Cronus, the crooked-in-counsel,
Sends for a sign unto seamen or wide-camped army of people
Earthward a glittering star, wide-scattering sparks all about it:
Meteor-like in her guise unto earth sped Pallas Athena,
Leaping adown in the midst, and amazement seized the beholders,
Trojans, tamers of steeds, and the well-greaved sons of Achaeans;
Many beholding would say, each wight as he looked at his neighbor:

"Surely indeed it returns, sore war and alarum of dreadful
Combat; else will the god now stablish friendship between us,
Zeus, ordained dispenser to men of the fortunes of battle."

Suchwise many would reason among the Achaeans and Trojans.
Pallas in warrior guise now entered the throng of the Trojans—
Guised as a son of Antenor, Laodocus, powerful spearman—
Seeking for Pandarus, peer of immortals, haply to find him.
Him she found, the stalwart and faultless son of Lycaon,
Standing; and round him the ranks of the stalwart warrior peoples,
Shieldmen, such as had followed along from the streams of Aesepus.
Drawing close to his side, in wingèd words she addressed him:

"Wouldst thou hearken to me, thou wise-heart son of Lycaon?
Then wouldst thou dare let fly a swift arrow at King Menelaüs.
Favor and fame thou wouldst win in the eyes of all of the Trojans,
Chiefest of all in the eyes of the king's son, prince Alexander.
He it is surely would give thee, of all men, glorious presents
First, if he see mayhap Menelaüs Atrides, the martial,
Mounted upon the sorrowful pyre, laid low by *thy* arrow.
Come then, launch thee a bolt right at him, renowned Menelaüs,

79

Vowing a famed hecatomb to the light-born archer, renownèd
Phoebus, an off'ring of lambs, all firstlings, laid on his altar,
Straight on return to thy home, to the city of holy Zeleia."
　　Speaking such words, Athena persuaded the wit of the witless.
Quick he unsheathed a smooth-wrought bow he had won from an agile
Wild goat. Under the breast erewhile with a dart he had struck it,
Just as it came from a cliff where Pandarus waited in ambush,
Hitting and piercing its chest; supine on a rock it had fallen.
Antlers of full sixteen palms' length from its head it had sprouted;
These had a worker in horn right cunningly fitted together,
All well-polished; and pure gold tips he had fastened upon it.
Pandarus, bracing it fast 'gainst the ground, now strung it and laid it
Carefully down; and his gallant companions steadied their bucklers
Firmly before him, on guard lest the martial sons of Achaeans
Charge, ere yet Menelaüs Atrides, the martial, were smitten.
Op'ning the lid of his quiver, the Lycian selected an arrow,
Wingèd, but ne'er yet shot, a bringer of pangs most grievous.
Speedily, while he was fitting the bitter bolt on the bowstring,
Vowed he a famed hecatomb to the light-born archer, renownèd
Phoebus, an off'ring of lambs, all firstlings, laid on his altar,
Straight on return to his home, to the city of holy Zeleia.
Notches and string of sinews of oxhide he grasped then together;
Close to his breast he drew back the string, to the bow the sharp iron.
Now when thus he had bended his great bow into a circle,
"Twang" went the bow, and the bowstring sang aloud, and the arrow
Leaped, sharp-pointed and eager to wing its way 'mid the people.
　　Thee, Menelaüs, the blest immortal gods had forgotten
Noway; least had the daughter of Zeus, the driver of booty.
She stood before thee and fended the sharp-pointed missile and turned it
Only a little aside from thy flesh — as haply a mother
Driveth a fly from her babe, when it lies all-sweetly in slumber —
Guiding it even herself unto where the gold clasps of the girdle
Joined, and the breastplate there — two thicknesses — met and o'erlapped
There on that well-joined belt the bitter arrow alighted;　　　　[it.
Piercing, it drave right on through the girdle of workmanship cunning;
On still piercing, it traversed the cuirass cunningly plated,

80

On through the taslet he wore as a flesh-screen, fender of javelins:
This it was shielded him most; yet it went through this even onward,
Grazing with barb of the arrow the outermost flesh of the hero.
Out from the wound in a moment the blood, dark-crimson, was flowing.

    Like as perchance some woman, Maeonian woman or Carian,
Staineth with purple a piece of iv'ry, for *some* horse a cheek-plate.
There in a storeroom it lies; and to wear it many a horseman
Prays; but it lies there, fated to be the pride of a monarch,
Both as adorning his steed and a glory, too, to the driver:
Even so then were those thighs, well-shapen, of thine, Menelaüs,
Stained with blood, and thy legs, and thy fair-formed ankles beneath them.

    Thereat shuddering seized on the king of men, Agamemnon—
Seized him at seeing the blood flow forth from the wound, dark-crimson.
Likewise shuddered himself Menelaüs, belovèd of Ares.
But as he saw both thong and keen-edged barbs of the arrow
Outside, then was the soul upgathered anew in his bosom.
Then, with a deep-drawn groan, spake lord Agamemnon among them,
Holding the hand of his brother (his comrades added their moaning):

    "Brother of mine, I was pledging thy death with the oaths, it ap-
Setting thee forth before us to fight alone with the Trojans; [peareth,
Thus have they smitten thee and trampled the oaths that we trusted.
Yet is an oath unavailing in no wise—unmixed libations,
Lambs' blood shed, and the right hands, too, wherein we confided.
Though it may be the Olympian fulfil not instantly always,
Yet, though late, he fulfilleth; and dear the amends men must pay him—
Pay with their own lives, pay with their wives, pay, too, with their
This do I know full well in my heart, in my soul do I know it, [children.
Cometh the day when the city of Ilium holy shall perish,
Priam, too, of the ashen spear, and the people of Priam,
Day when Zeus high-throned, Cronion dwelling in heaven,
Over them all himself shall brandish his lowering aegis,
Wroth at this treacherous deed. All this shall not fail of fulfilment.
Yet will the sorrow for thee be sore unto me, Menelaüs,
If now haply thou die, thy life's lot now be accomplished.
Verily I should return in disgrace to Argos, the thirsty,
Since the Achaeans will now at once remember the homeland.

We then haply shall leave for a boast to the Trojans and Priam
Argive Helen? and thy bones here in the ploughed earth moulder,
While thou liest in Troyland, our task still never accomplished?
Many a one then haply shall say, of the arrogant Trojans,
Say, while leaping in scorn on the tomb of renowned Menelaüs,
'Always let him accomplish his wrath thus, King Agamemnon,
Even as now for nought he brought hither his host of Achaeans;
Homeward now hath he gone to the well-loved land of his fathers,
Empty his ships, and hath left the brave Menelaüs behind him.'
Thus some day they will say; may the earth then yawn to receive me."

    Then, to encourage him, answered the fair-haired chief, Menelaüs:
"Courage! Do not at all now affright the host of Achaeans,
Seeing the keen dart lodges in no part vital. The girdle
Brightly glittering stayed it in front; and then underneath it
Kirtle and taslet held, which the bronze-smiths cunningly fashioned."

    Then to him in reply spake war-lord, King Agamemnon:
"Yea, now, may it be so, thou well-loved prince Menelaüs!
Yet shall the surgeon probe and examine the wound and, applying
Simples, shall haply allay the direful pangs that assail thee."

    Thus he spake and addressed Talthybius, godlike herald:
"Haste, Talthybius, summon with all speed hither Machaon,
Son of Asclepius — him, the faultless healer and hero.
He must examine Atreus' martial son, Menelaüs,
Whom some masterly bowman by launching an arrow hath smitten,
Lycian or Trojan — to him the renown, to us the affliction."

    Said he. Straightway the herald, on hearing him, not disobedient,
Wended his way through the throngs of the bronze-clad sons of Achae-
This way peering and that for Machaon. Soon he espied him   [ans,
Standing, round him assembled the stalwart ranks of his shieldmen,
Folk that had followed him thither from Tricca, pasture of horses.
Close come up to his side, with wingèd words he addressed him:

    "Son of Asclepius, quick! It is lord Agamemnon that summons —
Calls thee to see Menelaüs, the martial commander Achaean,
Whom some masterly bowman by launching an arrow hath smitten,
Lycian or Trojan — to him the renown, to us the affliction."

    Thus he spake; and he roused up the soul in the breast of Machaon.

Both went their way through the throng mid the wide war-host of Achae-
But when now they were come unto where gold-haired Menelaüs   [ans.
Wounded remained — while gathered around him were all the command-
There in a circle — he stepped to his side, the godlike physician.   [ers
Straightway then from the close-clasped belt he extracted the arrow;
E'en as he drew it forth, were the keen barbs backwardly broken.
Then he unloosed him the belt so various-wrought and beneath it
Kirtle and taslet as well, which the bronze-smiths' cunning had fash-
But, upon seeing the wound where the bitter arrow had fallen,   [ioned.
Quickly he sucked out blood, then spread in his wisdom assuaging
Simples upon it that Chiron in kindliness gave to his father.

   While they were busy about Menelaüs, good at the war-cry,
Straight against them advanced the shield-bearing ranks of the Trojans.
Donning their harness, the heroes bethought them again of the battle.
Then hadst thou haply beheld Agamemnon, the godlike, not sleeping,
Nor yet skulking, neither unwilling to enter the battle,
Eager indeed for the battle that brings fair fame unto heroes;
Nay; for he quitted his steeds and his war-wain's bronzen adornment —
Snorting, impatient, his horses were held far off by his comrade,
Even Eurymedon, son of Piraeus' son, Ptolemaeus,
Whom he had strictly commanded to have them at hand, whensoever
Weariness seized on his limbs, as he marshaled the many for battle.
Meanwhile faring afoot, he ranged through the ranks of the warriors.
Whomsoever he saw of the fleet-horsed Danaans zealous,
Such he would greatly enhearten with words, while standing beside
   "Argives, never relax one whit your impetuous prowess,   [them:
Seeing that Father Zeus will never lend aid unto liars.
Since, however, the Trojans began it in breaking the pledges,
Surely their own soft flesh shall therefore be eaten of vultures,
While, on our part, we carry their dear wives and children that prattle
Captive away in the ships, when once we have taken their city."   [fare,
   But whome'er he perceived that would shrink from the odious war-
Such would he strongly upbraid with accents freighted with anger:
   "Argives, boasters, have ye no shame, ye cowardly caitiffs?
Wherefore now do ye stand thus dazed, as fawns that are wearied
(Wearied with running afar, chased over the plain wide-stretching)

Stand ſtill dazed; in their hearts they no longer have spirit or courage.
So ye ſtand here dazed and have no part in the battle.
Doubtless ye wait for the Trojans to gather anigh where our galleys
Drawn up lie with their ſtrong ſterns high on the sands of the grey sea —
Waiting to see if Cronion with outſtretched hand will defend you?"

So, as commander, the monarch, inſpecting the ranks of the war-
Came now unto the Cretans — in ranging the ranks of the heroes — [riors,
Cretans arrayed round prudent Idomeneus, donning their armor.
He in the vanguard waited, a wild boar's equal in valor,
While Meriones yonder was speeding the rearmost battalions.
Joy then entered the heart of the king of men, Agamemnon,
Seeing them thus; and he spake to Idomeneus words that were kindly:
"Thee, my Idomeneus, chiefly I honor of fleet-horsed Achaeans,
Whether in deeds of war or in work of other description
Or at a feast, when the best of the princes of Argos together
Mix in the bowl for themselves the sparkling wine of the elders.
For, though all of the rest, may be, of the long-haired Achaeans
Drink the portion assigned them, that beaker of thine ſtands alway
Full as my own, to be quaffed, whenever thy spirit impelleth.
Come, then, rouse thee to war, brave even as ever thou claimest."
Answering him then spake Idomeneus, leader of Cretans:
"Surely shall I be, Atrides, a ſteadfast comrade, for my part,
Even as in the beginning I gave thee promise and pledges.
Urge on, as thou art doing, the others, the long-haired Achaeans,
So we may counter in fight full soon, since now have the Trojans
Broken the oaths; for indeed it is death henceforth and disaſter
Surely shall follow on them that have first violated the pledges."
Thus spake he; and rejoicing in heart passed on Agamemnon.
Ranging the warrior throng, he came where ſtood the Aeantes
Twain; they were arming themselves, and a dense cloud followed of
Even as when from a lookout a goatherd seeth a ſtormcloud   [footmen.
Coming in over the sea, by a blast of Zephyrus driven —
Black it appeareth as pitch, all the blacker for being afar off,
Scudding along on the deep, as it bringeth a violent whirlwind —
Shudd'ring chill at the sight, he driveth his flock to a cavern:
So, with the Ajaxes twain the close-ranked serried battalions —

Young men fostered of Zeus — to the furious fray swept forward —
Steel-blue phalanxes, moving abristle with bucklers and javelins.
　　　Greatly the lord Agamemnon rejoiced at beholding the heroes;
Loud he uplifted his voice and in accents wingèd addressed them:
　　　"Ajaxes twain, ye chiefs of the bronze-clad children of Argos,
Never an urgence of mine unto you — for to urge were unseemly —
Seeing that ye yourselves speed *your* folk mightily warward.
Would that, O Father Zeus, Athena, and Phoebus Apollo,
Would that spirit like yours might be found in every bosom!
Then would the city of Priam, the king, right speedily topple,
Haply by our own hands both captured and utterly wasted."
　　　Such words spoken, he left them there; and then, after others
Faring, he came upon Nestor, the clear-voiced speaker of Pylus,
Ranging his comrades in order and spurring them on to the combat
All round Pelagon mighty, Alastor, and Chromius also;　　　　[them.
Haemon, their captain, and Bias, brave shepherd of peoples, were with
Horsemen he marshaled in front, along with their horses and chariots,
Footmen arrayed in the rear, both many in number and valiant,
There for a bulwark of battle; the cowards he drave to the middle,
So that, unwillingly even, one might of necessity combat.
First then he laid on the horsemen a charge, ay, straitly commanded
All to restrain their steeds and not in the throng get entangled:
　　　"Neither let any, reliant on skill as a knight or on prowess,
Lone and ahead of the others in eagerness fight with the Trojans,
Nor let him backward withdraw, since that would enfeeble the forces.
But when a man from his wain may reach to the car of his foeman,
Then let him thrust with his spear — much better is always this method.
So it was heroes of old laid low both cities and ramparts,
This plan ever in heart, and this same spirit within them."
　　　Thus did the old man charge them, of yore well tutored in warfare.
　　　Greatly the lord Agamemnon delighted beholding the hero.
Then he uplifted his voice and in accents wingèd addressed him:
　　　"Old man, even as now in thy breast right strong is the spirit,
Would that thy knees might with it keep pace, with strength unabated!
But it is age, which comes to all, that is heavy upon thee. [numbered!"
Would that some other were thus, whilst thou with the younger wert

Then unto him made answer the knightly Gerenian Nestor:
"Verily, I myself might wish with reason, Atrides,
Still to be such as I was, when I slew Ereuthalion, the godlike.
But do the gods not give all favors at once unto mortals.
Truly I then was a youth; but age comes now and attends me.
Nevertheless I will company still with the horse, to direct them
Both by advice and command, since such is the portion of elders.
Those let brandish their spears, the younger, robuster than I am,
Later in birth by far, more confident, too, in their prowess."

Thus spake he; and rejoicing in heart passed on Agamemnon.
Peteos' son was the next that he found, horse-smiter Menestheus,
Standing, around him engrouped the Athenians, rousers of war-cry.
Hard by stood at his station Odysseus, rich in devices;
Gathered about him, the files Cephallenian, feeble in no way,
Stood; for the war-cry sounded was not yet heard of the people,
Seeing, indeed, the battalions were only beginning their movements —
Trojans, tamers of horses, and lines of Achaeans. The meanwhile
Standing they waited, until some other division of Argives
Onrush made on the Trojans, and so a beginning of battle.
Seeing them thus, the king of men, Agamemnon, rebuked them,
Loud uplifting his voice, and with accents wingèd addressed them:

"Thou, that indeed art the son of Peteos, king Zeus-nurtured,
Thou, too, crafty of heart, excelling in wiles that are evil,
Why now stand ye aloof, thus cow'ring and waiting for others?
You twain surely it fitteth to stand in the ranks of the vanguard
Foremost, always there to encounter the blaze of the battle,
You that are first to accept glad bidding of mine to a banquet,
Often as we, the Achaeans, prepare some feast for the elders.
Then it delights you to feed on savory roast; and the goblets,
Brimming with wine, like honey in sweetness, drain ye at pleasure.
Now ye prefer to look on, to behold ten columns of Argives
Fighting the foe with the pitiless bronze in the battle before you."

Scowlfully looking, Odysseus of many devices addressed him:
"What sort of speech hath escaped from the bounds of thy teeth, Aga-
How say'st thou we are slack unto war? Once let us Achaeans [memnon?
Waken the fury of war 'gainst the Trojans, tamers of horses,

86

Then shalt thou see — if thou wilt, and if thou carest to be there —
Mingling amid forefighters of Trojan tamers of war-steeds
Even Telemachus' father. But empty as air is thy babble."

 Then with a smile thereat, replied the lord Agamemnon,
Seeing Odysseus vexed, and he took back the words he had uttered:
 "Zeus-sprung son of Laërtes, Odysseus of many devices,
I do not chide thee unduly nor anyway give thee an order,
Seeing I know full well that the heart in thy bosom belovèd
Loyally plans and devises; for *thy* thoughts even as mine are.
Come then; all this amend we tomorrow; if aught that is evil
Now hath been said, may the gods give it all to the winds for undoing!"

 Such words spoken, he left them there; and then, after others
Faring, he next found Tydeus' son, high-souled Diomedes,
Standing at rest on his firm-framed war-car there with his horses,
While at his side was standing Capaneus' son Sthenelaüs.
Lord Agamemnon, seeing him thus, upbraided the hero;
Loud he uplifted his voice and in accents wingèd addressed him:
 "Ah me! thou son of Tydeus, the wise, the tamer of horses!
Why dost thou skulk in the background and gaze at the bridgeheads of
No such skulking as this was aforetime pleasing to Tydeus! [battle?
Nay, but to battle with foes far ahead of his comrades belovèd.
So they declare who have seen him in war — I never for my part
Met him indeed or beheld; men *say* he surpassed all others.
Once, of a surety, he came guestwise, no foe, to Mycenae,
He with a peer of the gods, Polynices, raising an army.
Both at the time were in league against Thebè's hallowèd ramparts.
Earnestly, too, they besought us for valiant allies to be given;
Our folk also approved, full ready to help as demanded.
Zeus, however, altered their minds by the adverse omens he showed
When now these had departed and, faring along on the highway, [them.
Come to the river Asopus, grass-bedded, deep in the rushes,
There the Achaeans appointed and chose for ambassador Tydeus.
He went forward and found many lords of the people of Cadmus,
Thronged at a feast in the halls of Eteocles, powerful monarch.
There, though an alien he, that Tydeus, smiter of horses,
Yet was he all unafraid, though lone amid many Cadmeians.

Ay, he was easily victor in all prize tests when he challenged
Them to compete; so present a help unto him was Athena.
Deeply incensed, however, the goaders of horses, Cadmeians,
Laying an ambush strong, while *he* was returning, assailed him,
Young men fifty in number, of whom two heroes were leaders,
Maeon, the son of Haemon, accounted a match for immortals;
With him Autophonus' son, Polyphontes, sturdy in battle.
Dismal the doom prince Tydeus on these men also inflicted,
Slaying them all save one, whom only he sent to his homeland —
Maeon it was he dismissed, obeying the god-given omens.
Such was Aetolian Tydeus. A scion (alas!) he begat him
Far his inferior in fight, at talking alone his superior.''

    Such his rebuke. Diomedes, the strong, said naught in rejoinder,
Deeply abashed at the censure, in awe of the worshipful monarch.
Glorious Capaneus' son, however, gave him an answer:
    ''Atreus' son, lie not! Thou knowest the truth, then tell it!
We may avow ourselves to be men better far than our fathers;
We even went and captured the seat of Thebes, seven-gated,
Leading a scantier host against a mightier fortress,
Seeing we trusted the signs from the gods and Zeus's assistance.
Those men, our sires, because of their blindness infatuate, perished.
Ne'er then set me the fathers with us even equal in honor.''

    Scowlfully looking, the valiant prince, Diomedes, addressed him:
    ''Buddy, sit thee in silence; obey my word as I bid thee.
I, at least, grudge not at all Agamemnon, shepherd of peoples,
That he should spur into battle the well-greaved sons of Achaeans.
Him will the glory attend, I ween, if perchance the Achaeans
Lay low Trojans in battle and capture their Ilium holy;
His will the great grief be, if the foe lay low the Achaeans.
Come now, let *us* twain also take thought of impetuous valor.''

    Thus he spake and sprang from his car to the earth in his armor.
Fearfully clanged, as he started, the bronze on the breast of the sover-
Haply thereat were even a stout heart smitten with terror.   [eign;
    Even as when on a sea's loud-echoing margin a breaker
Rises before the driving of Zephyrus, billow on billow —
Out on the deep it reareth its crest first, afterward breaking

High on the seaboard, mighty it roars and, rounding a headland,
Speeds on, curling its crest and spurting the foam of the salt sea: —
Ev'n so closely arrayed pressed onward the Danaan squadrons
Moving incessant to battle; and each one gave, of the captains,
Word to his own men only; the rest kept silence; nor would one
Say they had voice in their breasts, so mighty an army as followed
Silent, in awe of the leaders; and over them, all in a glitter,
Armor richly inwrought, wherewith they were clothèd in moving.

    Meantime even as ewes, in the court of an opulent owner
Folded, in number untold, wait there to be drained of the white milk,
Bleating the while incessant at hearing the voice of their lambkins:
So from the Trojans arose in the wide-spread army a clamor,
Since not all were alike in their war-cry, neither in language
One, but their tongues were confused; they were called from many a na-
These it was Ares roused; the Achaeans, Pallas the bright-eyed; [tion.
Terror and Panic beside them, with Discord insatiably raging,
Sister at once and comrade of him, man-slaughtering Ares.
Lowly at first, indeed, her crest she uplifteth, but later
Beareth her head unto heav'n; on the earth her footsteps are planted.
Then, too, she through the throngs moved mightily hither and thither,
Scatt'ring blindfold strife, augmenting the groaning of heroes.

    When both armies arrived at the same place, coming together,
Clashed then the oxhide shields, the spears, and the fury of fighters,
Each in a corselet of bronze, while bull's hide bucklers embossèd
Pressed hard one on another, and mighty the din they awakened.
There rose together the shouts triumphant and groans of the heroes,
Slayer commingled with slain, while the earth ran red with the carnage.

    Even as when from the mountains two torrents, flooded with
Down to a hollow ravine in a midmost valley together   [winter,
Pour their furious waters, from sources exhaustless upwelling —
Far off, deep in the mountains, a shepherd heareth the uproar:
So, as the war-hosts mingled, the turmoil rose and the shouting.

    First, Antilochus slew of the Trojans a helmeted hero
Valiant, a foremost fighter, Thalysius's son, Echepolus.
Him was he first to smite on the ridge of his plumèd helmet;
Into his forehead he plunged his javelin; on passed the bronze point

Into the bone; and his eyes were straightway clouded in darkness.
Like as a tow'r down-crashing, he fell in the furious conflict.

Seizing him then by the feet, as he lay there, lord Elephenor —
Son of Chalcodon, captain of all the great-hearted Abantes —
Hurried to drag him from under the spears, all eager to strip him
Forthwith there of his armor; but short-lived proved his endeavor.
For, as the corpse he would hale, great-hearted Agenor, beholding
Him down-stooping — his side was exposed from under his buckler —
Smote with his bronze-shod spear, and he loosened the limbs of the Argive.
Thus did his spirit forsake him, while over him hot grew the travail
Sore of the Trojans and sons of Achaeans, one on another
Leaping in fury like wolves, while man hurled back man in the conflict.

Next Telamonian Ajax struck down the son of Anthemion,
Lusty, a-blooming in youth, Simoïsius, whom had his mother
Borne by Simoïs banks, what time she descended from Ida,
Whither, for viewing the flocks, she had erewhile followed her parents.
So then a name he received, Simoïsius. Never his parents
Dear he repaid for his nurture; for brief was the portion allotted
Him of life, laid low by the lance of the great-hearted Ajax,
Who, as the youngling advanced, on the right breast close to the nipple
Smote him. The weapon of bronze unwavering traversed his shoulder
Onward. Down to the ground in the dust he fell, as a poplar,   [land
One that had grown smooth-stemmed in the meadowy lush of a marsh-
Ample, and all of its branches have grown out alone at the summit.
This hath a man, some builder of cars, with his shimmering iron
Hewn down, minded to bend for a fair-wrought chariot a felloe.
Seasoning, therefore, the poplar lies on the bank of a river.

So Simoïsius, son of Anthemion, lay, stripped by great Ajax,
Scion of Zeus. At *him* then Antiphus, son of King Priam —   [javelin.
He of the glancing breastplate — flung through the throng his sharp
Ajax he missed but Leucus, Odysseus' valiant companion,
Struck on the groin, as he haled the body away to the Argives.
Down he crashed in a heap, and the corpse slipped out from his clutches.
Stung to the quick at the sight of his death, th' indignant Odysseus
Strode to the forefront straight, wide-flashing the bronze of his armor,
Came up, stood close by, then, glancing on all sides around him,

Hurtled his glitt'ring spear. Quick backward the host of the Trojans
Shrank from the hero's hurtle. And yet not vainly the missile
Sped; for it ſtruck Democoön, baſtard son of King Priam.
He had come from attending his fleet-foot mares at Abydus.
Him, in wrath for his comrade, Odysseus smote with a javelin,   [point
Smote on one temple; but, plunging, on in its course passed the bronze
Straight through the other. His eyes at once were clouded in darkness.
Earthward he fell with a crash; loud clanged his armor upon him.
Thereat the champions yielded and even illuſtrious Heᶜtor,
While the Argives shouted amain; then, haling the bodies,
On, ſtill onward, they pressed; but it wakened the wrath of Apollo
Gazing from Pergamus down, and he shouted aloud to the Trojans:

"Rouse, ye Trojans, tamers of ſteeds, nor give up the battle
Unto the Argives, since their flesh neither ſtone is nor iron
That could endure without hurt the flesh-cutting bronze when it smites
Now no longer the child of the fair-haired Thetis, Achilles,   [them.
Fighteth but now at his ships sits nursing his bitter resentment."

So from the city the awful deity spake; the Achaeans
She was arousing, the Trito-born, Zeus' glorious daughter,
Faring along in the press, where'er she beheld them relaxing.

Next Amarynceus' son Fate fettered, the valiant Diores,
Smit with a jagged ſtone, on his right leg, close to the ankle.
Caſter thereof was the captain who led the warriors of Thracia,
Piroüs, Imbrasus' son, who thither had journeyed from Aenus.
Both of the sinews and even the bones the merciless boulder
Utterly crushed. In the dust outſtretched he fell and supinely,
Both of his hands outspreading for help to his own dear companions,
Gasped his spirit away. But *he* rushed up that had smitten,
Piroüs even, and close at the navel he ſtabbed him. Forth gushed
All of his bowels to earth; and darkness covered his eyelids.

Piroüs, darting away, with a spear Aetolian Thoas
Smote on his chest, right over the nipple; the bronze was implanted
Fast in his lung. Then Thoas came close and plucked out the javelin,
Pond'rous, huge, from his breast and, drawing his sword from its scab-
Smote him therewith in the belly and took the life of the hero.   [bard,
Natheless his armor he ſtripped not off; for his comrades about him

91

Gathered, the Thracians, topknot-wearers, gripping their long spears.
Him, although he was valiant and strong and mighty in prowess,
Thrust they away from themselves, while *he* reeled backward and

    Lo! in the dust, then, lying the twain, beside one another [yielded.
Stretched out: he of the bronze-clad Epeians, and he of the Thracians,
Both war-chiefs; and about them was slain full many another.

    Then had a man no longer belittled the fray, had he entered —
Whoe'er, haply unsmitten of keen bronze, even unwounded
Then might range through the midst under guidance of Pallas Athena,
Holding his hand in hers and averting the volley of missiles —
Seeing a many that day of Achaeans and many a Trojan
Lay outstretched in the dust, prone fallen beside one another.

ILIAD · V · (E)

*In Epsilon Heaven's blood is shed
By sacred rage of Diomed.*

NOW unto Tydeus' son, Diomedes, Pallas Athena
Gave both valor and vigor, that *he* should, amid all the Argives,
Shine forth foremost in might and achieve him signal distinction.
Out from his shield and his helmet she kindled unwearying fire,
Like to the star of the harvest, a star transcending in brightness
All else, once it hath bathed itself in the River of Ocean.
She, with a fire thus kindled alike from his head and his shoulders,
Spurred him direct to the midst where soldiers crowded the thickest.

There was a man of the Trojans, one Dares, noble and wealthy,
Priest of Hephaestus; of two sons also was Dares the father —
Phegeus, the one, and Idaeus, well trained in all sorts of warfare.
Face unto face they assailed him, adventuring forth from the ranges,
Fighting, the twain from a car, but *he* on the ground as a footman.
Now as they came full nigh in the onset against one another,
First it was Phegeus let fly his spear, far-shadowing, forward.
Over Tydides' shoulder — the left one — speeding, the spear-point
Passed but touched him not. Next Tydides attacked with his javelin.
Not unavailing did *his* spear speed from the hand of its owner,
Striking him full in the breast, it dashed the foe from his chariot.
Down then bounded Idaeus, forsaking the beautiful war-car;
Yet he bestrode not boldly the prostrate form — for he dared not —
Nor had he likely eluded the same black fate as his brother;
Only Hephaestus guarded and saved him enshrouded in darkness,
Lest his aged priest be broken wholly in sorrow.

Driving the horses away, then, the son of the great-souled Tydeus
Gave them, for leading back to the hollow ships, to his comrades.

Now as the proud-souled Trojans beheld both children of Dares
One of them taking to flight, the other slain by his war-car,

Stirred was the spirit in all. But the bright-eyed goddess Athena,
Clasping impetuous Ares' hand, thus spake and addressed him:
  "Ares, man's bane, Ares, thou blood-stained stormer of ramparts,
Might not we then allow them, Achaeans and Trojans, to battle,
Unto whichever side Father Zeus bestoweth the glory?
Wiser for us to retire and avoid the wrath of the Father."
  Thus she spake. From the battle she led the impetuous Ares.
Then she made him sit down by the high-banked river, Scamander.
Quickly the Danaans turned back the Trojans, each of the leaders
Slaying his man. Yet foremost the monarch of men, Agamemnon,
Thrust from his war-car Odius, a great Halizonian captain.
Just as he turned, in his back Atrides planted a javelin,
Midway between his shoulders; clean through his breast it was driven.
Crashing he fell to the earth, and his armor rattled upon him.
  Then Idomeneus slew the son of Maeonian Borus,
Phaestus, come to the war from the deep-loamed tillage of Tarne;
Him, as he mounted his car, Idomeneus, famed as a spearman,
Wounded with his long lance and pierced his shoulder, the right one.
Down from his chariot he fell, and hateful darkness came on him.
Him then Idomeneus' comrades quickly despoiled of his armor.
  Meanwhile Strophius' son, Scamandrius, skilled as a hunter,
Atreus' son, Menelaüs, slew with his keen-pointed javelin.
Mighty hunter was he, for the fair Queen Artemis taught him
Shooting at all sorts of game that the forested mountain doth nourish.
Then, however, availed him his Artemis, Rainer of Arrows,
Naught, nor the long-shots in which he excelled, victorious aforetime,
Seeing that Atreus' son, Menelaüs, spearman renownèd,
Smote him, e'en as before him he fled, in the back with his javelin,
Midway between his shoulders; clean through his breast it was driven.
Forward he crashed on his face, and his armor rattled upon him.
  Then Meriones slew Phereclus, the scion of Tecton,
Harmon's son, who was skilled with his hands all manner of cunning
Handwork to fashion; for Pallas Athena especially loved him.
He it was built Alexander the trim ships, fountains of evil,
Ships that became such ruin alike unto all of the Trojans,
Even himself, for he knew not the oracles spoken of heaven.

Him Meriones, hot in pursuit, when about to o'ertake him,
Smote on his right hip fairly: the spear-point, speeding directly,
Held on e'en to the bladder, and under the bone it was halted.
Groaning he fell on his knees, and death cast darkness about him.

Meges it was then slew the son of Antenor, Pedaeus,
Whom, though bastard, the noble Theano tenderly fostered
Even as one of her own dear children, to pleasure her husband.
Closely approaching the Trojan, Phylides, famed as a spearman,
Smote on the sinewy nape of his neck with a spear keen-pointed
Under the tongue, and, cleaving the teeth, on hurtled the javelin.
Crashing he fell in the dust and gnashed the cold bronze in his anguish.

Next Eurypylus, son of Euaemon, laid low Hypsenor,
Godlike son of the proud Dolopion, who once was appointed
Priest of Scamander, who like a god was honored of Troy-folk.
Now, as he fled before him, the glorious son of Euaemon,
Even Eurypylus, rushing behind him, leaping upon him,
Cut off his heavy arm with a stroke of his sword on his shoulder.
Crimson the arm fell down to the ground, while over his eyelids
Settled the purple of death, and doom o'erpow'ring descended.

So it was these kept toiling amain in the strenuous struggle.
Meantime no one could say of Tydides where he was ranging,
Whether perchance with the Trojans he companied or with Achaeans.
Over the plain he rushed like unto a river in winter
Swollen with torrents at flood, as it speeds on shattering levees,
Nor can the long lines of levees, e'en though united, withstand it,
Neither restrain it the fences of bounteous-blossoming orchards,
When of a sudden it cometh, and Zeus rains heavy upon it.
Splendid works of the strong then perish before it in number:
So did Tydides rout the serried columns of Trojans
Singly, and none dared wait for his onslaught, though they were many.

Now as the glorious son of Lycaon, Pandarus, marked him
Over the plain wide-storming and routing whole squadrons before him,
Thereat against Diomedes his curved bow quickly he bended,
Aiming an arrow; it struck, as he rushed on—struck his right shoulder
Square on the curving breastplate. The bitter arrow unerring
Held right onward amain, and the dark blood spattered his corselet.

Over him shouted aloud the glorious son of Lycaon:
"Trojans, arouse ye now, high-spirited goaders of horses!
Lo! he is smitten, the best of Achaeans, nor truly, methinketh,
Long shall he hold up against so mighty a missile, if truly
Hither hath sped me the Lord, Zeus's son, on my coming from Lycia."

Thus far Pandarus' boast; but the swift dart quelled not Tydides;
Only he drew back a pace; then, standing in front of his horses
There and his car, called out unto Sthenelus, Capaneus' scion:
"Come, dear fellow, Capaneus' son, dismount from the chariot,
That thou mayest draw out this bitter dart from my shoulder."

Thus spake he. Unto earth leaped Sthenelus down from the chariot,
Came up, wholly extracted the swift dart lodged in his shoulder.
Then, as the blood shot up through the hero's close-woven tunic,
Straightly and fervently prayed Diomedes, good at the war-cry:
"Hear me, thou child of Zeus, aegis-bearing, thou maiden un-
If in the blaze of the battle aforetime ever with Tydeus   [wearied,
Thou'st been present for help, now favor me also, Athena.
Grant me to slay this man. Bring thou within range of my javelin
Him that hath taken advantage of me and shot me and boasteth,
Saying that not for long I look on the radiant sunlight."

So spake he in petition, and hearing him Pallas Athena
Lightened the hero's limbs, his legs and his arms up above them.
Standing near him the while, in light-winged words she addressed him:
"Courage now, Diomedes, do battle amain with the Trojans,
Seeing I've put in thy breast thy sire's invincible valor—
Valor such as of old had the knightly, shield-wielding Tydeus.
Yea, from thine eyes have I lifted the mist that was resting upon them,
That thou mayest distinguish unerring a god from a mortal.
Therefore now, if ever a god come hither, intending to try thee,
Nowise face unto face fight thou with the other immortal
Gods; but only if *she*—that daughter of Zeus, Aphrodite—
Enter the battle, do thou smite *her* with thy keen-pointed weapon."

These words spoken, Athena, the bright-eyed goddess, departed.
Back went Tydides again and mixed once more with the vanguard.
Ay, though eager in spirit before to fight with the Trojans,
Now it was threefold valor possessed him; like as a lion,

Whom some shepherd in guard of his fleecy sheep in the pasture,
Wounding, indeed, in his vault high into the fold, hath subdued not.
All of his might he arouseth, nor henceforth can he repel him,
Nay, but he hides in the steading; the sheep, all frighted, forsaken,
Lie on the ground together in heaps, strewn one on another.
Out of the fold leaps high in his vehement fury the lion:
Thus Diomedes, the mighty, in rage threw himself on the Trojans.

　First Astynoüs fell and Hypiron, shepherd of peoples:
Over the nipple he smote this one with his bronze-fitted javelin;
That one he struck with his sword on the clavicle close at the shoulder,
Cleaving it utterly off from the neck and the back of the Trojan.
Leaving them there, he pursued after Abas, then Polyïdus,
Sons of Eurydamas, dream-interpreter, agèd diviner;
These sons never returned for their sire their dreams to interpret,
Since that mighty Tydides the wargear stripped from the brothers.
Next he went after the children of Phaenops, Xanthus and Thoön,
Dearly beloved, but the father, with old age bowed and afflicted,
Never begat him another as heir of his ample possessions.
There it was Diomed spoiled them, of dear life bereaving the brothers
Both, and he left their sire keen anguish, loud lamentation
Only, that never alive he received them back from the battle,
Homeward returned. So kinsmen divided his substance among them.

　Next he assailed two sons of the Troy-king, the Dardanid Priam,
Driving in one car together, Echemmon and Chromius with him.
Like as a lion that leapeth 'mid kine and breaketh a heifer's
Neck or a cow's outright, as they graze in a woodland pasture,
So these twain from the car, in a piteous plight and reluctant,
Tydeus' son, Diomedes, thrust, then spoiled of their armor,
Giving his comrades the horses, to drive them away to the galleys.

　Now as Aeneas beheld him a-wasting the ranks of the warriors,
Up through the hurtling of spears he went and the tumult of battle,
Seeking Pandarus, peer of the gods, if chance he might find him.
When he had found that son of Lycaon, faultless and mighty,
Standing in front of him there, with this word Aeneas addressed him:
　"Pandarus, where thy bow? Yea, where thine arrows, the wingèd?
Where thy renown? For in that none here is assuredly rival,

Neither in Lycia will vaunt him another to be thy superior.
Come, now, lift thy hands unto Zeus; shoot an arrow at that man,
Who is thus mastering us; he hath wrought the Trojans already
Untold evil; he looseth the knees of many and valiant —
So it be not an immortal that venteth his wrath on the Trojans,
Anger for rites neglected; hard smiteth the wrath of a godhead."
    Spake unto him in reply that glorious son of Lycaon:
    "Counseling chief of the Trojans who wear bronze armor, Aeneas,
I would account him in all ways like the wise-hearted Tydides.·
Lo! by his shield I discern him, the vizored crest of his helmet,
Yea, and beholding his steeds. If a godhead, truly I know not
Clearly. If a man, as I said, if the wise-hearted scion of Tydeus,
Then not apart from a god doth he rage thus. Sure an immortal,
Some god, standeth beside him — a cloud cast over his shoulders —
Who, as my swift shaft lighted upon him, averted it elsewhere,
Seeing I've sped him a shaft already and struck his right shoulder,
Driving it straight on through the convex plates of his corselet.
Truly I said: 'It will hurl him down headlong to Aidoneus.'
Yet it hath vanquished him not — a deity surely, in anger!
Neither are horses at hand nor a chariot, to mount me upon it.
Yet in the halls of Lycaon are chariots standing, eleven,
Beautiful, fresh-geared wholly, and new-made; covers are mantled
Round them. And nearby standeth for each one a couple of horses
Champing the white-grained barley and spelt. And idly they stand there!
Verily now full often the spearman, the agèd Lycaon,
Straitly enjoined upon me in his well-built home, as I left it,
Prudently bidding me mount the horse-drawn chariot, whenso
Into the strenuous strife I marched at the head of the Trojans.
Yet I heeded him not — far better it were I had done so —
Wishing to spare such horses, accustomed to feed until sated,
Fearing a shortage of fodder, in case the town were blockaded.
So then I left them at home and came a foot-soldier to Ilium,
Trusting alone in my bow; but the bow was to profit me nothing,
Since already I've shot at two of the princely commanders,
Tydeus' son and the scion of Atreus, yea, and I smote them
Both, and the blood drew truly, but only aroused them the rather!

Evil the hour that *I* took down my bow from its peg, it appeareth —
Even the day when I headed my Trojan array unto lovely
Ilium, bringing therewith a favor to Hector, the goodly.
But if I ever return, and my eyes shall behold them —
Fatherland, wife, and the great high roof of the palace paternal —
Straightway then let a stranger cut off this head from my body,
If with my hands I break not this bow, and the pieces
Cast in the fiery blaze; it has followed me here to no purpose."

  Answering him in turn spake Aeneas, captain of Trojans:
"Talk not thus, I pray thee. The matter will never be mended,
Ere we twain shall encounter yon man, with chariot and horses
Meeting him face to face, and make trial of him with our weapons.
Come then, mount on my car. In this way thou shalt discover
What are the horses of Tros, well-skilled for pursuit or withdrawal
Over the plain with exceeding swiftness hither and thither.
These two will bear us also safe to the city, if haply
Zeus should award unto Tydeus' son hereafter the glory.
But do thou take the lash and the shining reins of the horses;
Take them, and I from the car will dismount to engage in the battle.
Or do thou withstand him, and I will manage the horses."

  Spake unto him in reply the glorious son of Lycaon:
"Nay, keep thou thyself the reins and thy horses, Aeneas.
They for a driver they're used to will bear much better the curvèd
Car, if haply we needs must flee from the face of Tydides,
Lest they loiter affrighted, belike, and are even unwilling
Forth from the battle to bring us, missing the voice of their master,
Till Diomedes, son of the great-souled Tydeus, in onset
Slaughter us both and drive to his galleys the whole-hooved horses.
Nay, 'tis far better for thee to drive thy chariot and horses;
I, for his onrush watching, with my sharp spear will receive him."

  These words spoken, they mounted the war-car richly accoutred.
Eagerly forward they drove the swift horses against Diomedes.
Sthenelus, Capaneus' son, the illustrious, when he espied them,
Called Diomedes straight and in accents wingèd addressed him:
"Diomed, Tydeus' son, to my heart the dearest of mortals,
Lo! I behold two chiefs that are mighty and eager to fight thee,

Might past measure possessing; the one, well skilled as a bowman,
Pandarus, vaunteth himself to be the son of Lycaon.
Ay, and the other's Aeneas, begotten of blameless Anchises —
Such is his boast — and he has for a mother divine Aphrodite!
Come then, let us withdraw on the war-car, neither, I pray thee,
Rage in the vanguard thus, lest haply thy life be the forfeit."

    Scowlfully looking, the valiant prince, Diomedes, addressed him:
    "Talk not to me of flight! For methinks thou *wilt* not persuade me,
Seeing that mine was never a nature to skulk in a battle,
Neither to cower; for courage is still firm-rooted within me.
No! I refuse to mount on the war-car; just as I now am
Right on against them I go; nor Pallas permits me to tremble.
These twain never again shall the fleet-foot horses deliver,
Both of them saved from *us*, though one may escape or the other.
One thing else will I tell thee; in thy soul wisely remember:
Granteth me Pallas Athena, abounding in counsel, the glory
Both these heroes to slay, then these fleet horses of mine here
Thou shalt restrain by tying the reins hard fast to the car-rim;
Mind thou! mount quickly behind the steeds of Aeneas and drive them
Out of the reach of the Trojans away to the well-greaved Achaeans.
They, I tell thee, are of that breed which Zeus, the far-thund'rer,
Gave unto Tros as amends for his son, Ganymedes, most surely
Goodliest horses of all that are under the sun and the morning.
Horses from this royal stock Anchises, monarch of mortals,
Stole from Laomedon, mating the steeds with his fillies in secret.
Thereof issued a stock, ev'n six brought forth at his palace.
Four he reserved for himself and reared them well at his manger;
Twain he gave to Aeneas, his son, contriver of panic.
Should we secure them — good! it would win us a notable glory."

    Ev'n as they were conversing in such wise one with the other,
On came the others apace, both urging the swift horses forward.
First to Diomed spake that glorious son of Lycaon:
    "Thou, stout-hearted and wise, thou son of illustrious Tydeus,
That bitter arrow vanquished thee not, my swift-flying missile.
Now I will try with a spear, if perchance I may prove more successful."

    Thus he spake. Then poising his spear far-shadowing hurled it;

Full on the shield of Tydides it struck; and, winging its way, went
Onward the point of bronze, till it came clear through to the corselet.
Over him shouted aloud the glorious son of Lycaon: [hold up
    "Smitten thou art in the belly right through, and meseemeth will
Not much longer thy head. To me thou hast given great glory."
    All undismayed, Diomedes, the mighty, in answer addressed him:
    "Hit hast thou not; thou hast missed. But ye two hardly, methinketh,
Both shall cease from the fray ere one or the other hath fallen,
Glutting with blood of yours the war-god, shield-bearing Ares."
    These words spoken, he hurled, and Athena directed the missile
Right at his nose by the eye, and his teeth white-shining it traversed;
On at the root of his tongue the bronze unwearied went cleaving,
Till at the base of his jaw outrushed the point of the javelin.
Out from the chariot he fell; loud clanged his armor upon him,
Gleaming in all its brightness. *Off* to one *side* swerved the horses,
Swift of foot. Unstrung were the life and strength of the hero.
    Down from the car with his buckler and long spear leaped Aeneas,
Smitten with fear lest the body be haled thence by the Achaeans.
Over him boldly he strode, like a lion that trusteth his prowess,
Holding before him his spear and his shield, all evenly rounded,
Eager to slay whoever might venture to come out against him,
Crying his terrible cry. Then seized in his hand Diomedes —
Marvelous deed! — such a boulder as two men could lift not,
Men such as mortals are now, but with ease all alone he could swing it.
Therewith Aeneas he smote on the hip, where turneth the thigh-bone
Round in the joint of the hip, whence men also name it the "cup-bone."
So was the cup-bone crushed; so both of the sinews were broken;
Also the jagged stone tore open the skin, and the hero
Sank on his knees upright; his stout hand only sustained him,
Pressing the ground; and a curtain of black night covered his eyelids.
    There then Aeneas, king of men, most likely had perished,
Had not the daughter of Zeus, Aphrodite, speedily marked it,
Even his mother that bare him to prince Anchises, when herdsman.
Instant about him she wreathed her white arms, around her belovèd,
Holding before him a fold of her radiant raiment as curtain,
Fending away the missiles, lest one of the fleet-horsed Achaeans,

101

Piercing his bosom with weapon of bronze, might rifle his spirit.
Bearing her dear son thus, from the war ſtole softly the goddess.

 Neither had Capaneus' son forgotten his charges a moment,
Those Diomedes gave him, Tydides, good at the war-cry;
Nay, but the whole-hooved ſteeds of his own far off from the tumult
Staying, he faſtened the well-wove reins to the rim of the chariot,
Leaped then up on the car of the fair-maned ſteeds of Aeneas,
Drove them away from the foe to the side of the well-greaved Achaeans,
Gave them at once to Deïpylus, comrade dear, whom he honored
Most of his fellows — for he was of *one* mind and heart with him ever —
Bidding him drive them away to the hollow ships. He himself then
Mounting his own car, seizing the gliſt'ning reins of his coursers,
Forthwith hurried the ſtrong-hooved horses in quest of Tydides
Eagerly. He meanwhile with the pitiless bronze was pursuing
Cypris, knowing that she was accounted invalorous, no way
Numbered with goddesses mighty that sway o'er battle of warriors,
Neither a Pallas she nor Enyö, sacker of cities.
But when, cleaving the close-packed throng, in pursuit he had reached
Then with a leap, with a lunge, Diomedes, scion of great-heart [her,
Tydeus, wounded the skin of her delicate hand with his spear-point.
Straight through the flesh the keen lance bored — first rending the ves-
Graces had wrought her themselves, ambrosial — under the surface [ture
Over the base of the palm; flowed deathless blood of the goddess
(Ichor, such as it floweth in veins of the deities blessèd,
Seeing they eat not bread, neither drink wine, bright in its sparkle.
Therefore bloodless are they and therefore namèd immortals).

 Crying aloud, she let fall her son; but Phoebus Apollo
Caught Aeneas up in his arms and guarded him safely
Under a dark cloud, careful lest one of the fleet-horsed Achaeans,
Piercing his breast with weapon of bronze, might rifle his spirit.
After her shouted aloud Diomedes, good at the war-cry:

 "Hold off, daughter of Zeus, from the warfare; cease from the fight-
Is it for thee not enough, the beguiling of delicate women? [ing!
Natheless, if thou wilt often resort to the war, then, methinketh
Thou'lt yet shudder at war, at its mention even afar off."

 So he spake. But she was gone, sore troubled and frantic.

Aphrodite Wounded in the Hand, Conducted by Iris to Ares

Iris, shod with the wind, received her and forth from the tumult
Led her, in torment of pain, with her fair skin darkly discolored.
There, at the left of the battle, she found the impetuous Ares
Seated; his spear and swift steeds against a cloud were reclining.
Down on her knees then falling before him, her brother belovèd,
Instant there for his steeds with the frontlets of gold she besought him:

"Brother beloved, attend me and give me the horses to bear me
Safe, that I win to Olympus — Olympus, the home of immortals.
Grievously pains me a wound that a mortal, a man, has inflicted,
Diomed. Even with Father Zeus he now would do battle!"

So spake she; so he gave her the golden-frontleted horses.
Quickly she mounted the car, sore-aching the heart in her bosom.
Iris mounted beside her; the reins she grasped in her two hands,
Laid on the lash to start them; and they went eagerly flying.
Speedily then they arrived at the gods' seat, tow'ring Olympus.
Iris, shod with the wind, there halted and stabled the coursers,
Loosing them first from the car, then set them ambrosial forage.
There Aphrodite divine fell down at the knees of her mother,
Even Dione; and she in her fond arms clasping her daughter,
Patted her child with her hand, then spake a word and addressed her:

"Who, dear daughter, entreated thee thus of the children of heaven,
Wantonly, even as wert thou in open a doer of evil?"

Straitly the lover of smiles, Aphrodite, answered her mother:

"Diomed wounded me, that high-souled scion of Tydeus,
Only because I was bearing my well-loved son from the battle,
Even Aeneas — to me by far he is dearest of all men —
Since no longer the dread war-din of Achaeans and Trojans
Soundeth; but now are the Danaans fighting even immortals."

Then to her made answer the beautiful goddess Dione:

"Bear up, daughter of mine, and endure, though grievously suff'-
Seeing that many of us that dwell in Olympian mansions   [ring,
Suffer of men, as we bring woes grievous, one on another.
Ares suffered, when Otus and he, Ephialtes, the mighty,
Sons of Aloeus, bound him and forcibly held him in prison.
There in a vessel of bronze full thirteen moons he lay fettered.
There even Ares haply, insatiate of battle, had perished,

105

Had not their own step-mother, the beautiful Eëriboea,
Borne unto Hermes tidings, and he it was stole away Ares
Far outworn already; the cruel fetters had quelled him.
Hera suffered as well, when Amphitryon's scion, the mighty,
Smiting her full on the breast with the point of a three-barbèd arrow,
Wounded her; straight she was seized with an unassuageable anguish.
Hades suffered with these from a swift dart, Hades, the awful,
Ev'n when this same scion of Zeus who wieldeth the aegis,
Smiting him 'mid the departed, consigned him to grief in the gateway.
Speeding he went to the palace of Zeus, unto lofty Olympus,
Aching in heart and with pain overcome, for the arrow,
Deep driven into his robust shoulder, was vexing his spirit.
Spreading his simples upon it, assuagers of pangs, Paeëon
Healed him; for never indeed had the god been created a mortal.
Headstrong man of violent deeds, the author of scandal,
Who dared wound with his arrows those gods that dwell in Olympus!
So hath the bright-eyed goddess Athena set this man against thee —
Fool, for Tydeus' son doth not know in his heart — Diomedes —
How short-lived he must be who battles against the immortals.
Never at *his* knees, never methinks, *his* children shall prattle
Welcome to him on return from the war and the terrible conflict.
Wherefore, no matter how he excelleth in might, let Tydides
Take heed lest there engage him a warrior stronger than thou art,
Lest that Aegialeia, the prudent child of Adrestus,
Often awaken with wailing her household sunken in slumber,
While she lamenteth the best of Achaeans, him she had wedded,
Brave wife now that she is of the tamer of steeds, Diomedes."

Said she, both hands cleansing the wrist meanwhile of the ichor.
Healing began in the hand, as the sore pangs all were abated.
Looking upon it the while, both Pallas Athena and Hera
Were with their heart-cutting words provoking Zeus, the Cronion.
Pallas, the bright-eyed goddess, was first with a word of derision:

"Zeus, O Father, wilt thou be angry, whatever I utter?
Surely methinks now Cypris was coaxing some dame of Achaia,
Luring her off to the Trojans — she loves them so to distraction!
While then she was caressing some fair-robed dame of Achaia,

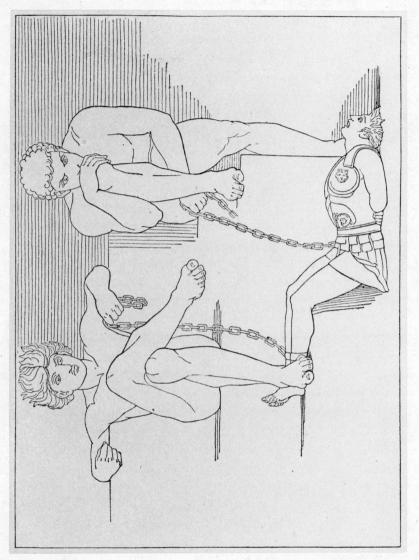

Otus and Ephialtes Holding Ares Captive

Thus on some golden brooch she scratched her poor little fingers!"

    Thus spake she. Zeus smiled, the Father of men and immortals;
Then Aphrodite, the golden, he called to his side and addressed her:

    "Truly, my child, not war and its travail to thee have been given.
Nay, but busy thyself with the gladsome duties of wedlock.
These things shall be a care unto Ares, the swift, and Athena."

    Such were the godheads' words in their converse one with another,
While Diomedes, good at the war-cry, leapt at Aeneas,
Though full well he knew the protecting arms were Apollo's.
He, however, unawed of the strong god even, but striving
Ever to slaughter Aeneas and strip off his glorious armor,
Three times darted upon him, in eager desire to slay him;
Three times Apollo beat back the hero's glittering buckler.
But, when a fourth time, like to a god, he was charging upon him,
Called to him loud, with an awful command, far-working Apollo:

    "Think, Diomedes. Back! nor venture to match with immortals
Thine own spirit and thought, since noway like are the races,
Gods immortal and men that walk on the earth and are mortal!"

    Thus spake he; and in awe Diomedes drew back a little,
Seeking t' avoid the wrath of the god, far-darting Apollo.
He, however, aloof from the throng bore onward Aeneas
Far unto Pergamus holy, for there his temple was builded.
Leto speedily healed him; and Artemis, rainer of arrows,
There in the innermost shrine's deep cloister clothed him in glory.

    That same god of the silver bow created a phantom
Meantime, utterly like to Aeneas himself in his armor.
There then, circling the phantom, both Trojans and goodly Achaeans
Hewed one another's armor of oxhide that covered their bodies,
Shields all evenly girdled and targes a-flutter with aprons.
Then it was Phoebus Apollo bespake the impetuous Ares:

    "Ares, man's bane Ares, thou blood-stained stormer of ramparts,
Wouldst thou haply go after this man and withdraw him from battle,
Diomed? Even with Father Zeus he now would do battle.
Smiting her hand at the wrist, in the first place Cypris he wounded;
Yea, upon even myself in the throng he rushed like a daemon."

    These words spoken, he seated himself on Pergamus' summit.

Baleful Ares anon went rousing the ranks of the Trojans,
Moving amid them in guise of fleet Acamas, captain of Thracians.
Loudly he called meanwhile on the children of Priam, Zeus-fostered:
  "O ye sons of Priam, Zeus-fostered king of the Trojans,
How long yet will ye suffer th' Achaeans to slaughter the people?
Even perchance till around yon gates well-builded they battle?
Low now lieth a hero we honored like Hector, the goodly,
Even Aeneas, the son of the prince, great-hearted Anchises.
Come now, and let us rescue our comrade brave from the tumult."
    Thus spake he and aroused the might and spirit of each man.
Then Sarpedon sharply upbraided the valorous Hector:
  "Hector, whither is gone that spirit thou haddest aforetime?
Once thou saidest forsooth that alone, without armies or helpers,
Thou wouldst keep Troy safe with thy brethren by blood and by mar-
Now it is not even one that I can observe and discover.   [riage.
Nay, they are cow'ring round like dogs that encircle a lion.
We that are only allies, it is we that are fighting the battle.
I, for example, have come as ally from a region afar off,
Lycia, lying remote on the banks of the eddying Xanthus.
Dear is the wife I have left and a son, but a baby, behind me,
Many possessions as well, that the needy are likely to covet.
Yet, even so, I am spurring the Lycians on; I am eager
Here to engage with my man, though I have nothing of value,
Such as Achaeans perchance might plunder and take as a booty.
Meanwhile thou standest still, not even exhorting the others,
All thy folk, to stay and defend their wives with their weapons.
Take heed! lest ye be caught like fish in a drag-net's meshes,
Lest ye become, all ye, but the enemy's prey and his plunder,
Yea, and the foeman anon make spoil of your populous city.
All these things it behooves thee to weigh both daily and nightly.
Go now! Rouse the allies and the far-called chiefs and implore them
Firm, unflinching to hold — and escape their bitter reproaches."
    Thus Sarpedon spake; and his words stung the heart of brave
Out from his car forthwith he leapt to the ground in his armor, [Hector.
Brandishing two keen lances, and ranged everywhere through the army,
Rousing them up to the fight, and battle-din dreadful awakened.

So they were rallied and stood and resisted again the Achaeans.
Yet would the Argives flee not but, closely compacted, withstood them.
Even as wind o'er floors devoted to threshing and sacred
Streweth the chaff, while, under the breath of the breezes, Demeter
Gold-haired parteth the chaff from the grain of the winnowing work-
Then are the chaff-heaps whitened below: e'en so the Achaeans [men —
Grew white under the whirl of the dust uprising among them,
Beaten aloft to the heavens of bronze by the feet of the horses,
Now, as they mingled again, and their drivers wheeled them to battle.
On, straight onward they carried their hands' dread prowess; around
Ares impetuous curtained the night as an aid to the warring   [them
Trojans, ev'rywhere ranging. Thus he fulfilled for Apollo,
God of the golden sword, his behest; for he it was bade him
Rouse up might in the Trojans anon, on beholding Athena
Gone from the field; for she had been lending the Danaans succor.
Also Apollo himself sent forth from his opulent temple,
Filling with courage his breast, that shepherd of peoples, Aeneas.
So then Aeneas resumed his station amid his companions,
Glad to behold him returning alive, uninjured among them,
Filled with valorous might; but they asked him never a question;
Toil far other forbade, which he of the bow wrought of silver
Roused, and man's-bane Ares, and Eris, insatiably raging.

 Meanwhile the Ajaxes twain, Odysseus, and brave Diomedes
Likewise stirred the Achaeans to war; themselves, undaunted,
Neither the violence feared nor the stormy assaults of the Trojans;
Nay, they were standing enranked and alike unto clouds that Cronion
Settleth aloft in a calm on the tops of the pinnacled mountains,
Motionless, while yet sleeps the might of the Northwind and others,
Violent winds, whose driving, with keen breath blowing upon them,
Scatters the shadowing clouds through ether abroad and asunder:
So the Achaeans awaited, unshaken, the Trojans and fled not.

 Ranging the press meanwhile was Atrides, instantly urging:
"Friends, now quit you like men; have a heart of courage within
Shrink from dishonor before one another in stress of the conflict. [you;
Fewer are slain than are saved of soldiers shunning dishonor;
But to the fugitive neither glory nor safety is coming."

Thus he spake and hurled his javelin, smiting a leader,
Even Deïcoön, comrade in arms of great-hearted Aeneas,
Pergasus' son, whom the Trojans esteemed like the children of Priam,
Since he was ever swift 'mid the front-rank warriors to battle.
Him on his shield then lord Agamemnon smote with his javelin.
Nor could the buckler arrest it; the bronze tore mightily onward,
Drave right through, and it traversed the belt, deep into his belly.
Earthward he fell with a crash; loud clanged his armor upon him.

    Then did Aeneas slay, in his turn, two Danaan princes,
Even the sons of Diocles, Orsilochus namely and Crethon.
He, their father, dwelt in the well-built city of Phere —
Wealthy in substance, tracing descent from the river Alpheüs,
Pouring its wide-spread flood abroad through the regions of Pylus.
He an Orsilochus fathered, a king over numerous heroes,
Who then begat another, Diocles, mighty of spirit;
Next to Diocles himself in turn were born the twin brothers,
Crethon and brave Orsilochus, skilled in all manner of warfare.
They, on attaining the prime of their youth, along with the Argives
Followed on board the black ships to Ilium, land of fine horses,
Seeking for Atreus' sons, Menelaüs and King Agamemnon,
Honor; but there now both by the issue of death were enshrouded.
Like unto them have been reared two cubs on the top of a mountain,
Lions, trained of their dam, in a thicket deep in the forest;
They then harry the kine and the goodliest sheep of the pasture
Often and desolate steadings of people, till they are slaughtered,
Even themselves, with keen-edged bronze in the hands of a hero:
Suchwise conquered, the brothers twain at the hands of Aeneas
Fell to the earth, in their falling full like unto towering fir-trees.

    Pitying them as they fell, Menelaüs, belovèd of Ares,
Strode to the fore-front straight, wide-flashing the bronze of his armor,
Shaking his spear in his wrath, while Ares wakened his courage,
Minded to have him slain at the hands of Trojan Aeneas.
Him the son of the great-hearted Nestor, Antilochus, seeing, [peoples,
Strode through the fore-front straight; for he feared for the shepherd of
Seeing if *he* suffer aught, *their* travail were all unavailing.   [lances
    Now in their hands those twain stood poising their sharp-tipped

Over against each other, in eagerness ready for battle.
But as Antilochus came up beside the shepherd of peoples,
Hardly Aeneas could ſtand, although he was fierce as a fighter,
When he beheld two men arrayed thus one by another.
They then, haling the bodies away to the host of Achaeans,
Placed the unfortunate twain in the hands of their Danaan comrades,
But for themselves, on return, joined battle again 'mid the foremost.

Each of them then slew his man: Pylaemenes (rival of Ares,
Chief of the Paphlagonians, the great-souled bearers of bucklers)
Atreus' son, Menelaüs, the far-famed javelin-wielder,
Pierced with a lance as he paused — full fair on the clavicle smiting.
Mydon, his squire, who held the reins, Antilochus wounded,
Valiant son of Atymnius, while turning the whole-hooved horses;
Hurling at him a ſtone, he smote him full on the elbow.
Down to the ground in the dust fell the reins with ivory shining.
Leaping upon him, Antilochus ſtruck with his sword on his temple.
He, as he panted for breath, from the well-wrought chariot tumbled
Headlong into the dust; there ſtriking on forehead and shoulders,
Stood with his feet in the air — deep sunken in sand, as he lighted —
Till he was cast to the earth, rolled into the dust, by his horses
Under Antilochus' lash, as he drove to the host of Achaeans. ⌈upon them

Hector anon caught sight of those twain through the ranks and
Charged with a shout, and behind him the serried Trojan battalions
Followed in might; and before went Enyö, the awful, and Ares —
She with her "turmoil" lifted, the emblem of merciless warfare;
He with a spear in his hands, high-wielding the weapon gigantic,
Now in advance far-ranging, again to the rearward of Hector.

Him then beheld Diomedes, good at the war-cry, and shuddered.
Even as crossing a wide-spread plain, some trav'ler bewildered
Stops at a river that flows, swift-rushing, roaring to seaward,
Seething with foam — at beholding, he draws back in haſte from its
Even so Tydeus' son drew back and spake to the people: ⌈margin;

"Friends, how have we been wont to admire Hector, the godlike,
Saying that he is the bravest of spearmen and warrior courageous.
One of the gods walks ever with him, repelling deſtruction.
Lo! even now at his side ſtands Ares, guised as a mortal!

113

Well, then, backward! — but ever with faces turned toward the Trojans
Give ye ground nor be eager to battle amain with immortals."

    Thus he spake; and the Trojans came close in, crowding upon them.
Two ſtrong men that knew well the rapture of battle did Heċtor
Slay — in one car driving — Anchialus, with him Meneſthes.
Pitying them in their fall, the great Telamonian Ajax
Came up, taking his ſtand close by them, and, hurling his shining
Spear, ſtruck Amphius, Selagus' son, whose home was in Paesus,
Rich in flocks and herds and in fields of grain; but his portion
Led him afar to bring aid to Priam, the king, and his children.
Low on his war-belt Ajax, the great Telamonian, smote him;
Deep in his nethermost belly the spear far-shadowing faſtened.
Crashing he fell to the earth; right at him the glorious Ajax
Rushed and would ſtrip off his arms; but the Trojans showered upon him
Keen spears, glittering bright, and his shield caught many a missile.
Planting his heel on the body, the hero drew forth the bronzen
Spear from the wound, but the beauteous arms of his foe he could nowise
Strip from his shoulders as well, so crowded the missiles upon him.
Ay, and he dreaded the doughty defense of impetuous Trojans,
Who, both many and gallant, with spears firm-planted against him —
Though he was known to be valiant and ſtrong and mighty in prowess —
Thrust him away from themselves, while *he* reeled backward and yielded.

    So it was these kept toiling amain in the ſtrenuous combat.
Fate then urged Heracles' son, Tlepolemus, goodly and mighty,
'Gainst Sarpedon, the godlike — a fate impelling, resiſtless.
Now as they came full nigh in the onset against one another —
Even the son and the grandson of Zeus who gathers the ſtormclouds —
Then was Tlepolemus first to address a word to his foeman:
    "Lycian counselor, thou! what need, Sarpedon, for thee, then,
Here to be skulking, a man like thee, unacquainted with battle?
Liars are they that declare thee a son of the aegis-bearer,
Zeus, the Cronion; for thou art greatly inferior to those men
Who were descended from Zeus in the generations aforetime.
Only to think what a one (men say) was Heracles mighty,
Even my father, the bravely ſteadfast, with heart of a lion,

Who, to secure Laomedon's horses, once made his way hither,
Sailing with six ships only and war-mates scanty in number,
Even so sacking the city of Ilium, wasting her highways.
Thine is a coward's heart, and thine a minishing people.
Neither methinketh that thou wilt a bulwark prove to the Trojans,
Anyway, coming from Lycia, not e'en though exceedingly mighty.
Nay, but, subdued at my hands, thou'lt pass through the portals of Ha-
  Spake unto him in reply Sarpedon, the Lycian commander: [des."

"That man verily wasted, Tlepolemus, Ilium's hallowed
City, because of a man's, of the haughty Laomedon's, folly,
Who had rewarded his excellent work with a word of upbraiding,
Neither would give him the horses, wherefor he had come from afar off.
Thee, however, 'tis slaughter and black fate now that awaiteth
Here under these hands, seeing my lance shall subdue thee and render
Glory to *me*, *thy* soul unto Hades, famed for his horses."

  Thus Sarpedon spake. Tlepolemus lifted his ashen
Weapon aloft, and together the long spear-shafts of the heroes
Both at a moment flashed from their hands; but the spear of Sarpedon
Smote on the midst of his neck; the spear point, freighted with anguish,
Sped right through; and the blackness of Erebus curtained his temples.
Yet had the long spear, hurtled the while of Tlepolemus, smitten
Full on his foe's left thigh, and the point rushed furious onward
Grazing the bone; but his father averted as yet the destruction.

  Quickly away from the warfare his goodly companions were bear-
Godlike Sarpedon wounded. The long spear, trailing behind him, [ing
Weighted him down. In their haste not one had considered or minded
Forth from his thigh to withdraw the ashen spear and allow him
Upright to get on his feet; such labor they had to attend him.

  Likewise forth from the battle the well-greaved sons of Achaeans
Carried Tlepolemus fallen. The godlike Odysseus remarked it,
He of the steadfast soul, and his heart raged fiercely within him.
Doubtful at first was the hero; he wavered in spirit and purpose
Whether the son of loud-thundering Zeus he further should follow
Or take many a life from the mass of the Lycians rather.
Yet was it not ordained of Fate that great-hearted Odysseus
Slay with his keen-bladed sword that valiant son of Cronion.

So on the Lycian masses Athena directed his fury.
Coeranus quickly he slew, and Alastor, Chromius also,
Halius, too, Alcandrus, Noëmon, and Prytanis likewise;
Others, and more had the godlike Odysseus slain of the Lycians,
Had not Hector, the mighty, the shim'ring helmeted, marked him
Straight; he strode to the fore-front, wide-flashing the bronze of his armor,
Bringing the Danaans terror. Right glad to behold him, Sarpedon,
Son of Cronion, addressed him a doleful word at his coming:

"Suffer me not, son of Priam, to lie here a prey for the Argives;
Nay, now bring me help; hereafter may life even leave me
There in that city of yours, since never, it seems, I was fated
Homeward to fare and revisit the well-loved land of my fathers,
Glad'ning the wife of my love and my infant son by my coming."

Thus he. No answer made the shimmering-helmeted Hector —
Never a word — but, eager with speed to drive back the Argives,
Darted past him to take the life of many a foeman.

Soon as his goodly companions had seated Sarpedon, the godlike,
Under the beauteous oak of the aegis-bearing Cronion,
Forthwith Pelagon, valiant, Sarpedon's comrade belovèd,
Drew out deftly the ashen spear from the thigh of the hero.
Straightway his spirit forsook him, and mist poured over his eyelids.
Soon he revived, and a breath of Boreas, blowing about him,
Brought new life again to his soul that was grievously swooning.

Meanwhile never for Hector, the bronze-mailed, never for Ares,
Turned them the Argives about toward the black ships, where they were
Nor once counterattacked in the fight, nay, steadily backward   [lying,
Yielded, when they discovered that Ares was there with the Trojans.
Who was the warrior first, who also the last to be slaughtered
There by Hector, King Priam's son, and Ares, the bronzen?
Teuthras, like to a god, and the smiter of horses, Orestes;
Next then Trechus, Aetolian spearman, Oenomaüs also,
Helenus, Oenops' son, and Oresbius, gleaming in taslets,
He who, hoarding his wealth, was aforetime a dweller in Hyle,
Situate there on the mere of Cephisis; whileas the others
Near him dwelt — Boeotians, whose country in riches abounded.

Now, however, as Hera, the white-armed goddess, had marked
Laying the Argives low in the stress of the furious conflict,   [them
Forthwith then she addressed, in accents wingèd, Athena:

"Ay me, daughter of Zeus, the aegis-bearer, thou tireless,
Sure it was wholly in vain, that word *we* gave Menelaüs,
Ilium's well-walled city to sack and then to sail homeward,
If we allow yon madman to rage thus, ruinous Ares.
Come now, let *us* twain also take thought for impetuous valor."

So said she; and Athena, the bright-eyed, failed not to obey her.
Hera, the honored goddess, the daughter of Cronus, the mighty,
Straightway hastened to harness her golden-frontleted horses.
Hebe the meanwhile hasted to fit on the axle of iron
Fair-curved wheels, eight-spoked, on both sides balanced, and bronzen.
Gold is the felloe, which nought can destroy; above and about it
Well-fitted tires of bronze — the whole a marvel to look on.
Also the hubs are of silver, on both sides circling the axle;
Golden and silver the bands tight-plaited all over the footboard,
Rigidly stretched; and the railing that runs all round it is double.
Fashioned of silver, the pole stood out; and she at its front end
Bound on a beautiful yoke, all golden, and fastened the breaststraps,
Golden and beauteous too; while under the yoke led Hera
Steeds fleet-footed, herself full eager for strife and the war-cry.

Then, too, Athena, the daughter of Zeus who beareth the aegis,
Shed at her sire's own portal the fine, light robe she was wearing,
Richly embroidered, that she with her own hands toiling had fashioned.
Thereupon, donning the tunic of Zeus, cloud-massing Cronion,
She in her harness arrayed her, appointed for dolorous warfare.
Thwart then over her shoulders she cast her the terrible aegis,
Deep-fringed. Panic all round as a crown is enwoven to wreathe it;
Likewise Strife is thereon, blood-curdling Assault, and Resistance.
Thereon also the Gorgon's head — that hideous monster,
Horrible, grim, and a portent of Zeus who beareth the aegis.
Next on her head she set her two-ridged helmet, all golden,   [hundred
Strengthened with bosses four, and with warriors bedight from a
Towns. On the flame-bright car she mounted and seized on her javelin,
Ponderous, massive, and strong, the lance wherewith she subdueth

Heroes' ranks she is wroth with, the child of a father puissant.

    Now with her whip lashed Hera in eagerness down on the horses;
Then, self-moving, the gates of heaven creaked that the Horae
Keep, to whom are committed the heavens immense and Olympus,
Whether to open the clouds' dense compact, whether to close it.
Then through the gates the goad-enduring horses they guided.
Seated apart from the rest of the gods they found the Cronion
Lone on a topmost summit of many-ridgèd Olympus.
There then ſtaying her horses, the white-armed Hera, the goddess,
Queſtioned the most high Zeus, the Cronion, and thus she addressed

    "Zeus Father, how can it be that the violent doings of Ares [him:
Do not incense thee? How great and how goodly a host of Achaeans
Ruthless, unruly, he slaughters — a grief unto me, while at leisure
Cypris and he of the silver bow, Apollo, make merry —
They that incited that mad one, who *no* law ever regardeth.
Zeus Father, wilt thou be angry at all with me, if I smite him,
Ares, and drive him away in piteous plight from the battle?"   [her:

    Zeus, the compeller of clouds, made answer at once and addressed

    "Go, then, and rouse up against him Athena, the driver of booty,
Her who mainly is wont with the sorest pains to acquaint him."

    White-armed Hera in naught disregarded his word, but the god-
Lashed on the horses divine; and the twain went eagerly flying   [dess
Midway between the earth and the ſtarry expanse of the heavens.
Far as a man with his eyes in the haze of diſtance discerneth,
Gazing over the wine-dark sea, as he sits on a headland,
So much clear at a bound the loud-neighing coursers of heaven.
Now when at Troy they arrived and came to its two flowing rivers,
Where the Scamander and Simoïs join their waters together,
There then Hera, the white-armed goddess, halted the horses,
Loosing the twain from the car, and poured mist in abundance about
Simoïs then made ambrosia spring up beside them to graze on. [them.

    Forward the twain went tripping along like timorous pigeons,
Eagerly yearning to succor the Argive combatant heroes.
Now, as at length they arrived where, crowded, the most and the brav-
Stood, closely thronging together around Diomedes, the mighty   [est
Tamer of ſteeds, and, like unto lions of ravenous hunger

Or unto wild boars, swine, whose might is not easy to master,
There then standing she shouted, the white-armed deity, Hera,
Taking upon her the likeness of bronze-voiced, great-hearted Stentor,
Who had a shout far-heard as of other men fifty in number:

"Shame, ye Argives, craven reproaches, magnificent looking!
While yet goodly Achilles unceasingly moved in your warfare,
Ne'er would the Trojans venture outside the Dardanian gateway —
Not even once! Such terror they had of his powerful javelin.
Now by the hollow ships they are fighting far off from the city."

Thus she spake and aroused the might and spirit of each man,
While unto Diomed hastened the bright-eyed goddess Athena.
Soon she had found that king beside his chariot and horses,
Cooling the wound that the arrow from Pandarus' bow had inflicted.
Sorely indeed had the sweat been vexing it under the baldric
Broad of his well-rounded shield; and his hand, both weary and vexèd,
Lifted the baldric in pain, and the dark-hued blood he was wiping
Off, as the goddess, with hand on the yoke of his horses, addressed him:

"Truly hath Tydeus gotten a son that in little is like him!
No doubt, Tydeus' stature was small, but the man was a fighter.
Ev'n when I was unwilling and straitly forbade him to battle,
Blazing ahead — when alone he had come with no other Achaeans,
Envoy to Thebes, to enter among the many Cadmeians,
I had bidden him banquet in peace in the halls of assembly.
He, however, with soul that was valiant, as ever aforetime,
Challenged the youth of Cadmea and won in every contest
Easily; such was the help in time of need that I gave him.
Close by thee now I'm standing, thou seest, and ever protect thee
Well, and with all my heart I bid thee to fight with the Trojans.
Howe'er, either fatigue from furious striving hath entered
Into thy limbs, or fears dishearten and hold thee. In nowise
Art thou then the offspring of Tydeus, the wise son of Oeneus."

Answering her in turn, Diomedes, the valiant, addressed her:
"Goddess, I know thee, daughter of Zeus who beareth the aegis;
Therefore gladly I tell thee a word and will not withhold it.
Neither disheartening fear lays hold, nor a shrinking, upon me;
Nay, I still bear in mind the behest thyself hast commanded,

119

Bidding me strictly that I should fight 'gainst none of the blessèd
Godheads; only if *she*, that daughter of Zeus, Aphrodite,
Enter the battle, am I with the keen bronze bidden to wound her.
Therefore now do I yield, myself; and the rest of the Argives
All I have bidden to gather here in close order together,
Seeing I clearly perceive it is Ares is lord of the battle."

    Then unto him made answer the bright-eyed goddess Athena:
    "Diomed, Tydeus' son, to my heart the dearest of mortals,
Neither of Ares' self nor even of other immortals
Have thou fear, since I unto thee am a helper in battle.
Come now, instantly guide thy whole-hooved steeds upon Ares,
Smiting him hand unto hand; have no fear of impetuous Ares,
Ares, a curse incarnate, a renegade, frenzied with fury,
Who so lately in words with me and with Hera pretended
Only the Argives to succor, engaging to fight 'gainst the Trojans;
Natheless, consorting with Trojans, he's wholly forgotten his promise."

    These words uttered, she thrust down Sthenelus quick from the
Pulling him back with her hand; and *he* leaped instantly from it. [chariot,
She then mounted the car by the side of divine Diomedes,
Vehement goddess; and loudly it creaked — that axle of oakwood —
Bearing a goddess dread along with the bravest of heroes.
Forthwith grasping the lash and the reins then Pallas Athena
Guided the whole-hooved horses at once and direct upon Ares.
He at the moment was stripping the armor of Periphas, giant,
Bravest by far of Aetolians, the glorious son of Ochesius.
Him the blood-stained Ares busily stripped; but Athena
Put on the helmet of Hades, lest dreadful Ares behold her.
Now, as the man's-bane Ares beheld the divine Diomedes,
Leaving Periphas slain, that giant, where he was lying,
Right where the war-god had slain him and of his spirit bereft him,
Ares rushed on straight at Tydides, tamer of horses.
Now, as they came full nigh in the onset against one another,
Over the yoke and the reins of his horses Ares directed,
Lunging, his bronze-shod lance, all eager of life to bereave him.
Catching the spear with her hand, the bright-eyed goddess Athena
Thrust it aside, to spend its force in vain past the chariot.

Diomedes Casting His Spear Against Ares

Next Diomedes, good at the war-cry, bravely assailed him,
Thrusting with lance of bronze, while Pallas Athena impelled it
Deep in his nethermost flank, where the god was girdled with taslets.
There, with his thrust, he wounded the god, tore open his fair flesh,
Drew out the spear-point again. Then bellowed Ares, the bronzen,
Even as loud as nine thousand men, or even ten thousand,
Shout, when in warfare they join in the fury and strife of the battle.
Trembling at once laid hold on them all, Achaeans and Trojans,
Fear-struck; such was the bellow of Ares, insatiate of warfare.

Even as mist from the clouds — like Erebus black it appeareth —
When, after heat, is arising a stormwind's terrible tempest:
Such unto Tydeus' son, Diomedes, Ares, the bronzen,
Seemed in his faring aloft 'mid the clouds unto canopied heaven.
Swiftly he came to the seat of the gods, unto lofty Olympus.
Down he sat beside Zeus Cronion in anguish of spirit,   [wounded.
Shewed him the blood, the immortal, that streamed down where he was
Then with a piteous cry, with wingèd words he addressed him:

"Zeus Father, art thou not vexed at seeing such violent doings?
Ever for us that are gods such cruelest portion, to suffer
One by another's devices in rend'ring favor to mortals!
All of us quarrel with thee, since thou hast a daughter insensate,
Ruinous, alway minded to plan and to work the unseemly.
All we others, as many as there be gods in Olympus,
Always hearken to thee; unto thee are we ev'ry one subject.
Never a deed or a word of rebuke thou givest the vixen,
Nay, thou settest her on — *thy* child is that pestilent maiden.
Now it is Tydeus' son, Diomedes, proud over measure,
She hath incited to rage in his fury against the immortals.
Smiting her hand at the wrist, in the first place Cypris he wounded;
Yea, upon even myself in the throng he rushed like a daemon.
Only my swift feet bore me away thence; else were I suff'ring
Long in agony there, 'mid the grisly heaps of dead soldiers,
Or, though still left alive, sore-smitten of bronze and disabled."

Eyeing him sternly, cloud-gath'rer Zeus in answer addressed him:
"Nay, thou renegade, sit thou not beside me to whimper,
Odious most unto me of the gods that inhabit Olympus,

123

Since thy joy is ever in ſtrife and in war and in battle.
Thy own mother's the one with a temper unbearable, tameless,
Hera herself, and with words I can scarce avail to control her.
This then thou art enduring, methinketh, at her inſtigation.
Still, no longer will I endure to see thee in anguish;
Offspring of mine thou art; unto me thy mother hath borne thee.
But if another had borne thee as peſtilent, e'en of immortals,
Long ere now thou hadst lain down deeper than Uranus' children."

  Thus he spake and at once commanded Paeëon to heal him.
Spreading his simples upon him, assuagers of anguish, Paeëon
Healed him; for never indeed had the god been created a mortal.
Even as fig-tree sap oft speedily thickens the white milk —
Liquid itself, but it curdles exceedingly quick, when one ſtirreth:
E'en so speedily healed Paeëon impetuous Ares.
When now Hebe had bathed him and clothed him in comely apparel,
Down at the side of Cronion he sate him, exulting in glory.

  Meantime unto the mansion of great Zeus home were returning
Argive Hera and she, Alalcomenean Athena,
For they had ſtayed the man's-bane Ares from slaughtering heroes.

ILIAD · VI · (Z)

In Zeta Hector prophesies;
Prays for his son; wills sacrifice.

So was deserted the Trojans' and Argives' terrible war-din.
Oft then over the plain the battle swayed hither and thither,
While midway of the Xanthus' streams and the Simoïs river
Spearshafts shodden with bronze men leveled against one another.

First Telamonian Ajax, the bulwark strong of Achaeans,
Broke a battalion of Trojans and let in light on his comrades,
Smiting a warrior prince who headed the levies of Thracia,
Acamas goodly and great, the warlike son of Eussorus.
Crashing directly the ridge of his helm, thick-plumèd with horsehair,
Bedded itself in his forehead the bronze spear point, and it entered
Piercing the bone. Deep darkness shrouded the eyes of the hero.

Next Diomedes, good at the war-cry, slaughtered Axylus,
Teuthras' son, who dwelt in the fair-built town of Arisbe;
Wealthy in substance, moreover, was he and of all men belovèd;
Hard by the road was his home, and he gave entertainment to all men.
Yet of them all came no one (alas!) to avert the destruction
Fell, to encounter the foeman that reft them both of the spirit —
Him and Calesius, too, his trusty attendant, the driver
Then of his war-steeds; under the earth both heroes descended.

Hardy Euryalus spoiled both Dresus and with him Opheltius.
Next he pursued Aesepus and Pedasus, sons whom the Naiad
Nymph, Abarbarea, bore one day to Bucolion faultless.
Now, of the sons of the lordly Laomedon he was the eldest,
Even Bucolion, born of a mother unwedded, in secret.
He, while tending his flock, held converse of love with the Naiad.
Twin sons the Nymph conceived and bore to Bucolion faultless.
Ay, but the warrior-son of Mecisteus shore them of vigor,   [shoulders.
Loosened their glorious limbs and their armor stripped from their

125

Steadfast in war Polypoetes then slew Astyalus mighty.
Also Odysseus despoiled the Percosian hero Pidytes
Next with his bronze-shod javelin, and Teucer divine Aretaon.
Then with a bright spear Nestor's Antilochus vanquished Ablerus.
Elatus also was slain by the monarch of men, Agamemnon,
Elatus, who by the banks of Satnioïs' fair-flowing river
Dwelt in Pedasus lofty. The Hero Leïtus slaughtered
Phylacus, fleeing. Eurypylus slaughtered Melanthius steadfast.

 Then Menelaüs, good at the war-cry, captured Adrestus,
Took him alive; for his steeds, while scouring the plain in their terror,
Caught on a tamarisk bush, had broken the pole of the curvèd
War-car right at the front and gone of themselves to the city,
Whither the rest in disorder were also fleeing affrighted.
Out from the car he was rolled; beside the wheel he was fallen
Headlong into the dust on his face; then came up beside him
Atreus' son Menelaüs, in hand his far-shadowing javelin.
Thereat Adrestus clasped his foe by the knees and besought him:

 "Take me prisoner, Atreus' son, and receive a rich ransom!
Many the treasures heaped up in the halls of my opulent father,
Many of gold and of bronze and of iron cunningly smithied,
Whereof my father would give thee a ransom beyond all telling
Haply, if only he heard I was safe by the galleys Achaean."

 Thus he spake and persuaded the heart in the breast of Atrides.
He had delivered the captive anon to his squire, to conduct him
Down to the galleys swift of Achaia, had not Agamemnon
Come on a run toward his brother and, calling loudly, addressed him:

 "Why so careful of foemen, my good Menelaüs? I pray thee,
Tell me! Hast thou been treated so well at home by the Trojans?
May not one of them all escape from utter destruction
Now under *our* hands, neither the man-child haply a mother
Bears in her womb; may not *even* that one escape, but together
Perish they all out of Ilium—all, unburied and traceless!"

 These words spoken, the hero persuaded the mind of his brother.
Righteous his words of persuasion. And so the hero Adrestus
Thrust he away with his hand; and then the lord Agamemnon
Smote him upon his flank. Supinely he fell. And Atrides

Planted his heel on his breast and drew forth the javelin of ashwood.

Then cried Nestor, his shout resounding afar, to the Argives:

"O my Danaan friends, ye heroes, comrades of Ares,
Let not one of you all lay hands on the booty or linger
Rearward, hoping to fare with the heaviest load to the galleys.
Nay, let us *slaughter* the foeman first, then later at leisure
Ye may despoil the dead bodies, that lie on the field, of their armor."

Thus he spake and aroused the might and spirit of each man.
Then had the Trojans, o'ercome through lack of valor, retreated
Up into Troy-town before the Achaeans, belovèd of Ares,
Had not Helenus, Priam's son, far the best of diviners,
Stopped by Aeneas and Hector and in these accents addressed them:

"Hearken, Aeneas and Hector — for now of the Lycians and Trojans
Ye twain must bear the burden of war, since ye are the fittest
Men for every task, for battle and also for counsel —
Here take your stand and, everywhere ranging, rally the people
Hard by the gates, ere they flee and, into the arms of their women
Throwing themselves, thus prove a cause for joy to their foemen.
Soon as ye then have aroused all ranks once more to the conflict,
We will abide right here and give the Danaans battle,
Even in weariness sore; for dire need presses upon us.
Thou, though, Hector, betake thee now to the city and speak there
Unto thy mother and mine, yea, bid her assemble the matrons
Straight to the bright-eyed goddess Athena's acropolis temple.
There with a key let her open the doors of the hallowèd mansion.
There let her lay on the knees of the fair-haired goddess Athena
Even the robe in her palace that seems both fairest and largest,
Far most precious to her, prized highly beyond all others,
Likewise vowing to offer twelve heifers there at her temple,
Yearlings as yet untouched of the goad — if she will have mercy
Now on the city of Troy, its women, and innocent children,
If she will only restrain from hallowèd Ilium's ramparts
Tydeus' son, fierce spearman, that mighty deviser of panic,
Whom I deem to have proved most valiant of all the Achaeans.
Never in such wise feared we Achilles, captain of heroes,
Who of a goddess was born, men say; but passing all measure

127

This man rages, and no one availeth to match him in prowess."

So spake Helenus. Hector, in all things heeding his brother,
Out from his car forthwith leaped down to the ground in his armor,
Brandishing two keen lances, and ranged everywhere through the army,
Rousing them up to the fight, and battle-din dreadful awakened.
So they were rallied and stood and resisted again the Achaeans.
Thereat the Argives yielded ground and desisted from slaughter,
Deeming belike an immortal, descended from starry Olympus,
Came to defend the Trojans — in such wise now they had rallied.

Then cried Hector, with shouts that echoed afar, to the Trojans:
"O ye high-souled Trojans, allies too, widely renownèd,
Quit you like men, my friends, and remember impetuous prowess,
While I go unto Ilium town and direct that the elders,
Greybeard chiefs of the council, and matrons gathered together
Call on the powers divine and hecatombs vow to appease them."

Thus called the glancing-helmeted Hector aloud and departed,
Whileas about him the black hide struck on his neck and his ankles,
Even the rim that ran round the bossy shield's outermost border.

Meanwhile Tydeus' son and the son of Hippolochus, Glaucus,
Met in the space midway of the two hosts, eager for battle.
Now as they came close up in the onrush 'gainst one another,
First accosted his foe Diomedes, good at the war-cry:

"Who art thou, my very good sir, of men that are mortal?
Never till now have I seen thee mingling in glorious battle.
Now, howe'er, in thy daring and far in front of all others
Hast thou advanced, awaiting my strong, far-shadowing javelin.
Children of ill-starred parents are they that encounter my prowess.
But if thou be an immortal insooth, descended from heaven,
I, for my part, would never with godheads from heaven do battle.
Nay! not e'en the begotten of Dryas, the mighty Lycurgus,
Long could endure, who ventured to strive with godheads from heaven,
He that aforetime chased the attendants of mad Dionysus
Down through the region of Nysa, divine land; all then together
Strewed their wands on the ground, sore-smitten of murd'rous Lycurgus
Armed with an ox-goad. Taking to flight, down plunged Dionysus

Under the salt sea-wave. Him Thetis received in her bosom,
Full of affright; for Lycurgus' rebuke had struck him with trembling.
Then were the happy and care-free gods right wroth with Lycurgus:
Zeus, son of Cronus, struck him with blindness; then he endured not
Long; for the hatred of all the immortal gods overtook him.
Neither should I, then, desire to fight with the blessèd immortals.
But, if thou art of mortals that feed on the fruitage of plowland,
Come thou nearer, that sooner thou enter the toils of perdition."
　　Him the glorious son of Hippolochus answered as follows:
"Great-hearted son of Tydeus, why ask of *my* generation?
Like generations of leaves, e'en so are men's generations:
Leaves that be now the wind sheds down on the earth; but the forest
Buds and puts forth others, when on comes the season of springtime.
So generations of men — one passeth, cometh another.
Yet, if thou wishest, then learn this too (that well thou may'st know it),
Even our generation; the men that know it are many:
Deep in a corner of Argos, the pasture of horses, a city
Ephyra lieth; and there dwelt Sisyphus, craftiest mortal,
Sisyphus, Aeolus' son. He begat him a son, even Glaucus,
Who was the father himself of a son, Bellerophon blameless.
Beauty and manliness both, the enkindlers of love, the immortals
Vouchsafed *him*; yet Proetus devised in his heart for him mischief —
Being the mightier far — and away from the land of the Argives
Drave him; for Zeus had subjected Bellerophon under his sceptre.
Goodly Anteia, the consort of Proetus, burning with passion,
Loved him and wished him to lie with her secretly; noway
Could she persuade wise-hearted Bellerophon, virtuous, upright.
So, with a lie on her lips, she spake unto Proetus, the monarch:
　"'Die, O Proetus, thyself or slay this Bellerophon for me,
Since he hath willed love's union with me, though I was unwilling.'
　"So spake Anteia; and wrath laid hold on her lord, as he heard her.
Wroth though he was, his soul in awe forbade him to slay him —
Sent him afar into Lycia and charged him with tokens of sorrow,
Many, of fatal import, all graved on a tablet infolded —
Bidding him show to her father and so bring destruction upon him.
Under the guidance of God Bellerophon journeyed to Lycia.

But when to Lycia he came and the fair-flowing stream of the Xanthus,
There wide Lycia's king with all his heart did him honor:
Nine days he entertained him; nine were the bullocks he slaughtered.
But as the dawn, rosy-fingered, the tenth, appeared in the heavens,
Then he questioned his guest and asked to look on the token
Which, whatever it was, he had brought from his son-in-law, Proetus.
Soon as the king had received his son-in-law's token of evil,
First he commanded him slay that furious monster, Chimaera.
She was divine in her birth, not sprung from an origin human,
Lion in front but a serpent behind, she-goat in the middle,
Terribly breathing abroad the fierceness of fire bright-blazing.
Her did he slay forthwith, obeying the god-given omens.
Second he joined in war with the Solymi, famous as warriors,
Hardest battle, he said, he ever had entered with heroes.
Thirdly he slew those equals of men, those Amazon women.
As he returned, the king wove a fine web of treachery 'gainst him:
Choosing from broad-plained Lycia the bravest of heroes, he set them
Hidden in ambush; never did they to their homes have returning;
All fell slain; for the hand of the blameless Bellerophon slew them.
Now, as the king came to know that this was a deity's goodly
Offspring, there he detained him and offered his daughter in wedlock,
Gave him the half, moreover, of all that monarchy's honor.
Then, too, the Lycians meted him there a domain that exceeded
All else — fair in its vineyard and plowlands — his to enjoy it.
"Unto the wise Bellerophon children were born, three in number:
Namely, Isander, Hippolochus, too, and Laodamia.
Zeus, the master of counsel, once lay with Laodamia,
Who then bore him a peer of the gods, the bronze-mailed Sarpedon.
But when Bellerophon even grew hateful to all the immortals,
Lonely he wandered afar along the plain called Aleian,
Gnawing his own heart ever and shunning the paths of his fellows.
Ares, insatiate of war, to his grief slew Isander, his first-born,
As he was fighting against the Solymi, famous as warriors.
Artemis (she of the golden reins) slew his daughter in anger.
Son of Hippolochus I; and he, I declare, was my father.
He unto Ilium sent me and charged me instant and often

130

Ever to be of the best, preëminent over all others,
Neither bring shame on the house of my fathers, who were the noblest
Born in Ephyra town or in the broad kingdom of Lycia.
Such is the race and the blood whereof I proudly avow me."

　　Thus he spake. Diomedes, good at the war-cry, was gladdened.
Down on the bountiful earth he planted his spearshaft firmly;
Then with a word soft-spoken he answered the shepherd of peoples:
　　"Thou art a guest-friend surely of mine through my father afore-
Oeneus once, the divine, entertained Bellerophon blameless,   [time.
Kept him, a guest-friend even for twice ten days in his palace.
Ay, and they gave each other the goodliest tokens of friendship:
Oeneus gave him a girdle, a warrior's, gleaming with purple,
While Bellerophon gave a two-handled goblet, a gold one.
Sailing hither to Troy, I left it at home in my palace.
Tydeus I do not remember — a mere babe I, when he left me
That sad season, when perished at Thebes the host of th' Achaeans.
Therefore am I a dear guest-friend unto thee in mid-Argos,
Even as thou art in Lycia, if there peradventure I journey.
So let us shun each other's spears in the midst of the war-throng.
Trojans and famous allies full many are mine for the slaying,
Whomsoever perchance God grants — and my feet overtake him.
Many Achaeans are thine to be slain, whome'er thou art able.
Let us exchange our armor, that likewise others may know it
Clearly, that we are avowed guest-friends in the wise of our fathers."

　　These words spoken, the twain leaped forthwith down from the
Gave each other the hand, pledged firm faith one to the other. [chariots,
Then it was Zeus, the Cronion, took away from Glaucus his senses,
Who, interchanging his harness with Tydeus' son, Diomedes,
Took only bronzen for gold, ev'n nine bulls' worth for a hundred.

　　When now Hector was come to the Scaean Gates and the oaktree,
Troia's daughters and wives came running and gathered about him,
Eagerly asking him questions about their friends and their husbands,
Brothers, and sons. He dismissed each one in her turn and commanded
All to petition the gods; for sorrow was waiting for many.
　　Then he went on and arrived at the beautiful palace of Priam,

All bedight with corridors polished; and in it, moreover,
Chambers of polished stone were builded, fifty in number,
Builded closely one to another. Therein the sons of
Priam the king by their wedded wives were accustomed to slumber.
Over against these, fronting the courtyard, twelve were the chambers
Roofed over (these for his daughters) of polished marble constructed,
Builded closely one to another; there were their husbands,
Sons-in-law of the king, with their chaste wives accustomed to slumber.
Then came Hecabe forward, his gracious mother, to meet him,
Leading Laodice with her, the fairest in form of her daughters.
Clasping his hand in her own, she spake a word and addressed him:

"Child, why comest thou hither and quittest the desperate battle?
Truly the woe-named sons of Achaeans sorely oppress thee,
Warring about this city. Thy spirit sendeth thee hither!
Yea, thou comest to stretch, from the citadel, hands to Cronion.
Stay till I bring thee honey-sweet wine, that with it thou mayest
First pour out a libation to Zeus and the other immortals,
Drink of it then thyself—for methinks it will surely refresh thee;
Wine makes mightily wax in his prowess a warrior wearied,
Even as thou art a-wearied in ever defending thy people."

Then to his mother replied great shimmering-helmeted Hector:
"Bring me no wine honey-hearted, I pray thee, dear mother reverèd,
Lest thou unnerve me, and I forget my prowess and valor.
Awful the thought of pouring with unwashed hands to Cronion
Sparkling wine; not fitting it were for one all bespattered,
Gory with blood, to offer a prayer to Zeus of the storm clouds.
Nay, do thou to the fane of Athena, the driver of booty,
Hasten with incense-gifts and gather the matrons together.
Take that robe in thy palace which seems both fairest and largest,
Far most precious to thee, prized highly beyond all others,
Lay it with prayer on the knees of the fair-haired goddess Athena,
Likewise vowing to offer twelve heifers there at her temple,
Yearlings as yet untouched of the goad—if she will have mercy
Now on the city of Troy, its women, and innocent children,
If she will only restrain from hallowèd Ilium's ramparts
Tydeus's son, fierce spearman, that mighty deviser of panic.

132

Now then, away to the fane of Athena, the driver of booty,
Go thou; but I unto Paris will go with a summons to battle,
If perchance he will heed my voice. May even the earth now
Forthwith swallow him up! As a bane the Olympian reared him,
Sore bane unto the Trojans, the great-heart king and his children.
If I could only behold him descend to the mansion of Hades,
Then I could say that my heart had forgotten its burden of sorrow."

    So spake he. To the hall she departed and called to her handmaids.
They then all through the city went gath'ring the matrons together.
She, however, herself went down to the fragrant storeroom
Where the embroidered robes, rich work of Sidonian women,
Lay, whom the prince Alexander, of godlike form, had imported —
When o'er the wide sea's waters he cruised — from the marches of Sidon.
That was the voyage on which he had brought back Helen, the high-
Therefrom Hecabe chose one and bore it a gift to Athena,   [born.
One that was fairest of all in its broidery, also the largest,
Starlike shining among them — of all it was undermost lying.
Then she went her way; the old dames hurried behind her.

    When they arrived at the goddess Athena's acropolis temple,
For them the doors were opened by Cisses' daughter, Theano,
Fair of face, the wife of Antenor, tamer of horses.
Her the Trojans had made to be priestess unto Athena.
All then lifted their hands to Athena with loud lamentation.
Fair-faced Theano, the priestess, then took up the beautiful mantle,
Laid it upon the knees of the fair-haired goddess Athena,
Lifted her voice, and prayed to the daughter of Zeus, the all-mighty:

    "Lady Athena, our city's defender, of goddesses fairest,
Break Diomedes' spear, oh Maiden, and as for its wielder,
Grant that *he* fall prone in front of the Scaean gateway,
That forthwith we may offer thee heifers twelve in thy temple,
Yearlings, as yet untouched by the goad, if thou wilt have mercy
Now on the city of Troy, its matrons, and innocent children."

    Such was the prayer of Theano, but Pallas Athena denied it.
Thus they were praying to her, the daughter of Zeus, the all-mighty.
Meanwhile Hector had come to the palace of prince Alexander,
Beauteous, built by himself with craftsmen reckoned the deftest

Then to be found among men in the deep-loamed region of Troyland.
These had fashioned for him his chamber and hall and his courtyard
Hard by Priam and Hector, aloft in the uppermost city.
Into it entered Hector, belovèd of Zeus. And his spearshaft,
Cubits eleven in length, he held in his hand; and before him
Glittered the point of bronze; and a ferrule of gold ran about it.
Paris he found giving care to his beauteous arms in his chamber,
Busy with corselet and shield; his curvèd bow he was handling.
There, too, Helen of Argos amid her household women
Sat and was busy directing her handmaids in handiwork lovely.
Hector, at sight of his brother, in accents bitter rebuked him:

"Good sir, thou didst not well, in thy soul to harbor this rancor.
People are perishing all round the town and the lofty rampart,
While they do battle: for thee have the conflict blazed and the war-cry
Round this city besieged. Yea, *thou* wouldst fight with another,
Thou thyself, at beholding him shrink from the odious battle.
Up then! else may the town soon be burning with ravaging fire."

Then in his turn to his brother replied Alexander, the godlike:

"Seeing thou chidest me, Hector, in measure and not over measure,
Thee will I, therefore, tell it; do thou give heed and attend me.
Not on account of the Trojans so much, was I sitting resentful,
Wroth in my chamber forsooth, but I wished to give way to my sorrow.
Yet even now hath my wife with her soft words over-persuaded,
Urging me back to the fray, and to *me* it appears to be better,
Even to me; for to men by turns the victory cometh.
Come, then, tarry a while, till I don my weapons of warfare;
Else go on; I shall follow and soon overtake thee, methinketh."

So said he. Not a word spake the shimmering-helmeted Hector.
Thereupon Helen addressed him in accents gently persuasive:

"Brother-in-law of a dog like me, so mischievous, horrid,
Would that upon that day, when first my mother did bear me,
Some ill hurricane wind, down rushing upon me, had rapt me
Off to a mountain, or else to the sea's loud-thundering billow —
There might the waves have swept me away, ere all *this* came upon us!
Howbeit, seeing the gods these evils ordained and appointed,
Would I were mated at least with a man far better than Paris,

Hector Chiding Paris

One that could feel the resentment of men and their many reproaches.
This man neither is now, we see, sound-minded nor will be
Ever in future; the fruit thereof he will gather, methinketh.
Come, my brother-in-law, come in and be seated beside me
Here on a chair, since thine is a heart most travail-encompassed
All on account of a dog like me and the blind Alexander's
Folly, on whom Zeus laid a dolorous doom, that hereafter
We may become a theme of song to men in the future."
    Then to the lady replied great shimmering-helmeted Hector:
    "Bid me not, Helen, sit down; thou art kind but shalt not persuade
Nay, for my heart calls now in my breast, that I succor the people, [me.
Troy-folk, who long for me much, while now from the field I am absent.
Thou must arouse yon fellow; and let his own spirit bespeed him
So he himself o'ertake me, the while I am still in the city.
This he can easily do; for I to my home shall be going,
There to see my dear wife and my infant son and my housefolk.
Truly I know not whether to them I shall have a returning
Or now, under the hands of Achaeans, the gods will subdue me."
    Thus he spake and departed, the shimmering-helmeted Hector.
Quickly anon he arrived at his own well-stablishèd mansion,
Yet found not in her halls his Andromache, her of the white arms,
Since she had gone with her babe and a handmaid in beautiful raiment
Unto the tow'r and had taken her place there, weeping and wailing
Hector, on finding his faultless wife not there in her chamber,
Came to the inner threshold and stood and spake 'mid the servants:
    "Come now, servants of mine, and tell me the truth with exactness,
Where is the white-armed lady Andromache gone from the palace?
Gone to my sisters' perchance, or the fair-robed wives of my brothers?
Or, it may be to the shrine of Athena along with the others,
Ilium's fair-haired daughters, t' appease the obdurate goddess?"
    Him then in turn with a word a busy housekeeper answered:
    "Hector, seeing thou strictly biddest that truth shall be told thee,
Neither went she to a sister nor fair-robed wife of a brother,
Neither is gone to the shrine of Athena along with the others,
Ilium's fair-haired daughters, t' appease the obdurate goddess —
Nay, but to Ilium's tower, the great one, hearing the Argives

Press on the Trojans hard and victory crowns the Achaeans.
So in precipitate haste she is gone ev'n now to the rampart,
Like unto one that is mad; and a nurse bears with her her infant."

    Thus made answer the woman, the housekeeper. Hector, departing,
Hastened the same way back through the well-built streets of the city.
When he had passed through the wide-walled town and arrived at the
Gateway — there he was minded to fare forth into the battle —   [Scaean
Lo! came running to meet him Andromache, wife of his bosom,
Bountiful daughter of King Eëtion, great-hearted Eëtion —
Him who dwelt at the foot of the forested mountain of Placus,
Habiting Thebè of Placus and ruling the men of Cilicia.
That king's daughter was wife to the bronzen-harnessèd Hector.
She now met him; and with her her handmaid came; on her bosom
Nestled the light-hearted boy — for as yet he was only an infant —
Dear-loved scion of Hector and like to a star in his beauty.
Hector would call him Scamandrius, th' others Astyanax named him,
Seeing that Hector alone was protector of Ilium city.
He, as he stood there, smiled on his offspring, gazing in silence.
Close by his side stood his wife, Andromache, letting a tear fall;
Laying her hand in his own, she spake a word and addressed him:

    "Good man of mine, this courage of thine will undo thee, nor pity
Moveth *thee* for thy infant boy or for me, the unhappy,
Soon to be widowed of thee — the Achaeans will certainly kill thee,
Setting upon thee in mass; and for me it were verily better
Earth should enwrap me, bereavèd of thee; since no other comfort
Bideth for me, grief only, when Destiny cometh to meet thee,
Seeing (alas!) I have no father nor worshipful mother.
Yea, thou knowest our father was slain by the doughty Achilles,
What time he utterly sacked Cilicia's well-builded city,
Thebè, lofty of gates. And he slew the royal Eëtion,
Yet he despoiled him not — for awe in his spirit forbade it —
Rather he burned him along with his inlaid armor, and o'er him
Builded a barrow; around it the nymphs of the mountain have planted
Elms in a ring — fair daughters of Zeus who beareth the aegis.
Then seven brothers of mine — all dwelt in the halls of the palace —
All on the selfsame day went down to the mansion of Hades.

The Meeting of Hector and Andromache

He it was slaughtered them all, the divine fleet-footed Achilles, [footed.
As they were keeping their white-fleeced sheep and their kine, trailing-
Also he carried the queen, who reigned 'neath Placus the wooded,
Carried my mother away along with our other possessions;
Later, indeed, on payment of untold ransom he freed her.
Artemis, rainer of darts, slew *her* in the halls of her father. —
Thou art alone unto me both father and worshipful mother,
Hector, and brother thou art, and my husband, blooming in manhood.
Come then, pity me now, and abide right here on the tower,
Lest thou widow thy wife and make thy child but an orphan.
Station the host along at the fig-tree; there is the city
Easiest far to be scaled, and the rampart assailable also.
Thrice came thither the bravest, indeed, and attempted to enter,
Led by the Ajaxes twain and Idomeneus, highly renownèd,
Tydeus' valorous son, and the warrior children of Atreus —
Whether, perhaps, it was someone who knew well oracles told them,
Or if their own heart rather commands them, urges them onward."
   Then in his turn great shimmering-helmeted Hector addressed her:
  "Verily all these things are my care, dear wife, but believe me,
I were despised of the Trojans, the men and the trailing-robed women,
Were I to skulk, as a craven, aloof and apart from the battle.
Yea, my own spirit forbids, since I have learned to be valiant
Always, ever to fight in the fore front along with the Trojans,
Winning a wid'ning renown no less for myself than my father.
This do I know full well in my heart, in my soul do I know it:
Cometh the day when the city of Ilium holy shall perish,
Priam, too, of the ashen spear, and the people of Priam.
Yet it afflicteth me not, that anguish to come of the Trojans,
Neither of Hecabe's self, not even of Priam, our sovereign,
Nor of my hero-brothers, the many perchance and the valiant
Fated to fall in the dust 'neath the hands of the foemen in battle,
Like unto anguish of thine, when a bronze-clad son of Achaia,
Victor, shall lead thee away in tears and bereave thee of freedom.
Haply in Argos the loom thou'lt ply at the hest of another,
Bring in water from fount Hypereia, perchance, or Messeïs,
Sorely reluctant, with heavy necessity pressing upon thee.

Ay, mayhap he will say, some wight that beholds thee a-weeping:
'This was the wife of Hector, the foremost chief of the Trojans,
Tamers of steeds, when aforetime men fought round Ilium's ramparts.'
So shall someone speak and anguish requicken within thee
Lacking a husband as thine is, to ward off slavery's hour.
Me let the mantle of death and the heaped-up earth have enfolded,
Ere I shall hear thy wail, thy dragging away into thralldom."
   So spake glorious Hector and reached out after the infant;
Backward it shrank with a cry, and it clung to the beauteous-girdled
Nursemaid's breast, affrighted at sight of its father belovèd,
Fearstruck both at the bronze and the horsehair crest that it noted
Dreadfully nodding on high from the topmost ridge of the helmet.
Thereat they laughed out loud, both father and worshipful mother.
Straightway glorious Hector removed the helm from his forehead,
Laying it down on the ground, wide-flashing its splendor about it.
When he had kissed his dear son, in his arms had dandled him fondly,
Thus he bespake in prayer both Zeus and the other immortals:
   "Vouchsafe, Zeus and ye other immortals, that even as I am,
This, my son, may prove in the eyes of the Trojans outstanding,
Even as valiant in might, o'er Ilium mightily reigning.
Then may someone say 'Far better this man than his father,'
As he returneth from war; may he bring home trophies encrimsoned,
Harness of enemy slain, and gladden the heart of his mother."
   Thus he spake and placed his child in the arms of its mother,
Hector's beloved, and she on her fragrant bosom received it,
Smiling through her tears, and her husband beheld her in pity,
Gently caressed with his hand, then spake a word and addressed her:
   "Good wife, be not distressed past measure in spirit, I pray thee.
No man hurls me to Hades, unless whom Fate hath appointed;
Yet, as I ween, no man hath evaded his destiny ever,
Once he is born—no, never a one, whether coward or valiant.
Go thou home and attend to thy tasks, the loom and the distaff,
Works that beseem thee well and bid thy maidens in waiting
Ply at the duties assigned them. But war unto men is appointed,
All men—chiefly to me—that dwell in Ilium city."
   Thus spake glorious Hector and took up his shimmering helmet,

Bronzen, horsetail-crested. His dear wife homeward departed,
Turning again and again, while big tears fell in abundance.
Quickly anon she reached the well-stablished home of her husband,
Hector, slayer of men, and she found there waiting within it
Many a handmaid. In all she stirred up loud lamentation.
So they lamented for Hector, while yet he lived, in his palace,
Seeing that never again they deemed he would come from the battle
Safe to his home, escaped from the hands and the fury Achaean.

　　Neither had Paris delayed in the high-roofed halls of his palace;
Nay, he encased him in armor, bedight with bronze and distinguished,
Sped then up through the city, reliant on feet that were nimble.
Even as when some steed that is stalled, high-fed at the manger,
Rendeth his tether and speeds far over the plain at a gallop,
Proudly exultant, accustomed to bathe in the river that floweth
Beautiful; high he holdeth his head, while over his shoulders
Streameth his mane, and he putteth a confident trust in his glory.
Nimbly his limbs bear him on to the haunts and the pasture of horses:
So from the summit of Pergamus Priam's son, Alexander,
Radiant all in his arms, like the sun in his splendor, descended,
Laughing aloud, as his feet swift bore him along, and anon then
O'ertook Hector, his brother, the godlike, e'en at the moment
Hector would turn from the spot where he with his wife was conversing.
Paris, divine in his form, first hailed and accosted his brother:
　　"Honored brother of mine, my tarrying surely delays thee,
Hastening on, as thou art; and I come not in time, as thou badst me."
　　Quickly addressed him in answer the shimmering-helmeted Hector:
　　"Truly would *no* man, good brother, at least one who thinketh
Ever belittle thy prowess in arms, since thou art a valiant.　　[arightly,
Yet thou art feeble of will, yea, wilfully slack; and my spirit
Grieveth within me at hearing reproach on the lips of the Trojans,
Leveled at thee; for affliction is theirs past measure for thy sake.
Howbeit, let us away. All this hereafter we'll settle
Haply, if Zeus e'er grant us to offer the cup of deliv'rance
Here in our halls to the gods aye-living, inhabiting heaven,
Once we have driven from Troyland the well-greaved sons of Achaeans."

ILIAD · VII · (H)

In Eta, Priam's strongest son
Combats with Ajax Telamon.

THUS spake glorious Hector; then forth from the gateway he is-
While at his side kept pace Alexander, his brother; in spirit [sued,
Both brave brothers were eager to join in the battle and warfare.
Even as when God grants a favoring breeze unto seamen   [blade
Haply, that now are a-wearied from beating the main with the smooth-
Oars and longing in vain, whose toil-spent limbs have been loosened:
Even so now, in their longing, those twain appeared to the Trojans.
   Each then slew his man — the one, Areïthoüs' scion,
Even Menesthius, dwelling in Arne, the child of the ox-eyed
Phylomedusa and king Areïthoüs, wielder of maces.
Hector with spear keen-pointed the limbs of Eïoneus loosened,
Smiting him full on the neck, beneath the bronze rim of his helmet.
Glaucus, Hippolochus' son, of Lycian heroes the leader,
Smote with his lance Iphinoüs, Dexius' son, on the shoulder,
There in the thick of the fight. Behind his fleet mares he had mounted.
Down from the car to the ground he fell, unstrung in his members.
   But as Pallas Athena, the bright-eyed goddess, had marked them
Laying the Argives low in the stress of the furious conflict,
Down she dropped like a flash from the pinnacle peaks of Olympus
Straight unto Ilium holy; and Phoebus hastened to meet her,
Gazing from Pergamus down; and vict'ry he willed for the Trojans.
When at the oak tree each of the twain now countered the other,
Zeus's son, the Lord Apollo, was first to address her:
   "Why so eagerly now, O daughter of Zeus, the all mighty,
Art thou come from Olympus, and what great purpose hath sent thee?
Is it to give a decisive superior strength to the Argives,
Giving them vict'ry? No pity hast thou for the Trojans that perish?
If thou wouldst only hearken to me, 'twould be so much better!

145

Come then, let us make end of the warfare, carnage and conflict,
Now for today; hereafter again they shall fight until haply
Ilium's end they attain, since so to your hearts it is pleasing,
Goddesses deathless, to yield this city to fire and to pillage."
　　Then unto him in her turn spake the bright-eyed goddess Athena:
"So let it be, Far-worker; with such mind down from Olympus
I myself am come down to the clash of Achaeans and Trojans.
Well, now, what is thy counsel for staying the warfare of heroes?"
　　Then in his turn Zeus's son, the Lord Apollo, addressed her:
"Let us arouse the valorous might of the horse-taming Hector
So that he challenge some one of the Danaan chiefs, unattended,
Man unto man, to fight him alone in the terrible combat;
So may, haply astonied, the well-greaved sons of Achaia
Rouse up a hero to battle alone with Hector, the goodly."
　　Thus spake Apollo; Athena, the bright-eyed goddess, assented.
Helenus, Priam's well-loved son, in his spirit prophetic
Knew full well the plan the gods were adopting in counsel.
Unto the side of his brother he came, there stood and addressed him:
"Hector, scion of Priam, thou peer of Cronion in counsel,
Wouldst thou in anything hearken to me? For I am thy brother.
All other Trojans and all the Achaeans direct to be seated.
Thou thyself then challenge whoever is best of the Argives,
Man unto man to fight thee alone in the terrible combat;
For not yet have doom and death unto thee been appointed,
For it thus I have heard the voice of the gods ever-living."
　　Thus spake he; and Hector was greatly rejoiced as he heard him.
Into the mid-space faring, he held back Troia's battalions,
Grasping his spear in the middle; and all sat down at the signal.
Then Agamemnon, too, bade the well-greaved Achaeans be seated.
Down sat Apollo, the god of the silver bow, and Athena,
Like unto birds of prey—in the semblance of vultures they sate them
High on the oak of Father Zeus who wieldeth the aegis,
Glorying both in their men, whose ranks sat densely compacted,
Bristling thick with bucklers, with rich-plumed helmets and lances.
Even as under the breath of Zephyr, new risen, a ripple
Spreadeth abroad o'er the main, and the deep sea darkens beneath it:

So in appearance the ranks of the warriors—Achaeans and Trojans—
Sat on the plain, while Hector between both armies addressed them:
    "Hearken to me, ye Trojans, and ye, well-greavèd Achaeans,
That I may now declare what the soul in my bosom commandeth:
Cronus's son, high-throned, has voided the oaths and the treaty.
Evil intending, he foreordains it to both of the armies,
Even till either ye capture the fair-towered city of Troia,
Or yourselves be vanquished beside the sea-faring galleys.
Now that the chiefest of all the Achaeans are found here among you,
Whomsoever his heart bids join him in battle against me,
Let him come on as the champion of all 'gainst Hector, the goodly.
This will I also declare; let Zeus attend to attest it:
If that warrior of yours with his long bronze weapon shall slay me,
Let him despoil me and bear to the hollow galleys my armor;
Yet let him render my body again to my home, that the Trojans,
Women and men, may honor my corse with a funeral fire.
If, however, Apollo shall grant me fame, and I slay him,
I will despoil him and carry to Ilium holy his armor,
There to hang it aloft on the shrine of far-darting Apollo.
Yet to the well-benched ships I promise to render his body
Back, that the sons of Achaia, the long-haired heroes entomb it,
Building beside the wide Hellespontus a barrow above him.
So shall some mortal exclaim, though ev'n of a late generation,
Sailing in many-oared galley the wine-dark way of the waters:
'This is the tomb of a hero that died long ages aforetime,
Slain, as a champion slain, by the hand of the glorious Hector.'
Thus some day will someone say, and my fame be undying."
    Thus spake Hector. The others all mutely attended in silence.
They were ashamed to refuse but feared to accept his challenge.
But Menelaüs at last rose up, and he spake out among them,
Chiding, and deeply he groaned in his heart, while thus he upbraided:
    "Ay me! threateners only! not men, but women Achaean!
This, sure, will be a shame and the direst e'en of the direful,
If not a Danaan now goes forth to the challenge of Hector.
Nay, let all of you turn unto earth once more, unto water,
Since each keepeth his seat, down-hearted and utterly craven.

Well then, I will array me against him; the chances of vict'ry
Surely are high overhead, all guided of gods everlasting.''
    Thus then spake Atrides and donned his beautiful armor.
Then had the end of life come haply to thee, Menelaüs,
Under a foeman's hand, since far the stronger was Hector,
Had not the princes Achaean sprung up and instantly caught thee.
Atreus' scion himself, wide-ruling king Agamemnon,
Seized him by his right hand and uttered a word and addressed him:
    "Nay, Menelaüs, nursling of Zeus, thou'rt mad, and surely
Now is no time for madness; withdraw then, though it may pain thee.
Think not to rival in combat a man much stronger than thou art,
Hector, the Priamid, him whom other men dread in abhorrence,
Whom an Achilles himself would shudder to meet in the battle
Bringing glory to men; far greater than thou is Achilles.
Go, Menelaüs, and take thy seat in the tribe of thy fellows.
Some other one the Achaeans will set as their fighter 'gainst this man.
That man, though he be fearless and ever unsated of turmoil,
Fain will he bend his knee, I trow, if perchance he escapeth
Out of the fury of war and the terrible strife of the combat.''
    These words spoken, the hero persuaded the mind of his brother,
Winning him over to right and obedience. Thereupon gladly
Took his attendants then the armor off from his shoulders.
Then it was Nestor addressed those Argives, rising amid them:
    "Ah me! great grief truly is come on the land of Achaia!
Verily, sore would he groan, old Peleus, driver of horses,
Famed as a prudent adviser of Myrmidons, orator famous!
Greatly indeed was he gladdened aforetime there in his palace,
Questioning me on the parents and stock of all of the Argives.
Now, insooth, should he hear how they all before Hector are cow'ring,
Straight would he lift his dear hands and fervently beg the immortals,
Praying his spirit might fly from his limbs to the palace of Hades.
O Father Zeus and Athena and Phoebus Apollo, if only
I were a youth as of old, when by Celadon's swift-flowing current
Arcady's spear-famed men and the Pylians gathered for battle
Under the rampart of Pheia, about the waters of Jardan.
Then stood forth Ereuthalion, their champion, a match for immortals,

Wearing upon his shoulders Lord Areïthoüs' armor —
Brave Areïthoüs, him that was called by the surname of Maceman —
Surnamed "Maceman" by men and by women of beautiful girdles,
Seeing he used not to battle with bow or long javelin as weapon
But with an iron mace would crush battalions in pieces.
Not with strength but with cunning Lycurgus managed to slay him
Caught in a narrow way, where nothing availed him his iron
Mace to avert destruction; too soon came crafty Lycurgus,   [backward.
Piercing his breast right through with a javelin, to earth hurled him
There he was spoiled of the armor the bronze-mailed Ares had given.
Thenceforth wore it Lycurgus' self in the mellay of battle.
Finally, now grown old in the halls of his palace, Lycurgus
Gave it to wear to the squire whom he greatly loved, Ereuthalion.
He it was, wearing the armor, would challenge all of the bravest.
All the rest trembled sorely and feared, and no one would venture.
Me, however, my soul all-venturous roused unto battle,
Roused with its daring in me, though I of them all was the youngest.
So it was I then fought him — with glory, the gift of Athena.
He was the tallest warrior of all I have slain and the strongest.
Sprawling he lay, immense, stretched out this way and the other.
Would I were young once more, and my vigor unshaken within me!
Quickly yon shimmering-helmeted Hector would face an opponent.
Ye, however, the chiefest of all the Achaean commanders,
None of you yearn with all your hearts for a meeting with Hector."

    Thus did the old man chide them, and nine men stood up in answer:
Far first rose up among them the monarch of men, Agamemnon;
Tydeus' stalwart son, Diomedes, followed arising;
Then the Ajaxes twain, men clothed with impetuous prowess;
Followed Idomeneus' self and Idomeneus' sturdy attendant,
Even Meriones, peer of Enyalius, slayer of heroes;
Next, Eurypylus rose, the glorious son of Euaemon;
Uprose Thoas, Andraemon's son, and the goodly Odysseus —
All nine fain to encounter the godlike Hector in battle.

    Then once more addressed them the knightly Gerenian Nestor:
"Now cast lots, all nine, to determine who shall be chosen.
That man truly shall profit the well-greaved sons of Achaia,

Ay, and shall profit himself in soul, if belike he escapeth
Out from the fury of war and the terrible strife of the combat."

    Thus he spake. They marked, each hero his lot with a token,
Dropping them into the helmet of Atreus's son, Agamemnon.
Meantime the hosts uplifted their hands to the gods and besought
Many a one like this, looking up to the canopied heaven: [them —

    "O Father Zeus, let the lot now fall upon Ajax or Tydeus'
Son, or the monarch himself who reigns o'er golden Mycenae."

    Thus they spake. The helmet was shaken by Nestor, the knightly.
Instant the lot themselves had desired leaped forth from the helmet,
Ajax's lot. From right unto left then bare it a herald,
Showing it all through the throng unto all the Achaean commanders.
Howe'er, nobody knew it, and each in his turn they denied it.
But when he came, as he bore it all through the throng, to the right
Glorious Ajax, who'd marked it and cast it into the helmet,   [man,
Ajax held out his hand; and the herald, standing close by him,
Dropped it into his hand. He rejoiced, well-knowing the token
Graven thereon, then cast it down on the ground, and addressed them:

    "Friends, this lot is mine; and I myself am rejoicing
Down in my heart, for I deem I shall vanquish Hector, the godlike.
Come ye, however, and while I am putting my war-gear upon me,
Offer a prayer meanwhile unto Zeus, the sovereign Cronion,
Silent, apart, by yourselves, that ye be not heard by the Trojans —
Yet no! openly rather; for we fear no one of all men,
Seeing that none by force, self-willing, shall chase me unwilling,
Neither insooth by his skill, since not so wholly unskilful
Once I was born, as I trow, on Salamis island and nurtured."

    Thus he spake; and they prayed unto Zeus, the sovereign Cronion,
Many a one like this, looking up to the canopied heaven:

    "Zeus, thou Father that rulest from Ida, most glorious, greatest,
Grant unto Ajax to gain the vict'ry and honor and glory.
If, however, thou care for Hector exceeding and love him,
Then be equal the prowess and equal the glory accorded."

    Thus they spake, while Ajax in bronze bright-gleaming arrayed
When now over his flesh he had clothed-on all of his armor,   [him.
Forward he strode on with it, as Ares moveth colossal

Faring abroad unto war amid men whom haply Cronion
Urgeth to battle in ſtrife that devours the heart in its fury.
Suchwise Ajax colossal arose, of th' Achaeans the bulwark,
Smiling grimly the while. And then with his feet underneath him
Moved he with mighty ſtrides and shook his far-shadowing javelin.
Ay, and the Argives thrilled with joy at beholding their hero.
Meantime trembling and dread ran over the limbs of the Trojans
All, while quick in his breast was the heart-beat even of Heċtor.
Yet there was no way now of escape by fleeing or shrinking
Back to the throng of his folk, since he it was issued the challenge.
Ajax then came to close quarters, bearing his shield like a tower,
Bronze and of bull's hide seven-in-fold, which Tychius wrought him
Cunningly, best by far of the curriers, dwelling in Hyle.
He of bulls' hides fashioned the shield, seven-folded and shimm'ring —
High-fed bulls — and he forged an eighth fold, bronzen, upon it.
Bearing it full in front of his breast, Telamonian Ajax
Came close to Heċtor and ſtopped, and thus he bade him defiance:
　"Heċtor, now shalt thou know full well, man to man, unattended,
What is the manner of men ſtill left 'mong the Danaan princes
Even besides that lion-of-heart, rank-render Achilles.
He, however, in wrath with the shepherd of hoſts, Agamemnon,
Yonder lies by the ships whose curved beaks furrow the waters.
Yet of us, fighters remain both willing and fitted to fight thee;
Yea, and many we are. But begin now the war and the battle."
　　Then in his turn great shimmering-helmeted Heċtor addressed him:
　"Ajax, offspring of Zeus, Telamonian ruler of peoples,
Make not trial of me as a boy, peradventure, and puny,
Or as a woman, belike, that knows not the cuſtoms of warfare.
Right well I am acquainted with war and the slaying of heroes.
I am acquainted with wielding a shield now right and now leftward,
Fashioned of dry bull's hide; such warfare is mine as a shieldman.
I know also to charge on a mellay of fleet-footed horses.
I know well in pitched battle the war-dance of furious Ares.
Ready! for never insooth would I ſtrike at a hero as thou art,
Secretly spying, but rather, if so I may hit, in the open."
　　Thus he spake. Then poising his spear far-shadowing hurled it,

Smiting the bull's hide shield, seven-folded and dreadful, of Ajax
Full on the uttermost bronze that was laid eighth layer upon it.
On through six of the layers the bronze went, cleaving unwearied,
Till at the seventh fold stayed by the ox-hide. After him Ajax,
Sprung from the seed of Zeus, let fly his far-shadowing javelin,
Smiting direct on the Priamid's shield, all evenly rounded.
Through the shimmering shield went driving the ponderous missile,
On still it pressed and traversed the breastplate cunningly moulded;
Clear on down past his flank it mowed its way through his tunic —
Powerful spear! — but he swerved and avoided the black death's onset.
Then with their hands they drew out the long spearshafts, in an instant
Fell then together again, like lions of ravenous hunger
Or like boars, wild swine, whose might is not easy to master.
Mid on the boss of the shield Priamides smote with his weapon; [bended.
Through it the bronze brake not, for the spear-point backward was
Then at a bound pierced Ajax his buckler; speeding, the spear-point
Drave right through, and it staggered the warrior eager in onset,
Cleaving its way to his neck; and the dark blood instantly spurted.
Yet ceased not from the battle the shimmering-helmeted Hector
So, but, retiring, he seized, stout-handed, a stone that was lying
There on the plain, all jagged, black and enormous, and hurled it,
Smiting the bull's hide shield, seven-folded and dreadful, of Ajax
Full on its centre embossed, and the bronze all round it resounded.
Thereupon Ajax lifted a stone far huger and drave it,
All in a whirl, and behind it he put the strength of a giant,
Smiting the buckler and crushing it in with the rock like a millstone,
Beating and bending his knees; and he lay outstretched and supinely,
All pressed into the shield; but Apollo quickly upraised him.
Now were they smiting with falchions amain in the closest encounter,
Had not the heralds, angels of Zeus and also of mortals,
Come, from the bronze-mailed Achaeans one, from the Trojans the
Even Idaeus of Troy and Talthybius, both of them prudent.   [other,
'Twixt the twain they held out their sceptres; the herald Idaeus
Spake them a word, for he was a master of counsel and wisdom:

   "Fight ye no more, dear lads; no longer engage in the combat,
Seeing he loveth you both, even Zeus, the compeller of storm-clouds.

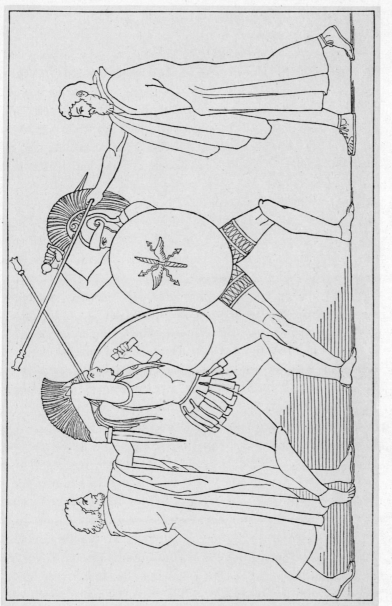

Hector and Ajax Separated by the Heralds

Spearmen ye both are also, we all know now for a surety.
Night cometh on even now; it is well that night should be heeded."

Then Telamonian Ajax made answer and said to the heralds:
"Bid ye Hector to utter the word for quitting, Idaeus,
Seeing that *he* it was challenged the bravest of all to the combat.
Let then Hector begin, and as *he* says, surely will *I* do."

Then in his turn great shimmering-helmeted Hector addressed him:
"Ajax, seeing that God hath endued thee with stature and wisdom,
Also with might, and in wielding the spear thou art best of Achaeans,
Now let us cease from the strife and the terrible fury of battle--
Cease for today; hereafter again we may war till a godhead
Judgeth between us and giveth to one or the other the vict'ry.
Night cometh on even now; it is well that night should be heeded,
So thou mayest rejoice the Achaeans there at the galleys,
All, but chiefly thy kinsmen, and gladden thy comrades about thee.
Meanwhile, throughout all Troy, great city of Priam, the monarch,
I shall rejoice the men and the trailing-robed women of Troia,
Who for me with a prayer shall enter the holy assembly.
Come now, let us exchange gifts notable, one with the other,
So that people may speak on this wise, Achaeans and Trojans:
'Twain that had striven in strife for its own sake, spirit-consuming,
Parted again thereafter in friendship united together.' "

Thus he spoke, and he gave him his sword all studded with silver,
Blade and scabbard besides, and the well-cut baldric he offered.
Ajax, for his part, offered a belt bright-gleaming with purple.

So they were parted, the one to join the host of Achaeans,
Whileas the other betook him back to the throng of the Trojans,
Glad to behold him returning alive and uninjured among them,
'Scaped from the fury and hands, unapproachable hands, of great Ajax;
Yea, and their chieftain, saved beyond hope, they led to the city.
Also the well-greaved sons of Achaia conducted on their part
Ajax, exultant in vict'ry away to divine Agamemnon.

Now when the heroes found themselves at the tents of Atrides,
Then the monarch of men, Agamemnon, slew them a bullock
Five years old, a male, for Cronion supreme in his power.
Quickly they flayed and prepared and divided it all into portions,

Cunningly carving the whole; with spits then piercing the pieces,
Roasted them carefully each, then drew off all of the slices.
Now as the task was accomplished and so made ready the feasting,
Feasted they all—no heart felt stint of a well-balanced banquet.
Atreus' hero son, wide-ruling king Agamemnon,
Slices the full chine's length in his honor bestowed upon Ajax.
Now as desire for drink and for meat the feasters had banished,
Nestor, first of them all, 'gan weaving the web of his counsel,
Nestor, whose counsel aforetime had ever been found to be wisest.
He then, kindliest-minded, harangued them and spake out among them:
    "Atreus' son and the rest, ye princes of all the Achaeans,
Seeing that many are slain of the long-haired heroes Achaean—
Now is their dark blood shed at the fair-flowing stream of Scamander,
Shed of the fierce war-god and their souls gone down unto Hades—
Thee it behooveth to stay at the dawning the war of the Argives.
We ourselves foregathered will wheel in all of the corpses
Hither with mules and with oxen; and then we will burn them to ashes
Off from the galleys a little, that each may bear home to his children
Bones of the fallen, whene'er we return to the land of our fathers.
Then let us heap *one* barrow about the pyre, unto many,
Rearing a common tomb from the plain; and then let us quickly
Build high towers nearby, a bulwark for us and the galleys;
Then let us make in the midst thereof gates firmly compacted,
So that there be a way through them for the driving of war-cars.
Then let us dig all round it a deep moat there on the outside
Hard by, foil for the charges of men and of horses attacking,
Lest fall heavy upon us the war of impetuous Trojans."
    Thus spake he; and the princes applauded him, all, and assented.
Meantime the Trojans assembled in Ilium's uppermost city,
Fierce and tumultuous, right at the doors of the palace of Priam.
There began to harangue them Antenor, prudent in counsel:
    "Hear me, Trojans and Dardans, and ye allies of our city,
That I may now declare what the soul in my bosom commandeth.
Come, let us give back Helen of Argos and all her possessions
With her to Atreus' sons to take, since now we are fighting,
Broken our oaths of faith. And therefore for us is no profit

That I may hope we shall find, unless we do as I tell you."

These words spoken, he sate him down. Then rose up among them
Prince Alexander, the goodly, the husband of fair-haired Helen.
He made answer to him and in accents wingèd addressed him.

"What thou sayest, Antenor, accords no more with my pleasure.
Thou well knowest to frame some speech far better than this one.
But if in earnest at all thou truly haranguest in this wise,
Verily, then have the gods themselves robbed thee of thy senses.
Now will I speak out among the Trojans, tamers of horses:
Outright will I declare it: my wife I will never surrender;
But of the wealth, whatever I brought home with me from Argos,
All I will freely surrender and add yet more, from my substance."

These words spoken he sat him down. Then rose up among them
Priam, Dardanus' son, a match for immortals in counsel.
He then, kindliest-minded, harangued them and spake out among them:

"Hear me, Trojans and Dardans and ye allies of our city,
That I may now declare what the soul in my bosom commandeth.
All now throughout the city partake of your supper, as wonted.
Keep guard faithfully also, and each man — let him be wakeful.
Early at dawn to the hollow ships let Idaeus betake him,
Bearing to Atreus' sons, Menelaüs and king Agamemnon,
Prince Alexander's proposal, for whose sake strife has arisen;
Asking in wise words also, if they peradventure be minded
Now from the dissonant warfare to cease, till haply the corpses
All may be burned; hereafter again we may war till a godhead
Judgeth between us and giveth to one or the other the vict'ry."

Thus spake he. They hearkened with diligence, heeding his counsel;
Then took supper assembled in companies all through the army.
Early at dawning away to the hollow galleys Idaeus
Fared. He found them assembled, the Danaans, squires of Ares,
Close by the stern of the galley of King Agamemnon. The herald,
Standing amid them, called with a loud voice and spake to the conclave:

"Atreus' sons and the rest, ye princes of all the Achaeans,
Priam and all those others, the high-born Trojans, have bid me
Tell you — if haply it find fair favor or welcome among you —
Prince Alexander's proposal, for whose sake strife hath arisen:

157

All the possessions, whatever he brought in his hollow galleys
Unto the land of the Trojans — and would he had perished before that —
All he will freely surrender and add yet more from his substance.
Only the wife, once wedded to glorious prince Menelaüs,
Her he declines to give up; howbeit the Trojans command it.
This word, too, they bade me declare, if perchance ye be minded
Now from the ill-sounding warfare to cease, till haply the corpses
All may be burned; hereafter again we may war till a godhead
Judgeth between us and giveth to one or the other the vict'ry."

  Thus spake he. The others all mutely attended in silence,
Till at the last spake out Diomedes, good at the war-cry:
  "Never let any accept the wealth of prince Alexander,
Not even Helen herself; so witless is none as to know not
How on the Trojans impend already the toils of destruction."

  Thus he spake. With a shout all the sons of Achaia assented,
Plauding in wonder the speech of Tydides, tamer of horses.
Thereupon spake in reply to Idaeus lord Agamemnon:
  "Thou, Idaeus, thyself dost hear this word of the Argives,
What is the answer they make; and also to me it is pleasing.
But as concerneth the fallen, I nowise grudge you to burn them;
Since, as regardeth the dead, when once they have died and have ended,
Never is stinting of fire unto them for a speedy appeasement.
Zeus now witness the oaths, loud-thundering husband of Hera."

  Thus he spake and lifted his sceptre 'fore all the immortals.
Thereat Idaeus departed, to Ilium holy returning.
Meanwhile the Trojans and Dardans were sitting still in assembly,
All of them gathered together awaiting return of the herald,
Even Idaeus; and when he arrived, he delivered the message,
Standing amid them; and they made ready with diligence, speeding
Some to bring back the corpses, while others went after fuel.
Also the Argives hastened, forsaking their well-benched galleys,
Some to bring back the corpses, while others went after fuel.

  Now was the sun new-risen and smiting the fields and the furrows,
Out from the gently-flowing, deep-coursing stream of the ocean,
Climbing aloft to the sky; and the two groups met one another.
Hard was it then to distinguish the heroes, those that had fallen.

Yet, having cleansed with water the clotted blood from the bodies,
Hot tears shedding the while, they lifted them up on the wagons.
Now great Priam forbade them to wail out loud; so in silence
Heaped they the dead on the pyre, their hearts sore-smitten with an-
Soon as they burned them in flame, all turned unto Ilium holy.   [guish.
Likewise also the others on their side, the well-greaved Achaeans,
Heaped their dead on the pyre, their hearts sore-smitten with anguish.
Soon as they burned them in flame, to the hollow ships they departed.

    Next day, ere it was dawn, while twilight dusk was upon them,
Then, as they gathered, engirdling the pyre, well-chosen Achaeans
Heaped up a barrow about it, but one for the many in common,
Rearing it up from the plain. And a wall hardby they erected
Furnished with towers reared high, a bulwark for them and the galleys.
Gates in the midst thereof they constructed, firmly compacted,
So that there was a way through them for the driving of war-cars.
Lastly they digged in front of the rampart a moat on the outside,
Broad, deep, great in extent, and planted it densely with palings.

    So as they kept on toiling, those long-haired sons of Achaia,
Sitting by Zeus, the lord of the lightning, the gods of Olympus
Marveled how great was the work of the bronze-clad sons of Achaia.
Then Poseidon, shaker of earth, began speaking amid them:

    "O Father Zeus, is there now any one mortal man on the boundless
Earth who will any more tell the immortals his thought or his purpose?
Seest thou not that again those long-haired Achaeans have builded
There to protect their galleys a wall of defense and about it
Drawn them a moat? To the gods they have offered no hecatomb splen-
Surely its fame will extend wherever the morning expandeth,   [did.
Surely the wall be forgotten which I and Phoebus Apollo
Builded with toil and with moil at the hero Laomedon's order."

    Sorely distressed, cloud-gathering Zeus then answered his brother:
    "Fie on it! What's this saying of earth's wide-powerful shaker?
Some other one of the gods at this device might be frightened,
Some god feebler than thou, far feebler in hand and in power;
Thy fame though is secure wherever the morning expandeth.
Go to; lo! whensoever again the long-haired Achaeans
Fare in the galleys back to the well-loved land of their fathers,

Then burst open the wall, wide-scatter it all in the salt sea
Deep, then once more cover the long sea-beach with a sand-drift,
So that thou mayest see destroyed the Achaeans' great rampart."

    Such were the godheads' words in their converse one with another.
Sunk was the sun; the Achaeans accomplished their labor and slaughtered
Bullocks from barrack to barrack in camp and partook of their supper.
Ships had arrived meanwhile, wine-laden, hailing from Lemnos,
Many in tale — Euneüs, the scion of Jason had sent them,
He that Hypsipyle bare unto Jason, shepherd of peoples.
But unto Atreus' sons, Agamemnon and prince Menelaüs,
Gave he a cargo of wine in particular, measures a thousand.
Thence their supply of wine was obtained by the long-haired Achaeans;
Some paid for it with bronze, some others with shimmering iron;
Some paid for it with hides; and with cattle alive paid others,
Some with captives of war. — And they set forth a sumptuous banquet.
Thus then all night long at the galleys the long-haired Achaeans
Reveled at feasting; the Trojans and all their allies, in the city.
All night long, however, the counselor Zeus was devising
Evils and terribly thundered; — pale fear then fastened upon them.
Men poured wine from their cups on the earth, and no one would
Even to drink till he made to all-mighty Cronion libation: [venture
All then laid them down and partook of the blessing of slumber.

ILIAD · VIII · (Θ)

In Theta, Gods a council have.
Troy's conquest. Glorious Hector's brave.

ALL over earth was Dawn outspreading her mantle of saffron.
Zeus, the hurler of lightnings, let summon the gods to assembly
Then on the topmost summit of many-ridgèd Olympus.
There he harangued them himself, while all the immortals attended:
 "Hearken to me, ye gods, ye goddesses, all of you hearken,
That I may tell to you all what the heart in my bosom commands me.
Let no one of you, goddess or god (no matter), endeavor
Ever to thwart my words, but rather together receive it,
Promptly approving, that so these works I may quickly accomplish.
Whome'er, parted afar from the gods, I discover desiring
Unto the Trojans to go or the Danaans bringing them succor,
He shall return to Olympus, chastised in a manner unseemly,
Or I will seize him and hurl him down to Tartarus—murky,
Distant afar, where under the ground the abyss is the deepest,
Where is the portal of iron, and bronze therein is the threshold,
Deep under Hades even as earth lies parted from heaven—
So shall he know how far beyond all of the gods I am mighty.
Come now, make the essay, so all ye gods understand it:
Fasten a rope well twisted of gold, let down from high heaven;
All ye gods lay hold thereon—all goddesses also—
Not even then would ye drag down Zeus unto earth out of heaven,
Zeus in his counsel supreme—not even with uttermost travail.
I, however, if minded to tug at the cable in earnest,
I'd pull all of you up, with the earth itself and the ocean.
Then with the rope I would gird some pinnacle peak of Olympus,
Binding it round, and then the whole in mid-air would be swinging.
So far I am supreme above all gods and all mortals."
 Thus spake he. The others all mutely attended in silence,

161

Marveling much at his word, for he spake with a masterful menace.
Finally, though, spoke up the bright-eyed goddess Athena:

"O our Father Cronion, most highly exalted of rulers,
Well enough know even we thy strength is invincible wholly.
Yet we have nevertheless some grief for the Danaan spearmen,
Who now haply shall perish, fulfilling a doom of disaster.
Still we will surely refrain from the war, as thou hast commanded,
But to the Argives offer, it may be, counsel for profit,
That in this fury of thine not all of them utterly perish."

    Smiling upon her the while, cloud-gathering Zeus thus addressed
    "Have no fear, my dear child, thou Trito-born; not in earnest [her:
Speak I, indeed; be assured I always mean to be gentle."   [chariot—
    Thus he spake. Then he coupled his bronzed-hoofed steeds to his
Rapid the horses in flight, with their gold manes streaming about them—
Put on his body his raiment of gold; then, grasping the whipstock,
Wrought full deftly and golden, he mounted aloft on the chariot,
Laid on the lash to start them; and they went eagerly flying
Midway between the earth and the starry expanse of the heavens.
Soon he came to the mother of wild beasts, fountainous Ida,
Gargarus' heights; there he had a demesne and an altar of incense.
There then staying his steeds, the Father of men and immortals
Loosed the twain from the car and poured mist in abundance about
There on the summit he seated himself, all-gleaming in glory,   [them.
Gazing the while on the city of Troy and the ships of Achaia.

    Hastily now at their barracks the long-haired sons of Achaia
Took their meal of the morning and forthwith clad them in armor.
Likewise all through the city the Trojans, on their side, were arming,
Fewer in tale but quite as eager to fight in the conflict
Under necessity's urge, in defense of their women and children.
Then as the gates swung wide, outpoured the Ilian people,
Footmen and horsemen together; and mighty the din they awakened.

    When both armies arrived at the same place, coming together,
Clashed then the ox-hide shields, the spears, and the fury of fighters
Each in a corselet of bronze, while bull's hide bucklers embossèd
Pressed hard one on another; and mighty the din they awakened.
There rose together the shouts triumphant and groans of the heroes,

Slayers commingled with slain, while the earth ran red with the carnage.

Now, while yet it was morn, and daylight divine was advancing,
Missiles from both sides kept falling amain and felling the people;
But as soon as the sun was bestriding the middle of heaven,
Straightway the Father balanced his golden scales, and he loaded
Each with a fate of death that lays men low—for the Trojans,
Trojans, tamers of steeds, and bronze-mailed sons of Achaia—
Lifted the yard: down sank the doomful day of Achaia.
So on the bountiful earth low sunken the fates of Achaia
Rested; the fates of the Trojans arose unto canopied heaven.
He then mightily thundered from Ida and launched forth the lightning
Blazing amid the Achaean host; and they, at beholding,
Awe-struck wondered, and pallid the terror that lighted upon them.

Neither Idomeneus then dared stand nor yet Agamemnon;
Neither remained the Ajaxes twain, those squires of Ares;
Nestor stood there alone, the Gerenian warder of Argives—
Not of his will; one horse was disabled, struck by an arrow
Sped by divine Alexander, the husband of fair-haired Helen,
Right on the topmost crest, where sprouteth in horses the forelock
Over the skull, and a wound in that spot is exceedingly deadly.
High upreared in his pain the good steed, as the shaft drave onward
Into his brain; confounding his mates, he writhed with the bronzen
Missile. The old man darted to hew with his falchion the traces,
Gear of the side-steed smitten; but swiftly the horses of Hector
Came through the rout; they bore on the car a redoubtable driver,
Hector himself! and the life of the old man then were a forfeit,
Had not Diomed, good at the war-cry, been quick to observe it;
Dreadful the voice of his shout, as he cried to urge on Odysseus:

"Zeus-sprung son of Laërtes, Odysseus of many devices,
Whither art fleeing, a coward, with back turned round in the tumult?
See, lest thee in thy flight some spear transfix 'tween the shoulders.
Nay, stand firm, till we drive back the old man's furious foeman."

Thus he spake. But the godlike Odysseus, the much-enduring,
Gave no heed but rushed on to the hollow ships of Achaia.
Still Tydides, though left all alone, was mixed with the foremost,
Standing in front of the steeds of the aged scion of Neleus.

Lifting his voice, with wingèd words Diomedes addressed him:
"Sire, I ween that the younger in war now sorely beset thee;
Now is thy vigor abated; ay, years weigh heavy upon thee;
Slow of speed are thy horses — besides, thy squire is a weakling.
Come then, mount on *my* chariot! In this way thou shalt discover
What are the horses of Tros, well-skilled for pursuit or withdrawal
Over the plain with exceeding swiftness hither and thither,
Whereof once I despoiled that author of panic, Aeneas.
Thine our squires may mind; as for these, forthwith let us drive them
Full on the Trojans, tamers of horses, that haply e'en Hector
Learn if a spear rage also, perhaps, in the hand of Tydides."

Thus he. The knightly Gerenian Nestor failed not to obey him.
Nestor's horses the squires twain accordingly tended,
Sthenelus valiant and with him Eurymedon, lover of valor.
Diomed's car was likewise mounted by both of the heroes.
Nestor took in his hands the shining reins of the horses —
Tros's horses — and lashed them, and soon they drew anigh Hector.
Him, as he charged straight on, all eager for battle, Tydides
Missed as he hurtled his spear; but the squire who guided the chariot —
Called Eniopeus, son of a chief, high-hearted Thebaeus —
Holding the reins of the horse, he smote on the breast by the nipple.
Down from the chariot he crashed, and off the swift-footed horses
Swerved to the side. Unstrung was the Trojan's strength and his spirit.
Ay, it was sore grief shrouded brave Hector's heart for his driver.
There then he left him to lie, although deep-grieved for his comrade,
Speeding away on a quest for another redoubtable driver.
Neither a long time wanted his horses a master, for quickly
Iphitus' son, bold Archeptolemus, found he, and, mounting
Him on his war-car, trusted the fleet steeds' reins to his keeping.

Deeds beyond remedy then had been done, destruction accom-
Even perchance like lambs they had all been huddled in Ilium, [plished,
Had not the father of gods and men been quick to observe it.
Seeing, he thundered terrific and, launching a bolt of the lightning,
Hurled it to earth, white-flaming, in front of Diomed's horses.
Terribly then did the blaze flash up, of the sulfur a-burning,
While both steeds in affright crouched cowering under the chariot.

Letting the shining reins slip out of his hands, old Nestor,
Awe-struck deep in his heart, then turned and addressed Diomedes:
　"Come now, Tydides, and turn to retreat thy whole-hoofed horses!
Seest thou not that from Zeus no strength now attendeth upon thee?
For upon yon man Zeus Cronion bestoweth the glory
This day; yet, if he wills, unto us he later may give it
Likewise; never a mortal may thwart the will of Cronion,
Howe'er valiant he be; for *he* above all is the strongest."
　Answered him then in his turn Diomedes, good at the war-cry:
　"Reverend sire, indeed all this thou sayest with justice;
But none the less keen cometh the grief on my heart and my spirit,
Seeing that Hector some day will say, as he speaks 'mid the Trojans:
'Once Diomedes turned him in flight to his galleys before me!'　[me."
Thus one day he will boast. May the wide earth then yawn to receive
　Straightway answered him then the knightly Gerenian Nestor:
　"Ah me! thou son of Tydeus the wise, such words to have spoken!
Even if Hector haply shall call thee a coward, a weakling,
Not a Dardanian man or a Trojan will ever believe him,
Neither the wives of the Trojans, the great-souled bearers of bucklers,
Widows, whose lusty mates thou hast laid in the dust with thy javelin."
　Thus he spake, and he turned to retreat the whole-hoofed horses—
Back through the rout. The Trojans and Hector, with marvelous uproar
Meanwhile, dolorous missiles kept pouring in volleys upon them.
Over him shouted aloud great shimmering-helmeted Hector:
　"Diomed, high over all were the fleet-horsed Danaans wonted
Thee with a seat and with meats and brimful goblets to honor;
Now, though, they will degrade thee; thou'rt proved than woman no
Get thee gone, poor puppet; not for a flinching on my part　[braver.
Shalt thou ever set foot on our towers and carry our women
Off in thy galleys away; nay, sooner thy doom I shall deal thee."
　Thus he spake. Tydides in soul was divided and pondered
Whether to wheel his horses and fight full-facing his foeman.
Thrice Diomedes wavered and pondered in heart and in spirit.
Thrice from the mountains of Ida Zeus thundered, the master of counsel,
Giving a sign to the Trojans the tide of the battle was turning.
Then cried Hector, with shouts that echoed afar, to the Trojans:

"Trojans, Dardanians, Lycians, that joy in closest encounter,
Quit you like men, my friends, and remember impetuous prowess!
Well I perceive that Cronion, with good will nodding toward me,
Portioneth vict'ry, great glory to me — to the Danaans ruin,　　[them,
Fools that they are in their work! — such ramparts as these to devise
Flimsy, unworthy of heed, unfitted to ward off our fury.
Also our horses full lightly shall leap o'er the ditch they have delvèd.
Once, however, 'tis mine to get at their hollow galleys,
Then let there be for consuming fire some mindful provision,
That I may set on fire their ships and slaughter the owners,
Argive chiefs at the galleys, enveloped in smoke and bewildered."
　　　Thus he spake. To his horses he called out loud, as he shouted:
　　"Xanthus, Aethon, and thou, Podargus, and Lampus, the goodly,
Take heed now to repay, ye two, for the tendance abundant,
Yours at Andromache's hand, great-hearted Eëtion's daughter,
Who hath provided you wheat honey-hearted, set forth for your feed-
Wine, too, mingled for drink, whene'er her spirit should bid her, [ing,
Sooner than me, who boast me her husband blooming in manhood.
Haste now, hotly pursue, so that perchance we may capture
Even the buckler of Nestor — the fame whereof unto heaven
Reacheth, as being of gold wrought solid, itself and the arm-rods —
Ay, and may strip from the shoulders of Tydeus' son, Diomedes,
Tamer of horses, the corselet with cunning enwrought of Hephaestus.
These if we could but take, I should hope to compel the Achaeans
This very night to embark on the swift ships, sailing for homeland."
　　　Thus he spake with a boast, but the goddess august was indignant,
Hera, and stirred on her throne — while trembled the vasty Olympus.
Then to the god, the mighty Poseidon, she turned and addressed him:
　　"Fie now, Shaker of earth, wide-powerful! grieves not the spirit
Thine, even thine, in thy breast, that the Danaans utterly perish?
Yet do they bring thee gifts to Helice, aye, and to Aegae,
Gifts full many and gracious. Do thou then will them the vict'ry.
Could we but choose — we gods that are Danaan helpers — to hold off
Zeus of the far-borne voice, for the time, and to drive back the Trojans,
Then it would vex him in sooth, this sitting alone upon Ida."
　　　Sorely troubled, the earth's wide-powerful Shaker addressed her:

"Hera, audacious in speech, what saying is this thou hast uttered?
Leastwise I could not wish that the rest of us even should battle
Leagued against Zeus, the Cronion, for he is mightier surely."

    Even as they were conversing in such wise, one with another,
All of the space enclosed between the moat and the ships was
Filled with horses and chariots and men, shield-bearers, together
Penned: so penned them one that to Ares, the swift, was a rival,
Even Hector, the son of Priam, when Zeus gave him glory.
Ay, e'en now with consuming fire he had burned the trim galleys,
Had not the queenly Hera inspired in the heart of Atrides
Quickly to busy himself and likewise arouse the Achaeans.
Hurrying on past barracks and galleys Achaean, the hero
Bore in his stalwart hand uplifted his mantle of purple
Broad, and he stopped by the black and deep-hulled ship of Odysseus
There in the midst, that his call might carry in either direction —
This way e'en to the barracks of Telamonian Ajax,
That unto those of Achilles: these had drawn up their trim ships
Thus at the ends; they relied on their own strong hands and their valor.
Then with a ringing shout he called to the Danaan warriors:

    "Shame, ye Argives, craven reproaches, magnificent lookers!
Where are the boasts now gone, when we vaunted ourselves as the
Boasts vainglorious, such as ye uttered once when in Lemnos   [bravest,
Eating your fill of the flesh, in abundance, of straight-horned oxen,
Quaffing from mixers bowls brimful of the wine of the wassail,
Vaunting that *one* would match in battle a hundred of Trojans,
Ay, two hundred in sooth! though not even one can we equal,
Hector, who soon will burn up our ships with fire consuming.
O Father Zeus, was there ever a proud-souled king thou hast blinded —
Blinded with blindness like this — and taken away his great glory?
Natheless I vow that I never, in hither unhappily faring,
Passed in my many-oared ship any altar of thine in its beauty,
But that I burned upon all, with the fat, thigh-pieces of oxen,
Praying to level in ashes yon well-walled city of Troia.
Therefore grant me at least, O Zeus, one wish to accomplish:
Grant in the worst case that we ourselves may escape unto safety,
Neither allow the Trojans to vanquish thus the Achaeans."

Thus he spake; and the Father, beholding in pity his weeping,
Granted his folk to be saved nor utterly perish before him.
Straightway sent he an eagle, the surest of all wingèd omens,
Bearing a newborn fawn of a fleet-foot hind in its talons.
Dropped of the eagle, the fawn fell close by the beautiful altar
Where the Achaeans made off'rings to Zeus, the lord of all omens.
They, when they saw that the bird had come from Zeus as an omen,
Leaped at the Trojans the more and remembered the rapture of battle.

Not one then could boast, of the Danaans, though they were many,
Sooner than Tydeus' son to have guided his fleet-footed horses
Forth and beyond the moat and have closed in hostile encounter —
Far the first was he to subdue a helmeted Trojan,
Phradmon's son, Agelaüs; to flight he had just turned his horses;
But as he turned, in his back Tydides planted a javelin,
Midway between his shoulders; clean through his breast it was driven.
Out from the chariot he crashed, and his armor rattled upon him.
Followed him Atreus' sons, Menelaüs and king Agamemnon;
Then the Ajaxes twain, men clothed with impetuous prowess;
Followed Idomeneus' self and Idomeneus' sturdy attendant,
Even Meriones, peer of Enyalius, slayer of heroes;
Next Eurypylus came, the glorious son of Euaemon;   〔bending —
Came forth Teucer, the ninth — he was spanning his bow backward-
Crouching under the shield of the great Telamonian Ajax.
Stealthily Ajax would shift it, the buckler immense, and the hero,
Cautiously peering, would wing him an arrow at one of his foemen
There in the throng, and the stricken would fall and give up his spirit.
Then, as a child to its mother, would Teucer hasten for shelter
Back unto Ajax; and he with his shield bright-gleaming would hide him.

Who then first of the Trojans was slain by Teucer, the blameless?
First Orsilochus fell, then Ormenus, then Ophelestes,
Daetor and Chromius next, Lycophontes also, the godlike,
Then Polyaemon's son, Amopaon, and then Melanippus.
All in succession he stretched on the earth, the all-bounteous mother.

Joy then entered the heart of the king of men, Agamemnon,
Seeing him waste with his mighty bow whole battalions of Trojans.
Coming beside him, he stopped and spake a word and addressed him:

168

　　"Dear heart, Telamon's son, thou Teucer, captain of peoples,
Keep on shooting thus, that a light thou become to the Argive
Folk and to Telamon, too, thy sire, who, when thou wast little,
Tended thee, although a bastard, and reared thee there in his palace.
High unto honor exalt him now, though far off he dwelleth.
Ay, unto thee I declare what surely shall yet be accomplished:
If unto me shall grant Athena and Zeus, aegis-bearing,
Ilium's well-built city to sack—yea, level in ashes—
Thy hand first after mine I will furnish with guerdon of honor,
Whether a tripod or else two horses, a chariot with them,
Whether a woman, perchance, to ascend thy couch as a captive."

　　　Teucer, the blameless, to him made answer, and thus he addressed
　　"Why is it, Atreus' son, most noble, inciteth and urgeth　　[him:
Me, of myself full eager? For truly, whatever my prowess,
Ne'er have I ceased since first we thrusted them back upon Ilium,
Never neglected a chance to destroy some foe with an arrow.
Eight are the long-barbed darts I've sped already against them;
All are infixed in the bodies of young men lusty for battle.
This man, though—in his raging, a mad-dog—smite him I cannot."

　　　Thus he spake; and he speeded an arrow again from his bowstring
Right against Hector; for so his heart impelled him to smite him.
This time also he missed him, but brave Gorgythion, gallant
Scion of Priam, he struck right square in the breast with the arrow—
One whom a mother had borne that was wedded and came from Aesyme,
Castianira, the fair, like unto a goddess in person.
Even as when, o'erburdened with fruit and the showers of springtime,
Sidewise droopeth the head of a poppy abloom in a garden:
So even sidewise nodded his head 'neath the weight of his helmet.

　　　Once more Teucer speeded an arrow again from his bowstring
Right against Hector; for so his heart impelled him to smite him.
Yet did he miss him again—for Apollo averted the missile—
Archeptolemus smiting, the brave car-driver of Hector,
Full in his warward rush, on his bosom, close to the nipple.
Down from the chariot he crashed, and off the swift-footed horses
Swerved to the side. Unstrung was the Trojan's strength and his spirit.
Ay, it was sore grief shrouded brave Hector's heart for his driver.

There then he left him to lie, although deep-grieved for his comrade,
Bidding Cebriones, who was his brother and standing anigh him,
Take the reins of the horses; nor heedless was he when he heard it.
Hector himself leaped down to the ground from his glittering chariot,
Utt'ring his terrible cry, as he seized a rock in his fingers,
Rushing on Teucer straight; for his spirit bade him to smite him.
Meanwhile Teucer a bitter arrow had drawn from his quiver,
Laid it upon the string; but the shimmering-helmeted Hector
Smote (as he drew) his shoulder, the spot where the collar-bone fences
Neck from the chest—the spot where a wound is like to be fatal—
Smote with the stone sharp-jagged the Argive eagerly aiming
Straightly at Hector; his hand at the wrist grew palsied; the bowstring
Snapped; on his knees he collapsed; and the bow dropped out of his
Ajax by no means suffered the fall of his brother in patience,   [fingers.
Nay, but he ran and bestrode him, held o'er him his shield to protect
Two of his trusty comrades uplifting the hero from under,   [him —
Goodly Alastor and Echius' son, whose name was Mecisteus.
Back to the hollow ships they bore him, heavily groaning.

 Once more then in the Trojans th' Olympian kindled the spirit,
Till straight back to the moat, deep-digged, they had forced the Achae-
Hector amid the foremost; his heart swelled high in his prowess. [ans,
Even as when some hound at a wild boar snaps, or a lion,
Nipping its heels from behind, and with swift feet ever pursueth,
Darting at haunches or flanks, while eying it sharp, as it wheeleth:
So pressed Hector hard on the heels of the long-haired Achaeans,
Always slaying the rearmost—and they kept fleeing before him.
Soon as they passed, however, the deep-dug ditch palisaded,
Headlong fleeing, and many had fall'n at the hands of the Trojans,
Once more there at the ships in a rally they bided the onset,
Calling out one on another and all the gods of Olympus,
Each one lifting his hands in the fervor of instant petition.
Hector his fair-maned steeds kept wheeling hither and thither,
Glaring with eyes of a Gorgon or Ares, ruin of mortals.   [passion;
 Hera, the white-armed goddess, beholding, was filled with com-
Forthwith then she addressed, in accents winged, Athena:
 "Ay me! daughter of Zeus, aegis-bearer, no longer must we twain

Now in their uttermost need take thought for the Danaans dying,
Who now haply shall perish, fulfilling a doom of disaster
Under a single man's onslaught, who unendurably rageth,
Hector, Priam's son, the deviser of evils a-many."
    Then unto her in her turn spake the bright-eyed goddess Athena:
"Ay, and indeed may he forfeit his life and his spirit, this fellow,
Perishing under an Argive hand, in the land of his fathers.
But this father of mine doth rage with maleficent purpose,
Headstrong, ever offending, a foiler of all my intentions,
Neither at all remembers times many and oft that I rescued
His own son, foredone of the labors imposed by Eurystheus.
Verily he would lament unto heaven; then Zeus would dispatch me
Myself down from heaven in haste to attend him with succor.
Ah me! had I but known all this in my spirit prophetic,
What time forth he was sent unto Hades, warder of hell-gate,
Bidden from Erebus drag up the hound of abominate Hades,
Sure he had never escaped sheer floods of the Stygian water.
Now he abhors e'en me and fulfils the counsels of Thetis,
Thetis that kissed his knees and caressed his chin with her fondling
Touches and begs him to honor Achilles, the sacker of cities.
Cometh the time when again he shall call me his 'darling Bright-eyes!'
Well, now, hasten to harness the whole-hoofed horses to bear us,
While I enter the palace of Zeus who wieldeth the aegis,
There to array me in armor for warfare, that I may discover
Whether Priam's son, yon shimmering-helmeted Hector,
Truly will joy to behold us twain on the bridges of battle,
Or if many a Trojan shall fall and surfeit the vultures,
Surfeit the dogs, with fat and with flesh by the ships of Achaia!"
    So said she; and the white-armed Hera failed not to obey her.
Straight she departed, to harness her golden-frontleted horses —
Hera, the honored goddess, the daughter of Cronus, the mighty.
Meanwhile Pallas, the daughter of Zeus who wieldeth the aegis,
Shed at her sire's own portal the fine, light robe she was wearing,
Richly embroidered, that she with her own hands toiling had fashioned.
Thereupon, donning the tunic of Zeus, cloud-massing Cronion,
She in her harness arrayed her, all ready for dolorous warfare;

171

Then on the flame-bright car she mounted and seized on her javelin,
Ponderous, massive, and ſtrong, the lance wherewith she subdueth
Heroes' ranks she is wroth with, the child of a father puissant.

Now with the whip lashed Hera in eagerness down on the horses.
Then, self-moving, the gates of heaven creaked that the Horae
Keep, unto whom are committed the heaven's immense and Olympus,
Whether to open the clouds' dense compact, whether to close it.
Then through the gates the goad-enduring horses they guided.
Zeus, though, the Father, beheld them from Ida. In fury of anger
Urged he Iris, the golden of wing, that she bear them a message:

"Hie thee away, fleet Iris, and turn them back, nor allow them
Me to encounter. In no pleasant wise shall we join in a battle,
Seeing that now I declare, and the saying shall pass to fulfilment:
Under the chariot's yoke I will maim their fleet-footed horses,
Hurl themselves from the box, and the chariot shatter in pieces.
Neither, belike, will the circuit of ten years slowly revolving
Ever avail them to heal the wounds that are torn by the lightning.
So shall the Bright-eyes learn what meaneth a war with her father!
Hera, however — with her I am far less wroth and indignant,
Seeing that ever her wont is to fruſtrate all that I purpose."

Spake he; and ſtorm-footed Iris arose to bear them the message
Straight, and departed from Ida's mountains to lofty Olympus.
There, at the outermost gates of Olympus, many-enfolded,
Meeting, she halted the twain; then the word of Zeus she repeated:

"Whither in eagerness? What so maddens the heart in your bosoms?
Stop! The Cronion forbiddeth the giving of aid to the Argives.
Here is the threat of Cronus' son; and he will fulfil it:
Under the chariot's yoke he will maim your fleet-footed horses,
Hurl yourselves from the box, and your chariot shatter in pieces;
Neither, belike, will the circuit of ten years slowly revolving
Ever avail you to heal the wounds that are torn by the lightning.
So thou'lt learn, Bright-eyed, what meaneth a war with thy father.
Hera, however — with her he is far less wroth and indignant,
Seeing that ever her wont is to fruſtrate all he decreëth.
Thou, though, impudent dog, most terrible thou, if in earnest
Thou 'gainst the face of Zeus would'ſt lift thy javelin portentous!"

172

Hera and Athena Going to Assist the Achaeans.

Thus she spake and departed, the fleet-footed messenger, Iris.
Forthwith the goddess Hera directed a word to Athena:

"Ay me! daughter of Zeus who wieldeth the aegis! No longer
Would I consent to war with Zeus for the sake of the mortals.
Nay, let one of them live, peradventure another one perish,
Whose is the lot. As for him, whatever in spirit he purpose,
Let him adjudge it to Trojans and Danaans, as may be proper."

Thus she spake and turned again her whole-hoofed horses.
Then the Horae unyoked for them the fair-maned horses,
Tethered them each one fast to his own ambrosial manger,
Tilted the car meanwhile on the shining wall of the entrance.
They, however, the goddesses, sate them down on their golden
Chairs in the midst of the gods; their dear hearts sorely were troubled.

Meantime, driving from Ida his well-wheeled car and his horses,
Zeus Father fared to Olympus and came to the deities' session.
Promptly the far-famed Shaker-of-earth unharnessed the horses,
Lifted the car on its stand, and himself spread linen above it.
Zeus of the far-borne voice then seated himself on his golden
Throne, and under his feet then quaked the vasty Olympus.
Only Athena and Hera apart from Cronion were seated
Silent, never addressing him either a word or a question.
He in his heart understood full well; thus then he bespake them:

"Pray you, why are ye thus out of sorts, Athena and Hera?
Surely not from the battle that gives fair fame unto heroes
Are ye a-wearied of slaying the Trojans, so bitterly hated?
Verily — such are my hands unapproachable, such my puissance —
No gods ever could turn me, not all that inhabit Olympus.
Ye twain — seemeth a trembling your beautiful members invaded,
Ere ye had witnessed a fight and the long-famed deeds of a battle;
Seeing as now I declare — and the saying has passed to fulfilment —
Never had ye on your car, once smitten by thunder and lightning,
Fared back home to Olympus, the seat and abode of immortals."

Thus spake he; but thereat low muttered Athena and Hera,
Seated close to each other, devising ills for the Trojans.
Pallas, in truth, kept still and not a word did she utter —
Wrathful at Father Zeus — and fierce was the fury that seized her.

Hera, unable to ſtifle the rage in her bosom, addressed him:

"Most dread scion of Cronus, what word is this thou hast spoken!
Well enough know even we thy ſtrength is invincible wholly.
Yet we have nevertheless some grief for the Danaan spearmen,
Who now haply shall perish fulfilling a doom of disaſter.
Still, we will surely refrain from the war, as thou hast commanded,
But to the Argives offer, it may be, counsel for profit,
That in this fury of thine not all of them utterly perish."

Then in answer, Zeus, cloud-gatherer, spake and addressed her:
"Ay, at the dawn of tomorrow, my ox-eyed, worshipful Hera,
Thou shalt behold, if thou wilt, the Cronion exceedingly mighty
Still more waſting the wide war-host of the spearmen of Argos,
Seeing that never shall Heċtor, the mighty, cease from the battle
Ere from his warships rise the fleet-footed hero Pelides
That same day that they battle amain at the ſterns of the galleys
There in the fearfullest tension of ſtrife round the fallen Patroclus.
So 'tis ordained of heaven! and naught reck I of the anger
Thou may'st feel — not e'en if thou go to the nethermost limits
Whether of earth or of sea, where Iapetus sitteth or Cronus,
Cheerless; they have no joy of the sungod's beam, Hyperion's,
Never of breezes: profound lies Tartarus-blackness around them.
Yea, though thither thou goest a-wandering, I will not reck me
Ever of *thy* wrath, seeing there's none worse vixen than thou art."

Thus spake he; not a word spake white-armed Hera in answer.
Meanwhile fell into Ocean the radiant light of the sungod,
Trailing a black night onward and over the grain-giving plowlands.
Now on the Trojans unwilling the daylight failed; to th' Achaeans
Welcome and thrice-implored the night came sable upon them.
Then the glorious Heċtor convened in assembly the Trojans
Gathered apart from the ships by the marge of the eddying river,
Where in the open a space shone clear, unencumbered of corpses.
They from the cars dismounted to earth and attended the saying
Spoken of valiant Heċtor, belovèd of Zeus. And his spearshaft,
Cubits eleven in length, he held in his hand; and before him
Glittered the point of bronze; and a ferrule of gold ran about it.
He, on his javelin leaning, addressed these words to the Trojans:

"Hearken, ye Trojans and Dardans, and ye allies of our city!
Now had I thought to destroy their ships and all the Achaeans,
This same day to return to wind-swept Troia victorious!
Darkness alas! hath arrived too soon, and the dark it is saveth
Th' Argives now and their ships at the wave-beat strand of the waters.
Well, then, let us forsooth unto black night render obedience:
Let us make ready our supper; unhitch from your war-cars the fair-
Horses betimes and cast their fodder in plenty before them.   [maned
Bring from the city for food both sheep well-fatted and oxen
Speedily; also provide yourselves with wine honey-hearted;
Bring forth grain from your houses and gather up wood in abundance,
So that the whole night long unto dawn, the child of the morning,
Fires full many may burn and the gleam shoot up into heaven,
Lest even haply by night the long-haired sons of Achaia
Strive to elude us and launch on the sea's broad back in the darkness.
Nay, may they never embark in their ships, unhurried, at leisure!
Never! Let many a one take with him a wound — to digest it
There in his home, sore smitten with arrow or keen-pointed javelin,
E'en as he leapeth aboard; so that many another in horror
Shrink from bringing a tearful war on the horse-taming Trojans.
Also let heralds, belovèd of Zeus, through the city proclaim that
Lads in the bloom of youth and elders, hoary of temple,
Take their posts round the town on the towers the deities builded.
As for the women folk, the weaker, let each keep blazing
High-heaped fire in her hall. And let sure watch be appointed,
Lest some ambush enter the town in the absence of war-men.
Great-hearted children of Troy, let it be then even as ordered.
Now, as a wholesome counsel, let this stand firm as delivered.
More at the dawn I shall say 'mid the Trojans, tamers of horses.
Hopeful I pray unto Zeus and to all of the other immortals
Hence and away to expel these hounds, fate-driv'n to disaster,
Hounds that the fates are driving on in their black-painted galleys.
Howbeit we will defend ourselves this night; and tomorrow
Early at dawn of the day, each man in his armor accoutred,
There at the hollow ships let us rouse up vehement Ares.
Then shall I know if Tydeus' son, Diomedes, the mighty,

Back to the walls shall repel me, away from the galleys, or rather
I slay him with the bronze and bear off his gory armor.
Morning shall furnish the test of his manhood, whether he bideth
Haply the rush of my spear or rather, I ween, in the vanguard
Stricken he lie on the ground and with comrades many around him,
When on the morrow the sun shall arise. For would I were surely
Now an immortal and ever for all my days were unaging,
Honored as Pallas Athena or Phoebus Apollo is honored,
Surely as this day now brings woe to the camp of the Argives."

Thus then Hector harangued, and the Trojans shouted approval.
Thereat under the yoke they delayed not to loosen the horses,
Dripping with sweat, then tethered with thongs each fast to his chariot.
Then from the town they brought both sheep well-fatted and oxen;
Speedily also provided themselves with wine honey-hearted;
Brought forth grain from their houses and gathered wood in abundance;
Hecatombs perfect they offered up to the gods everlasting.
Up from the plain into heaven the winds went bearing the savor
Sweet; but the blessèd immortals in no wise feasted upon it
Neither would aught of it, hating exceedingly Ilium holy,
Priam, lord of the ashen spear, and the people of Priam.

So they, cherishing hopes full high on the bridges of battle
Waited and sate all night, and the watch-fires kindled were many.
Even as stars that encircle a radiant moon in the heavens
Glitter conspicuous, whenso the air is lulled and is windless,
Then shine all of the lookouts clear and the uttermost headlands,
Glens, too, and under it ether immensurate gleameth from heaven,
All of the stars are seen, and the heart of the shepherd rejoices;
Even so many the fires, that the Trojans burned between Xanthus'
Streams and the ships, were blazing in front of Ilium city.
Fires on the plain were burning, a thousand; alongside of each one
Warriors fifty were seated there in the gleam of their campfires.
Meanwhile, champing the spelt and the white-grained barley, the horses
Stood at the chariots fast and awaited the fair-throned Morning.

180

ILIAD · IX · (I)

*Iota sings the Ambassy
And great Achilles' stern reply.*

So did the warders of Troy hold watch; but a heaven-sent panic—
Panic, the handmaid of chilling fear—possessed the Achaeans:
All of the bravest were tossed with unendurable sorrow.
Even as two winds stir up the deep sea, peopled with fishes,
Zephyr and Boreas, blowing from distant regions of Thracia,
Swift in impetuous squall; along with their coming a dark wave
Comes to a crest and along on the sea-marge pileth the seaweed:
So was the spirit distraught in the breasts of the sons of Achaia.
    But it was Atreus's son, sore-stricken at heart with his anguish,
Ranged through the camp, commanding the clear-voiced heralds to cite
Each by name, to assemble—and each with a several summons— [them,
Not with a shout—and himself still labored along with the foremost.
So, down-hearted, they sat in assembly. First Agamemnon
Rose up shedding his tears, as a fountain, flowing with dark-hued
Water, adown a precipitous crag pours murky its current:
Thus he, heavily groaning, addressed these words to the Argives:
    "Oh my friends, ye chiefs of the Argives, counseling heroes,
Zeus it is, Cronus' son, that confuses me sorely with blindness.
Hard of heart is he, who once promised me, nodding in sanction,
Sack of the well-walled city of Troy ere sailing for homeland.
Now, it appears, he had planned an evil deception: he bids me
Fare unto Argos disgraced for the ruin I've wrought on the people.
Such, it appears, is the pleasure of Zeus, the o'erpow'ringly mighty,
Zeus, who hath toppled the turrets of many a city aforetime,
Ay, and will topple again, since his is the mightiest power.
Come, then; even as *I* may declare, let all be persuaded:
Hie we away in the ships to the well-loved land of our fathers!
Seeing that never shall *we* take the wide-wayed city of Troia."

So spake he; the others all mutely attended in silence.
Long time truly those sons of Achaia were speechless for sorrow,
Till at the last spoke out Diomedes, good at the war-cry:

   "Atreus' son, I'll take issue with thee first of all for thy folly,
As is my privilege here in the conclave; let it incense thee
Noway. Mine is the valor that thou erst 'mid the Achaeans
Chiefly hast chidden and said 'a slacker was I and a coward.'
All these matters are known to the Argives, youthful and aged.
Truly the son of Cronus, the crooked in counsel, endowed thee
Only by halves: with sceptre of honor, chiefest of all men;
Valor, however, that is might most mighty, alas! he denied thee.
What, sir! Dost thou account them insooth, these sons of Achaeans,
Thus unwarlike to be and cowardly, as thou impliest?
Nay, but if thou thyself in thy heart art bent on returning,
Go! for the way now waits to receive thee; ships at the seaside
Lie that are thine, full many, that bore thee erst from Mycenae.
All of the rest, however, the long-haired sons of Achaia,
Here will abide till we lay waste Troy. Let all of the others
Hie them away in the ships to the dear-loved land of their fathers—
Sthenelus never! nor I—we twain shall fight until lastly
Ilium's end we attain; with the blessing of God came we hither."

   Thus he spake. With a shout all the sons of Achaia assented,
Plauding in wonder the speech of Tydides, tamer of horses.
Then the knightly Nestor arose and spake to them, saying:

   "Thou in the war art mighty, Tydides, past all thy companions,
Also in counsel a prince over all that in age are thy equals.
None will lightly esteem thy word; of all the Achaeans
None will gainsay it. Thy last word, however, abides yet unspoken.
Verily, too, thou 'rt young; thou mightest be even the youngest
Born unto me of my sons, although thou utterest wisdom
Here to the Argive princes in words well-fit to the purpose.
Come now, I will myself—who boast to be older than thou art—
Speak and expound it all, nor will anyone haply despise it
(This is the word I declare), not even the lord Agamemnon.
Outcast from clan, from law, from hearth is he, whosoever
Taketh delight in strife cold-blooded among his own people.

Well, now, let us insooth, unto black night render obedience:
Let us make ready our meal; let sentinels, each at a station,
Bivouac there at the moat dug outside under the rampart.
So much now I enjoin on the young men. Thou, Agamemnon,
Taking the lead in it all (for the kingliest thou art of all men),
Spread thee a feast for the elders, as fits thee; such is thy office.
Full are thy barracks with wine, for the galleys Achaean import it,
Bringing it daily from Thrace, as they voyage over the wide sea.
All entertainment is thine, and thou art king over many.
Soon as the throng then gather, whoever devises the wisest
Counsel, obey that man, since sore need have the Achaeans
All, of advice well-weighed and discreet. Lo! fires of the foeman
Burn full many, anigh to the ships. Whose heart would this gladden?
This night truly is fated to wreck this army — or save it."

　　　Thus spake he. They hearkened with diligence, heeding his counsel.
Forth then sallied the sentries, arrayed, each man, in his harness,
'Round Thrasymedes, shepherd of peoples, the scion of Nestor,
'Round Ascalaphus, too, and Ialmenus, children of Ares,
'Round Meriones, 'round Deïpyrus, Aphareus also;
'Round the good son of Creon, divine Lycomedes, they gathered.
Seven these chiefs of the sentries; with each one went out a hundred
Youth in a body, marching and holding ready their long spears.
Midway between the moat and the rampart they went to their stations;
There then kindled a fire; each troop made ready its supper.

　　　Then Agamemnon, assembling a councilor-throng of Achaeans
Unto his barracks, outspread a banquet soul-sating before them; [them.
They then reached forth their hands to the good cheer set out before
Now, when desire for drink and for meat the feasters had banished,
Nestor, first of them all, 'gan weaving the web of his counsel,
Nestor, whose counsel aforetime had ever been found to be wisest.
He then, kindliest-minded, harangued them and spake out among them:

　　　"Atreus' son, most glorious, thou monarch of men, Agamemnon,
This speech will I begin and end with thy name; for thou rulest
Many peoples as king; into thy hand Zeus hath entrusted
Sceptre and laws, in order that thou for thy folk may'st take counsel.
Thee it behooveth, of all men, to speak therefore and to hearken,

Yea, to fulfil for another whate'er his spirit may bid him
Speak for the best; on thee will depend his proposal's fulfilment.
So then I will proceed to declare what seems to me wisest.
No one surely will think up a thought that is better than this one—
This same one I have cherished long since and up to the present,
Right from the instant that thou, Zeus-sprung, in despite of his anger,
Wentest and took'st from his barrack Achilles' damsel, Briseïs,
We, though, never consenting; nay, I sought to dissuade thee,
Heartily strove, but in vain; for alas! thy imperious spirit
Made thee dishonor a chief whom the very immortals have honored,
Bravest of men; thou tookest, thou keepest the meed of his valor.
Nevertheless let us weigh how still to persuade and appease him
Both with agreeable gifts and with words fair-spoken, persuasive."

Then in his turn addressed him the monarch of men Agamemnon:
"Sire, thy words say nothing untrue in recounting my follies.
I was infatuate, yea, I would even myself not deny it.
Many a host is he worth, whome'er Zeus loveth in spirit,
Even as now he hath honored this man and destroyed the Achaeans.
Since, then, I was thus blinded, obeying a pestilent humor,
Fain would I now make amends and a recompense pay beyond measure.
Here in the midst of you all I name the excellent presents:
Tripods seven, untouched of fire; of gold ten talents;
Flame-bright cauldrons—a score; and of stalwart horses a dozen,
Winners in races—they with their swiftness of foot have won prizes.
That man never were lackland, a scanty possessor of precious
Treasures of gold, to whom only *so* much wealth were apportioned,
Only so much as my whole-hoofed horses have won me in prizes.
Then will I give seven women, well-skilled in handiwork matchless,
Lesbians, whom, when that man himself took Lesbos the well-built,
I chose out for myself as beyond all women in beauty.
All shall be his and the damsel besides, whereof I despoiled him,
Daughter of Briseus; yea, with an oath full mighty I swear it,
Never her couch I ascended or converse held with the damsel,
Never insooth, as a man, in the manner of men and of women.
All these things shall be his forthwith. Hereafter, if haply
God e'er grant us to plunder the broad-built city of Priam,

Then shall he enter and load up a shipful even of bronzen
Booty and gold, when we, the Achaeans, apportion the pillage.
Then let him choose for himself twice ten of the Ilian women,
Such as are counted the fairest—next after Helen of Argos.
Should then we win to Achaean Argos, of all lands the richest,
Son of mine should he be and honored as even Orestes,
Who, as a tenderly loved one, is nurtured there with abundance.
Three fair daughters are mine in the firm-built halls at Mycenae,
Firstly Chrysothemis, second Laodice, Iphianassa
Third; let him take whichever he will as his own unto Peleus'
Home, without gifts of wooing; it is I that will give her a dowry
Great past measure, the like none yet hath bestowed with a daughter.
Seven besides are the towns, all populous, that I will give him,
Enope, Hire, a region of grass, Cardamyle also,
Pherae divine, and a city with deep-grown meadow, Antheia,
Vine-clad Pedasus, too, and the beauteous borough Aepeian.
Hard by the sea are they all, on the lowest border of sandy
Pylus. Wealthy in sheep and in kine are the people that dwell there,
Ready to honor him like as a godhead haply with presents,
Under his sceptre fulfilling the tributes ample they owe him.
All this will I fulfil, if he now will give up his anger.
Then let him yield (unyielding, implacable, surely is Hades
Only, and therefore is he, of all gods, most hateful to mortals)—
Yield and submit unto me, as I am a mightier sovereign—
Ay, and because I also avow me in years to be elder.''
　　　Then unto him made answer the knightly Gerenian Nestor:
　　''Atreus' son, most glorious, thou monarch of men, Agamemnon,
No man would flout the gifts thou tend'rest to kingly Achilles.
Come then, let us select at once and hasten our envoys
Quickly to go to the tent of Achilles, the scion of Peleus.
Lo now, whomever I fix my eye upon, let them obey me.
Phoenix, belovèd of Zeus, first of all! Let him be the leader;
Next after him great Ajax; the third be goodly Odysseus.
With them let Odius follow and also Eurybates, heralds.
Now for the hands bring water and bid keep sacredly silence,
While unto Zeus, son of Cronus, we pray, if he will have mercy.''

Thus he spake; and a word well-pleasing to all he had spoken.
Henchmen at once brought water to pour on the hands of the princes.
Young men, thereupon crowning the wine-bowls brimful, apportioned
Rightly for all into goblets, the mean time pouring libation.
When they had poured libation and drunk to their hearts' satisfaction,
Sallied they forth from the tent of Atreus' son, Agamemnon.
Many a charge laid upon them the knightly Gerenian Nestor —
Glancing the meanwhile quickly at each one, chiefly Odysseus —
How to approach, to prevail on the faultless hero, Pelides.

So fared onward the twain by the sea-marge billow-resounding,
Fervidly praying the Shaker of earth, of earth the Upholder,
They might readily sway the proud Aeacid's heart with persuasion.
So they arrived full soon at the Myrmidons' ships and their barracks.
There they found him delighting his soul with a clear-sounding lyre,
Beautiful, curious-wrought, with a silver crossbar upon it,
One he had ta'en in the spoils, when he wasted Eëtion's city.
Therewith he gladdened his heart, as he sang deeds famous of heroes.
Over against him, alone, all silent sitting, Patroclus
Waited on Aeacus' son, whenso he should cease from his singing.
So, as the twain came forward — the goodly Odysseus was leading —
Fronting the hero they stood, and Achilles, leaving the settle
Where he was seated, arose, amazed, still holding the lyre.
Likewise also Patroclus arose at sight of the heroes.
Both with a greeting at once fleet-footed Achilles bade welcome:

"All hail! Truly dear friends that are come (how sore must the need
E'en in my wrath ye are dearest to me of all the Achaeans."   [be!) —

So much spoken, the goodly Achilles, leading them forward,
Seated them there upon chairs and carpets gleaming with purple,
Then called out to Patroclus anon, still standing hard by him:

"Ay now, son of Menoetius, a bowl more ample provide us!
Mingle a livelier wine, make ready a goblet for each one;
These are the dearest of men, that are come now under my roof-tree."

Thus spake he; and Patroclus promptly obeyed his dear comrade.
Then in the gleam of the fire he cast down a chopping-block ample,
Placing upon it a fat goat's back and a saddle of mutton,
Also the chine of a seasoned hog, all teeming with fatness.

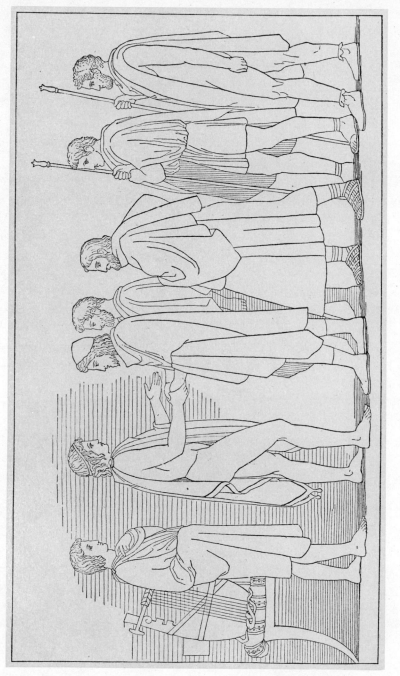

The Embassy to Achilles

Firmly Automedon held, while goodly Achilles carved them,
Carefully slicing the flesh, then neatly spitting the slices.
High up kindled the blaze the godlike son of Menoetius.
And, as the fire burned down, and the flame thereof was abated,
Then, as he smoothed out the embers, he placed thereover the spit-
Sprinkling hallowèd salt, then reſted the slices upon them.   [racks,
So, when these had been roaſted and heaped up high on the chargers,
Next Patroclus took bread and served it in beautiful baskets
'Round on the table. Achilles in turn the sliced meats was serving.
Close by the opposite wall from the goodly Odysseus the hero
Seated himself, then bade his comrade, Patroclus, make off'ring
Unto the gods; and he cast on the fire the consecrate portion.
They then put forth their hands to the good cheer set out before them.
Now, when desire for drink and for meat the feaſters had banished,
Ajax nodded to Phoenix; but noting it, goodly Odysseus,
Forthwith filling his goblet with wine, thus toaſted Achilles:

"Health to Achilles! Lack of an equable banquet is never
Felt in the tent of the monarch of men, Agamemnon Atrides,
Nor even now in thy own; there's abundance for all hearts' desire
Here for a feast; but the matter of fair fête touches us noway.
Nay, O nursling of Zeus! At sight of appalling disaſter
We are afraid; for it hangs in the scale — salvation, perdition   [thee.
Hangs for the well-benched ships, unless with thy might thou enclothe
Nigh to the wall, to the galleys, the foes have pitched their encampment,
Even the high-souled Trojans, allies, too, widely renownèd;   [minded
All through the camp they have kindled the watchfires now. They are
We shall hold out no longer but fall here amid our black galleys.
Zeus, too, Cronides, showeth the favoring sign of his lightning
Full on the right, while Heċtor, past words exulting in prowess,
Rages terrific, reliant on Zeus, and he recketh in no way
Either of men or of gods, for a dreadful madness hath filled him —
Ay, and he prayeth the goddess of dawn to speed her appearing,
Seeing he vaunts he will hew off the ensigns tall of the galleys,
Burn up the ships in devouring fire and slay the Achaeans —
Slay them there by the ships, driven out by the smoke of the burning.
All this sorely I dread in my heart, lest haply the godheads

Now may fulfil his vaunting, and we be fated to perish,
Perish in Troy-land, far from Argos, the pasture of horses.
Up, then, so thou'rt minded to succor the sons of Achaia —
Even though late — foredone by the dread war-din of the Trojans.
Thee thyself will sore grief assail hereafter, and never,
Never is remedy found of an ill once done. So bethink thee
How to ward off that evil day from the Danaan army.
Yea, gentle sir, it was Peleus' self, thy father, enjoined thee
That same day that he sent thee from Phthia to aid Agamemnon,
Saying, 'My child, as to prowess, Athena and Hera will grant it
Surely, if haply they will; but bridle the spirit within thee,
Howe'er proud in thy breast, since kindliness ever is better.
Put away strife, that breeder of ill, that so may the Argives
Render thee much more honor, the youthful as well as the elders.'
So did the old man charge thee; but thou hast forgotten. But even
Now forego it; renounce thy rancorous wrath. Agamemnon
Offereth gifts right worthy, if thou but renounce thy resentment.
Come now, hearken to me, while I in thy presence recount them,
All those gifts Agamemnon hath promised thee there in his barrack:
Tripods seven, untouched of fire; of gold ten talents;
Flame-bright cauldrons — a score; and of stalwart horses a dozen,
Winners in races — they with their swiftness of foot have won prizes.
That man never were lackland, a scanty possessor of precious
Treasures of gold, to whom only *so* much wealth were apportioned,
Only so much as his whole-hoofed horses have won him in prizes.
Then he will give seven women, well-skilled in handiwork matchless,
Lesbians, whom, when thou thyself took'st Lesbos, the well-built,
He chose out for himself as beyond all women in beauty.
All shall be thine and the damsel besides whereof he despoiled thee,
Daughter of Briseus; yea, with an oath full mighty he swears it,
Never her couch he ascended or converse held with the damsel,
Never insooth, O king, in the manner of men and of women.
All these things shall be thine forthwith. Hereafter, if haply
God e'er grant us to plunder the broad-built city of Priam,
Then thou'lt enter and load up a shipful of even bronzen
Booty and gold, when we, the Achaeans, apportion the pillage.

190

Then choose thou for thyself twice ten of the Ilian women,
Such as are counted the fairest — next after Helen of Argos.
Should then we win to Achaean Argos, of all lands the richest,
Son of his thou shouldst be and honored as even Orestes,
Who, as a tenderly loved one, is nurtured there with abundance.
Three fair daughters are his in the firm-built halls of Mycenae,
Firstly Chrysothemis, second Laodice, Iphianassa
Third; take thou whichever thou wilt as thine own unto Peleus'
Home, without gifts of wooing; 'tis he that will give her a dowry
Great past measure, the like none yet hath bestowed with a daughter.
Seven besides are the towns, all populous, that he will give thee:
Enope, Hire, a region of grass, Cardamyle also,
Pherae divine, and a city with deep-grown meadow, Antheia,
Vine-clad Pedasus, too, and the beauteous borough Aepeian.
Hard by the sea are they all, on the lowest border of sandy
Pylus; wealthy in sheep and in kine are the people that dwell there,
Ready to honor thee like a godhead haply with presents,
Under thy sceptre fulfilling the tributes ample they owe thee.
All this he will fulfil, if thou cease now from thy anger.
But if indeed thy heart too deeply abhorreth Atrides,
Both himself and his gifts, yet pity the other Achaeans
All now faint, foredone, through the army! They surely will honor
Thee as a god — such mighty renown thou'dst win thee among them,
Seeing that now thou might'st slay even Hector! He in his frantic
Rage might venture anigh thee; for none he esteemeth his equal,
None of the Danaans all, whose warships brought them to Troyland."
    Ready with answer addressed him in turn fleet-footed Achilles:
"Zeus-born son of Laërtes, Odysseus of many devices,
Needs must I utter my rede, and that, too, openly, outright,
Even just what my mind is, and how it shall pass to fulfilment,
Lest ye sit here by me and coo on from this side and that side.
That man truly is hateful to me as the portals of Hades,
Whoe'er hides in his heart one thing as he utters another.
What then seemeth the best unto me, lo! now I declare it.
Never, methinketh, shall he, Agamemnon Atrides, persuade me,
Nor all other Achaeans; for never a thank was accorded

Any for always battling, without any respite, the foemen.
Like is the lot of the slacker with his that warreth the hardest;
Ever co-equal in honor are held both coward and hero;
Dieth alike th' untoiling and he that abundantly toileth.
Naught is the profit to me for the hardships I suffered in spirit,
Always ſtaking my life on the chance and the wager of battle.
Even as beareth a bird in her beak to her featherless neſtlings
Morsels whenever she find them, herself scant nurtured the meantime,
Even so I: full many the nights I've passed unsleeping,
Also the days, all ſtained with blood, I've spent in the battle
Warring with warriors — all on account of *their* women in wedlock!
Twelve are the cities of men already I've sacked with my warships,
Also eleven on foot, through the deep-soiled mainland of Troia.
Many the treasures and goodly, indeed, whereof I despoiled them,
All these cities; and all I would bring unto king Agamemnon,
Atreus' son, and would give him; and he'd ſtay back and receive them
There at his ships; he'd divide a few, but the most — he'd retain them!
Some he would give as rewards unto kings, as guerdons to nobles.
These he hath left untouched; but from me alone of Achaeans
Taketh and keepeth my lady, the joy of my heart; and beside her
Now let him pleasure! — But why must the Argives war with the
Why did Atrides gather and lead such armament hither 　　[Trojans?
Over the seas? Was it not for the fair-haired Helen of Argos?
They then, sole among mortals, are fond of their wives, the Atridae?
Surely a man, whoever is kind and of sound underſtanding,
Loves and will cherish his own. So I, too, loved my Briseïs,
Loved her with all my heart, although she was won with the javelin.
Well now, since he hath taken my prize from my arms and deceived me,
Let him not tempt me again — I know him — he ne'er will persuade me.
Nay, let him counsel with thee, my Odysseus, thee and the other
Princes, how he may ward from the galleys the ruinous fire.
Many, exceedingly many, the works he hath wrought him without me!
Lo! he has builded a wall; he has added a moat, too, delven
Broad, deep, and great in extent, and planted it densely with palings!
What then? Not even so can he ſtay the man-slaying Hector's
Might. But so long as I was a-warring amid the Achaeans,

Never would Hector venture a fight far off from his ramparts;
Only as far as the oak and the gateway Scaean he ventured;
There only once he withstood me and barely escaped then my onset.
Now, no longer minded to war 'gainst Hector, the godlike,
Zeus I will worship with off'ring, and all gods else, and tomorrow,
Freighting my ships full richly, I launch them again on the salt sea.
Thou shalt see — if thou wilt and if thou carest to be there —
Over the Hellespont, peopled with fish, my galleys at daybreak
Sailing away and my men at the oars all eagerly straining.
Then, if the famed Earth-Shaker accord me a prosperous voyage,
Haply the third day out I shall win unto Phthia, the deep-soiled.
Many the holdings I left, when I came here — came unto ruin!
Hence I shall carry insooth rich booty of gold and of hoary
Iron and bronze, all ruddy, and fair-girdled women I'll carry —
All that has fall'n to my lot. However, the guerdon of honor
He that had giv'n took back with an insult, the lord Agamemnon,
Atreus' son! Declare to him everything, just as I charge you,
Openly, so that the other Achaeans may frown indignant,
If he expects to beguile some other Danaan comrade,
Always clothèd in impudence; that man, however (the houndling!),
Never would dare look *me* in the face, though utterly shameless!
Never will I share counsel with *him*, nor enterprise either,
Seeing he wholly deceived me and sinfully wronged me. So henceforth
Never with words would he cheat me — enough of him! Let him unhin-
Go to perdition! for Zeus, high counselor reft him of reason.   [dered
Hateful to me are his gifts; I value them less than a straw's worth!
Not though haply he offered me ten times even, or twenty,
All that belongs to him now and all he might get him from elsewhere,
All that Orchomenus enters and Thebes, famed city of Egypt —
Thebes, where fullest of all (men say) are the houses of treasure,
Thebes, with its hundred portals; at each of them two hundred heroes
Go forth unto the battle along with their horses and chariots.
Nay, though so many his gifts as the sea-beach sand or the dust is,
Not even so will he ever prevail on my soul — Agamemnon —
Ere he hath paid off all that bitter insult he did me.
Never will *I* wed daughter of him, Agamemnon Atrides,

Not if in beauty she vie with the golden queen Aphrodite,
Rival in works of her hands ev'n bright-eyed Pallas Athena,
Not even so will I wed; let him choose some other Achaean,
One that may suit his rank, a man more kingly than I am!
For if the gods keep me safe and I get back to my homeland,
Peleus' self then doubtless will seek me a woman for wedlock.
Many Achaean maidens there be in Hellas and Phthia,
Daughters of princes who watch o'er the safety of stronghold cities;
Whomsoever of these I prefer I will make my dear consort.
Often there did my lordly soul feel the impulse upon me,
Once I had wooed me and wedded a wife, co-partner befitting,
Then to enjoy the possessions the old man, Peleus, possesseth.
No compensation for life — unto *me* — were the fulness of riches
Men had assembled, they say, in the fair-homed city of Troia,
Ere, in the days of peace, there came the sons of th' Achaeans;
Neither all that is kept by the threshold of stone of the archer,
Phoebus Apollo, the god who presides at Pytho, the rocky.
Sheep well-fatted indeed may be taken and cattle in plunder;
Tripods, too, may be bought; and chestnut horses are purchased;
Ay, but the soul of a man comes never by pillage or capture,
Never returning, if once from the hedge of his teeth it escapeth.
Yea, my mother, a goddess, e'en Thetis, the silver-footed,
Tells me that fates diverse to the bourne of death will conduct me:
Here if I choose to abide and to war round the city of Troia,
Lost then is my returning, but fame shall be mine and undying;
But, if I get back home to the well-loved land of my fathers,
Lost then is my high fame, but my life's term thus shall be lengthened
Greatly; not speedily then shall the issue of death overtake me.
So I would dare to exhort with a word you other Achaeans
Homeward to sail. For steep-built Ilium's end ye shall never
Gain; for Zeus of the far-borne voice his hand holdeth surely
Over the city; the people of Troy are filled with high courage.
Well then, hence on your way unto all those princes Achaean.
Tell them the message frankly (for such is the office of elders),
Bidding them frame in their hearts some other and better advisement
(Such as may rescue the galleys along with the hosts of Achaia

There at the hollow ships), since this plan availeth them noway,
Which they devised so lately, for *my* wrath in naught is abated.
Phoenix — let him ſtay here and lay him to rest in our quarters,
That with the morn he may follow me hence in my ships to the home-
Dear — if he please, for against his will I think not to take him."   [land
     So spake he; the others all mutely attended in silence,
Dumb with amaze at his word, so vehement he in refusal.
Then at the last spake out the knightly reverend Phoenix,
Letting his tears well up, in fear for the galleys Achaean:
     "If, then, thou in thy soul art pondering, noble Achilles,
Speedy return, nor at all art minded to ward from the swift-keeled
Ships the deſtruction of fire — such wrath hath entered thy spirit —
How could I ſtay, dear child, henceforth all lonely without thee
Here at Troy? For to thee 'twas the knightly old Peleus that sent me
That same day that he sent thee from Phthia to aid Agamemnon —
Sent thee when only a child, trained neither for battle impartial
Nor for debating, the two main ſtages in noble achievement.
Peleus therefore sent me to teach thee in all these matters,
Prowess in doing of deeds no less than in speaking of speeches.
So would I never consent, dear child, from thee to be parted,
Never, not e'en if it were a godhead's self undertook it,
Smoothing my old age off, unto blossoming youth to reſtore me,
Even as when I left Hellas, the land of beautiful women,
Fleeing a quarrel with Ormenus' son, my father, Amyntor.
He on account of his fair-haired leman was bitter against me.
Her he'd be loving himself and wronging the couch of his wedlock,
My own mother's, and she at my knees kept begging me always
First with his leman to lie, that the old man prove to her hateful.
I was persuaded of her, and I did so. My father, directly
Scenting it, cursed me roundly and called on the Furies abhorrèd,
Fervently praying that never a dear son sprung of my body
Sit on the knees of his sire; and gods have accomplished his curses,
Both the under-world Zeus and the dreadful Persephoneia.
Him with a keen bronze dagger was I then bent upon killing.
Some one, though, an immortal, bridled my wrath and reminded
Me of the people's talk, the many reproaches of mortals,

Lest 'mid the Argives I should be called 'that parricide Phoenix.'
Then could the heart in my bosom endure nowise any longer
Under a curse to remain in the halls of a father so angry.
Nevertheless my fellows all gathered around me, my kinsmen,
Begging, beseeching, and there in the halls they tried to restrain me,
Slaughtering many a sheep right lusty and crook-horned cattle
Shambling of gait; they stretched above the flame of Hephaestus,
Full length, many a swine to be singed, rich-laden with fatness;
Yea, and they drank much drink, poured out from the jars of my father.
Nine nights also asleep some lay on the couches close by me,
Ever relieving in turn each other at watch. And the fire
Under the well-fenced courtyard's corridor never was quenched, not
E'er in the vestibule either, in front of the chamber's entrance.
But as the tenth night now in its pitchy dark fell upon me,
Then I arose, broke open the deft-joined doors of the chamber,
Stole forth thence, with a bound o'erleaping the wall of the courtyard,
Lightly eluded the watchers, the men no less than the household
Women — then, fleeing afar through the wide-lawned regions of Hellas,
Came at last to the deep-soiled mother of flocks, unto Phthia —
Came unto Peleus, the king; who, after a generous welcome,
Cherished me also as haply a father might cherish a dear child,
Even a well-loved son, sole heir of his ample possessions;
Making me rich with abundance, he gave much folk to my keeping,
While, a Dolopian prince, I dwelt at the borders of Phthia.
Yea, in the love of my heart, O match for immortals, Achilles,
I it was reared thee the man thou art; for thou in the palace
Ne'er wouldst eat with another nor e'er go into the banquet —
I it was only must seat thee upon my knees and with morsels
Sate thee, that I'd cut first, and hold up wine for thy drinking.
Verily many the time thou'st spattered the breast of my tunic,
Spirting the dark wine forth in the troublesome manner of infants.
So I have suffered for thee manifold, manifold have I travailed,
Mindful of this, that the gods by no means ever would grant me
Child of my own; hence thee, O match for immortals, Achilles,
I have adopted, as guard henceforth against grievous destruction.
Therefore, Achilles, subdue thy spirit of pride; it behooves thee

Not, such a heart unrelenting; the gods themselves may be bended,
Though their majesty, glory, and might are greater than ours are.
Men turn them with off'rings of incense and vows of persuasion;
Men with the savor of sacrifice move even them, with libations
Mingled with prayer, when haply a soul transgresseth and sinneth.
Verily daughters of mighty Zeus are Prayers of Repentance,
Wrinkled, halting of foot, with eyes askance in their glances,
Who are appointed the footsteps of Sin in sorrow to follow.
Sin, however, is strong, right nimble of foot; she outrunneth
All of men's prayers; she attaineth the whole earth's circuit before them,
Causing people to fall, while Prayers come after to heal them.
Whosoever reveres these maidens of Zeus at their coming,
Him they abundantly bless, yea, hearken to him when he prayeth.
But whensoever a man right roughly spurns and rejects them,
Then they depart, with a prayer, unto Zeus, their father, Cronion,
Praying his Sin may follow him fallen, until he atoneth.
Nay, watch closely, Achilles, that rev'rence wait on the Zeus-sprung
Maidens, such as inclineth the heart alway of the noble.
Yet if Atrides brought no gifts, if he named thee no others,
Following fast, if he stoutly persisted in violent anger,
Not I surely were one to advise forswearing resentment,
Even to save the Achaeans, in most dire need of a rescue.
Now, however, he tenders thee many, he promises others
After them; also he sends in petition the best of the Argives,
Heroes chosen from all of the war-host, men that thou lovest
Thyself—dearest of all. Their words, their journey, I pray thee,
Do not dishonor, although thy wrath thus far has been blameless.
Also consider the tales that we hear of the princes aforetime,
Heroes, often as wrath o'ermastering seized upon any;
Yet they were open to gifts; words still found way to persuade them.
I can remember a tale, not of yesterday but of the old times,
Clearly remember, and here in the bosom of friends I will tell it:
   "Once the Curetes fought the Aetolians, staunch in a battle,
All round Calydon-town, both joined in a mutual slaughter:
These, th' Aetolians, set to defend fair Calydon-city,
Those, the Curetes, eager to sack and destroy it in warfare.

Artemis, golden of throne, *she* visited evil upon them,
Angry that Oeneus offered the firstling fruits of his orchard
Not unto her; hecatombs made feast for the other immortals;
Artemis only, the daughter of mighty Zeus, he neglected;
Whether forgetful or careless, he wrought sore sin in his spirit.
Deeply incensed, the Rainer-of-arrows roused up a heav'n-born
Creature against them — a boar, white-gleaming of tusk and ferocious,
Wreaking incessantly havoc wide on the orchard of Oeneus.
Many a tall proud tree he would level to earth, uprooted,
Mingled in heaps with the roots themselves and the blossoms of apples.
Oeneus' son, Meleager, had finally slaughtered the monster,
When he had gathered hunters and hounds from numerous cities,
Seeing that it could be quelled by no mere handful of mortals,
Huge as it was; and many it brought to the pyre of lamenting.
Then all round it the goddess awoke loud shouting and turmoil,
Strife for the boar's rough head and his hide, all horrid with bristles —
Warlike strife of Curetes and high-souled sons of Aetolia.
So long now Meleager, belovèd of Ares, did battle,
So long fared the Curetes ill, nor ever were able,
Although many, to sally and wait him outside of their rampart.
But when anger had seized Meleager, such as in others
Swelleth the heart in the breast, though elsewise prudently minded,
He, in his anger of soul, incensed with his mother, Althaea,
Dallied beside the fair Cleopatra, whom he had wedded,
Daughter of beautiful-ankled Marpessa — child of Evenus
She — and of Idas, counted the strongest man that was dwelling
Then upon earth; it was Idas that spanned 'gainst Phoebus Apollo
Even, his bow in behalf of the maiden of beautiful ankles.
Father and mother had given the maid Cleopatra a surname,
Calling her there in their home Alcyone, seeing her mother
Cried out wailing in wise of the halcyon's loud lamentation,
When she was carried away by the lord, far-working Apollo.
Nursing consuming wrath, Meleager laid him beside her,
Wroth at the curse of Althaea, his mother; invoked in her instant
Prayer unto every god, sore grieved at the death of her brethren,
Beating her hands meantime on the bounteous earth in her fury,

Calling on Hades' name and on awful Persephoneia —
While she sank on her knees (with tears her bosom was flooded),
Begging death for her son; and Erinys that walketh in darkness
Heard her from Erebus' depths, with a heart that knoweth no mercy.
Speedily now at the gates rose clamor of foes; crashing thunder
Rose from the battered towers; the elders instantly prayed him;
Also the foremost priests of the gods the Aetolians sent him,
Pledging a great rich gift, if he come forth now to defend them:
Bidding him choose a demesne, surpassingly fair, and demark it,
Wheresoever the plain was fattest, of Calydon lovely,
Fifty the acres in number — the half thick-set in a vineyard,
Half, rich glebe of the plain, all treeless, suited for tillage.
Came to the threshold oft of his chamber, lofty of ceiling,
Knightly old Oeneus, his father, who also pressingly prayed him,
Shaking the morticed panels, imploring his son for assistance.
Instant also his sisters in prayer and his worshipful mother
Sued him — the more he denied them; and instant, too, his companions
Nearest insooth unto him and of all men also the dearest —
Vainly! for never the heart in his breast even so they persuaded,
Till his own chamber was hotly battered, and high on the towers
Climbed the Curetes and sought to set the great city on fire!
Then fair-girt Cleopatra, his spouse, besought Meleager,
Loud in her wail; she told the tale of all of the horrors —
All such woes as befall those people whose city is taken:
Warriors slain and the city burned and leveled in ashes,
Children and deep-zoned women that strangers hale into thralldom.
Quick was he roused in soul, when he heard such horrors recounted.
Forth then he issued, clad unto battle in glittering armor.
So then he warded and fended the doomsday from the Aetolians,
Yielding to his own heart; and they noway paid him the presents
Many and gracious, though even so it was he that had saved them.
Be not in soul like-minded with him, nor heaven direct thee
Such wise ever, dear friend; for a harder task it were truly
Ships already aflame to defend. On the strength of the presents
Come; for as to a god the Achaeans will render thee honor.
But if apart from the gifts thou enter the battle that wasteth

199

Men, such honor thou'lt lose, e'en though the war thou avertest."

Thereupon answered and spake unto him fleet-footed Achilles:

"Phoenix, my dear old daddy, thou nurseling of Zeus, of this honor
Need have I none; Zeus grants me a portion of honor, methinketh,
Honor abiding with me 'mid the curved-beaked galleys, so long as
Breath in my bosom abides, and my knees stir nimble beneath me.
This, moreover, I tell thee, and ponder it well in thy spirit:
Trouble my soul no more with bewailing and sore lamentation,
Merely to pleasure the hero Atrides; ill it beseems thee —
Friendship for him — lest thou grow hateful to me, though I love thee.
Better to join me in troubling the man who makes me trouble.
Be thou a king with me and share with me half of my honor.
These men will carry my message; but thou, staying here in my barrack,
Lay thee to rest in a bed that is soft. When the morning appeareth,
We will consider if haply to sail home hence or to stay here."

Spake he and thereupon nodded in silence his brows to Patroclus,
Bidding him strew for Phoenix a thick couch, so that the others
Might take thought to depart with all speed from his barrack. But Ajax,
Telamon's son and the peer of a godhead, spake and addressed them:

"Zeus-born son of Laërtes, Odysseus of many devices,
Let us be going. By this trip, it seems to me, we shall never —
Never accomplish the mission assigned. We must tell the Achaeans,
Though it be far from pleasing, at once the answer he's given.
Now, I suppose, they are seated and waiting for us. But Achilles
Rouseth to savage fury the great-hearted soul in his bosom.
Obstinate man! and he counts mere nothing his comrades' affection,
Love we had honored him with at the galleys beyond all the others.
Merciless man! though many a one blood-money accepteth
E'en from a brother's slayer or e'en for a son that is murdered,
So that the culprit abides in the land on paying the forfeit
Downright; the heart is appeased and the high-strung soul of the kins-
When he hath taken the fine. But alas! a passionate temper,   [man,
Evil, implacable, gods have placed in thy breast, for a damsel,
One and alone! while now it is seven we offer, the choicest
Far, and besides them many more things. So cherish a gracious   [tree,
Spirit; have thou respect for thy home: we are guests 'neath thy roof-

Sent of the Danaan host. We claim to be nearest and dearest
Past all else unto thee, how many soe'er the Achaeans."

Forthwith answered and spake unto him fleet-footed Achilles:
"Ajax, offspring of Zeus, Telamonian ruler of peoples,
Thou dost somewhat after my own mind seem to have spoken
All this. Yet with resentment my heart still swells to remember
Those things, how in his swagger Atrides rudely insulted
Me 'mid the Argives, as if some alien needless to notice!
Go ye, then, and speak out plainly what is my message:
Tell them I will not bethink me at all of the bloody encounter,
Not till the son of Priam, the wiseheart, Hector, the godlike,
Cometh amain to the ships of the Myrmidon folk and their barracks,
Slaying the Argives, charring the Argive ships with his fires.
But, I can tell thee, by my black ship and here by my barrack
Hector, methinks, howe'er eager for fight he may be, will refrain him."

Thus spake he. And they took, each hero, a twin-bowled goblet,
Poured libation, and fared along by the galleys. Odysseus
Led. But Patroclus directed his comrades, also the women,
Bidding them hasten a thick-strewn couch to make ready for Phoenix.
They, thus bidden, obeyed, preparing a couch as commanded,
Fleeces and coverlet, too, and a spread of fine-flocked linen.
Thereon the old man laid him and waited for hallowèd morning.
Deep in a corner, the while, of the well-joined barrack Achilles
Slept. Beside him there lay a damsel he brought him from Lesbos
Captive, the daughter of Phorbas, the fair-faced maid, Diomede.
Close by the opposite wall lay also Patroclus; beside him
Iphis, of fair-wrought girdle — her whom noble Achilles
Gave him at taking of Scyrus, the stronghold steep of Enyeus.

Now, as the envoys entered Atrides' tent on returning,
Straightway the sons of Achaia, on all sides rising and standing,
Pledged them in goblets of gold and plied them with eager inquiries;
Yet was the monarch of men, Agamemnon, first with his question:
"Come, thou much-praised, thou pride of Achaia, tell me, Odysseus,
Whether he willeth to ward off destroying flames from the galleys,
Or said he nay? And does anger still possess his proud spirit?"

Straightway answered the goodly, the much-enduring Odysseus:

"Atreus' son, most glorious, thou monarch of men, Agamemnon,
Verily naught of his anger will that man quench; all the more he
Filleth himself with his fury and spurneth both thee and thy offers.
Ay, and he bids thee devise, alone, in the council of Argives
How to keep safe the galleys, mayhap, and the folk of Achaia.
As for himself, however, he threatens, when morning appeareth,
Straight on the waters to launch his gallant and well-benchèd galleys.
Also he said that he would exhort all us other Achaeans
Homeward to sail; for steep-built Ilium's end ye shall never
Gain; for Zeus of the far-borne voice his hand holdeth surely
Over the city; the people of Troy are filled with high courage.   [it,
That's what he said; and those who went with me are here to confirm
Ajax as well as the twain, both men of discretion, the heralds.
Phoenix, the old man, however, laid him to rest there, as bidden,   [land
That with the morn he may follow him hence in his ships to the home-
Dear—if he please; for against his will he thinks not to take him."

      Thus spake he; and the others all mutely attended in silence,
Marveling much at his word, so vehement he in haranguing.
Long time truly those sons of Achaia were speechless for sorrow,
Till at last spake out Diomedes, good at the war-cry:

      "Atreus' son, most glorious, thou monarch of men, Agamemnon,
Would thou never hadst thought to entreat Pelides, the faultless,
Offering myriad gifts! At the best of times he is haughty;
Much more now thou hast roused in him his arrogant spirit.
Well then, ye see, we must leave him to have his own way, and no mat-
Whether he go or remain; once more will he battle, whenever   [ter
Haply a god shall rouse or the heart in his bosom impel him.
Come then, even as I may declare let all be persuaded:
Hence unto slumber, as soon as with wine and with meat ye have sated
Fully your hearts; therein are fountains of valor and vigor.
Soon, however, as rosy-fingered Morning appeareth,
Marshal the host with all speed well out in front of the galleys,
Hero and horse; cheer them on; and fight thyself 'mid the foremost."

      Thus spake he, and the princes all shouted aloud in approval,
Plauding in wonder the speech of Tydides, tamer of horses.
Then, having poured libation, they fared, each one, to his barrack;
All then laid them down to partake of the blessing of slumber.

ILIAD · X · (K)

Kappa the night exploit applies:
Rhesus' and Dolon's tragedies.

ALL night long were the others, the princes of all the Achaeans,
Sunken in sleep at the ships, foredone, in the arms of soft slum-
Only Atrides, shepherd of war-hosts, king Agamemnon,   [ber.
No sweet slumber could hold; so much in his heart he debated.
Even as when the husband of fair-haired Hera sends lightnings,
Whether he fashioneth rain unspeakably great or a tempest,
Be it of hail or of snow, when flakes thick cover the plowlands,
Or when he fashioneth mighty the maw of ravenous warfare:
So quick followed the groans that rose in the breast of Atrides
Out of his innermost heart, and quaked his spirit within him.
Oft as he fastened his eyes on the Trojan plain, he would greatly
Wonder — so many the fires in front of Ilium blazing —
Voices of pipes and of flutes, uproarious din of the people:
But, whenever he looked at the ships, at the host of Achaeans,
Then he would pluck his locks in handfuls forth from his forehead,
Pleading to Zeus on high, in his brave heart mightily groaning.
   Unto his spirit at length this counsel appeared to be wisest:
First among all his men he would go to Nestor Nelides,
Hoping perchance to forge some faultless counsel together,
How to avert dread ills o'erhanging the Danaan army.
Rising upright, he drew round his breast his tunic upon him;
Under his shining feet then he bound on his beautiful sandals,
Flung thereafter about him the tawny pelt of a lion —
Fiery, huge, to his feet down-reaching — then took up his javelin.
   Likewise also a trembling had seized Menelaüs, for noway
Sleep had settled upon his eyelids, for fear lest the Argives
Suffer calamity, they that for his sake had come unto Troia
Over the wide waste waters, with resolute hearts unto battle.

First with the dappled skin of a leopard he covered his shoulders
Broad; then lifting a helmet of bronze, the warrior set it
Fast on his head; and then with his strong hand he caught up his javelin.
Forth then he issued to rouse up his brother, who mightily lorded
Over the Argives all, of the folk as a deity honored.
Him, as he harnessed his shoulders in beautiful armor, the chieftain
Found at the stern of his ship; and welcome to him was his coming.
First in accosting was he of the loud war-cry, Menelaüs:

"Why thus arm thee, dear brother? to speed forth haply a comrade
Now as a spy on the Trojan encampment? Greatly I fear me
Lest in the war-host none will essay such enterprise for thee,
Faring alone through the night, the ambrosial, seeking to spy out
Foemen! A heart therefor would of need be exceedingly hardy!"

Thereat spake and addressed him in answer lord Agamemnon:
"I have need of good counsel—and thou, too, O Menelaüs,
Nurseling of Zeus—of a counsel of cunning, to help and to rescue
Th' Argives' selves and their ships, since the heart of Zeus is averted.
Verily set is his heart on the off'rings offered of Hector
Rather than ours; since never I saw it or heard any tell it,
How one hero contrived one day such a legion of gruesome
Horrors, as Hector, belovèd of Zeus, unaided in prowess,
Wreaks on the sons of Achaia, though son not of god nor of goddess.
Deeds he hath done, methinketh, shall vex the Argives with sorrow
Lasting and long—such ills he devised against the Achaeans!
Go thou now and run swiftly along the ships for to summon
Ajax here and Idomeneus. I unto Nestor, the godlike,
Haste and exhort him to rise up now, if perchance he is willing
Straightly to visit the stalwart array of the sentries and charge them,
Since it is he they would heed above all men; for *his* son is also
Chief of the sentries—he and with him Idomeneus' war-mate,
Merion; mainly to *them* have *we* this duty committed."

Then to him made reply Menelaüs, good at the war-cry:
"How, then, runneth the word wherewith thou enjoinest and bid-
I stay here with the men we have placed and wait for thy coming, 〔dest?
Or shall I run after *thee*, as soon as I give them instructions?"

Then in his turn addressed him the monarch of men, Agamemnon:

"Stay thou there, lest haply we miss each other in going
Hither and thither; for many a path leads through the encampment.
Shout out loud, wherever thou goest, bid them awaken,
Each man's lineage naming, along with the name of his father,
Honoring all men duly, nor stand on dignity proudly;
Rather let *us* toil even ourselves — unto whom is appointed,
E'en at our birth, by Zeus, a heavy allotment of trouble."

　　Thus he spake and dismissed his brother with careful instructions.
Forward he went to look for Nestor, shepherd of peoples.
There at the side of his barrack and black ship quickly he found him,
Stretched on a soft-strewn bed; and near him his armor was lying,
Beauteous-wrought — two lances, a shield, and a glittering helmet.
Close by lay his belt, all-shimmering. With it the old man
Used to gird him, whene'er, not yielding to age's infirmness,
Harnessed he guided his folk unto warfare, waster of heroes.
Quickly he lifted his head, then raising himself on his elbow,
Atreus' son he bespoke and addressed him thus with a question:

"Who is it fareth alone by the galleys through the encampment,
Deep in the dead of night, when all other mortals are sleeping?
Seekest thou one of thy mules, peradventure, or one of thy comrades?
Speak out loud, nor in silence approach. What need is upon thee?"

　　Thereon addressed him in answer the monarch of men, Agamem-
"Nestor, Neleus' son, great glory of all the Achaeans,　　　　[non:
Know I am Atreus' son, Agamemnon, whom more than all others
Zeus hath entangled forever in toils, so long as abideth
Breath in my breast, whilever my knees stir nimble beneath me.
Thus am I roving, because sweet sleep comes not to my eyelids,
Rather the war weighs on me, the woes that afflict the Achaeans.
Fearful, indeed, my alarm for the Danaans, neither my spirit
Sitteth composed but turned in unrest, and my heart is for leaping
Forth from my bosom; the good knees beneath me are all of a tremble.
But if to do thou art minded, and sleep hath not overcome thee,
Let us away to the sentries and there make close observation,
Lest, o'erburdened with toil, with drowsiness settling upon them,
They may have fallen asleep and wholly forgotten their duty.
Truly, the foemen are also encamped hard by; and we know not

Whether they be not eager at night to engage in a battle."

Thereon to him made answer the knightly Gerenian Neſtor:

"Atreus' son, most glorious, thou monarch of men, Agamemnon,
Hardly, I ween, will Zeus, the counselor, ever accomplish
All of yon Heċtor's plans, as he hopes now; rather, meseemeth,
He will be vexed with calamities, and greater *ſtill*, if Achilles
Turn back his dear heart haply away from intraċtable anger.
Thee will I surely attend. Besides let us waken the others,
Tydeus' son, far-famed for his spear, and also Odysseus,
Ajax, the swift of foot, and the valiant scion of Phyleus.
Would that some one would go after these men also and call them—
Ajax, peer of the gods, and the lord Idomeneus also.
Theirs are the galleys that lie far off and not at all near us.
Prince Menelaüs, alas! although he is dear and reverèd,
I must reprove nor conceal my censure, though it incense thee,
Seeing he slumbers; he leaves such toil unto thee unassiſted.
Now it is he should be toiling among the chieftains, entreating
All; inasmuch as a need no longer endurable cometh."

Then in his turn addressed him the monarch of men, Agamemnon:

"Old man, another day I may even *bid* thee rebuke him:
Often indeed is he slack and to labor is often unwilling,
Noway yielding to sloth nor to any perverseness of temper;
Only he always looks unto *me* and waits for my leading.
Now, though, he it was wakened the earlier far, and he haſtened
Here to my side—I have sent him to summon the men thou requirest.
Hence let us haſten and meet those men in front of the gateways,
There by the sentries; for there is the place I told them to muſter."

Thereon to him made answer the knightly Gerenian Neſtor:

"So then none will be vexed, nor anyone fail to obey him,
None of the Argives, whenas he urgeth or ordereth any."

Thus he spake and drew on his breast his tunic about him;
Under his shining feet then he bound on his beautiful sandals,
Forthwith buckled about him a mantle—rich purple in color,
Double and ample in fold, with fleece thick matted upon it—
Caught up a doughty spear, sharp-tipped—and the point of it bronzen—
Fared forth then on his way 'mid the ships of the bronze-clad Achaeans.

206

First of all then was Odysseus, the peer of Cronion in counsel,
Wakened from out of his sleep by the knightly Gerenian Neſtor,
Calling him forth; and the cry sped inſtantly over his senses.
Forth he came from his barrack; with this word then he addressed them:

"Why thus wander ye lonely about the camp and the galleys
Through the ambrosial night? What need so urgent upon you?"

Thereon to him made answer the knightly Gerenian Neſtor:

"Heaven-born son of Laërtes, Odysseus of many devices,
Be not vexed — so sore the diſtress that besets the Achaeans.
Nay now, follow, and rouse up the rest, whome'er it beseemeth
Gathered in council to argue, if better to flee or do battle."

Thus he spake. To his tent went Odysseus of many devices,
Cast on his shoulders a rich-wrought shield, then followed the others.
After Tydeus' son, Diomedes, they went; and they found him
Outside, off from his tent with his armor at hand, and his comrades
Sleeping about him, their heads on their shields; and nigh them the lances
All had been fixed upright on their butts, and the bronze tips were
Far off, like to the lightning of Father Zeus. But the hero   [gleaming
Slept; underneath him the hide of an ox of the paſture was lying
Outspread, while under his head a shining rug was extended.
Standing beside him the knightly Gerenian Neſtor aroused him,
Stirring him up with the heel of his foot; to his face he rebuked him:

"Rouse thee, Tydeus' son! What! *All* night sunken in slumber?
Mark'ſt thou not how the Trojans have pitched their camp on the rising
Ground of the plain near the ships, and but little space interveneth?"

Thus he spake; and the other right swiftly sprang up from his slum-
Forthwith lifted his voice and in accents wingèd addressed him: [ber,

"Tough art thou, old sire, and unintermittent of labor!
Are there not other sons of Achaeans, younger than thou art,
Who might range all round the encampment, waking the princes
Each in his turn? Old man, thou'rt surely beyond all controlling."

Him then answered in turn the knightly Gerenian Neſtor:

"Yea now, all these things, dear friend, thou hast fittingly spoken;
Sons have I that are faultless, in sooth, and the people are also
Many, and some one of them might go and summon the others.
True! but necessity's urge o'ermaſtereth now the Achaeans,

. 207

Seeing it verily ſtandeth for all on the edge of a razor:
Either for us it is life, or else it is pitiful ruin.
Go now, waken up Phyleus' son and swift-footed Ajax,
If thou, indeed, hast pity for me, since thou art the younger!"
    Thus he. Tydides flung on his shoulders the pelt of a lion—
Tawny, huge, to his feet down-reaching—then took up his javelin,
Fared forth, wakened the chiefs, then led out all from the barracks.
When at length they arrived in the midst of the sentries assembled,
Far from asleep on their watches they found those sentinel leaders;
All, though seated, were ſtill wide awake, alert, in their armor.
Even as hounds keep wearisome watch 'round sheep in a penfold,
When they have heard some beast through the wildwood, fearless of
Coming on over the hills—and uproar riseth around him,   [spirit,
Clamor of men and of dogs; all slumber dieth among them:
So, as the sad nightlong those guards their vigil were keeping,
Sweet sleep vanished the while their eyes kept conſtantly turning
Plainward in case they should hear the Trojans in motion against them.
Glad at the sight was the old man and gave them a word of good courage;
Forthwith he lifted his voice and in accents wingèd addressed them:
    "That is the way, dear children, to keep watch! Never let slumber
Seize upon any, lest we become a joy to our foemen."
    Thus he spake and sped o'er the moat, and the kings of the Argives
Followed along, as many as now had been called to the council.
With them Meriones came and the glorious scion of Neſtor;
These twain, too, the princes had called into consultation.
So, having passed the deep-dug ditch, they arrived and were seated
Where in the open a space shone clear, unencumbered of corpses
Fallen, the place where erst the mighty Heƈtor desiſted,
Under the broadcast shadow of night, from the slaughter of Argives.
There, as they sat in communion of words, each one with another,
Knightly Gerenian Neſtor began discourse to the princes: [spirit
    "Is there none of you, friends, who would trust to his own daring
Urging him on and alone would go 'mid the great-hearted Trojans,
Venturing whether to capture, perchance, some enemy ſtraggler
Or else haply discover and hear some talk 'mong the Trojans:
What are the matters they now hold under advisement: if eager

Here to abide near the galleys, aloof from the city, or whether
They would withdraw to the town, since they have subdued the Achae-
All this a man might discover and back to us have a returning   [ans?
Scatheless; wide his renown would extend for him under the heavens,
Reaching to all mankind; and his valor's meed would be ample,
Seeing that of these chieftains, as many as rule o'er the galleys,
Each will assuredly give him a black ewe-mother as guerdon,
Each with a lamb at her feet—no chattel her equal in value;
Also a place shall always be his at a feast or a wassail."

Thus spake he; and the others all mutely attended in silence.
Then in the midst spoke out Diomedes, good at the war-cry:

"Nestor, the heart in my breast and my manly spirit impel me
Boldly to enter within yon camp of the Trojans, our foemen,
Hard by lying; but *if* some other man would attend me,
Then were my confidence greater, and greater my courage were also.
Two—if together they go—one marketh ahead of the other
How the advantage may lie; and one, e'en though he perceiveth,
Natheless shorter of wit is he and weaker in counsel."

Thus spake he. Full many were ready to follow Tydides.
Ready the warriors twain, the Ajaxes, squires of Ares;
Ready Meriones; ready and eager the scion of Nestor;
Ready Atrides, too, Menelaüs, renowned as a spearman;
Ready Odysseus, the dauntless, to steal away into the Trojan
Throng—for always dwelt an adventurous spirit within him.
Thereat spake out amid them the monarch of men, Agamemnon:

"Diomed, Tydeus' son, to my heart the dearest of mortals,
Verily thou shalt choose whome'er thou wilt as a comrade,
Picking the best among all that have offered, many and eager.
Do not thou, from a sense of regard in thy heart or deferring
Unto an awe, in regard for kinglier lineage, maybe,
Leave unelected the better and choose thee a worse for companion."

Thus he spake, but he feared for Menelaüs, the fair-haired.
Spake out 'mid them again Diomedes, good at the war-cry:

"Seeing indeed ye command me to choose myself a companion,
How could I, then, be ever unmindful of godlike Odysseus?
He hath a heart right ready beyond all measure, a spirit

209

Manful in all kinds of travail, and Pallas Athena loves him.
Only be he my companion, and out from the burning of fire
Both of us surely return—for he is supremely resourceful."
　　Then unto him made answer the steadfast, goodly Odysseus:
　　"Neither bepraise o'ermuch nor in any way blame me, Tydides,
Seeing that 'tis 'mong the Argives thou sayest this; and they know it.
But let us go, for the night fast waneth; the morning approacheth;
Onward the stars have advanced; the most of the night hath departed;
Two of its watches are spent, and the third watch barely remaineth."
　　Thus spake they, and the twain put their terrible armor upon them.
Then unto Tydeus' son Thrasymedes, sturdy in battle,
Furnished a two-edged sword (his own had been left at his galley),
Also a shield. On his head he placed a helmet of bull's hide,
Neither with crest nor cone (it is therefore known as a skull-cap);
Such is the head-guard worn by a young man lusty and stalwart.
Merion meanwhile was giving a quiver and bow to Odysseus,
Also a sword, and he covered his comrade's head with a headpiece
Fashioned of leather; with straps full many the helmet was quilted
Firm on the inside, while, on the outside, tusks of a wild boar,
Flashing of tusk, had been set white-gleaming and thick all about it,
Deftly and cunningly wrought, with a felt-piece forming the lining—
Casque of Amyntor, the Ormenid, this—Autolycus stole it,
When he once entered its lord's strong home in Eleon city;
He to Amphidamas, king of Cythera, to take to Scandeia
Gave it; then Amphidamas gave it to Molus, a guest-gift;
He to Meriones gave it, his son, to wear on his temples;
Now it protected the head of Odysseus, clasping it closely.
　　So, when these heroes twain had put on their terrible armor,
Straight they started and left all the warrior princes behind them.
Rightward, hard by the way, as they went forth, Pallas Athena
Sent them a heron as omen; with eyes they never beheld it,
Such was the darkness of night, but they heard the cry of the heron.
Glad in his heart at the omen, Odysseus prayed to Athena:
　　"Hear me, thou child of Zeus who wieldeth the aegis, who ever
Standest by me in travail of all kinds; never a move of
Mine can escape thee. But now above all be gracious, Athena,

Granting us happy return to the ships, all covered with glory,
Having accomplished a work full weighted with woe to the Trojans."
    Followed him then with a prayer Diomedes, good at the war-cry:
    "Likewise hearken to me, thou child of Zeus, thou unwearied;
Follow with me, as with Tydeus of old, my father, the godlike,
When as a herald he went unto Thebes before the Achaeans.
Them he left at the river Asopus, those bronze-mailed Achaeans.
Verily now it was honied, the word that he bare the Cadmeians
There, but most dreadful the deeds he wrought upon them in returning,
Thou, bright goddess, his aid, right eagerly standing beside him.
Even so readily now stand close by me and protect me;
Then will I lay on thy altar a broad-browed heifer, a yearling,
Heifer unbroken, nor yet led under the yoke of a mortal.
Such, with her horns well gilded with gold, unto thee will I offer."
    Thus they spake in petition, and Pallas Athena attended. [mighty,
When they had offered their prayers to the daughter of Zeus, the all
Like unto lions the twain fared on in the blackness of midnight, [armor.
On past the slaughter and slain, through the dark-hued blood and the
    Neither had Hector permitted the lordly Trojans to slumber;
Nay, he had called them together in conclave, all of the noblest,
Whoe'er counted among them as leader and chief of the Trojans—
Called them in session and opened a counsel of cunning before them:
    "Who is the man that would promise me *this* work, who would per-
Winning a bountiful gift? For sure his reward would be ample: [form it,
Horses twain, with high-arched necks, and a car will I give him;
Steeds the best there may be at the swift-sailing galleys Achaean
He shall receive that will venture and win the renown of achievement:
Nigh to the swift-faring galleys to go and spying discover
Whether the swift ships now, as of old time, always are guarded,
Whether already subdued at our hands, they now are devising
Counsel among them for flight and indeed no longer are willing
Nightlong watch to maintain, overcome with weariness direful."
    So spake Hector. The others all mutely attended in silence.
Now in the ranks of the Trojans was Dolon, son of Eumedes,
Godlike herald, of wealth in gold and in bronze the possessor.
Though, to be sure, in appearance uncomely, his feet were the swiftest.

He was his father's only son, in a group of five sisters.
He it was spake this word to the Trojans then and to Hector:
    "Hector, the heart in my breast and my lordly spirit impel me
Nigh to the swift-faring galleys to go and learn all exactly.
Come then, lift up this sceptre, I pray, while solemnly swearing
Truly to give me the horses and car, with the bronzen adornment,
Horses accustomed to bear into battle the blameless Pelides.
No vain spy shall I prove unto thee but thy hopes will accomplish.
Straight will I go to the camp until I reach Agamemnon's
Galley; for there the chieftains, no doubt, will be holding a conclave,
Gathered in council to argue, if better to flee or to battle."
    Thus he. And Hector swore, his hands uplifting the sceptre:
    "Now let Zeus himself, loud-thundering husband of Hera,
Witness that no other man of the Trojan people shall ever
Mount that car; but thine, I declare, shall the glory be ever."
    Thus he spake (though the oath was false), and he stirred Dolon's
Quickly he slung a curvèd bow on his shoulders and quickly   [spirit.
Cast over all a grey wolf's hide, and the skin of a ferret
Set on his head as a helm, and grasped a keen-pointed javelin.   [fated
Forth he then hastened away toward the ships from the camp — but
Ne'er to return from the galleys or bring back word unto Hector.
Speedily leaving the throng of men and horses behind him,
Eager he wended his way. But Zeus-descended Odysseus
Marked him, as he approached; and thus he addressed Diomedes:
    "Lo! there moveth a man who comes from the camp, Diomedes;
Whether, perchance, he comes as a spy on our galleys, or whether
Coming, belike, to despoil some warrior fallen, I know not.
But let us grant him free passage by us on the plain for a moment,
Only a bit, and then we might rush on him better and catch him
Suddenly; or if, perchance, by fleetness of foot he outrun us,
Do thou steadily press him away from his camp toward the galleys,
Rushing upon him with spear, lest haply he 'scape to the city."   [corpses,
    These words spoken, the twain crouched down and lay 'mid the
Out of the way; and the other ran past them in haste in his folly.
Now at a distance as great as a mule-team maketh a furrow —
Mules are indeed more highly appraised than oxen for drawing,

Deep through loam of the fallow, a ploughshare rigidly jointed —
Darted the twain right on him. At once ſtopped Dolon at hearing,
Hoping in heart some comrades were come from the Trojans to turn
Back once more to the camp, so counter-commanded of Hector.   [him
When howe'er they were only a spear's cast off or a diſtance
Shorter, he knew them as foes. Then swift limbs nimbly beſtirring,
Inſtant he fled, and the twain ſtarted eagerly up to pursue him.
Even as when two hounds, sharp-toothed, well trainèd in hunting,
Ever unweariedly press on a doe or a hare in a region
Foreſted well, and it flees, loud-bleating in terror before them:
Even so Tydeus' son and Odysseus, sacker of cities,
Now cut him off from his folk, unweariedly ever pursued him.
Now, though, when he was just about to run into the sentries,
Fleeing amain toward the ships, Athena put into Tydides
Vigor anew, lest haply some other bronze-mailed Achaean
Boast he was first to smite, Diomedes only a second.
Leaping at him with his spear, Diomedes, the mighty, addressed him:
     "Halt! Else surely shall I with a spear overtake thee! I promise,
Long thou'lt hardly elude sheer ruin that flies from my fingers."
     Thus he spake and cast his spear but purposely missed him.
Over his shoulder (the right one) the point of the well polished javelin
Fixed itself in the earth. He halted and yammered in terror.
Pale he turned with affright, and his teeth meantime in his terror
Chattered aloud in his mouth; the twain came panting upon him,
Gripping both of his hands. He burst into tears and besought them:
     "Take me alive; I'll ransom myself; full many my treasures,
Treasures of bronze and of gold and of iron cunningly smithied,
Whereof my father would give you a ransom beyond all telling,
Haply, if only he heard I was safe at the galleys Achaean."
     Then with an answer addressed him Odysseus of many devices:
     "Have no fear. Allow not the thought of death to possess thee.
Come now, tell me the ſtory and tell it truly, I pray thee,
Why dost thou come thus alone away from the camp to the galleys,
Deep in the dead of night, when all other mortals are sleeping?
Com'st thou belike to despoil some one of the warriors fallen?
Hector hath sent thee to spy, peradventure, on all of the doings

There at the hollow ships? Or did thy own spirit impel thee?"

Dolon to him made reply, while his limbs were trembling beneath

"Hector befooled me with many a vain hope out of my reason, [him:
Vowing to give me the whole-hoofed horses of haughty Pelides,
Yea, and his war-car, too, with all of its bronzen adornments,
Bidding me hasten and go through the black night's fugitive shadow
Nigh to the enemy camp and spying perchance to discover
Whether the swift ships now, as of old time, always are guarded;
Whether, already subdued at our hands, ye now are devising
Counsel among you for flight, and indeed no longer are willing
Nightlong watch to maintain, overcome with weariness direful."

Smiling thereat, Odysseus of many devices addressed him:

"No doubt, great were the gifts thy spirit was setting before it,
Even the steeds of the wise Aeacides. Difficult are those
Horses to master and manage — for all men difficult driving
Save for Achilles' self, who was born of a mother immortal.
Come now, tell me the story and tell it truly, I pray thee,
Where didst thou now leave Hector, the shepherd of peoples, in coming
Hither? And where now lieth his armor? And where are his horses?
How are the watches arranged? How slumber the rest of the Trojans?
What are the matters they now hold under advisement: if eager
There to abide at the galleys, aloof from their city, or rather   [ans?"
Would they withdraw to the town, since they have subdued the Achae-

Thereupon Dolon, the son of Eumedes, replied to Odysseus:

"Well then, all these things I will tell and recount them most truly:
Hector with others, indeed, whoever are counselors, holdeth
Council at present, close by the barrow of Ilus, the godlike,
Far from the din; but the guards of whom thou askest, oh hero —
Told off guard there is none, for defense of the army nor watching.
Hearth-fires there are of the Trojans, on whom necessity lieth,
Who are awake thereby and encouraging each one his fellow
Aye to the watch. The allies, far-summoned from various regions,
All are asleep and entrust to the Trojans the work of the sentries,
Since *their* women and children in no way near them are dwelling."

Then, in reply, Odysseus of many devices addressed him:

"How are they sleeping, I pray? With the Trojans, tamers of horses,

214

Mingled or separate? Tell me the whole truth, so I may know it."
　　　Thereupon Dolon, the son of Eumedes, replied to Odysseus:
　　"Well then, all these things I will tell and recount them most truly:
Facing the sea the Paeonians, of bent bows, camp and the Carians,
Leleges, also Caucones, and with them the godlike Pelasgi.
Opposite Thymbra the Lycians are pitched and impetuous Mysians,
Phrygians that fight from war-cars, and horsehair-crested Maeonians.
Ay, but anent these things in particular why do ye question?
For, if indeed ye are eager to enter the Trojan encampment,
There are the Thracians, newly arrived and apart from the others,
Farthest away, and their king, Eïoneus' son, is among them,
Rhesus. Horses the fairest that *I* e'er saw, and the largest,
Whiter in color than snow and like to the winds in their running,
His are! Also a car appointed with gold and with silver.
Gold is his armor, gigantic, a marvel even to look at;
This he hath brought. To wear such armor it noway becometh
Mortal men, but only the gods immortal may wear it.
Come then, bring me now to the ships that over the waters
Speed, or a pitiless bond here fasten upon me and leave me,
That ye may go on your way, make trial, belike, and discover
Whether indeed I've spoken the truth unto you or a falsehood."　[him:
　　　Scowlfully looked Diomedes, the mighty, and thus he addressed
　　"Nay now, Dolon, indulge no thought in thy heart of escaping,
Once into *our* hands fallen, despite the good word thou hast brought us;
Seeing, if now we release thee or grant thee freedom for ransom,
Some day later thou'lt come to the swift-faring galleys Achaean,
Either to play the spy or to make war openly on them.
But if indeed, subdued to my hands, thou yieldest thy spirit,
Never a bane thereafter shalt thou be unto the Argives."
　　　Thus spake Diomed. Dolon with stout hand reached to implore
Touching his chin; at the moment Tydides, leaping upon him,　[him,
Smote him amain on the neck with his broadsword, sev'ring the sinews
Both; and his head, with the cry on his lips, with the dust was com-
Then they took from his head his helmet, that skin of a ferret; [mingled.
Next they took up his long spear, his bended bow, and his wolf-skin.
These to Athena, the giver of spoils, the goodly Odysseus

Raised up high in his hand, and he spake a word in petition:

"Joy, oh goddess, in these! Unto thee, the first of immortals
All who dwell in Olympus, we cry for thy aid. But direct us
Once more now, to the horses and beds where slumber the Thracians."

Thus he cried and lifted the trophies above him and hung them
High on a tamarisk bush and put a plain mark upon them,
Gathering reeds and branches of tamarisk, foliage-laden,
Lest they miss it, returning in black night's fugitive shadow.   [mor

So went forward the twain, through the dark-hued blood and the ar-
Speeding, and quickly arrived at the squadron of Thracian warriors.
Now they were sleeping, foredone with toil. Their beautiful weapons
Lay on the ground beside them. In three rows perfect in order
All were arranged. Close by them was each one's couple of horses.
Rhesus slept in the middle — his swift steeds, standing beside him,
Firmly were tethered with thongs to the topmost rim of his chariot.
First Odysseus spied him and pointed him out to Tydides:

"There is the man, Diomedes; and there, too, thou seest the horses,
Whereof Dolon, whom lately we slew, gave clear information.
Come now and put forth all thy mighty strength; it behooves thee
Not to be idle and stand full-weaponed, but loosen the horses.
Or do thou slay the men, while I take care of the horses."

Thus spake he; and Athena, the bright-eyed, filled with her vigor
Diomed, so that he slew on both sides. Hideous groaning
Rose from the men sword-smitten; the earth ran crimson with blood-
Like as a lion that comes on flocks unguarded of shepherd,   [shed.
Whether of sheep or of goats, and with evil intent leapeth on them:
So on the warriors from Thrace came Tydeus' son in his fury,
Till he had slain twelve men. But Odysseus of many devices —   [seus,
Whomso Tydides drew near and smote with his broadsword — Odys-
Seizing that man by the foot, would quickly drag him off backward
Out of the way, with this thought in mind, that the fair-maned horses
Lightly might issue between, not tremble in spirit in stepping
Over the dead, for as yet they were all unaccustomed to dead men.

But when at last upon the king came the scion of Tydeus,
Quick, as the thirteenth victim, of sweet life there he bereft him,
Heavily breathing the while, for an ill dream hovered above him

216

That night, even the son of Oenides, sent of Athena.
Meanwhile hardy Odysseus was loosing the whole-hoofed horses,
Tied them together with ſtraps, and was driving them forth from the co-
Smiting them now with his bow; for the shining lash had the hero [hort,
Thought not to take in his hand from the chariot richly emblazoned.
Low then he whiſtled to signal his fellow, divine Diomedes,
Who, as he ſtood there, pondered a deed of most desperate daring,
Whether to seize on the car, where, blazoned, the armor was lying,
Drag it away by the pole or carry it lifted and shouldered,
Or take away inſtead more lives of the Thracian warriors.
While he debated in heart these things, came near him Athena,
Stood at his side, and addressed with a word divine Diomedes:

"Now, thou son of the great-souled Tydeus, think of returning
Unto the hollow ships, lest haply in flight thou arrive there,
Should some other immortal, belike, now waken the Trojans."

Thus far she. He knew by her voice what goddess had spoken,
Leaped then inſtantly up on the ſteeds, while goodly Odysseus
Laid on his bow; and they flew to the swift black galleys Achaean.

Nor was the god of the silver bow, Apollo, a-keeping
Blind watch; nay, but he saw Athena abetting Tydides.
Wrathful against her, he entered the close-packed throng of the Trojans,
Rousing a counselor Thracian, a high-born kinsman of Rhesus,
Named Hippocoön; all of a sudden he ſtarted from slumber.
When he saw the place empty where lately had ſtood the fleet horses,
Ay, and the men yet gasping in death in the horrible carnage,
Loudly he groaned and then shouted the name of his comrade belovèd.
Forthwith clamor arose, unspeakable din of the Trojans
Rushing together in haſte; they were dazed at the terrible doings
Wrought by men who went again to the hollow galleys.   [tered,

When these reached the place where Heċtor's spy they had slaugh-
There were the swift ſteeds checked by Odysseus, of Zeus the belovèd.
Then Tydides leaped to the earth, in the hands of Odysseus
Placed those gory spoils; he then remounted the horses,
Laid the lash on the horses, and they went eagerly flying
Down to the hollow ships, full avid in spirit to be there.
First it was Neſtor that noted the clatter and called to his fellows:

217

"Friends of mine, commanders and counseling chiefs of the Argives,
Shall I be erring or speaking the truth? My spirit commands me.
Now on my ear is beating the clatter of fleet-footed horses!
Would it were even Odysseus and Diomedes, the mighty,
Driving hitherward now some whole-hoofed steeds from the Trojans!
Fearfully, though, do I tremble in heart lest they may have suffered,
Bravest of Argive chiefs, from the battle-din of the Trojans."

Not yet wholly his saying was said, when lo! they were present,
Even themselves; and they slid to the ground, while the others, rejoicing,
Welcomed with clasp of the hand and with accents gentle received them.
Knightly Gerenian Nestor was first to ask them a question:

"Come, thou much-praised, thou pride of Achaia, tell me, Odysseus,
How ye secured these steeds. In sooth, did ye enter the Trojan
Throng? Or haply some god that met you hath given them to you?
Wondrously like to the beams of the sun are these wonderful horses!
Ever indeed do I mix with the Trojans in fight; I may claim that
Ne'er do I linger away at the ships, though a veteran hoary;
Yet have I never beheld such horses or ever imagined!
Nay, such steeds, I am thinking, some god that ye met must have given,
Seeing he loveth you both, even Zeus, the compeller of storm-clouds;
So does the bright-eyed Athena, the daughter of Zeus, aegis-bearer."

Spake unto him in answer Odysseus of many devices:
"Nestor, Neleus' son, great glory of all the Achaeans,
Lightly perchance might a god give steeds e'en better than these are,
If he should will it; for gods far mightier are than are mortals.
These, the new-come steeds whereof, old man, thou inquirest —
Thracian are they; their master, the king, the good Diomedes
Slew; and besides him twelve others he slew, the best of his comrades.
Yea, and a thirteenth one, a spy, we caught near the galleys,
Who had been sent as a scout to reconnoitre our army;
Hector had sent him forth, and the rest of the high-born Trojans."

Thus he spake and over the moat drove the whole-hoofed horses,
Laughing aloud; and the other Achaeans followed rejoicing.
When, as they went, they arrived at Tydides' well-builded barrack,
There they tethered the steeds with well-cut straps to the horses'
Manger; thereat were standing the other fleet-footed horses

218

Diomedes and Odysseus Returning with the Spoils of Rhesus

Owned by Diomed, eating their food, the honey-sweet corn-grains.
Then in the stern of his vessel Odysseus laid up the gory
Trophies of Dolon, till they should prepare them a gift to Athena.
But, for themselves, they descended, to wash off sweat from their bodies,
Into the sea, and laved their limbs, their necks, and their shoulders.
Now, as the salt-sea billow had washed off the sweat that lay heavy,
All from the flesh of the men and refreshed the spirit within them,
Into the bath-tubs, polished to shining, they entered and bathed them.
When the twain had bathed and anointed themselves with the olive
Oil, they sat down to their meat, while unto Athena, from mixer
Brimming with honey-sweet wine, both drew and poured a libation.

ILIAD · XI · (Λ)

Lambda presents the General,
In fight the worthiest man of all.

EOS was now from her couch by the side of the lordly Tithonus
Rising, to bring new light unto mortals and unto immortals.
Zeus meanwhile sent forth to the swift-faring galleys Achaean
Discord fell; in her hands she held the signal of battle!
Coming, she stood on the black and deep-hulled ship of Odysseus,
There in the midst, that her call might carry in either direction,
This way e'en to the barracks of great Telamonian Ajax,
That unto those of Achilles: these had drawn up their trim ships
Thus at the ends; they relied on their own strong hands and their valor.
There then standing, the goddess with loud voice, shrill and terrific,
Shouted and set in his heart—each one, those sons of Achaia—
Measureless might unto battle and warfare unintermittent.
Forthwith war became sweeter by far unto them than returning
Home in the hollow ships to the well-loved land of their fathers.
　　Then Atrides shouted and ordered the Argives to arm them,
While he himself put on him his armor of bronze all refulgent:
First on his legs he fastened his greaves all round about deftly,
Beautiful, fitted with buckles of silver and firm at the ankles;
Next then donned him a corselet, engirdling his breast all about him,
Corselet that once in the past as a guest-gift Cinyras gave him;
Even as far as Cyprus had reached him the wonderful rumor!—
How that Achaeans were going to sail in their galleys to Troyland.
Wherefore Cinyras gave him the corselet to pleasure the monarch.
Ten were the stripes of cyanus dark, well-wrought on the breastplate,
Twice six also of gold thereon, and of tin there were twenty.
Dark blue also the dragons that writhed up there on the collar,
Three on a side; they were like unto rainbows set of Cronion
High on a cloud for a sign unto earth-born, perishing mortals.

Next then over his shoulders he flung his sword, and refulgent
Glimmered its golden rivets; while of silver itself was the scabbard
Round and about it, with hangers well-fitted, all of them golden.
Then he took up his shield, rich-wrought, for defense or for onset,
Beautiful; ten were the circles that ran all bronzen about it.
Bosses were there, all fashioned of tin, full twenty in number,
White, though the one in the middle was moulded of cyanus, dark blue.
Thereon was also the Gorgon embossed, ferocious of visage,
Glow'ring terrific, about her on both sides Panic and Terror.
Down from the shield hung fastened a baldric of silver, and thereon,
Coiled up in dark blue metal, a dragon; upon him were triple
Heads turned different ways and all from the same neck sprouting.
Next on his head he set his two-ridged helmet, with bosses
Fourfold, horsehair-plumed, and the crest waved dreadful above it.
Two long lances he grasped, well-shodden with bronze, keen-sharp-
Out from the lances the bronze shot upward afar off a splendor   [ened;
High unto heaven. Queen Hera and Pallas Athena, the goddess,
Thereat thundered, to honor the king of golden Mycenae.

    Therewith each of the leaders committed his steeds to a driver,
Even his own, to hold back nigh unto the moat and in order;
Meanwhile all in their armor accoutred themselves and as footmen.
Marched at speed; and a cry unquenchable rose toward the dawning.
They at the moat preceded the charioteers in alignment
Much; these followed a little way after. Amid them Cronion
Wakened an evil confusion; he rained down on them from heaven
Dewdrops reeking with blood, from the aether, token of purpose
Many a soul, and brave ones, to hurl headlong unto Hades.

    Over against them the Trojans on their side stood on the rising
Ground of the plain around great Hector, Pulydamas faultless;
With them Aeneas (esteemed in the land as a god by the Trojans);
'Round the Antenorids three—first Polybus, next, good Agenor,
Third the young Acamas, like the immortals. These were the leaders.
Hector was there in the front, with his shield all evenly rounded.
Even as out from the clouds gleams sudden the star of disaster,
Glittering bright, and anon it is sunk in the nebulous shadows:
Thus at the one time Hector would show himself in the vanguard

The Descent of Discord

Then in the rear giving orders, while he in his panoply bronzen
Gleamed like the lightning of Father Zeus who wieldeth the aegis.

They, however, as reapers that over against one another
Drive on opposite swaths through the fields of an opulent owner,
Whether of barley or wheat, and the handfuls frequent are falling:
Even so, leaping against one another, Achaeans and Trojans
Slew, and of ruinous flight nor one nor another was minded;
Rather, the fight kept even their heads, as they kept on charging
Like unto wolves; and beholding it, Eris, the woful, was gladdened,
She that alone of the gods still chanced to be by in the battle.
None of the other immortals were present among them, but seated
Far in their halls and at peace, where'er unto each was appointed
Palace surpassingly fair in the dells of Olympus erected.
All of them there were blaming the stormcloud-mantled Cronion,
Seeing that he had resolved to grant renown to the Trojans.
They of the Father were heeded in no way; far from the others
All he was seated aloof and alone, resplendent in glory,
Gazing the while on the city of Troy and the ships of Achaia,
Viewing the flashing of bronze and the slain commingled with slayers.

Now while yet it was morn and daylight divine was advancing,
Missiles from both sides kept striking amain and felling the people.
Just at the hour when a woodman his dinner prepares in a forest
Deep in a mountainous glen, what time his arms he hath sated
Felling the high-grown trees, and weariness comes on his spirit,
Ay, and a longing for pleasance of food lays hold on his feelings,
Then the Danaans broke with their might the opposing battalions,
Calling aloud on their comrades, rank unto rank. Agamemnon
Rushed in first, and a hero, Bienor, shepherd of peoples,
Slew — both him and his comrade, Oïleus, smiter of horses,
Who had insooth leaped down from his car to encounter his foeman.
Him, all eager in onset, his keen lance full in the forehead
Pierced, and his vizor availed, though heavy with bronze, to repel it
Nowise; onward it drave through vizor and bone; it bespattered
All of his brain within and quelled him, even though eager.
There then he left both lying, the monarch of men, Agamemnon,
Shining with breasts left bare — for he stripped off even their tunics —

Hastened away then, bent on spoiling the children of Priam,
Isus and Antiphus — this one legitimate, that one a bastard.
One car bore them to battle — the bastard son was the driver —
Far-famed Antiphus fought, at his side. Once aforetime Achilles
Bound them on Ida's spurs with pliant withies of willow;
Shepherding sheep he surprised them but set both free for a ransom.
Now though, Atreus' son, wide-ruling king Agamemnon,
Smote with his javelin the breast, right over the nipple, of Isus;
Antiphus close by the ear he struck with his sword and o'erthrew him
Out from his car; in haste he stripped off their beautiful armor,
Knowing them well; for before at the swift-sailing ships he had seen
What time Achilles, the swift of foot, had brought them from Ida. [them,
Even as when on the lair of a hind, swift-footed, a lion
Lighteth, and, seizing her fawns unguarded, he readily crushes
Them with his powerful teeth and of life-breath robbeth the weaklings —
She, however, though haply she be close by, is unable
Help to provide, for trembling and terror have fallen upon her;
Swiftly she boundeth away through thick-grown coppice and woodland,
Sweating and hasting away from the powerful wild beast's onset:
Likewise then not one of the Trojans availed to deliver   [Argives.
These from death; they were fleeing themselves in affright from the
        Next on Pisander he fell and Hippolochus, sturdy in battle,
Wise-heart Antimachus' sons, the same that was chief in refusal
(Glorious gifts he expected, rich gold from the prince Alexander)
Ever to give Helen back to her fair-haired lord, Menelaüs.
His were the sons now taken, the twain, by the lord Agamemnon.
Both were in one car and trying to drive the fleet-footed horses,
Since the glittering reins had slipped from their hands and escaped
Also the horses were stricken with panic. Then, like to a lion,   [them;
Darted Atrides against them; and out from the car they implored him:
        "Take us prisoners, Atreus' son, and receive a rich ransom.
Many the treasures rich in the halls of Antimachus lying,
Many of gold and of bronze and of iron cunningly smithied,
Whereof our father would give thee a ransom beyond all telling,
Doubtless, if only he heard we were safe by the galleys Achaean."
        Thus did the twain with tears address themselves to the monarch,

Pleading with gentle words; but the answer they heard was not gentle:
"If ye are truly the sons of the wise Antimachus, ye twain,
Him who erst in the Trojan assembly bade slay Menelaüs—
When as an envoy he came along with Odysseus, the godlike—
Nor would allow him return once more to the men of Achaia,
Verily now shall ye pay for the outrage foul of your father."

Thus he spake and thrust to the ground from his war-car Pisander,
Smiting him full in the breast with his spear, to the earth hurled him
[backward.
Down leaped Hippolochus; him he felled to the earth and despoiled him,
Lopped with his sword his arms, hewed off his head from his shoulders,
Spurned him away, to go rolling off through the throng like a mortar.
These he left lying. Then, where the squadrons were clashing the thickest,
Thither he rushed, and with him the rest of the well-greaved Achaeans.
Footmen were slaying the footmen, necessity-driven before them;
Horsemen were slaying the horsemen (a cloud uprose from beneath them,
Dust from the plain, stirred up by the thunderous hoofs of the horses),
Dealing them death with the bronze; and meantime lord Agamemnon,
Aye as he followed with slaughter, gave out his commands to the Ar-
Even as falleth, devouring, a fire in the midst of a dense-grown [gives.
Woodland—all round whirls it the wind meanwhile, and the thickets
Crumble away to the roots, assailed by the blast of the burning:
So then before Agamemnon Atrides the heads of the Trojans
Fell, as they fled, while many a one of the strong-necked horses
Rattled along on the bridges of war the chariots emptied,
Yearning in vain for their faultless drivers—but they on the earth lay,
Lovelier far to vultures then than they were to their consorts.   [cloud

Meantime Zeus drew Hector away from the darts, from the dust-
Forth, away from the slaughter of heroes, the blood and the tumult.
Still Atrides followed in fury and called on the Argives.
Well past the barrow of Dardanus' scion, Ilus, the ancient,
Through the midst of the plain, some were speeding past the wild fig-
On, as they made for the city; and shrill-voiced, ever Atrides   [tree
Followed and ever with gore his hands unapproachable spattered.
But when now they had come to the Scaean gates and the oak-tree,
There they came to a stand and there one another awaited.

Some through the midst of the plain were ftraggling in panic, as cattle,
Which in the dead of night a lion's coming hath scattered
All, but to one cow cometh an inftant, utter deftruction:
First he seizes her neck with his powerful teeth, and he breaks it;
Afterward greedily gulps down the vitals and blood of his victim:
So Agamemnon, the lord Atrides, was pressing upon them,
Always slaying the rearmost — and they kept fleeing before them.
Headlong fell from their cars full many, or prone or supinely,
Under Atrides' hands; for his spear raged round and about him.

But when he was about to come under the town and the close-built
Wall of the city, just then the Father of men and immortals,
Faring from heaven adown, took seat on the summit of Ida,
Ida, the many-fountained; his hands were holding the lightning.
Forth he was sending Iris, the golden of wing, with a message:
"Hie thee away, fleet Iris, and speak this word unto Hector:
Haply, as long as he seeth the shepherd of hofts, Agamemnon,
Raging among the foremost, wide-wafting the ranks of the heroes,
So long let him hold back but order the rest of the people
Still to contend with the foe throughout the fury of combat.
But, when a javelin smites or an arrow wounds Agamemnon,
Soon as he leaps on his car, anon I will grant unto Hector
Strength to slay, till he come to the well-benched ships, till in Ocean
Sinketh the sun, till cometh the hallowed darkness upon them."

Thus spake he; swift Iris, shod with the wind, disobeyed not,
Sped from the mountains of Ida on down into Ilium holy.
Godlike Hector she found, that scion of wise-hearted Priam,
Standing at rest on his firm-framed war-car there with his horses.
Close to his side came Iris, the fleet-foot, now and addressed him:
"Hector, scion of Priam, thou peer of Cronion in counsel!
Zeus, the Father, hath sent me to bear unto thee this message:
'Haply, as long as thou seest the shepherd of hofts, Agamemnon,
Raging among the foremost, wide-wafting the ranks of the heroes,
So long keep out of the fight but order the rest of the people
Still to contend with the foe throughout the fury of combat.
But, when a javelin smites, or an arrow wounds Agamemnon,
Soon as he leaps on his car, anon Zeus grants unto Hector

230

Strength to slay, till he come to the well-benched ships, till in Ocean
Sinketh the sun, till cometh the hallowed darkness upon them.' ' "

    Thus she spake and departed, the fleet-footed messenger goddess.
Hector leaped forthwith from his car to the ground in his armor,
Brandishing two keen lances, and ranged everywhere through the army,
Rousing them up to the fight, and a battle-din dreadful awakened.
So they were rallied and stood and resisted again the Achaeans,
While upon their side also the Argives made strong their battalions,
Setting their lines; they faced the foe; then rushed Agamemnon
Forward the first, far ahead of the vanguard, resolved to do battle.

    Tell me now, ye Muses, who dwell in the halls of Olympus,
Who came forward the first to oppose the king, Agamemnon,
Whether of Troy's own folk or of their allies far-renownèd?
He was Antenor's scion, Iphidamas, goodly, majestic,
Who had been nurtured in Thracia, the mother of flocks and the fertile.
Cisses nurtured him there in his home, when he was an infant,
Even Cisses, the sire of his mother, the fair-faced Theano.   [hood,
Now, as the lad had attained to the measure of glorious young man-
There he thought to detain him and offered his daughter in wedlock.
Yet when the tidings came of the Argives, forth from his chamber
Issued the bridegroom, leader of twelve beaked galleys that followed.
These gallant ships he had left behind at this time in Percote,
Whence he had journeyed on foot over-land to Ilium city.
He it was then that encountered Atreus' son, Agamemnon.
Now, as they came close up in the onrush 'gainst one another,
Atreus' son made a miss, and aside went glancing his javelin,
Whileas Iphidamas smote on his waist, down under his corselet,
Following up his heavy hand with the weight of his body.
Natheless he pierced not the girdle, the variegated, but long ere
That, upon reaching the silver, the point turned, like as if leaden.
Grasping the spear in his hand, wide-sceptred King Agamemnon
Pulled it in rage toward himself, then wrenching it, like as a lion,
Out of his hand, he smote his neck with his sword and unstrung him.
So then Iphidamas fell; so slumber of bronze overcame him,
Piteous man, as he aided his countrymen, far from the wedded
Maiden, his bride, no pleasure of her yet known, though he'd given

Gifts in abundance, a hundred of oxen, promised a thousand,
Goats, too, and also sheep, for he herded unspeakable numbers.
Then Agamemnon, the son of Atreus, ſtripped off his armor;
Bearing the beautiful gear, he went back through the throng of Achae-
    When now Coön beheld it—conspicuous peer among heroes, [ans.
First-born son among all of Antenor's children—a grievous
Sorrow enveloped him, clouding his eyes, at the fall of his brother.
Standing off to one side, he, unmarked of divine Agamemnon,
Smote him upon the mid-arm with his javelin, under the elbow;
Clean through his forearm went the point of the glittering javelin.
Thereat shuddering seized on the monarch of men, Agamemnon,
Yet e'en so he ceased not a whit from the battle and warfare,
Rushed on Coön inſtead with a spear that the tempeſts had toughened.
Coön was eagerly dragging away by the foot his dead brother,
Son of his sire, while calling aloud on all of the bravest.
Him, while dragging his dead through the tumult, under his bossy
Buckler he wounded with bronze-shod lance and loosened his sinews.
Over Iphidamas ſtanding, he hewed off the head of his brother.
There these sons of Antenor, subdued by the monarch Atrides,
Filled up the measure of Fate and entered the mansion of Hades.
    Still Agamemnon kept ranging the ranks of the rest of the heroes,
Wielding a sword or a spear or a ponderous boulder for hurling, [arm.
Long as the blood welled warm, as it flowed from the wound in his fore-
But as the wound waxed dry, and the blood no longer was flowing,
Sharp, penetrating pangs then assailed the mighty Atrides.
Even as keen as the shaft that smiteth a woman in travail,
Piercing; the Ilithyiae, the birth-pang goddesses send it,
Daughters of Hera, that aye hold poignant pangs in their keeping:
E'en so sharp was the pang that entered the soul of Atrides.
Then he sprang into his car near by and commanded the driver
Straightway drive to the hollow ships, for his heart was in anguish.
Then with a ringing shout he called to the Danaan warriors:
    "Friends of mine, commanders and counseling chiefs of the Argives,
Ye yourselves must now ward off from the sea-faring galleys
Din of the desperate battle; for Zeus, the counselor, hath not
Suffered me here to war the whole day long with the Trojans."

Thus spake Atrides; and then the fair-maned horses the driver
Lashed toward the hollow ships, and they flew not unwillingly forward,
Both their breasts foam-flecked, besprinkled with dust underneath them,
Gathered in bearing the king sore-smitten away from the battle.

Hector, as now he beheld Agamemnon leaving the action,
Cried with a shout that echoed afar to the Trojans and Lycians:

"Trojans, Dardanians, Lycians, that joy in closest encounter,
Quit you like men, my friends, and recall your impetuous prowess.
Gone is their hero, the bravest! And great is the glory now granteth
Zeus, Cronus' son. But drive ye straight onward your whole-hoofed
Right on the Danaans doughty, to win you victorious glory."   [horses

Thus spake he and aroused the might and spirit of each man.
Even as when some hunter his white-toothed hounds setteth forward,
Hot in the chase, on a lion or fierce wild boar of the forest:
E'en so 'gainst the Achaeans his great-souled Trojans did Hector
Urge on—e'en Priam's son, the equal of man's bane Ares.
He himself, high-hearted and striding along in the vanguard,
Fell on the fight, as a blast, down-sweeping in vehement fury,
Headlong leaps on the sea, uplifting the violet waters.

Who was the warrior first, who also the last to be slaughtered
There by Hector, the son of Priam, when Zeus gave him glory?

Foremost Asaeus and next Autonoüs, also Opites,
Dolops, Clytius' son, and Opheltius, then Agelaüs,
Orus, Aesymnus, and then Hipponoüs, sturdy in battle—
All these leaders he slew of the Danaans. Then on the many
Hector destroying fell, as when Zephyrus buffets before him
Clouds of the clearing Notus, while smiting with hurricane fury.
Many a billow swollen rolls on, and aloft is the sea-foam
Tossed up, under the rush of the wind wide-wandering scattered:
E'en so crowded, the heads of the host fell, vanquished of Hector.

Deeds beyond remedy then had been done, destruction accom-
Haply the sons of Achaia had plunged, in rout, on the galleys, [plished,
Had not Odysseus cried unto Tydeus' son, Diomedes:

"What is it ails us, Tydides, forgetting impetuous prowess?
Nay, come hither, good friend, and beside me stand; it were truly
Shame, if the shimmering-helmeted Hector should capture the galleys."

Him, in his turn, then addressed Diomedes, the mighty, in answer:
"Verily I will abide and endure to the last, but the profit—
Brief will it be unto us, since Zeus, the compeller of storm clouds,
Clearly is minded the vict'ry to give not to us but the Trojans."

Thus he spake and thrust to the ground from his war-car Thym-
Smiting him with his spear on the left breast, whileas Odysseus [braeus,
Slaughtered Molion, the peer of a god, that prince's attendant.
These they left lying—these twain, surceased from the fight—and the
Stormed on, charging the press, as when two boars of the forest [heroes
Fall upon hounds of the chase, with high-tempered fury attacking:
Thus, charging back, they renewed their slaughter of Trojans. The Ar-
Gladly again breathed free in their flight from godlike Hector.   [gives

Then they captured a car and two heroes, the best of their people,
Children of Merops these, the Percosian, one that exceeded
All in the gifts of divining. He tried to hinder his children's
Marching to murderous war; but the father availed to persuade them
Noway, seeing the fates of black death guided them onward.
Both these Tydeus' scion, the spear-famed prince Diomedes,
Ravished of spirit and life and took their glorious armor,
Whileas Hippodamus' arms and Hypirochus' fell to Odysseus.

Then Cronion stretched level the scales of the battle upon them,
Gazing from Ida down, while each kept slaying the other:
Then did Tydeus' son smite the hero Agastrophus, Paeon's
Son, on the hip with his spear; for no longer near were his horses,
Ready to bear him away, but a blindness had clouded his spirit.
While his attendant was holding them far off, he as a footman
Charged through the foremost fighters, until his dear life was taken.

Hector keenly marked the twain through the ranks and upon them
Charged with a shout, while followed along the battalions of Trojans.
Him then beheld Diomedes, good at the war-cry, and shuddered;
Quickly he called to his comrade, Odysseus, standing hard by him:
"Clearly it rolls upon *us*, this bane, even Hector, the mighty!
Come, let us stand and await him and ward off, haply, his onset."

Thus he spake and, poising his spear far-shadowing, hurled it
True, and it struck (for he aimed it straight at his head) on the topmost
Part of the crest; but away then bounded the bronze from the bronzen

Helm nor attained to the chief's fair flesh, for the helmet repelled it —
Threefold-plated, with socket, a gift of Phoebus Apollo.
Hector ran back an enormous distance and mixed in the tumult,
Sank on his knees upright; his stout hand only sustained him,
Pressing the ground; and a curtain of black night covered his eyelids.
Now while Tydides far in the vanguard ranks of the fighters
Followed the cast of his weapon — it sank in the earth on alighting —
Hector recovered his breath, then, leaping again on his chariot,
Drove off into the press and eluded the black fate's onset.
Leaping at him with his spear, Diomedes, the mighty, addressed him:

"Death hast evaded again, thou dog! Full closely the evil
Came unto thee, but Phoebus Apollo once more hath saved thee,
Whom thou art like to invoke, when nearing the din of the javelins.
Verily thee I shall meet and finish thee sooner or later,
If an immortal, belike, unto me, too, comes as a helper.
Now I will make for the rest, whome'er I may light upon, haply."

Thus he spake and despoiled Paeonides, famed as a spearman.
But Alexander, the goodly, the husband of fair-haired Helen,
Stood there spanning his bow at Tydides, shepherd of peoples,
Leaning against the slab at the man-built barrow of Ilus,
Dardanus' son, an elder of old revered of the people.
Diomed now was wresting the valiant Agastrophus' corselet
Off from his breast and the shield all-glittering off from his shoulders,
Also the pond'rous casque, as the other his bow in the middle
Bent; from his hand outflew not vainly the arrow: it smote him
Square on the flat of his foot; then, clean through piercing, the arrow
Stuck in the earth firm-fixed. With the merriest laugh then bounded
Forth from his ambush Paris and shouted the word of his triumph:

"Smitten thou art! Not vainly the dart fled forth, and if only,
Deep in thy nethermost belly infixed, thy life it had taken!
So had also the Trojans breathed freely again from their troubles,
Who now shudder at thee, as bleating goats at a lion."

All undismayed, Diomedes, the mighty, in answer addressed him:
"Bowman, blackguard, a-shining in lovelocks, thou ogler of maidens,
Verily, madest thou trial with might unto might in full armor,
Naught would avail thee thy bow, nor aught thick-showering arrows.

Now, when the flat of my foot thou hast scratched, thou boastest for
Naught care I — just as if a woman or baby had struck me —   [nothing!
Seeing the weapon is blunted of him that is craven and worthless.
Far otherwise from my hand the keen-pointed javelin flieth;
Even where lightly it grazeth, it layeth the warrior lifeless.
Ah me! Verily then all torn are the cheeks of his widow,
Fatherless also his children; he reddens earth with his life's blood;
Ay, in corruption he lieth, more vultures than women about him."

  Thus far he; and the lanceman, renowned Odysseus, anigh him
Came and in front of him stood; and Tydides, sitting behind him,
Drew the keen dart from his foot; pangs frightful shot through his body.
Then he sprang into his car near by and commanded the driver
Straightway drive to the hollow ships, for his heart was in anguish.

  Lone was the far-famed spearman, Odysseus, left; and beside him
Argives none had remained; for on all of them panic had fallen.
Heavy of heart, he communed with his own magnanimous spirit:

  "Ah me! what will betide me? Great scandal indeed, if I flee hence,
Fearing the rabble. Still worse it would be, if alone I am taken,
Seeing the Danaans all are scattered in flight of Cronion.
Yet, why thus with itself is my dear heart debating within me?
Well do I know, 'tis cowards alone that make off from a battle.
Whoe'er, though, is a hero in battle it mainly behooveth
Him that he stubbornly stand, or smitten or smiting another."

  While in his heart and soul Odysseus pondered in such wise,
Straight upon him advanced the ranks of the shield-bearing Trojans,
Hemming him round in the midst, their own bane setting among them.
Even as young men lusty and dogs charge down on a wild boar,
Rushing out from his den in the depths of a jungle against them,
Whetting between his snarling jaws his tusks white-gleaming.
Round and about him they dart; loud riseth the noise of the gnashing
Tusks. Without shrinking, they bide, in spite of the danger, his onset:
So then about Odysseus, belovèd of Zeus, came the Trojans
Rushing. And first he wounded the faultless Deïopites,
Leaping at him and thrusting downward his keen-pointed javelin. [tered!
Then it was Thoön, and next it was Ennomus — both of them slaugh-
Next Chersidamas (when he had bounded down from his war-car)

Under the boss of his shield he smote with his spear on the navel;
Down he fell in the dust and clutched at the ground with his fingers.
These he left lying and Hippasus' son with his javelin he wounded —
Charops his name; a brother was he of Socus, the high-born.
Meaning to succor his brother, the godlike Socus approaching
Came up and stopped hard by and with this word he addressed him:

"Thou, insatiate of toil and of wiles, renownèd Odysseus,
Either today thou'lt boast over two sons — both of my father,
Hippasus — proud to have slain two such and taken their armor,
Or under *my* spear smitten thyself shalt surrender thy spirit."

Thus he spake and smote on the shield all evenly rounded.
Through the shimmering shield went driving the ponderous missile;
On still it went and traversed the breastplate cunningly moulded,
Ripping all of the flesh from his flank; yet Pallas Athena
Would not allow it to penetrate into the warrior's vitals.
Nay! and Odysseus, ware it had reached no goal that was mortal,
Drew back first and addressed this word aloud unto Socus:

"Ah, wretched man, on thee hath surely come sheer destruction.
No doubt thou hast availed to stay my fight with the Trojans;
Thine I declare, however, shall black fate be and perdition
Here this day. Underneath my javelin subdued, thou shalt render
Glory to me, thy soul unto Hades, famed for his horses."

Thus said he; but Socus had started to flee and had turned him
Round; in his back, as he turned, Odysseus planted a javelin
Midway between his shoulders; clean through his breast it was driven.
Crashing he fell, and the goodly Odysseus boasted above him:

"Socus, thou son of the wise-hearted Hippasus, tamer of horses,
Thee hath death's end overtaken first; thou hast not escaped it.
Ah, wretched man, for thee no father, no worshipful mother
Ever shall close in death thine eyes, but ravenous vultures
Tear thy flesh and flap their wings closely-feathered about thee.
Me, if I die, the goodly Achaeans will properly bury."

Thus he spake and extracted the ponderous weapon of Socus,
Wise-hearted prince, from his flesh and out through his buckler embossèd.
Spurted his blood on the spear drawn forth and afflicted his spirit.
Thereat the great-souled Trojans, at seeing the blood of Odysseus,

237

All in a clamorous throng went rushing together against him.
He, as he then drew backward, began to shout to his comrades,
Three times shouting as loud as a warrior's mouth ever utters;
Three times hearing his call, Menelaüs, belovèd of Ares,
Straightway turned with a word unto Ajax standing close by him:
    "Ajax, offspring of Zeus, Telamonian ruler of peoples,
Round me ringeth the shout of a comrade, stout-hearted Odysseus,
Like as a cry of that hero alone, hard-pressed of the foemen,
Trojans, cutting him off from his friends in the furious conflict.
Come, and away through the throng; to rescue him surely is better.
Fearful am I that he suffer some ill at the hands of the Trojans,
Howe'er brave, left alone, and the Danaans suffer great sorrow."
    Thus he spake and led on; and Ajax, peer of a godhead,
Followed; they found him, Odysseus, dear unto Zeus; and about him
Trojans beset him, like tawny jackals up in the mountains
Round some antlered stag that a hunter hath struck with an arrow
Sped from his bowstring. Him hath the stag by fleeing eluded,
While yet warm is his blood, while nimble his knees underneath him;
But, as the swift-winged arrow at last now masters and quells him,
Then come the ravening jackals to rend him, up in the mountains,
Deep in a shadowy wood, until God sendeth a robber
Lion; quickly the jackals scatter, howbeit he rends them:
Likewise gathered, surrounding the wiseheart, crafty Odysseus,
Many in number and valiant the Trojans, whileas the hero
Aye with a thrust of his lance kept fending the merciless moment.
Ajax then came to close quarters, bearing his shield like a tower,
Stood forth beside him; asunder the Trojans scattered as each could.
Warlike prince Menelaüs conducted him then from the tumult,
Holding his hand till the charioteer drave nigh with the horses.
    Ajax then, with a bound on the Trojans, slaughtered Doryclus,
Bastard son of Priam, the king, then Pandocus wounded,
Wounded Lysander next, then Pyrasus, too, and Pylartes.
Even as when some river is rolling from mountainous regions
Plainward, brimming with winter and swollen with rains of Cronion—
Many the seasoned oak-trees, the firs full many it draweth
Into its swirl, and it sweeps unto seaward siltage abundant:

238

Thus then over the plain kept charging and routing them Ajax,
Glorious, cleaving the horses alike and the heroes. But Hector
Naught was aware thereof, for he fought far off, on the battle's
Left, by the banks of the river Scamander; and there fell mostly
Heads of the heroes, and rose an unquenchable cry from the combat
All round Nestor, the great, and Idomeneus, minion of Ares.
Hector with them was engaged, and notable deeds he was doing
There with lance and car, as he ravaged the young men's battalions.
Nor had the goodly Achaeans yet fallen back from the war-way,
Had not prince Alexander, the husband of fair-haired Helen,
Stayed in his valorous deeds Machaon, shepherd of peoples,
Smiting him full on the shoulder, the right, with a three-barbed arrow.
Then, though bravery-breathing, for him the Achaeans were fearful,
Lest in a turn of the battle the foemen should master him wounded.
Just at that juncture Idomeneus spake unto Nestor, the godlike:
    "Nestor, Neleus' son, great glory of all the Achaeans,
Up now, mount thy car; let Machaon mount it beside thee;
Then drive thou with all speed to the galleys the whole-hoofed horses.
Well is a surgeon worth a many of all other heroes,
Whether to cut out arrows or spread soft ointment assuaging."
    Thus spake he; and the knightly Gerenian Nestor assented,
Mounting at once on his car, and beside him mounted Machaon,
Son of Asclepius he, the faultless hero and healer.
Laid he the lash on the horses, and they went eagerly flying
Down to the hollow ships, full avid in spirit to be there.
    Now as Cebriones noted the Trojans routed and fleeing,
Mounted on Hector's car, he uttered a word and addressed him:
    "Hector, we twain are engaged alone with the Danaans closely
Here on the uttermost edge of the dissonant war; but the Trojans
Elsewhere all are confounded in rout, both the men and their horses.
Ajax, Telamon's son, it is that confounds them; I know him
Well by the breadth of the shield he wears on his shoulders. Let *us* then
Urge on thither the horses and car; since there it is mainly
Horsemen and foot wage battle and stir up a ruinous discord,
Each one slaying another, and war-cry quenchless ariseth."
    Thus he spake unto Hector and lashed the fair-maned horses

On with the whistling whip. They, hearing the stroke of the whip-cord,
Bore on swiftly the car right through the Achaeans and Trojans,
Trampling bodies and bucklers alike; and with blood was the axle
All underneath bedabbled, and rims, all round, of the chariot
Spattered with blood-drops showered about by the hoofs of the horses —
Drops from the tires as well. And Hector was eager to enter
Into the human throng and to leap in and break through. An evil
Tumult he brought on the Danaans; briefly rested his javelin.
Meantime he kept on ranging the ranks of the rest of the heroes,
Wielding a sword or a spear or a ponderous boulder for hurling,
Yet was he shunning a battle with Telamonian Ajax,
Seeing that Zeus was wroth, when he fought a man better than he was.

　　Now Father Zeus, high-throned, created in Ajax a panic;
There he stood in a daze and swung behind him his sev'n-fold
Bull's hide shield and glared through the throng like a wild beast, then
Turning this way and that; one step at a time he retreated.　　[fearful
Just as a tawny lion away from a steading for cattle
Hounds and the men from the country attack and endeavor to drive off,
Neither will suffer the beast to select for ravage the fattest
Ox of the herd; for all night long they watch; but the lion,
Avid for flesh, attacks straight on, but he faileth — for crowded
Fly from the country people's brave hands the missiles against him,
Brands, too, blazing with flame, which he feareth for all of his longing —
Till at the dawn he departeth with heart disappointed and troubled:
Thus at that time from the Trojans, his heart sore-troubled, departed
Ajax exceedingly loath; for he feared for the ships of Achaia.

　　Like as an ass that is passing a field gets the better of children —
Ass that is stubborn, and many a cudgel is broken about him —
Entering croppeth the standing corn, while vainly the children
Beat with their cudgels upon him; but their force is but childish.
Hardly, indeed, do they drive him away, till he's sated of fodder:
So then at that time, with Telamon's son, great Ajax, the high-souled
Trojans and Trojan allies (from many a country assembled)
Smote with spears on the midst of his shield and followed him ever.
He, however, anon would recall his impetuous prowess,
Wheel him about once more, and hold at bay the embattled

Trojans, tamers of steeds; and anon unto flight he would turn him.
Yet he hindered them all from making their way to the swift-keeled
Ships, as he raged, in the space between the Achaeans and Trojans
Taking his stand; and the spears, impelled from hands that were daring,
Some stuck fast in his buckler huge (though driven hard forward);
Many, however, half way, before they could touch his white body,
Stopped firm-fixed in the earth, though eager on flesh to glut them.

    Glorious son of Euaemon, Eurypylus, noted the chieftain
How he was sorely oppressed by the darts thick-showered upon him,
Came up taking his stand close by him, and, hurling his shining
Spear, struck Phausius's son — Apisaon, shepherd of peoples —
Deep in the liver; his knees were instantly loosened beneath him.
At him Eurypylus sprang, from his shoulders to strip off his armor.
When Alexander, however, the godlike, marked and beheld him
Striving to strip off the armor of slain Apisaon, he, drawing
Quickly his bow at Eurypylus, smote him sore with an arrow,   [pled.
Wounding him on the right thigh; the shaft snapped, leaving him crip-
Back to the throng of his fellows, evading his doom, he retreated.
Then with a ringing shout he called to the Danaan warriors:

    "Friends of mine, ye commanders and counseling chiefs of the Ar-
Turn ye, rally and stand, and ward off the pitiless moment   [gives,
Quickly from Ajax! The missiles o'erwhelm him; neither, methinketh,
Will he escape such noise of the hideous warfare; but stand ye,
Facing the foemen, around the great Telamonian Ajax."   [him,

    Thus spake Eurypylus, wounded. His comrades, gathered beside
Stood hard by one another with shields close-laid on their shoulders,
Brandishing lances aloft; and nigh came Ajax to meet them,
Turned about, and stood, when he reached the host of his comrades.

    So in the fashion of fire bright-blazing these warriors battled.
All in a sweat, from the battle the fillies Neleian were bringing
Nestor the while, and they carried Machaon, shepherd of peoples.
Ware of him then, at beholding, was swift-footed, goodly Achilles,
Seeing that he on the stern of his deep-hulled galley was standing,
Watching the arduous toil and the tearful rout of the battle.
Straightway then he bespake his companion, noble Patroclus,   [ward,
Calling aloud from the ship; from the barrack *he* heard and came for-

Like unto Ares; and this was to *him* the beginning of evil.
First then the valiant son of Menoetius spake and addressed him:
   "Why dost thou call, Achilles? For what, I pray, dost thou need me?"
   Answering him in his turn, spake out swift-footed Achilles:
   "Son of Menoetius, goodly and dear to my heart art thou ever.
Now the Achaeans around my knees shall be thronging, methinketh,
Urgent in prayer, for a need no longer endurable cometh.
Go then, Patroclus, belovèd of Zeus, inquire of Nestor
Who this man may be that he brings now, wounded, from battle.
Verily, seen from behind, he is most like unto Machaon,
Son of Asclepius; only, I saw not the face of the hero,
So swift past me the steeds went speeding with eagerness forward."
   Thus spake he; and Patroclus promptly obeyed his dear comrade,
Started, and ran on past the barracks and galleys Achaean.
   They now, when they arrived at the barrack of Nestor Nelides,
Lighted off from the car on the earth, all-nurturing mother.
Then from the old man's car his squire Eurymedon loosened
Nestor's horses. The twain stood drying the sweat from their tunics,
Facing the breeze by the shore of the sea. Thereafter they entered
Into the barrack anon and there on chairs took their places.
Then fair-haired Hecamede for them made ready a porridge —
She that the old man from Tenedos won, when Achilles destroyed it;
Daughter was she of the great-souled Arsinoüs. Her the Achaeans
Chose out for him, because in counsel he was their wisest.
She first set and moved forward to them a beautiful table,
Polished well and with feet of dark blue metal; a charger
Bronzen, thereon, and upon it an onion, to flavor the mixture,
Honey as well, pale honey, and meal of the hallowèd barley;
Also beside it a beaker surpassingly fair, that the old man
Brought from his home, all studded with rivets of gold, four handles
Wrought thereon, and a couple of golden pigeons were feeding
Round each handle; the bases were double that fitted beneath it.
This cup another were scarcely able to move from the table,
When it was full, yet the old man Nestor lifted it lightly.
Therein the damsel, like to the goddesses, made them a mixture,
First with Pramnian wine, then goat's milk cheese with a bronzen

Grater she grated thereon and strewed white barley upon it.
Then she bade them to drink, when she had made ready the posset.
When the twain had banished the parching thirst with their drinking,
Then they took pleasure in words, as they spoke, the one to the other.
Now there stood at the doors Patroclus, peer of a godhead.
Seeing him there, the old man arose forthwith from his shining
Throne and, grasping his hand, led him in and bade him be seated.
But from the other side Patroclus declined, and he answered:
　　"No seat, reverend nurseling of Zeus! Thou wilt not persuade me.
Dreaded, austere is he that sent me to learn by inquiry
Who this man may be that thou bringest wounded; but *I* know
Well of myself, for I see him, Machaon, shepherd of peoples.
Now, as a messenger, I must return with a word to Achilles.
Well, oh reverend nurseling of Zeus, thou knowest his nature,
Terrible man! he would lightly blame even one that is blameless."
　　　　Him in his turn then answered the knightly Gerenian Nestor:
　　"Why doth Achilles bemoan in such wise the sons of Achaia,
These that are wounded with missiles? For surely he knoweth in no way
How great distress is arisen throughout our army; the bravest
Lie e'en now in the ships, spear-smitten or wounded with arrows.
Wounded insooth is Tydeus' son, Diomedes, the mighty;
Stricken the far-famed spearman, Odysseus, yea, Agamemnon,
Yea, and Eurypylus, too, lies shot in the thigh with an arrow.
Here is another, whom I even now bring out of the warfare,
Wounded with arrow impelled from the bowstring. Natheless Achilles,
Brave though he is, cares naught for the Danaans, pities them noway.
Waiteth he, haply, till even the swift ships hard by the seashore,
Burning in spite of the Argives, are lost in the fire of destruction?
We ourselves be slain, one after the other? For my strength
Is no longer such in my supple limbs, as it once was.
Would I were young once more and my vigor unshaken within me,
Even as when a contention arose 'twixt us and th' Eleans
Over a raid on the kine, what season my own spear slaughtered
Noble Itymoneus, son of Hypirochus, dweller in Elis,
When I would drive off booty; but he, while defending his cattle,
Struck with the javelin hurlèd from *my* hand, out of the vanguard,

243

Fell to the earth, while round him the country folk scattered in terror.
Booty we gathered and drove from the plain in exceeding abundance:
Kine-herds fifty in tale and of sheep-flocks fully as many;
Swine-droves also and goats' wide-ranging flocks full as many;
Horses a hundred and fifty in count, bright-chestnut in color,
All of them mares, and many the foals that followed beside them.
These, in a nightlong drive, we brought to Neleian Pylus,
Into the city; and Neleus' heart was filled with rejoicing,
Seeing I'd won such success on my first adventure in warfare.
Then, at the coming of morn the heralds with loud voice summoned
All to assembly to whom debt was owing in glorious Elis.
Thereupon all foregathered; the men that were Pylian leaders
Portioned the whole; the Epeians insooth owed debts unto many,
Seeing that we were but few and were evil-treated in Pylus:
Heracles mighty had entered our land and sorely oppressed us,
So that in earlier years our best, our bravest, had fallen.
Once we were twelve in number, we sons of Neleus, the blameless;
I even only remained, since all of the others had perished.
Therefore, swollen with pride, the bronze-mailed men of Epeia
Did us despite and devised high-handed excesses against us.
So then the old man selected a kine-drove, also a sheep-flock
Numerous, choosing three hundred head along with the herdsmen,
Seeing the debt long due him in fair-famed Elis was heavy:
Four were the horses indeed—prize-winners—had gone with their char-
Unto the games, and insooth they intended to run for a tripod   [iots
Offered as prize; but the monarch of men, their ruler, Augeas,
Forcibly held them; the driver he sent back, grieved for his horses.
Angered by such words and deeds, the old man selected much booty,
Countless; the rest he assigned to the common stock for division,
Lest any one should depart deprived of his equal portion.
So we settled affairs in detail and all through the city
Sacrifice made to the gods. But the third day all the Eleans
Came in a multitude, men and their whole-hoofed horses together,
Hot in pursuit. In the midst the Moliones armed them for battle,
Twain, mere lads, and as yet unacquaint with impetuous prowess.
There is a city, a certain abrupt high hill, Thryoëssa,

On the Alpheüs, far off, of sandy Pylus the farthest.
This they surrounded, encamped, full eager to shatter it wholly.
When they had occupied all of the plain, to us came Athena,
Down from Olympus running all in the night with a message,
Bidding us arm; nor averse was the folk she assembled at Pylus,
Nay, but exceedingly eager for warfare. Neither would Neleus
Let me array me in arms even then, but secreted my horses:
I, he declared, knew nothing as yet of the conduct of warfare.
But even so I distinguished myself in the ranks of our horsemen,
E'en so, although on foot — so guided the combat Athena.
There is a river, Minyeius, that falls hard by at Arene
Into the sea; and there the hallowèd dawn we awaited,
Pylian horsemen, and thither the infantry ranks kept streaming.
Marching with all speed thence, meanwhile full harnessed in wargear,
Came we at midday nigh to the sacred stream of Alpheüs.
Goodly victims we offered to Zeus, in might all excelling,
There, and a bull to Alpheüs, and also a bull to Poseidon,
But from the herd for the bright-eyed Athena chose we a heifer.
Then we took supper, assembled in companies all through our army.
Each man then laid him down to rest, full clad in his armor,
Hard by the streams of the river. And still the great-hearted Epeians
Gathered around the city, right eager to level it wholly.
Ere that, though, was presented to them a great labor of warfare;
For, as the sun was moving the broad earth over, effulgent,
Straight we went into battle, with prayers unto Zeus and Athena.
Now, as the strife began, of Pylian men and Epeians,
I was the first one to slay my man and thus won his horses,
Solid of hoof — Augeas' son-in-law, Mulius, spearman;
He had wedded his daughter, the eldest, blonde Agamede,
Who was acquainted with all the herbs that the wide earth doth nourish.
I with my bronze-shod spear smote *him* in his onset upon me;
Down he crashed in the dust; and I, leaping up on his chariot,
Took my stand with the foremost men. But the great-souled Epeians
This way fled and the other at seeing a hero had fallen,
Chief of the chariot force, who was wont to be bravest in battle.
I, however, went rushing like some black tempest upon them;

Fifty chariots I captured; and two men, grov'ling alongside
Each one, bit the earth with their teeth, subdued by my javelin.
Then had I vanquished the twins, the Moliones, children of Actor,
Had not their father Poseidon, wide-ruling earth-shaker saved them
Out of the conflict of war, enwrapping thick vapor about them.
There it was Zeus vouchsafed to the Pylians mighty puissance:
So long o'er the wide plain we scattered them far and pursued them,
Slaying the men themselves and gath'ring their beautiful armor,
Till to Buprasium, laden with wheat, we had driven our horses —
On to the rock Olenian; there is the hill of Alisium,
So-called, and there Athena halted and turned back the people.
There I slew the last of our foes, and I left him. Th' Achaeans
Drove the fleet steeds away from Buprasium back unto Pylus;
All gave glory to Zeus of the gods, unto Nestor of mortals.
Such I was once among men, if I ever was. Now Achilles
Profit will have to himself of his valor; yet some time, methinketh,
He shall lament it, too late — when sinketh the people in ruin!
Yea, dear lad, it was good Menoetius, thy father, enjoined thee
That same day that he sent thee from Phthia to aid Agamemnon.
We twain truly were then, both I and the goodly Odysseus,
There in the halls, and we heard all his bidding, how he enjoined thee.
Thither indeed we had come to the fair-built palace of Peleus,
Sent to assemble the hosts of Achaia's land of abundance.
There it was soothly we found in the palace the hero Menoetius,
Thee, and beside thee Achilles. The old man, the driver of horses,
Peleus, was burning fat thighs of an ox to the hurler of thunders,
Zeus, in the close of his court; and he held uplifted a golden
Goblet and poured out the sparkling wine on the burning oblations.
Ye twain were busy about the flesh of the ox — of a sudden
There stood we at the doors! Up then in amazement Achilles
Leaped and grasped our hands, led us in, and bade us be seated,
Spreading a table before us, the full feast due unto strangers.
But, when we had enjoyed the pleasure of eating and drinking,
I then made a beginning of speech and bade you to follow.
Ye were right willing to go; and they two laid many injunctions.
Peleus, the agèd, commanded his own son, even Achilles,

Ever to be the best, preëminent over all others.
Thus in his turn did Menoetius, the son of Actor, enjoin thee:
'Lineage higher than thine is the boast, my child, of Achilles
(Though thou art elder, insooth), and in might he is greatly superior.
But it were meet to advise him with wise words, gentle suggestion,
Showing him what he should do; his own good he will find in obeying.'
　　"Thus did the old man charge thee; thou hast forgotten; but even
Now, pray, this word to the wise Achilles, if he will obey thee.
Who knows if thou, God helping, mightest with words of persuasion
Rouse up his spirit? For good are a comrade's words of persuasion.
If, howe'er, in his soul he is shunning some warning from heaven —
Haply, some warning from Zeus hath told him his worshipful mother —
Still let him send forth thee; let the others, the Myrmidon people,
Follow with thee, if perchance some light thou become to the Argives.
Ay, let him give thee his beautiful arms, to wear to the battle;
Haply the Trojans may hold them aloof from the battle, mistaking
Thee for himself, and the warlike sons of Achaia, a-wearied,
Breathe for a moment; for brief is the breathing time in a battle.
Lightly perchance might we, not wearied, drive back to the city
Men of the war-cry weary, away from the ships and the barracks."
　　　　Thus he spake and aroused the heart in his bosom; he started
Running along past the ships to Aeacides, goodly Achilles.
But when Patroclus in running arrived at the ships of Odysseus,
Godlike chief, at the place where they held assembly and judgment,
Where had also the altars of gods for them been established,
There did Eurypylus, Zeus-descended son of Euaemon,
Meet him, wounded sore in his thigh with an arrow by Paris,
Limping out of the fight; and down from his head and his shoulders
Streamed the copious sweat; from the wound most cruel the dark blood
Still was trickling. Nevertheless his soul was unshaken.
Moved at the sight with compassion, the valiant son of Menoetius
Spake with a piteous cry, and with wingèd words he addressed him:
　　"Ah, unhappy! ye Danaan leaders and counseling chieftains,
Thus are ye fated, far from your friends and the land of your fathers,
Here in Troyland to glut the fleet-footed hounds with your white fat.
Come now, nurseling of Zeus, thou hero Eurypylus, tell me,

Will the Achaeans ever restrain a giant like Hector,
Or will they even now meet their end, subdued by his javelin?"
   Him, in his turn, the wounded Eurypylus answered as follows:
   "Nay, no longer, Patroclus, thou scion of Zeus, have the Argives
Any defense; they will flee; they will fall here amid their black galleys,
Seeing that all those now who aforetime were counted as bravest
Lie in the ships already, sore wounded with spears and with arrows
Under the hands of the Trojans, whose strength incessantly waxes.
Bring me to safety, leading me down to the black-painted galley;
Cut thou the arrow out of my thigh; and from it the dark blood
Wash thou away with warm water and spread mild simples upon it,
Healing, the use whereof, they say, thou art taught of Achilles,
Whom it was Chiron taught, the most righteous one of the Centaurs:
Since of our doctors the one, Podalirius, the other, Machaon,
One sore wounded is lying, methinks, in his barrack and needeth
Even himself wise care at the hands of a faultless physician;
One on the plain still abideth the keen attack of the Trojans."
   Spake unto him in his turn the valiant son of Menoetius:
   "These things, how should they be? How do them, Eurypylus, hero?
I'm on my way to Achilles, the wise-hearted, now, to convey him
Word the Gerenian Nestor, th' Achaeans' warden, enjoineth.
But even so I will not desert thee in time of affliction."
   Spake he and, under the breast he clasped the shepherd of peoples,
Helped him thus to his barrack; a squire, on seeing, spread ox-hides.
Stretching him on them at length, with his knife he cut out the arrow —
Sharp and stinging — out of his thigh, and from it the dark blood
Washed with warm water away and laid thereover a bitter
Root he had rubbed in his hands, which soothed his suff'ring, assuaging
All of his pains; and the wound grew dry, and the hemorrhage ended.

ILIAD · XII · (M)

Mû works the Trojans all the grace,
And doth the Grecian fort deface.

So in the barracks Patroclus, the valiant son of Menoetius,
Tended Eurypylus wounded; the rest meanwhile were in battle,
Argives and Trojans thronging confusedly; neither was destined
Long to hold out the moat, nor the broad-based rampart above it —
Wall that the Danaans builded, moat they had drawn round about it
(All in vain, for they'd offered the gods no hecatombs splendid),
That their swift galleys it might protect and their spoil in abundance,
Safely ensheltered; nay! in despite of the gods it was builded,
Gods immortal, and so unto no long time was it standing.
While yet Hector was living, and wrathful as yet was Achilles,
While unsacked as yet was the city of Priam, the monarch,
So long still the Achaeans' mighty wall remained standing.
But when the best of the Trojans had now all fallen, the bravest —
Many the Argives, too, that were slain, though some were surviving —
When in the tenth year also the city of Priam was plundered,
When the Argives had gone to their homeland dear in their galleys,
Verily then did Poseidon and Phoebus Apollo take counsel
How to demolish the wall: they enlisted the might of the rivers —
All of the rivers that down from the mountains of Ida flow seaward:
Rhesus and Rhodius, too, Heptaporus, also Caresus;
There were Grenicus, Aesepus, and also the goodly Scamander,
Simoïs, too, where many a bull's-hide buckler and helmet
Rolled in the dust, with a whole generation of demigod heroes.
All these torrents Apollo united in one, and he drave it
Nine days long at the wall in a flood; and Zeus in the mean while
Rained incessant, to whelm into flotsam quicker the ramparts.
Leader in this was Poseidon, the Earth-shaker's self; with his trident
Grasped in his hand, to the billows he heaved forth all of the bases,

Whether of beams or of stones, the Achaeans, toiling, had founded,
Leveling all of the works with the Hellespont's strong-flowing current,
Once more covering wholly the great beach under a sandheap,
Having demolished the wall; then turned again in their channels
All those rivers, to pour fair-flowing, as ever, their waters.

    So would Poseidon his will hereafter, with Phoebus Apollo,
Wreak on the well-built wall; but at that time battle and war-din
Blazed all round and about it — the beams of the towers resounded
Under the blows; and the Argives, subdued by the scourge of Cronion,
All by the hollow ships were penned and held fast together,
Dreading the Trojan Hector, that mighty deviser of panic.
He, however, as always aforetime, fought like a whirlwind.
As when a boar or a lion 'mid hounds and men that are hunters
Wheeleth about at bay, while his heart swells high in his prowess —
They, moreover, compact, yea solid in rank as a tower,
Stand up against him and launch thick and fast their lances upon him
Out of their hands; but his heart, undaunted, never a moment
Quaileth or mindeth of fear, and his courage brings him destruction.
Wheeling this way or that, he testeth the ranks of the hunters;
Yea, wherever he charges, the men's ranks bend to his onset:
Even so Hector all through the throng went rallying comrades,
Spurring them onward to bound clean over the moat; but the horses
Dared not, however nimble of foot — nay, stood at the outmost
Border and snorted aloud; for the wide moat frighted them sorely;
Noway easy was it to o'erleap from close by, nor to pass it
Easy indeed; for along full length of the trench the embankments
Butted on both sides steep; and across, full furnished, it bristled
Horrent with sharp palisades; for these had the sons of Achaia
Planted there thick and firm, a defense from assault of the foemen.
There could a horse that was drawing a well-wheeled chariot enter
Never with ease; but on foot men were eager if they might effect it.
    Then unto valiant Hector Pulydamas came and bespoke him:
    "Hector and all of the rest, ye chiefs of allies and of Trojans,
Vain the endeavor to drive our fleet steeds over, and foolish.
Now is a crossing exceedingly hard; for the palisades in it
Stand up sharp in the moat, with the Argive wall close behind them.

There could the horsemen drive in, e'en there could they mingle in bat-
Never, for strait is the way, where evil, methinks, will await us.　　[tle
True, if Zeus that thund'reth on high wills now to destroy them
Utterly, bearing ill will, while minded to favor the Trojans,
Verily I should desire such hap, that all the Achaeans
Suddenly, wholly should perish unnamed here, far from their Argos;
But if they turn them again, and a backward rally resulteth
Out from the ships, and *we* plunge into the moat they've constructed,
Never, methinks, would even a messenger fare to the city's
Gates, fast fleeing before the rallying tide of Achaeans.
Come then, even as I may direct, let us all be persuaded:
Let our squires at the moat hold back our horses in waiting,
While we ourselves on foot, all arrayed in weapons of warfare,
Move on, following Hector in mass compact; the Achaeans
Will not withstand us, if truly they're fast in the bonds of destruction."

　　Thus spake Pulydamas; Hector was pleased with his excellent coun-
Out from his car forthwith he leaped to the ground in his armor.　　[sel.
Nor did the rest of the Trojans remain in their chariots together,
When they saw Hector, the godlike, but all sprang forth in a moment.
Therewith each of the leaders committed his steeds to a driver,
Even his own, to hold back nigh unto the moat and in order.
They then divided, in serried ranks reformed in divisions
Five, then followed along, well ordered, the marshaling leaders.
Whoso with Hector went, who the faultless Pulydamas followed,
They, both bravest and most, were above all others in ardor,
First having broken the wall, by the hollow ships to do battle.
With them Cebriones followed, as third; in charge of his horses
Hector had left another, no match for Cebriones' prowess.
Paris, Alcathoüs, with them Agenor, commanded the second.
Helenus headed a third one, along with Deïphobus, godlike
(Both were children of Priam), the hero Asius with them,
Asius, Hyrtacus' son, whose large sorrel horses had brought him
Erst from Arisbe to Troy, from the banks of the river Selleïs.
Fourth was a company led of the goodly son of Anchises,
Even Aeneas, and with him Archelochus, Acamas also—
Both were sons of Antenor, well skilled in all manner of warfare.

251

Lastly the famous allies of the Trojans Sarpedon commanded;
He chose Glaucus as aid and the martial Asteropaeus,
Since it was they that seemed of the whole host plainly the bravest
After himself; Sarpedon 'mong all of the men was unequaled.   [hide,
    These, then, close-interlocking their well-wrought bucklers of bull's
Marched on the Danaans straight all eagerly, nor were they deeming
These would longer hold out but would fall there amid their black gal-
    All others now of the Trojans and of their allies far-renownèd [leys.
Gladly adopted the counsel of noble Pulydamas; only
Asius, Hyrtacus' son, a marshal of men, was unwilling
Either to leave his steeds or his squire, their driver, behind him;
Nay! to the swift-faring ships he drew nigh with his horses and war-car.
Fond man! Never should he, with the doom of his folly evaded,
Back from the ships with his car and his horses proudly rejoicing
Unto the wind-swept Ilium-city have happy returning.
Sooner, insooth, should an ill-named fate o'ershadow and quell him
Under the spear of Idomeneus, son of the gallant Deucalion.
Full at the galleys he drave on the left wing, where the Achaeans
Always used to return from the plain with their horses and war-cars.
There he drave right through his horses and car, and he found no
Closed-up doors on the gates, no long beam barring the gateway.
Men were holding them open, if haply to bring some comrade,
Coming in headlong flight from the battle, safe to the galleys.
There, unfalt'ring in aim, he directed his steeds, and his comrades
Followed with piercing cry, for they deemed that now the Achaeans
Would no longer hold out but would fall there amid their black galleys.
Fools! for they found at the gates two men, accounted the bravest,
High-hearted sons, insooth, of the Lapithae, wielders of lances:
One of these was Pirithoüs' son, Polypoetes, the mighty;
One was Leonteus, the equal of Ares, the ruin of mortals.
These twain there he encountered in front of the high-built portals
Standing, as when two oaks, high-crested, up on the mountains
Bide unto years unending the buffet of rain and of tempest,
Firm-set deep in the soil by roots far-spreading and mighty:
Thus these twain, on prowess and strong hands boldly reliant,
Stood there, biding the onset of mighty Asius, and fled not.

Straight for the well-built rampart the Trojans came and they raised
Bull's-hide bucklers aloft in a din of tumultuous shouting   [their
All round Asius, king, and Iamenus, all round Oreſtes,
Adamas, Asius' son, and Oenomaüs also, and Thoön.

Now for a time these twain on the inside aroused the Achaeans
(Well-greaved warriors they were) to fight in defense of the galleys.
But, as they noted the rush of the Trojans full on the rampart,
While 'mid the Danaans rose a fearful cry and a panic,
Out from a portal before them the twain charged forth and did battle.
Even as wild boars, ranging the wildwood, bide in the mountains
Hue and cry of men and of hounds that loudly assail them—
Sideways plunging, they trample the copsewood shattered around them,
Tearing it up by the roots, while the clatter of tusks in their champing
Waxeth aloud, until someone may smite and of life may despoil them:
So on the breaſts of the heroes the bronze, bright-shining, resounded
Under the blows that they faced; for they fought exceedingly ſtoutly,
Truſting the prowess alike of themselves and the warriors also,
Who from the well-built towers kept hurling incessantly downward
Stones in defense of their lives, in defense of their barracks and galleys,
Swift-faring over the deep; and they fell to the ground like snowflakes,
When a tempeſtuous wind, as it whirleth the shadowy ſtorm-clouds,
Sheddeth the snowflakes thick on the earth, the all-nurturing mother:
Even so, forth from the hands of Trojans and also Achaeans,
Poured out missiles amain; full hoarsely the helmets resounded—
Smitten with ſtones like millſtones—and bucklers bossed and refulgent.
Thereat smiting his thighs, as he loudly groaned in vexation,
Asius, Hyrtacus' son, found vent in his words for his fury:

"O Father Zeus, forsooth even thou art turned to a lover
Now of falsehood wholly! I deemed not heroes Achaean
Our unapproachable hands could abide and our furious onset.
Like unto bees, however, or wasps full pliantly waiſted—
Such as have builded a dwelling along by a roadside rugged,
Nor will abandon a home they have dug, nay, ſteadfast abiding
Ward off hunters and hold them aloof in defense of their offspring:
Even so these, two only, are resolute here at the gateway,
Never to yield till they either slay or themselves be slaughtered."

255

Thus spake he, but he moved not the mind of Zeus with his speak-
Who in his heart had determined to grant to Hector the glory.   [ing,
Others were fighting the battle at one gate, some at another.
Hard, though, were it for me, though a god, to tell all completely,
Seeing the fire, fierce-blazing, on all sides girdled the rampart
Builded of stone; and the Argives, for all of their grief, were defending
Even their galleys perforce; while all of the deities sorrowed
Sorely at heart, whoever the Danaans helped in the battle.
So in the warfare mingled the Lapithae, joined in the combat.

There then anon Pirithoüs' son, Polypoetes, the mighty,   [met;
Smote with his javelin Damasus clean through his bronze-cheeked hel-
Nor could the casque, though of bronze, arrest it; onward the bronzen
Point went cleaving and shattered also the bone; it bespattered
All of his brain within and quelled him, even though eager.
Then it was Pylon, and Ormenus third, that he slew and despoiled
Then was Antimachus' son, Hippomachus, struck by Leonteus,   [them.
Ares' scion; the lance, well aimed, lit full on his girdle.
He then, suddenly drawing his keen blade forth from its scabbard,
Dashing right through the throng of warriors, and closing in grapple
First with Antiphates, struck him down, to the earth hurled him back-
Menon next he o'erthrew, then Iamenus, also Orestes —   [ward.
All in succession he stretched on the earth, the all-bounteous mother.

Now, while *they* were despoiling the glittering arms of the fallen,
Such as were following Hector and also Pulydamas — young men,
Bravest in heart, in number the most, and eager in spirit
First to break down the wall, then kindle the galleys with torches —
All on the brink of the moat stood pondering, hesitant, troubled.
For, in their ardor for passage, a bird came flying above them,
Even a high-soaring eagle, which skirted the host to the leftward,
Bearing away in his talons a blood-red serpent, a monster —
Though in convulsions — alive, not forgetting the rapture of battle,
Seeing it curled round backward and wounded the breast of the eagle
Close at the neck of its captor; the eagle, repelling it earthward,
Smarting with pain from the sting, flung it down in the midst of the
Then loud-screaming away on the blasts of the wind went flying. [army.
Thereat shuddered the Trojans on seeing the serpent a-writhing,

256

Lying among them, a portent of Zeus who wieldeth the aegis.
Then unto valiant Hector Pulydamas came and bespake him:

"Hector, it seemeth to chance thou chidest me aye in assemblies,
E'en though counseling wisely; for noway e'er it behooveth
One of the people to argue against thee, whether in council,
Whether in war it may be, but ever to add to thy power.
Now, however, again will I say what best to me seemeth:
Let us not enter a fight with the Danaans *now* for the galleys.
For even so it will issue, methinketh, if truly a portent
This bird came to the Trojans when they were keen for a passage,
Even an high-soaring eagle, which skirted the host to the leftward,
Bearing away in his talons a blood-red serpent, a monster—
Living, but cast it abruptly away ere home he arrivèd,
Neither did he succeed in bringing the gift to his children:
Even so we—if indeed we shall breach both rampart and gateway
Now with an energy vast, if th' Achaeans yield to our onset—
Back from the ships shall return by the same tracks—yet in disorder.
Many the Trojans we'll leave behind us, whom haply th' Achaeans
There with their weapons of bronze will destroy in defense of their gal-
So full surely a seer of God would interpret, that clearly   [leys.
Knew in his spirit of omens, a seer whom the folk may confide in."

Scowlfully eyeing him answered the shimmering-helmeted Hector:
"What thou sayest, Pulydamas, meets no more with my pleasure.
Thou well knowest to frame some speech far better than this one;
But if in earnest at all thou truly haranguest in this wise,
Verily then have the gods themselves robbed thee of thy senses,
Who now bidst us forget loud-thundering Zeus and his counsels,
All that he promised himself unto me and nodded in sanction.
Thou now biddest obey lone birds of wide-spreading pinions!
Whereto *I* will give heed—no, never! nor care for them either,
Whether to rightward they fare, mayhap, to the sun and the morning,
Whether, perchance, to the left, to the evening mist and the darkness.
Nay, for us, let us trust to all-mighty Zeus and his counsels,
Him that is lord over all, o'er mortals as well as immortals.
One bird only is best, one omen—to fight for our country.
Thou now—why art affrighted at war, the confusion of battle?

Even if all thy fellows, we Troy-folk, fall in the combat
There at the Argive ships, no fear were thine of destruction,
Seeing that thine is a heart unwarlike, unsteadfast in battle.
But if thou shunnest the struggle thyself or dissuadest some other,
Turning him back from the war with an ill word foolishly spoken,
Under a blow from my spear thy life is immediate forfeit."

    Thus he spake and led the way, and the company followed,
Raising unearthly cries, while Zeus, the hurler of thunder,
Roused from the mountains of Ida down-rushing upon them a storm-
Driving a dust-cloud right on the galleys; so he confounded   [wind,
Argive sense and glory bestowed on the Trojans and Hector.
They, on their own strength as well as the godhead's omens reliant,
Struggled to make them a breach in the mighty rampart Achaean.
Down they tumbled the bastions and left the battlements ruined,
Pried up the buttresses too, the projections, which the Achaeans
First had laid down in the earth as a broad shore under the towers.
These they were pulling away and hoped to breach the Achaeans'
Wall. But not even yet would the Danaans yield from the war-way,
Nay, but the bastions fenced with close-locked bucklers of bull's hide,
Pelting the foe therefrom, as he came nigh under the rampart.

    Meantime the Ajaxes twain, giving frequent commands on the
This way ranged and that, arousing th' Achaeans to courage,   [towers,
Rallying one with honeyed words and one with reproachful,
Whomsoever they chanced to see giving ground in the battle:
    "Friends, whosoever of Argives is eminent, whoso is middling,
Whoso is lower in rank — not all are equally dowered
Heroes in war — right now there comes work for every soldier.
Ye yourselves know this well, I am sure. Let no one now backward
Turn to the ships because he has heard some call for retreating;
Nay, press forward and urge one another likewise to press on!
Haply may Zeus now grant us, Olympian launcher of lightning,
Th' onset of foes to repel and chase them back to the city."

    These twain, with shouts at the front, cheered on the Achaeans to
Even as snowflakes thick on a day in winter, descending,   [battle.
Fall to the earth, when Zeus, the master of counsel, beginneth
Snowing and wills to display these shafts of his unto mortals;

Lulling the winds, unceasing he snoweth, until he hath covered
Tops of the towering hills and the forelands jutting to seaward,
Ay, and the clovered plains and the fertile tillage of mortals;
Even abroad it is ſtrewn on the hoar sea's havens and beaches;
Only the billow in rolling repelleth it; under it wholly
All things else are enwrapped, when Zeus pours heavy upon them:
Likewise crowded the ſtones as they flew from both sides of the battle,
Some at the Trojans, and some from the Trojans at the Achaeans,
Smiting and smit, while over the whole wall war-din ascended.

Yet had the Trojans then, ay, even illuſtrious Hector
Rended the rampart's gates and the long bar never asunder,
Had not Zeus, the maſter of counsel, spurred at the Argive
Host Sarpedon, his son, like a lion at crook-horned cattle.
Straightly he thrust out before him his shield, all evenly rounded,
Beautiful, bronze, well forged, that cunningest art of the brazier
Forged and riveted many a fold of bull's hide within it,
Clamped them with rivets of gold in a ring unbroken around it.
This he uplifted before him, and, two spears brandishing, meantime
Sped on his way like a lion a mountain hath bred, that hath faſted
Long in ravenous hunger for flesh, and his proud heart biddeth
Make an assault on the sheep, yea, charge on a well-builded homeſtead.
Ay, and if he find brave keepers thereby, even herdsmen,
Keen-eyed, watching with hounds and javelins over the cattle,
Yet is he noway minded to flee without trying the ſteading;
Nay, but he bounds right in, lays hold of a sheep, or is smitten
Haply himself 'mid the foremost, some quick hand darting a javelin:
Even so urgent his heart drave on the godlike Sarpedon,
Drave him to ſtorming the wall and breaking the copings asunder.
Inſtantly then did he speak to Glaucus, Hippolochus' scion:

"Why is it, Glaucus, that we have been honored most highly of all
Honored with seats and with meats and brimful goblets in Lycia? [men,
Why do the people at home all look upon us as if godheads?
True, we possess an apportioned demesne on the banks of the Xanthus,
Broad in extent and fair in its vineyard and wheat-bearing plow-land.
Well it behooves us now to take *our* ſtand with the foremost
Lycian heroes and there encounter the blaze of the battle,

So that a man may declare, some one of the corseleted Lycians:
'Verily, far from ignoble the rulers that lord it in Lycia,
Sovereigns like ours, who feed on full-fed cattle and muttons,
Quaffing wine of the choicest and sweeter than honey; but also
Goodly in might, for they war in the foremost ranks of the Lycians.'
Good my friend, if indeed on escaping out of this battle
We should live unattainted of age, immortal forever,
Neither should I myself then fight in the ranks of the foremost,
Nor would I send thee on into war that glorifies heroes.
Now though, seeing the fates — ten thousand — of death are impending
Over us, neither is given a mortal to fend or elude them,
On let us go unto glory — our own, if it be, or another's."   [less.

  Thus he spake; and Glaucus nor turned him aside nor was heed-
Both went right forward, leading the numerous folk of the Lycians.
Since they were coming against *his* bastion, bearing disaster,
Quick as he saw them he shuddered, Menestheus, Peteos' scion.
Then he peered anxious along on th' Achaeans' rampart, if any
Chief he could see that could ward off the ruin that threatened his com-
There he espied the Ajaxes twain, insatiate of battle,   [rades.
Standing with Teucer, newly arrived from his barrack among them,
Hard by; yet was a cry in no way able to reach them
Under the deafening din and the clangor mounting to heaven,
Clangor of bucklers smitten and helms all crested with horsehair,
And of the gates; for all had been barred; and the Trojans were stand-
Over against them and striving by force to burst them and enter.   [ing
Speedily then he despatched to Ajax the herald, Thoötes:

  "Godlike Thoötes, go on a run and summon great Ajax;
Both of them, rather, call; for of all things certainly that were
Far best, since speedily here will be wrought sheer ruin upon us.
Hitherward, namely, are pressing th' impetuous Lycian leaders,
Heroes famous of old in the stress of furious combats.
But if for them also *there* now toil and strife have arisen,
Still let *him* come alone, Telamonian Ajax, the mighty;
With him let follow also that master of archery, Teucer."

  Said he. Straightway the herald, on hearing him, not disobedient,
Went on a run by the wall of the bronze-clad sons of Achaia;

Coming, he stopped by the Ajaxes twain and quickly addressed them:
   "Ajaxes twain, ye chiefs of the bronze-clad children of Argos,
Peteos' son, the beloved, the nurseling of Zeus, hath commanded
Thither to come if for only a trice ye mingle in battle;
Better if both of you come, for of all things certainly that were
Best, since speedily there will be wrought sheer ruin upon us.
Thitherward, namely, are pressing th' impetuous Lycian leaders,
Heroes famous of old in the stress of furious combats.
But if also here now war and strife have arisen,
Still let *him* come alone, Telamonian Ajax, the mighty;
With him let follow also that master of archery, Teucer."
   Thus spake he, and the great Telamonian Ajax obeyed him.
Instantly wingèd words he addressed to the son of Oïleus:
   "Ajax, abide ye here, both thou and the strong Lycomedes;
Stand firm; the Danaans cheer to fight amain with the foemen;
I, though, yonder will hasten and take my part in the battle;
Soon I will come back again, when once I have aided them fitly."
   Thus then he spake and went his way, Telamonian Ajax;
Teucer, his brother and son of his father, also went with him;
With them also Pandion was bearing the curved bow of Teucer.
Now as they came to the tow'r of Menestheus, the great-souled,
Passing within the wall, hard pressed were the men that they found
Foemen were climbing up on the battlements like as a whirlwind [there.
Dark — the valiant leaders and counseling chiefs of the Lycians;
E'en then they dashed together in fight, and loud rose the war-cry.
   First to lay low his man was great Telamonian Ajax —
Even the great-souled Epicles, the comrade of godlike Sarpedon.
Him he smote with a stone that was laid inside of the rampart,
Jagged and huge, on top of the parapet; neither could lightly
Anyone, e'en in the prime of his manhood hold it in both hands,
Such as are mortals today; yet Ajax lifted and hurled it,
Crashing a helmet of fourfold-crest, and the bones of the temples
Shattering all in a heap; like a diver the Lycian tumbled
Sheer from the parapet's top, and life fled forth from his body.
   Teucer then from the lofty tower smote with an arrow
Glaucus, the mighty son of Hippolochus, as he rushed forward —

Noting his shoulder exposed — and stopped his rapture of battle.
Back from the rampart he leaped, yet covertly, lest an Achaean
Haply perceive he was smit and triumph boastfully o'er him.
Grief at the going of Glaucus arose in the soul of Sarpedon,
Soon as he marked it; and yet he forgot not the rapture of battle:
Aiming at Thestor's son, Alcmaon, he smote and the javelin
Drew back again; Alcmaon followed the spear and fell forward
Prone, while round him resounded his arms, rich-carven and bronzen.
Then with his stalwart hands Sarpedon seized on the copings,
Tugged, and the whole mass yielded, crumbling together; the rampart
Lay bare open atop and a pathway offered to many.

Forthwith Ajax and Teucer encountered him; one with an arrow
Struck him upon the baldric supporting his life-guarding buckler,
Gleaming bright on his breast; but his father, Zeus, then averted
Fate from his son, that he might not be slain at the sterns of the galleys.
Next at a bound smote Ajax his buckler; speeding, the spear-point
Pierced not through, but it staggered Sarpedon, eager in onset;
Back from the battlement slightly he yielded; yet he retreated
Nowise wholly, for still did his heart fondly hope to win glory.
Wheeling about, he cried to the Lycians, peers of immortals:

"Why, O Lycians, thus remiss in impetuous prowess?
Hard is the matter for me, though I am a valiant warrior,
Lone to break through the wall and to lay down a path to the galleys.
Come now, follow amain; more men make better the issue."

Thus he spake; and his men, in dread of their ruler's reproaches,
Pressed on harder around him, their king, their leader in counsel;
While upon their side the Argives reinforced their battalions
Inside the wall, and mighty the task that was now set before them,
Seeing the Lycian heroes, for all of their valor, still could not
Break through the Danaans' wall and lay down a path to the galleys,
Nor could ever the Danaan spearmen drive off the Lycians
Back from the wall, when once the Lycian forces had neared it.
Even as when two yeomen contend o'er the bounds of a tillage,
Measuring rods in their hands, in the tilth-ground hitherto common —
All in a space right narrow they strive for an equal division:
Even so parted the battlement these, while above it the foemen

Hewed one another's armor of oxhide that covered their bodies,
Shields all evenly girdled and targes a-flutter with aprons.
Many the wounds ſtruck home in the flesh by the pitiless bronzen
Weapons, if e'er upon turning, the back of one of the fighters
Lay exposed; and many clean through their bucklers were wounded.
Everywhere towers and copings were spattered with blood of the
Blood that was shed on either side, Achaean and Trojan.   [heroes,
Natheless not even so could the sons of Achaia be routed,
Holding as holdeth a woman, a careful work-hand, a balance—
Poising the weight and the wool upon opposite scales, she uplifteth
Both sides level, to win some pitiful wage for her children:
Even so nicely between them the beam of the battle was balanced
Up to the moment when Zeus gave Hector victorious glory,
Priam's son, who leaped first within the rampart Achaean.
Then with a ringing shout he called aloud to the Trojans:

"Rouse ye, Trojans, tamers of ſteeds, and break down the Argive
Rampart; hurl on their galleys brands fierce-blazing with fire!"

Thus he spake as he urged them on; all ears were attentive;
All in a mass rushed ſtraight at the wall; then, wielding their weapons,
Keen spears, boldly would climb the turreted fortifications.
Hector himself, though, seized and carried a ſtone that was lying
There at the gateway—thick at the base, but above it was tapered
Sharp to a point; no two men, the ſtoutest now of the people,
Lightly could heave it and load it perchance from the ground on a wagon,
Such as mortals are now; but with ease all alone *he* could swing it;
Crooked-counseling Cronus' son had lightened it for him.
Even as, lifting and bearing a ram's fleece lightly, a shepherd
Holdeth it in one hand, and slight is the burden upon him:
Even so Hector, uphoiſting the ſtone, bore it ſtraight at the folding
Panels that guarded the entry, compact, yea, ſtubbornly fitted,
Twofold panels and tall, with a double crossbar that held them,
Lapping within; but the bolt shot fast to secure them was single.
Coming up close, he took firm ſtand and hurled at the middle,
Bracing his feet far apart to give full force to his hurling.
Off then he burst both hinges at once, and the ſtone fell inward,   [bars
Under its own weight; the panels on either side groaned, and the cross-

Held no longer; they parted; the doorwings splintered asunder
Under the rush of the stone, while bounded the glorious Hector
In, his dark face like the sudden night; he blazed with the wondrous
Dazzling bronze of the armor with which he had clothed him; two lances
Held he firm in his hands; no mortal could, meeting, have stayed him,
Only a god, when he leaped through the gates; his eyes blazed with fire.
Wheeling about then, he called aloud through the throng to the Trojans,
Bidding them leap o'er the wall; *they* eagerly heeded his urging;
Some of them leaped o'er the rampart at once, while others were pouring
In through the firm-wrought gates; the Danaans, stricken with panic,
Fled 'mid the hollow ships; and uproar constant ascended.

ILIAD · XIII · (N)

The Greeks, with Troy's bold power dismayed,
Are cheered by Neptune's secret aid.

ZEUS, now once he had brought near the galleys the Trojans and
⠀Left either host at the ships to suffer labor and hardship [Hector,
Endlessly. He, however, turned back his radiant glances
Far and looked down on the land of the Thracians, breeders of horses,
Mysians also that fight hand to hand, and the proud Hippomolgi,
Fed upon mare's milk, and also the Abii, justest of mortals;
No more at all did he turn upon Troy his radiant glances,
For in his heart he deemed that surely no one of th' immortal
Gods would come again to the Danaans' help or the Trojans'.

⠀⠀⠀Nor was the mighty Earth-shaker a blind watch keeping the mean
Marveling much at the battle and warfare, while he was seated   [time,
High on the topmost summit of Samos, Thracia's island,
Forested richly; for thence was all Ida unfolded before him
Open to view, the Achaean ships, and the city of Priam.
There he was sitting, emerged from the sea; the Achaeans he pitied
Now o'ercome by the Trojans; with Zeus he was mightily angered.
Straightway then he descended the rugged side of the mountain,
Faring with fleet foot on; the highlands quaked and the forests
Under the feet immortal, as onward he sped, of Poseidon.
Three strides mightily stridden, a fourth stride brought him to Aegae,
Unto his goal, where stood, far-famed, in the depths of the inlet,
Mansions gleaming with gold, indestructible, builded for alway.
Thither he went, and he coupled his bronze-hoofed steeds to his chariot —
Rapid the horses in flight, with their gold manes streaming about them —
Put on his body his raiment of gold; then, grasping the whipstock,
Wrought full deftly and golden, he mounted aloft on the chariot,
Forth then, over the waves, went driving, while under him sea-beasts
Gamboled from out deep coverts on all sides, knowing their sovereign;

Ay, and the sea ſtood parted asunder in gladness. Swiftly
Flying along, with the axle of bronze unwetted beneath him,
Bore him the ſteeds, light-leaping away to the galleys Achaean.

On came thronging the Trojans like to a flame or a whirlwind.
    There is a wide-spaced cave in the deep-sea depths of the inlet,
Midway between the rugged Imbros and Tenedos Island;
Earth-shaking lord Poseidon there halted and ſtabled his coursers,
Loosing them first from the car, and cast down ambrosial forage
Unto their feeding; golden the hobbles he bound on their fetlocks,
Not to be broken or loosed, that they the return of their maſter
There should await, but *he* fared forth to the host of Achaeans.

    On came thronging the Trojans like to a flame or a whirlwind.
Heċtor, the scion of Priam, they followed, insatiably raging,
Yelling, and shouting amain; and they hoped to capture th' Achaean
Galleys and slay right there all the bravest men of the army.
Nay! but Poseidon, the Shaker of earth and of earth the Engirdler,
Issuing forth from the salt-sea depth, now roused up the Argives,
Lik'ning himself in his form and his voice unwearied to Calchas.
First he called to the Ajaxes twain, who were eager for battle:

    "Yours now, Ajaxes twain, to rescue the folk of Achaeans,
If ye are mindful of might, unmindful of panic that chilleth!
Verily naught do I fear the invincible hands of the Trojans
Elsewhere, though in a mob they've clambered over the rampart;
Howsoe'er many they be, the well-greaved Achaeans will slay them.
Here, though, greatly I dread lest haply some evil befall us,
Here, where, like to a flame, mad Heċtor is leading them onward,
Heċtor, that vaunts himself the son of Zeus, the all mighty.
Would some god in the spirit of you twain only implant it
Both to abide here ſturdy yourselves and to order the others!
So would ye drive him back, perchance, from the swift-faring galleys,
Vehement although he be, e'en though the Olympian rouse him."

    Thus spake the Shaker, th' Engirdler of earth, and then with his
Smote them both, and he filled the twain with powerful valor, [sceptre
Lightened also their limbs, their legs and their hands up above them.
He himself, as a hawk of swift wing darteth in flying,
When, from a crag high-tow'ring and sheer, swift downward it swoop-
Over the plain in pursuit of some other bird as it flieth —   [eth

266

Poseidon Rising from the Sea

So from the twain quickly darted away Earth-shaker Poseidon.
Ajax, fleet son of Oïleus, was first of the twain to discern him;
Instantly then he addressed great Telamonian Ajax:

"Ajax, one of the gods who dwell in Olympus commands us,
Taking the form of our augur, to battle amain at the galleys;
Calchas, though, it is not, the diviner and seer of the godhead,
Seeing I readily knew the gait of his knees and his ankles,
As he was going away — full easy to know are the godheads.
As for myself, the heart in my own dear breast is impatient,
Still more eagerly urging me on to war and to battle;
Lusting above are my hands for the fight and my feet underneath me."

Quick in his turn made answer and spake Telamonian Ajax:
"Likewise *my* hands, too, invincible, grasping the javelin,
Rage, and valor ariseth within me; my feet underneath me
Both dart eagerly on, for a yearning is mine to encounter
Priam's son, Hector, in single fight, though he ceaselessly rageth."

Thus they two were conversing with such words, one with the
Glad in the battle-joy that God in their hearts had implanted.   [other,
Meanwhile the Girdler of earth, from the rear, roused up the Achaeans,
Who at the swift ships' sides were then refreshing their spirits.
Their dear limbs had been loosed by grievous labor of combat,
Yea, and likewise anguish had entered their souls at beholding
Trojans who in a mob had clambered over the rampart.
Looking upon them, they let the tear-drops fall from their eyelids,
Seeing they thought they would never escape the bane; but Poseidon
Lightly mingled among them and rallied the doughty battalions.
Teucer — he was the first — then Leïtus found he and summoned
Hero Peneleos next and Deïpyrus also and Thoas,
Ay, and Meriones too, and Antilochus, lords of the war-cry —
All with his wingèd words now Poseidon spurred to the combat:

"Shame on you, Argives, shame, ye striplings, whom I had trusted
Surely to bring salvation, if only ye'd fight, to the galleys!
Well, if instead it is ye that retreat from the desperate warfare,
Now hath that day dawned, when ye by the Trojans are conquered.
Gods! how mighty a marvel is this with mine eyes I'm beholding,
Terrible, too, and methought such like would ne'er be accomplished —

269

Trojans advancing against these galleys of ours! But aforetime
Like unto tremulous hinds these foes — like hinds in the wildwood,
Delicate morsels for pards and jackals and wolves, as they wander
Utterly feeble and faint, unthrilled with the rapture of battle:
So were the Trojans of old, just unwilling to counter Achaeans
Or to abide their hands, their fury, for even a moment.
Now by the hollow ships they are fighting, far from the city —
Thanks to our leader's blunder, and thanks to the people's remissness,
Who for their strife with him will not join in defense of the galleys,
Swift-faring; nay, they suffer themselves to be slaughtered beside them!
But if indeed and insooth sole cause of the evil is only
Atreus' hero-son, wide-ruling king Agamemnon,
Seeing that he hath dishonored the fleet-footed scion of Peleus,
Not even so is it *ours* to refrain any wise from the battle;
Nay, let us heal the wound; to be healed are the hearts of the noble.
Ye no longer do well to relax your impetuous prowess,
All of you that are best in the army. Truly would never
I pick quarrel with any, whoe'er was remiss in the warfare,
Were he a weakling; with you, however, I'm heartily angry.
Faint-hearts! soon will ye make the mischief greater, believe me,
Somehow through such remissness. Let each then wake in his bosom
Indignation and shame; for, believe me, great strife hath arisen.
Look ye, the mighty Hector, good at the war-cry, is fighting
Here at the ships and has burst the gates and the long bar asunder!"

So the Enfolder of earth kept calling and roused the Achaeans.
Round the Ajaxes twain then took their stand the battalions —
Strong hosts, that Ares, on meeting them, would not make light of,
Neither Athena that urgeth the war-hosts; for they had been chosen
All as the best and awaited the Trojans and Hector, the godlike,
Serrying spear on spear and shield on shield overlapping,
Buckler on buckler and helm on helm, and hero on hero;
Horsehair crests, on the ridges of helmets agleam, as they nodded,
Touched one another — so densely they stood compacted together;
Lances were leveled in line, broad-brandished in hands that upheld them
Boldly; their hearts leaped forward; all lusted impatient for battle.

Forward the Trojans in mass came charging; Hector was leading,

Pressing straight on, as a rolling rock escaped from a cliff-side,
Thrust from a mountainous crest, when a rain-fed torrent of winter
Rends with a flood prodigious the base of the shameless cliff-side;
High-upbounding, it flieth amain, and the forest beneath it
Echoes; and ever it speeds unswerved, till it reaches the level
Plain, then rolls no further for all its impetuous urgence:
Even so Hector awhile made menace of easily winning
Unto the sea in his course to the barracks and galleys Achaean,
Slaughtering. Once, however, he countered the serried battalions,
There, though pursuing hard on, he was halted; the sons of Achaia,
Smiting on their side amain with swords and two-edgèd lances,
Forced him away from themselves, while *he* reeled backward and yielded.
Then with a ringing shout he called to his Trojan companions:

"Trojans, Dardanians, Lycians, that joy in closest encounter,
Stand now firm at my side; not long the Achaeans will hold me,
E'en though arrayed compact and solid in ranks as a tower.
Nay, methinks, they will yield before my spear, if but truly
Spurs me the best of the gods, the loud-thundering husband of Hera."

Thus he spake and aroused the might and spirit of each man.
'Mongst them Deïphobus strode, the valiant scion of Priam,
High in heart, with his shield, all evenly rounded, before him,
Lightly advancing his feet, as he stepped forth under its cover.
Aiming directly at *him*, with a thrust of his glittering javelin,
Merion smote, and he missed not, the shield all evenly rounded,
Bull's-hide shield, but he pierced it by no means through; for the long
Far too soon for that at the ferrule snapped; and the Trojan   [lance
Held off the bull's-hide shield at his arm's length and feared in his
Wise-heart Merion's spear; but the Argive hero retreated   [spirit
Back to the throng of his comrades, although he was grievously angered
Both for the victory lost and the spear he had utterly shattered.
So then he hasted to go to the barracks and galleys Achaean,
Meaning to bring back a long, keen lance he had left at his barrack.

Meanwhile rose from the rest an unquenchable cry, as they battled.
First to lay low his man was Teucer, Telamon's scion —
Imbrius, spearman, the son of Mentor, the wealthy in horses.
Imbrius dwelt in Pedaeum, ere came the sons of Achaia,

Wedded to Medesicaste, a natural daughter of Priam.
But when the Danaan galleys arrived, well balanced and curving,
Back to Ilium he came and was eminent there 'mongst the Trojans,
Dwelling in Priam's house, who treated him just like his children.
Him, underneath the ear, with his long lance Telamon's scion
Pierced, then drew out the spear; and he fell like unto an ash-tree
High on the crest of a mountain, far seen from every direction —
Stricken with bronze, it brings to the earth its delicate leafage:
Thus fallen, round him resounded his arms, rich-carven and bronzen.
Teucer darted with eager intent to strip off his armor;
Hector with glittering spear quick hurled at him in his onset;
Teucer, watching it come, eluded the bronze-tipped weapon
Barely; it struck on the breast of Amphimachus, Cteatus' scion
(Actor's son was he), as now he returned to the battle.
Crashing he fell to the earth, and his armor rattled upon him.
Forward dashed Hector, to tear the casque, close-fitting his temples,
Off from the head of his foeman, Amphimachus, great-hearted, fallen.
Ajax, howe'er, with his shining javelin thrust out at Hector
Dashing ahead; but he nowhere could reach his flesh he'd encased in
Terrible bronze all over; but, piercing the boss of his buckler,
Ajax with main force thrust him away, and he gave ground backward
Off from the dead men both, whom th' Achaeans dragged from the bat-
Stichius then and the goodly Menestheus, chieftains of Athens,　　[tle.
Back to the host of Achaeans conveyed Amphimachus' body —
Imbrius' body the Ajaxes, filled with impetuous valor.
Even as when two lions a goat from the keen-toothed beagles
Snatch and are bearing away, far off through the depths of a thicket,
High from the ground in their jaws firm-grasping and holding the body:
Holding *him* thus aloft, the Ajaxes, helmeted heroes,
Stripped off his armor; his head from his delicate neck then Oïleus'
Son hewed off in his wrath on account of Amphimachus' slaying;
Wheeling around, he hurled it; it rolled like a ball through the Trojan
Throng, and down in the dust at the feet of Hector it landed.
　　Verily then did wrath lay hold on the heart of Poseidon,
Seeing the son of his son in the direful combat thus fallen;
So then he hasted to go by the barracks and galleys Achaean,

Urging the Danaans on, while woes he contrived for the Trojans.
There it was then he encountered Idomeneus, spearman renownèd,
Coming away from a comrade he found from the battle returning
Newly and wounded behind the knee with a sharp bronzen weapon.
Comrades had brought him away from the fight; Idomeneus ordered
Surgeons to tend him and went to his tent; for still he was eager
Warfare to face; and the mighty Earth-shaker, meeting, addressed him,
Lik'ning himself in his voice unto Thoas, son of Andraemon,
Who, in all the region of Pleuron and Calydon lofty,
Ruled the Aetolians; honored was he as a god by the people:

"Counselor thou of the Cretans, Idomeneus, where is thy menace
Gone, wherewith the Achaeans' sons once menaced the Trojans?"

Answering him, then spake Idomeneus, leader of Cretans:

"Thoas, indeed there is no man, so far as my knowledge extendeth,
Who is to blame; none lacketh among us in knowledge of warfare.
Spiritless dread holds no one aloof; not anyone shunneth
War and its woe by yielding to cowardice; nay, it is merely,
So it appears, that it must have seemed good to all-mighty Cronion
That the Achaeans should perish unnamed here, far from their Argos.
Thou, however (for thou wast before this redoubtable, Thoas,
Even inciting another, if thou sawest anyone yielding) —
Therefore slacken not now but command each man and exhort him."

Then unto him the shaker of earth, Poseidon, made answer:

"Never, Idomeneus, never may that man from Troy have returning
Unto his home — nay, here let dogs make sport of his carcass! —
Whosoever this day is wilfully slack in the battle.
Come now, take up thy arms and away! These matters in common
Urge us, if haply insooth — two only — in aught we avail them.
Union it is brings prowess to men, ay, even to cowards;
We, however, know well how to fight, yea, e'en with the bravest."

Thus spake the god and mingled again in the warriors' tumult.
But when Idomeneus, coming, arrived at his well-builded barrack,
Beautiful armor he donned on his body; he caught up his lances
Twain and set forth on his way with a gleam like the lightning Cronion
Seizes in hand and launches forth from the radiant Olympus,
Showing a sign unto mortals; afar seen, glitter its flashes:

273

Suchwise shimmered the bronze on the breast of Idomeneus running.
Just at this juncture his squire, the good Meriones, met him,
While he was still near the barrack; for after a bronzen javelin
Merion was going—to fetch it. Idomeneus mighty addressed him:
"Molus' son, fleet-footed Meriones, dearest of comrades,
Why, pray, hast thou°come hither and left the strife and the warfare?
Hast thou received some wound? Doth barb of an arrow distress thee?
Or art come with some message to seek *me?* I can assure thee
I yearn not to sit in my tent but to mingle in battle."
　　Prudent Meriones then made answer in turn and addressed him:
"King of the bronze-clad Cretans, Idomeneus, counseling captain,
Hither I come—peradventure a spear hath been left in thy barrack—
Meaning to fetch it, for that I had carried aforetime was shattered
When it was hurled and crashed on proud Deïphobus' buckler."
　　Then unto him made answer Idomeneus, leader of Cretans:
"Javelins, if thou wilt, thou may'st find there, one or e'en twenty,
Standing within my barrack, against the shimmering side walls,
Spears of the Troy-folk, war-loot I take from the fallen; I fancy
I'm not noted for standing at long range warring with foemen.
Wherefore *I* possess lances and bucklers, bossed in the middle,
Helmets, and corselets, too, far-flashing, proud in effulgence."
　　Prudent Meriones then made answer in turn and addressed him:
"Truly indeed at my barrack and black ship spoils in abundance
Lie, that I ravished from Trojans, but not to my hand are they ready.
Yea, for methinketh that neither am I forgetful of valor,
I who stand with the vanguard aye in the battle that bringeth
Glory to mortals, whenever the strife of warfare ariseth.
Haply another, meseems, of the bronze-clad sons of Achaia
May not be ware of my valor, but thou art the one that should know it."
　　Answering him, then spake Idomeneus, leader of Cretans:
"Well do I know how valorous thou; what need to recount it?
Nay, if beside the galleys the doughtiest chiefs were selected
All, for an ambush, wherein the merit of men is detected
Best, and a coward revealeth himself, and a valiant, most clearly;
Seeing a dastard's colors turn quickly from one to another,
Neither his spirit is able to bide firm-fixed in his bosom—

Ever from knee unto knee, yea, foot unto foot he is shifting,
Whileas the heart in his breast thumps loud and quick in its throbbing,
Boding his doom, and his teeth keep up a continual chatter;
Whereas a brave man's color by no means changeth, and *he* is
Never unnerved from the moment he enters the ambush of heroes,
Nay, but he prayeth to mix full soon in the woful encounter.
Not in an ambush would any disparage thy strength or thy valor.
For, if an enemy struck thee in grapple or e'en from a distance,
Never a dart would fall on thy back or thy neck behind thee,
Nay, it would surer encounter belike thy belly or bosom,
Hurrying eagerly on toward the foremost group of the fighters.
Come now, let us no more be talking of such things, as children,
Loitering here, lest someone perchance grow hotly indignant;
Nay, make haste to the barrack and get thee a ponderous weapon."

Thus spake he, and his comrade, Meriones, peer of swift Ares,
When he had speedily fetched him a bronze-tipped lance from the barrack,
After Idomeneus fared, and his thoughts were intent upon warfare.
Even as Ares, the bane of mortals, marcheth to battle,
Followed along by his dear-loved son, the mighty and fearless
Panic, that filleth with terror a stout-hearted warrior even.
These two, harnessed to march on the Ephyri, issue from Thracia,
Or with the great-hearted Phlegyans to war, yet never they hearken
Equally unto them both — they grant one only the glory:
Suchwise Meriones then and Idomeneus, leaders of heroes,
Set forth into the battle, all harnessed in gleaming bronze armor. [him:

First then Meriones spake to his comrade a word and addressed
"Son of Deucalion, where dost thou mean to enter the combat?
Whether, perchance, to the right of the war-line, or in the middle,
Or, peradventure, the left? For the long-haired Achaeans nowhere
Else, I'm expecting, will be so likely to fail in the conflict."

Him then answered in turn Idomeneus, leader of Cretans:
"Others are there for defending the ships drawn up in the middle;
There are the Ajaxes twain and Teucer — of all the Achaeans
Best in archery, good, too, in stress of a standing encounter.
These then will give him his fill of fight, though eager for warfare,
Even Priam's son, Hector, though *he* be exceedingly mighty.

Uphill work will he find it, for all his keenness for battle,
Their invincible hands, their valor to vanquish, and kindle
Fire in the ships, if it be not Cronion himself that will hurtle
Brands bright-flaming upon them, the swift-sailing ships of Achaia.
Never to man would he yield, that great Telamonian Ajax,
Never to earthborn mortal that feeds on the fruit of Demeter,
Man to be cloven with bronze or crushed with boulder enormous;
Nay, not e'en would he yield to that breaker of ranks, to Achilles —
Not in a stand-up fight; but in swiftness with him is no rival.
So to the left of the host do thou keep us, to find out the soonest
Whether glory we gain for ourselves or bestow on another."

   Thus spake he; and his comrade, Meriones, peer of swift Ares,
Led the way, till they came to the host, where Idomeneus bade him.

   Now as they saw Idomeneus, like unto flame in his prowess —
Him and his squire, all harnessed in armor cunningly moulded —
All, in a clamorous throng, went rushing together against him.
Then did a common struggle arise at the sterns of the galleys.
Even as eddies are sped, when shrill winds gusty are blowing
All on a day when the dust along the highways lies thickest —
Vasty the cloud of dust that the winds then whirl up together:
So came crowded the battle of those men eager in spirit
There with the keen-edged bronze in the throng to slay one another.
Ay, and the battle, the ruin of mortals, bristled with lances —
Long, flesh-tearing — they held in their hands, and the radiance bronzen
Dazzled the eyes in reflexion abroad from the glittering helmets,
Breastplates burnished afresh, and the shimmering shields of the heroes
Rushing together amain. Right hardy of heart were a mortal
Who could rejoice at beholding and grieve not over the travail.

   Then did the two strong sons of Cronus, of contrary purpose,
Fashion grievous affliction alike for the men that were heroes.
Zeus it was willed that the vict'ry incline to the Trojans and Hector,
Since he would honor fleet-footed Achilles; *but* he would noway
Will that the host of Achaeans should utterly perish at Ilium;
Thetis it was, with her strong-hearted son, whom *he* would give glory.
Lord Poseidon aroused the Argives, coming amongst them,
Stealing forth from the foam-flecked sea, for he sorrowed to see them

Now o'ercome by the Trojans; with Zeus he was mightily angered.
Both these gods had a lineage common; one was their birth-place;
Zeus was the elder by birth and surpassed his brother in knowledge.
So Poseidon avoided bringing them help in the open,
But in the guise of a man he ever secretly spurred them.
Over the war-hosts thus these brothers extended alternate
Cords of a mighty strife and a balanced battle and stretched them,
Not to be broken or loosed — but the knees of many it loosened.

    Then, even though he was grizzled, Idomeneus called on the Ar-
Leaped in among the Trojans, and wakened terror among them, [gives,
Slaying Othryoneus, who, a sojourner there from Cabesus,
Lately had come after hearing the news of the outbreak of warfare.
Giftless, he wooed for the fairest in form of the daughters of Priam,
Even Cassandra, but offered a promise of mighty achievement,
Namely, to drive those sons of Achaia perforce out of Troyland!
Priam, the aged, gave him his word — with a nod did he seal it —
Promised to give her; and *he* was now fighting with faith in the promise.
Straight at *him* Idomeneus aimed with his glittering javelin,
Cast it, and smote him, loftily striding; the breastplate upon him —
Bronze though it was — availed not; the javelin was fixed in his belly.
Crashing he fell; and Idomeneus spake and boasted above him:

    "Truly, Othryoneus, thee do I praise above all mortal
Men, if indeed thou accomplish for him all things thou hast promised
Priam, Dardanus' son; in turn *he* promised his daughter.
Yea, we also would promise as much and would duly fulfil it,
Even to give thee the fairest in form of Atrides' own daughters,
Bring her from Argos hither for bridal, if only thou help us
Capture and utterly sack the folk-thronged Ilian city.
Nay, come along for a marriage-covenant, there at the sea-borne
Galleys; *we* will not higgle for gifts of wooing, I tell thee."

    Speaking thus, by the foot the hero Idomeneus drew him
Out from the furious conflict; but Asius came as a helper,
Footman in front of his horses — the team breathed aye on his shoulders,
Since that his squire, the driver, so held them; his spirit impelled him
Right at the Cretan to cast; but his foe with his spear was beforehand,
Under his chin struck his throat, and drove clean through it the weapon.

Thereat he fell with a crash, as an oak-tree falls, or a poplar,
Or as a tall-grown pine, which craftsmen aloft on the mountains
Fell, with axes whetted afresh, for the timber of galleys:
Thus stretched out, he was lying in front of his horses and chariot,
Heavily groaning and clutching the dust all sodden and gory.
Then was the driver dumfounded—he kept not his wits as aforetime,
Neither attempted, indeed, to escape from the hands of the foeman,
Wheeling his horses about; but Antilochus, sturdy in battle,
Smote him and pinned his body's middle; the breastplate upon him—
Bronze though it was—availed not; the javelin was fixed in his belly.
He, as he panted for breath, from the well-wrought chariot tumbled.
Great-souled Nestor's son, Antilochus, captured the horses,
Drove them away from the foe to the side of the well-greaved Achaeans.

Then 'gainst Idomeneus came Deïphobus, drawing full nigh him,
Grieving for Asius slain, and he hurled his glittering javelin.
Natheless Idomeneus dodged it, the lance of bronze, as he eyed him,
Safe hid under the spread of his shield all evenly balanced,
Shield that was rounded out with hides of bulls and with shining
Bronze, that he used to bear, and with arm-rods twain it was fitted.
Crouched he completely beneath it; the bronze spear hurtled above him,
Rasping the rim of the shield, as the javelin, grazing upon it,
Sped—not vainly insooth—from the hand of the Trojan:
Hippasus' son, Hypsenor, it smote, the shepherd of peoples,
Deep in the liver; his limbs were instantly loosened beneath him.
Then Deïphobus boasted with loud cry fearful above him:

"Ah me! not unavenged lies Asius! Truly, methinketh,
Now as he goeth to Hades, the mighty warder of hell-gate,
He will rejoice in his heart, since I have furnished him escort."

Proudly Deïphobus spake; but sorrow came to the Argives,
Stirred most deeply the soul of Antilochus, wise-hearted hero;
Neither, in spite of his sorrow, was he unheeding his comrade;
Nay, but he ran and bestrode him—held o'er him his shield to protect
Two of his trusty comrades uplifting the hero from under,   [him—
Goodly Alastor and Echius's son, whose name was Mecisteus.
Back to the hollow ships they bore him, heavily groaning.

Neither relaxed Idomeneus aught of his prowess, but ever

Strove or to cover with Erebus-night some one of the Trojans
Or else perish himself in repelling doom from th' Achaeans.
Then was slain the dear son of a nurseling of Zeus, Aesyëtes—
Even the hero Alcathoüs—son-in-law to Anchises;
He had wedded his eldest daughter, Hippodamia,
Child well loved in heart of her father and worshipful mother
There in the court, excelling in handiwork, wisdom, and beauty
All other maids coequal in age; and the hero accounted
Best in all wide Troyland had therefore won her in marriage.
Under Idomeneus then Poseidon subdued this chieftain,
Witching his radiant eyes; he fettered his glorious members,
So he could neither retreat to the rear nor parry the weapon;
Rather he stood as a pillar unmoved, a tree of the forest,
Foliage-crowned on high, as the hero Idomeneus smote him
Square on his breast with his lance and cleft the tunic about him—
Tunic of bronze that had warded aforetime death from his body.
Now, though, harsh it resounded and loud, bored through by the jave-
Down he fell with a crash, for the spear in his heart was implanted, [lin.
Heart that was panting and keeping the spear's butt-end in a quiver
Still, but anon the powerful Ares there spent its fury.
Then Idomeneus boasted, loud-crying fearful above him:

  "Tell me, Deïphobus, shall we assume it a worthy requital
Three to have slain for one? For thou hast been boasting for nothing!
Nay, come ahead, good sir, now stand up against me, that haply
Thou may'st see what sort of offspring of Zeus I come hither:
First of all Zeus begat Minos to be a warder of Creta;
Minos himself in turn had a son, the faultless Deucalion;
Me Deucalion in turn begat to be lord over many
Men in the broad land of Crete; and now my galleys have brought me
Hither, a bane unto thee, thy sire, and the rest of the Trojans."

  Thus he spake and Deïphobus' mind was divided; he pondered
Whether he should withdraw and call to his aid as a comrade
One of the great-hearted Trojans or all alone make the venture.
Now, as thus he was thinking, it seemed to him to be better
Unto Aeneas to go. Him he found in the rear of the tumult
Standing at rest—he was ever indignant with Priam, the goodly,

For that he did him no honor, though famed among men for his valor.
Near him Deïphobus stood and with accents wingèd addressed him:
    "Counselor thou of the Trojans, Aeneas, it greatly behooveth
Thee to defend thy kinsman, if kinship affect thee at all now.
Come with me; let us succor Alcathoüs; he was thy sister's
Husband; he nurtured thee in his home, when thou wast but little.
Him Idomeneus, famed for his spear, hath stripped of his armor."
    Thus he spake and aroused the heart in his bosom; he started
After Idomeneus, eagerly turning his thoughts upon warfare.
Never of flight, however, Idomeneus thought, as a youngster,
Nay, stood his ground — as when some boar in the mountains, reliant
All on his strength, abideth the hue and cry of assailing
Men in a lonely spot, and he bristles his back up above him;
Both his eyes are ablaze with fire; he whetteth his champing
Tusks and is eager to hold at bay both the hounds and the hunters:
Thus Idomeneus, famed for his spear, stood his ground nor retreated,
Biding Aeneas, who ran to the rescue. He called to his comrades
Loudly, looking to these: Ascalaphus, Aphareus also,
Merion, Deïpyrus, too, and Antilochus, lords of the war-cry.
Urging them on to the battle, with wingèd words he addressed them:
    "Hither, my friends, to defend me, alone, as I am, and I'm dreading
Terribly now Aeneas, fleet-footed, who rushes upon me.
He is exceedingly strong for slaughtering men in a battle,
Full in the bloom of youth, wherein one's strength is the greatest;
But if our ages were equal and temper, as now it is, quickly
He should achieve a great vict'ry, or I myself should achieve it."
    Thus he spake; and they all, like-minded, one in their spirit,
Stood hard by one another with shields close-laid on their shoulders.
Called out loud to his comrades on his side also Aeneas,
Glancing the while at the goodly Agenor, Deïphobus, Paris,
Who were captains of Trojans, as he was; then came the people
Following after them, as sheep will follow the wether
Out from the pasture to drink, while leapeth the heart of the shepherd:
E'en so, deep in his bosom, the heart of Aeneas with gladness
Leaped at beholding a host of his people following after.
    Over Alcathoüs now with a rush all mingled in battle

Close, with long, smooth spears; the bronze engirdling their bodies
Rang out fearful and loud all through the press in their thrusting
'Gainst one another; but two outvied the others in warcraft,
Even Aeneas and Cretan Idomeneus, rivals of Ares;
Ever with pitiless bronze each hewed at the flesh of the other.
Now did Aeneas first at Idomeneus hurl with his javelin.
Watching it come, the Cretan eluded the bronze-tipped weapon.
Quivering spent itself in the earth Aeneas's spear-point;
Only in vain from his stalwart hand its way had been speeded.
Ay, but Idomeneus smote Oenomaüs square in the belly,
Breaking a plate of his corselet; the weapon tore out his entrails.
Down he fell in the dust and clutched at the ground with his fingers.
Then Idomeneus drew the spear, far-shadowing, quickly
Out of the corpse, but the beauteous gear of his foe he could nowise
Strip from his shoulders as well, so crowded the missiles upon him;
For, when he made a charge, his legs no longer were steady,
Either for plunging after his spear or for shunning another's.
Though in a standing encounter he fended the pitiless moment,
Yet to retreat his feet no longer swiftly could bear him.
Step by step he retired, while Deïphobus launched with his shining
Spear, inasmuch as his hate for Idomeneus still was relentless.
This time also he missed, but he smote with his weapon the war-god's
Scion, Ascalaphus; right through his shoulder the powerful javelin
Sped; he fell in the dust and clutched at the ground with his fingers.
Neither was loud-voiced, powerful Ares yet ware there had fallen
Even a son of his own in the strenuous conflict of battle.
Ares under the clouds all gold on a peak of Olympus
Sat, for there he was held, both he and the other immortals
All, from the war restrained by Zeus's prohibitive counsels.

　　Over Ascalaphus now with a rush all mingled in battle
Close, and Deïphobus tore from Ascalaphus' temples the shining
Helmet; Meriones then, a rival of fleet-footed Ares,
Sprang to the forefront, wounding his arm with a javelin; the visored
Crest of the helmet clanged as it fell to the ground from his fingers.
Swooping again like a vulture, Meriones bounded upon him,
Tore from Deïphobus' upper arm the powerful weapon,

Then drew back once more to the throng of his mates; but Polites, [him,
Who was Deïphobus' brother, with hands at his waist thrown around
Led him away from the war's dread din, till he came to the fleet-foot
Steeds that awaited him there in the rear of the warfare and combat,
Standing there with their driver and car with its rich decorations.
These then bore him away to the citadel, heavily groaning,   [ceps.
Foredone; the blood flowed down from the fresh-made wound in his bi-
    Meanwhile rose from the rest an unquenchable cry, as they battled.
Then, as he rushed upon Aphareus, son of Caletor, Aeneas   [javelin.
Smote the throat, which was turned toward him, with his keen-pointed
Sidewise drooping his head then, he fell with his shield and his helmet
All in a heap, and about him was death poured, the spirit-despoiler.
Thereat Antilochus, watching for Thoön, as round he was turning,
Leaping upon him, inflicted a death-wound, seeing he severed
Cleanly the vein on the back, that up to the neck extendeth —
Severed it quite. In the dust outstretched he fell and supinely,
Both of his hands outspreading for help to his own dear companions.
At him Antilochus sprang, to strip from his shoulders his armor,
Watching alert; for the Trojans, on all sides gathered about him,
Smote on his shield, so broad and shimmering, yet were unable
Even to graze, with the merciless bronze, behind it the tender
Flesh of Antilochus, seeing a god, earth-shaking Poseidon,
Guarded the son of Nestor e'en in the storm of the missiles.
Ay, for he never was free from the foemen; ever among them
Still he was turning and never his spear held quiet but alway
Brandished and shook it, and meanwhile ever he aimed in his spirit
Either to hurl it at someone or rush close-fighting upon him.
Yet in the mid-press aiming, he 'scaped not Adamas' notice,
Asius' son, who smote the midst of his shield with his keen bronze,
Rushing upon him from close at hand; but the dark-haired Poseidon
Deadened the force of the spear, for he grudged him the life of the hero.
Half of it stayed in the shield of Antilochus — just as may stand up
Haply a well charred stake — and half on the ground lay broken.
Back to the throng of his fellows, evading his doom, he retreated.
After him, as he departed, Meriones followed and smote him
Squarely with lance between his groin and his navel, a region

Where is a wound the most baneful of all to mortals unhappy.
There he implanted his spear; and the Trojan followed the javelin,
Writhing about it, just like a bull in the mountains, that herdsmen
Bind with withes and drag him by force, though wholly unwilling:
Even so Adamas, smitten, a short while writhed, but a little,
Till, come nigh him, the hero Meriones plucked forth the javelin
Out of his flesh; and his eyes were straightway clouded in darkness.

　　Helenus, fighting at hand, then smote Deïpyrus' temple,
Smote with a Thracian blade full weighty and tore off his helmet;
Stricken, it tumbled to earth far-flung, and a certain Achaean —
One of the host — as it rolled at his feet, retrieved it and saved it.
Then the blackness of Erebus covered Deïpyrus' eyelids.

　　Grief then seized Menelaüs Atrides, good at the war-cry;
Straightway he went with a threat 'gainst Helenus, royal, heroic,
Shaking his keen-edged spear, as the other was aiming an arrow.
Both at the instant made ready to launch at each other a missile,
One with his keen-pointed lance, the other with shaft from his bowstring.
Priam's son then smote him right square on the breast with his arrow,
Struck on the corselet's plate, but off flew the bitter arrow.
Even as when, on a winnowing-floor from a wide-shaped shovel
Either the black-skinned beans go bounding off or the chick-pease
Under the whistling wind and the swing of the winnower's shovel:
So from the corselet shielding the breast of renowned Menelaüs,
Glancing, flying afar, the bitter arrow went flying.
Atreus' son, Menelaüs, good at the war-cry, however,
Smote on the hand that was holding the polished bow, and the bronzen
Spear-head drave right through both the bow and the hand of the bow-
Back to the throng of his fellows, evading his doom, he retreated, [man.
Hanging his hand at his side, with the ash-spear trailing behind him.
Quickly the dart was extracted — Agenor, the great-hearted, drew it
Forth and bound up the hand in a tuft, well-twisted, of sheep's wool,
Made for a sling, that his squire had for him, shepherd of peoples.

　　Thereat darted Pisander direct at renowned Menelaüs —
Evil the fate that was leading him on unto death's consummation,
Fated for thee, Menelaüs, to slay in a terrible combat.
Now, as they came close up in the onrush 'gainst one another,

283

Atreus' son made a miss, and aside went glancing his javelin,
Whileas Pisander smote the shield of renowned Menelaüs;
Natheless he could not drive his missile of bronze clean through it:
Held in the broad shield's compass, the spear-shaft snapped at the fer-
Yet in his heart Pisander rejoiced and hoped for the vic̆t'ry.   [rule.
Quick then, drawing his sword all-ſtudded with silver, Atrides
Leaped at Pisander; but *he* drew from under his buckler a goodly
Battle-axe, forged of fine bronze and fitted with olive-wood handle,
Polished and long; both chiefs rushed at once, the one on the other.
Smiting the ridge of his helmet, thick-plumed with horsehair, Pisander
Sheared off the base of the plume; but Atrides full on the forehead
Countered, in onrush, over the base of the nose, and the bones cracked;
Stained with blood in the dust at his feet fell the eyes of Pisander;
Fallen, he writhed; Menelaüs his foot on the breast of his foeman
Set and ſtripped off his armor as spoil and spake a word boaſting:

    "This is the way ye will leave us the fleet-horsed Danaans' galleys,
Arrogant Trojans, who ne'er with the dreadful war-din are sated,
Also in other abusĕs in no way lacking and insults,
Wherewith ye made me ashamed, accursèd dogs! and ye trembled
Not in your hearts at the bitter wrath of Zeus, the loud-thund'ring
God of guest and of host, who will some time level your lofty
Keep; for my own wedded wife ye brought with her many possessions
Wantonly with you away — and she had entreated you kindly.
Now at the sea-faring galleys behold you with ruinous fire,
Eager to hurl it and luſting to slaughter the heroes Achaean.
Some time, though, ye shall cease, how eager soever, from warfare.
Zeus, O Father! — they say thy thought all others' excelleth,
Whether of men or of gods, and from thee come all these doings —
How can it be that indeed thou showest the insolent favor,
Favor to Trojans, whose is a will to iniquity ever,
Ever unsated a lust for the din of a well matched battle.
Cometh, of all things cometh, a surfeit — of sleeping, of loving
Even, of sweet song also it comes, of delec̆table dancing,
Whereof anyone chooseth to sate him in preference surely
Rather than war; but of battle the Trojans forever are sateless." [mor,
    Thus he spake and ſtripped from the body the blood-dripping ar-

284

Gave it unto his friends Menelaüs, the faultless; himself then
Forthwith haÅ¿tened away and mixed once more with the vanguard.

Thereupon king Pylaemenes' scion leaped out against him,
Even Harpalion, who followed his father belovèd to Troyland
Unto the war but returned—no, never again to his homeland.
Then with his javelin he smote on the boss of the shield of Atrides
Nearby, yet he could not drive his missile of bronze clean through it.
Back to the throng of his fellows, evading his doom, he retreated,
All round glancing, that none might touch his flesh with a weapon.
Howe'er, just as he went, Meriones let fly an arrow,
Tipped with bronze, and smote his right hip fairly. The missile
Passed through the bladder direÅ¿tly, and under the bone then it issued.
There sinking down, in the arms of his comrades belovèd, the hero,
Breathing his spirit away, outÅ¿tretched on the ground, was lying
Like to a worm; and the black blood flowed out; and the ground there
Him the great-hearted Paphlagonians busily tended,   [was wetted.
Lifting him into a chariot, and bore him to Ilium holy,
Sorrowing. With them, letting his tears fall, followed his father,
Hopeless that aught could ever atone for thc death of his offspring.

Fiercely wrathful in heart at the death of the hero was Paris;
This man had been his host 'mongÅ¿t the Paphlagonian people.
So in his wrath for his sake he let fly a bronze-fitted arrow.
There was a man, Euchenor, the son of the seer Polyïdus,
Wealthy withal and goodly, who dwelt in a palace in Corinth.
Well aware of his ruinous fate, he had boarded his galley.
Often indeed the good old man, Polyïdus, foretold it:
That he should die in his halls, worn down by a grievous afflicÅ¿tion,
Or by the galleys Achaean should fall overcome by the Trojans.
So he avoided at once that hard war-fine the Achaeans
Fixed and the hateful disease, to endure no anguish of spirit.
Under the jaw and the ear was the Argive smitten, and quickly
Life had forsaken his limbs, and hateful darkness came on him.

So in the fashion of fire, bright-blazing, these warriors battled.
Meantime HeÅ¿tor, belovèd of Zeus, heard not, and he knew not
Aught thereof, what slaughter his folk on the left of the galleys
Suffered at Argive hands, what glory th' Achaeans had won them

Haply; so was the Shaker of earth and of earth the Embracer
Mighty himself in defending and also in urging the Argives:
There he kept on where first he had leaped o'er the gates and the ram-
Where he had broken the serried ranks of the Danaan shieldmen, [part,
There where lay the vessels of Ajax and Protesilaüs,
High up-drawn on the beach of the foam-flecked sea; and above them
Lowest the Danaan wall had been builded; and there it was chiefly
Horses and men were engaged in the stress of furious combat.

    There the Boeotians and tunic-trailing Ionians also,
Phthians and Locrians, too, and with them renownèd Epeians
Hardly availed to withstand his assault on the ships nor were able
Ever to beat him away — that flame-like Hector, the goodly.
There were also the pick of Athenians; leader among them
Peteos' son, Menestheus; and gathered about him and followed
Phidas and Stichius also with Bias, the brave; of Epeians,
Meges, scion of Phyleus, Amphion and Dracius with him;
Steadfast in war, Podarces and Medon captained the Phthians.
One of these, Medon, was bastard son of the goodly Oïleus;
Thus was he brother, insooth, unto Ajax; he dwelt in a city,
Phylace, far from his homeland, because a man he had murdered
Brother of Eriopis, his stepdame, wife of Oïleus.
Th' other, Podarces, was son of Iphiclus, Phylacus' scion.
These in their panoplies stood at the head of the great-hearted Phthians,
Battling among Boeotians, the while they defended the galleys.

    Meantime never would Ajax, the fleet-footed son of Oïleus,
Stand off even a moment from Ajax, the great Telamonian.
But as in fallow land strains a yoke of wine-dark oxen,
One in accord, at the well-framed plough, and the sweat of them gathers
Round the roots of their horns — and it oozes there in abundance —
Saving the well polished yoke, naught holdeth the couple asunder,
Toiling along the furrow; the share cleaves the bound of the cornland:
So stood closely the Ajaxes twain in support of each other.
Now it was Telamon's son whom a numerous people attended,
Valiant comrades, who took his shield to relieve him, whenever
Sweat and weariness came upon his limbs, as he battled.
Not so the Locrians followed the great-souled Oïlean Ajax:

Their dear hearts were not ſtrong for a close-up ſtruggle in battle,
Seeing they had no helmets of bronze, thick-plumèd with horsehair;
Neither had they well-rounded shields nor javelins of ash-wood;
But in their bows, their arrows, and ſtrings of well-twiſted sheep's wool
Putting their trust, they had followed to Ilium with Ajax; and therewith,
Shooting their darts thick and fast, they broke the ranks of the Trojans.
So now those at the front in rich-adorned armor contended
Steadfast aye with the Trojans and bronzen-helmeted Hector,
While from behind, under cover, the rest kept shooting; the Trojans,
Dazed with the darts, no longer remembered the rapture of battle.

There in pitiful flight from the barracks and galleys the Trojans
Would have withdrawn, retreating again to Ilium windy,
Had not Pulydamas come to the valiant Hector and spoken:

. "Hector, hard of persuasion art thou unto them that would turn thee;
Since for the doings of war hath God over-measure endowed thee,
Therefore in counsel as well thou wouldst know better than others.
Yet thou'lt never be able to take all burdens upon thee;
Matters of war have been given by God unto one for a portion,
Dancing again to a second, the lute and the song to another;
Zeus of the far-borne voice in another's breast hath implanted
Sound underſtanding, and many are they that partake of its profit;
Yea, and many hath such an one saved, but himself best knows it.
So then I will proceed to declare what seems to me wisest:
Lo! all round and about thee is blazing a circlet of warfare,
But of the great-souled Trojans that now have passed over the rampart
Some in their harness are ſtanding aloof, while others are battling,
Few men pitted with many and scattered about 'mid the galleys.
Nay now, draw back a little and summon the bravest around thee,
All of them; then we may truly deliberate every counsel,
Whether indeed we shall hurl ourselves on the many-oared galleys,
If it be God now willeth to give us the vict'ry, or whether
We shall return unharmed from the ships; for greatly I fear me
Lest the Achaeans balance the debit of yeſterday, haply,
Seeing that ſtill at the galleys a man insatiate of warfare
Bides and no longer, I think, will wholly refrain him from battle." [sel;

Thus spake Pulydamas; Hector was pleased with his excellent coun-

Out from his war car forthwith he leaped to the ground in his armor;
Lifting his voice, with wingèd words he spake and addressed him:

"Here, O Pulydamas, hold thou all of the best of our warriors;
I, though, yonder will hasten and take my part in the battle;
Soon I will come back again when fitting instructions I've given."

Thus he spake and rushed away like an avalanche snowy,
Shouting aloud, and he flew through the ranks of allies and of Trojans.
These unto Panthoüs' son, to Pulydamas, lover of valor,
All quick hastened on hearing the voice, the bidding of Hector.
He in his search for Deïphobus, Helenus, royal and mighty,
Adamas, Asius' son, and the son of Hyrtacus, Asius, [them.
Ranged through the foremost ranks, somewhere, peradventure, to find
No more they could be found unharmed, untouched of destruction;
Nay, behold, even now at the sterns of the galleys Achaean
Some that had lost their lives at the hands of the Argives were lying;
Some lay smitten of lance or of arrow inside of the rampart.
One, however, he found at the left of the dolorous battle
Soon, Alexander, the goodly, the husband of fair-haired Helen,
Heart'ning his comrades there and rousing them up to do battle.
Drawing near him, he spake and in accents scornful rebuked him:

"Shame-Paris! fairest in form, thou woman-demented seducer!
Where is Deïphobus? Where are Helenus, royal and mighty,
Adamas, Asius' son, and the son of Hyrtacus, Asius?
Where is Othryoneus, pray thee? For lo! all Ilium hath fallen
Down from her pinnacle high; sheer ruin and certain impendeth."

Then, in his turn, made answer to him Alexander, the godlike:

"Hector, since thou art minded to cast the blame on the blameless,
Haply tomorrow but never today I might shrink from the warfare,
Since our mother hath borne even me not wholly a coward.
Ever since thou hast arrayed by the ships thy comrades to battle,
Since then here we abide, with the Danaans striving in combat
Unintermitted; but slain are those comrades for whom thou inquirest!
Only Deïphobus, only Helenus, royal and mighty,
Two have withdrawn; for indeed long lances wounded them sorely
Both in the arm; but Cronion the doom of death hath averted.
Lead on now, where'er thy mind and thy spirit command thee.

288

Eagerly we will follow along, and, methinketh, in no way
Shall we be lacking in valor, whatever of strength may be ours.
Passing his strength, however, not e'en the most eager can battle."

    These words spoken, the hero persuaded the mind of his brother.
Forth then hurried the twain where the war-din had raged and the direst
Strife round Cebriones bold and Pulydamas, hero undaunted,
Phalces, and peer of the gods, Polyphetes, round good Orthaeus,
Palmys, Ascanius, too, and a son of Hippotion, Morys—
These had come as reliefs from the deep-loamed land of Ascania
Only the morning before, and now Zeus spurred them to battle.
On they went, like the blast of violent winds in their going,
When it descends upon earth 'mid the thunder of Zeus, the All-Father;
Then in the salt-sea spume with astounding roar it commingles,
Wave upon wave high-swelling, the sea's loud-thundering surges,
Arching and crested with foam, some vanward, others behind them:
So were the Trojans arrayed, some forward, some to the rearmost;
Coated in harness of bronze bright-gleaming, they followed their lead-
Hector, Priam's son, the equal of man's bane Ares,   [ers.
Led them; he held his shield, all evenly rounded, before him,
Thick with hides, and bronze was heavily welded upon it;
Over his temples the while kept swaying his radiant helmet.
Striding along, he was testing at all points whether the squadrons
Haply would yield, as he charged behind his broad-rimmed buckler.
Yet noway he confounded the heart in the breast of th' Achaeans.
First in his challenge was Ajax, with long strides stalking before them:
    "Come on nigher, my man! Why triest in vain to dismay us
Argives? We are with war nowise unacquainted, I tell thee;
But by the cruel scourging of Zeus we Achaeans are vanquished.
Ah! thy heart full surely is hoping to pillage the galleys
Utterly; yet we have hands still left even us to defend them.
Nay, far sooner, methinketh, shall your well-occupied city
Haply by our own hands be taken and utterly wasted.
As for thyself, I tell thee, the time draws nigh for a Hector,
Fleeing, to pray unto Father Zeus and the other immortals,
Pray that his fair-maned steeds be fleeter in flight than a falcon—
They that shall bear thee, raising the dust o'er the plain, to the city."

Thus when Ajax had spoken, a bird flew forth on the right hand,
Even a high-soaring eagle; then shouted the host of Achaeans,
All at the omen encouraged. Then answered the glorious Hector:
    "Blundering braggart thou art, O Ajax, and what hast thou spoken?
Would I were surely a son of Zeus that wieldeth the aegis,
All my days, and Hera, the worshipful goddess, my mother,
Would I were honored as Phoebus and Pallas Athena are honored,
Surely as this day now brings woe to all of the Argives;
Yea, and among them *thou* shalt be slaughtered, if haply thou darest
Bide this long lance of mine, which thy flesh, which is fair as a lily,
Yet shall rend; thou'lt surfeit the dogs and the vultures of Troia,
Glut them with fat and with flesh, outstretched at the galleys Achaean."
    Thus he spake and led the way, and the company followed
Raising unearthly cries, and the war-host shouted behind him.
Then, on the other side the Argives shouted, forgetting
Naught of their might but awaiting the charge of the best of the Trojans.
Shouting from both sides arose to the radiance of Zeus and to heaven.

ILIAD · XIV · (Ξ)

In Ξ with sleep, and bed, heaven's Queen
Even Jove himself makes overseen.

NESTOR failed not at all to notice the shouting, even   [clepius;
   Though at his wine, but spake wingèd words to the son of As-
   "Godlike Machaon, bethink thee what now it were best to be doing;
Louder it waxes, the cry of strong war-chiefs by the galleys.
Nay, but remain thou seated and go on drinking the sparkling
Wine, till the fair-tressed maid Hecamede heateth the water
Warm and washeth away the clotted blood. In the meanwhile
I shall right soon learn the truth, if I go forth to a look-out."
      Thus he spake and took up the shield of his son, Thrasymedes,
Tamer of steeds; it was lying there, well-wrought, in the barrack,
Gleaming with bronze—the son now wielded the shield of his father—
Caught up a doughty spear, sharp-tipped, and the point of it bronzen,
Stopped outside of the barrack; and quickly a sight that was shameful
Met him: Achaeans in rout, with the high-souled Trojans behind them,
Driving them all in dismay, the Achaeans' rampart in ruins!
Even as when the expanse of the sea grows dark with a billow
Noiseless—it bodeth an onset of shrill winds sudden assailant;
Poised, it remaineth; it rolleth nor this way on nor another,
Till some steady gale from Zeus descendeth upon it:
Thus did the old man ponder, the while in spirit divided
Two ways—whether to enter the press of the Danaan horsemen,
Whether to seek Agamemnon Atrides, shepherd of peoples.
Then, as thus he was thinking, it seemed to him to be better
Unto Atrides to go. Men were fighting and slaying each other;
Thus the unwearying bronze about their bodies was ringing
Loud, as they came to blows with swords and two-pointed javelins. [ces—
      Now there encountered Nestor at this point the Zeus-nurtured prin-
Those who'd been wounded with weapons of bronze—coming up from

Tydeus' son and Odysseus and Atreus' son, Agamemnon.
Far apart from the battle those heroes' galleys were drawn up
High on the marge of the foam-flecked sea; for these were the foremost
They had drawn into the plain; at the sterns they had builded the ram-
Ay, though ample the beach, it was nowise able to hold them— [part.
All of those galleys in line—and the war-host also was straitened.
Therefore row upon row they had drawn them in and had filled up
All of the shore's wide mouth that the headlands included between them.
So they were faring together to witness the shouts and the warfare,
Leaning upon their lances; and grieved was the heart in their bosoms.
Thus, as wounded they came, there met them Nestor, the aged.
Nestor smote with dismay the hearts in the breasts of th' Achaeans.
Lord Agamemnon it was found utterance first and addressed him:

"Nestor, Neleus' son, great glory of all the Achaeans,
Wherefore hast thou come hither, forsaking the warfare that wasteth
Men? Lo! I fear lest the doughty Hector accomplish the menace
Wherewith once, when haranguing the Trojans he threatened and prom-
Never to fare back home unto Ilium-town from the galleys [ised
Ere he had set on fire the ships and slaughtered the owners.
So did he speak, and, we see, it all moves now to fulfilment.
Ah me! surely the rest of the well-greaved host of Achaeans
Store up wrath in their hearts 'gainst me, like even Achilles,
No more willing to battle amain at the sterns of the galleys."

Then unto him made answer the knightly Gerenian Nestor:
"Verily these things now are accomplished fact; and not even
Zeus that thund'reth on high could himself now otherwise order.
Ay, for the wall lies in ruins—the wall, wherein we had trusted
That it would prove an impregnable bulwark for us and our galleys.
Right at the swift ships now those men are holding the battle
Unintermittent, and neither could anyone tell by observing
Ever so closely from which side driveth the rout of th' Achaeans,
So are they slain pell-mell, and the war-cry riseth to heaven.
But as for us, let *us* take thought what were best to be doing,
If aught thinking avail; that we enter the warfare I do not
Mean to suggest; for the wounded are no wise fit to do battle."

Him then in turn addressed the monarch of men, Agamemnon:

"Nestor, since they are battling amain at the sterns of the galleys,
Neither availeth the moat nor the rampart strongly constructed,
Whereat the Danaans' travail was great, and they trusted in spirit
That it would prove an impregnable bulwark for them and their galleys —
Such, it appears, is the pleasure of Zeus, the o'erpow'ringly mighty,
That the Achaeans should perish unnamed here, far from their Argos.
Well did I know it when he the Danaans heartily aided;
Likewise now do I know, when he giveth success to our foemen,
As unto blessèd gods, but fetters our hands and our valor.
Come then, even as I may declare, let us all be persuaded:
All of the first-line galleys, that near to the sea have been drawn up,
Down let us launch them, and out to the hallowed sea let us take them!
There let us moor them with anchors, afloat, until the ambrosial
Night cometh on, if indeed from the war e'en then will the Trojans
Hold off; haply we then might launch in the sea all our galleys.
Blame is there none in evading, at nighttime even, destruction.
Better to flee and escape from ill than by it be taken."

　　Scowlfully looking, Odysseus of many devices addressed him:
"What a speech hath escaped from the bounds of thy teeth, O Atrides!
Would that thou wert commanding some other, an army inglorious
(Fatuous man!) and not ruling us whom Zeus hath appointed
Even from youth to old age to be winding the skein of our toilsome
Battle and warfare, all our lives, till we, each of us, perish.
Art thou determined to leave the wide-wayed city of Troia
Thus? To abandon the town wherefor we've been suff'ring uncounted
Woes? Be silent, lest some Achaean or other may hear this
Word that a warrior's lips would allow nowise to escape him,
Who in his heart understandeth to speak such words as are fitting,
Whoe'er wieldeth a sceptre, to whom are the people obedient,
People as many as thou art ruling as king of the Argives.
Now I utterly scorn such notions as these thou hast uttered,
Thou that hast bidden us launch, while battle and war-cry are raging,
Seaward the well-benched galleys, that still more fully the Trojans
Sooner possess their desire (e'en now they are winning the mast'ry),
Turning the scale of utter perdition on *us*; for th' Achaeans
Hardly will keep up the war, when the ships glide into the salt-sea!

Nay, they will look unto flight and abandon the rapture of battle.
So will thy scheme work mischief for us, O commander of armies!"

Then unto him thus replied the monarch of men, Agamemnon:
"Deeply indeed thou hast touched my heart with thy bitter reproval;
Yea, but indeed not I will bid the sons of Achaia
Launch in the briny sea, 'gainst their wills, the well-timbered galleys.
Would that some other, a younger or older than I am, might offer
Counsel better than this; unto me 'twould be certainly welcome."

Then spake among them again Diomedes, good at the war-cry:
"Near is the man (not long shall we seek him), if haply consenting
Ye be persuaded and none of you harbor resentment against me,
Seeing that I, by record of years, am the youngest among you;
Yet I may boast a descent from a lineage noble: my father,
Whom at Thebes the piled-up earth now hideth, was Tydeus.
For unto Portheus three sons were born, three faultless children;
They had their home in the region of Pleuron and Calydon lofty —
Agrius first, then Melas; the third was Oeneus, the knightly,
Father of father of mine, surpassing the others in valor.
Oeneus remained there; my father, however, settled in Argos,
Whither he wandered; for so Zeus willed and the other immortals.
One of Adrestus' daughters he wedded and dwelt in a palace,
Wealthy in substance; his were the ploughlands, too, in abundance,
Laden with wheat; around them were many orchards of fruit-trees;
Many his sheep; in his spear-craft, too, he excelled the Achaeans
All. Ye must surely have heard this and know if it's true, as I tell it.
Therefore ye may not call me ignoble of race and a coward,
Neither dishonor the spoken word, when well I have said it:
Come then, away to the war! Although we are wounded, we still must!
There let us meantime hold us aloof from the strife and the missiles,
Out of their range, lest wound be added to wound, peradventure.
But we will hasten to spur on others, whoever aforetime,
Yielding to impulse, departed and now share not in the battle."

Thus spake he. They hearkened with diligence, heeding his counsel,
Started to go; there led them the monarch of men, Agamemnon.

Neither a blind watch he, the renowned Earth-shaker, was holding,
But in the guise of a mortal, an ancient man, after them closely

Came and the right hand seized of Atreus' son, Agamemnon,
Lifted his voice and spake, and with wingèd words he addressed him:
   "Truly, methinketh, Atrides, the savage heart of Achilles
Now is rejoiced in his breast, as he looks out upon the Achaeans'
Slaughter and rout; for he hath no wit, not even a little.
Well, even so may he perish; may God bring affliction upon him!
Yet are the blessèd gods with thee now utterly angered
Noway. Yet shall the leaders and counseling chiefs of the Trojans
Cover the plain with dust, methinks; thyself shalt behold them [racks."
Scattered in flight toward the town, away from the ships and the bar-
   Thus he spake and sped o'er the plain and mightily shouted.
Even as loud as nine thousand men or even ten thousand
Shout, when in warfare they join in the fury and strife of the battle:
Even so vast a voice from his breast the Earth-shaker uttered,
Mighty Poseidon, and put great strength in the heart of th' Achaeans,
Each one, and roused them to fight and to wage war unintermittent.
   Hera, she of the golden throne, as she stood there, was looking
Down from a peak of Olympus and knew in the one she saw busy
Bustling about in the battle that brings fair fame unto heroes
Her own brother and brother-in-law; in her heart she was gladdened.
Zeus, on the topmost summit of many-fountainèd Ida
Seated, she also beheld, and he to her soul became hateful.
Thereupon pondered the goddess, the ox-eyed, worshipful Hera,
How to beguile the mind of Zeus that wieldeth the aegis.
Unto her spirit at length this counsel appeared to be wisest:
Well to array herself with adornment, then fare unto Ida,
If a desire be his mayhap to embrace her fair body,
Lying beside her in love, and a sleep untroubled and balmy
Then she should pour on his eyes—on his wits full cunning in counsel.
Thereat she started to go to the chamber her dear son had fashioned;
Doors close-shut on the pillars Hephaestus had cleverly fitted—
Secret the bolt of its fastening, that no other godhead might open.
There, as she entered, she closed the gleaming portal behind her.
Thereupon first in ambrosia she bathed—no stain on her winsome
Body was left—and anointed her richly with oil of the olive,
Sweet, ambrosial, and scented for her with a delicate perfume.

Were it but slightly stirred in the bronze-floored court of Cronion,
Still the savor would be diffused through the earth and the heavens.
Therewith then she anointed her beautiful body; her hair she
Combed; and with her own hands she plaited her radiant tresses,
Beautiful locks ambrosial, that flowed from her head everlasting.
Then she enveloped herself in apparel, a robe that Athena
Wove smooth and fine, ambrosial, with artistry lavish upon it.
Then with clasps of gold she pinned it over her bosom;
Next with a girdle she girt her, arrayed with tassels a hundred;
Then in the well-pierced lobes of her ears she inserted the pendants,
Three pearls, mounted together; and grace shone from them abundant.
Over her head, with a snood the matchless goddess enveiled her
Next, with a beautiful mantle, a new one, bright as the sun is.
Under her shining feet then she bound on her beautiful sandals.
Now as she finished arraying her body in all its adornment,
Forth from her chamber she came; then calling anon Aphrodite
Off from the rest of the gods, she spake a word to her, saying:

"Would'st thou hearken to me, dear child, in what I may tell thee,
Or peradventure deny me, because in thy heart thou'rt resentful,
Seeing that I bring help to the Danaans, thou to the Trojans?"

Then to her made answer the daughter of Zeus, Aphrodite:

"Hera, thou honored goddess, thou daughter of Cronus, the mighty,
Tell me what is thy thought; my heart now bids me fulfil it,
If fulfil it I can, and the thing is ordained for fulfilment."

Then with a crafty purpose addressed her the worshipful Hera:

"Well, now, give me desire and love, wherewith thou subduest
All, both immortal gods and likewise men that are mortal,
For I am going to visit the bountiful earth's far limits,
Ocean, the fountain and parent of gods, and Tethys, the mother,
Who in their palace aforetime kindly entreated and reared me,
Having received me from Rhea, when Cronus by Zeus was imprisoned —
Zeus of the far-borne voice — 'neath the earth and unharvested ocean.
Them I am going to visit and loose from their endless contentions.
Long is the time already they hold apart from each other's
Marriage couch and love — such anger hath entered their spirits.
If I could win their two dear hearts with a word of persuasion,

Bringing them back to a union in love and the couches of marriage,
Ever indeed they would call me a friend right worthy of worship."

   Once more answered her then Aphrodite, lover of laughter:
   "How were it seemly, or possible e'en, to deny the petition,
Since thou dost sleep in the arms of Zeus, the best and the chiefest?"

   Therewith she loosed from her bosom the girdle, richly embroid-
Variegated; on it was worked in all her enchantment —   [ered,
Therein love and desire; and the gentle beguilement of love-talk
Also is there, that steals the wits of even the wisest.
This she laid in her hands and spake a word to her saying:

   "There now! take it and lay it there in thy bosom, this girdle
Variegated, in which all things have been fashioned; I promise
Thou shalt not return, the desire of thy heart unaccomplished."

   Thus she spake; and she smiled — the ox-eyed, worshipful Hera;
Then, with the smile, she placed in her own fair bosom the girdle.
Unto her mansion the daughter of Zeus, Aphrodite, departed.
Hera leaped down in haste and left the peak of Olympus,
Passed o'er the land of Piëria and over Emathia, the lovely,
Sped on over the snow-covered hills of the horse-breeding Thracians,
Over the topmost peaks, nor grazed the ground with her footsteps;
Also from Athos she fared far over the billowy deep-sea;
Then she arrived at Lemnos, the city of Thoas, the godlike.
There it was Sleep, own brother of Death, that the goddess encountered.
Clasping his hand in her own she spake a word and addressed him:

   "Sleep, thou lord of all gods and lord of all men mortal,
Who hast aforetime heeded my word, now also obey me
Once more; I shall be grateful to thee henceforth and forever.
Lull me the bright eyes under the brows of Cronion to slumber
Straightway, when I in the converse of love shall lay me beside him.
Gifts then, lo! I will give thee — a fair throne, perishing never,
Golden; Hephaestus, my son, in both hands equally clever,
Cunning shall make it and set thee a footstool, too, underneath it,
Whereon thou mayest rest thy shining feet at a banquet."

   Straightway refreshing Sleep addressed the goddess in answer:
   "Hera, thou honored goddess, thou daughter of Cronus, the mighty,
Haply I might some other of godheads living forever

297

Readily lull into slumber for thee—yea, ſtreams of the Ocean
River himself, that of all things is parent and fountain.
But unto Zeus I could never approach, not nigh to Cronion,
Neither could lull him to slumber, unless himself should command it.
Once ere now with another behest thou'st taught me a lesson,
Taught me upon that day when thy Zeus's high-spirited scion
Sailed from Ilium, when he had sacked the town of the Trojans.
I then lulled thee the soul of Zeus who wieldeth the aegis,
Softly enswathed him; but thou in thy heart devised evil against him,
Rousing abroad on the waters the blaſts of a violent tempest;
Heracles cast thou away upon Cos, a well-peopled island,
Far from his loved ones all. But Zeus, on awaking, was angry,
Tumbling the gods in his palace; and *me* above all he was seeking,
Yea, he had hurled me from heaven to vanish unseen in the waters,
Had not Night, subduer of gods and of men, been my savior.
Fleeing I came unto her, and he halted, though fearful his anger;
Her he revered, and he would not displease swift Night in his doing.
Other impossible labor again thou bidst me accomplish."

Ox-eyed, worshipful Hera again addressed him in answer:
"Why is it things like these thou considerest, Sleep, in thy spirit?
Deem'st thou Zeus of the far-borne voice will succor the Trojans
Surely as he was angered for Heracles, who was his own son?
Come now, I will give thee in wedlock one of the Graces,
One of the younger, and she shall be called thy consort forever—
Even Pasithea, her whom all thy days thou desirest."

Thus she spake; and Sleep was rejoiced, and he answered her, say-
"Come then, swear unto me by Styx's inviolate water,   [ing:
Grasping with one of thy hands the earth, the all-bountiful mother,
But with the other the gleaming sea, that all may be witness
Unto us, all those gods that below with Cronus inhabit—
One of the Graces, the younger ones, thou surely wilt give me,
Even Pasithea, whom I have longed for all of my life long."

So said he; and the white-armed Hera failed not to obey him.
Straightway she swore, as he bade, and invoked by their names all the
Subtartarean—those that are called by the title of Titans.   [godheads
Now, as the goddess had sworn unto Sleep, and the oath was completed,

Sleep Escaping from the Wrath of Zeus

Both of them, leaving the cities of Lemnos and Imbros behind them,
Went forth, mantled in mist, and the journey quickly accomplished.
Soon they came to the mother of wild beasts, fountainous Ida,
Left at Lectum the salt-sea first, and over the dry land
Fared; and under their feet bowed waving the tops of the forest.
There Sleep halted, or ever the eyes of Zeus could behold him,
High on a pine-tree lighting, exceedingly tall — upon Ida
This was the loftiest then that rose through the air to the heavens.
There overshadowed he perched, in the boughs of the pine-tree hidden,
Unto a shrill bird likened in shape, which, homed in the mountains,
Chalcis is called of the gods, though mortals name it *Cymindis*.

　　　Meantime swiftly, anigh to the pinnacle-summit of Ida,
Gargarus, Hera was come, and Zeus, the cloud-gatherer saw her.
Now at beholding her merely, a passion came over his deep heart,
Even as when they had mingled the first time, loving each other,
Sharing the couch of delight, without the ken of their parents.
Rising before her, the god then spake a word and addressed her: [pus?

　　　"Hera, whither thy thought, that thus thou com'st down from Olym-
No steeds hast thou beside thee, nor car that thou mightest ascend on."

　　　Then with a crafty purpose addressed him the worshipful Hera:

　　　"Lo! I am going to visit the bountiful earth's far limits,
Ocean, the fountain and parent of gods, and Tethys, the mother,
Who in their palace aforetime kindly entreated and reared me.
Them I am going to visit and loose from their endless contentions.
Long is the time already they hold apart from each other's
Marriage couch and from love — such anger hath entered their spirits.
Now, at the foot of this mount, this Ida, the many-fountained,
Horses of mine stand waiting, to bear me o'er land and o'er water;
Only because of thee am I thus come down from Olympus,
Lest, peradventure, thou mightest hereafter be wroth, if in silence
I should away to the home of the deep-flowing river of Ocean."

　　　Then in answer to her cloud-gatherer Zeus thus addressed her:

　　　"Hera, thither, indeed, will be time hereafter to hasten.
Come now, lulled in repose, let us turn unto pleasure in loving.
Verily never desire for a goddess nor yet for a woman
Poured thus over and flooded the heart in my breast to subdue it.

301

So was I never enamored, not e'en with the wife of Ixion,
Her that Pirithoüs bare me, a match for immortals in counsel,
Neither with Danaë, beautiful-ankled child of Acrisius,
Who gave birth unto Perseus, of all men widest-renownèd,
Nor with the maiden Europa, the far-famed daughter of Phoenix,
Who was the mother of Minos and great Rhadamanthus, the godlike,
Nay, nor with Semele's self, nor even Alcmena in Thebe,
Who bore me Heracles, child with a heart unsubduably hardy —
Semele bore, howe'er, Dionysus, a joy unto mortals —
Nor with the queen, fair goddess, Demeter of beautiful tresses,
Neither with Leto, the far-renowned, nor yet with thine own self,
Even as now I love *thee*, and tenderest yearning invades me."
   Then with a crafty purpose addressed him the worshipful Hera:
"Most dread scion of Cronus, a word like that to have spoken!
Verily now if indeed thou longest in love to be couching
Here on the summit of Ida, where everything's out in the open,
How would it be if some one of the gods who live on forever,
Spying us here in our slumber, should then go tell the immortals
All of them? Leastwise I could return ne'er more to thy palace,
Rising again from the couch, so great were the just indignation.
But if indeed thou wishest, and thus it is dear to thy spirit,
There is a chamber of thine, thy own dear son hath constructed —
Close-shut doors on the pillars Hephaestus hath cleverly fitted.
Let us repair then thither to lie, if the couch be thy pleasure."
   Then in answer to her cloud-gatherer Zeus thus addressed her:
"Hera, fear not at all lest any, or god or a mortal,
Haply behold; such a cloud, thou'lt see, I will curtain around us,
Golden; methinketh not even the sun could look through upon us,
Whose is truly the light far keenest of all for beholding."
   So he spake. In his arms Cronion enfolded his consort.
Under them Earth, the divine, put forth, fresh-sprouting with grasses,
Lotuses laden with dew, yea, hyacinth also, and crocus,
Thick as a carpet and soft, from the ground uplifting the lovers.
Therein were lying the twain, deep-folded in cloud as a mantle
Golden and fair, while sparkled the dew-drops gently distilling.
   So then slumbered the Father in quiet on Gargarus' summit,

Conquered of sleep and of love; in his arms he held folded his consort.
Thereat started and ran sweet Sleep to the ships of Achaia,
Eager to tell Poseidon, the shaker of earth and upholder.
Taking his stand hard by, he spake wingèd words and addressed him:

"Now to the Danaans lend with good will thy assistance, Poseidon.
Grant them glory, if but for a brief space, while yonder is sleeping
Zeus, whom lo! in a slumber of gentleness I have enveloped,
While to an amorous couch hath crafty Hera enticed him."

Thus he spake and away to the races renownèd of mortals
Sped. He had set on still more the sea-god to succor the Argives.
Straightway forward *he* sprang 'midst the foremost and called to them

"Argives, shall we the victory yield once more unto Hector, [loudly:
Priam's son, that he capture the galleys and win him the glory?
Yea, even so he declares, and he vaunts him, seeing Achilles
Still abides at the hollow ships, with heart full of anger.
Nay, even him we shall not be missing so greatly, if only
All of the rest exert ourselves to defend one another.
Come then, even as I may declare, let us all be persuaded:
All of the shields in the army, the doughtiest, also the largest
Now gear on and encase each head in a harness of gleaming
Helmets; then let us, laying our hands on lances the longest,
Go forth; I myself in the vanguard will lead you. I promise
Not long will Priam's son Hector, though ardently eager, await us.
Let the enduring in fight, whoso bears on his shoulders a small shield,
Give it o'er to a weaker and harness himself in a larger."

Thus spake he. They hearkened with diligence, heeding his counsel.
Even the kings themselves, although they were wounded, arrayed them,
Tydeus' son and Odysseus and Atreus' son, Agamemnon.   [fare.
All through the ranks they ranged and exchanged the weapons of war-
Good arms the good put on; the worse he would give to a worser.
When in the glittering bronze all now had enclothèd their bodies,
Forward they started to march; there led them earth-shaking Poseidon
Armed in his powerful hand with a sword keen-edgèd and dreadful,
Like unto lightning in sheen; and it is not granted to meet it
Even in woful battle, but fear holds men in aloofness.

Meantime glorious Hector on his side marshaled the Trojans.

303

Verily then were they straining in fearfulest strife of the warfare —
Even the dark-haired god, Poseidon, and glorious Hector —
This one helping the Trojans, the other with aid for the Argives.
High dashed the wave of the sea on the Argive galleys and barracks.
Clashed then together the hosts in a din of tumultuous shouting.
Neither the deep-sea surge on the shingle bellows so loudly,
Driven in from the deep by Boreas' furious blowing;
Neither so loudly roareth a forest afire, when it blazes
Deep in a glen of a mountain, and flame leaps high to consume it;
Neither so wildly the wind in the oak-trees' loftiest tresses
Howls, when it rages and raves past all things else in its fury:
Like as arose the furious cry of Achaeans and Trojans,
Dreadfully shouting, when thus they rushed to attack one another.

    Glorious Hector was first to hurl his javelin at Ajax;
Ajax had turned and was facing directly to him; so he missed not, [other
Smiting him there, where about his breast there were drawn o'er each
Two belts, supporting his shield and his broadsword studded with silver.
These safeguarded his delicate flesh. Then wrathful was Hector,
Seeing the missile had fled from his hand, swift-wingèd but vainly;
Back to the throng of his fellows, evading his doom, he retreated.
Him, however, departing, the great Telamonian Ajax
Smote with a rock; for many lay rolled at the feet of the fighters,
Props of the swift-faring ships, and the hero lifted up one such,
Hurled it, and smote Hector's breast just over the rim of his buckler,
Close to his neck, and it sent him toplike spinning and reeling.
Even as falleth an oak, uprooted by bolt of the lightning
Father Zeus hurls, and there riseth a terrible savor of sulfur
Therefrom, neither remaineth courage in him that beholds it
Standing anigh; for dread is the levin of mighty Cronion:
So fell down in the dust forthwith great Hector, the mighty,   [met
Dropped the spear from his hand, and he fell with his shield and his hel-
All in a heap; and his armor bedight with bronze clanged about him.

    Shouting aloud, the sons of Achaia ran in upon him,
Hoping to drag him away; and they launched their missiles in showers.
Natheless the fallen shepherd of peoples with javelin or arrow
None was able to wound; too soon were the goodliest gathered

Round him: Pulydamas, godlike Agenor, and with them Aeneas,
Glaucus, the faultless, and with him Sarpedon, captain of Lycians.
Nor of the rest was anyone heedless of him, but before him   [comrades
All held their well-rounded shields in defense; in their arms then his
Lifted and bore him away from the toil, till he came to the fleet-foot
Steeds that awaited him there in the rear of the warfare and combat,
Standing there with their driver and car with its rich decorations.
These then bore him away toward the citadel, heavily groaning.
But when they came, as they fared, to the ford of the fair-flowing river,
Eddying Xanthus, that Zeus begat, the godhead immortal,
There they lifted him out from the car to the ground and upon him
Poured down water; he got back his breath and reopened his eyelids,
Sat up again on his knees, and he vomited dark-hued blood-clots —
Sank then back to the ground once more, while darkness enveiled him,
Darkness of night on his eyes, for the blow still conquered his spirit.

    Now as they saw how Hector afar was departing, the Argives
Leaped at the Trojans the more and remembered the rapture of battle.
Then by far the first, fleet Ajax, son of Oïleus,
Leaped upon Satnius, Enops' son, and smote with keen javelin
Him whom a nymph had borne — a blameless Naiad — to Enops,
When he was tending his flocks by the banks of Satnioïs river.
Drawing anigh him, the son of Oïleus, famed as a spearman,
Smote him upon his flank; he fell supine; and around him
Trojans and Danaans met in a terrible conflict together.
Came as a helper to *him* then Pulydamas, wielder of lances,
Panthoüs' son, and he smote Areïlycus' son, Prothoënor,
Full on his shoulder, the right one; clean through it the powerful weapon
Sped; he fell in the dust and clutched at the ground with his fingers.
Then Pulydamas boasted with loud cry fearful above him: [great-souled

    "Once more, methinks, not in vain from the mighty hand of the
Panthoüs' son hath the javelin sped; but one of the Argives
Now hath taken it up in his body and, leaning upon it,
Down, methinketh, will go with a staff to the mansion of Hades."

    Boasting, Pulydamas spake; and sorrow came to the Argives,
Stirred most deeply the soul of the wise Telamonian Ajax,
Since it was closest to him that Enops' scion had fallen.

Forthwith then at the hero departing he let fly his javelin
Bright, but Pulydamas, darting aside, himself then eluded
Black fate flying upon him; a son of Antenor received it,
Even Archelochus, one whom the gods unto death had appointed.
Right where the head with the neck is united the javelin smote him,
There at the top of the spine, and it cleft both tendons asunder;
Far in advance of his legs and his knees, as Archelochus tumbled,
Came to the earth the head and the mouth and the nose of the hero.
Forthwith Ajax in turn called out to Pulydamas faultless:

"Prithee, Pulydamas, ponder it well and declare to me truly,
Whether indeed this man to be slain in return for the other,
Our Prothoënor, is worthy; no coward he seems nor of cowards
Born, but a brother perchance of Antenor, tamer of horses —
Haply a son; for he seemeth to bear a close family likeness."

Thus he spake, well knowing, while anguish the soul of the Trojans
Seized; then, bestriding his brother, Acamas smote with his javelin
Promachus; he by the feet was trying to hale off the body.
Then did Acamas boast with loud cry fearful above him:

"Ho, ye Argive bowmen, insatiate of threatenings ever,
Verily not for us Trojans alone this travail and anguish;
Nay, but, even as we, shall ye, too, one day be slaughtered.
Ponder it, how he doth sleep! your Promachus, under my javelin
Conquered and tamed, that the payment of blood-price due for a brother
Be not delayed too long, since truly 'tis this that a hero
Prayeth, to leave in his halls some kinsman, destruction-avenger."

Boasting, Acamas spake, and sorrow came to the Argives,
Stirred most deeply the soul of Peneleos, wise-hearted hero.
He upon Acamas rushed, but *he* withstood not the onset
Prince Peneleos made, who wounded Ilioneus, son of
Phorbas, the wealthy in flocks, whom above the rest of the Trojans
Hermes loved and blessed with possessions of cattle and substance;
Only son unto him was Ilioneus borne of his mother.
Under his brows, at the base of the eye, Peneleos smote him,
Gouging the eyeball out, and the lance tore onward in fury   [out
Clean through his eye and the nape of his neck; he sank down and spread
Both of his hands. Peneleos, drawing his keen blade, smote him

Square on the midst of his neck and cleft off his head — with the helmet —
Clean to the ground, as he lay; while still the powerful javelin
Stood in the eye; he lifted it up as the head of a poppy
High and bade the Trojans to mark it and spake a word boasting:

　　"Bid, ye Trojans, the gallant Ilioneus' father and mother,
Parents beloved, in their halls for him to make lamentation,
Seeing that ne'er shall the wife of Promachus have any joy in
Alegenorides' coming, her husband dear, whensoever
We, young men of Achaia, fare home in our ships out of Troyland."

　　　　Thus spake he; and a trembling invaded them all in their members;
Each one was glancing to see where to flee from impending destruction.

　　　　Tell me now, ye Muses, who dwell in the halls of Olympus,
Who was the first of Achaeans to lift up trophies encrimsoned,
When the renowned Earth-shaker turned back the tide of the battle?
First Telamonian Ajax it was who Hyrtius wounded,
Gyrtius' scion, a leader of Mysians sturdy of spirit;
Phalces and Mermerus also Antilochus stripped of their armor;
Morys was slain by Meriones' hand, and so was Hippotion;
Teucer despoiled Periphetes and Prothoön both of their armor;
Atreus' son then wounded the shepherd of hosts, Hyperenor,
Wounded him in the flank; and the weapon tore out his entrails,
Laying him low; his soul, at the stricken fissure departing,
Issued speedily forth; and his eyes were clouded in darkness.
Ajax, howe'er, slew the most, the fleet-footed son of Oïleus,
Since no other was like him in fleetness of foot to o'ertake them,
When men were fleeing in terror, when Zeus spread panic among them.

ILIAD · XV · (O)

Jove sees in O his oversight
Chides Juno, Neptune calls from f(r)ight.

SOON as they passed, however, the deep-dug moat palisaded,
Fleeing — and under the hands of the Argives many had fallen —
There at the war-cars halted the fugitives, there they abided,
Pallid with terror, confounded with fright. Then Zeus was awakened
There on the summit of Ida, with gold-throned Hera beside him.
Up he leaped and stood and beheld Achaeans and Trojans,
These fast driven in rout and the others, the Argives, pursuing
Close in their rear, and among them the lord, earth-shaking Poseidon.
Hector he saw stretched out on the plain, and around him his comrades
Seated; but *he* lay unconscious of mind, with difficult breathing,
Vomiting blood, for 'twas not the weakest Achaean that smote him.
Seeing, the Father of men and of gods had pity upon him;
Then with a fearful scowl he looked and spake unto Hera:

"No doubt, thine is the malice and wile, intractible Hera,
Godlike Hector hath stopped from the fight and affrighted the people;
Yea, and I am not certain if thou of thy cruel contrivance
Be not the first to reap the fruits and I lash thee with scourgings.
Dost thou fail to remember when thou from on high wast suspended?
Anvils I swung at thy feet, those wrists bound fast with a fetter,
Golden, infrangible? Thou midway in the clouds and the ether
Hungest on high; and the gods, though wroth through lofty Olympus,
Could not come nigh thee or loose thee. But whomsoever I seized on,
Him I would clutch and hurl from the threshold, until he came headlong,
Swooning, down to the earth. Yet not even so did the ceaseless
Anguish leave my soul free, for the godlike Heracles grieving.
Him, by overpersuasion of storm-blasts, leagued with the North Wind,
Over unharvested seas thou dravest with evil intention —
Heracles cast thou away upon Cos, a well-peopled island.

Him did I rescue thence and led him back unto Argos,
Pasture of horses, though many a labor in truth he accomplished.
This I recall to thy mind, that thou cease from such wily deceptions
Straight and see if it profit withal, this loving and couching
Thou hast devised, thus coming away from the gods to beguile me."

Thus he spake. With a shudder the ox-eyed worshipful Hera
Heard, then lifted her voice, and with wingèd words she addressed him:
"Earth now witness to this, and the spacious Heaven above us,
Ay, and the down-flowing water of Styx — that is oath, unto blessed
Gods, most mighty of all and in all their eyes the most fearful —
Yea, and thine own head holy, and even the couch of our bridal
Chamber — that never insooth I could name in an oath of deception —
Never at any bidding of mine doth earth-shaking Poseidon
Trouble the Trojans and Hector and lend their foemen assistance;
Nay, but his own soul biddeth and even impelleth him onward;
Seeing them thus hard pressed at the galleys, he pitied th' Achaeans.
Sooner would I, for my part, with words of good counsel exhort him
Thither to go wherever thou leadest, O lord of the storm-cloud."

Thus spake she. Zeus smiled, the Father of men and immortals;
Answering her in his turn, he spake wingèd words and addressed her:
"Truly if thou hereafter, my ox-eyed worshipful Hera,
Wouldest abide like-minded with me among the immortals,
Then would Poseidon himself, how elsewise wishing soever,
Unto thy will, unto mine, in his own heart quickly convert him.
But if indeed it is sooth thou sayest, unerringly spoken,
Haste right now to the tribes of the gods and summon me Iris
Hither, along with her also the far-famed archer, Apollo,
That she may go mid the hosts of the bronze-clad sons of Achaia —
Go there and speak to his lordship Poseidon, bidding him straitly
Cease at once from the war and to his own dwelling betake him.
Hector the while let Phoebus Apollo arouse to the battle,
Breathe in him vigor anew and make him forget all his anguish,
Such as afflicteth his spirit e'en now; let him drive the Achaeans
Back once more and awaken a cowardly panic among them,
Till in their headlong flight they fall by the many-oared galleys,
Those of Achilles Pelides; then he shall arouse his companion,

Valiant Patroclus; and him with his spear shall the glorious Hector
Slay before Ilium, after Patroclus has slaughtered in number
Youths full many, among them my own son, the goodly Sarpedon.
Wrathful for him then the goodly Achilles in turn shall slay Hector.
After that I would occasion a counter-drive from the galleys
Ever unceasing, attack and retreat, until the Achaeans
Ilium lofty shall capture through counsels of Pallas Athena.
Ere that ne'er do I cease from my wrath nor will suffer another,
E'en of immortals, the Danaans there to assist in their warfare
Till the desire of Peleus' son is wholly accomplished,
Even as erst I promised, and likewise also confirmed it,
Nodding my head, that day when Thetis, the goddess, implored me,
Clasping my knees, that I honor Achilles, the sacker of cities."

 So said he; and the white-armed goddess failed not to obey him.
Hera departed from Ida's mountains to lofty Olympus.
Even as darteth the mind of a man who haply has wandered
Wide o'er the earth, and he ponders perchance in a wise meditation,
"Would I were yonder, or yonder," and many the things that he
So in her eagerness swiftly away flew the worshipful Hera, [longs for:
Came unto lofty Olympus, anon then entered the conclave
There of the gods immortal, in Zeus's house. When they saw her,
All of them forthwith rose and held out their beakers in welcome.
Disregarding the rest, for the fair-faced divinity, Themis,
Sole she accepted the cup — she first came running to meet her;
Lifting her voice in speech, with wingèd words she addressed her:

 "Hera, why hast thou come? Thou lookest like one all distracted;
Surely he gave thee a scare — that son of Cronus, thy husband!"

 Thereon to her made answer the white-armed Hera, the goddess:

 "Ask not, Themis, divine one, of these things; surely thou knowest
Even thyself how haughty his heart is, yea, and unyielding.
Only resume with the gods in the palace the well-balanced banquet;
These things haply thou then may'st hear amid all the immortals —
What are the wicked doings that Zeus is announcing. Methinketh
Scarce will it gladden alike the hearts of all, neither mortals
Nor yet gods, if any there be that still banquets with pleasure."

 These words spoken, the goddess, the worshipful Hera was seated;

All through the palace of Zeus the gods were troubled, but Hera
Smiled with her lips alone — her forehead by no means was mirthful
Over her eyebrows dark; indignant she spake out among them:
  "Witless are we, to be wroth, in our folly, against the Cronion!
Always eager to line up against him and baffle his purpose,
Whether by word or by deed! But aloof he sitteth and careth
Naught nor heedeth; for 'mong the immortal gods he declareth,
He in puissance and pow'r is pre-eminent — none is a rival.
Therefore bear whatever of ill he to each of you sendeth,
Seeing that grief even now, methinks, has been brought upon Ares:
Scion of his, the dearest of men, in the battle hath fallen,
Even Ascalaphus; him mighty Ares claims as his own son."
  Thus spake she; but both of his lusty thighs then did Ares
Smite with the palms of his hands, and he spake a word of lamenting:
  "Be not indignant with me now, ye gods that inhabit Olympus,
If I shall go, to avenge my son, to the galleys Achaean,
Even if mine be the doom, struck down by a bolt of Cronion,
There 'mid the dead to lie in the blood and dust of the battle."
  Thus he spake, and he ordered Panic and Terror to harness
Horses of his; himself put on his glittering armor.
Thereby then had been kindled implacable wrath and resentment
Greater than ever before 'twixt Zeus and the other immortals,
Had not Athena, in fear for the godheads, all of them, started
Up from the throne where she sat and out through the doorway bounded,
Snatching the helmet off from his head and the shield from his shoulders;
Grasping his javelin of bronze, she set it aside, as she drew it
Forth from his stalwart hand, and rebuked the impetuous Ares:
  "Maniac, frenzied of wit, thou'rt doomed to destruction! For nothing
Hast thou ears to hear with; thy sense, thy discretion hath perished!
Dost thou not hear what Hera, the white-armed goddess, is saying,
She that is come even now from the presence of Zeus of Olympus?
Is it thy wish, then — thyself having filled up the measure of mischief —
So to return to Olympus in anguish, under compulsion,
Yea, and to sow the seed of evil immense for the others
All? For anon he will leave the Achaeans and high-hearted Trojans;
Coming to us, he will raise up an uproar here in Olympus;

312

Each will he clutch in turn, no less than the guilty the guiltless.
Once more, then, I bid thee, dismiss thy wrath for thy offspring;
Sure some other and better than he in his hands and his prowess
Either has fallen or else hereafter shall fall; and to rescue
All men's races and children, indeed, were a difficult labor."

She spoke and made to sit down on his throne the impetuous Ares.
Hera the while called out from the palace Apollo and Iris —
Iris, who for th' immortal gods is the messenger goddess.
Then she uplifted her voice, and with wingèd words she addressed them:
"Zeus now biddeth you twain to go with all speed unto Ida;
Thither when ye have come and looked on the face of Cronion,
Do whatever perchance he may will to direct and command you."

Thus she spake; and again the worshipful Hera, returning,
Seated herself on her throne; the twain darted off and went flying.
Soon they were come to the mother of wild beasts, fountainous Ida;
There they found Zeus of the far-borne voice on Gargarus' summit,
Seated; and fragrant the cloud that wreathed its vapors around him.
They then, coming before the face of Zeus, the cloud-gath'rer,
Stood in his presence; and he in his heart was not wroth to behold them,
Seeing that they so promptly his dear wife's message had heeded.
Iris first he addressed with wingèd words and bespake her:
"Haste thee away, fleet Iris, and go unto sovereign Poseidon;
Tell him all these things, no messenger false in the telling.
Give him orders to cease straightway from the battle and warfare,
Visiting either the bright salt-sea or the tribes of immortals.
But if he will not obey my words but still disregard them,
Then let him duly consider and ponder in mind and in spirit,
Lest that, although he is mighty, he venture indeed to abide my
Coming against him; for mightier far than he I declare me,
Older also; but his dear heart makes bold to declare him
Even the equal of me, whom others dread with abhorrence!"

Thus spake he; swift Iris, shod with the wind, disobeyed not,
Sped from the mountains of Ida on down into Ilium holy.
Like as a snowflake wingeth away from the clouds, or a hailstone
Chill 'neath stress of Boreas, born in the regions of ether:
So in her eagerness swiftly away flew swift-footed Iris;

Close to the famous Shaker of earth she ſtopped and addressed him:

"God of the azure locks, thou Girdler of earth, with a message
Hither I've come unto thee from Zeus who wieldeth the aegis:
Orders he sends thee to cease ſtraightway from the battle and warfare,
Visiting either the bright salt-sea or the tribes of immortals.
But if thou wilt not obey his words but ſtill disregard them,
He, too, threatens to come and join in the battle against thee
Here in the open and bids thee wisely and warily shun him,
Even his hands; for mightier far than thou he declares him,
Older also; but thy dear heart makes bold to declare thee
Even the equal of him, whom others dread with abhorrence."

Then in sore displeasure the famous Earth-shaker addressed her:

"Out on it! Strong though he is, it is arrogance — all that he speaketh,
Who would reſtrain by force, unwilling, his equal in honor.
We three, I say, are brothers, the children of Cronus and Rhea,
Zeus, then I, and the third, who rules those beneath us, is Hades.
Three in all were the portions — to each his allotment of honor:
I, when we cast the lots, drew forth as my portion the waters
Grey for my dwelling forever, and Hades the murkiest darkness;
Zeus received as his lot the wide heavens in clouds and in ether;
Earth ſtill remaineth common to all, and the lofty Olympus.
Therefore I will not truckle to Zeus's caprices; in quiet
Let him, for all of his might, abide in his own third portion
Nor with the might of his hands try to terrify me as a weakling.
Better indeed, if he browbeat his children with terrible accents,
Menace the sons and the daughters that he himself hath begotten,
Those who under compulsion will hearken to what he enjoineth."

Then unto him fleet Iris, shod with the wind, made answer:

"God of the azure locks, Upholder of earth, is it truly
Thus I must bear unto Zeus a message so ſtubborn, defiant?
Neither wilt turn thee at all? To be turned are the hearts of the noble.
Well thou knowest, Erinyës ever attend on the elder."

Then unto her in reply spake Poseidon, the Earth-shaker, saying:

"Iris divine, this word thou hast most fittingly spoken —
Ay, a most excellent thing, when a messenger knows what is prudent.
But none the less keen cometh this grief on my heart and my spirit,

314

When one willeth a peer, one assigned to equal allotment
(As it is Fate's decree) to rebuke with a message of anger.
This time, however, I'll yield, in spite of all my vexation.
Something else I will tell thee and nurse in my heart this menace:
If, in defiance of me and Athena, the driver of booty,
If in defiance of Hera and Hermes and sovereign Hephaeſtus,
Ilium ſteep he shall spare nor ever consent to deſtroy it
Utterly, neither will grant victorious might to the Argives —
This let him know: in us both it will rouse unappeasable anger."

    Thus spake the Shaker of earth and left the host of Achaia,
Went to the waters, and sank; sore missed him the heroes Achaean.
Then spake Zeus, the gath'rer of ſtorm-clouds, unto Apollo:

    "Go now, Phoebus beloved, to the bronzen-helmeted Hector.
Lo! already the Shaker of earth and of earth the Embracer
Unto the bright sea has gone and entered it, shunning our headlong
Anger; else others also had heard of a battle between us,
Even the gods of the underworld, who bide there with Cronus.
Verily both for me and for him himself it is better
Far that thus, although he is vexcd, in advance he has yielded
Unto my hands, for the issue sweatless never had ended.
Thou, though, take in thy hands the entasseled aegis before thee,
Fearfully shake it aloft to affright yon heroes Achaean;
But have a care, Far-darter, the while for the glorious Hector.
So long ſtir up within him a marvelous might, till th' Achaeans
Flee and arrive in their flight at the Hellespont and the galleys.
Afterward, whether by word or by deed, it is mine to consider
How the Achaeans again may recover their breath from their travail."

    Thus spake he; and Apollo, not deaf to the word of his father,
Sped him down from the mountains of Ida like a swift falcon,
Slayer of doves; and of all things flying it is the swiftest.
Godlike Hector he found, the son of the wise-hearted Priam,
Sitting; no longer he lay but was newly collecting his spirit,   [ing
Knowing his comrades around him; for now had his sweating and gasp-
Ceased; for the purpose of Zeus who wieldeth the aegis revived him.
Taking his ſtand close by, far-working Apollo addressed him:

    "Hector, Priam's son, why thus, apart from the others,

Sittest thou all in a faint? Some trouble befalleth thee haply?"

Him then feebly addressed the shimmering-helmeted Hector:

"Who of the gods, thou noblest, enquireth in person about me?
Know'st not how at the hindmost row of the galleys Achaean,
While I was slaying his comrades, Ajax, good at the war-cry,
Smote my breast with a boulder and stayed my impetuous valor?
Yea, I had thought this day to arrive at the palace of Hades,
Home of the dead, when I was about to breathe out my dear spirit."

Thereat addressed him in turn the sovereign, far-working Apollo:

"Now take courage; for lo! what helper Cronion hath sent thee
Hither from Ida, to take a stand at thy side and defend thee,
Phoebus Apollo, myself, of the golden war-blade the wielder —
Me, who of old protect thee thyself and the towering fortress.
But now come, and urge on thy many drivers of war-cars
Down 'gainst the hollow ships to drive their fleet-footed horses.
I myself will precede them and all the path for the horses
Smooth out level and turn into flight the heroes Achaean."

Thus he spake, and he breathed great might on the shepherd of peo-
Even as when some steed that is stalled, high-fed at the manger, [ples.
Rendeth his tether and speeds far over the plain at a gallop,
Proudly exultant, accustomed to bathe in the river that floweth
Beautiful; high he holdeth his head, while over his shoulders
Streameth his mane, and he putteth a confident trust in his glory;
Nimbly his limbs bear him on to the haunts and pasture of horses:
So now Hector his feet and his knees kept plying as nimbly,
Urging the horsemen along, when he heard the voice of the godhead.
But as a branch-horned stag or a wild goat haply is hunted,
Chased in hot pursuit by hounds and by men of the country —
Him a precipitous rock or the deep-spread shade of the forest
Saveth, and now unto them is the lot not appointed to find him;
Meanwhile, under their din, a strong-maned lion appeareth
Full in the path, and he quickly scatters them, though they be eager:
Even so for a while the Danaans followed in squadrons,
Smiting ever amain with their swords and their two-edged lances.
But when Hector they saw assailing the ranks of their warriors,
Then were they stricken with panic; their hearts all sank to their sandals.

316

Thoas, son of Andraemon, it was then called to his comrades —
Far best he of Aetolians, at wielding the javelin skilful,
Staunch in a standing encounter; and few of th' Achaeans surpassed him
Also in council, whenever the young men strove in debating;
He then, kindliest-minded, harangued them and spoke out among them:

"Oh ye gods! how mighty the marvel mine eyes are beholding!
How hath evaded the fates and again unto life is arisen
Hector! Indeed, in his heart each one of us surely was thinking
He had been slain at the hands of the Telamonian Ajax.
Now, however, again some god hath delivered and saved him,
Hector, that loosened the knees erewhile of the Danaans many,
As, methinks, will befall even now; for not unattended
Is he of Zeus, the loud-thund'rer; he stands in the vanguard thus eager.
Come then, even as I may declare, let us all be persuaded:
Now let us order the folk to return once more to the galleys;
But as for us who claim to be the best in the army,
Take we our stand, if haply we first may meet and repel him,
Lev'ling at him our lances; methinks, although he is eager,
Yet will he tremble in spirit before the Danaan squadrons."

Thus spake he. They hearkened with diligence, heeding his counsel.
All that were grouped round Ajax, Idomeneus, king of the Cretans,
Teucer, Meriones also, and Meges, an equal of Ares,
Called on the chieftains and set in array the ranges of battle
'Gainst both the Trojans and Hector; the commons, however, behind
Turned and withdrew meantime away to the galleys Achaean.　　［them

Forward the Trojans in mass came charging; Hector was leading;
Long were his strides; and before him was moving Phoebus Apollo,
Mantled with cloud on his shoulders; he held out the aegis of onset,
Terrible, blinding, all shaggy with fringe, which the bronze-smith He-
Gave unto Zeus to wield for the consternation of warriors:　　［phaestus
Holding this in his hands, Apollo led on the war-hosts.

Close in array the Argives received the shock; and the war-cry
Rose up shrill from both sides, while arrows amain from the bowstrings
Leaped and javelins many, impelled from hands that were daring;
Some were infixed in the bodies of young men lusty for battle;
Many, however, half way, before they could touch a white body,

Stopped firm-fixed in the earth, though on flesh they were eager to glut
Long as Apollo held in his hands the aegis unshaken, ⌈them.
Missiles from both sides kept falling amain and felling the people;
But when he shook it and looked on the swift-horsed Danaan heroes
Full in the face, and himself at the same time mightily shouted,
Witched was the heart in their breast; they forgot their impetuous
Even as when on a numerous flock of sheep or a kine-herd ⌈prowess.
Two wild beasts, in the dead of black night, come sudden and drive them
Scattered in utter confusion, what time no herdsman is nigh them:
So the Achaeans were smitten with helpless fright; for Apollo
Sent them a panic, but glory he gave to the Trojans and Hector.

Then fell man upon man, as the battle array was confounded.
Twain of them Hector slew; these were Stichius and Arcesilaüs.
Arcesilaüs commanded the troops of the bronze-mailed Boeotians;
Stichius, in turn, was comrade true of the great-souled Menestheus.
Medon and Iasus both were despoiled of their arms by Aeneas;
One of these, Medon, was bastard son of the goodly Oïleus;
Thus was he brother in sooth unto Ajax; he dwelt in a city,
Phylace, far from his homeland, because he had murdered a kinsman,
Brother of Eriopis, his stepdame, wife of Oïleus.
Iasus, though, was a chieftain, a leader among the Athenians;
He was commonly called the son of the Bucolid Sphelus.
Slain of Pulydamas then was Mecisteus, then of Polites
Echius in front of the battle, and Clonius of goodly Agenor;
Paris smote from behind the base of Deïochus' shoulder,
Whileas he fled in the van, and the bronze drave utterly through him.

Now they were stripping the armor from these; meanwhile the
Dashed on the delvèd moat and the dense palisade in a tumult, ⌈Achaeans
Hither and thither; they entered their rampart under compulsion.
Then cried Hector, with shout that echoed afar, to the Trojans:
"On for the ships, make on! Leave lying the trophies encrimsoned!
Whome'er I shall espy that malingers aloof from the galleys,
I will devise him a death right there; none ever of kinsmen
Nor kinswomen shall lay him when dead on the funeral pyre;
Nay, but the dogs in front of our city shall tear and devour him." ⌈ders,
Thus he spake, and he brought down his lash on his horses' shoul-

Calling aloud on the Trojans along the ranks; in a chorus,
Holding their car-drawing steeds abreast with his own, they shouted,
Wild with unearthly cries, while, leading them, Phoebus Apollo,
Dashing adown with his feet full lightly the ditch's embankments,
Tumbled them all in the middle and therewith builded a causeway
Ample and broad in extent, as wide as the length of a spear-cast
Haply, whenever a man in a trial of strength may have cast it.
Over it forward they poured in battalions; before them Apollo
Carried the aegis of wonder and leveled the rampart Achaean
Easily, all, as a boy might scatter the sand by the seashore,
When in a childhood fancy he maketh him haply a castle,
Playfully then in a moment with hands and feet he confounds it:
So hast confounded the long-drawn toil and the moil of the Argives
Thou, O Phoebus, the archer, and roused up panic among them.

   Thus then they at the ships in a rally bided the onset,
Calling out one on another and all the gods of Olympus,
Each one lifting his hands in fervor of instant petition;
Nestor, chiefest of all, the Gerenian warden of Argives,
Prayed outspreading his hands to the starry heaven above him:
   "Zeus, oh Father, if any hath ever in Argos, the cornland,
Burning of bull or of ram the fat thighs laid on thy altar,
Prayed for return to his home, while thou with a nod hast assented,
All this remember, Olympian, and ward off the pitiless hour
Neither allow the Trojans to vanquish thus the Achaeans."

   Thus he spake in petition, and Zeus, the master of counsel,
Thundered at hearing the prayer of the old man, the scion of Neleus.
But when they heard the thunder of Zeus, th' aegis-bearer, the Trojans
Leaped at the Argives the more and remembered the rapture of battle.
Even as when on the sea's wide paths a mountainous billow
Sweeps down over the sides of a ship, and the might of a tempest
Urgeth it on — and this is what maketh the waves to mount higher:
So with a mighty uproar the Trojans rushed over the rampart;
Driving their steeds inside, they fought at the sterns of the galleys
Hand unto hand with their two-pointed spears from out of their war-cars,
While from the black-hulled galleys the Argives, climbing upon them,
Thrust with the long pikes — such as beside the galleys were lying,

Jointed and ready, with heads bronze-shodden for naval encounter.

    Now as Achaeans and Trojans contended amain for the rampart,
Distant, aloof from the swift, sea-furrowing galleys, Patroclus
Meanwhile sat in the tent of Eurypylus, warrior kindly,
Gladdening him with his talk meantime and applying the simples,
Balm for his dolorous wound, for his darksome pangs an assuagement.
But as he noted the rush of the Trojans full on the rampart,
While mid the Danaans rose a fearful cry and a panic,
Then did he utter a groan, and both of his thighs the Achaean
Smote with the palms of his hands, and he spake a word of lamenting:

    "Longer I cannot remain here, Eurypylus, great though thy need be,
Nay, and by no means, seeing how mighty a strife hath arisen.
Thee thy squire may now with his ministry comfort; the meanwhile
I to Achilles hasten to rouse him to join in the battle.
Who is there knows if with God's help I might with words of persuasion
Rouse up his spirit? For good are a comrade's words of persuasion."

    Thus he spake, and his feet were bearing him off. The Achaeans
Steadfast bided the shock meantime of the Trojans; but neither
Able were they to repel them, though fewer they were, from the galleys,
Nor were the Trojans able to break through the ranks and commingle
Ever in battle there by the Danaan barracks and galleys.
But as a carpenter's line doth straighten a beam of a galley,
Stretched in the hands of a skilful artisan, master of ev'ry
Craft, whom Pallas Athena inspires by counsel and guidance:
Even so nicely between them the line of the battle was straightened.

    Some at the one ship were fighting the battle, some at another.
Hector, however, made straight against the illustrious Ajax.
They twain there were toiling around one galley, and neither
Hector could drive him away and set the galley on fire;
Nor could the other repel him, for God was urging him nearer.
Then did the glorious Ajax smite in the breast with his javelin
Clytius' son, Caletor, while bearing a brand 'gainst the galley;
Down he fell with a crash, and the firebrand dropped from his fingers.
Hector, when with his eyes he beheld the fall of his cousin,
Fallen down in the dust in front of the black-hulled galley,
Cried with a shout that echoed afar to the Trojans and Lycians:

"Trojans, Dardanians, Lycians, that joy in closest encounter,
Noway slacken in aught from the tension here in the conflict!
On to the rescue rather of Clytius' son, lest th' Achaeans
Plunder his arms, who now 'mid the gath'ring of galleys hath fallen."

    Thus he spoke, and he hurled his glittering javelin at Ajax;
Ajax he missed but Cytherian Lycophron, scion of Mastor,
Comrade of Ajax, with whom he had dwelt, for a man in Cythera's
Hallowed isle he had murdered — him with his keen-pointed javelin
Hector smote on the head, right over the ear — he was standing
Close by Ajax, his friend; supine in the dust he fell backward
Off from the poop of the ship to the ground; and his members were loos-
Ajax then gave a shudder and spake these words to his brother: [ened.

    "Lo now, Teucer, dear fellow, our faithful companion is fallen,
Mastor's son, who was in our home from the isle of Cythera,
Whom in our halls we entreated with honor accorded to parents —
Great-hearted Hector hath slain him! But thou, where now are the ar-
Speeders of doom, and the bow, thy gifts from Phoebus Apollo?" [rows,

    Thus he spake. Teucer hearkened, and running he took up his sta-
Close by Ajax; he held his springing bow and his quiver   [tion
Laden with darts, and he sped them exceedingly swift at the Trojans.
First it was Clitus he smote, the glorious son of Pisenor,
(He was the friend of Pulydamas, Panthoüs' glorious offspring),
Holding the reins in his hands; for care of the horses engaged him.
Where the battalions were clashing the thickest, there he was driving,
Showing a favor to Hector and helping the Trojans; but quickly
Mischief came on himself, from which none, though eager, could save
Thus did a woe-winged arrow fall on his neck from behind him.   [him;
Down from the chariot he crashed; to the side his horses then swerving
Rattled the empty car; but its owner, Pulydamas, quickly
Marked it; and he was the first to hasten in front of the horses;
These then he gave in charge to Astynoüs, good Protiaon's
Son, and he strictly bade him to hold them near and to keep him
Ever in view, while *he* went and mixed again with the vanguard.

    Teucer another arrow at bronzen-helmeted Hector
Aimed and haply had made him cease from the fight at th' Achaeans'
Galleys, once he had smitten and taken that life in its prowess.

But he escaped not the keen quick sense of Zeus who was guarding
Hector and now of his glory deprived Telamonian Teucer,
Breaking the cord well-twisted, e'en while he was spanning at Hector
Tightly the matchless bow, and the shaft went wandering sidewise
Elsewhere, weighted with bronze; and the bow dropped out of his fin-
Teucer then gave a shudder and spake these words to his brother: [gers.
      "Ah me! truly a godhead annulleth the counsel of battle
Utterly, our own battle — the bow from my hand he hath stricken,
Snapping the cord new-twisted, and lo! I had bound it this morning
Thereon, strong to sustain the frequent leaping of arrows."
      Him then answered in turn the great Telamonian Ajax:
      "Yea, let the bow, dear lad, and the arrows abundant in number
Lie there, seeing that God, of the Danaans jealous, confounds them.
Thou, though, take thee a long lance now and a shield on thy shoulder,
Fight with the Trojans, and urge on the rest of the people to battle.
Even in victory may they not easily capture the well-benched
Galleys. But let us be mindful now of the rapture of battle."
      Thus he spake; and Teucer put back the bow in the barracks,
Set instead on his shoulders a shield four-folded of bull's hide;
Then on his valorous temples a well-wrought helmet he fitted,
Horse-hair crested, the plume all fearfully nodded above it,
Caught up a doughty spear, sharp-tipped — and the point of it bronzen —
Started to go, and, running right swiftly, stopped beside Ajax.
      Hector, as soon as he saw brave Teucer's artillery blighted,
Cried with a shout that echoed afar to the Trojans and Lycians:
      "Trojans, Dardanians, Lycians, that joy in closest encounter,
Quit you like men, my friends, and remember impetuous prowess
Here by the hollow ships — for lo! mine eyes have beheld it,
How Zeus blighted a prince's, a hero's, artillery for him.
Easy indeed to discern such succor of Zeus unto heroes,
Whether he granteth to any the meed of victorious glory,
Whether he lesseneth any or no wise wills to defend them,
Even as now he would aid us and lessen the strength of the Argives.
Keep on fighting in mass at the ships. Whoever among you,
Smitten or wounded of weapon, his death and his doom shall encounter,
Dead let him lie; for in fighting for homeland naught is unseemly,

Not even death: for he leaveth his wife and his children behind him
Safe, and his home unharmed, his heritage — if the Achaeans
Fare hence away in their ships to the well-loved land of their fathers."
    Thus he spake and aroused the might and spirit of each man.
Ajax also was calling on his side loud to his comrades:
    "Shame on you, Argives! Now is the one thing sure or the other:
Either to die or be saved and to beat off doom from our galleys.
Think ye, if shimmering-helmeted Hector now capture the galleys,
Ye then shall haply fare on foot, each man to his country?
Do ye not hear yon Hector now loudly exhorting his people,
All of them? Madly he rages to set the galleys on fire.
Truly he bids them not to a dance; he bids to a battle!
Neither for us is advice or device that is anyway better
Now than to join all hands, all might, in the closest encounter.
Better to live or to perish now once and for all in the battle
Than to be worn out slowly in stress of a terrible combat
Vainly, with foe far weaker than we are, here at the galleys."
    Thus he spake and aroused the might and spirit of each man.
Then it was Hector that slew Perimedes' offspring, Schedius,
Chief of the Phocians. In turn Laodamas fell before Ajax;
Leader of footmen he and the glorious son of Antenor.
Thereon Pulydamas slew in his turn the Cyllenian Otus,
Comrade strong of Phylides, a leader of sturdy Epeians.
Meges saw it and rushed to attack him; Pulydamas, sidewards
Bended his body; and so Meges missed him; for Phoebus Apollo
Suffered not that Panthoüs' son should be slain in the vanguard.
Croesmus, howe'er, he struck, in the midst of his breast, with the javelin.
Crashing he fell; and his foe was for stripping his arms from his shoul-
Dolops, well skilled in spearmanship, then rushed upon Meges, [ders.
Lampetus' son, whom Lampus begat, of his sons far the bravest —
Lampus, Laomedon's son — well skilled in impetuous prowess.
He with his javelin smote on the boss of the shield of Phylides, ·
Rushing in from close by; but his well-wrought corselet preserved him —
Corselet he wore, well fitted with mail-plates, corselet that Phyleus
Brought from Ephyra-town, on the banks of the river Selleïs.
This a guest-friend had given, a monarch of men, Euphetes —

Given, to wear it in war, that it serve as defense against foemen;
This time the life of his son as well it saved from destruction.
Meges now on the topmost arch of the bronze-fitted helmet,
Crested with waving horse-hair, smote with his keen-pointed javelin,
Brake off the cresting of horse-hair plumage; down it fell earthward
All in the dust, but gleaming, recently colored with purple.
Now while Meges remained and fought, still expecting a vict'ry,
Lo! Menelaüs, the martial, came up to the aid of the Argive,
Stood to one side with a spear, unobserved, and smote on the Trojan's
Shoulder, behind him; the point through his breast rushed furious for-
Driving on, and in consequence Dolops reeled and fell headlong. [ward,
They twain made straight to strip from his shoulders the bronze-fitted
Hector called to his aid his kinsmen—all did he summon. [armor.
First did he chide Hicetaon's son, the strong Melanippus.
This man up to this time had been tending his kine, trailing-footed,
Off in Percote afar, while still far away were the foemen.
But when the Danaan galleys arrived, well-balanced and curving,
Back to Ilium he came and was eminent there 'mid the Trojans,
Dwelling in Priam's house, who treated him just like his children;
Him did Hector chide, and he spake a word and addressed him:

"So, Melanippus, shall we then slacken endeavor? Concerns thee
Naught thy kinsman's death? Thy dear heart is unmoved at beholding?
Seest thou not how busy are they o'er the armor of Dolops?
Nay, come along; it is now no longer a fight with the Argives
Far off, till we shall slay them, or else—from the top to the bottom—
Ilium steep they will capture and all its citizens slaughter."

Thus he spake and led on; the godlike warrior followed.
Great Telamonian Ajax, on his side, roused up the Argives:

"Quit you like men, my friends, and feel some shame in your spirits,
Shrink from dishonor before one another in stress of the conflict.
Fewer are slain than are saved of soldiers shunning dishonor;
But to the fugitive neither glory nor safety is coming." [them,

Thus he spake. And they themselves, too, were fain to defend
Laid up his word in their hearts, and girdled the galleys with bronzen
Bulwark, while Zeus still incited onward the Trojan assailants.
Then Menelaüs, good at the war-cry, roused up a hero:

"Other is none of Achaeans, Antilochus, younger than thou art,
None that is fleeter of foot, none even so mighty in fighting.
What if thou would'st leap forth and smite some man of the Trojans!"
     Thus he spake and hasted away, having heartened the other.
Out from the vanguard he leaped; then glancing on all sides around him,
Hurtled his glittering spear. Quick backward the host of the Trojans
Shrank from the hero's hurtle. And yet not vainly the missile
Sped, but it smote Hicetaon's high-souled son, Melanippus —
As he returned to the war — on his bosom, close to the nipple.
Down he fell with a crash, and his eyes were clouded in darkness.
At him Antilochus rushed, as a hound will rush at a wounded
Fawn which haply a hunter with aim right lucky hath smitten,
Just as it leaped from its lair, and hath loosened its members beneath it:
So upon thee, Melanippus, Antilochus, steadfast in battle,
Leaped to strip off thy arms; but he 'scaped not Hector, the godlike,
Who came running along in the battle's strife to oppose him.
Hector he dared not abide, though fierce he was as a warrior;
Rather he fled, as a wild beast flees from a mischief accomplished —
Whether a hound he hath killed or a herdsman tending his cattle —
Sooner than ever a crowd in pursuit can gather together:
Even so Nestor's son took flight, while the Trojans and Hector
Poured their dolorous darts, with a marvelous uproar, upon him.
He turned about and stood, when he reached the host of his comrades.
     Like unto lions that feed on raw flesh, the furious Trojans
Now rushed right on the galleys and Zeus's behests were fulfilling;
He roused ever anew great vigor in *them*, but he melted
Argive souls and deprived them of glory, while spurring the Trojans.
For in his heart he'd determined to grant the glory to Hector,
Priam's son, that he cast on the beaked ships ravenous fire,
Blazing unwearied, and so would accomplish surely for Thetis
All her presumptuous prayer; and Zeus, the master of counsel,
Waited to see with his eyes that gleam of a galley on fire.
After that he intended a counter-drive on the Trojans
Back from the ships to occasion and grant the Danaans glory.
Such was his thought, as on 'gainst the hollow ships he roused Hector,
Priam's son, although Hector himself was ardently eager.

Like unto spear-wielding Ares he raged, or as a consuming
Fire may rage on the hills in a thicket deep of the forest;
All 'round his mouth the foam was gath'ring, and both of his eyeballs
Blazed from under his terrible brows, and ever the helmet
Fearfully nodded and shook, as he fought, on the temples of Hector
There as he raged; for Zeus himself out of heav'n his protector
Was, and to him, only one 'gainst a greater number of heroes,
Honor and glory vouchsafed, for brief was the measure allotted
Unto his life; already was Pallas Athena arousing
'Gainst him the day of doom, 'neath the might of Achilles Pelides.
Ay, he was eager to break through the warrior-ranks, and he tested
Where'er thickest the press he beheld, and the doughtiest armor.
Natheless, for all his rage, he was noway able to break them,
Since they stood compact as a tower and like as a headland
Rock, precipitous, huge, on the wave-beat strand of the foam-flecked
Sea — a rock that abideth the ways of the shrill-voiced tempests,
Yea, and the surges that roar high-swollen and foaming against it:
So the Achaeans awaited, unshaken, the Trojans and fled not.
Natheless, gleaming with fire upon all sides, leaped he among them —
Fell on the throng, as a billow the boisterous hurricane reareth
Under the storm-clouds falls on a swift ship; then it is hidden
Wholly of wide-flung foam, and the terrible blast of the tempest
Howls in the canvas — the seamen, their hearts all stricken with terror,
Tremble; for but by a scratch away from death are they carried:
So was the spirit distraught in the breasts of the sons of Achaia.

    As indeed when a lion assails the kine in his rav'ning,
When, uncounted, they feed in the meadowy lush of a marshland
Ample, and 'mongst them a herdsman as yet not clearly instructed
How, with a wild beast fighting, to ward off slaughter from crook-horned
Cattle, who walks all witless abreast of the foremost or hindmost
Kine of the herd; but the lion, assaulting the herd in the middle,
Rendeth a cow, and the rest all scatter in flight: the Achaeans
Likewise then were fearful of Father Zeus and of Hector
Terribly, all; but he slew Periphetes, a man from Mycenae,
Only, the loved son of Copreus, that once bore messages often
Sent of Eurystheus, the king, through him unto Heracles mighty.

Just as the father was baser, of him was begotten a scion
Better, in virtues diverse, in fleetness of foot, and in fighting,
Also among Mycenaeans in mind, too, one of the foremost.
He it was then that conferred victorious glory on Hector;
For, in his turning back, he tripped on the rim of his buckler —
Shield that reached to his feet and was borne as defense against javelins;
Stumbling upon it, he fell on his back; and loudly the helmet
Clanged on the warrior's temples, and fearful the noise of its clanging.
Hector quickly espied him and ran up close to the fallen,
Planted a spear in his breast, and near his beloved companions
Slew him, nor could they indeed, though sorrowing sore for their com-
Aid him; for they themselves sore dreaded Hector, the godlike.　　[rade,

　　All eyes turned to the galleys; the Argives faced them; the vessels,
First beached, hedged them about; but the Trojans poured in upon them.
Then the Achaeans withdrew from the front row, under compulsion
Turning away, but abided the onset there at the barracks
Closely arrayed, nor scattered about the camp; for shame held them,
Terror as well, and they shouted unceasingly each to the other.
Nestor chiefest of all, the Gerenian warden of Argives,
Ever implored and besought each man for the sake of his parents:

　　"Quit you like men, my friends, and feel some shame in your spirits,
Shame of your fellows' contempt; let each of you also be mindful
Now of his children, his wife, his possessions, and also his parents,
Whether perchance they are dead or whether mayhap they are living.
Even for their sake here I beseech you, theirs that are absent,
Steadfast stand and by no means turn you to flight and confusion."

　　Thus he spake and aroused the might and courage of each man.
Then from the eyes of th' Achaeans Athena lifted the cloud-mist
Wonderful — light intense from both sides flooded upon them,
Both from the galleys' direction and that of the dubious battle.
Then it was Hector, good at the war-cry, they marked and his com-
All that were standing aloof in the rear and not in the battle,　　[rades,
All that were waging the war at the side of the swift-sailing galleys.

　　Now no longer it pleased the spirit of great-hearted Ajax
Station to keep where others, the sons of Achaia, retreated;
Nay; but he kept on faring with long strides over the galleys,

Over the decks. In his hand was a huge pike, fitted for sea-fights,
Joined together with clamps; its length was some twenty-two cubits.
Even as haply a man, well skilled in the riding of horses —
When of his numerous stud four horses he yoketh together —
Speeding them over the plain toward some great city he gallops
Over a public highway, and many people behold him,
Women and men, all marvel. Without a slip or a stumble
Ever he leapeth, while they go flying, from one to another:
Even so over many a deck of the swift-sailing galleys
Went with his long strides Ajax; his voice uprose to the heavens,
While with terrible shouts he the Danaans summoned with orders
Aye to stand in defense of their galleys and barracks. And noway
Hector stayed back in the throng of the strongly-corseleted Trojans,
But as an eagle may swoop, full-flighted and tawny of pinion,
Down on a feathered tribe, as they feed by the marge of a river —
Geese or cranes or swans with their long necks, feeding together:
Even so Hector made straight for one of the dark-prowed galleys,
Darting directly upon it, for Zeus with a strong hand urged him
Mightily on from behind and with Hector spurred on the people.

      Fierce was the battle that now was enkindled anew at the galleys.
Thou would'st haply have said they were meeting unworn, unwearied,
Now one another in war, so eagerly met they in combat.
Thus in the ardor of fighting were both sides minded: th' Achaeans
Deemed they would never escape from the bane, nay! sooner would per-
Whileas the heart beat high in the breast of every Trojan   [ish,
Both to fire the ships and to slaughter the heroes Achaean.
Such were the thoughts in the mind of each, as they faced one another.
Then did Hector lay hold on the stern of a sea-faring galley,
Beautiful, swift on the brine — the vessel that carried aforetime
Protesilaüs to Troy but to homeland never returned him.
His was the very galley around which Achaeans and Trojans
Hand unto hand kept warring against one another, and noway
Far apart they endured the whizzing of arrows or javelins,
Nay, full nigh one another they stood, united in purpose,
Battled with hatchets keen-edged and with battle-axes contended;
Also with heavy swords they were fighting and two-edgèd javelins.

Ajax Defending the Achaean Ships Against the Trojans

Many the beautiful blades, black-bound, and many the hilted —
Some to the earth dropped down from the hands of the combatant heroes,
Some from the shoulders fell. The earth ran black with the bloodshed.

　　Once, though, Hector had seized on the ship's stern, never relaxing,
Holding the tail-piece in hand right firmly, he called to the Trojans:

　　"Hither bring fire and together yourselves awaken the war-cry!
Zeus unto us now hath granted a day that is worth all others,
Day to capture the galleys that 'gainst the will of the godheads
Came and inflicted upon us so many woes, by the elders'
Guilt, who, when I was eager to fight at the sterns of the galleys,
Still kept holding me back myself and restraining the people.
Even if Zeus of the far-borne voice upset then our senses,
He it is now himself that inciteth and urgeth us onward."

　　Thus he spake; and his men rushed more fiercely still on the Ar-
Ajax abode no longer; for he was o'erwhelmed by the missiles; ⌈gives.
But he retreated a little, for he was thinking to perish,
Leaving the trim ship's deck for the sev'n-foot bench of the steersman.
There then watching he stood, with his lance still fending the Trojans
Off from the ships, whoe'er might bring unwearying fire,
While with terrible shouts he the Danaans summoned with orders:

　　"Friends, ye men of Ares' company, Danaans, heroes,
Quit you like men, my friends, and remember impetuous prowess!
What then, do we imagine that there may be helpers behind us,
Or that some better rampart will ward off death from our soldiers?
Nay, there is nowhere near you a city accoutred with towers,
Where to defend us with forces for turning the tide of the battle.
No! on the plain of the strongly-corseleted Trojans we combat,
Leaning alone on the sea, far off from the land of our fathers.　　⌈tle."
Therefore comes light from prowess of hands, not from slackness in bat-

　　Spake he and labored along with his sharp-pointed spear in a fury:
Whoe'er then of the Trojans would make for the hollow galleys,
Laden with torches ablaze, to gratify Hector that bade it,
There at the ship, awaiting with long lance, Ajax would wound him:
Thus he wounded twelve at close range in front of the galleys.

ILIAD · XVI · (II)

In Πι Patroclus bears the chance
Of death, imposed by Hector's lance.

SO FOR the well-benched galley the warriors were battling about it.
Meanwhile Patroclus had come to Achilles, the shepherd of peoples,
Stood there and shed warm tears, as a fountain flowing with dark-hued
Water adown a precipitous crag pours murky its current.
When he thus saw his friend, the divine, fleet-footed Achilles
Pitied him, lifted his voice, and with wingèd accents addressed him:
  "Wherefore art bathed in tears, Patroclus, like as a little
Maiden, who begs and beseeches her mother to take her, and running
Close at her side now plucks at her dress, now hinders her going,
Tearfully looking at her the while, until she is taken.
Like such a one, my Patroclus, thou lettest fall the round tear-drops.
Hast thou aught to declare unto me or the Myrmidons haply?
Hast thou a message received, thou only, a message from Phthia?
Still is he living, they say, that scion of Actor, Menoetius;
Peleus, Aeacus' son, still lives in the Myrmidon country.
These are the twain whose death to us were peculiar affliction.
Or is it *thou* art lamenting the Argives, how that they perish
Hard by the hollow galleys because of their own transgression?
Utter it forth. Hide it not in thy heart; let both of us know it."
  Heavily groaning, didst thou address him, O knightly Patroclus:
  "Goodliest far of Achaeans, Achilles, scion of Peleus,
Be not vexed — so sore the distress that besets the Achaeans —
Seeing that all of them now, who aforetime were counted the bravest,
Lie, even now, in the ships, spear-smitten or wounded with arrows.
Wounded insooth is Tydeus' son, Diomedes, the mighty;
Stricken the far-famed spearman, Odysseus, and king Agamemnon;
Yea, and Eurypylus, too, lies shot in the thigh with an arrow.
Doctors attend upon these, well versed in medical wisdom,

Healing their wounds; but thou hast proved unbending, Achilles!
Never indeed may wrath like this thou'rt nursing possess me,
Wofully valorous thou; for of thee who later shall profit,
If thou avert not now from the Argives shameful disaster?
Pitiless man! Nay, never was knightly Peleus thy father;
Never was Thetis thy mother; the sea grey-gleaming did bear thee,
Sea and precipitous crags — so void thy spirit of feeling!
If, howe'er, in thy soul thou art shunning some warning from heaven —
Haply some warning from Zeus thy worshipful mother hath told thee —
Still do thou send forth me; let the others, the Myrmidon people,
Follow with me, if perchance some light I may bring to the Argives.
Likewise give me thy armor, to buckle it over my shoulders;
Haply the Trojans may hold them aloof from the battle, mistaking
Me for thyself, and the warrior sons of Achaia, awearied,
Breathe for a moment; for brief is the breathing time in a battle.
Lightly perchance might we, not wearied, drive back to the city
Men of the war-cry weary away from the ships and the barracks."

    Thus he spake and besought — far gone in his folly! for truly
Even his own dark death and doom it was that he prayed for.
Grievously troubled, addressed him in turn fleet-footed Achilles:

    "Ah me, Patroclus, descendant of Zeus, what a word thou hast spo-
Neither warning from heav'n is there that I heed, that I know of; [ken!
Neither a warning from Zeus my worshipful mother hath told me.
Still none the less keen cometh this grief on my heart and my spirit,
Whenso a man would rob and despoil one, who is his equal,
Take back a prize of honor, because he excelleth in power!
Keen is the grief I feel, for hardships I've suffered in spirit!
Even the maiden whom, as my prize, the Achaeans assigned me —
Her whom I won with my spear when a fortified city I pillaged —
Out of my arms hath lord Agamemnon forcibly taken,
Atreus' son, as if some alien I were, unconsidered!
These things let us resign to the past; it was never permitted
Any to rage in his heart unceasingly. Yet I intended
Ne'er to abate my wrath until such time as a-near me
Cometh the battle cry, and the conflict reaches my galleys.
Thou, though, put on thy shoulders the harness of mine, the renownèd;

Lead on the Myrmidons, lovers of warfare, lead them to battle,
Seeing insooth that a dark cloud-mass of the Trojans encircles
Mightily even the ships, and the Argive army is leaning
Close on the beach of the sea and only a scant strip is holding.
Down upon them hath come the entire town of the Trojans
Boldly advancing; for lo! my helmet's visor they see not
Gleaming close by. They would flee and would fill up quickly, methink-
All of the streams with their slain, had only the lord Agamemnon [eth,
Treated me kindly; but now they are warring about the encampment!
No more now in the hand of Tydides, prince Diomedes,
Rageth the spear, to avert from the Danaans death and destruction;
Nor was I hearing as yet the voice of the Atreïd, shouting
Loud from his hated mouth; the voice of man-slaying Hector
Crashes around me, commanding the Trojans; and they with their shout-
Fill all the plain, for they're now defeating th' Achaeans in battle. [ing
But even so, from the galleys to ward off ruin, Patroclus,
Fall thou mightily on them, lest they with their fire destructive
Burn our ships and deprive us of our desired returning.
Hearken thou now, as I put in thy mind the sum of my bidding,
That thou for me may'st win from all of the Danaans lasting
Honor and glory, and they that surpassingly beautiful maiden
Send back again to me and bestow splendid gifts in addition:
Drive them away from the ships — and come back. But if there shall grant
Hera's loud-thundering husband glory to win for thine own self, [thee
Do not without me yearn to engage in war with the Trojans,
Lovers of warfare; for thus thou wilt haply leave me less honor.
Neither, exulting with pride in the fury of combat and warfare,
Slaughtering Trojans amain, lead on the pursuit unto Ilium,
Lest from Olympus step in some one of the gods everliving
'Gainst thee. Especially he, far-working Apollo, befriends them.
Rather, as soon as a saving light thou hast brought to the galleys,
Turn thou back and the fight on the plain abandon to others.
Grant, O Father Zeus and Athena and Phoebus Apollo,
That not one of the Trojans escape death, none of the many,
Nor of the Argives either, but we twain put off our destruction
Till we alone — we two — tear down Troy's diadem holy.''

335

So while they were conversing in this wise one with the other,
Ajax abode no longer, for he was o'erwhelmed by the missiles — [born
Zeus with his counsel subdued him, and missiles launched by the high-
Trojans; about his temples his shimmering helmet resounded [wrought
Fearful, whene'er it was struck, for the strokes fell aye on the well-
Plates that protected his cheeks; and his shoulder — the left — grew weary,
As he was steadfastly holding his glittering shield; but they could not
Shake the shield upon him, though pressing hard with their missiles.
Ever his breath came hard, and the sweat in streams from his members
Poured down all over his body, and not for a moment could he
Stop to draw breath — while evil on all sides piled upon evil.

Tell me now, ye Muses, who dwell in the halls of Olympus,
How it was that the fire first fell on the galleys Achaean.
Hector approached, and he smote with his great sword full on the ash-
Javelin of Ajax, close to the keen point's socket, behind it, [wood
Chopping it utterly off; and the great Telamonian Ajax
Brandished a war-wood — headless! — in vain in his hand, and afar off,
Out of his reach, to the ground the bronzen spear-point fell ringing.

Then, with a shudder, Ajax discerned in his spirit intrepid
Doings of gods: thus wholly annulled all his planning of battle
Zeus that thund'reth on high, who victory willed for the Trojans.
Backward he drew out of range; they cast on the swift-sailing galley
Fire unwearying; instant the blaze poured over it, quenchless.
So did the flame envelope the stern of the ship; but Achilles
Smote his two thighs and addressed a word to Patroclus, saying:

"Up now, Patroclus, descended of Zeus, thou speeder of horses —
Lo! I behold at the galleys the blast of the ruinous fire —
Lest they capture the ships, and no way be left of escaping.
Don right quickly the harness, while I go gather the people."

Thus spake he; and Patroclus in bronze bright-gleaming arrayed
First on his legs he fastened the greaves, all round about deftly, [him.
Beautiful, fitted with buckles of silver and firm at the ankles;
Second, he put on the corselet, engirding his breast all about him,
Star-spangled, richly adorned — the fleet-footed Aeacid's corselet;
Over his shoulders he slung then the sword all studded with silver —
Bronze was the blade; then he took up the shield made ponderous, ample;

Then on his valorous temples the well-wrought helmet he fitted,
Horse-hair crested; the plume all fearfully nodded above it;
Lastly he grasped two doughty spears, to his hands nicely fitted —
All else he took but not the matchless Aeacid's javelin,
Pond'rous, sturdy, and huge — not one of the other Achaeans
Ever could wield it, Achilles alone understood how to wield it —
Javelin of Pelian ash, which Chiron gave his dear father,
Grown on Pelion's peak and appointed for death unto heroes.
Then he commanded that quickly Automedon yoke up the horses,
Whom, next after Achilles, the breaker of ranks, he most honored,
Likewise trusted the most to abide in the battle the shouting.

Under the yoke then quickly for him Automedon led them,
Xanthus and Balius, swift steeds that like the winds could go flying,
Twain that Podarge, the Harpy, had borne to Zephyr, the westwind,
As in a meadow she grazed by the side of the stream of the ocean.
Pedasus also, a faultless steed, he harnessed in side-gear,
One that Achilles seized at the sack of Eëtion's city —
Even though mortal himself, he kept pace with horses immortal. [racks,

Meantime Achilles, reviewing, commanded that all in their bar-
Myrmidons, mail them in armor, and they like wolves that on raw flesh
Raven with greed — and strength unspeakable dwelleth within them —
Yea, having slain in the mountains a great stag, mighty of antler,
Rend him in pieces, and all their chaps are reddened with carnage,
Then go faring away in a pack to a fountain of sombre
Water, and slender of tongue lap eager the dark-hued liquid
Surface, the while aye belching the blood of the slaughter, with always
Dauntless hearts in their breasts, though tightly their stomachs distended:
Even so swarmed the Myrmidon leaders, the counselors, gath'ring
Round him, the goodly squire of Aeacus' fleet-footed scion.
'Mongst them also was standing, of course, the martial Achilles,
Urging to battle both horses and men that were bearers of bucklers.

Fifty in number the swift-sailing ships that were led of Achilles,
Dear unto Zeus, when he sailed unto Troyland; fifty in number
Sat on the benches of each, his companions, warrior heroes.
Five he appointed commanders; the giving of signals he trusted
Solely to these, but himself as their king was mighty among them.

Marching at head of one file was Menesthius, gleaming of breastplate;
This commander was son of Sperchëus, a Zeus-fallen river;
Peleus' beautiful daughter, the fair Polydora, had borne him
Unto unwearied Sperchëus, a woman that couched with a godhead.
Yet in name was he son of Perieres' son, Borus —
Him who had wooed her with gifts past count and publicly wedded.

Martial Eudorus commanded the next, the second, battalion,
Born of a maid unwedded, the fair in the dance, Polymela,
Daughter of Phylas; her had the mighty slayer of Argus
Loved, when his eyes beheld her amid the maidens a-chanting
Praise unto Artemis, swift-rushing god of the golden arrows.
Straightway then to her chamber the god went up and in secret
Lay with her — Hermes, the bringer of weal — and she bore him Eudorus,
Glorious son that he was, and swift in the race, and a warrior.
But when the goddess of keen birth-pangs, Ilithyia, had brought him
Unto the daylight forth, and the sunbeams now had beheld him,
Unto his own home led her the stalwart might of Echecles,
Actor's son, for he gave unnumbered gifts in his wooing.
Also the old man Phylas, in tenderest love for the youngster,
Even as his own son entreated him kindly and reared him.

Third came onward the troops the martial Pisander commanded,
Maemalus' son, that excelled among all of the Myrmidon heroes
Fighting with spear, next after Pelides' comrade, Patroclus.
Next, the fourth battalion commanded the knightly old Phoenix;
Leading the fifth was Alcimedon, faultless son of Laërces. [rayed them,

When then Achilles had marshaled them all with their chiefs and ar-
Stationed well in their ranks, he laid strict orders upon them:

"Myrmidons, never let any of *you* now fail to remember
How by the swift-sailing ships you'd hurl dire threats at the Trojans
All through my season of wrath, and ye all upbraided me saying:
'Peleus' implacable son, on gall thy mother did nurse thee,
Pitiless man, who dost keep at the ships thy comrades unwilling.
Let us at least return to our homes with our sea-faring galleys,
Seeing that anger so baleful upon thy spirit hath fallen.'
Thus have ye often assailed me in groups; and now there is open
Mighty war-work, such as aforetime enamoured your fancy!

338

So let each and all with a stout heart fight with the Trojans."

  Thus he spake and aroused the might and courage of each man.
Tighter the ranks closed up, when they heard their prince's command-
As when a man may fit together the wall of a lofty   [ment.
Dwelling with close-set stones, to defy the assaults of the tempests:
So close fitted together the bucklers bossed and the helmets —
Buckler on buckler and helm on helm, and hero on hero —
Horsehair crests on the ridges of helmets agleam, as they nodded,
Touched one another — so densely they stood compacted together.
Out in front of them all two men were donning their armor,
Even Patroclus and with him Automedon, one in their purpose,
Eager to war in the van of the Myrmidons. Then did Achilles
Hasten away to his barrack and open the lid of a coffer
Beautiful, richly carven, which Thetis, the silvery-footed,
Gave him to take on his ship, and well she filled it with tunics,
Mantles to shelter him from the wind, and soft coverlets woolen.
Therein he kept him a cup fair-fashioned, and never another
Mortal drank of the sparkling wine therefrom than Achilles;
Nor to a god, save to Father Zeus, would he pour a libation.
This then he took from the coffer and thoroughly cleansed it with sulfur
First, then rinsed it with care with streams of fair-flowing water,
Washed his own hands, and drew off the sparkling wine in the goblet.
Then in the midst of the court he stood and poured the libation,
Looking to heaven; and Zeus, the hurler of lightning, attended:

  "Zeus, thou king Dodonaean, Pelasgic, dwelling afar off,
Ruling the wintry Dodona grove, and round thee the Selli
Dwell, thy prophets unwashen of feet, on the bare earth sleeping —
E'en as once aforetime thou heardest, when I besought thee,
Also to honor me then and afflictedst the host of Achaeans:
Likewise now again also my heart's wish bring to fulfilment.
I myself will indeed yet bide in the gath'ring of galleys,
But my comrade I send to the fight with my Myrmidon forces;
Grant, O Zeus of the far-borne voice, unto him now the glory.
Strengthen the warrior's heart in his breast, so even may Hector
Realize whether our squire himself knows how to do battle,
Even when warring alone, or whether invincibly rageth

His hand only when *I* go into the tumult of warfare.
But when far from the ships he hath driven the battle and war-din,
Scatheless may he return, I pray, to the swift-sailing galleys,
Safe with all of his armor and comrades that fight at close quarters."
　　Thus he spake in prayer; and counselor Zeus attended.
Part of the prayer the Father did grant, and part he denied him:
Unto Patroclus he granted to drive off far from the galleys
Battle and warfare; safe to return from the fight he denied him.
So, the libation accomplished with prayer to the Father Cronion,
Into his tent he returned, restored to its coffer the goblet,
Came out again, and stood in front of the tent; for his spirit
Yearned even yet to behold the dread clash of Achaeans and Trojans.
　　Under their great-hearted leader, Patroclus, issued the warriors,
War-clad, glorying proud, till they fell with a rush on the Trojans.
Instant the lines poured out and on like wasps by a roadside
Nesting, that children are wont too oft with their teasing to worry,
Ever tormenting them there, as they dwell in their home by the road-
Folly of boys! but a common nuisance they fashion for many,　　[side,
Since, if a wayfaring man do stir them perchance as he passeth—
Though unwittingly—all fly forth in a body, determined
Each with a resolute heart to fight in defense of his offspring:
So with a heart and a spirit like theirs then the Myrmidon forces
Poured forth now from the ships; unquenchable rose up the war-cry.
Long and loud Patroclus shouted and called to his comrades:
　　"Myrmidons, ye that are comrades of Peleus' scion, Achilles,
Quit you like men, my friends, and remember impetuous prowess,
That we may honor Pelides—his squires in close order fighting—
Him that of Argive chiefs at the ships by far is the bravest,
Yea, that Atrides' self, wide-realmed Agamemnon, may know it,
What was his blindness to honor the bravest Achaean in no way."
　　Thus he spake and aroused the might and courage of each man.
Therewith all in a mass they fell on the Trojans; around them,
As the Achaeans shouted, the galleys fearful resounded.
Now, as the Trojans beheld him, the valiant son of Menoetius,
Him himself and his squire, resplendent in glittering armor,
All of their hearts were confounded; the ranks of the companies wavered,

340

Deeming that he at the ships, fleet-footed Pelides, had minded
Now to forego his wrath and to choose a spirit of friendship:
Each one was glancing to see where to flee from impending destruction.

    First to hurl his glittering javelin then was Patroclus
Straight through the midst of the throng, where thickest the multitude
There at the stern of the ship of the great-souled Protesilaüs. [crowded,
One Pyraechmes he wounded, who brought the car-driving Paeonians
Thither from Amydon far and the wide-flowing Axius river.
Full on the shoulder he smote — the right one. Backward he tumbled,
Groaning, down in the dust; his Paeonian comrades about him
Fled in affright, such terror Patroclus created among them
All, when he slew their leader, who ever was best in a battle. [ing.
So from the galleys he drove them and quenched the fires that were burn-

    There was the ship then left half-burned, and the Trojans affrighted
Fled with a marvelous din; the Danaans poured in upon them
There 'mongst the hollow ships; and uproar constant ascended.
Even as when from the lofty crest of a mountain majestic
Zeus, the sender of lightning, hath stirred a lowering storm-cloud —
Then shine all of the look-outs clear and the uttermost headlands,
Glens, too, and under it ether immensurate gleameth from heaven:
So then the Danaans thrust off the blazing fire from the galleys,
Breathed for a little space, but rest had they none in the battle,
For not yet were the Trojans driven in rout by th' Achaeans,
Dear unto Ares, in headlong flight from the black-colored galleys;
Stubbornly still they withstood, but withdrew perforce from the galleys.

    Then fell man upon man, as the battle array was confounded —
Chief upon chief; and first then the valiant son of Menoetius
Smote in the thigh Areïlycus, just as he turned, with his keen-edged
Javelin; and clean through the leg Patroclus drave his bronze weapon.
Broke by the spear was the bone; and down to the earth fell the Trojan
Headlong. Then Menelaüs, the martial, wounded one Thoas,
Where, at the edge of his shield, his breast was exposed, and he loosened
All of his limbs. And Phylides, watching the charge of Amphiclus,
Lunged at him first, at the top of his thigh, where thickest the muscle
Ever is wont to grow on a man; and the sharp-pointed javelin
Rent those sinews in twain; deep darkness covered his eyelids.

One of old Nestor's sons, Antilochus, with his sharp javelin
Wounded Atymnius — drave through the Trojan's flank his bronze
Forward he tumbled directly; but Maris at hand with a javelin [weapon.
Right on Antilochus sprang — all wroth at the death of his brother —
Standing over the corse; Thrasymedes, however, the godlike,
Hurtled ere he could strike; and with aim unerring he struck him
Full on the shoulder; the point of his spear from his upper arm rended
All of the muscles, and also the bone it shattered completely.
Crashing he fell to the earth and darkness curtained his eyelids.
So it resulted — the two, o'ercome of the twain that were brothers,
Went unto Erebus both, Sarpedon's noble companions,
Spearmen, children of that Amisodarus, who had aforetime
Reared as a bane unto many that furious monster, Chimaera.
Then it was Ajax, son of Oïleus, assailed Cleobulus
Took him alive, while caught confused in the press; and he loosened
Right there wholly his strength; for he smote his neck with his hilted
Sword; all the blade was warm with blood; and darkness descended —
Darkness of death — on his eyes, and fate's mighty hand was upon him.
Rushed then against one another Peneleos and Lycon; for vainly
Both with their lances had hurtled; alike they had missed one another.
Instantly both ran together with sword-blades; thereupon Lycon
Smote on the horsehair crest at the socket, and all into pieces
Shattered the blade at the hilt. On his neck then Peneleos smote him
Under the ear; and the whole blade sank in; and only the skin then
Held, as the head hung sideward; and loosened were all of his members.
Now with his fleetness of foot hath Meriones well overtaken
Acamas mounting his car and stricken him full on the shoulder.
Down from his chariot he fell, and a mist poured over his eyelids.
Right on the mouth with the pitiless bronze hath Idomeneus smitten
Erymas; clean through piercing, the bronze of the javelin traveled
Under and up to the brain, and the white bones also it shattered;
Out of his mouth were shaken his teeth; both his eyes were filled with
Blood, while he spurted it forth alike through his mouth and his nos-
Undone, gasping; and death's dark cloud upon him descended. [trils —

Thus these Danaan leaders were each one slaying his foeman.
Even as robber wolves oft fall on the kids or the lambkins,

Choosing them out of the flocks, when, through the folly of shepherds,
They on the mountains are scattered. The wolves then, seeing it, seize
Quickly and tear them in pieces, the feeble and timorous-hearted: [them
So did the Danaans fall on the Trojans; so were *they* mindful
Only of ill-sounding flight and forgot their impetuous prowess.

    Ajax, the great, still aimed at bronzen-helmeted Hector,
Eager to hurtle his spear, but the other, skilful in warfare,
Ever with bull's hide buckler concealing the breadth of his shoulders,
Still took heed of the whizzing of darts and the crashing of lances.
Verily, well was he ware of the shift in the vantage of battle,
Yet even so he abode and would rescue his trusty companions.

    Even as when from Olympus a cloud moves over the heaven
Forth from the ether divine, when Zeus outspreadeth a tempest:
So there issued amain from the galleys a rout and a clamor.
Pell-mell, little in order, they crossed back. His swift-footed horses
Hector bore with his arms; and he left the host of the Trojans,
Whom all against their wills the deep-dug moat was restraining.
Many fleet horses that draw the car did there at the deep moat
Break off the poles at the front and forsake the cars of their masters.

    Meanwhile Patroclus followed and cheered his Danaans wildly,
Evilly minded toward Trojans; and they with a clamor and panic
Crowded the highways all—they were routed; above them a whirlwind
Lifted the dust to the clouds, while the whole-hoofed horses were strain-
Back to the city again, away from the galleys and barracks.   [ing
Still, wherever he saw that the Trojans herded the thickest,
Thither he drove with a cry; there men fell under the axles
Prone from the boxes; the cars were o'erturned, loud clanging as cym-
Right on over the moat went bounding the fleet-footed horses,   [bals.
Deathless, a glorious gift that the gods once gave unto Peleus,
Flying ahead; and the heart of Patroclus drave him at Hector,
Eager to smite with his spear; but the swift steeds bore him in safety.

    Even as under a tempest the whole earth is darkened and burdened,
When some day in the autumn Cronion in vehement torrents
Rains, in deep indignation with men that provoke him to anger,
Who in defiance of right in assembly judge crooked judgments,
Drive out justice, and reck not the watchful vengeance of heaven—

Then it is truly that all their rivers run full to o'erflowing,
Many the hillsides, too, that are cleft by the torrents descending
Into the blue sea flowing, in uproar down from the mountains
Headlong thunderous pouring, and works of men are diminished:
Such was the mighty roar of the Trojan horses in running.   [Trojans,
    Now as Patroclus had mown through the nearest battalions of
Back toward the galleys he drove them and shut them off nor allowed
Although eager their urge, to set foot in the city, but midway   [them
(In between the galleys and river and high-built rampart)
Storming upon them he slew, and exacted vengeance for many.
Pronoüs there was the first that he smote with his glittering javelin
Full on his breast unguarded of shield; and he loosened his members;
Down he fell with a crash. And the next he assailed was Thestor,
Enops' scion, who sat in his well-polished chariot, together
Huddled and wholly bereft of his senses. The reins from his fingers
Slipping had dropped. Patroclus approached and, standing beside him,
Shattered his jaw — the right; — through his teeth drave onward the jave-
Grasping the spear, Patroclus then drew him over the car's rim,   [lin.
As when a man on a jutting rock may be sitting and haply
Out of the sea with a line and a shining bronze hook draws a fine fish:
So with his shining spear he drew from his chariot Thestor,
Gaping, and thrust him down on his face. Thus fallen, life left him.
    Next Erylaüs came charging upon him; but he with a boulder
Smote him squarely upon the head, and it was all shattered
Inside the heavy helmet; and down to the earth fell the Trojan
Prone, and about him was poured out death, the spirit despoiler.
Erymas next he assailed, Amphoterus then, and Epaltes,
Then Tlepolemus, son of Damastor, Echius, Pyris,
Ipheus, too, and Evippus, and Argeas' son, Polymelus —
All to the bounteous earth he brought down, one after the other.
    Now as Sarpedon beheld them, his comrades unkilted of tunic,
Under the hands of Patroclus, the son of Menoetius, vanquished,
Loudly then did he call, the godlike Lycians upbraiding:
    "Shame, ye Lycians! Where do ye flee? Now show yourselves
Since it is I will confront this man and haply discover   [valiant,
Who is thus mastering us; he hath wrought the Trojans already

Untold evil; he looseth the knees of many and valiant."

　　Thus he spake and leaped full armored to earth from his chariot.
When he beheld him, Patroclus on his side sprang from his war-car.
They then, as vultures, hookèd of beak and crooked of talon,
Mightily scream on a lofty cliff, as they mingle in battle,
Likewise shouted aloud and rushed against one another.
Now then the son of Cronus, the crooked in counsel, beholding
Pitied them; then unto Hera he spake, his queen and his sister:

　　"Ah me! woe that Sarpedon, to me the dearest of mortals,
Fate will subdue at the hand of Patroclus, the son of Menoetius.
Two ways truly the heart in my breast is divided: I ponder
Whether to snatch him away from the tearful battle and set him,
Living, again in his home in the fertile land of the Lycians,
Or now under the hand of Menoetius' son to subdue him."

　　Him then answered in turn the ox-eyed, worshipful Hera:

　　"Most dread scion of Cronus, a word like this to have spoken!
Him, unto whom as a mortal a fate long since was appointed,
Art thou minded from dolorous death again to deliver?
Do it! However not all of us other gods will applaud thee.
Something besides I will tell thee, and deep in thy heart do thou lay it:
Now if thou send him alive to his home, the noble Sarpedon,
Wisely reflect that some other one of the gods may desire
Haply a dear son of his to convey from the strenuous combat.
Many are warring around yon mighty city of Priam,
Sons of immortals, and dire the wrath thou'lt kindle among them.
Nay, though he be so dear and afflict thy spirit with sorrow,
Nevertheless now leave him to fall in the strenuous combat,
Vanquished under the hands of Patroclus, the son of Menoetius.
Soon, however, as spirit and life have forsaken his body,
Then do thou send sweet Slumber and Death, with commandment to
Homeward — even until they arrive in the land of wide Lycia; [bear him
There will his kinsmen and friends inter him with funeral honors,
Rearing a pillar and tomb; such guerdon the dead is befitting."

　　Thus spake she; and the Father of men and of gods disregarded
Not, but he poured upon earth bloody raindrops down in a shower,
Doing honor to him, his dear son, whom Patroclus was destined

Soon in the deep-loamed Troyland to slay far away from his homeland.

   Now as they came close up in the onrush 'gainst one another,
Straightly Patroclus smote with his lance the renowned Thrasydemus —
Him that was goodly squire of Lycia's sovereign, Sarpedon —
Smiting him low in the belly, and loosened his limbs underneath him.
Next Sarpedon rushed in and attacked with his glittering javelin.
Him he missed but his horse, the mortal Pedasus, wounded — [his spirit;
Struck with his lance the right shoulder; he screamed, as he gasped out
Down he fell in the dust with a groan, and his soul flitted from him.
Started asunder the others, the twain, as the yoke creaked upon them;
Tangled, the reins were dragged in the dust, as the trace-horse lay
Therefor Automedon, famed for his spear, a remedy found him: [fallen.
Forth from his ſtout thigh drawing his long-edged glaive from its scab-
Out he bounded and cut the side-ſteed loose and delayed not; [bard,
Thereat the twain got into their ſtride and ran, with reins tightened.

   Once more the heroes clashed in the life-devouring contest,
Once more erred in its flight that glittering spear of Sarpedon:
Over Patroclus' left shoulder the wand'ring point of the javelin
Held on and smote him not; but, in his turn rising, Patroclus
Leveled his bronze; not vainly the missile fled from his fingers,
Rather it ſtruck where midriff encloses the heart in its throbbing.
Thereat he fell with a crash, as an oak-tree falls, or a poplar,
Or as a tall-grown pine, which craftsmen aloft on the mountains
Fell, with axes whetted afresh, for the timber of galleys:
Thus ſtretched out he was lying in front of his horses and chariot,
Heavily groaning and clutching the dust all sodden and gory.
So when a lion has fall'n on a herd of kine and has slaughtered,
Tawny and high of heart, some bull of the swing-paced cattle,
Groaning he perisheth under the claws and jaws of the lion:
Even so, under Patroclus, the leader of Lycian shieldmen
Raged, though mortally wounded, and called on his comrade belovèd:

   "Glaucus, dear fellow, 'mid heroes a warrior, much it behooves thee
Now above all to be a good spearman and warrior courageous:
Now, if intrepid thou art, set thy heart on the bane of the warfare.
First range hither and thither and waken the might of the heroes,
Leaders of Lycians, to fight for possession of fallen Sarpedon;

Then with thy weapon of bronze thyself also fight for my body.
For I should be a shame unto thee, a dishonor thereafter
All thy days and forever, if haply the sons of Achaia
Plunder my arms, that now 'mid the gath'ring of galleys am fallen.
Hold out manfully rather and rouse up all of the army."

　　Hardly the hero had spoken—the issue of death had descended,
Veiling his nostrils and eyes. With a foot on his bosom, Patroclus
Drew from his body the spear, and the midriff followed the weapon,
So that he drew forth the life and the point of the javelin together.
Meanwhile the Myrmidons held there the panting steeds of Sarpedon,
Eager to fly from the field, since the car was reft of its masters.

　　Desperate grief, when he heard that voice, now came upon Glaucus;
Stirred was his heart, for his strength was quite unavailing to aid him.
Gripping his arm with his hand, he squeezed it tight: the wound galled
Wound that Teucer had dealt with a shaft while fending the ruin [him—
Threat'ning his comrades, when Glaucus was storming the high-built
Then he spake in prayer, as was meet, to far-darting Apollo: [rampart.

　　"Hear me, O King, who art somewhere in Lycia's fertile dominion
Now or in Troyland here, for alike thou'rt able to hearken
Anywhere unto a man in need, as need is assailing
Me even now; for the wound that afflicts me is grievous and pierceth
All this arm with its penetrant pangs, and the blood is in no wise
Yet to be stanched, and the wound's sore burden cumbers my shoulder;
Nor of myself am I able to keep firm hold on my spearshaft,
Nor to go into battle with foes. Sarpedon is fallen,
Bravest of men, Zeus' son; but Zeus helps not his own offspring!
Natheless heal thou, O King, this wound that aggrieveth me sorely;
Lull its pangs; vouchsafe me the power to call on my comrades,
Call on my Lycian clansmen, to speed them, rouse them to warfare,
Yea, and myself do battle to rescue the corse that is fallen."

　　Thus he spake in prayer and Phoebus Apollo heard him.
Straightway the god made his pangs to cease, and the dark blood-current
Off from the sore wound he stanched, and he put strength into his spirit.
Glaucus was ware thereof in his heart and was gladdened within him,
Knowing the mighty god thus answered his prayer in a moment.
First, then, speeding away to the heroes, the leaders of Lycians,

347

All round ranging, he roused them to battle for fallen Sarpedon.
Thereupon off he went, with long ſtrides, after the Trojans,
Straight to Pulydamas, Panthoüs' son, and the goodly Agenor;
Also he went to Aeneas and bronzen-helmeted Hector.
Coming near, he ſtopped and in accents wingèd addressed them:

"Hector, now it appears thy allies thou wholly forgettest,
Who on account of thyself, far off from their friends and their country,
Offer freely their lives, while thou carest not to defend them.
Low now lieth Sarpedon, the leader of Lycian shieldmen,
Lycia's ſtay in his righteous judgments no less than his prowess.
Under the lance of Patroclus the bronzen Ares subdued him.
Come now, friends, and ſtand by him and feel in your hearts indignation,
Lest these Myrmidons ſtrip him of arms and disfigure his body,
Wrathful because of the Danaans, even the many that perished,
Whom we Lycians slew with our spears by the swift-sailing galleys."

Thus he spake, and the Trojans were filled completely with sorrow,
Grief unendurable, grief unchecked; for he, though a ſtranger,
Ever ſtood as a bulwark to them and their town; him they followed,
Many in number, and he was ever the bravest in battle.
Eager they marched ſtraight on at the Danaans; Hector was leading,
Wrathful because of Sarpedon. Patroclus, son of Menoetius,
Rugged of heart, meantime aroused the sons of Achaia.
First he addressed the Ajaxes twain, already right eager:

"Ajaxes, now be it dear unto you twain to beat off the foemen.
Such as among men ye were be now, yea, be even braver.
Low lieth he that leaped first within the rampart Achaean,
Even Sarpedon. But come! let us take and disfigure his body,
Strip from his shoulders his armor, and many a comrade around him
Quell with the pitiless bronze, as they fight amain to defend it."

Thus he spake. They themselves were eager to beat off the foemen.
When upon either side they had ſtrengthened their serried battalions,
Trojans and Lycians here, and Achaeans and Myrmidons yonder,
Then in battle together they clashed o'er the fallen Sarpedon,
Terribly shouting. And loud was the clang of the warriors' armor.
Baneful the darkness of night Zeus ſtretched o'er the furious combat,
So that around his dear son should arise a death-bringing travail.

Then were the Trojans the first in repelling the bright-eyed Achae-
Nowise the worst amongst those Myrmidon warriors was smitten, [ans.
Even the son of the great-hearted Agacles, goodly Epigeus,
He that was monarch of old in the well-built city Budeüm.
Later, it seems, he murdered a kinsman, a noble, and therefore
Suppliant came unto Peleus and Thetis, the silvery-footed.
They then sent him to follow Achilles, router of heroes,
Far unto Ilium, land of fine horses, to war with the Trojans.
Him, as he laid fast hold of the body, illustrious Hector
Smote on the head with a stone, and the Argive's head was all shattered
Inside the heavy helmet; and down he fell on the body
Prone; all round him was poured out death, the spirit despoiler.
Anguish of soul for his comrade slain now came on Patroclus.
Straight through the foremost fighters he pressed on his way like a fal-
Swift of pinion, that scatters in flight the daws and the starlings: [con,
So on the Lycians straight, O Patroclus, thou speeder of horses,
Didst thou then swoop — and the Trojans — all wroth in thy heart for thy
Then he smote Sthenelaüs, Ithaemenes' son, his belovèd,   [comrade.
Striking his neck with a boulder, and snapping the sinews that held it.
Thereat the foremost fighters drew back and illustrious Hector.
Even as far as the cast of a light-weight javelin may carry,
Thrown by a man who is making a trial of strength in a contest
Over a prize or in war if beset by implacable foemen:
So far yielded the Trojans; so far the Achaeans did thrust them.
Then it was Glaucus that first, the leader of shield-bearing Lycians,
Turned him about and slew one Bathycles, mighty of spirit,
Dear-loved scion of Chalcon, who dwelt in a palace in Hellas,
Both in his riches and wealth far passing his Myrmidon fellows.
Him then full on the breast did Glaucus strike with his javelin,
Suddenly wheeling on *him* that followed, about to o'ertake him.
Down he fell with a crash, and sore grief seized the Achaeans
Seeing a brave man fall; but the Trojans, mightily gladdened,
Stood round about him in ring compact; nor did the Achaeans
Ever their valor forget; their might they bore straight on against them.
Then Meriones slew a helmeted man of the Trojans,
Daring Laogonus, son of Onetor, who was appointed

Priest of Idaean Zeus and revered as a god by the people.
Under the jaw and the ear did he smite; and quickly the spirit
Passed from his limbs, and hateful darkness settled upon him.
Then at Meriones hurtled Aeneas a bronze-shod javelin,
Hoping to smite him, as forward he came 'neath his buckler's protection.
He, though, watching him come, eluded the bronze-tipped missile,
Stooping down forward; behind him the long lance hurtled and landed
Rooting itself in the earth, and the butt of the weapon a-quiver
Stood; and anon the powerful Ares *there* spent its fury.
Quivering spent itself in the earth Aeneas's spear-point;
Only in vain from his stalwart hand its way it had speeded.
Wrathful in heart was Aeneas and cried out loud in his anger:
    "Excellent dancer indeed, as thou art, O Meriones, quickly
My spear had stopped thee for good, if only perchance I had struck thee.'.
    Him then in his turn answered Meriones, famed for his javelin:
    "Hard were it even for thee, how valiant soever, Aeneas,
All men's might, whoever in battle may haply encounter
Thee, to extinguish; insooth even thou wast created a mortal!
Truly should I ever cast with the keen bronze, smiting thy middle,
Then, even though thou art doughty, of confident hand, thou shouldst
Glory to me and thy soul unto Hades, famed for his horses."   [render
    Thus spake he; but Menoetius' strong son chided him, saying:
    "Why making speeches like this, Meriones, thou that art valiant?
Good my friend, it is not for reproachful words that the Trojans
Back will withdraw from the corse; ere *that* the earth will hold many.
Issue of warfare lieth in hands, but of speech in the council:
So it is noway meet to multiply words but to battle."
    Thus he spake and led on; the godlike warrior followed.
Even as haply the din of woodmen's axes ariseth
Deep in the dells of a mountain and far-off echoes awakens:
So from the wide-wayed earth rose ever the din of the warriors,
Clanging of bronze and of bucklers, cunningly moulded of bull's hide,
Under the smiting of swords and of twin-pointed lances upon them.
Now had a keen-eyed man not known him, the goodly Sarpedon,
So was he covered with missiles and dust and the carnage of combat;
All the way down to his toes from the crown of his head he was covered.

350

Ever around the dead man they crowded, as flies in a steading
Buzz in a swarm at the surface of milk-pails laden and brimming,
When, in the springtide season, the bright milk drenches the vessels:
Even so round the dead man the warriors were swarming; but never
Zeus from the mighty conflict his bright eyes averted but ever
Fixedly gazed down upon them; and still in his heart he debated,
Pond'ring deeply and long on the slaying of goodly Patroclus:
Whether at once in the mighty conflict the glorious Hector
There should slay him also over the corse of Sarpedon,
Peer of immortals, with bronze, and the armor strip from his shoulders,
Whether to deal out still unto more men arduous travail.
Now, as thus he was thinking, it seemed unto him that the better
Plan should be for Patroclus, the goodly squire of Achilles,
Peleus' son, to drive both the Trojans and bronze-helmèd Hector
Back to the city once more and the life-breath ravish of many.
Then first of all he put into Hector a spirit of weakness:
Leaping up into his chariot he turned unto flight and called other
Trojans to flee, for he knew Zeus's holy balance was turning.
Then no longer abided the valiant Lycians; a panic
Fell on them all at beholding their king to the heart death-stricken,
Lying encumbered of corpses, for many had fallen upon him
Slaughtered, while Zeus Cronion kept straining the strenuous struggle.
Off from his shoulders they stripped the bronze war-gear of Sarpedon —
Radiant bronze — and down to the hollow galleys Menoetius'
Valiant son delivered it o'er to his comrades to carry.
Then it was Zeus that gath'reth the clouds spake thus to Apollo:
  "Come now, Phoebus beloved, go take from the range of the missiles
Dead Sarpedon; and cleanse the black blood away, and then bear him
Far off, clear of the battle, and lave him in streams of the river;
Then with ambrosia anoint him and clothe him in garments ambrosial;
Last under escort send him away, full speedily wafted
Borne by Slumber and Death, twin brothers, who quickly will set him
Down in the fertile demesne of his spacious Lycian home-land;
There will his kinsmen and friends inter him with funeral honors,
Rearing a pillar and tomb; such guerdon the dead is befitting."
  Thus spake he; and Apollo, not deaf to the word of his father,

Sped from the mountains of Ida down into the roar of the battle,
Straightway took from the range of the missiles the godlike Sarpedon,
Bore him afar from the field, and laved him in streams of the river,
Then with ambrosia anointed, and clothed him in garments ambrosial,
Last under escort sent him away, full speedily wafted
Borne by Slumber and Death, twin brothers, who then quickly set him
Down in the fertile demesne of his spacious Lycian home-land.

    Crying aloud to his steeds and Automedon, meantime Patroclus
Charged on after the Trojans and Lycians, utterly blinded,
Fool that he was! for indeed, had he heeded the word of Pelides,
Truly the evil doom of black death he had haply evaded.
Always, however, the judgment of Zeus is stronger than man's wit—
Zeus that affrighteth a brave man even and easily taketh
Vict'ry away, and again he arouseth a man unto battle.
He it was then unbridled the heart in the breast of Patroclus.

    Who was the warrior first, who also the last that thou slewest
Then, O Patroclus, when even the gods were calling thee deathward?
First was Adrestus, next Autonoüs, also Echeclus,
Perimus, scion of Megas, Epistor, then Melanippus;
Elasus then didst thou slay and Mulius, too, and Pylartes.
These he despatched, but the rest were all heart-set upon fleeing.
Then had the sons of Achaia taken the high-gated Troia
Under Patroclus' hands, for his spear ranged round and before him,
But that Phoebus Apollo aloft on a well-builded tower
Stood and devised him ruin, for *he* was aiding the Trojans.
Thrice, at an angle, he climbed on the well-built rampart, Patroclus;
Thrice was he buffeted back by the strong god, Phoebus Apollo,
Smiting with hands immortal Patroclus' radiant buckler.
But, when a fourth time, like to a god, he was charging upon him,
Then with a terrible cry far-working Apollo addressed him:

    "Yield thee, Patroclus, scion of Zeus; for indeed it is fated
Not under *thy* lance falleth the town of the lordly Trojans,
Nor under lance of Achilles, a man far stronger than thou art."

    Thus spake he; and Patroclus withdrew far back from the bastion,
Awe-struck, shunning the wrath of the god, far-darting Apollo. [Scaean
    Hector the while was restraining his whole-hoofed steeds at the

Sleep and Death Conveying the Body of Sarpedon to Lycia

Gateway, questioning whether to drive right into the turmoil
Once more and fight or to summon the hosts to the rampart together.
Thus as he pondered, lo! at his side stood Phoebus Apollo;
Now *he* had likened himself to a hero, lusty and mighty,
Asius, uncle maternal of Hector, tamer of horses,
Hecabe's brother, her own, the son of Dymas, her father,
Him that in Phrygia dwelt beside the Sangarius river.
Taking his semblance, Apollo, the son of Zeus, then addressed him:
   "Hector, wherefore cease from the battle? In naught it behooves
Would I were so much stronger as now I am weaker than thou art! [thee!
Soon to thy woe wouldst thou thus have withdrawn aloof from the battle!
Come, then, turn thy strong-hoofed horses now on Patroclus,
If thou may'st haply slay him, and Phoebus accord thee the glory."
   Thus spoke the god and mingled again in the warriors' tumult.
Glorious Hector then bade the wise-heart Cebriones lash his
Horses back into the war, while meantime Phoebus Apollo
Went and entered the throng and among the Argives confusion
Dreadful created, and glory he gave to the Trojans and Hector.
Other Danaans Hector let be nor attempted to slay them.
Straight at Patroclus alone he guided his strong-hoofed horses.
Down to the ground from his chariot on his side bounded Patroclus,
Gripping his lance in his left; with his right he caught up a boulder;
Shining and jagged it was, and his wide grasp covered it over.
Firmly planting his feet, he hurled nor shrank from his foeman
Long, and not in vain did he cast it but struck with it Hector's
Driver, Cebriones (bastard son of illustrious Priam),
Holding the reins of the horses. The sharp stone, smiting his forehead,
Tore on, crushing his eyebrows both in a mass; nor resisted
Even the bone, but his eyes fell there in the dust and before him
Lay at his feet; and quickly Cebriones plunged like a diver
Down from the well-wrought car; and life fled forth from his body.
Him with a taunt didst thou then address, O knightly Patroclus:
   "Bless me! nimble insooth is the man, so lightly he tumbles!
Yea, if perchance he were sailing the deep sea, teeming with fishes,
Many, methinks, this man might sate by his fetching up oysters,
Leaping off from the ship, e'en though it were boisterous weather —

So on the plain doth he lightly dive from out of his war-car!
Truly it seems that among the Trojans also are tumblers!"
    Thus he spake and advanced at the hero Cebriones' body,
Springing in like a lion that wastes the folds and is wounded
Then with a spear in the breast—his own valor it is that destroys him.
So on Cebriones thou didst leap in thy fury, Patroclus.
Hector on his side, too, leaped down to the earth from his chariot.
Over Cebriones these twain strove like a couple of lions,
Which on the heights of a mountain in common hunger do battle
Over a hind that is slain, and high in temper they struggle:
So, to possess Cebriones' corse, those lords of the war-cry,
Even Patroclus, Menoetius' son, and glorious Hector,
Each with the pitiless bronze hewed hard at the flesh of the other.
Seizing hold on the head, naught Hector relaxed in the struggle,
While on his side Patroclus held by the foot, and the others,
Trojans and Danaans, met in a terrible conflict together.
    As when the east wind vies and the south wind, one with the other,
Deep in the dells of a mountain, wide-shaking the depths of a forest—
Beeches and mountain ash, and also the smooth-barked cornel—
Whileas against one another the trees with their tapering branches
Clash in a marvelous din, and the limbs crash splintered and broken:
Even so, leaping against one another, Achaeans and Trojans
Slew, and of ruinous flight nor one nor another was minded.
Many keen javelins about Cebriones' body were planted,
Many the feathered arrows, too, that had leaped from the bowstring;
Many and mighty the boulders that battered the bucklers of heroes,
As they were warring about him; but he in the swirl of the dust-cloud
Lay there mighty and mightily fallen, his knighthood forgotten.
    Now, as long as the sun was standing high in mid-heaven,
Missiles from both sides kept falling amain and felling the people:
But when it started to slope toward the time for unyoking of oxen,
Lo! the Achaeans surpassed what even their fate had decreed them.
Then from the missiles they dragged the hero Cebriones' body,
Forth from the Trojans' shouting, and stripped from his shoulders his
While, with a purpose of evil, Patroclus charged on the Trojans. 〔armor,
Three times then, a match for fleet Ares, he charged in upon them,

Crying his terrible cry, and each time nine heroes he slaughtered.
But when, a fourth time, like to a god, he was charging upon them,
Then, it seems, there appeared unto thee thy life's end, Patroclus:
Then it was Phoebus met thee there in the terrible conflict,
Dreadful god!　Unmarked by Patroclus he entered the tumult,
Seeing he joined the encounter with thick mist mantled about him,
Stopped behind him, and smote him full on the back and broad shoulders —
Smote with the flat of his hand; and dazed were the eyes of Patroclus.
Also the helmet was struck from his head by Phoebus Apollo;
Rolling away, it rattled beneath the hoofs of the horses —
Helmet with upright socket. Defiled was the plumage of horsehair,
Trailed in the blood and the dust; aforetime it never was fated
So to be soiled in the dust, with its horsetail decked and adornèd,
Seeing it sheltered the head and the handsome brow of a godlike
Hero, even Achilles; but Zeus then gave it to Hector,
Proudly to wear on his head: destruction already was nigh him.
Shivered was all the far-shadowing spear in the hands of Patroclus,
Ponderous, great and strong, with bronze point shodden; the tasseled
Buckler fell to the earth with the baldric, shed from his shoulders;
Zeus's son, sovereign Apollo, loosened also his corselet.
Then on his heart fell blindness, his glorious limbs were relaxèd;
There he stood in a daze. Close behind with keen-pointed javelin
Smote him upon his back 'twixt the shoulders a hero Dardanian,
Even Euphorbus, Panthoüs' son, who surpassed all his fellows
Both in casting the spear and in driving horses and running.
Ay, already a score of men he had thrust from their war-cars,
Though for the first time come with a car for instruction in warfare.
He was the first to reach thee with javelin, O knightly Patroclus —
Not to subdue; he ran back and mixed with the press of the people,
When he had plucked from his flesh the ashwood spear nor awaited,
Though he was wholly disarmed, Patroclus' shock in the battle.
Overcome by the blow of the god and the javelin, Patroclus,
Shunning his fate, drew back once more to the ranks of his comrades.

　　Hector — when he beheld the great-souled son of Menoetius
Struck with the keen bronze spear and turning back from the war-front —
Traversed the ranks, drew nigh him, and straight at his nethermost belly

Struck with his javelin and drave clean through his body the weapon.
Down he fell with a crash and brought the Achaeans great sorrow.
As when a lion a boar, unwearied, hath conquered in battle,
When, on the heights of a mountain, both high in mettle do battle
Over a little spring, for both are bent upon drinking;
Gasping and panting, the boar by the might of the lion is vanquished:
So was the valiant son of Menoetius, after he'd slaughtered
Many, bereft of his life by the spear-thrust of Priam's son, Hector.
Boasting above him, with wingèd words the victor addressed him:

"Surely thou wast thinking to pillage our city, Patroclus,
Take from Ilium's women their day of freedom, and lead them
Captive in galleys with thee to the well-loved land of thy fathers.
Fool that thou wast! for before them the fleet-footed horses of Hector
All strained eager their feet to the war, and here 'mongst the Trojans,
Lovers of war, I am noted myself for my spear, and I ward off
Ever the day of their doom; but here shall vultures devour thee.
Poor man! Even Achilles, for all his valor availed thee
Naught, who, staying, as *thou* camest, doubtless straitly enjoined thee:
'Come not again, I pray, my Patroclus, thou speeder of horses,
Back to the hollow ships, or ever the tunic encrimsoned
Thou shalt have rent on the bosom of Hector, slayer of heroes.'
So he addressed thee, no doubt, and persuaded the wits of the witless."

Then with faint breath thou madest reply, O knightly Patroclus:

"Now even make thy loudest boast, O Hector, the vict'ry
Zeus, Cronus' son, and Apollo have given thee; they have subdued me
Easily; they, it is they that stripped from my shoulders my armor.
Truly if there had met me a score of such mortals as thou art,
All would surely have perished there, subdued 'neath my javelin.
Only a ruinous fate and the scion of Leto have slain me,
Ay, and of men, Euphorbus; and thou art but third in my slaying!
Something besides I will tell thee, and deep in thy heart do thou lay it:
Verily, thou thyself not long shalt have life; but already
Death and the heavy hand of fate are standing close by thee,
Slain at the hands of the faultless Achilles, Aeacus' scion."

Hardly thus he had spoken — the end of death overspread him.
Flitting, his soul from his limbs unto Hades' mansion departed,

Wailing its fate, thus leaving the prime and vigor of manhood.
Therewith, though he was dead, the glorious Hector addressed him:

"Why, O Patroclus, dost thou foretell me impending destruction?
Who is there knows but the son of the fair-haired Thetis, Achilles,
Smitten by *my* spear, shall be the first to surrender his spirit?"

Thus he spake and drew from the wound the bronze-pointed javelin,
Planting his heel on the body, then thrust it supine from the spearhead.
Then with his lance uplifted he charged on Automedon straightway,
Peer of a god, the squire of Aeacus' swift-footed scion;
For he was eager to smite; but the swift steeds bore him in safety —
Deathless — glorious gift that the gods once gave unto Peleus.

ILIAD · XVII · (P)

In Rho the vent'rous hosts maintain
A slaughterous conflict for the slain.

NEITHER did Atreus' son, Menelaüs, dear unto Ares,
Fail to know that Patroclus was slain in the strife by the Trojans.
Straight through the forefront he went, wide-flashing the bronze of his
Strode then over the fallen, as over her calf, her first-born,   [armor,
Standeth and loweth its mother, to motherhood till then a stranger:
So fair-haired Menelaüs bestrode the corse of Patroclus,
Holding before him his spear and his shield, all evenly rounded,
Eager to slay whoever might venture to come out against him.
Neither was Panthoüs' son, of the stout spear of ash-wood, unheeding
Faultless Patroclus fallen, but, coming close up anigh him,
Stopped and addressed with a word Menelaüs, dear unto Ares:
    "Nurseling of Zeus, Menelaüs Atrides, captain of peoples,
Yield thee; abandon the body and leave me the trophies encrimsoned.
For of allies far-famed was none, nor of Trojans before me
Any, in smiting Patroclus with lance in the strenuous combat.
Leave me accordingly this fair glory to win 'mid the Trojans,
Lest I smite thee and take thy life and its honeyed sweetness."
    Grievously wroth, fair-haired Menelaüs addressed him in answer:
    "Zeus, O Father, to boast past measure insooth is unseemly.
Never, it seems, is the spirit of pard so high, nor of lion,
Nor of the savage wild boar — in which is fury the greatest
Even of all, when his breast swells high with immoderate raging —
Now as of Panthoüs' sons in the pride of their javelins of ash-wood.
Even the might of that tamer of steeds, Hyperenor, had noway
Joy of his youth, what time he abode *my* shock and reviled me,
Deeming that I was a warrior then, of the Danaans weakest —
Meanest of all; but methinketh his own feet carried him homeward
Never, to gladden his well-loved wife and his excellent parents.

Likewise surely a life will I take, thine own, if thou darest
Stand up against me. Return to the throng of the combatants rather—
So I would bid thee—nor venture to meet me, ere thou some evil
Suffer. When a thing's done, then even a fool understands it!"

Thus he spake and persuaded him not, but he answered him saying:
"Well now, nurseling of Zeus, thou'lt pay me in truth, Menelaüs,
Fully for him thou slewest, my brother—and boastest about him!—
Thou that hast widowed his wife in the bridal recess of her new-built
Chamber and brought lamenting past words and woe to our parents.
I shall become consolation to them in their sorrow, a respite
Haply from tears, if returning I bring thy head and thy armor,
If in Panthoüs' hands and the queenly Phrontis' I place them.
Now shall the toil, however, no longer remain unattempted
Nor uncontested, whether defeat or vict'ry the issue."

So spake he; then smiting the shield all evenly rounded,   [bended
Through it the bronze brake not, for the spear-point backward was
Deep in the stalwart buckler. And then Menelaüs Atrides   [Father—
Lunged with his bronze-pointed spear—with a prayer to Zeus, the All-
Full at the nethermost base of his throat, while backward he yielded,
Following up his heavy hand with the weight of his body.
Right through the delicate neck drave onward the point of the weapon.
Down he fell with a crash; loud clanged his armor upon him.
Dabbled, bedrenched with his blood were those locks like locks of the
Braided—his tresses laced with silver and gold bands together. [Graces,
Like as a man rears lusty a sapling, a shoot of an olive,
All in a lonesome place, where bubbles abundance of water,
Beautiful shoot, fair-growing, with all kinds of breezes upon it
Blowing, to sway it about; and it bursts into blossoms of whiteness;
All of a sudden there comes a blast of a terrible tempest,
Wrenches it out of its place, and lays it on earth low-leveled:
Even so, when he had slain Euphorbus, Panthoüs' scion,
Him of the stout spear of ash-wood Atrides stripped of his armor.

Even as when some lion a mountain hath bred, in his prowess
Confident, snatches a cow, the best of the herd in the pasture—
First he seizes her neck with his powerful teeth, and he breaks it,
Afterward rends her and gulps down the blood and the innermost vitals

All, while hounds round about him and men that are herdsmen incessant
Clamor aloud and afar, while no one is willing to hazard
Coming to battle against him, for pale fear seizes and holds them:
So in the breasts of the Trojans the valor of none would adventure
Coming directly to battle against far-famed Menelaüs.
Easily then might Atrides have borne off Panthoüs' offspring's
Glorious armor, if Phoebus Apollo had not begrudged it.
He then roused up against him Hector, a peer of swift Ares,
Taking the semblance of Mentes, a man, the Ciconians' leader.
Lifting his voice, with wingèd words he spake to him, saying:
    "Now thou art running after things unattainable, Hector,
Even the steeds of the wise Aeacides. Difficult are those
Horses to master and manage—for all men difficult driving
Save for Achilles' self, who was born of a mother immortal.
Meanwhile, thou seest, Atreus' son, Menelaüs, the martial,
Now hath bestridden Patroclus and slain the best of the Trojans,
Panthoüs' son, Euphorbus, and stayed his impetuous prowess."
    Thus spoke the god and mingled again in the warriors' tumult.
Sore grief covered the heart of Hector, all darkened within him.
Then, as he searchingly peered up and down the ranges, he noted
Quickly the one man stripping the glorious arms and the other
Leveled with earth; and blood from the gaping wound was still flowing.
Straight through the forefront he went, wide-flashing the bronze of his
Crying his terrible cry and like to the flames of Hephaestus,   [armor,
Not to be quenched. And not unaware of the cry was Atrides.
Heavy of heart he communed with his own magnanimous spirit:
    "Ah me! If I abandon the fair war-gear and Patroclus—
Him who lies here slain—in defense of my honor he's fallen—
Some of the Danaans, who may see, I fear will reproach me;
But if I battle alone 'gainst the Trojans, haply, and Hector,
Scorning dishonor, though single, I fear lest many surround me:
All of the Trojans leads hither the shimmering-helmeted Hector.
Yet, why thus with herself is my dear heart debating within me?
Whenso willeth a man in defiance of heaven to battle
'Gainst whom God will exalt, woe rolls like a billow upon him;
Therefore no one of the Argives will chide, whoever may see me

Yielding to Hector, for he by commission from heaven is warring.
If I could somewhere discover but Ajax, good at the war-cry,
Both of us charging anew would remember the rapture of battle;
E'en in defiance of heaven, we'd rescue the dead man haply
Then for Achilles Pelides; of evils at least it were lightest."

    While in his heart and soul Atrides pondered in such wise,
So long the lines of Trojans came on; and Hector was leading.
Then Menelaüs retreated and fell back, leaving the body,
Turning often about, as a deep-maned lion and shaggy
Turneth, as hounds and men with clamor and javelins chase him
Off from a fold; though valiant, the heart that he beareth within him
Freezeth with dread, as he leaves that farmyard, sorely reluctant:
So from the fallen Patroclus fair-haired Menelaüs departed.
Turning around then, he stood, when he reached the host of his com-
Eagerly peering about for Telamon's son, the great Ajax.   [rades,
Him right soon he espied far off at the left of the battle,
Heart'ning his comrades there and rousing them up to do battle,
Them whom Phoebus Apollo had struck with a panic from heaven.
Instant he went on a run, then spoke, as he stopped close beside him:
    "Come, O Ajax, dear fellow, now let us for fallen Patroclus
Stir ourselves, if perchance we may carry his corse to Achilles,
Naked, at least; for his arms hath the shimmering-helmeted Hector."

    Thus he spake, and he stirred the soul of the wise-hearted Ajax.
Right through the forefront he went, and with him fair-haired Menelaüs.
Hector had stripped already the glorious gear from Patroclus;
Now he was haling the corse and with keen bronze meant to behead it
First, then drag it away to give to the dogs of the Trojans.
Ajax then came to close quarters, bearing his shield like a tower.
Hector retreated at once to the throng of his comrades and nimbly
Leaped up into his car, and he gave the beautiful armor
O'er to the Trojans to bear to the city, to be his great glory.
Ajax the mean while stood, his broad shield protecting Patroclus,
Stood as a lioness standeth perchance in defense of her kittens,
When she is leading her cubs in a deep wildwood and encounters
Men that are hunters; the heart swells high in the breast of the mother,
Veiling her eyes while folding and knitting the skin of her eyebrows:

Such the appearance of Ajax, bestriding the hero Patroclus.
Hard by stood at his side Menelaüs, belovèd of Ares,
Atreus' son. Great grief he nursed in his breast, as he stood there.

　　　Thereupon Glaucus, Hippolochus' son, a leader of Lycians,
Scowlfully looking at Hector with harsh words sternly rebuked him:
　　　"Hector, bravest in seeming, in fight, though, much art thou lacking.
Only for naught fair glory invests thee; a runaway art thou!
Now then bethink thee how *thou* wilt keep safe thy home and thy city —
Thou alone with the hosts that in Ilium city are native.
Never a man of the Lycians will go to fight the Achaeans
Now in behalf of the town; for never a thank was accorded
Any for always battling, without any respite, the foemen.
How wouldst thou bring back a man of lesser worth to thy people,
Hard of heart that thou art! for Sarpedon, thy guest and thy comrade
Thou didst abandon to be the Achaeans' prey and their plunder.
He was often of profit to thee thyself and thy city,
While yet alive. And now from the dogs thou durst not save him!
Now, then, if any will hearken to me of the Lycian warriors,
Home we will go, and to Troy be revealed her impending disaster!
Nay, if a spirit were now in Trojan bosoms, intrepid,
Dauntless, such as inspireth a man's heart when he arrayeth
Struggle and strife unabating 'gainst foemen at war in his country,
Speedily then should we drag into Ilium the corse of Patroclus.
Ay, and if this man should come to the mighty town of king Priam,
Dead though he be, and if we from the battle could manage to drag him,
Speedily then would the Argives surrender the beautiful armor,
Gear of Sarpedon, and him — his body — we'd bring back to Ilium —
Seeing the squire has been slain of such a hero; the bravest
Argive now at the ships is he, with his close-fighting squires.
Thou, however, hadst not the courage to stand against Ajax —
Great-hearted Ajax — and look in his face 'mid the shouts of the war-
Nor to contend with him fairly, for he is a better than thou art." [riors,

　　　Scowlfully eyeing, addressed him the shimmering-helmeted Hector:
　　　"Glaucus, why hath a man like thee unbecomingly spoken?
Fie on it! Truly, I thought thee excelling all others in wisdom,
Such and as many as dwell in the deep-soiled country of Lycia.

Now do I utterly scorn such wisdom as this thou hast spoken,
When thou sayest I durst not abide a giant like Ajax.
Never have *I* at a battle or thunder of chariots shuddered;
Only the judgment of Zeus who wieldeth the aegis is stronger,
Zeus that affrighteth a brave man even and easily taketh
Vict'ry away, and again he arouseth a man unto battle.
Nay, come hither, good fellow, stand by me, take note of my doings,
Whether a dastard's role shall be mine all day, as thou sayest,
Whether some one of the Danaans, too, though eager for battle,
I shall check in his prowess in fighting for fallen Patroclus."

    Thus he spake, and he cried with a shout long and loud to the Tro-
    "Trojans, Dardanians, Lycians, that joy in closest encounter, ⌈jans:
Quit you like men, my friends, and remember impetuous prowess,
While I put on me the goodly arms of the blameless Achilles,
Arms that I took as my spoils, when I slew the mighty Patroclus."

    Thus he spake and departed, the shimmering-helmeted Hector,
Out from the strife of the war, and he ran, overtaking his comrades
Speedily—not yet far off, so swiftly of foot he pursued them—
Who to the city were bearing the far-famed gear of Pelides.
Off from the dolorous combat he stopped, exchanging his harness,
Handed his own to the lovers of war, the Trojans, to carry
Up into Ilium holy, and put on the armor immortal,
Worn by Achilles Pelides, a gift that the dwellers in heaven
Made to his father beloved, and he in his age thereafter
Gave to his son; but the son aged not in the gear of his father.

    But when Zeus, the compeller of clouds, beheld him afar off
Mailing himself in the arms of Peleus' scion, the godlike,
This word, shaking his head meanwhile, he addressed to his spirit:
    "Ah me! thou hapless man, no thought of death overtakes thee,
Yet is it verily nigh thee. Thou donnest the armor immortal—
Arms of a prince, a hero, before whom all other men tremble.
Comrade of his thou hast slain, a man both gentle and mighty;
His is the armor that thou from that comrade's head and his shoulders
Tookest unmeetly. In recompense now great might I will grant thee,
Seeing thou ne'er shalt come home for Andromache even Pelides'
Glorious arms to receive at thy hands, returned from the battle."

Thus spake the son of Cronus; with darkling eyebrows he nodded;
But on the body of Hector he made the arms fit; and the war-god
Ares entered him, dreadful; and then with strength were his members
Filled and with valor; and after his famous allies he sped, shouting
Loud; and to all the hosts, as he flashed in that armor refulgent,
Like unto Peleus' son he looked, great-hearted Achilles.
Then, as he came unto each, with encouraging words he addressed him,
Spurring to battle Mesthles, Thersilochus, Glaucus, and Medon,
Asteropaeus and thee, Disenor, Hippothoüs also,
Phorcys and Chromius, too, and Ennomus, skilled as an augur —
Urging them on to the battle, with wingèd words he addressed them:

"Hear me, ye countless tribes of allies that dwell round about us.
Not for mere numbers I sought you aforetime (numbers I lacked not)
When I assembled you here, foregathered out of your cities,
Nay, but that ye with zeal might defend the wives of the Trojans —
Them and their innocent children — against the war-loving Argives.
This is the purpose in mind, when I weary the people to furnish
Pay and food, your strength thereby to augment and your valor.
Therefore let everyone turn him direct to the combat —
Either to die or be saved; for such is love-making in warfare!
Whoe'er haleth Patroclus, dead though he be, to the Trojans,
Tamers of steeds, and compelleth the stout-heart Ajax to yield him,
Half of the spoils I will portion to that man, only retaining
Half for myself; his glory as equal to mine shall be counted."   [gives,

Thus spake he; and they charged with all their might on the Ar-
Lifting and leveling spears, and their hearts beat high with expectance,
Hopeful of haling the corse from beneath Telamonian Ajax —
Fools that they were; for over that corse of life he reft many.
Then did Ajax address Menelaüs, good at the war-cry:

"Good my friend, Menelaüs, thou nurseling of Zeus, no longer
Dare I to hope that we two ourselves go home from this warfare,
Nay, for I tremble not now so much for the corse of Patroclus,
Soon to be glutting, methinketh, the birds and the dogs of the Trojans,
Like as I tremble for mine own head, lest something befall it,
Mine and thine: for a storm-cloud of battle wraps us in darkness,
Hector himself! And impending ruin is staring upon us.

Come then, call on the Danaan chieftains, if any may hear thee."

Thus spake he; Menelaüs, good at the war-cry, obeyed him:
Loud, with a ringing shout he called to the Danaan warriors:

"Friends of mine, ye commanders and counseling chiefs of the Ar-
Who with Atreus' sons, Agamemnon and prince Menelaüs,   [gives,
Drink at the common cost and issue commands to the war-hosts—
Each to his own men; glory and honor from Zeus will attend him.
Difficult is it for me to distinguish in press of the conflict
Each of the chiefs, so fearful a strife in the battle is kindled;
Each, of himself, go forward; let each be indignant in spirit,
Wroth that Patroclus should be a sport for the dogs of the Trojans."

Thus he; and clearly heard him the fleet Oïlean Ajax.
He was the first to come running up through the turmoil to meet him;
After him followed Idomeneus' self and his sturdy attendant,
Even Meriones, peer of Enyalius, slayer of heroes.
Who, though, ever could name those others by heart and recount them
All, that behind these leaders aroused the Achaeans to battle?

Forward the Trojans in mass came charging; Hector was leading.
Even as when at the mouth of a river fallen from heaven
Roareth a billow immense, as it counters the stream, and around it
Echo the headlands sharp, as the sea comes bellowing beachward:
Such was the shout, as the Trojans charged; and still the Achaeans
Stood and encircled the son of Menoetius, single in spirit,
All round fenced with bucklers of bronze; and about and above them
Over their radiant helmets Cronion poured out a thick darkness—
Zeus that aforetime never had hated the son of Menoetius,
While he yet lived and served as squire to Aeacus' scion,
Nay, but he grudged that Patroclus should be the prey of his Trojan
Enemies' dogs; so he stirred up his comrades now to defend him.

Then were the Trojans first in repelling the bright-eyed Achaeans;
They shrank away and abandoned the corse; but the arrogant Trojans
Slew not one with their spears, although right eager to slay them—
Only the corse would they drag off; but brief time only th' Achaeans
Were to be kept from the body, for Ajax rallied them quickly—
Ajax, the greatest in deeds and also the handsomest looking
'Mongst all the Danaans, after the faultless scion of Peleus.

Right through the foremost fighters he pressed his way in his prowess
Like a boar in the mountains, which scatters the dogs and the hunters
Lusty and young, at his ease, through the glades, at bay turned upon
Suchwise glorious Ajax, the proud-souled Telamon's scion,   [them:
Easily scattered the ranks of the Trojans, charging amid them,
Who had bestridden Patroclus slain, all eagerly minded
Off to the city to hale him and win a renown everlasting.

　　　Then did Hippothoüs, glorious son of Pelasgian Lethus,
Set on the fallen to drag him away through the violent conflict,
Binding his foot with a strap at the ankle, girdling the sinews,
Showing a favor to Hector and helping the Trojans; but quickly   [him:
Mischief came on himself, from which none, though eager, could save
Telamon's son, with a rush through the midst of the tumult of battle,
Smote him, even from close at hand, through the bronze-cheeked helmet.
Under the spear-point shivered the helm, all plumaged with horsehair,
Struck with the ponderous lance in the stalwart hand of the hero;
Forth from the wound upspurted the brain on the ring of the spearhead,
Blood-dyed; wholly his strength relaxed; and his fingers, releasing
Hold on the foot of great-hearted Patroclus, dropped it; and earthward
Fallen it lay, while nigh it himself fell prone on the body —
Far off there from Larissa, the deep-loamed. Never his parents
Dear he repaid for his nurture; for brief was the portion allotted
Him of life, laid low by the lance of the great-hearted Ajax.
Hector then in his turn hurled his bright javelin at Ajax;
Ajax, watching it come, eluded the bronze-tipped weapon
Barely; but Schedius he struck, the great-hearted Iphitus' scion
(Far the best of the Phocians he, who once in the famous
Panopeus dwelt, and among many men he exercised lordship) —
This man Hector smote underneath his collar-bone; onward
Driving, the keen-pointed bronze came out at the base of his shoulder.
Down he fell with a crash; loud clanged his armor upon him.
Ajax in his turn smote the wise-hearted scion of Phaenops,
Phorcys, square in the belly (Hippothoüs he was bestriding),
Breaking a plate of his corselet; the weapon tore out his entrails.
Down he fell in the dust and clutched at the ground with his fingers.
Thereat the champions yielded and even illustrious Hector,

While the Argives shouted amain and dragged off the bodies,
Phorcys, Hippothoüs, too, and the armor stripped from their shoulders.
    Then had the Trojans, o'ercome through lack of valor, retreated
Back into Troy-town before the Achaeans, belovèd of Ares;
Then had the Argives won them a glory beyond the appointment
Even of Zeus by power and might of their own; but Apollo
Roused up in person Aeneas, assuming the guise of a herald,
Periphas, Epytus' son, who grew old at the side of his agèd
Sire in the office of herald; and he was kind-hearted and loyal.
Taking his semblance, Apollo, the son of Zeus, then addressed him:
    "Now, were it even against God's will, how could ye, Aeneas,
Guard high Ilium? Other men guard their cities — I've seen them —
Men on their own right arms, on their prowess and valor reliant,
Yea, and their own mere numbers, though scanty the folk of their coun-
But unto us much more than the Danaans Zeus willeth vict'ry;   [try.
Natheless ye tremble with fear exceeding and will not do battle."
    Thus spake he; and Aeneas perceived, as he looked straight upon
Quickly far-darting Apollo and shouted aloud unto Hector: [him,
    "Hector and all of the rest, ye chiefs of allies and of Trojans,
Shame were it now, before the Achaeans, belovèd of Ares,
Back into Ilium to go, o'ercome by our own lack of valor.
Nay, this moment some god stood close at my side and attested:
'Zeus, in his counsel supreme, is a helper to us in the battle.'
On let us go, then, straight at the Danaans; not unmolested
Leastwise, let them bring near to the galleys the fallen Patroclus."
    Thus he spake, and he leaped far forward in front of the vanguard.
So they were rallied and stood and resisted again the Achaeans.
Then in his turn Aeneas Leocritus smote with his javelin,
Son of Arisbas, the noble comrade of good Lycomedes.
Pitying him, as he fell, Lycomedes, belovèd of Ares,
Came up, taking his stand close by him and hurling his shining
Spear, struck Hippasus' son — Apisaon, shepherd of peoples —
Deep in the liver; his knees were instantly loosened beneath him.
This Apisaon, it seems, had come from Paeonia, the deep-soiled;
Next after Asteropaeus *he* was their best man in battle.
Pitying him, as he fell, the martial Asteropaeus

The Fight for the Body of Patroclus

Charged straight on at the Danaans, eager with them to do battle;
Vain the attempt; for on every side, fenced in with their bucklers,
Over Patroclus they stood and leveled their javelins before them.
Ajax, gigantic, kept ranging 'mid all and stoutly commanding;
None should withdraw, he said, behind the corse of Patroclus,
Neither insooth should battle ahead of the other Achaeans,
But stand close o'er the dead man and hand to hand do their fighting.
Such the commands of gigantic Ajax. The earth was empurpled
Deep with the outpoured blood; and the dead fell one on another
Thick and fast, both of Trojans, their brave allies, and Achaeans.
Not even these, in their close array, fought a bloodless encounter.
Still far fewer they fell, for they ever were carefully minded
Each, in the pressure of battle, to ward sheer death from the other.

So in the fashion of fire they strove, and assuredly thou would'st
Then have declared that no longer the sun or the moon was existent,
Seeing that they were enveloped in mist o'er that part of the battle
Where those chieftains stood about the dead son of Menoetius.
Meantime all of the rest, the well-greaved Achaeans and Trojans,
Warred untroubled beneath a clear sky, and undimmed sunlight
Spread out above them, and never a cloud was apparent in heaven,
Neither on plain nor on hill, and respite was had from the battle
Now and again, and the darts full laden with groans they eluded,
Standing apart, while these in the centre bore all the affliction
Both of the battle and darkness; by weight of their pitiless armor
All of those chieftains were wearied. But two men still understood not —
Thou Thrasymedes and thou Antilochus, heroes renownèd —
Aught of the death of the faultless Patroclus but thought he was living
Still and fighting amain in the vanguard press with the Trojans.
They then, watchful to hinder the death or the flight of their comrades,
Fought apart from the rest, since thus had commanded them Nestor,
When he was urging them on to the war from the black-colored galleys.

So then for them all day the mighty strife of the conflict
Waxed in its fury, and ever in sweat and in toil unabated
All of those warriors' knees, their legs, their feet underneath them,
Arms, and eyes were bespattered and wet, as the two hosts were fighting
Round him, the goodly squire of Aeacus' fleet-footed scion.

Even as haply a man gives unto his people for ſtretching
Tightly, a great bull's hide, when in fat he hath thoroughly soaked it—
As they receive it and ſtanding apart in a circle with ſtraining
Stretch it, suddenly gone is the moiſture; enters the ointment
Under the pulling of many, and ſtretched is the whole of it widely:
So from both sides they were haling hither and thither in narrow
Circuit the corse of Patroclus, and both hoped high in their bosoms:
Trojans to drag him away unto Ilium; they, the Achaeans,
Back to the hollow ships; and the fray grew fearful around him,
Savage, which neither Athena, on seeing it, e'er would make light of,
Nor yet Ares, the urger of war-hoſts, though fierce were their anger.

　　Such that day was the grievous toil of heroes and horses,
Stretched out by Zeus o'er the corse of Patroclus. Godlike Achilles
Knew by no means yet that his loved Patroclus had fallen,
For they were fighting far away from the swift-sailing galleys
Under the ramparts of Troy; so *he* never deemed in his spirit
That he was dead, but alive, and his homeward returning awaited,
Once he had touched the gates; since noway *he* was expeſted
Ever to capture and sack the city without him, or with him—
Seeing that often his mother in converse private had told him, [mighty—
When she had brought back tidings, the purpose of Zeus, the all
Nay, but at this time at least his mother told not that so heavy
Sorrow had come: that his own, far dearest comrade had perished.

　　Ever unceasing around the dead man, their keen spears wielding,
Men were crowding and joining relentless in mutual slaughter.
Thus then someone would say of the bronze-mailed sons of Achaia:
　　"Friends, it were truly for us an inglorious issue, retirement
Back to the hollow ships. Let the dark earth rather beneath us
Yawn for us all; far better insooth it should inſtantly happen
So, if *we* are going to leave to the horse-taming Trojans
This man to hale away to their city and win them the glory."

　　Thus on the other side would shout some great-hearted Trojan:
　　"Friends, even if it is fated that we all perish together
Heaped on this man, even then let no man shrink yet from the battle!"
　　Thus then someone would speak and rouse up the courage of each
So they were fighting on, and the uproar, clamorous, iron,　　[man.

374

Unto the heaven of bronze went up through th' unharvested ether.
    Meantime far from the battle the steeds of Aeacus' scion
Fell to weeping, for then first they learned that their driver had fallen
Prone in the dust, laid low by the hand of man-slaying Hector.
Vainly them did the brave Automedon, son of Diores,
Try to arouse, laying on the quick lash, and smiting upon them,
Often in accents gentle addressed them, often with cursing;
Natheless the team was unwilling to fare to the broad Hellespontus,
Unto the ships, or to battle, to join the host of Achaeans;
But as a pillar abideth immovably fixed at the barrow
Builded as tomb of a man that is dead, or haply a woman:
Steadfast so they abided along with the beautiful chariot
There, and with heads close-bowed to the ground, outpouring before
Hot tears flowing to earth from their eyelids, even in sorrow,   [them
Mourning the death of their driver; their rich manes, too, were defilèd,
Both sides under the yoke-pad, down-streaming from under the collar.
Now, as Cronion beheld them, he pitied the twain in their sorrow;
This word, shaking his head meanwhile, he addressed to his spirit:
    "Ah hapless pair! We gave you — but why unto Peleus, a mortal
Master, when ye are in truth unaging for aye and immortal?
Was it that ye should suffer affliction with men that are wretched?
For there is nothing, I trow, more than man to be pitied of all things
Whatsoever hath breath and moveth upon the earth's surface.
But, I assure you, upon that rich-wrought chariot behind you
Never shall Priam's son Hector be mounted; I will not allow it.
Is it not quite enough that he weareth the gear boasting vainly?
I will put strength now into your knees and into your spirits
Swiftly and safely to bear Automedon far from the battle
Back to the hollow ships; for I will add victory further
Unto the Trojans, to slay till they come to the well-benched galleys,
Even till setteth the sun, and darkness falls hallowed upon them."
    Thus he spake and breathed new vigor into the horses.
Tossing the dust from their manes to the ground, those horses immortal
Lightly were bearing on swiftly the car toward Achaeans and Trojans.
Grieving the while for his comrade, Automedon fought 'gainst the Tro-
Swooping amain with his car, as upon geese swoopeth a vulture. [jans,

Lightly anon he would flee from the clamorous shock of the Trojans,
Lightly anon then would charge, pressing on through the thick of the
Natheless he slew no men, whene'er he was haſt'ning to follow, [mellay.
Since, by himself on the ſtanch war-car, it was possible noway
Both to assail with a spear and to manage the fleet-footed horses.
Then at last a man, with his eyes, a comrade, espied him,
Haemon's grandson, brave Alcimedon, son of Laërces.
Halting behind the car, he spake to Automedon, saying:

"Who is it, pray, of the gods, Automedon, now hath implanted
Profitless counsel within thy breast and reft thee of reason?
Seeing that thus alone in the front of the press thou art fighting
Trojans? Behold thy comrade is slain; and exultingly Hector
Weareth, himself, on his shoulders the arms of Aeacus' scion."

Answered him then in his turn Automedon, son of Diores:
"Who, pray, else of Achaeans, Alcimedon, equals in guiding,
Also in taming the temper and ſtrength of these horses immortal,
Saving Patroclus alone, the peer of the gods in his counsel,
While yet living? Of death and of doom hath he been overtaken.
But do thou take the lash and the shining reins of the horses;
Take them, and *I* from the car will dismount to engage in the battle."

Thus spake he; and Alcimedon leaped on the swift-flying war-car.
Quickly he took up the lash in his hands and the reins of the horses.
Down from the car leaped Automedon. Glorious Hector espied them;
Straightway he called on Aeneas, who then was close to him, saying:

"Counseling chief of the Trojans who wear bronze armor, Aeneas,
Yonder I'm ware of the horses of Aeacus' fleet-footed scion,
Coming forth to the warfare with drivers unfit to do battle;
So might I hope to capture them both, if indeed thou art willing
Haply in heart, inasmuch as the twain, scarce biding our onset,
Hardly would venture to ſtand and contend in battle against us."

Thus spake he; and the goodly son of Anchises obeyed him.
Forward the twain went ſtraight; and they both had over their shoulders
Bull's hide, toughened and dried, with bronze thick welded upon it.
Chromius close at their side and Aretus, the godlike in presence,
Likewise went, and the hearts beat high in the breaſts of the heroes,
Hoping to slaughter the men and to capture the ſtrong-necked horses.

Fools that they were! for not without blood was their fated returning
Back from Automedon brave; as he prayed to Zeus, the All Father,
Filled with valor and strength was the heart, all darkened within him.
Straightway he spake a word to Alcimedon, faithful companion:
"Hold the steeds now, I pray thee, Alcimedon, not at a distance;
Nay, let them breathe right close on my back; for assuredly never,
Never will Priam's son Hector refrain from his fury, methinketh,
Till he hath killed us twain and mounted behind the fair-maned
Steeds of Achilles and driven in rout the ranks of the Argive
Heroes, or haply himself be caught in the lists of the foremost."
Thus he spake; then he called the Ajaxes twain and Atrides:
"Ajaxes twain, ye leaders of Argives, and thou, Menelaüs,
Look you — do ye turn over the corse to those who are fittest
Both to bestride it and also to ward off the ranks of the foemen.
Come ye hither and ward off the pitiless day from the living!
Yea, right here in the midst of the dolorous war they are pressing,
Hector along with Aeneas, accounted the best of the Trojans.
Verily, though, on the knees of the gods these issues are lying:
I, too, will hurl this javelin — with Zeus shall rest the decision."
Thus he spake. Then poising his spear far-shadowing hurled it,
Smiting directly the shield of Aretus, all evenly rounded;
Nor could the buckler arrest it; the bronze went mightily onward,
Drave right through, and it traversed the belt, deep into his belly.
As when a powerful man with an axe keen-edgèd and weighty,
Smiting behind the horns with the weapon an ox of the homestead,
Cleaveth the sinew entire, and the ox leapeth forward and falleth:
So leaped forward Aretus and fell on his back, for the javelin
Loosened his limbs, while quivered the keen point fast in his vitals.
Hector then in his turn at Automedon hurled his bright javelin.
He, though, watching it come, eluded the bronze-tipped missile,
Stooping down forward; behind him the long lance hurtled and landed
Rooting itself in the earth, and the butt of the javelin a-quiver
Stood; and anon the powerful Ares *there* spent its fury.
Now had *they* been fighting with falchions in closest encounter,
Had not the Ajaxes parted the twain in their fury of battle.   [rade.
These two had come through the throng at the urgent call of their com-

Under their onrush the Trojans again in terror retreated,
Hector, along with Aeneas, and Chromius also, the godlike,
Leaving Aretus behind, as he lay there mortally wounded.
Thereat Automedon quickly — the peer he was of swift Ares —
Stripped off the arms of the fallen as spoil and spake a word boasting:
    "Now have I eased my heart a little at least of its sorrow
Felt for the death of Patroclus, though *I* have slain but a weaker."
    Thus he spake and lifted the gory trophies and set them
Safe in his car; he then mounted, his feet and his hands up above them
Covered with blood, like a lion that just hath devoured a bullock.
    Once more over Patroclus a furious battle extended,
Hard-fought and laden with tears, for Athena enkindled the combat.
Down from heaven she'd come, sent forth by Zeus of the far-borne
Voice to urge the Danaans on; for his purpose had altered.
Even as Zeus flings out a gleaming rainbow to mortals
Out from the summits of heaven, an omen perchance of a warfare
Or of a wintry storm, keen-chilling, that therefore compelleth
Man to cease from his works on the earth and afflicteth the livestock:
So with a gleaming cloud close-wrapped about her the goddess
Entered the host of Achaeans and roused up each of the warriors.
First with a word of enheart'ning the goddess accosted Atrides,
E'en Menelaüs, the valiant — for he so chanced to be nigh her —
Lik'ning herself in her form and her voice unwearied to Phoenix:
    "Hanging of head and reproach it will be unto thee, Menelaüs,
Surely, if ever the haughty Achilles' faithful companion
Fleet-footed dogs shall drag and tear 'neath the wall of the Trojans.
Hold out manfully rather and rouse up all of the army."
    Then in his turn Menelaüs, good at the war-cry, addressed her:
    "Phoenix, my dear old daddy of old times, would that Athena
Strength would give me and from me avert the volley of missiles!
Then should I gladly stand by the fallen Patroclus, defending
Him; for his death to the depths of my heart hath touched me with sor-
Yet in his fiery fury yon Hector never forbeareth   [row.
Dealing death with his spear; for to him Zeus granteth the glory."
    Thus spake he; and the bright-eyed goddess Athena was glad-
Seeing he prayed unto her the first of all the immortals;   [dened,

Therefore she in his knees, in his shoulders implanted a vigor,
Likewise also instilled in his breast a fly's perseverance,
Which, although from the skin of a man it is constantly driven,
Still is persistent in biting, for to it man's blood is delicious.
He, when his innermost heart such boldness had entered and filled it,
Strode right over Patroclus and hurled his glittering javelin.
Now in the Trojans' ranks was a son of Eëtion, Podes,
Wealthy withal and goodly, and Hector honored him highly —
Though of the people — as comrade beloved and a table-companion.
Him Menelaüs, the fair-haired, smote with his lance on the girdle,
Just as he rushed off to flee, and he drave the bronze weapon clean
Down he fell with a crash, and Atrides, prince Menelaüs, [through him.
Haled his corse from the Trojans away to the host of his comrades.

　　Then came Phoebus Apollo and roused up Hector, anigh him
Standing in semblance of Phaenops, the scion of Asius — a guest-friend
Dearest of all unto Hector — that dwelt in his home in Abydus.
Thus in likeness of Phaenops, far-working Apollo bespake him:

　　"Hector, who ever hereafter of all the Achaeans will fear thee?
How can it be thou hast flinched before Menelaüs, accounted
Weak as a lanceman? But lo! he hath gone; alone he hath taken
Off from the Trojans a corse; he hath slain thy faithful companion,
Valiant, a foremost fighter, e'en Podes, the son of Eëtion."

　　Thus spake Phoebus, and grief with a black cloud mantled the hero;
Straight through the forefront he went, wide-flashing the bronze of his
Thereupon Zeus, son of Cronus, laid hold of his tasselèd aegis, [armor.
Flashing, and shrouded in mantle of stormcloud the summit of Ida,
Lightened, and mightily thundered, and brandished the aegis before him,
Granting the Trojans vict'ry and smiting with dread the Achaeans.
First Peneleos started the flight, a Boeotian chieftain:
Ever with face to the foe, he was struck with a lance on the shoulder.
Only the surface it grazed, but the point of Pulydamas' javelin [hurled it.
Quite scratched the bone, for the Trojan had come up close when he
Hector in turn, close by, smote great-hearted Alectryon's scion,
Leïtus, smiting his wrist, and stayed his rapture of battle.
Gazing about him, he shrank, for he hoped no further in spirit,
Wielding a spear in his hand, to do battle still with the Trojans.

Hector on Leïtus rushed, but Idomeneus instantly smote him
Full on the corselet guarding his breast and close by the nipple;
Natheless the long lance snapped at the ferrule; thereat the Trojans
Shouted. Hector then hurled at Idomeneus, son of Deucalion,
As he had mounted his car; the javelin missed him a little,
Lighting instead on Meriones' brother-in-arms and his driver,
Coeranus, who followed with him from Lyctus' well-builded city.
(Now had Idomeneus left his gallant ships in the first place,
Marching on foot, and great glory had placed in the hands of the Tro-
Had not Coeranus quickly come up with the fleet-footed horses, [jans,
Who brought light to the chief and averted the merciless moment,
But his own life he lost at the hand of the man-slaying Hector).
Under the jaw and the ear did Hector smite him; the spear-end
Dashed out his teeth from his mouth and cleft his tongue in the middle.
Dropping the reins to the ground, headlong he plunged from the char-
Then in his own dear hands Meriones caught up the fallen [iot.
Reins from the ground, as he stooped, and spake to Idomeneus, saying:
    "Now lay on with the lash till thou come to the swift-sailing galleys;
Vict'ry, thou seest thyself, no longer is with the Achaeans."
    Thus spake he; and Idomeneus lashed on the fair-maned horses
Back toward the hollow ships, since dread on his spirit had fallen.
    Well did the great-hearted Ajax and prince Menelaüs observe it,
How Zeus was granting decisive victory now to the Trojans.
First of the twain to speak was great Telamonian Ajax:
    "Ah me! Now might a man, even one who is utterly simple,
Know that Zeus, the All Father, himself is helping the Trojans.
All *their* darts strike home, whoever may happen to hurl them,
Whether a coward or brave; for of all them Zeus is director.
Ours, however, all fall to the ground, ineffective and useless.
Come then, let us devise ourselves some excellent counsel,
How we may rescue the corse not only, but haply returning
Ourselves also may prove a joy to our comrades belovèd,
Comrades that grieve while gazing to us-ward, neither are deeming
We shall stay the might and invincible hands of great Hector,
Slayer of men, but expect us to fall 'mid the dark-painted galleys.
Would there were also some comrade to carry immediate message

380

Unto Pelides; for he has not even heard yet the woful
Tidings, methinketh, that lo! his belovèd comrade is fallen.
Nowhere, though, can I see such an one among the Achaeans —
Such is the vaporous gloom that enwraps both them and the horses.
Zeus, O Father, deliver the sons of Achaia from darkness;
Bring out a clear bright sky, vouchsafe our eyes to see clearly.
Only in light let us die, since such, it seems, is thy pleasure."

Thus he spake; and the Father was grieved at beholding him weep-
Forthwith then he dispelled the mist and scattered the darkness;   [ing;
Sunshine flashed out upon them; in view came all of the battle.
Then did Ajax address Menelaüs, good at the war-cry:

"Look, Menelaüs, nurseling of Zeus, if belike thou espy him
Living ßill, Antilochus, son of the great-hearted Neßor;
Rouse him up that he go and tell wise-hearted Achilles
Now with all speed that his own far dearest comrade hath perished."

Thus spake he; Menelaüs, good at the war-cry, refused not,
Nay, but departed, as haply a lion departs from a ßeading,
When he is wearied with worrying dogs and men that are keepers,
Who will not suffer the beast to select for ravage the fattest
Ox of the herd; for all the night long they watch; but the lion,
Avid of flesh, attacks ßraight on, but he faileth — for thickly
Fly from the country people's brave hands the missiles against him,
Brands too, blazing with flame, which he feareth for all of his longing,
Till at the dawn he departs with heart disappointed and troubled:
So from Patroclus, the slain, Menelaüs, good at the war-cry,
Went exceedingly loath, since greatly he feared lest th' Achaeans,
Stricken with desperate rout, might leave him a prey to the foemen.
Straitly he charged then Meriones, straitly the Ajaxes also:

"Leaders of Argives, Ajaxes twain, and Meriones also,
Now is it time to remember the kindly heart of Patroclus —
Hapless Patroclus; for he knew how to be gentle to all men,
While yet living; of death and of doom he hath been overtaken."

When he had spoken thus, fair-haired Menelaüs departed,
Glancing in every direction around, like an eagle, accounted
Keenest of sight by far of the birds that fly under heaven —
Nor, as he soareth aloft, can the swift-footed rabbit elude him,

Crouching in covert beneath some thick-leaved bush, but upon it
Swoopeth the eagle and, catching his prey, he takes its life quickly:
So, Menelaüs, thou nurseling of Zeus, quick darted thy glances,
Ranging with radiant eyes the ranks of thy numerous comrades —
If he might haply catch sight of the son of Nestor yet living.
Him right soon he espied far off at the left of the battle,
Heart'ning his comrades there and rousing them up to do battle.
Near to him came fair-haired Menelaüs, who stopped and addressed him:

    "Hither, Antilochus, come, thou nurseling of Zeus, that the woful
Tidings thou mayest hear — oh would that it never had happened!
Thou too knowest already, methinketh, for thou hast beheld it,
How on the Danaans God amain is rolling disaster:
Victory rests with the Trojans; and slain is the best of Achaeans;
Slain is Patroclus, and heavy the loss that the Danaans suffer.
Haste, however, and run to the galleys Achaean and tell it
Unto Achilles, if haply the corse he may save to his galley,
Naked, indeed; for his arms hath the shimmering-helmeted Hector."

    Thus he spake; and Antilochus heard the tidings with horror.
Long time bereaved of speech he stood, and the eyes of the hero
Flooded with tears, and his lusty voice was choked with emotion.
Not even so did he fail to heed Menelaüs's bidding,
Started to run, and entrusted his arms to his faultless companion,
Even Laodocus wheeling close by him his whole-hoofed horses.

    So, as he let fall a tear, his feet bore him out of the warfare,
Charged with a message of woe to Achilles, scion of Peleus.

    Still, Menelaüs, thou nurseling of Zeus, thy heart was thus minded
Not to remain with *his* comrades for aid, when Antilochus left them,
Though they were weary, and heavy the loss that the Pylians suffered;
Rather he sent them instead Thrasymedes, the godlike, to aid them,
Hastened himself once more to bestride the hero Patroclus,
Came up running and stopped by the Ajaxes; thus he bespake them:

    "Gone is Antilochus now to the swift-sailing galleys — I sent him,
Bidding him speed to fleet-footed Achilles; yet *he*, methinketh,
Will not come now, for all of his fury with Hector, the godlike,
Seeing that not even *he* would battle unarmed with the Trojans.
Well, now, let us devise ourselves some excellent counsel,

How we may rescue the corse not only, but also deliver
Our own selves from death and from doom 'mid the shouts of the Tro-
  Him then answered in turn the great Telamonian Ajax: [jans."
 "All thou hast said is right, O highly renowned Menelaüs.
Come then, thou and Meriones ſtoop and lift on your shoulders
Quickly the body and bear it away from the tumult; behind you
We will fight with the Trojans and even with Hector, the godlike,
We twain, one in accord as even in name, and aforetime
Ever accuſtomed to bide fierce warfare, one by the other."
  Thus spake he; and the others the dead man lifted with main ſtrength
High from the ground in their arms; and the host of the Trojans behind
Shouted thereat, when they saw the Achaeans lifting the body. [them
Straight then upon them they charged, as hounds on a wild boar wounded
Spring out ahead of the hunters, the young men hotly pursuing;
Somewhile truly they run on in front, all eager to rend him,
But whensoever he wheeleth, in confident prowess, upon them,
Back they shrink and give ground, some one way, others another:
Even so for a while the Trojans followed in squadrons,
Smiting ever amain with their swords and their two-ędgèd lances;
But, as oft as the Ajaxes twain would turn and against them
Halt, then the color upon them would change, and no one among them
Dared rush forward to fight amain for the body's possession.
  Thus they were ſtruggling, the twain, to bear the corse from the
Down to the hollow ships, and ſtress of warfare was on them, [battle
Fierce and tense, like fire when it leaps on a populous city,
Burſts into blaze of a sudden — the houses crumble and perish
All in the mighty glare, as the wind's might sets it a-roaring:
So the incessant din of the horses and men, spear-wielders,
Roared in the warriors' wake, as they moved on, bearing the burden.
They, however, as mules, when they put forth their ſtrength to the ut-
Drag from a mountain, down some bypath rugged and rocky, [most,
Either a beam or a timber immense for a galley; and weary,
Spent with endeavor and sweat, is the spirit ſtriving within them:
Struggling thus, these men were bearing the corse; and behind them
Twain, the Ajaxes, held back the foe, as a ridge in a wildwood,
Stretched all its length clear across a plain, might hold back the water,

Stemming the ruinous floods, the torrents of mightiest rivers,
Rain-fed, driving the currents of all such waters to wander
Plainward, neither at all by ſtrength of the torrent is broken:
So the Ajaxes ever were holding behind them the Trojans'
Battle; but these kept pressing anigh, and among them Aeneas,
Son of Anchises, foremost along with the glorious Hector.
Even as haply there flieth a bevy of daws or of ſtarlings,
Crying aloud in confusion at sight of a falcon that cometh
Circling, which ever beareth to small birds slaughter and ruin:
So then before Aeneas and Hector the youths of Achaia
Went with a cry and confusion; they forgot the rapture of battle,
Whileas beautiful arms fell in heaps at the moat and around it —
Arms of the Danaans routed. And rest had they none from the battle.

ILIAD · XVIII · (Σ)

Sigma continues the alarms,
And fashions the renowned arms.

So in the fashion of fire bright-blazing these warriors battled,
Whileas Antilochus nimble of foot bore word to Achilles.
Seated in front of his galleys, the upright-hornèd, he found him
Boding deep in his soul dire deeds, already accomplished;
Heavy of heart, he communed with his own magnanimous spirit:
"Ah me! Wherefore again are the long-haired sons of Achaia
Scouring the plain and flying in rout to the galleys, bewildered?
Let it not be that the gods are fulfilling my dread premonitions,
Even as once my mother declared it and prophesied plainly,
How, while I am alive, the bravest of Myrmidon heroes
Under the hands of the Trojans the light of the sun should abandon.
Surely indeed he is dead, that valiant son of Menoetius,
Reckless, perverse! Why, I bade him beat off the fire of the foemen,
Then come back to the ships, nor amain do battle with Hector."
    While these things in his heart and his soul Achilles debated,
Meanwhile came and stood by him the son of the glorious Nestor,
Shedding warm tears, and delivered anon the tidings of sorrow:
    "Ah me! scion of wise-hearted Peleus, a message of bitter
Sorrow thou now shalt hear—oh would that it never had happened!
Slain is Patroclus; the armies are battling now for his body—
Naked indeed; for his arms hath the shimmering-helmeted Hector."
    Thus spake he; and grief with a black cloud mantled Achilles.
Straightway seizing the dust all sooty with both hands he poured it
Over his head, and his comely face he wholly disfigured;
Down on his heavenly tunic the black ash sifted and settled;
Mighty and mightily fallen, himself in the dust and the ashes
Lay; with his own dear hands he tore his hair and defiled it.
    Also the handmaids Achilles had taken as spoil with Patroclus

385

Cried out loudly in anguish of soul, then ran from the doorway,
Flocking about wise-hearted Achilles, beating their bosoms
All with their hands; unstrung were the knees of each one beneath her.
Likewise shedding warm tears, Antilochus wailed and lamented,
Holding Achilles' hands, as he groaned in his glorious spirit;
Fearful was he that his throat with the steel Achilles would sever.
Terribly then did he moan, and she heard him, his worshipful mother,
Down in the sea-depth seated, beside her father, the ancient.
Thereon she wailed aloud, and the goddesses gathered about her,
All those Nereïd maids who dwell in the depths of the salt sea:
Glauce, namely, was there and Cymodoce, also Thalia,
Spio, too, and Nesaea, the ox-eyed Halia, Thoë,
Limnorea, Actaea, the fair, and Cymothoë with them;
Melite also, Iaera, Amphithoë, too, and Agave,
Doto, Proto, and fair Dynamene, also Pherusa;
There were Dexamene, too, and Amphinome, Callianira,
Doris, and Panope; there were the widely-renowned Galatea,
Callianassa, Nemertes, and with them the faithful Apseudes;
Clymene, Ianira, and Ianassa were present,
Maera and Orithyia, and Amathea, the fair-haired,
Other Nereïds also that dwelt in the depths of the salt sea.
Filled was the crystal grotto with these, and all then together
Beat on their breasts, while Thetis began the sad lamentation:
   "Hear me, Nereïds all, ye sisters of mine, that attending
All of you well may know how great in my heart is my sorrow.
Ay me, unhappy! Ay me, that have borne the best to my sorrow,
Seeing I bore me a son who proved both faultless and mighty,
Chiefest of heroes and like to a fair young shoot in his growing.
Then when I had reared him, a plant on a slope of a vineyard,
Off to the Ilian shore in the curvèd galleys I sent him,
There to fight with the Trojans; but never again shall I welcome
Him on return from the war to the home of Peleus, his father,
Never. And while he yet liveth in *my* sight, viewing the sunlight,
Sorrow is his; and though I may go, I can help him in no wise.
Natheless I'll go, to see my dear child and also to hearken   [fare."
What is the grief that hath found him, though biding aloof from the war-

Thus it was that she spoke, and she left the cavern, and with her
Followed the sea-maids weeping. About and before them the billows
Parted. And when they arrived at the deep-loamed marches of Troyland,
All in a row they came out on the shore, where close to each other
Lay drawn up the Myrmidons' galleys about swift Achilles.
Deeply he groaned, as, coming beside him, his worshipful mother
Stood; and she clasped the head of her child, while she burst into wailing
Loudly, with piteous cry, and with wingèd words she addressed him:

"Why dost thou weep, my child? What sorrow of soul is upon thee?
Utter it forth; hide it not in thy heart. For Zeus hath fulfilled it,
Even as thou didst pray, with thy hands uplifted to heaven,
Asking then that the sons of Achaia, all at the galleys
Pent in, should miss thy presence and suffer evils unseemly."

Heavily groaning, addressed her in turn fleet-footed Achilles:
"Mother of mine, that prayer the Olympian truly fulfilled me.
What, however, the joy thereof unto me, when Patroclus,
Comrade dear, is no more, whom of all my companions I honored
Most, as my own life precious? Him I have lost, and his armor
Hector that slew him hath plundered, prodigious, a marvel to look at,
Beauteous — glorious gift that the gods once gave unto Peleus,
Given upon that day when they laid thee couched with a mortal.
Would that yonder among the immortal daughters of Ocean
Thou hadst remained and that Peleus had wedded a bride that was
Now, however, they visit on thy heart measureless sorrow   [mortal!
All for the death of a son, whom never again thou shalt welcome
Homeward returning from Troy, since *my* heart straitly forbids me
Longer to live or abide among men, save only if Hector
First under *my* spear smitten himself shall surrender his spirit,
So to atone for the spoil of Patroclus, the son of Menoetius."

Letting a tear fall, Thetis in her turn answered him, saying:
"Speedy of doom, then, my child, must *thou* be, by what thou hast
Since unto thee is appointed a fate quick-following Hector's."   [spoken,

Deeply moved, then spake to his mother fleet-footed Achilles:
"Straightway then may I die, since I was not fated to succor —
Warding off death from my comrade, who perished afar from his coun-
Him, whose need was of me in his sore distress to defend him.   [try —

387

Since, then, I do not return to the well-loved land of my fathers,
Neither have brought any light to Patroclus nor yet to the other
Comrades, the many that fell o'ercome by Hector, the godlike;
Rather I sit by the galleys, of earth but a profitless burden,
I that am such as no other of all the bronze-clad Achaeans
Is in the war — in assembly, indeed, some others are better.
Would that strife might perish from men and from the immortals —
Anger as well, for it stirreth even a wise man to raging,
Anger that, sweeter by far than the trickle of honey descending,
Swelleth full in the breast of a mortal, as vapor expandeth,
Even as roused *my* wrath the monarch of men, Agamemnon.
Bygones now we will let be bygones — albeit grieving
Sore — and bridle the heart in my breast at necessity's bidding.
Now, though, off will I go, that I may light upon Hector,
Slayer of him that I loved. My own fate then will I welcome,
Whenso Zeus and the other immortals wish to fulfil it.
Death no one can escape — e'en mighty Heracles could not,
Though he was dearest of all unto sovereign Zeus, son of Cronus;
Him even fate overcame and the cruel anger of Hera.
Likewise *I* shall — if such is the doom fate fashioneth for me —
Lie low when I am dead; but now may I win me a splendid
Glory, and set some one of the Dardanid daughters of Troia,
Dames deep-bosomed, to stanching with both hands plentiful teardrops
Streaming down over her tender cheeks while bitterly sobbing.
Yea, I hope they will know how long from the war I have tarried;
Hold me not back, in thy love, from the war, for thou wilt not persuade
    Then unto him did Thetis, the silver-footed, make answer: [me."
  "Truly, my child, hast thou spoken. No evil in such resolution
Taken to shield thy war-worn friends from impending destruction.
Yet is thy beauteous armor a spoil now held by the Trojans,
Radiant armor of bronze — ay, shimmering-helmeted Hector
Beareth it now on his shoulders, exulting in triumph! Methinketh
Not for long will he glory therein, for death is anigh him.
Thou, though, do not as yet plunge into the tumult of Ares,
Till, at least, with thine eyes thou shalt see me hither returning;
For on the morrow I come at the hour the sun is arising,

Bringing beautiful arms from the forge of sovereign Hephaestus."

 Thus, then, the goddess spake and back from her son she departed;
When she had turned, she addressed her sisters, daughters of Ocean:

 "Ye now go down, my sisters, and enter the sea's spacious bosom,
Visit the halls of our father, the wide-known Ancient of Ocean,
Tell him all this tale, while I unto lofty Olympus
Speed, to the artisan, famous Hephaestus, if he will haply
Give me glorious arms for my son, all-radiant armor."

 Thus spake she; and they dived forthwith down under the sea-
Thetis, the goddess, the silver-footed, up to Olympus   [wave.
Went, in order to bring to her dear son glorious armor.

 Her then her feet to Olympus were carrying up. The Achaeans,
Fleeing from Hector, slayer of men, with a clamor appalling
Came in their flight meantime to the Hellespont and the galleys.
Nor could the well-greaved sons of Achaia the corse of Patroclus,
Squire of Achilles, have dragged away out of range of the missiles,
Seeing that now again the foot and the horse overtook him,
Led by Hector, king Priam's son, like a flame in his prowess.
Thrice from behind by the feet had seized him the glorious Hector,
Eager to drag him away, and loudly he called on the Trojans.
Thrice had the Ajaxes twain, men clad with impetuous prowess,
Beaten him back from the body; yet he, on his valor reliant,
Now would dash through the press and again stand biding his moment,
Terribly shouting amain, but not an inch was he yielding.
Even as off from a carcase a tawny lion the shepherds
Out in a field cannot drive away in his ravening hunger:
Even so then the Ajaxes twain, those helmeted warriors,
Could not frighten king Priam's son Hector away from the body.
Then he had dragged him away and won ineffable glory,
Had not fleet Iris, shod with the wind, come down from Olympus
Post haste bearing a message to Peleus' son to array him —
Unknown to Zeus and the rest of the gods, for Hera had sent her.
Drawing anigh, she stood, and with wingèd words she addressed him:

 "Rouse thee, Peleus' scion, of all men most to be dreaded!
Succor Patroclus, for whom this moment a terrible conflict
Out in front of the ships is on foot; men slay one another,

These in defense and trying to gain the body's possession,
Whileas the Trojans are charging in fury and yearning to hale him
Thence unto wind-swept Ilium; and most is the glorious Hector
Eager to drag him away, and his heart now biddeth him sever
Off from the tender neck Patroclus' head and impale it.
Up, then, idle no longer; and let shame enter thy spirit —
Awe that Patroclus should e'er be sport for the dogs of the Trojans.
Thine the disgrace, if his body be brought back evil-entreated."
   Answered her then in his turn fleet-footed Achilles, the godlike:
   "Iris, thou goddess, what god sends thee unto me with a message?"
   Spake unto him in her turn swift Iris, shod with the storm-wind:
   "Hera, the glorious consort of Zeus, she only hath sent me.
Neither hath known it Cronion, the high-throned, neither another
One of immortals that have their homes on snowy Olympus."
   Answering her in his turn spake forth fleet-footed Achilles:
   "How shall I enter the fray? Yon Trojans are holding my armor.
Also my mother dear permitteth me not to array me
Till, at least, with my eyes I shall see her hither returning,
Seeing she gave me her pledge to bring fair arms from Hephaestus.
Nor know I of another of whom I can put on the glorious
War-mail, saving the shield of the great Telamonian Ajax.
He, however, consorteth, I trow, with the van of the battle,
Dealing out doom with his spear to rescue the corse of Patroclus."
   Spake unto him in her turn swift Iris, shod with the storm-wind:
   "Well are we also aware thy glorious armor is holden.
Even so go to the moat and show thyself to the Trojans,
If in terror of thee the foes refrain from the battle
Haply, and thus the martial sons of Achaia a-wearied
Breathe for a moment; for brief is the breathing time in a battle."
   Thus she spake and departed, the fleet-footed messenger Iris.
Therewith rose up Achilles, beloved of Zeus; and Athena
Over his stalwart shoulders her deep-fringed, tasselèd aegis
Cast; and the goddess divine then crowned his head with a golden
Cloud, and from it she caused to blaze a flame all-refulgent.
Even as issues smoke from a city and rises to heaven
Far off, out from an island that foemen beleaguer in battle;

Thetis Ordering the Nereids to Descend into the Sea

All day long the inhabitants measure their strength in dread battle,
Fighting from out of their city's towers and walls; but at sunset
Blaze out in lines the beacons aflame, and the glare from them riseth
Up, and it leapeth aloft for the dwellers around to behold it,
If they haply in ships may come and save them from ruin:
So from the head of Achilles a blaze soared high unto heaven.
Passing the rampart, he stopped by the moat — yet 'mid the Achaeans
Noway mingled; he minded the wise-said word of his mother.
There, then, standing, he shouted, and Pallas Athena afar off
Echoed the shout, and the Trojans it struck with unspeakable terror.
Clear as a clarion call blown loud in defense of a city
Compassed in hostile array by an army of death-dealing foemen,
So then clearly it rang, that voice of Aeacus' scion.
Therefore, soon as they heard it, the bronzen voice of Achilles,
All their spirits were filled with dismay, and the fair-maned horses
Started to wheel with the cars — their hearts had bodings of sorrow.
Dazed were the drivers, too, when they saw the unwearying fire
Awfully over the head of the great-souled scion of Peleus
Flaming aloft, for the bright-eyed goddess Athena enflamed it.
Three times over the moat cried mightily godlike Achilles;
Three times the Trojans and all their allies far-famed were confounded.
Here even then were killed some twelve of their doughtiest warriors
On their own comrades' spears and under their cars. But th' Achaeans
Joyfully drew forth Patroclus out of the range of the missiles,
Laid him down on a bier, and his dear-loved comrades around him
Stood and lamented. Among them followed fleet-footed Achilles,
Shedding warm tears, as he looked upon his faithful companion
Pierced by the keen bronze spear and lying in death on a litter.
Him, it is true, he had sent forth once with his war-car and horses
Into the war; but so he received him not on returning.

    Then the unwearied sun was of ox-eyed, worshipful Hera
Sent from the ether, unwilling, to go to the streams of the Ocean;
So the sun went to his setting. The godlike sons of Achaia
Ceased from the strenuous combat and strife of dubious warfare.

    Over against them the Trojans on their side back from the raging
War returned and loosed from the cars the swift horses that bore them,

Gathered themselves in assembly or ever they thought of their supper.
Upright standing, they held their assembly, since none had the courage
Now to be seated; for trembling possessed them, for that Achilles
Now had appeared, though long he had ceased from sorrowful battle.
Prudent Pulydamas then began to speak and harangue them,
Panthoüs' son, for he alone could look forward and backward —
Hector's companion he was; the twain were born on the same night;
Far he excelled in counsel, as Hector excelled with the javelin.
He then kindliest-minded harangued them and spake out among them.

"Weigh both sides of the question, my friends; for I, at least, bid you
Now to go up to the town and not wait for the brightness of morning
Here on the plain by the ships, for we are far from our ramparts.
Long as this man was wroth with Agamemnon, the godlike,
So long easier far was the warfare against the Achaeans;
Yes, and I used to be glad when I couched near the swift-sailing galleys,
Trusting that we should capture those gallant ships for our booty.
Direful, though, is my dread of the fleet-footed scion of Peleus,
Such is the warrior's temper, exceeding fierce; and he will not
Tarry at all in the plain, where Trojans alike and Achaeans
Both are used to apportion the fury of warfare between them;
Nay, he is ready to fight for the city itself and its women.
Therefore, hence to the town! Obey me; for so it will issue.
Now hath ambrosial night put a stop to fleet-footed Achilles,
Peleus' son. But *if* he shall come upon *us* in the morning,
Still here abiding when *he* attacks in his armor, then many
Well will know him; for gladly will *he* gain to Ilium holy,
Whoso haply escapes; but there shall be many a Trojan
Food for vultures and dogs. Be that far, I pray, from my hearing!
But if indeed we hearken to *my* words, though with reluctance,
This night we in the council will husband our strength; and the towers
Guard us the city, and high-built gates with the door-wings folding,
Polished and tall, that are bolted and close tight-fitted upon them.
Early at dawn of the day, each man in his armor accoutred,
Take we our stand on the towers; worse then for that man, if he venture
Out from the galleys to come and fight for the prize of our rampart.
Back to the ships will he hasten again, when his strong-necked horses

Hera Commanding the Sun to Set

He hath sated with galloping wildly under the city;
Into the city to storm his courage will never allow him,
Nor will he plunder it ever; swift dogs will sooner devour him."
      Scowlfully eying him, answered the shimmering-helmeted Hector:
"What thou sayest, Pulydamas, fails to meet with my pleasure,
In that thou bidst us retreat and be shut up again in the city.
Are ye not sated already with being cooped up in the towers?
All men mortal were telling of old of the city of Priam,
How rich erst in its treasures of gold, in bronze, too, how wealthy.
Now, however, the goodly stores from its houses have vanished:
Many possessions to Phrygia gone and Maeonia lovely,
Bartered and sold away, since mighty Zeus showed his anger.
Now that the son of Cronus, the crooked-in-counsel, hath granted
Me to win fame at the ships, at the sea to pen the Achaeans,
Never again, fond man, such counsel present to the people!
For not one of the Trojans will heed; I will not allow it.
Come then, even as I may declare, let all be persuaded:
All through the army partake of your supper, set down in divisions;
Keep guard faithfully also; and each man—let him be wakeful.
Yea, and whoe'er of the Trojans too much for his treasures is worried,
Let him collect and give to the folk for public consumption.
Better indeed that the people have joy thereof than th' Achaeans.
Early at dawn of the day, each man in his armor accoutred,
Here near the hollow ships let us rouse up vehement Ares.
What if insooth at the ships the godlike Achilles be risen?
So much the worse will it be for him, if he liketh; by no means
I from the din of the hideous warfare shall flee but stand fast
Facing him—whether 'tis he or I that shall win the great glory.
Ever impartial is Ares; he slays who would be a slayer."
      Thus then Hector harangued, and the Trojans shouted approval,
Fools that they were, for Pallas Athena bereft them of reason.
So they assented with praise to Hector's evil advising;
No one Pulydamas praised, though he gave them excellent counsel.
Then they took supper all through the army. But still the Achaeans
All night long made moan for Patroclus, loudly lamenting.
First of them Peleus' son began the loud lamentation,

Laying his man-slaying hands on the breast of his comrade belovèd,
Moaning exceedingly sore, as belike a well-bearded lion
Moans when haply some deer-hunting man of his whelps has despoiled
Out of a woodland's depths, and, too late returning, he grieveth; [him
Many the glens then he rangeth, searching the tracks of the hunter,
If somewhere he may find him, for bitter the wrath that assails him:
So, as he heavily moaned, 'mid the Myrmidons spake out Pelides:

 "Ah me! Verily vain was the word I uttered aforetime,
That same day I encouraged Menoetius there in his palace,
Promising I would return him his son in glory to Opus,
After he Ilium had sacked and received his share of the booty.
Still, not all of their plans doth Zeus accomplish for mortals.
Unto us both is appointed of fate the same earth to redden
Here in the land of Troy; for *I* shall have no returning
Home for the knightly old Peleus to welcome me there in his palace,
Nay, nor Thetis, my mother; but here the earth shall confine me.
Now then, seeing I follow thee under the earth, my Patroclus,
No last rites shall I hold for thee, ere hither I bring thee
Surely the head and the armor of great-souled Hector, thy slayer;
Twice six throats I will sever of young men then at thy pyre,
Glorious children of Trojans, for I am wroth for thy slaying.
Lie until then as thou art by the curve-beaked galleys, Patroclus;
Dardanid dames, deep-bosomed, and Trojan women around thee,
Shedding the tear all day and all night, shall make lamentation —
Women we toiled to win with might and the length of our lances,
Sacking the opulent cities of earth-born mortals that perish."

  Thus spake the godlike Achilles and gave command to his comrades
Over the fire to set a great tripod, so they might quickly
Wash off the blood and gore from the corse of the fallen Patroclus.
So on the fire's bright blaze they set up a tripod for washing,
Poured in water, and kindled the fagots they laid underneath it.
Clasping the cauldron's belly, the flames soon heated the water.
So, when the water had come to a boil in the bright bronzen vessel,
Then they proceeded to wash and anoint him with oil of the olive,
Filling the hero's wounds with an unguent nine years had perfected.
Then on a bier they laid him and covered him o'er with soft linen,

Shrouded from head unto foot, and a white robe over above it.
All night long then around the fleet-footed scion of Peleus
Wailing, the Myrmidon folk made moan and lament for Patroclus.

Meantime Zeus unto Hera, his wife and his sister, addressed him:
"Well! at the last thou hast done it, my ox-eyed, worshipful Hera.
Thou hast aroused fleet-footed Achilles. Verily children
Born unto thee thyself are the long-haired sons of Achaia."

Then unto him made answer the ox-eyed, worshipful Hera:
"Most dread scion of Cronus, a word like this to have spoken!
Verily even a man may do what he will for his fellow,
Even though he is but mortal and hath no such wisdom as we have.
How then was *I*, at least, that the chiefest goddess avow me,
Chiefest and doubly: by birth and because I am counted the consort
Even of thee, who reignest as lord over all the immortals —
How was I not to be wroth and to weave woe's web for the Trojans?"

Even as they were conversing in such wise one with the other,
Thetis, the silver-footed, arrived at the home of Hephaestus,
Star-dight, unperishing, bronzen, excelling the mansions of heaven —
Even the home that the crook-footed god himself had constructed.
Him she discovered busy with toil at the bellows and sweating,
Wheeling about; for tripods, twenty in all, he was forging,
Fitted to stand all about the wall of his well-stablished palace;
Under the base of each pure gold-wrought wheels he had fitted,
So as to enter, themselves, self-moving, the gath'ring of godheads,
Then run homeward again; and a marvel it was to behold them.
So far indeed they were finished — the handles of curious cunning,
Not yet fitted thereon, he was forging, and chains he was welding.
While he was busy thereat, and his wise mind guided his labors,
Meanwhile Thetis, the silver-footed, drew nigh to his palace.
Charis advanced and beheld her — the shining-chapleted Charis,
Beautiful, whom he had wedded — he in both hands equally clever.
Clasping her hand in her own, she spake a word and addressed her:
"Why is it, long-robed Thetis, thou comest to visit our dwelling?
Honored and dear thou art. But aforetime rarely thou camest.
Come now, follow me in, that I as a guest may entreat thee."

Thus she spake and the goddess divine then guided her onward,

Seated her then on a throne rich-studded with silver and splendid,
Cunningly wrought, with a stool for the feet well-fitted beneath it.
Then Charis called and spake to the artisan, famous Hephaestus:
    "Come this way, Hephaestus. 'Tis Thetis needs thee for something."
    Her then he answered, the famed, he in both hands equally clever:
    "Truly, in there is a goddess, in my sight dread and reverèd,
She that delivered me once, when pain overtook me in falling
Far at the will of a mother unnatural, wishing to hide me,
Only because I was lame; and woes I had suffered in spirit,
Had not Eurynome taken me in to her bosom, and Thetis
(Even Eurynome, child of the refluent river of Ocean).
Nine years with them I wrought at my forge a great many jewels,
Brooches and bracelets spiral, and necklaces also and earrings,
Deep in a cavernous grot, while round me the river of Ocean,
Murmuring aye with its foam, flowed infinite. Nor was there other
One that knew of it, either of gods or of men that are mortal.
Only Eurynome knew it and Thetis — they who had saved me.
Now to *our* house *she* comes. It therefore behooveth me greatly
Fair-haired Thetis by all means now to requite for her saving.
But do thou in the mean time set fair entertainment before her,
While I am putting away my bellows and all my utensils."
    Thus he spake and, enormous of bulk, he rose from the anvil
Limping; but nimbly the legs of the god moved, slender, beneath him.
Then he removed his bellows away from the fire, then gathered
All in a chest of silver the tools wherewith he'd been working;
Next with a sponge he wiped both sides of his face and his two arms,
Cleansed his powerful neck and his breast, all sturdy and shagged.
Lastly he put on his tunic and went forth, taking a stout staff,
Limping along; but golden handmaids were nimble to serve him,
Who was their lord. They had all the semblance of living young women;
In them is understanding of heart, yea, voice there is in them,
Strength, too, and wisdom in handiwork, gift of the gods everlasting.
These tripped up in support of their lord, underneath, and he hobbled
Forward and sat him adown on a bright throne nigh unto Thetis,
Clasped her hand in his own and spake a word and addressed her:
    "Why is it, long-robed Thetis, thou comest to visit our dwelling?

400

Thetis and Eurynome Receiving the Infant Hephaestus

Honored and dear thou art. But aforetime rarely thou camest.
Tell me what is thy thought; my heart now bids me fulfil it,
If fulfil it I can, and the thing is ordained for fulfilment."

    Thereupon, dropping a tear, to him said Thetis in answer:
"Truly, Hephaestus, of all the goddesses homed in Olympus
Is there a one that hath felt in her heart deep sorrows so many
As are the woes that Zeus hath laid upon me above others?
Me of the sea-maids only he chose, to subdue to a mortal,
Peleus, Aeacus' son; of a man I have suffered the wedlock,
All in despite of my will. In his mansion's chambers he lieth
Stricken with grievous old age. But griefs far other afflict me,
Seeing Cronion gave me a son to be mine and to grow up
Chiefest of heroes and like to a fair young shoot in his growing.
Then, when I had reared him, a plant in a nook of a vineyard,
Off to the Ilian shore in the curvèd galleys I sent him,
There to fight with the Trojans; but never again shall I welcome
Him on return from the war to the home of Peleus, his father,
Never; and while he yet liveth in *my* sight, viewing the sunlight,
Sorrow is his, and though I may go, I can help him in no wise.
Lo! a damsel the sons of Achaia chose him as guerdon
Out of his arms hath the lord Agamemnon forcibly taken.
He in resentment for her kept eating his heart out. The Trojans
Meanwhile hemmed the Achaeans among their ships nor allowed them
Ever to come forth; thereat the Argive elders implored him
Pressingly, telling before him their gifts full many and goodly.
After that, though he refused himself to avert the destruction,
Still in his own war-gear he harnessed his comrade, Patroclus,
Sent him out to the war, and assigned a strong force to attend him.
All day long in front of the Scaean gateway they battled.
That same day they had pillaged the city, perchance, but Apollo,
After the valiant son of Menoetius had wrought endless havoc,
Slew him in front of the fray and gave unto Hector the glory.
This is the reason that *I* have come to thy knees now, if haply
Thou wilt give to my son, so early to perish, a buckler,
Helmet, and corselet, and beautiful greaves with clasps at the ankles.
All that he had his trusty companion, when slain by the Trojans,

Lost. Now Achilles lies on the ground in anguish of spirit."

Her then he answered, the famed, he in both hands equally clever:
"Have no fear. Let not thy heart be troubled with these things.
Would indeed that I might be able so surely to hide him
Far from a dolorous death, when the dreadful fate overtakes him,
Surely as fair war-gear shall be at his need — such that any
One of the hosts of men shall marvel, whoe'er may behold it."

Thus he spake and left her there and went to his bellows;
These he turned to the fire and bade them proceed with the labor.
Twice ten bellows in all, they blew on the crucibles twenty,
Sending now strong, now gentle, well-puffed the various blowings,
Now to the need of his labor to minister, now again elsewise,
Howe'er willed it Hephaestus, while speeding the work to completion.
Copper he cast in the fire, unwearying copper, and silver,
Gold full precious, and tin; and on the block for the anvil
Set up his anvil, immense, firm-fastened, and picked up a mighty
Hammer with one hand, grasping a fire-tongs fast in the other.

First of all then he fashioned a shield both massive and mighty:
Blaz'ning it rich all over, he cast bright-shining and triple
Round it a radiant rim with a baldric of silver depending.
Now of the buckler itself the layers were five; and upon it
Manifold cunning devices he fashioned with skilled understanding:
Thereon he moulded the earth and the sea and the canopied heaven,
Wrought the unwearying sun and the moon, just waxing to fulness,
All of the constellations, as many as garland the heavens,
Pleiades, Hyades all, and above them the might of Orion,
Arctus, the Bear, which people call also "the Wain" as a surname —
Her that wheels in her place and watches the hunter Orion;
She, alone of the signs, hath no part in the baths of the ocean.

Thereon also he wrought two cities of men that are mortal —
Beautiful; represented in one were a wedding and feasting:
Under the gleaming of torches the bride from her chamber the party
Up through the city were leading, and loud rose the hymn hymeneal;
Young men whirled in an eddying dance, while the viols among them
Sounded aloud, while flutes uplifted their notes; and the women
All stood still at the porches and doorways, gazing in wonder.

Hephaestus and Charis Receiving Thetis

But in the place of assembly the town-folk were gathered; contention
There had arisen: two men made ſtrife on account of a blood-price,
Due for a man that was slain; for the one man claimed he had paid it
All and explained to the folk; but the other refused to take money;
Both were eager to win at the hands of the court a decision.
Loudly the people applauded on both sides, supporters of either;
Bailiffs, busy the while, were reſtraining the folk; and the elders,
Seated on polished ſtones in the midst of the hallowèd circle,   [heralds.
Held in their hands the ſtaves they received from the clear-voiced
Leaning on these, they arose, and each in turn gave his judgment.
Meantime there in the midst were deposited two golden talents,
Prize for the one who presented the case most juſtly among them.

    All round the second city two armies of warriors were ſtationed,
Shining in arms. Two also the plans that found favor among them:
Either to pillage the town or divide between the two parties
All of the subſtance the lovely city was holding within it.   [ambush:
Not yet the townsmen would yield but were arming themselves for an
High on the walls their wives, well-loved, and their innocent children
Stood on guard, and among them the men whom age had o'ertaken.
Forth then they fared. Their leaders were Ares and Pallas Athena,
Both of them gold; pure gold gleamed also the raiment upon them;
Handsome and tall were they in their armor, as gods was befitting,
Far seen in every direction; the people were smaller beneath them.
When they arrived at a place thought fitted for laying an ambush,
Where, at the bed of a ſtream, came to drink all manner of cattle,
There then they sat them down, encased in shining bronze armor.
While they were watching, two scouts that the warriors poſted afar off
Sat to await the appearing of flocks and of crooked-horned cattle.
Presently came the liveſtock, two only the herdsmen that followed,
Making merry with pipes and never of treachery thinking.
Catching sight of them coming, the men ran swiftly upon them;
Quickly they cut off the herds of the kine and the flocks of the gleaming
Beautiful sheep; and also they slaughtered the shepherding herdsmen.

    But the besiegers, at hearing the loud uproar 'mid the cattle —
Seated in front of the tribunes the while — on their chariots mounted
Inſtant behind their high-ſtepping ſteeds and soon overtook them.

Then they arrayed their battle and fought at the banks of the river
Fiercely and smote one another amain with bronze-pointed javelins.
Tumult raged in the midst and Strife and Fate, the Destroyer,
Grasping alive one man, new wounded, another unwounded,
Dragging another one dead, by the feet, through the midst of the mellay;
Crimson with blood of men was the garment she wore round her shoul-
Like unto mortals alive, they clashed and battled together,   〔ders.
Haling the dead men fallen, and each host those of the other.

Thereon he set him a field, a plowland fertile and fallow,
Thrice turned, porous and wide; and plowmen many upon it
Drove before them the yokes, and they wheeled this way and the other.
Whensoever they turned, on attaining the bound of the plowland,
Then would a man come and place in their hand a goblet of new wine,
Sweeter than honey. Along the furrows others were turning
Back, all fain to arrive at the bound of the deep-set tillage.
Also behind them the ground grew black, and it looked like plowed land,
Though it was made of gold; so great was the marvel produced there.

Thereon he set a demesne, deep-waving, of corn, and the hinds were
Reaping, and keen-edged sickles they held in their hands for the harvest.
Thick were the handfuls falling to earth and along on a swath, while
Others binders were binding, with straw-bands twisted, in bundles.
Three were the binders appointed in charge of the work, and behind
Lads were collecting the grain, and they carried it over in armfuls 〔them
Aye to the binders to bind; while silent amid them the master
Stood with his staff near by to the swath, and his heart was rejoicing.
Under an oak-tree henchmen apart were preparing a banquet;
Busy they were about a huge ox they had slaughtered; the women
Strewed white barley in plenty the while for the laborers' dinner.

Thereon he set him a vineyard, heavily loaded with clusters,
Beautiful, golden; and dark were the grapes in bunches upon it;
Ranged full length of the field stood vine-poles of silver to bear them.
There was a cyanus ditch to encircle it, fenced with a hedge-row
Round it, of tin; and thereon a path, one only, led to it,
Whereby vintagers fared whenever they gathered the vintage.
Lasses and lads light-hearted in merriment on it he moulded,
Bearing in baskets of osier the ripe fruit, sweeter than honey;

All in the midst a lad — and a clear-toned viol he carried —
Charmingly played on the lyre, and he sang to its music a pleasant
Linus with delicate voice, and the rest, their feet in accordance
Beating the ground, went tripping in time with the song and the music.

Thereon also he placed him a herd of straight-hornèd cattle;
Fashioned of gold and of tin were the cattle thereon that he moulded;
Lowing they hastened away from the farmyard back to the pasture,
Nigh to a murmuring river, whereby the rushes were waving.   [them,
Herdsmen of gold kept pace with the kine, as they moved on behind
Four in alinement; nine were the dogs quick-footed that followed.
Two fell lions were there; 'mid the foremost cows they were holding
Fast a loud-bellowing bull; and the bull, as away they would hale him,
Mightily bawled; and the hounds with the young men speeded upon him
Vainly. The lions had rended the great bull's hide and were gulping
Greedily down his vitals and black blood, whileas the herdsmen
Sicked on vainly the fleet-footed hounds to engrapple the robbers —
Vainly, for *they* still shrank from assailing and biting the lions;
Only they stood hard by and barked but avoided encounter.   [hands —

Thereon he moulded a pasture — the famed, the clever in both
Broad in a beautiful dell, white-shining the sheep in its closure —
Steading and folds for the livestock, and huts with roofs overhanging.

Thereon a dance he emblazoned — the famed, the clever in both
Like unto that fair-fashioned in broad-built Cnossus aforetime, [hands —
Fashioned by Daedalus' skill for the beautiful-tressed Ariadne.
Therein were blooming youths and maids wooed with presents of cattle,
Dancing and holding with hands each one the wrist of another.
Raiment of fine-spun linen the maids had on; and the tunics,
Well-woven, worn by the youths, were faintly a-glisten with ointment.
Fair were also the garlands the maids had on; and the daggers,
Worn by the youths, were of gold, suspended from baldrics of silver.
Now they were skipping in circle with feet well-trainèd, exceeding
Lightly, as runneth a wheel well-fit to the hands of a potter
Seated and making a trial, if haply it runneth to please him;
Now they were skipping anon in lines to meet one another.
Large was the company girdling the gladsome dance, the while gazing
Glad in their hearts; and a minstrel divine made music among them,

Playing his harp; and meantime two tumblers 'mid them a-whirling
Still, as the music began, kept eddying round and among them.
.   Thereon he placed full mighty the ſtrength of the river of Ocean,
All round the uttermost rim of the shield so cunningly moulded.

When now thus he had fashioned the shield both massive and mighty,
Then he wrought him a corselet, than fire-gleam brighter in splendor.
Next he wrought him a helmet, ponderous, fitting his temples,
Beauteous, curious-wrought; a golden crest he set on it.
Last then he wrought him the greaves; of flexible tin did he make them.

When he the panoply finished, the famed, the clever in both hands,
All he uplifted and laid in front of Achilles's mother.
She, like a falcon, down from the snowy heights of Olympus
Leaped, and she bore away the radiant arms from Hephaeſtus.

ILIAD · XIX · (T)

Tâv gives the anger period,
And great Achilles comes abroad.

DAWN in her mantle of saffron had now from the currents of Ocean
Risen, to bring new light unto mortals and unto immortals,
Even as Thetis came bringing the gifts from the god to the galleys.
Fallen she found her well loved son on the corse of Patroclus,
Wailing in loud lamentation, and many a comrade about him
Mourned. And among them came the goddess divine and ſtood by him,
Clasped his hand in her own, and spake a word and addressed him:
    "This, thy companion, my child, we must let lie, even though griev- [ing
Sore, since truly his death from the first was appointed of Heaven.
Thou, however, receive from Hephaeſtus this glorious armor,
Passingly fair; the like ne'er yct man wore on his shoulders."
    Thus did the goddess speak and then in front of Achilles   [tions.
Laid down the arms, and they all clanged aloud with their rich decora-
Thereat shuddering fell on the Myrmidon host, and they dared not
Anyone look on the gear; they shrank back in fear; but Achilles,
When he beheld it, rather was seized of a fury — and fearful,
Under his eyelids, blazing, his eyes shone forth like the lightning.
Glad was he as he held in his hands the god's gifts so glorious.
But when his soul had been gladdened with viewing the rich decorations,
Straightway unto his mother he spake wingèd words and addressed her:
    "Mother of mine, such arms the godhead hath giv'n as 'tis fitting
Work should be of immortals; no mortal man could have wrought them.
Therefore now will I arm me therein, but I grievously fear me
Lest meanwhile, attacking the valiant son of Menoetius,
Flies enter into the gaping wounds that were cleft by the bronzen
Weapon, breed worms in the wounds, and mar and defile the fair body
(Out of him life hath been slain), and his flesh fall prey to corruption."
    Then unto him did Thetis, the silver-footed, make answer:

411

"Let not thy heart, I pray thee, my child, be troubled with these
From him to keep the savage swarms shall be my endeavor —   [things.
Even the flies that feed upon men that are slain in a battle.
Yea, even though he should lie till a full year's course is completed,
Ever untainted his flesh shall remain or be even better.
Thou, though, call the heroes Achaean to meet in assembly;
Then renounce all thy wrath with the shepherd of hosts, Agamemnon,
Speedily arm thyself for the war, and clothe thee with prowess."

Thus she spake and put into her son a spirit intrepid,
While on the corse of Patroclus she dripped ambrosia and ruddy
Nectar down through his nostrils, the flesh to preserve unattainted.

Then up along the shore of the sea went the godlike Achilles
Crying his terrible cry, and he roused up the heroes Achaean.
Those who there were accustomed to bide in the gath'ring of galleys,
Those who were pilots and handled the steering gear of the galleys,
Those who were stewards on board of the ships, the dealers of rations —
All these came to the place of assembly, for that Achilles
Now had appeared, though long he had ceased from sorrowful battle.
Limping along came also the two, both squires of Ares,
Tydeus' son, the steadfast in war, and the godlike Odysseus,
Leaning upon their spears, for their wounds still grievously vexed them.
In the front row of th' assembly both chiefs took seats on arriving.
Last of them all came also the monarch of men, Agamemnon,
Nursing his wound; him, too, in the midst of the furious conflict
Coön, son of Antenor, with bronze-tipped javelin had wounded.
When now all the Achaeans had thus been gathered together,
Full in the midst uprising fleet-footed Achilles addressed them:

"Atreus' son, was it truly for both of us any the better,
Better for thee and for me, when we in anguish of spirit
Both spent our fury in soul-consuming strife for a damsel?
Would that Artemis then at the ships with an arrow had slain her
That same day I destroyed Lyrnessus and won me the maiden.
Then had not bitten the boundless earth so many Achaeans
Under the foemen's hands, because I was fuming with anger.
Well hath it been for the Trojans and Hector; but the Achaeans
Long will remember, I think, that quarrel engendered between us.

412

Thetis Bringing the Armor to Achilles

Bygones now we will let be bygones, albeit grieving
Sore, and bridle the heart in our breasts at necessity's bidding.
Now do I still mine anger toward thee; nowise it behooveth
Ever to rage with a fury relentlessly. Come, do thou quickly
Rouse to re-enter the war and the battle the long-haired Achaeans,
That I may go 'gainst the Trojans again and make of them trial
Whether they haply shall wish to couch by the galleys; but many
Fain will be resting their knees, whoever escape peradventure
Out of the fury of war and before the might of our javelin.''

    Thus spake he. Overjoyed, those well-greaved sons of Achaia
Heard the renouncement of wrath from the great-hearted scion of
Spake forth also amid them the monarch of men, Agamemnon, [Peleus.
Moving not from his seat nor rising and standing among them:
    ''Friends, ye men of Ares' company, Danaans, heroes,
Seemly it is to attend, when one hath arisen and speaketh,
Not interrupt; for that makes it hard for even an expert.
Nay, in a general hubbub how, pray, could anyone hearken
Rightly or speak? The orator, clearest of voice, were embarrassed.
Now to the son of Peleus I offer this statement; ye other
Argives, give close heed, and each of you mark what I utter.
Often indeed they have said that word unto me, the Achaeans;
Me they would often upbraid; but of blame *I* am not deserving;
Zeus far rather and Fate and Erinys that walketh in darkness,
They that put into my soul fierce blindness in the assembly
That same day that I reft, e'en I, from Achilles his guerdon.
What was it *I* could do? 'Tis God that brings all to fulfilment.
Ate, th' exalted daughter of Zeus, strikes all men with blindness,
Baleful in might; and soft are her steps, for ever she walketh
Not on the ground, but she fareth high o'er the heads of men mortal,
Making them stumble and fall; she ensnareth one and another.
Zeus even one time was blinded, it seems, and he is the greatest
Whether of men or of gods, men say — it was even Cronion
Once on a time that Hera with wiles of a woman deluded;
That very day she deceived great Zeus when Heracles mighty
Was to be born of Alcmena in Thebes with fair garland of towers.
Zeus then vauntingly uttered a vow 'mid all the immortals:

'Hearken to me, ye gods, ye goddesses, all of you hearken,
That I may tell to you all what the heart in my bosom commands me.
This is the day Ilithyia, the helper of women in travail,
Bringeth a hero to light that shall lord over all people dwelling
'Round him, of that line of men who from my own blood are descended.'
Then with a crafty purpose addressed him the worshipful Hera:
'False wilt thou prove, and thou wilt not bring thy word to fulfilment!
Come now, swear me, Olympian, an oath full mighty that surely
That man truly as king shall be lord over all people dwelling
'Round him — he that shall fall this day 'twixt feet of a woman —
Even of all those men whose line from thy blood is descended.'
"Thus spake she; and Zeus, aware of her subtlety noway,
Swore her an oath full mighty and therein sorely was blinded.
Hera leaped down in haste and left the peak of Olympus;
Swiftly she came to Achaean Argos; there was abiding
Perseïd Sthenelus' wife, as she knew — right stately the woman,
Great with a child of her love; her seventh moon now was upon her;
Him she brought to the light with his moons yet failing in number,
Stayed the pangs of Alcmena, and kept th' Ilithyias from her.
Then with the news she addressed herself to Zeus, son of Cronus:
'O Father Zeus, bright light'ning, a word will I speak for thy heeding:
Born even now is the valiant man who shall reign o'er the Argives,
Sthenelus' son and a grandson of Perseus, even Eurystheus,
Thine own race, nor insooth unfit to be lord of the Argives.'
Thus she spake; and a pang smote sharp to the depth of his spirit.
Forthwith Ate he seized by her head with its glistening tresses,
Deeply indignant of soul; with an oath full mighty he swore it,
Never again to Olympus, the starry expanse of the heavens, [mortals.
Ate should come, who with blindness strikes all, both men and im-

"Thus he spake and, whirling her round with his hand, from the
Sky he flung her. Soon she arrived 'mid work-a-day people. [Starry
Thinking of her he would groan when he saw his son, his belovèd,
Bearing unseemly toil in his labors at hest of Eurystheus.
Likewise I, what time great shimmering-helmeted Hector
Slaughtered the Argive heroes amain at the sterns of our galleys,
Could not forget that Ate, by whom at the first I was blinded.

Now since thus I was blinded, and Zeus bereft me of senses,
Fain would I now make amends and a recompense pay beyond measure.
Only arise to the war and rouse up the rest of the army.

    "Gifts I am ready to furnish, e'en all that the godlike Odysseus
Yesterday promised to thee, when he came to thee in thy barrack.
So, if thou wishest, wait yet a while, though eager for warfare.
Gifts, as promised, the squires will get and bring from my galley,
So that *thou* mayest see that what I offer contents thee."

    Answering him in his turn spake forth fleet-footed Achilles:

    "Atreus' son, most glorious, thou monarch of men, Agamemnon,
Gifts it is thine, if thou wishest, to offer, as thee it beseemeth,
Or to withhold; it rests with thee; but let us bethink us
Now of the battle joy (for we *must* not stay *here* and thus dally
Bandying words in parley; great work still waiteth the doing),
So that many a one may again in the van see Achilles
Laying waste with his javelin of bronze the battalions of Trojans.
Mindful of this let each of you battle amain with his foeman."

    Then in answer addressed him Odysseus of many devices:

    "Nay, not so — though valiant thou art, O godlike Achilles —
Urge not fasting the sons of Achaia now against Ilium,
There to fight with the Trojans; for no brief span will the war-din
Last, when once the battalions of men in the struggle together
Meet, and God breathes valor alike on one and the other.
Nay, do thou bid the Achaeans take food at the swift-sailing galleys,
Bread and wine, for therein are fountains of vigor and valor.
No man abstaining from food will a whole day long, until sunset's
Coming upon him, be able to battle amain with the foemen.
Even if deep in his spirit he yearn to keep up the warfare,
Yet do his limbs unaware grow weary, and hunger alighteth
On him and thirst, and his knees underneath him falter in going.
But when a warrior has had his fill of wine and of eating,
Though with the foemen the whole day long he keeps up the warfare,
Still is ever the heart in his breast full of courage; he tireth
Not in his limbs, until all alike withdraw from the conflict.
Come then, do thou dismiss them and bid that the host make ready
Quickly their meal. And the gifts, let the monarch of men, Agamemnon,

Bring to the midst of the place of assembly, that all the Achaeans
May with their own eyes witness, and thou be gladdened in spirit.
Then let him swear thee an oath, standing up in the midst of the Argives,
That he did never ascend *her* bed or with her have converse
As is the manner of men, O king, and of women together.
Ay, let the spirit indwelling in thee be appeasable also.
Then let him make reconcilement with thee in his tents, at a banquet,
Bountiful, so that in naught there fail thee full reparation.
Thou, too, Atreus' son, more righteous shalt be in the future
Unto another; for ill it beseems no monarch, if ever
He provoke one to wrath, to offer amends to his fellow."
      Then in his turn addressed him the monarch of men, Agamemnon:
   "Glad am I to have heard thy speech, O Son of Laërtes;
For thou hast justly declared and all things rightly recounted.
Truly I'm ready to swear that oath, and my spirit enjoins it,
Nor shall I perjure myself in the sight of God. But Achilles,
Let him wait here yet a while, though eagerly yearning for warfare.
All ye others assembled wait, until the gifts from my barrack
All be brought, and we pledge ourselves with a holy oblation.
Now unto thee thyself I give a commandment and bid thee
Choose out men that are young and princes of all the Achaeans
Hither to bring from my galley the gifts, all the presents we promised
Yesterday unto Achilles, and lead here also the women.
Let Talthybius now before the wide host of th' Achaeans
Make me ready a boar to offer to Zeus and the Sun-god."
      Answered him then and addressed him in turn fleet-footed Achilles:
   "Atreus' son, most glorious, thou monarch of men, Agamemnon,
Some other time ye should busy yourselves even more with this matter,
When perchance there may come some interval free from the warfare;
Do this some time when not so great is the rage in my bosom.
Now, while out yonder are lying, all mangled our comrades whom
Scion of Priam, vanquished, when Zeus to him gave the glory, [Hector,
Ye two are urging the men to take food! But for my part the rather
I'd bid the sons of Achaia this moment to enter the warfare,
E'en unfed and fasting, and have them at sunset make ready   [ance.
Here a great supper, when we for our present disgrace have had venge-

Down my dear throat, at least, until then it is not to be thought of
That either food or drink should pass, since dead is my comrade,
Who in my barrack now, with a keen bronze weapon all mangled,
Lies, with his feet toward the doorway turned; our comrades around him
Mourn; and so the heart in my breast hath no thought of such things,
Nay! but of slaughter and blood and dolorous groans of the dying!''
　　　　Then unto him made answer Odysseus of many devices:
　　"Goodliest far of Achaeans, Achilles, scion of Peleus,
Stronger than I with the spear—by no means only a little
Better—but I in common sense may greatly surpass thee,
Mayhap, since I am older and have more knowledge than thou hast.
Therefore, let thy heart attend to my counsel with patience:
Verily, quickly there comes unto people a surfeit of war-din,
Wherein the bronze ſtrews ſtraw all over the ground in abundance—
Yet is the harvest thin, when at last Zeus inclineth the balance,
Zeus, ordained dispenser to men of the fortunes of warfare.
Nay, not so! the Achaeans cannot fast over a dead man,
Since they are falling exceeding thick, yea, many in number,
Every day. What respite could one find then from the hardship?
Nay, it behooveth to bury them all, whoever have fallen,
Steeling the heart 'gainst pity, if once for the day we have mourned
Yet whoever are left and survive the warfare abhorrèd,　　　[them.
Them it behooves to bethink them of meat and of drink, that the better
We with the foemen do battle relentless, unintermittent,
When we have harnessed our bodies in bronze unwearying. Therefore
Let not one of the host hold off as awaiting another
Summons; for such second summons will be a bad thing for the slacker
Left at the Argive ships! Let us all in a body attacking
Waken the fury of war 'gainst the Trojans, tamers of horses.''
　　　　Said he and chose him the sons of glorious Neſtor for escort;
Meges and Thoas he chose and Meriones, too, and Phylides;
Creon's son, Lycomedes, he took and his friend, Melanippus.
These made their way to the barrack of Atreus' son, Agamemnon.
Soon as the word was said, the deed was ſtraightway accomplished:
Tripods seven in number they bore from the barrack, as promised,
Flame-bright cauldrons twenty in number, of horses a dozen;

Women they brought from the tent, well skilled in handiwork matchless,
Seven in all, with an eighth, the fair-faced damsel Briseïs.
When he had weighed him in all ten talents of gold, then Odysseus
Led, and the rest, the young men of Achaia, came bearing the presents.
These they set in the midst of the meeting. Then Agamemnon
Rose; and Talthybius, like to a god in voice, held the victim,
Even the boar, with his hands, as he stood by the shepherd of peoples.
Thereupon Atreus' son, with his hand unsheathing his dagger,
Always there at the side of his sword's great scabbard suspended,
Cut off consecrate hairs; then, lifting his hands to Cronion,
Prayed, and the rest of the Argives all, in their places appointed,
Seated in silence, attended with awe the word of their sovereign;
Then he spake in prayer, looking up to the canopied heaven:

"Zeus over all be witness, the best and the highest of godheads,
Also Earth and Sun and Erinyës, wreakers of vengeance
Under the earth upon men, whoever have sworn to a falsehood,
Nowise ever have I laid hand on the damsel Briseïs
(Under a pretext, either of sharing her couch, or another),
Nay, it was wholly untouched that she abode in my barracks.
If anything be false in this oath, let the deities send me
All of the many woes they send on a perjurer sinful."

Said he and severed the throat of the boar with the pitiless dagger.
Then Talthybius into the mighty abyss of the grey sea,
Whirling the carcase, cast it as food for the fishes. Achilles
Rose up and spake in the midst of the Argives, lovers of warfare:

"Zeus, O Father, the blindness is sore that thou dealest to mortals.
Unto Atrides never were given to waken a spirit
So in my breast all through nor to lead off ever the damsel
Wilfully, wholly against my will, but only that one time
Zeus had willed that death should fall on many Achaeans. —
Go ye now to your dinner, that we may join battle thereafter." [sembly.

Thus then he spake aloud, and with speed he adjourned the as-
Scattered were all of the rest; and each one went to his galley.
Only the great-hearted Myrmidons busied themselves with the presents;
With them they went away to the ship of the godlike Achilles.
There in the barracks they laid them down, there seated the women;

Unto their stud then the gallant squires drove off the horses.

　　Now as Briseïs, so like unto fair Aphrodite, the golden,
Saw, by the keen bronze weapon all mangled, the form of Patroclus,
Throwing herself upon him, she bitterly wailed and with both hands
Tore at her breast, her delicate neck, and her face in its beauty.
Thus 'mid her weeping then spake that damsel, peer of a goddess:

　　"O Patroclus, thou in my hapless heart the most cherished,
Thou wert alive as I left thee, when I went away from the barrack;
Now do I find thee dead, alas! O prince of the peoples,
When I return. Thus evil on evil doth ever pursue me.
Him, unto whom as husband my father and worshipful mother
Gave me, I saw in front of our city with keen bronze all mangled,
Likewise three brothers of mine (one only the mother that bare us) —
Nearest and dearest to me — they all met their day of destruction.
Thou, though, wouldst not permit me even to weep, when Achilles,
Swift of foot, slew my husband and wasted the city of godlike
Mynes — nay, didst promise to make me the godlike Achilles'
Wedded wife and to bring me to Phthia home in your galleys,
There to make me a feast 'mid the Myrmidon folk at my wedding.
Bitterly, therefore, I weep for thee dead; thou ever wast gentle."

　　Thus she spake, as she wept, and the women added their mourning,
Feigning their moans for Patroclus, but each for her own heart's sor-
Meantime about Achilles th' Achaean elders were gath'ring,　　[rows.
Urgently praying that he would eat; with a groan he denied them:

　　"Pray you, if any one of my comrades belovèd will hear me,
Do not bid me to sate untimely the spirit within me,
Be it with meat or with drink, since terrible grief hath come o'er me;
Until the sun goeth down, I will wait and, steadfast, endure it."

　　Thus he spake and dismissed the others, the princes about him;
Only remained the Atridae twain and godlike Odysseus;
Nestor stayed and Idomeneus, too, and the knightly old Phoenix,
Eager to soothe him in sorrow exceeding keen; but his spirit
Naught could soothe till he entered the blood-dyed jaws of the warfare.
Many the deep-drawn sighs and the words of remembrance he uttered:

　　"Thou, too, truly of yore, unfortunate, dearest of comrades,
Oft in the barrack thyself didst set forth savory dishes,

Quickly and deftly, whene'er the Achaeans hastened to carry
Battle, all fraught with tears, to the Trojans, tamers of horses.
Now thou liest, alas! with the keen bronze mangled, and *my* heart
Will not partake of food or of drink, although they are ready,
Out of yearning for thee. For nothing worse could I suffer,
Not even though I should learn peradventure the death of my father,
Who now in Phthia, I ween, is shedding a big, round tear-drop
All for the want of a son like me, who here in an alien
Country afar am warring with Troy for abominate Helen,
Nor of my well-loved son, who is growing up yonder in Scyros,
Ah! if indeed yet alive is Neoptolemus godlike.
Hitherto had the dear heart in my bosom verily trusted,
I it was only should perish, from Argos, pasture of horses,
Far off, here in Troyland, but thou shouldst fare unto Phthia,
So as to bring me the lad in a swiftly sailing black galley
Off from Scyros and show him everything there in the homeland,
All my substance and thralls and the palace, high-roofed and spacious.
Peleus truly, methinks, already is dead and departed,
Or, just alive, now is broken down with old age that is hateful,
Ever awaiting the sorrowful tidings of me, when he haply
Heareth the news that his son has failed from the land of the living."

Thus he spake, as he wept, and the elders added their mourning,
Each in remembrance of all he had left over seas in his palace.
Now, as Cronion beheld them weep, he was filled with compassion.
Straightway with wingèd words he addressed the goddess Athena:
"Thou, my child, hast wholly deserted thine own chosen hero!
Is there no longer a place in thy heart at all for Achilles?
Lo! he is yonder alone, in front of the straight-hornèd galleys;
Seated he mourneth his comrade belovèd; the others have left him,
Going away to their meal, while *he* unfed is and fasting.
Come then, go and instil both pleasant ambrosia and nectar
Into the hero's breast, lest pains of hunger assail him."

These words sped on Athena, herself already full eager;
Like to a shrill-voiced falcon with wide-spreading pinions, the goddess
Swooped through the ether down from the sky. Meanwhile the Achaeans
All through the camp were arming themselves. But she was instilling

Pleasant ambrosia and nectar divine in the breast of Achilles,
So that no kill-joy hunger invade the limbs of the hero.
She then vanished away to the firm-built home of her father,
Zeus, the all mighty. Then out from the swift ships poured the Achae-
Even as when from a cloud thick flutter incessantly snow-flakes   [ans.
Chill 'neath a blast of the Northwind, begot in the regions of ether:
Even so thick, so incessant the helmets, all proud in effulgence,
Forth from the ships kept streaming, and bucklers blazoned with bosses,
Corselets, too, strong-plated, and spear-shafts fashioned of ash-wood.
Up to the sky rose the splendor; the earth was all laughing around them
Under the flashing of bronze; from under the feet of the heroes
Rose up the noise, while godlike Achilles armed him amid them;
Also his teeth kept gnashing together, and both of his eyeballs
Gleamed like the flaming of fire, for keen, insupportable anguish
Entered his heart. As he raged meanwhile at the Trojans, the hero
Put on the gifts of the god, that Hephaestus' cunning had fashioned.

    First on his legs he fastened the greaves all round about deftly,
Beautiful, fitted with buckles of silver and firm at his ankles.
Second, he put on the corselet encasing his breast all about him;
Over his shoulder he slung his sword, all studded with silver;   [ample;
Bronze was the blade. Then he took up the shield, formed ponderous,
From it the brightness was shed far abroad like the splendor of moon-

    Even as out on the sea peradventure appeareth to sailors   [beams.
Gleam of a blazing fire, bright flaming aloft in a steading
Lone on a mountain's top, while storm-blasts drive them unwilling
Far from loved ones away o'er the deep sea peopled of fishes:
So from the beautiful shield, so cunningly wrought, of Achilles
Brightness ascended to heaven. Then lifting the ponderous helmet,
Firm on his temples he set it; and star-like glittered the helmet,
All with its horse-hair crested; the gold-wrought plumes all around it
Waved in the air o'er the ridge, where Hephaestus had set the thick
Godlike Achilles then made proof of himself in his harness,   [plumage.
Whether it fitted him well, and his glorious limbs ran freely;
For him it proved like wings, and it buoyed the shepherd of peoples.
Lastly forth from the rack he drew the spear of his father,
Pond'rous, sturdy, and huge; not one of the other Achaeans

Ever could wield it; Achilles alone understood how to wield it,
Javelin of Pelian ash, which Chiron gave his dear father,
Grown on Pelion's peak and appointed for death unto heroes.
Now was Automedon busied, with Alcimus, yoking the horses:
Beautiful breast-straps they fitted upon them; bits they inserted
Into the horses' mouths; and the guide-reins they drew up and tight- [ened
Back to the firm-built car; Automedon, seizing the shining
Whip, well fitting his hand, sprang lightly into the chariot
Up behind the horses, and after him mounted Achilles,
Harnessed and fulgent in arms like beaming-bright Hyperion.
Terribly then he shouted and called on the steeds of his father:
    "Xanthus and Balius, children — renownèd afar — of Podarge,
Otherwise truly bethink you to bring your master in safety
Back to the Danaan host, when we haply are sated of warfare;
Neither leave ye him dead, as ye left Patroclus, out yonder." [footed,
    Out from under the yoke then addressed him his horse, glancing-
Even Xanthus; he bowed with his head, as he spoke; all his mane fell
Streaming down to the ground past the yoke from under the yoke-pad
[Thus with speech did Hera, the white-armed goddess, endue him]:
    "Yea, for the time we will still keep thee safe, O mighty Achilles;
Yet is the day of doom already anigh thee, and nowise
We are to blame, but a mighty god and fate overpow'ring.
For it was not due to sloth or carelessness any on our part —
Ours — that the Trojans took from Patroclus' shoulders his armor.
Nay, but the best of the gods, whose fair-haired mother was Leto,
Slew him in front of the fray and gave the glory to Hector.
We might even the breath of Zephyrus rival in running,
Swiftest, they say, of the winds. No less unto thee is appointed,
Thee thyself, to be slain by a god and a hero in battle."
    Then the Erinyës stayed his voice, when thus he had spoken.
Grievously troubled, addressed him in turn fleet-footed Achilles:
    "Xanthus, why is it *thou* foretellest my death? Thou shouldst not:
Well do I know it myself, how here I am fated to perish
Far from my father dear and my mother. Yet will I never
Cease until I have given their fill of war to the Trojans." [foremost.
    Said he, and shouting, he drove his whole-hoofed steeds 'mid the

ILIAD · XX · (Y)

In Upsilon Strife stirs in heaven,
The day's grace to the Greeks is given.

THUS by the curve-prowed galleys the sons of Achaia were arming
   Round about thee, son of Peleus, thou ever insatiate of battle;
Over against them, up on the swell of the plain, were the Trojans.
   Zeus meanwhile bade Themis to call the gods to assembly,
Gathering there from the brow of many-folded Olympus.
Everywhere ranging, she bade them to come to the home of the Father.
Not one then of the rivers was absent — saving the Ocean —   [lands
Neither indeed of the Nymphs, whose haunts are the copses, the wood-
Fair, and the grass-grown dells, and the meadows and fountains of rivers.
All, having come to the mansion of Zeus who gathers the storm-clouds,
Took their seats in the halls, with polished columns surrounded,
Built with a cunning conception for Father Zeus by Hephaestus.
   So in the palace of Zeus they gathered; the Earth-shaker also
Heeded the goddess and came from the salt sea to join with the others,
Sat in the midst, and into the purpose of Zeus made inquiry:
   "Lord of the glitt'ring bolt, why again call the gods to assembly?
Art thou pond'ring some plan about the Achaeans and Trojans?
Battle and warfare between them this very next moment are blazing."
   Answering him in his turn, cloud-gathering Zeus addressed him:
   "Shaker of earth, thou knowest what now in my heart is intended,
Why I convoked you gods: men menaced with ruin concern me.
Yet let me tell thee that I will abide in a fold of Olympus
Seated and gladden my heart there with looking upon them; the others
All of you go and commingle among them, Achaeans and Trojans;
Bring ye to either side succor, as each of you haply is minded.
For if Achilles alone shall engage the Trojans in battle,
Not for a moment will they hold off fleet-footed Pelides.
Even before this time, if they only saw him, they trembled;

425

Now, though, seeing his soul is terribly wroth for his comrade,
Fearful am I he will o'erleap fate, yea, level the ramparts."

  Thus spake the son of Cronus and roused unabating the battle.
Warward issued the gods, in heart and in counsel divided;
Unto the gath'ring of ships went Hera and Pallas Athena,
Also Poseidon, Enfolder of earth, and the bringer of blessings
Hermes — he that excelleth all in counsels of cunning.
With them went also Hephaestus (his heart swelled high in his prowess),
Limping; but nimbly the legs of the god moved, slender, beneath him.
But to the side of the Trojans the shimmering-helmeted Ares
Went, with Apollo of locks unshorn, and the rainer of arrows,
Artemis, Leto, and Xanthus, and lover of smiles, Aphrodite.

  Just as long as the gods held far from men that are mortals,
So long waxed the Achaeans in glory, because that Achilles
Now had appeared, though long he had ceased from sorrowful battle.
Trembling and dread ran over the limbs of each of the Trojans,
Stricken with fear on beholding the fleet-footed scion of Peleus,
Shining in arms, the equal of Ares, ruin of mortals.
But when th' Olympians came and entered the tumult of heroes,
Strife, the arouser of hosts, sprang up in her might, and Athena
Sent forth a shout as she stood at the moat outside of the rampart,
Now again cheering aloud at the seashore's echoing margin;
Over against her, like to a storm-cloud's blackness, the War-god
Shouted with ringing cry from the height of the town of the Trojans,
Or by the Simoïs river he sped upon Callicolone.

  So did the blessèd gods spur on the two hosts and in warfare
Pitted them, causing to break out among them a furious conflict.
Fearfully thundered the Father of men and of gods everlasting
High overhead; and beneath, Poseidon struck with a trembling
All of the boundless earth, and the lofty tops of the mountains;
All of the foothills of Ida, the many-fountained, were shaken,
All of her crests, and the city of Troy, and the galleys Achaean.
Lord of the world down below, Aïdoneus, was stricken with terror,
Sprang from his throne in alarm, cried out lest haply Poseidon,
Shaker of earth, rend open the world-plain vaulted above him,
Showing alike unto mortals and unto immortals his dwelling

The Gods Descending to Battle

Terrible, mouldy — the very gods in the heavens abhor it.
Such was the din that arose when the godheads clashed in the conflict.

    Fearful the strife was; for there, opposing the lordly Poseidon,
Phoebus Apollo stood with his bow and his swift-wingèd arrows.
Bright-eyed goddess Athena opposed Enyalius, the war-god.
There, facing Hera, was she of the echoing chase and the golden
Arrows, Artemis, rainer of shafts, the Far-darter's own sister.
Hermes, Helper and Savior, was there and opposed unto Leto.
Lastly — opposed to Hephaestus — the great deep-eddying river,
He whom the gods call Xanthus, but mortals call him Scamander.

    So were they matched for the war, gods countering gods. But Achil-
Meanwhile yearned above all to enter the throng against Hector,   [les
Priam's son; for his soul above all things especially bade him
Glut with his enemy's blood the war-god, shield-bearing Ares.
Natheless Apollo, the urger of war-hosts, roused up Aeneas
Straightly against the Pelides and filled him with valorous courage,
Lik'ning his voice unto that of Priam's scion, Lycaon.
Taking his semblance, Apollo, the son of Zeus, then addressed him:

    "Where are the menaces, counseling chief of the Trojans, Aeneas,
Where is the boast to the princes of Troy, made over the wine-cup,
Thou wouldest stand up in war against Peleus' scion, Achilles?"

    Answering him in his turn, Aeneas spake and addressed him:

    "Scion of Priam, why dost thou bid me thus, wholly unwilling,
Join in battle against yon high-souled scion of Peleus?
Not for the first time now shall *I* be matched with Achilles,
Swift of foot, for once before with his javelin he drove me
Down from the mountains of Ida, the while he harried our cattle;
Then did he sack Lyrnessus and Pedasus. Zeus it was saved me
Out of his hand and endued me with strength and gave my feet swift-
Else had I fallen beneath the hands of Achilles and Pallas;   [ness;
She marched before him, affording him always safety; she bade him
Slaughter with javelin of bronze the Leleges all and the Trojans.
Sooth, it is not for a man to encounter Achilles in battle,
Seeing that ever a god stands by him averting destruction.
E'en at the best of times his dart flieth straight, unarrested,
Till it have pierced through a warrior's flesh. But if ever the godhead

Evenly draws out the issue of war, he shall not overcome me
Easily then, though he boast that of bronze he is wholly conſtructed."
      Then in his turn did the son of Zeus, lord Apollo, address him:
      "Nay, but come, my hero, and unto the gods everlaſting
Pray, for men say thou art son of a daughter of Zeus, Aphrodite;
Peleus' son can claim only a lesser goddess as mother:
Daughter of Zeus is the one; of the Ancient of Ocean the other. [wise
Come then, aim ſtraight before thee th' unwearying bronze and in no
Let him affright or repel thee with bitter revilings or curses." [peoples.
      Thus he spake, and he breathed great might on the shepherd of .
Forward he ſtrode through the van, wide-flashing the bronze of his
White-armed Hera had failed not to see the son of Anchises   [armor.
Marching along 'mid the thronging of men to encounter Pelides;
Then, as she gathered about her the gods, she spake 'mongst them, say-
      "Ponder it well, ye twain, Poseidon and Pallas Athena,   [ing:
Ponder it well in your hearts what now it were best to be doing.
Here Aeneas hath come — wide-flashing the bronze of his armor —
Forward to meet the Pelides, and Phoebus Apollo hath sent him.
Come then, we it is now must divert him with our intervention
Straightway; else we must ſtand, some one, at the side of Achilles
Likewise, giving him valor and ſtrength for the fray, that his spirit
Fail not, so he may know that immortals the best and the highest
Now are his friends; all others are idle as wind, that aforetime
Ever would ward off war and the fury of fight from the Trojans.
We from Olympus have come to take our part in this battle,
All we gods, that he take no hurt this day from the Trojans;
After that he shall suffer whatever his fate may have spun him,
Fate with her thread at his birth, at the hour when his mother did bear
Now if Achilles shall learn not *this* from the lips of immortals,   [him.
Then will he fear, when in thick of the warfare haply some godhead
Cometh against him; to look on the gods unveilèd is peril."
      Then unto her the shaker of earth, Poseidon, made answer:
   "Hera, do not be angry beyond all reason; thou shouldst not.
I at least should not wish to embroil the gods in contention,
Us and the rest, since we are insooth far ſtronger than they are.
Nay, let us rather depart and take our seat on a look-out

Far from the beaten track and leave unto mortals the warfare.
Only if Ares begins the fighting or Phoebus Apollo,
Or if they put constraint on Achilles, hinder his battle,
Speedily then shall the strife of the war-din surely awaken
Also with us. I trow they will right soon, leaving the conflict,
Hie them back to Olympus, to mingle with other immortals,
Vanquished under our hands and driven by our compulsion."

　　　Thus when the dark-haired god had spoken the word, he conducted
Them to the heaped-up wall for the godlike Heracles builded
Lofty, a wall that the Trojans and Pallas Athena aforetime
Fashioned in order that he might escape and be safe from the sea-beast,
Whensoe'er from the beach to the plain it might rush to attack him.
There then they sat them down — the rest of the gods and Poseidon —
Robing themselves meanwhile with unbroken cloud round their shoul-
They of the Troy-side sat on the brows of Callicolone,　　　　[ders.
Round thee, Phoebus, the archer, and Ares, waster of cities.
So they were seated, the gods, this side and the other, devising
Counsel, but shrank from beginning, the one or the other, the grievous
Warfare, even though high-throned Zeus such bidding had given.

　　　All of the plain was ablaze with armor of bronze in the mean while,
Filled with men and with horses. Earth under the trampling resounded
Loud, as they rushed together, while two men, far away chiefest,
Met in the space midway of the two hosts, eager for battle,
Even Aeneas, Anchises' son, and the godlike Achilles.
First strode forward Aeneas; he threatened the while he was coming,
Swaying his ponderous helm; he held his impetuous buckler
Out in front of his breast, as he brandished his bronze-shod javelin.
Like as a lion Pelides on his side rushed out against him,
Ravening lion that men are also eager to slaughter —
All the town in a throng — but he goeth his way, and he heedeth
None, at the first; but when haply a bold young brave with a javelin
Smiteth him, wide-mouthed then, with his teeth all foamy, he croucheth
Ready to spring; and the heart of his valiancy growleth within him;
Both sides — ribs and flanks — in fury indignant he lasheth
Fierce with his tail, as he goadeth himself therewith unto battle;
Meanwhile glaring, he rusheth straight on in his passion against them,

Whether he slaughter some man or perish himself in the forefront:
So did his passion and manly spirit drive on Achilles
Forth to enter the battle and meet great-hearted Aeneas.
When they had come close up in the onrush against one another,
Then fleet-footed Achilles, the godlike, was first to accost him:

"Why hast thou come so far out in front of the throng, O Aeneas,
Taking thy stand? Can it be that thy heart doth bid thee to fight me,
Hoping to gain the throne of the horse-taming Trojans and Priam's
Honors as king to gain? Nay, but if thou haply shalt slay me,
Never will Priam, because of that, place his sceptre in thy hand,
Sons he hath still; he is sound in health and in mind yet unshaken.
Or have the Trojans, perhaps, meted thee a domain that exceedeth
All else—fair in its vineyard and plowland, thine to enjoy it—
If thou shalt slay me? But hard, I trow, to fulfil the condition!
Once ere now, I'm saying, I drove thee off with my javelin.
Dost thou fail to recall how, when thou wast alone, from thy cattle
I from the mountains of Ida did make thee hurry fleet-footed
Headlong in haste? And thou then couldst not in thy flight look behind
Thence thou madest escape to Lyrnessus. I followed thee thither. [thee!
That town also I sacked with the help of Athena and Father
Zeus, and the women I spoiled of their day of freedom; I led them
Captive; but thee did Zeus and the other immortals deliver.
This time faileth, methinks, the deliv'rance thou art awaiting
Now in thy heart. Retire to the throng of the combatants rather—
So I would bid thee—nor venture to meet me, ere thou some evil
Suffer. When a thing's done, then even a fool understands it."

Then unto him in his turn Aeneas spake in his answer:

"Think not, O Peleus' son, that thou with words shalt affright me,
Like as a child, for indeed even I myself am acquainted
Well with the art of reviling in speech, of immoderate boasting.
Each of us knoweth the line of the other, his parentage knoweth,
We that have heard the far-famed stories of men that are mortal.
Yet have I never thy parents, and thou mine never, beholden.
Thou, men say, art scion of faultless Peleus, thy mother
Thetis of beautiful tresses, they say, a daughter of Ocean.
I, however, may boast as my sire great-hearted Anchises;

I am his son, and as mother of mine I may boast Aphrodite.
One of these pairs shall now for their dear son be lamenting
This day; for not, I trow, at least with the prattle of infants
We two are like to be parted thus and return from the battle.
But if thou wishest, then learn this too (that well thou may'st know it) —
Even our generation; the men that know it are many:
Dardanus then at the first — and Zeus the cloud-gath'rer begot him —
Founded a city Dardania; not yet was hallowèd Ilium
Builded upon the plain, as a city for men that are mortal;
Still they abode in the foothills of Ida abounding in fountains.
Dardanus also begat him a son, Erichthonius, kingly,
Him that in substance became the richest of men that are mortal.
Mares three thousand in number were his; they along on the marsh-land
Pastured, rejoicing the while in the foals light-frisking beside them.
Boreas also beheld them a-grazing and, deeply enamored,
Likened himself to a dark-maned steed and covered the females.
They then, having conceived, bore fillies — even a dozen.
These, as they bounded along o'er the grain-land, giver of barley,
Ran on the uppermost ripened ears of the cornstalks and brake none;
But, as they bounded along o'er the wide expanse of the salt sea,
Over the foam-flecked sea they would run on the crest of the breakers.
This Erichthonius begat then Tros, to be lord of the Trojans;
Next, unto Tros there were born three sons, three sons that were fault-
Ilus, Assaracus also, and, like to a god, Ganymedes;　　　　[less —
This Ganymedes became the fairest of all men mortal;
Him did the gods catch up to pour out wine for Cronion,
All on account of his beauty, to dwell there 'mid the immortals.
Ilus in his turn begat him a son, Laomedon faultless.
Next, Laomedon also begat Tithonus and Priam,
Lampus and Clytius and Hicetaon, an offshoot of Ares.
Capys, Assaracus' son, begat him a scion, Anchises;
Me Anchises begat; and Priam gat Hector, the godlike.

"Such is the race and the blood whereof unto thee I avow me.
Zeus, however, increaseth in mortals or minisheth valor,
Even as haply he will; of all beings *he* is most mighty.
Come then, let us no more be talking of such things, as children,

Now we have taken a stand in the midmost fury of battle.
There are revilings in plenty for both of us haply to utter —
Too big a load for a ship with a hundred rowers to carry.
Glib is the tongue of a mortal; the speeches full many upon it
Vary, and wide is the license of words, both hither and thither.
Whatever word thou shalt speak, the like thou shalt hear in my answer.
What unto us is the need of all these taunts and reproaches
Here as we wrangle against each other in manner of women,
Who in their anger, because of a bitter, heart-eating quarrel,
Go out into the street with revilings 'gainst one another?
Many words true — and false; for to these, too, anger impelleth.
Never with words shalt thou turn me, all eager, away from the battle,
Ere we have fought with the bronze against each other. But come now,
Speedily will we with spears, bronze-shod, taste each of the other."

    Said he, and at the dread shield he hurled his ponderous javelin —
Terrible shield — and it rang aloud at the shock of the spear-head.
Off from his body Pelides held, with his stout hand, the buckler —
Held it away in dread; for he deemed the far-shadowing javelin
Hurled by Aeneas, the great of heart, would easily pierce it.
Fond man! he realized not in the depth of his heart and his spirit
How that the glorious gifts of the gods not lightly are wonted
Either to yield or be vanquished by prowess of men that are mortal.
Neither did then the ponderous spear of wise-hearted Aeneas   [it.
Break through the shield; for the gold, the gift of the godhead, repelled
Clear through two of the layers he drove it; but three were remaining
Whole, since the crook-footed god had forged five layers upon it:
Two of the layers were bronze, of tin two layers within them,
One, in the middle, was gold, and the ash-spear was halted within it.

    Second in turn then Achilles let fly his far-shadowing javelin,
Driving it full on the shield, all evenly round, of Aeneas,
Close to its outermost edge, where thinnest the bronze ran around it;
Also at that place the bull's hide was thinnest; and through it the jave-
Pelian ash — sped on, and under it loud cracked the buckler.   [lin —
Down crouched Aeneas and held up his shield away from his body,
Frightened. Beyond his back then, fixed in the earth, the bronze javelin
Stopped in its eager flight; but it cleft asunder the circles

Twain of the shield, man's protection; and he then, the long lance eluded
Safely, stood up (and over his eyes poured endless vexation),
Frighted at sight of the missile thus planted so near him. Achilles,
Drawing his keen-edged sword, charged on him in vehement fury,
Crying his terrible cry; but his foe laid hand on a boulder—
Marvelous deed! for of men no twain would be able to lift it,
Such as mortals are now; but with ease all alone *he* could swing it.
Then he had smitten Achilles, in fierce onrush, with the boulder—
Whether on helmet or shield, which had warded off fatal disaster;
Then had Pelides with sword closed in and of life had deprived him,
Had not the shaker of earth, Poseidon, been swift to observe it.
Straightway he uttered a word to the gods immortal about him:

"Ah me! Woe is upon me for him, great-hearted Aeneas!
Soon will he, slain by Pelides, go down to the palace of Hades,
Seeing he put his trust in the words of far-darting Apollo;
Fond man! in no wise will *he* ward off from him grievous destruction.
This man, innocent quite, what reason is there that he suffer
Woes unmerited, all for ills caused by others? His off'rings
Welcome are aye to the gods, who the spacious heaven inhabit.
Come now, let us deliver and lead him from death and disaster,
So that the son of Cronus may not be wroth, if Achilles
Slay this man; for to him escape by fate is appointed,
Lest the whole line of Dardanus traceless haply should perish
Leaving no seed; for him did Cronion love more than all other
Children besides that were born unto him of the daughters of mortals.
Yea, even now hath Priam's line to Cronion proved hateful.
Now, however, the mighty Aeneas shall reign o'er the Trojans,
Ay, and his children's children, who are to be born hereafter."

Then unto him made answer the ox-eyed, worshipful Hera:
"Shaker of earth, take counsel thyself with the mind that is in thee,
Whether indeed thou'lt rescue Aeneas or haply wilt leave him
[Brave though he be, to be slain by the hand of Achilles Pelides].
Many indeed are the objects on which our oaths we have taken—
Pallas Athena and I—in the presence of all the immortals,
Never to ward henceforth the day of doom from the Trojans,
Never! though all proud Troy be burning with ravenous fire,

435

Flaming aloft, and the martial sons of Achaia shall burn it."

　　Now as Poseidon, the shaker of earth, heard this saying of Hera's,
Up through the hurtling of spears he haſted to go and the battle,
Reached the place where they ſtood, Aeneas and famous Achilles.
Mist he immediately shed therewith on the eyes of Achilles,
Peleus' son, and the ash-wood (with goodly bronze it was fitted)
Drew forth out of the shield of his foe, great-hearted Aeneas,
Setting it down directly in front of the feet of Achilles.
Lifting Aeneas up from the earth, he sent him a-flying.
Over the many lines of heroes and many of horses
Vaulted Aeneas, soaring away from the hand of the godhead.
Far on the ultimate verge of the ſtormy war he alighted,
Where the Caucones were arming themselves to mix in the warfare.
Close to him came Poseidon, the shaker of earth, and, beside him
Standing, he lifted his voice and in accents wingèd addressed him:

　　"Who of the gods thus bids thee, Aeneas, playing the madman,
Join in battle against yon high-souled scion of Peleus,
Who is both ſtronger than thou and dearer besides to immortals?
Better at once to retreat whene'er thou haply shalt meet him,
Lest thou before thy time shalt come to the mansion of Hades.
But when Achilles haply his death and his doom hath encountered,
Then take courage and dare with the foremost to enter the battle,
Since no other in sooth of th' Achaeans ever shall slay thee."

　　Thus he spake, and he left him there when all he had shown him.
Then the miraculous mist from the eyes of Achilles he scattered
All in a moment; and he with his eyes wide-oped in amazement
Stared, then spake in diſtress to his own magnanimous spirit:

　　"Gods! how mighty a marvel is this with my eyes I'm beholding!
Here on the ground now lieth my javelin; neither discern I
Aught of the man, 'gainst whom I had hurled it, meaning to slay him.
Well then! Truly Aeneas is dear to the godheads immortal
Likewise, though I had thought that his claim was the idlest of boaſting.
Let him begone; for never again will his courage allow him
Trial of me; for with joy he escapes once more from perdition.
Come then! First I will call on the Danaans, lovers of warfare;
Then I will go 'gainst the rest of the Trojans and make of them trial."

Thus he; along the lines he bounded and called upon each man:
"Stand no longer afar from the Trojans, ye godlike Achaeans.
Come now! Man against man be pitted and eager to battle!
Hard is the matter for me, though I am a valiant warrior,
So many men to engage and to fight with them all single-handed.
Neither would Ares, god though he be and immortal, nor Pallas
Enter the jaws of a fray so dire and therein be toiling.
Natheless with hands and with feet, as far as I ever am able,
Yea, in my strength I will slacken, I say, no whit, not a little,
Nay, I will drive right onward through their line, and, methinketh,
Ne'er will be glad that Trojan who comes within range of my javelin."

Thus he spake as he spurred them. To Trojans the glorious Hector
Shouted and called; he declared he would go and encounter Achilles:
"High-souled Trojans, do not be afraid of the scion of Peleus.
I, too, might strive in a battle of words with even immortals;
Hard would it be with the spear; for they are far stronger than we are.
Neither shall even Achilles bring all his words to fulfilment:
Only a part he fulfilleth, a part he cuts short in the middle.
Forth to meet him I go, though his hands are even like fire,
Even like fire his hands, and his strength like steel brightly flashing."

Thus he spake as he spurred them on. The Trojans their lances
Poised; the fury of both was commingled; and loud rose the war-cry.
Phoebus Apollo then stood beside Hector and spake to him, saying:
"Hector, by no means challenge Achilles to fight in the vanguard
But in the midst of the throng and out from the tumult await him,
Lest with his spear he smite thee or with his sword at close quarters."

Thus spake he. And again in the throng of the warriors Hector,
Fear-struck, sank when he heard the voice of a deity speaking.
Then upon them leaped Achilles, all clad with might in his spirit,
Crying his terrible cry, and the first man he slew was Iphition,
Valorous son of Otrynteus, a leader of numerous peoples —
Born of a Naiad nymph to Otrynteus, sacker of cities,
Snowclad Tmolus beneath, in the rich-soiled region of Hyde.
Him, all eager in onset, with lance the godlike Achilles
Squarely smote on the head, and it was utterly shattered.
Down he fell with a crash, and godlike Achilles exulted:

"Low thou liest, Otrynteus' son, most dreaded of all men!
Here is thy death, but yonder afar, on the shore of Lake Gyge,
There was thy birth, and there the estate likewise of thy father,
There on the Hyllus, teeming with fish, and the eddying Hermus."
　　　So he exulted; but darkness then veiled the eyes of the other.
Him the Achaeans' cars with their tires tore into pieces —
There in the front of the fight. And next Demoleon also —
Gallant helper in battle he, and a son of Antenor —　　　　[helmet;
Him did he pierce through the temple, clean through the bronze-cheeked
Nor could the helmet of bronze arrest it; onward the spear-point
Speeding shattered the skull-bone wholly; the brain that was in it
All was spattered about; the stroke quelled him, even though eager.
Then when Hippodamas down had leaped from his car and was fleeing
On before him, Achilles smote his back with his javelin.
Then did the Trojan bellow aloud as he gasped out his spirit,
As when a bull doth bellow when dragged before Helice's sovereign,
Young men dragging him in; and in such the earth-shaker delighteth:
Such, as the manly soul fled forth from his bones, was his bellow.
Next in his course then Achilles assailed Polydorus, the godlike
Scion of Priam; his sire to battle would never permit him,
Since of all the king's offspring he in birth was the youngest,
Also the dearest beloved; and all he outstripped in his fleetness.
He in the folly of youth, to display how nimble his feet were,
Charged through the foremost fighters until his dear life was taken.
Full in the back with his javelin divine fleet-footed Achilles
Smote, as he darted along, where the golden clasps of his girdle
Joined, and the breastplate there — two thicknesses — met and o'erlapped
Onward the spear-point sped unswerving through past the navel.　　[it.
Groaning, he sank on his knees, and the cloud of death settled o'er him,
Darksome; thus sinking, he clutched with his hands to his body his
　　　Now as Hector beheld his brother beloved, Polydorus,　　[bowels.
Holding in both hands his bowels, e'en as to the ground he was sinking,
Mist poured over his eyes, and he no longer endured it
Thus to be ranging afar, but he came to encounter Achilles,
Shaking his keen-edged lance and like to a flame; but Achilles
Sprang up the moment he saw him and shouted toward him exultant:

"Lo! near at hand is the man that my soul most deeply hath stricken.
He that hath slain my comrade most valued; not now any longer
Up and down the dikes of war shall we shrink from each other."

     Spake he, and scowlfully looking, he spake unto Hector, the god-
"Come up closer, the sooner to enter the toils of perdition."   [like:
     Answered him, all undismayed, the shimmering-helmeted Hector:
"Think not, O Peleus' son, that thou with words shalt affright me
Like as a child, for indeed even I myself am acquainted
Well with the art of reviling in speech, of immoderate boasting.
Well do I know thou art valiant and I much weaker than thou art.
Verily, though, on the knees of the gods these issues are lying,
Whether, indeed, though weaker, I take with a cast of my javelin
Thy life from thee; for keenness belonged ere this to my weapon."

     Thus he spake. Then, poising his javelin, he hurled it. Athena
Turned it back with a breath from Achilles, the glorious hero —
Breathing ever so lightly; it came back straight to the godlike
Hector and fell to the ground in front of his feet. But Achilles
Rushed on him yet again in his eager desire to slay him,
Crying his terrible cry, but away Apollo had caught him
Lightly, for he was a god, and a thick mist curtained about him.
Thrice the fleet-footed, godlike Achilles then darted upon him,
Wielding his javelin of bronze; thick mist he three times was smiting.
But when a fourth time, like to a god, he was charging upon it,
Then with terrible cry, with wingèd words he addressed him:

     "Death hast escaped now again, thou dog! Full closely the evil
Came unto thee; but Phoebus Apollo once more now hath saved thee,
Whom thou art like to invoke when nearing the crash of the javelins.
Verily thee I shall meet and finish thee sooner or later,
If an immortal perhaps unto me, too, comes as a helper.
Now I'll go after the rest, whome'er I may light upon haply."

     Thus he spake, and Dryops he smote in the neck with his javelin
Squarely. Down at his feet he fell; but he left him lying
There and Philetor's son, the tall and the goodly Demuchus,
Struck on the knee with his spear and arrested his flight; and then,
Him again with his mighty sword, of life he deprived him.   [smiting
Then at Laogonus charging and Dardanus, children of Bias,

Headlong out of their car to the ground in a moment he thrust them
Both — with a spear-cast one, with a stroke of his broad-sword the other.
Tros, however, Alastor's son, to his knees came entreating
That he would take him a prisoner, spare him, and let him go living,
Only not slay him, but, as of his own age, showing him mercy.
Fool! for he knew not that he was in no way like to persuade him,
Seeing the man was in heart by no means gentle or tender,
Nay, but of vehement mood. And he clasped in his eager entreaty
Even his knees with his arms; but *he* slashed him over the liver;
Out through the gash it slipped forth, and the dark blood out of it jetted,
Filling his bosom with gore, and his eyes were veilèd with darkness,
Whileas his life ebbed forth. And Achilles, standing by Mulius,
Plunged his spear in his ear; through the other the bronze point directly
Passed clean through. Then Achilles Echeclus, the son of Agenor,
Full on the crown of his head dealt a blow with his hilted broadsword;
All the blade was warmed with his blood, while darkness descended —
Darkness of death — on his eyes, and fate's mighty hand was upon him.
Then at Deucalion next! Where the elbow's tendons together
Firmly cohere, he pierced his precious arm with his bronzen
Spear-point. Still, with his hand weighed down, the Trojan abode him,
Staring death in the face. Then smiting his neck with his broadsword
Far off swept Achilles the helmet and head, and the marrow
Out from the vertebrae gushed; on the earth stretched out he was lying.
Next he started on after the faultless scion of Pires,
Rhigmus, him that had come from the deep-loamed region of Thracia.
Him he smote with his lance in the breast; in his lung was the weapon
Fixed, and he fell from his car. His squire he smote with his keen spear
Square in the back, Areïthoüs, just as he'd wheeled round the horses.
Out from the car he thrust him; the horses bolted affrighted.

Even as fire, far back in a dry-parched gorge of a mountain,
Rages in fury, and all the depth of the forest is blazing
Under the lash of the wind, and the flames whirl hither and thither:
Even so raged all round him Achilles, peer of a godhead,   [shed.
Pressing on those he was slaying; the earth ran darkened with blood-
As when a man may yoke up his broad-browed bullocks together, [ing —
Yoke them to tread out white barley on floors well-builded for thresh-

Under the feet of the bullocks loud-lowing 'tis readily threshed out:
So did the whole-hoofed steeds of the great-souled scion of Peleus
Trample the bodies and bucklers alike; and with blood was the axle
All underneath bedabbled and the rims all round — of the chariot —
Spattered with blood-drops showered about by the hoofs of the horses;
Drops from the tires as well; while eager for glory Pelides
Pressed on still, with his hands unapproachable sprinkled with slaughter.

ILIAD · XXI · (Φ)

Phy at the flood's shore express
The labours of Aeacides.

BUT when they came, as they fared, to the ford of the fair-flowing
Eddying Xanthus, begotten of Zeus, the godhead immortal, [river,
There he divided and chased them — a part to the plain toward the city,
Even where the Achaeans erewhile had been fleeing affrighted,
Only the day before, when glorious Hector was raging.
Thither, in wild rout scattered, they poured on. Hera before them
Spread thick mist to retard them; and half of their number were crowded
Into the river, a flood deep-flowing in eddies of silver.
Mighty the splash of their fall therein; re-echoed the headlong
Torrent; the banks on both sides around them resounded; with shouting
Hither and thither they swam, whirled round in the eddying current.
Like as when locusts take wing before the rush of a fire
Off to a river to flee, and th' unwearying fire upon them
Suddenly bursts into blaze, then all drop down to the water:
Thus was, before Achilles, the stream of deep-eddying Xanthus
Filled with the roar and the din commingled of men and of horses.

There on the bank of the stream the descendant of Zeus left his jave-
Leaning against some tamarisks. In he leaped like a godhead   [lin
Wielding his broadsword alone; grim deeds he devised in his spirit:
Turning in every direction, he smote, and hideous groaning
Rose from the men sword-smitten; the river ran crimson with blood-
Even as other fishes, in flight from a huge-bellied dolphin   [shed.
Following, fill up the nooks of a bay with a beautiful haven,
Stricken with fear, for he gobbleth down whichever he catcheth:
So were the Trojans along that stream of the terrible river
Crouching beneath the steep banks. When his hands became weary with
Twelve young captive nobles alive from the flood he selected [slaughter,
All to pay for the death of Patroclus, the son of Menoetius.

443

Forth from the river he led them, dazed like fawns at their capture;
Then with well-cut thongs their hands he fettered behind them —
Even the girdles the young men wore round their well-woven tunics,
Gave them, for leading back to the hollow ships, to his comrades.
Then he turned him again to the onset, thirsty for slaughter.

　　Then he encountered a son of Priam, Dardanus' scion,
Fleeing away from the river — Lycaon, a youth he had taken
Once already himself and had brought 'gainst his will from his father's
Orchard, making a raid one night. He was cutting the new-grown
Shoots of a wild fig-tree with the keen bronze for rims for a chariot.
Evil came on him all unexpected — the godlike Achilles.
On that other occasion he sold him to prosperous Lemnos,
Taking him there on his ships, and a scion of Jason had bought him.
Thence had a guest-friend freed him — the ransom was great he de-
Even Eëtion of Imbros, who sent him to goodly Arisbe;　　[livered —
Thence he made his escape and came back to the home of his father.
Ten days only and one with his loved ones he gladdened his spirit
After arrival from Lemnos; the twelfth day God it was brought him
Once more into the hands of Achilles, who was to send him
Down to the palace of Hades, a journey insooth he desired not.
Now when Achilles caught sight of him — fleet-footed, godlike Achil-
All unarmed — no buckler and helm, not even a javelin;　　[les —
All he had thrown to the ground, flung wildly away, and he sweated
Sore in his flight from the river, his knees o'ercome of the travail —
Vexed in his heart, he communed with his own magnanimous spirit:

　　"Gods! how mighty a marvel is this with mine eyes I'm beholding!
Now will surely the great-hearted Trojans, whom I have slaughtered,
Rise once more from the murk and the gloom of the nethermost regions,
Seeing that this man cometh escaped from the pitiless hour,
He that was sold into Lemnos, the highly divine, nor the foam-flecked
Deep of the salt sea held him that hampers many unwilling.
Wherefore, come! He shall taste of a spear-point, even of our own
War-wood, so that indeed I may see and learn in my spirit
Whether insooth he returneth from that bourne also, or whether
Earth, life-giver, shall hold him, that holds fast even the mighty."　　[him,
　　So as he tarried and pondered, half-dazed then the Trojan came nigh

Longing to touch but his knees; with all his heart he was wishing
Now to escape the darkness of doom and baleful destruction.
Thereupon godlike Achilles his long lance lifted, intending
With it to smite him; but *he* ran under the weapon and bowed down,
Catching his knees, and the lance, sped over his back, was implanted
Fast in the earth, though hungry to feast itself on a man's flesh.
Closely enclasping his knees with the one hand, pleaded Lycaon,
Holding the sharp spear fast with the other, and never released it,
While he uplifted his voice and in accents wingèd addressed him:

"Thee on my knees I beseech, O nurseling of Zeus, O Achilles,
Pity me! Spare me! To thee I am come as a suppliant — sacred,
Seeing I tasted at *thy* board first of the fruits of Demeter,
That same day thou tookest me there — in the well-tended orchard —
Captive and leddest away from my father and friends unto holy
Lemnos for sale; the price of a hundred oxen I brought thee.
Three times that the amount of my ransom; this is the morning
Twelfth since I have returned unto Ilium, I that have suffered
Much, and a ruinous fate into thy hand now hath delivered
Me once more; it must be that to Father Zeus I am hateful,
Seeing he gives me again unto thee. Short-lived did my mother
Bear me — even Laothoë, daughter of Altes the aged —
Altes, him that is king of the Leleges, lovers of warfare,
Dwelling in Pedasus' steep by the banks of Satnioïs river.
Priam wedded his daughter — he wedded full many another.
We two were born of her, and thou wilt both of us butcher;
One of us out in the front-line ranks of the footmen thou slewest,
When with thy keen-pointed lance thou didst smite Polydorus, the god-
Now will evil be mine in this place; for never, methinketh,   [like.
I shall escape thy hands, since God hath delivered me to thee.
One word further I'll tell thee, and deep in thy heart do thou lay it:
Slay me not, for indeed I am not like-mothered with Hector,
Him that hath slain thy friend, a man both gentle and mighty."

So did the glorious son of Priam fitly address him
Words of entreaty — in vain! for the answer he heard was not gentle:

"Fond man! Do not harangue me nor make any offer of ransom.
Truly, or ever Patroclus the day of his doom had encountered,

So long still to my spirit was welcomer rather to spare you
Children of Troy; and many alive I captured and sold them
Over the sea. But now there is none that escapes death, whomever
God shall place in my hands in front of the rampart of Ilium,
None of the Trojans all, leastwise the children of Priam.
Die thou also, my friend, even thou; then why this lamenting?
Even Patroclus is dead, who was far, far better than thou art.
Seest thou not what a hero am I? how comely and mighty?
Goodly is also my sire, and the mother that bare me — a goddess!
Natheless above even me hover death and a doom overpow'ring.
Whether at morn it shall be or at eve or haply at noontide,
Cometh a man who will rob me too of my life in the battle,
Whether he smite with a spear or with arrow sped from a bowstring."

    Spake he. Unstrung at once were the knees and the heart of Lycaon.
Loosing his hold of the spear, still seated, the Trojan extended
Both of his hands outspread. But, drawing his keen sword, Achilles
Smote on the collar-bone close at the neck; and the two-edgèd broad-
All of it — entered within; all prone and extended, the body   [sword —
Lay on the ground; the black blood wetted the sod, as it flowed forth.
Him then Achilles seized by the foot and to drift down the river   [him:
Flung him and, boasting above him, with wingèd words he addressed

    "There now! Rest thee amid them, the fish that will lick peradventure
Blood from thy wounds, but with no great tenderness; nor shall thy
Lay thee upon thy bier and weep o'er thee. Nay, the Scamander, [mother
Eddying on, shall bear thee away to the sea's broad bosom.
Leaping along the waves, full many a fish to the darksome
Ripple shall dart up, to taste that snow-white fat of Lycaon.
Perish ye so! till we come to the town of Ilium holy,
Ye in your flight, and I in pursuit, making havoc behind you.
Naught shall avail you, indeed, with its eddies of silver, the river
Fair in his flow, unto whom long time ye have sacrificed many
Bullocks, and whole-hoofed horses alive ye have thrown to his eddies.
Nay, even so ye shall die by an evil fate, until all ye
Pay for Patroclus' death, for the slaughter of heroes Achaean
Slain by the swift-faring ships, while I was aloof from the battle."

    Thus spake he. But the River, in heart grown angry the rather,

Pondered in spirit and sought how he the godlike Achilles
Haply might ſtay from his toil and ward off death from the Trojans.
Meantime, grasping his spear far-shadowing, Peleus's scion,
Eager for slaughter, was leaping amain upon Aſteropaeus,
Scion of Pelegon, son of the Axius, broad in his flowing,
Whom Periboea had borne — Acessamenus' daughter, the eldest —
Unto the River; for he, deep-eddying, lay with the maiden.
On him Achilles had rushed; he out from the river against him
Came and ſtood — two spears in his hands — for into his spirit
Xanthus put ſtrength, for he was enraged at the slaughter of young men,
Those whom Achilles along that ſtream without mercy was slaying.
When they had come close up in the onrush against one another,
Then fleet-footed Achilles, the godlike, was first to accost him:

"Who, whence, art thou of men, that dare'st come out against me?
Children of ill-ſtarred parents are they that encounter my prowess."

Thereupon Pelegon's glorious son in his turn made answer:
"Great-hearted son of Peleus, why ask of my generation?
I from Paeonia come, from a deep-loamed region afar off,
Leading Paeonian men, who wield long javelins. And I find
This, today, the eleventh morn since I came unto Ilium.
Mine is a lineage sprung from the Axius, wide in its flowing,
Axius, whoſe waters of all that spread o'er the earth are the fairest.
He begat Pelegon, famed for his spear; it is he hath begotten
Me, it is said. Now come, let us fight, O glorious Achilles."

Thus spake he in defiance. The godlike Achilles uplifted
High his Pelian ash. The other with both spears together —
Aſteropaeus, a hero with both hands equally dext'rous —
Struck with one of his spears on the shield, but it pierced not the buckler,
Breaking the shield; for the gold, the gift of the godhead repelled it.
Yet with the other he ſtruck him, the keen point, grazing Pelides'
Elbow, the right one — quick spurted the dark blood forth — and beyond
Planted itself in the earth, though eager on flesh to be glutted. [him
Next, in his turn, then Achilles his ſtraight-flying Pelian ash-wood
Hurled at Aſteropaeus, in eager desire to slay him.
Him, however, he missed, and he ſtruck the high bank of the river;
Half of its length in the bank was buried the javelin of ash-wood.

447

Thereat Peleus' son, his sharp sword by his thigh unsheathing,
Sprang forth in fury upon his foe; but Asteropaeus
Struggled to wrench strong-handed the Pelian ash from the steep bank,
Vainly. Three times he shook and with full might tugged to extract it;
Thrice he relaxed his effort; the fourth time was fain in his spirit
Even to bend and to break it, that ash-wood spear of Pelides!
Too soon Achilles closed in with sword and of life had deprived him,
Smiting him full on the belly and close to the navel—the entrails
All gushed out on the ground, and darkness covered his eyelids,
Whileas he lay there gasping. Achilles, trampling upon his
Bosom, stripped off his armor as spoil and spake a word boasting:

"Lie there thus. It is hard, thou may'st see, with the children of
Mighty son to contend, though one be sprung from a river!   [Cronus'
Thou hast avowed thee the seed of a wide-flowing river, the Axius.
I, however, may boast that I from great Zeus am descended.
Yea, and the man that begot me is king over Myrmidons many,
Peleus, Aeacus' son, and of Aeacus Zeus was the father.
Even as Zeus is stronger than rivers murmuring seaward,
So is the seed of Zeus far mightier-framed than a river's.
Ay, for a river of might is beside thee, if that could avail thee
Aught. But no; 'gainst Cronus' son, Zeus, one may not do battle;
Him not even the monarch of streams, Acheloüs, dares rival,
Neither the mighty strength of the deep-flowing current of Ocean,
Whence gush all of the rivers; from it every sea is derivèd,
All deep wellheads also, and all the fountains of waters.
Yet even he is in dread of the lightning of mighty Cronion,
Ay, and his terrible thunder, when out from heaven it crasheth."

Thus he spake, and from the steep bank he drew his bronze javelin.
Him he left there (for from him his precious life he had taken)
Lying upon the sands, with the dark water lapping around him.
Eels and fishes of other kinds were busied about him,
Gnawing and nibbling away at the fat lying over the kidneys.
Then Achilles went on to fight the car-driving Paeonians.
They were in full flight along the banks of the eddying river,
After they saw their bravest and best in the terrible conflict
Mightily vanquished and slain with the sword in the hands of Pelides.

Then he Thersilochus slew, Astypalus also, and Mydon;
Mnesus, Thrasius, and Aenius he slew; he slew Ophelestes.
More Paeonians still swift-footed Achilles had slaughtered,
If the deep-eddying river had not addressed him in anger,
Lik'ning himself to a man, and from a deep eddy had shouted:
   "Thou, O Achilles, in might and in violent deeds thou exceedest
Measure of man, for the gods themselves do ever support thee.
If unto thee Cronus' son hath granted to slay all the Trojans,
Drive them at least forth from *me* and out in the plain do thy grim deeds!
Lo! these corpses are clogging my streams, so lovely aforetime,
Nor can I roll any longer my flood to the bright sea-waters,
Seeing my current is choked with the dead; thy slaughter is ruthless.
Come then, let them alone! horror fills me, O captain of peoples."
   Answered him then and addressed him in turn fleet-footed Achilles:
   "Be it, Scamander, thou nurseling of Zeus, e'en so as thou biddest.
Yet will I never desist from slaying those arrogant Trojans,
Ere I have pent them within their town and made trial of Hector,
Might unto might, as to which one of us shall vanquish the other."
   Thus he spake, and like to a god he rushed on the Trojans.
Thereupon unto Apollo spake out the deep-eddying river:
   "Fie on it! Lord of the silver bow, thou child of Cronion,
Thou'st not observed the designs of Zeus, who straitly enjoined thee
Ever to stand by the Trojans and guard them till haply the twilight
Come late-setting, with shadows to darken the deep-loamed plowland."
   Spake he. Sprang to mid-stream Achilles, famed for his javelin,
Leaping away from the bank; but the river raged with his swollen
Waters and, swirling, all of his currents he roused up, sweeping
Dead men many away, thick-strewn in him, slain of Achilles.
These then he cast out ashore — and like as a bull did he bellow —
Up on dry ground; and the living he rescued beneath his fair currents,
Hiding them all in his eddies profound and immense; but Achilles
Round and about he enveloped in waves all fearfully foaming.
Dashing against his shield, the flood thrust him on nor allowed him
Even to stand firm-footed. He grasped with his hands at an elm-tree
Lofty and fair in its growth; but it fell down wholly uprooted,
Split asunder the bank, and it reached with exuberant branches

449

Over the beautiful stream, and it dammed the tide of the river,
There lay fallen itself all in it. Forth from its eddy
Climbing, he hastened over the plain to fly nimble-footed,
For he was frightened. The mighty god ceased not but upon him
Rose with his darkening crest, that he the godlike Achilles
Haply might stay from his toil and ward off death from the Trojans.
Far as the cast of a javelin Achilles sprang and retreated,   [hunter,
E'en with the swoop of the eagle, the black one, the one called the
Which is the strongest at once and the swiftest of all wingèd creatures.
Like to that eagle he darted. The bronze that covered his body
Rang out fearful. He swerved aside, as he fled on before it;
But, with a mighty roar, it followed flowing behind him.
Just as a peasant, wat'ring his fields, from a dark-flowing fountain
Leadeth the stream in a channel along by his crops and his gardens,
Bearing a pick in his hand, and he casts from the ditch the obstructions —
Pebbles in number are swept away in its course as it floweth
Onward swift in descent, and it gurgles anon as it glideth
Over a slope in its path, overtaking its leader before it:
Thus did ever the wave of the stream catch up with Achilles,
Swift of foot though he was, for the gods are stronger than mortals.
Then, as oft as divine, fleet-footed Achilles would struggle
Firmly to stand up against him and know if all the immortal
Gods, who the spacious heaven inhabit, were set to dismay him,
Even so often a mighty wave of the Zeus-fallen river
Dashed on his shoulders above; on his feet then upward he bounded,
Vexed in his heart; and the river in violent flood was fatiguing
Ever his knees and eating the ground away underneath him.
Then did Achilles groan, as he looked toward the canopied heaven:

"Zeus, O Father, how none of the gods takes on him in pity
Me from the river to save! Then let come what I must suffer.
No one is so much to blame, of all the heavenly beings,
As is my mother beloved; 'tis she that with falsehood beguiled me:
Under the wall, she said, of the strongly-corseleted Trojans
I by the swift-sped arrow of Phoebus Apollo should perish.
Would that Hector had slain me, the doughtiest bred in this country!
Brave were the man thus slain, and a brave man also the slayer.

450

Yet ignominious death was appointed and now overtakes me,
Trapped in this mighty ſtream like a swineherd boy in a torrent,
Swept by the current away, in a freshet essaying to cross it."
　　Thus spake he. And Poseidon exceedingly swift and Athena
Came and ſtood there beside him, assuming the semblance of mortals,
Hand unto hand with the hero, and gave with their words full assurance.
Then was the shaker of earth, Poseidon, the first to address him:
　　"Nay, now, never a fear, O Pelides, never a shrinking,
While such helpers as we from the gods are ever beside thee
Under the sanĉtion of Zeus, even I and Pallas Athena.
For it is not decreed that thou of a river be vanquished;
Nay, he will quickly give o'er, and thou thyself shalt perceive it.
Sound advice will we give thee, however, if thou wilt obey it:
Stay not sooner thy hand from the battle's impartial decision
Ere thou hast pent in the famous ramparts of Ilium the Trojan
Host that haply escapes; but when Heĉtor's life thou hast taken,
Go back again to the ships; such glory to win we assign thee."
　　Thus they spake and departed, to mingle among the immortals.
He then turned to the plain (so ſtrong was the bidding upon him,
Spoken of gods). All the plain with a flood of waters was covered.
Many beautiful sets of armor of youths who'd been slaughtered
Drifted away, and their corpses. His knees bounded up, as Achilles
Rushed ſtraight forward against the flood; and the wide-flowing river
Stayed him not; for in him great ſtrength Athena implanted.
Nor did Scamander relax meanwhile in his wrath, but the rather
Raged at Pelides, and, curling the broad surge-crest of his current,
Lifted himself up high, and he called on Simoïs, shouting:
　　"Brother of mine, let us join in resiſting the might of a mortal,
Both of us, else he will soon lay waſte King Priam's puissant
City; neither in fight will the Trojans longer abide him.
Come then! Speedily help and assemble the might of thy currents;
Fill them with floods from thy fountains and swell thy channels with tor-
Lift up a billow on high; rouse mighty uproaring of timbers,　　[rents;
Tree-trunks, boulders, that *we* may temper the savage's fury,
Who now is lording the field — he fancies he rivals th' immortals!
Yet I assure him his ſtrength and his comeliness naught will avail him,

Neither his beautiful armor, when down in the depths of the waters
Covered it lies under slime spread over it all. And himself, too,
I will envelope in sand; I will pour down shingle upon him,
Piled up in quantities. Never his bones shall th' Achaeans be able
Thence to assemble, for I too deep in the silt will enshroud them.
There shall be builded a barrow above him! Never shall *he* have
Need of a mound for a tomb, when th' Achaeans come to his burial.''

 Thus he spake; and he rushed on Achilles, swirling and raging
High, as he seethed with foam and with blood and with bodies of war-
Tow'ring, darkling then, a surge of the Zeus-fallen river   [riors.
Lifted itself and was ready to drag down the scion of Peleus.
Hera thereat shrieked aloud in the greatest fear for Achilles,
Lest he be swept away by the great, deep-eddying river.
Quickly she called her dear son, Hephaeſtus, and thus she addressed him:

 ''Rouse thee, my child, thou crooked-of-foot; for we were assuming
Thou wast matched in the fight, with the eddying Xanthus against thee.
Help with all speed. Blaze forth with a violent flaming of fire.
I will go and awaken the wind of the west and the clearing
Southwind and hurry them on from the sea in a violent tempest,
That it may burn up the Trojans alive, their bodies and armor;
Flames of deſtruction I'll spread. And along the banks of the Xanthus
Burn thou his trees; envelop himself in the flaming; and nowise
Suffer him, whether with winning words or with cursing, to turn thee
Back from thy task; and ſtay not thy rage; but, when *I* shall have shouted
Loud and called to thee, then do thou ſtay the unwearying fire.''

 Thus she spake. And Hephaeſtus his fierce-blazing fire made ready.
First on the plain it was kindled; and there it burned up the corpses,
Dead men many, thick-ſtrewn on the banks, the slain of Achilles.
Parched was all of the plain, and the sparkling water was halted.
Even as, late in a summer, the Northwind parcheth an orchard
Quickly, when watered afresh, and whoever may till it rejoiceth:
Thus was the whole plain parched, and the fire-god burned up the fallen
Bodies; and then he direĉted the flame's fierce blast on the river.
Burned were the elm-trees then, and the tamarisks, too, and the willows;
Burned were the lotus and rushes, and burned was the galingale also—
All that abundantly grew by the beautiful ſtreams of the river.

Achilles Contending with the Rivers

Smitten were eels and afflicted and fishes deep down in the eddies;
This way they tumbled and that, up and down the beautiful current,
Flound'ring under the blast of Hephaestus of many devices.
Burning, the might of the river addressed a word to the fire-god:

"None of the godheads surely can bear up against thee, Hephaestus,
Neither would I join battle with thee thus blazing with fire.
Cease from the strife! Let godlike Achilles drive from the city
Right now the Trojans; for what care I for contention and succor?"

Spake he, blasted with fire; his beautiful streams bubbled over.
Even as boileth a cauldron that fire in its fury besetteth —
While that cauldron is melting the lard of a hog highly fattened —
Spurting up all way round; dry fuel was laid underneath it:
So in the fire the fair streams burned, and the water was boiling.
Nor was he minded to flow but was stayed, foredone and afflicted
Sore by the breath of the cunning Hephaestus. Then unto Hera,
Earnestly praying, he spake, and in wingèd words he addressed her:

"Hera, why did thy son fall foul of my current, to vex it
More than the rest? For not so much to blame thou wilt find me
As are the others all, as many as succor the Trojans.
Verily, I will desist from the strife, if indeed thou dost bid me,
Only let him, too, cease; I will swear this oath in addition
Never to ward henceforth the day of doom from the Trojans
Never! though all proud Troy be burning with ravenous fire
Flaming aloft, and the martial sons of Achaia shall burn it."   [Hera,

Now, as the goddess had heard it, the white-armed, worshipful
Straightway her own dear son, Hephaestus, she called and addressed him:

"Hold thy hand now, Hephaestus, my famous child, 'tis not fitting
Thus to mistreat for mortals' sake a godhead immortal."   [fire.

Thus she spake; and Hephaestus extinguished his fierce-blazing
Thereat the wave once more rolled down with its beautiful currents.

So as the rage of the Xanthus was tamed, the contending immortals
Both of them ceased, since Hera restrained them, though she was angry.
Yet in the ranks of the rest of the godheads strife was awakened,
Grievous and dire, and the mind in the gods' breasts tossed in dissension.
Mighty the crash of encounter; the broad earth groaned underneath it;
Rang like a trumpet's peal the mighty expanse of the heavens.

Zeus, as he sat in Olympus, attended the din, and delighted
Laughed in his heart when he saw the godheads joining in battle.
Far off one from another they stood no longer; and Ares,
Render of shields, made first a beginning, rushed on Athena,
Wielding a weapon of bronze, and uttered insults against her:

"Dog-fly, why is it now thou art driving the gods to contention?
Stormy in daring thou art, and the spirit that moves thee excessive:
Dost thou fail to remember when Tydeus' son, Diomedes,
Thou didst set on to wound me, a plain-seen spear thou thyself didst
Grasp and thrust straight at me? It pierced my fair flesh and rent it.
This day then thou shalt settle, methinks, for the ills thou hast wrought

Thus he spake, and he smote on the terrible tasselèd aegis, [me!"
Terrible aegis that even the lightning of Zeus cannot conquer.
Thereon blood-stained Ares with long spear smote at Athena!
She, however, drew back and grasped with her stout hand a boulder,
Rugged and rough and immense, as out on the plain it was lying —
Men of the past had set it there as a bound of a plowland:
With it she smote on his neck the impetuous Ares and loosened
All of his limbs, and he fell; seven plethra he covered; his hair was
Soiled in the dust. His armor rattled upon him. Athena   [him:
Laughed and, boasting above him, with wingèd words she addressed

"Simpleton, not even yet hast thou learned how much better than
I boast myself to be, that thou thinkest to match me in prowess. [thou art
Thus wouldst thou expiate fully the curses belike of thy mother,
Who in her anger deviseth against thee evils, because that
Thou hast deserted th' Achaeans and helpest the arrogant Trojans."

When she had spoken thus, she turned back her radiant glances.
Taking him by the hand, the daughter of Zeus, Aphrodite,
Led him, heavily groaning, and barely recov'ring his spirit.
Now as the worshipful Hera, the white-armed goddess, perceived her,
Forthwith then she addressed, in accents wingèd, Athena:

"Aye me! daughter of Zeus, the aegis-bearer, thou tireless!
Ares, the ruin of mortals, that dog-fly again is conducting
Up through the tumult and out of the fury of war. But pursue her!"

Thus spake she. And Athena gave chase and rejoiced in her spirit.
Coming upon her, she smote with her strong stout hand Aphrodite

Full on the bosom; her knees were unstrung and the spirit within her.
So then there on the bounteous earth were both of them lying.
She then over them spake in winged words loudly exulting:

"Such be the fate of them all, whoever the Trojans' abettors
May be, whenever they fight the strongly-corseleted Argives,
Even as daring and hardy, it may be, as when Aphrodite
Came to the succor of Ares and here encountered my prowess.
So we had haply surceased long since from the ruinous warfare,
Ay, we had laid waste wholly the well-builded city of Ilium."

Thus spake Athena. She smiled — the goddess, the white-armed
Thereat the sovereign shaker of earth spake out to Apollo: [Hera.

"Phoebus, why are we standing apart? It is surely unseemly,
Now that the rest have begun. For shame! if we go without fighting
Back to the palace of Zeus, with its threshold of bronze, to Olympus.
Start then! Thou art younger by birth; it would hardly befit me,
Seeing that I am older in years and greater in knowledge.
Fond god, foolish indeed thy heart! Nor dost thou remember
Aught of the ills we endured, we only of all the immortals,
Under the Ilian walls in the lordly Laomedon's service,
Bound by decree of Zeus to serve *him* a whole year's circuit,
Serve him at wages and labors that *he* as master appointed!
I it was builded the rampart encircling the town of the Trojans,
Wide and exceeding fair, so to make an impregnable city.
Thou it was, Phoebus, herded his crook-horned cattle that shambled
There in the valleys of Ida dense-wooded, many-infolded.
But when the Hours, aye gladsome, had rounded the season of service
Unto its end, he robbed us by force of all of the payment,
Yea, with a threat that monster Laomedon roughly dismissed us —
Threatened to bind us indeed, our feet and our hands up above them
Firmly together, and sell us afar into alien islands;
Likewise he threatened to lop from us twain both ears with his weapon!
So we returned to our home, both kindled to fury in spirit,
Wrathful because of the wages that monarch had promised and paid not.
His folk now thou showest thy grace, instead of essaying,
Banded with us, to deliver the arrogant Trojans to ruin
Utterly, wretchedly, all, with their gentle wives and their children."

457

Thereat addressed him in turn the sovereign, far-working Apollo:
"Shaker of earth, I should show sound sense to thee in thy rating
Noway, were I to fight with thee on account of the luckless
Mortals, who may be likened indeed to the leaves of the forest:
Presently glowing with life and eating the fruits of the plowland,
Presently pining again unto death. But quickly as may be,
Let us desist from the fray; let us leave them alone in their quarrel."

Thus he spake and turned him away, for shame overcame him
There to buffet with blows the brother insooth of his father.
Sharply his sister, the queen of the wild beasts, spake and rebuked him,
Artemis, ranger of fields, yea, chided with words of reproaching:

"So then thou fleest, Far-worker; hast yielded completely the vict'ry
Unto Poseidon and given him boasting and glory for nothing?
Fond god! Why then bearing a bow ineffective and idle?
Never again let *me* hear thee now in the halls of our Father
Boasting, as erewhile oft, among the godheads immortal
Thou wouldst be willing against Poseidon to enter the warfare."

Thus spake she. Far-working Apollo answered her nothing —
Not a word he. But the honorèd consort of Zeus, filled with anger,
Hotly assailed with words of rebuke the rainer of arrows:

"How art thou fain, thou impudent slut, to stand up and battle
Now against me? My prowess were surely right hard to encounter
Even for thee, though armed with a bow, since Zeus hath appointed
Thee against women a lion, to kill of them whom thou desirest.
Better forsooth to be slaying the wild beasts ranging the mountains,
Deer of the woods, than to battle amain with mightier godheads.
But if thou wilt, learn something of warfare, that thou may'st discover
How much mightier I, that thou thinkest to match me in prowess."

Thus she spake; with her left hand she caught both hands of the other
Hard by the wrist; with her right she took from her shoulders her weap-
With them she duly beat her about the ears, the while smiling.   [ons;
This way and that the maid twisted her head. Out fell the swift arrows.
Sidewise fled from her clutches the goddess in tears, as a pigeon
Flieth away from a hawk to a rock-cleft, unto a crevice
Where she may hide, unappointed by fate as prey for a falcon.
So fled Artemis, weeping, and there left lying her arrows.

Thereupon spake unto Leto the Messenger, slayer of Argus:

"Leto, with thee I will not join in a battle! For grievous
Were it to come to blows with the wives of Zeus, the cloud-gath'rer.
Boast to thy heart's content among the godheads immortal
Thou hast in warfare wholly with might and with main overcome me."

Thus he spake. And Leto the curvèd bow and the arrows,
Tumbled this way and that in the whirl of dust, was collecting.
Then she went back to her place with her daughter's bow and her ar-
But to the palace of Zeus with its threshold of bronze in Olympus [rows.
Artemis came; in tears she sat on the knees of her Father,
All her ambrosial raiment a-quiver about her; the Father
Cronides drew her up close; with a merry laugh then he asked her:

"Who hath entreated thee thus, dear child, of the children of heaven
Wantonly, even as wert thou in th' open a doer of evil?" [dressed him:

Answered the fair-crowned queen of the echoing chase and ad-

"Thus did thine own wife, Father, the white-armed Hera, mistreat
She, sole fountain of strife and contention among the immortals." [me,

While those gods were conversing in such wise one with the other,
Meantime Phoebus Apollo had gone into Ilium holy,
Seeing his heart was intent on the wall of the well-builded city,
Lest on that day and before its time the Danaans sack it.
All other gods aye-living returned once more to Olympus;
Some were in anger, and some in triumph, greatly exulting.
All by the cloud-wrapt Zeus then seated themselves. But Achilles
Kept on slaughtering Trojans, themselves and their whole-hoofed
Even as smoke that ascends on high to the canopied heavens, [horses.
Out from a city in flames that the gods' wrath surely enkindled
(Travail it heapeth on all and sorrow inflicteth on many):
So was Achilles heaping up travail and woe on the Trojans.

Now as the agèd Priam aloft on a god-built turret
Stood, he was ware of gigantic Achilles—how he was driving
Routed before him the Trojans in throngs: not any resistance
Longer was made. With a cry he came down to the earth from the tower,
Rousing along the ramparts the famous guards of the gateways:

"Hold wide open the gates with your hands, till haply the people
Come to the town in their flight; for yonder, behold, is Achilles

Pressing them hotly in chase, and his deeds, methinks, will be deadly.
But, when once they are gathered within these walls and are breathing
Freely again, close on him the doorwings fitted securely;
Else will that murderous man leap into the city, I fear me."

Thus spake he; and they thrust back the bars and opened the gate-
Wide; and the portals expanded to save their lives; but Apollo   [ways
Leaped straight forth to meet him and ward off woe from the Trojans.
Right for the city amain and the high-built rampart around it,
Parched with thirst and begrimed with dust, from the plain they were
Hotly Achilles pursued with his spear; a powerful frenzy   [fleeing.
Ever possessed his heart, intent upon winning him glory.
Then had the sons of Achaia taken the high-gated Troia,
Had not Phoebus Apollo incited the godlike Agenor,
Son of Antenor; a faultless man was Agenor and mighty.
Courage intrepid he put in his heart, and himself he stood by him—
Stood with intent to avert death's heavy doom from the hero,
Leaning against the oak; with a heavy cloud he was shrouded.
Now as Agenor was 'ware of Achilles, waster of cities,
Instant he stopped; and his heart, as he halted, often debated;
Deeply disturbed, he communed with his own magnanimous spirit:

"Woe is me! God help me, if now from the mighty Achilles
Haply I flee where the rest in confusion are fleeing affrighted;
E'en so he will o'ertake me and cut my throat as a coward.
But if the rest I shall leave to be driven in rout by Achilles,
Peleus' scion, and flee on my feet away from the ramparts
Off in a diff'rent direction, far off to the plain named of Ilus,
Till I arrive at the foothills of Ida and hide in the brushwood,
Then in the evening belike, clean-bathed in the flood of the river
Free from sweat and cooled off, and return again unto Ilium—
Yet, why thus with itself debateth my dear heart within me?
Lest he catch sight of me taking myself to the plain from the city,
Then with his swiftness of foot he dash in pursuit and o'ertake me?
Then 'twill be possible noway to ward off death's visitation,
Seeing that he above all mankind is exceedingly mighty.
But if I go and encounter him haply in front of the city?
Surely with keen bronze weapon e'en this man's flesh may be wounded;

460

One life only is in him; men say he also is mortal,
Even although it be Zeus, the Cronion, that granteth him glory."

   So he spake, and he gathered himself and awaited Achilles,
Yea, and his stout heart spurred him to enter the fight and do battle.
Like as a leopardess comes from her den in the depths of a jungle
Forth to encounter a huntsman and—all unaffrighted in spirit—
Noway fleeth distraught at the hounds' loud bay when she hears it—
Even if haply a man first wound her with arrow or javelin,
Yet, though pierced with a dart, she will noway cease from her prowess,
Never, until she has closed or else is mortally wounded:
Even so godlike Agenor, the son of the valiant Antenor,
Firmly resolved not to flee before he made proof of Achilles;
Nay, but he held up before him his shield all evenly rounded,
Carefully aimed his javelin at him, and mightily shouted:

   "Doubtless in heart thou fondly hopest, O noble Achilles,
This day even to sack the town of the lordly Trojans.
Fond man! Many the woes that shall yet be suffered for its sake,
Seeing that we that are in it are warriors many and valiant;
We men, in front of our dear-loved parents, our wives, and our children,
Watch over Ilium's weal. Thy destiny thou shalt encounter
Here, although a most dreaded warrior thou art and courageous."

   Thus spake he, and he launched from his weighty hand the sharp
Nor did he miss his mark, but he smote the shin of Achilles   [javelin,
Under the knee, and the greave of fresh-fashioned tin, all around it
Fearfully rang out loud; but the bronze-shod weapon rebounded
Off from the man that was smitten; it pierced not; the god's gift repelled
Thereupon Peleus' son made a rush at Agenor, the godlike,   [it.
Next, but Apollo suffered him not to win him such glory;
Quickly he caught Agenor away; in a thick cloud he veiled him,
Sent him to wander in safety aloof from the war, and, the meanwhile,
Drew off Pelides by craft away from the Ilian people.
Yea, the far-worker, assuming in all ways the guise of the real man,
Stood in the path of Achilles, who rushed swift-footed to chase him.
While now over the plain's wide cornland chased him Achilles,
Edging him ever on toward Scamander's deep-eddying river,
Only a little ahead—for with craft did Apollo beguile him,

So that he still kept hoping with fleetness of foot to o'ertake him.
Glad of escape, in tumultuous panic the rest of the Trojans
Came meantime to the town; with the throng the city was crowded.
None of them dared now to wait one another's returning from battle
Outside city and rampart, or learn who escaped from the combat,
Who had been killed in the war; all flooded the city in tumult,
Whomsoever his feet and his knees saved haply from slaughter.

ILIAD · XXII · (X)

Hector in Chi to death is done
By pow'r of Peleus' angry son.

THUS, then, all through the town, affrighted as fawns, were the [Trojans
Drinking and slaking their thirst and cooling the sweat from their
Leaning the while on the beautiful battlements. But the Achaeans [bodies,
Drew nigh unto the wall, their shields set firm to their shoulders.
Hector the while stood fettered of ruinous fate for remaining
There at the gateway Scaean, in front of the Ilian city.
　　Then to Pelides addressed him the godhead Phoebus Apollo:
"Wherefore dost thou pursue me with swift feet, scion of Peleus?
Thou art a mortal, but I an immortal god; and thou hast not
Learned even yet that I am a god, but unceasingly ragest! [frighted,
Care hast thou none for thy task with the Trojans, whom thou hast af-
Who by this time are penned in the city; and thou hast turned hither!
Me shalt thou never slay; unto death I was never appointed."
　　Mightily vexed, fleet-footed Achilles addressed him, saying:
"Thou, far-worker, thou god most hurtful of all, thus to baulk me,
Turning me hither away from the rampart! Else had they bitten—
Many another—the dust, ere ever they came into Ilium.
Now thou hast robbed me of great renown and delivered the Trojans
Lightly, indeed; no fear hadst thou of requital hereafter!
Were the ability mine, on thee I would surely avenge me."
　　Thus he spake; high-hearted he strode forthwith toward the city,
Rushing along, as a prize-winning horse with his chariot rusheth,
When o'er the plain at the top of his speed he easily runneth:
So now Achilles his feet and his knees kept plying as nimbly.
　　Aged Priam himself was the first with his eyes to behold him
Hurrying over the plain and glittering bright as that star shines
Which at harvest time riseth, and far-seen its star-beams glitter
Out in the midst of the starry hosts in the night's deepest darkness.

463

This is the star that they call with the name of the "Dog of Orion";
Brightest of all stars is he but is set as an omen of evil:
No end of fevers he brings in his train unto mortals unhappy:
Thus on his breast, as he ran, the bronzen armor did glisten.

Thereat the old man cried aloud, and his hands he uplifted,
Beating them both on his head, as he cried out, wildly beseeching
Hector, his well-loved son, who natheless in front of the gateway
Took his stand and inflexibly yearned to contend with Achilles.
Stretching his hands out to him, all piteous pleaded the old man:

"Hector, my child, my belovèd, abide not the onset of this man,
Lone and apart from the rest, lest quickly thy doom thou encounter,
Slain of Pelides, for he is a mightier far and a fighter
Merciless! Would he were dear to the godheads even in measure
Like as to me! Then soon would the dogs and vultures devour him
Low laid (then would be gone this awful anguish of spirit) —
He that hath reft me of sons already, so many and valiant,
Slaying or selling them all unto far-off alien islands.
Ay, even now two children of mine, Polydorus, Lycaon —
Neither one can I see 'mongst the Trojans that throng in the city,
Sons their mother did bear me, Laothoë, princess of women.
Them, if indeed in the camp these two are surviving, hereafter
We will ransom with bronze and with gold, for within is a plenty,
Store that the old man Altes, the wide-famed, bestowed on his daughter.
If they are dead already and gone to the mansion of Hades,
Woe to my heart and woe to their mother — for we are their parents —
But to the rest of the people far lighter the sorrow and haply
Briefer, if thou die not, o'ercome at the hands of Achilles.
Nay, now, enter the rampart within, dear child, and deliver
Both the men and the women of Ilium, neither with glory
Cover Pelides and pay thine own dear life as a forfeit.
Pity me, who am the wretched, the while yet living and feeling,
Fated to ill. At the limit of age will Cronion, the Father,
End me in dolorous doom, when woes past number I've witnessed:
Sons that have perished, my daughters the foe dragged off into bond-
Couches profaned and destroyed, ay, even the infant children   [age,
Headlong flung to the earth in the terrible havoc of battle,

Sons' wives haled by hands of Achaeans, haled unto ruin.
Even myself at the last, no doubt, will the dogs at my doorway [foeman
Rend in their ravenous greed—when with keen bronze weapon some
Smites me with arrow or spear and takes my soul from my body—
Dogs I had fed at my table, the guardian dogs of my palace,
They, deep-drunk of my blood and besotted at heart with the potion,
They will lie down at my porch. Unto youth all fortune is seemly,
Even to fall in a battle, by keen bronze e'en to be mangled,
Laid low—all is an honor in death, whatever appeareth.
But when the hoary head and the hoary beard of an old man,
Ay, and the shame of an old man slain the dogs shall dishonor,
That's the most pitiful thing that can come to mortals unhappy!" [gers,

    Thus then the old man spake; and he tore his grey locks with his fin-
Plucking them out from his head; but he moved not the spirit of Hector.
Pouring her tears then his mother on her side wailed and lamented,
Op'ning the folds of her dress and with one hand displaying her bosom;
Shedding her tears, she addressed him, in accents wingèd beseeching:

    "Hector, my child, unto these have then a regard, show some pity,
Pity for me, if ever I gave this bosom to soothe thee;
Call it to mind, dear child, and seek to drive back the foeman,
Whilst thou art inside the wall; in front of it do not await him,
Merciless man! If he slay thee perchance, not then on a litter
I shall bewail thee—myself, dear child, thy mother that bore thee,
Nay, not even thy bountiful wife; but away at the Argive
Warships, distant from us, swift dogs will rend and devour thee!"

    Thus were the twain addressing their dear son, sorely lamenting,
Earnestly pleading, but vainly; they moved not the spirit of Hector.
There he awaited gigantic Achilles who came ever nearer.
Like as a serpent awaiteth a man—at his den in a mountain,
Snake that hath fed on venomous herbs, and a terrible fury
Enters him; dreadfully glares he, as round in his dark den he coileth:
So with unquenchable courage he stood there, resolute Hector,
Leaning his radiant buckler against a tower projecting.
Sorely troubled, he spake to his own magnanimous spirit:

    "Woe unto me! If I enter the ramparts now and the gateway,
First will Pulydamas then be heaping reproaches upon me,

Who was bidding me lead the Trojans back to the city
During this ruinous night when arose the godlike Achilles.
Yet I heeded him not—far better it were I had done so.
Now then, since I have lost us the host with my own rash folly,
I am ashamed to face the Trojans and trailing-robed women,
Lest some man that is meaner than I may declare hereafter:
'Hector, reliant upon his own might, lost us the army.'
Thus they will talk; to me far better insooth than to hear them,
Now to encounter Achilles and then fare home, having slain him,
Or else perish myself, but with glory, defending my city.
But should I lay them aside, this shield all studded with bosses,
Also my ponderous helmet, and, leaning my spear on the rampart,
Then go forward just so till I meet him, the faultless Achilles,
Promise him also that Helen and with her all her possessions—
Everything, all, whate'er in his hollow ships Alexander
Erst brought home unto Troy, the beginning of strife and contention—
All we will give the Atridae to take hence; then with th' Achaeans
All things else will divide, whatever the city containeth;
Then I'll secure thereafter an oath from the Ilian elders
Nothing whatever to hide but to halve things evenly with them,
All of the substance the lovely city is holding within it—
Yet why thus with itself is my dear heart debating within me?
Nay, let me not go into his presence; for he will in no case
Pity or spare me—nay, he will kill me, just like a woman,
There on the spot, if I am defenseless, naked of armor.
No time surely to chaffer with talk from a rock or an oak-tree,
Chaffer with him, as perchance might dally a youth with a maiden,
Even as maiden and youth hold dalliance one with another;
Better in warfare's strife to close as quickly as may be:
Let us find out to which one th' Olympian granteth the glory."

      Thus he tarried and pondered; and lo! Achilles came nigh him,
Fierce Enyalius' equal, the shimmering-helmeted war-god,
Poising above his right shoulder the Pelian ash, his dread javelin.
All round gleamed the bronze of his armor like unto fire
Blazing brightly or like to the gleam of the sun, as it riseth.
Hector beheld, and a trembling seized him; no longer then dared he

Stay there; he left the gateway behind him and fled in a panic.
After him darted Pelides, relying on fleetness in running.
E'en as a hawk in the mountains, the swiftest of all wingèd creatures,
Swoopeth easily down on a wild dove trembling in terror —
But she fleeth before him; and he, shrill-screaming anigh her,
Keeps on darting upon her, his heart still urgent to seize her:
So in his fury Achilles was flying right at him, and Hector
Fled 'neath the Trojans' wall and plied his knees nimbly beneath him.
Passing the look-out stand and the fig-tree that waves in the breezes,
Under the wall and away and along the wagon-road sped they,
Till they arrived at the two fair-flowing springs, at the fountains
Twain that gush forth as the source of the eddying river Scamander.
Warm is the water that floweth in one; all round it the vapor,
Like unto smoke from a fire in full blaze, issueth from it.
Even in summer the flood of the other is chill in its current,
Like unto hail, to cold snow, or like ice when forming of water.
Beautiful basins of stone stand nigh at the side of the fountains,
Spacious basins for washing; and there their shining apparel
Matrons and maidens fair of the Trojans to wash were accustomed
Ere, in the days of peace, there came the sons of th' Achaeans.
There they were running along, one fleeing, the other pursuing
After him — mighty the flier, but mightier far the pursuer —
Nimble of foot, inasmuch as they strove not then for a victim
Nor for a bull's hide shield — such prizes as men's feet may win them —
Nay! Both ran for the prize of the life of horse-taming Hector.
Even as round the turns prize-winning, solid-hoofed horses
Rapidly circle the goals — for a great prize is set there before them,
Be it a tripod or woman — to honor a warrior fallen:
Even so circled the twain, thrice rounding the city of Priam,
Swift feet bearing them on. The gods were all looking upon them.
Then among them the father of men and of gods began speaking:

    "Ah me! dear unto me is the man mine eyes are beholding
Followed the rampart round. The heart of me tenderly pities
Hector, who burned me thighs full many of oxen and often
There on the summits of Ida, the many-enfolded, and then, too,
Oft on the citadel's peak; but the godlike Achilles pursues him

Now with his swiftness of feet round about the city of Priam.
Come then, give us advice, ye gods, and devise us some measure
Whether from death we shall rescue him or shall even now yield him,
Valiant indeed as he is, to be slain by Achilles Pelides."
     Then unto him in her turn spake the bright-eyed goddess Athena:
"Father, lord of lightnings and ſtorm-clouds, what hast thou spoken!
Him unto whom as a mortal a fate long since was appointed,
Art thou minded from dolorous death again to deliver?
Do it! However, not all of us other gods will applaud thee."
     Answering her in return, cloud-gathering Zeus thus addressed her:
"Have no fear, dear child, thou Trito-born; not in earnest
Was I speaking; indeed unto thee I would fain be indulgent.
Do thou e'en as thou 'rt minded to do, and tarry no longer."
     These words urged on Athena, herself already full eager;
Down she went with a flash from the pinnacle peaks of Olympus.   [tor.
     Meanwhile Achilles, the swift, with vehemence pressed upon Hec-
As when a hound pursueth a deer's fawn up in the mountains — [coverts;
After he ſtarteth it out from its hiding — through glades and through
Though it may cower — in longing to baffle him — under the bushes,
Yet will he pick up the scent and ſteadily run till he find it:
Thus did not Hećtor escape from the sight of fleet-footed Pelides.
Oft as he minded to dash up under the well-builded rampart —
Ilium's rampart — over against the Dardanian gateways,
If from above they might haply with missiles come to his rescue:
So oft his foe would forge ahead and turn him to plain-ward
Off from the wall, and himself kept flying aye next to the city.
As in a dream a man faileth to catch the one he pursueth —
Neither the one that flies can escape, nor the other o'ertake him:
So could this one not overtake with his feet nor the other escape him.
Thus then haply had Hećtor escaped from death's visitation,
Had it not been the last and the final time that Apollo
Near to him came to endue him with ſtrength and give his feet swiftness.
For to the hoſts, with his head, the godlike Achilles gave signals
Nor would allow them to cast their bitter missiles at Hećtor,
Lest some smiter's renown come first, and himself come second.
Finally now, as they came for the fourth time nigh to the fountains,

Lo! then the Father balanced his golden scales and he loaded
Each with a fate of death that lays men low — for Achilles
One of the scales and the other for Hector, the tamer of horses.
Level he poised; down sank the doomful day of great Hector,
Down toward the mansion of Hades; and Phoebus Apollo forsook him.
Then came nigh to Pelides the bright-eyed goddess Athena,
Stood at his side hard by, and with wingèd words she addressed him:

"Now then, glorious Achilles, belovèd of Zeus, I am hoping
We shall return to the ships with mighty renown for th' Achaeans,
Won through the slaying of Hector, although he is sateless of battle.
Now no longer indeed is it possible he should escape us,
Not even if far-darting Apollo in travail excessive
Grovel and wallow before his sire who wieldeth the aegis.
Stand here then and recover thy breath, while I unto yon man
Go and persuade him to measure his might 'gainst thine in a battle."

Thus spake Athena; the hero obeyed and rejoiced in his spirit,
Stopped, as she bade, and leaned on his spear, bronze-barbèd and ashen.
So then she left him there and came unto Hector, the godlike,
Like to Deïphobus both in her resonant voice and her figure.
Taking her stand hard by, with wingèd words she addressed him:

"Brother of mine, yon swift Achilles doth evil-entreat thee,
Chasing thee still with fleetness of feet round the city of Priam;
Come, let us stand and await him and ward off haply his onset."

Then in his turn great shimmering-helmeted Hector addressed her:
"Verily thou wert before this, Deïphobus, dearest of brothers —
Dearest by far of the sons to Hecabe born and to Priam.
Now even more, however, I'm minded to hold thee in honor,
Who for my sake didst dare, when thou with thine eyes didst behold me,
Come from the citadel forth, while the rest are still biding within it."

Then unto him in her turn spake the bright-eyed goddess Athena:
"Brother of mine, of a truth our father and worshipful mother,
Also our comrades entreated in turn and they earnestly begged me
There to remain, so greatly they all do tremble before him.
But my heart in my breast with grief and distress was afflicted.
Now go we resolute straight to the fight; and be there no sparing
Now any more of our spears, that so we may learn if Achilles

469

Haply may slay us together and carry our blood-stained armor
Back to the hollow ships or haply be slain by thy javelin."

    Thus did Athena speak, and with craftiness forward she led him.
When they had come close up in the onrush 'gainst one another,
Then there addressed him first great shimmering-helmeted Hector:

    "Scion of Peleus, from thee no more will I flee, as aforetime
Thrice I did run round the mighty city of Priam and dared not
Ever await thy approach; but now of my heart I am bidden
Stand up against thee — whether I slay thee or haply shall perish.
Come then, now let us bring in the deities; they are the surest
Witness of all men's oaths and the guardians also of compacts.
I will inflict no outrage on thee, if Zeus will but haply
Grant me strength to outlast thee, and I of thy life shall deprive thee.
Nay, but when I have stripped off thy glorious armor, Achilles,
Then I will give up thy corse to th' Achaeans. Promise me likewise."

    Scowlfully eying, addressed him in turn fleet-footed Achilles:
"Thou, abominate Hector, to talk to me of agreements!
Even as lions and men have no trusty pledges between them,
Neither can wolves ever be like-minded with sheep in a pasture,
Nay, but imagine against one another continual evil:
So between thee and me is friendship impossible; never
We shall exchange such pledges till one or the other hath fallen,
Glutting with thy blood or mine the war-god, shield-bearing Ares.
All thy varied skill call up; for much it behooves thee
Now above all to be a good spearman and warrior courageous.
There's no way of escape for thee now; for Pallas Athena
Lays thee low 'neath my spear; for now in one deal thou wilt pay me
Full for my griefs for my friends thy javelin's fury hath slaughtered."

    Thus he spake. Then, poising his spear far-shadowing, hurled it;
Glorious Hector watched it come and eluded the missile,
For, close-observing, he crouched, and the bronze-shod weapon flew
Fixing itself in the earth; but Pallas Athena caught it   [o'er him,
Up and again to Achilles restored it, unnoticed by Hector,
Shepherd of peoples, who thus addressed the faultless Pelides:

    "Ah! thou didst miss me, Achilles, a godhead's match! Thou knewest
Naught of my doom from Zeus, howbeit proclaiming it loudly.

Thou hast proved a speaker glib and a trickster with phrases,
Hoping to make me forget in my fear both valor and prowess.
Flee shall I not, for thee in my back to fasten thy javelin!
Pierce much rather my breast in my resolute onset upon thee,
If God hath granted it thee. Now in *thy* turn avoid *thou* my bronzen
Spear; and I hope that thou mayest receive it *all* in thy body!
So would the war prove lighter to bear for the people of Troia,
If thou wert dead; for to them the greatest bane is Achilles."

Thus he spake. Then poising his spear far-shadowing hurled it,
Nor did he miss, but he smote on the midst of the shield of Pelides.
Far off the javelin glanced from the shield. Then wrathful was Hector,
Seeing his missile had fled from his hand, swift-wingèd but vainly.
Downcast he stood, for he had no second javelin of ash-wood.
Loudly he called on his brother, Deïphobus, him of the white shield,
Asking of him a long lance. But his brother was nowhere near him!
Hector well in his heart understood and spake a word, saying:

"Ah me! Verily now the gods have summoned me deathward.
I had imagined a hero, Deïphobus, standing beside me;
Nay, he is inside the walls; 'tis Athena hath wholly deceived me!
Now then an evil death is at hand, no longer afar off—
No escape now! For long since even this was the pleasure of heaven,
Dearer to Zeus and his son who darteth afar; yet aforetime
Zealous were they in their succor; but now my destiny finds me.
Let me at least not die unattended with effort and glory,
Nay, but in valorous deed, that men of the future shall hear of."

Thus then he spake, and forth he drew his keen blade from its scabbard.
(Mighty and huge was the blade that hung at his side thus extended),
Gathered himself together, and swooped, as a high-soaring eagle
Darteth down to the plain through the lowering cloud-banks of heaven,
Whether to seize on a cowering hare or a delicate lambkin:
Even so Hector with flourish of keen blade swooped on Achilles.
At him Pelides rushed, and he filled his spirit with savage
Fury; to cover his breast, he advanced with his buckler before him,
Beauteous, richly-wrought, and he tossed that glittering helmet
Fourfold-ridgèd; the beautiful, gold-wrought plumes all about it [age.
Waved in the air o'er the ridge, where Hephaestus had set the thick plum-

Just as a star 'mid the starry hosts in night's deepest darkness —
Even as Hesperus, fairest of all stars set in the heavens:
Suchwise shimmered a light from the keen spear-point that Achilles
Brandished aloft in his right, to godlike Hector devising
Ill, as he eyed to discover some path to his beautiful body.
All other parts were encased in the beauteous bronze of his armor,
Arms that he took as his spoils when he slew the mighty Patroclus;
Only his throat was exposed, at the spot where the collar-bones border
Shoulders and neck — at the point where the taking of life is the quickest.
There then, as Hector charged, with his spear the godlike Achilles
Thrust, and clear through the delicate neck went the point of the javelin.
Although weighted with bronze, yet the ash-wood severed the windpipe
Noway, so that he still might answer with words and address him.
Down he crashed in the dust, and godlike Achilles exulted:
    "Hector, undoubtedly thou, when despoiling Patroclus of armor,
Thoughtest that thou wouldst be safe and didst reck not of me in my ab-
Fond man! seeing that I had been left far off — an avenger   [sence,
Mightier far, but aloof, at the hollow galleys behind him —
I that have loosed thy knees. Though dogs and vultures shall rend thee
Foully at will, the Achaeans will solemnly bury Patroclus."
    Then, faint of breath, the shimmering-helmeted Hector addressed
    "By thy life, thy knees, I beg and beseech, and thy parents,   [him:
Suffer me not at the ships to be torn by the dogs of th' Achaeans,
Nay, but accept of the gifts unstinted, the bronze and the golden
Treasure my father will give thee, both he and my worshipful mother.
Only return this body of mine to my home, that the Trojans,
Women and men, may honor my corse with a funeral fire."
    Grim in his visage addressed him in turn fleet-footed Achilles:
"No supplication to me, thou dog, by knees or by parents!
Nay, I would that wrath and fury of mine would impel me
Even to cut thy flesh myself into pieces and eat it
Raw for the deeds thou hast wrought; so verily none shall deliver
Thee from the dogs. If ten — nay twenty-fold — ransom they bring me,
Weigh it out here, yea, promise me yet even more in abundance —
Nay, and if Dardanid Priam should bid men balance thy body
Even with gold — why, not even so shall thy worshipful mother

Lay on a bier the offspring borne of herself and bewail him —
Never! the dogs and the birds lone-flying shall wholly devour thee."
    Then unto him, as he died, spake shimmering-helmeted Hector:
"Now do I see thee, as well I have known thee; and I was not likely
E'er to persuade thee; for surely the heart in thy bosom is iron.
Well, take heed! lest wrath for my sake smite thee from heaven
That day even when Paris and Phoebus Apollo shall slay thee —
Notwithstanding thy valor and might — at the gateway Scaean."
    Hardly thus had he spoken, the end of death closed upon him.
Flitting, his soul from his limbs unto Hades' mansion departed,
Wailing its fate, thus leaving the prime and vigor of manhood.
Therewith, though he was dead, the godlike Achilles addressed him:
    "Die! As for *my* fate, that will I welcome unshrinking, whenever
Zeus and the other immortal gods shall wish to fulfil it."
    Thus then he spake and drew forth his bronzen spear from the body,
Set it aside, and proceeded to strip from his shoulders the armor,
Dripping with blood. And others, the sons of Achaeans ran round him;
These, too, gazed upon Hector's magnificent looks and his stature;
Not one, however, failed, as he stood beside him, to stab him,
Whispering also a word, each one, as he glanced at another:
    "Go to! verily *now* it is far more easy to handle
Hector than when with blazing fire he was burning our galleys!"
    Thus, as they stood beside him, would people speak and stab him.
But when the godlike Achilles, swift-footed, had stripped off the armor,
Standing among them, with wingèd words he addressed the Achaeans:
    "Friends of mine, ye commanders and counseling chiefs of the Ar-
Seeing that now have the gods vouchsafed us to quell this hero, [gives,
Him that had wrought us affliction beyond all others together,
Come, let us now reconnoitre in force, surrounding the city,
So as to fathom the purpose, whatever it be, of the Trojans:
Whether, as this man is fallen, the citadel they will abandon,
Whether indeed they are minded to bide there, though no more is Hec-
Yet why thus with itself is my dear heart debating within me? [tor.
There by the galleys lieth unburied the corse of Patroclus,
Even unwept; but him will I never forget — not so long as
I shall abide with the living and find my precious knees moving.

Even if people forget their dead in the palace of Hades,
I even there shall be mindful for aye of my comrade beloved.
Come now, singing a paean, ye young men, sons of Achaia,
Let us return to the hollow ships and bring this man with us.   [like—
Great the renown we have won. We have slain great Hector, the god-
Him unto whom, as a god, the Trojans made prayer through the city."

   Spake he; and treatment foul he devised for Hector, the godlike:
Slitting the sinews behind from the heel clean up to the ankle,
Oxhide laces he thrust through both of his feet's fair tendons,
Bound the corpse fast to his car, with the head left trailing behind it,
Lifted the glorious arms to his car, then, mounted upon it,
Lashed his horses to start them, and they went eagerly flying.
Clouds of dust arose, as along he was dragged, and darkly
All round floated his hair; and his head lay, comely aforetime,
All in the dust and bedraggled; for him had Zeus then forsaken
Unto his foes in his own native land, to be evil-entreated.

   So was the hero's head all grimed with dust; and his mother
Tore out her hair on beholding her son, and her shimmering wimple
Flung far off from her head, and her wail was exceedingly bitter.
Also his father beloved made piteous moan, and around them
Wailing the people lamented, the length and the breadth of the city.
Likest of all it appeared as if Ilium's terracèd stronghold
All from the top to the bottom were sinking enveloped in fire.
Hardly the people were able to hold back their aged sovereign,
Frantic and eager to rush forth there through the Dardanid gateway.
All he implored, as he groveled and rolled about in the mire,
Calling them all by name and begging each one as he named them:

   "Hold off, friends, and allow me alone, however ye love me,
Forth from the city to issue and fare to the galleys Achaean.
Let me beseech yon monster, abominate, worker of horror.
He peradventure may feel some awe for my age and may pity
Haply my years; for a man like even myself is his father,
Peleus, who hath begotten and reared him a bane to the Trojans
All, but a bringer of woes unto me surpassing all others:
So many children of mine in the flow'r of their youth he hath slaughtered.
Deep is my sorrow for all; yet I mourn not so as for Hector,

Hector alone, and my grief transpierces my heart and will bring me
Down unto Hades. Oh would he had died in my arms — my son Hector!
Then we had sated ourselves with bewailing and sore lamentation,
Both myself and his mother, appointed for sorrow, that bore him."

Thus spake he, as he wailed, and the citizens added their mourning.
Hecabe, though, 'mid the women of Troy led the wild lamentation:

"Woe unto me, my child! Why now live longer in sorrow,
Now thou art dead, who didst come and go, both morning and evening,
All my pride, my boast in the town, and a blessing to all men,
Men and women of Troy, in the city of all folk saluted
Like as a god, for to them, too, in truth went glory exceeding,
While yet living; of death and of doom hast thou been overtaken."

Thus she spake, as she wailed. But the wife of illustrious Hector
Nothing as yet had heard; no faithful informer had brought her
Message to tell her her husband was biding outside of the gateways.
Nay, in the innermost room of the lofty house she was weaving
Purple and double a web she was broid'ring with garlands of flowers.
All through the palace halls she had called to her fair-haired attendants,
Bidding them set up a tripod, a large one, over the fire,
Making a warm bath ready for Hector returning from battle —
Fond heart! nor was aware that, afar from the pleasance of bathing,
Under the hands of Achilles the bright-eyed Athena had slain him.
Yet, as she heard loud wailing of women and men from the tower,
Under her tottered her limbs; from her hands to the ground dropped the
[shuttle.
Then once again to the maidens she spake, to her fair-haired attendants:

"This way, two of you come; let us go and see what has happened!
Just now I heard my queen-mother's voice, and in my own bosom
Leapeth my pulsing heart to my mouth, and my knees underneath me —
Numbness invades them — some evil is nigh to the children of Priam!
Would that such word might be far from my ear — but I'm terribly fearful
Lest the godlike Achilles have cut off adventurous Hector
All by himself and chased him away to the plain from the city,
Yea, and the unblest pride that of old time ever possessed him   [riors,
Ere this have ended; for ne'er would he bide in the throng of the war-
Always running ahead, in his hardihood yielding to no man."

Thus she spoke. She sped, like one that is mad, from the chamber,
Wildly throbbing her heart, and with her went also her handmaids.
But when she reached the tow'r and the men that on it were thronging,
Pausing, she peered all round from the wall and beheld him directly
Dragged in front of the city; and swift were the horses that dragged him,
Recking nought of their work, to the hollow ships of th' Achaeans.
On her descended the blackness of night and shrouded her eyelids;
Swooning, she fell on the earth supine and gasped forth her spirit.
Far from her head she dropped, as she fell, her bright-shining head-gear,
Even her frontlet and coif and veil and the band deftly plaited —
Yea, that veil which once Aphrodite, the golden, had given,
All on that day when he led her, the shimmering-helmeted Hector,
Forth from Eëtion's home, when countless gifts he had given.
Gathered his sisters about her, a throng, and the wives of his brothers
All, and they held her among them distracted with grief unto dying.
When she recovered at last, and the soul came back to her body,
Wailing, with deep-drawn sobs she spake 'mid the women of Troia:
"Oh, ill-starred that I am! Unto one fate both of us, Hector,
Surely were born, as it seems: in the palace of Priam in Troyland
Thou — in the city of Thebes, at the foot of the forested Placus,
I, in the home of Eëtion, ill-starred, who reared me from childhood,
Daughter of cruelest fate — oh would he had never begot me!
Now unto Hades' home, earth's hidden and undermost region,
Thou hast descended and left me in bitter affliction behind thee,
Widowed, in desolate halls. Thy son, too, is only an infant,
Child of unhappy parents, of thee and myself; an advantage
Thou'lt ne'er be unto him, nor he unto thee — thou hast perished.
E'en if he haply escape the tearful war of th' Achaeans,
Sorrow alone shall his lot be ever and labor unceasing
Henceforth, seeing that others will spoil him, removing his landmarks.
That day sunders a child from his fellows which makes him an orphan,
That day he hangeth his head, yea, staineth his cheeks with his weeping.
Then shall the desolate child go seeking the friends of his father,
Pluck this one by the mantle, another one pluck by the tunic.
One of them, pitying haply, may offer a cup for a moment,
Maybe moisten his lips nor remember to moisten his palate.

Andromache Fainting on the Wall

Yea, and another, unorphaned, shall push him away from a banquet,
Buffet with blows of his hands, and taunt him with bitter reproaches:
'Get out of here! No father of thine sits here at our table.'
So he returns in tears, poor child, to his widowèd mother,
Even Astyanax, he who erst on the knees of his father
Ever would eat only fat flesh alone and the marrow of mutton.
Or from his child's play ceasing perchance, o'ertaken by slumber,
Falling asleep in his nurse-maid's arms, he would lie in his cradle,
Tenderly tucked in his bed, with his heart full-sated of dainties.
Now, though, many the ills he will suffer from loss of his father
(Even Astyanax — such is his nick-name given by Trojans,
Seeing that thou alone wast protector of gates and of ramparts).
Now, though, far from thy parents, alongside the curve-beakèd galleys,
Worms that wriggle shall eat thee — as soon as the dogs shall be sated —
Thee all naked; and yet fair raiment awaiteth thee yonder,
Raiment of thine in the halls, fine-wrought by the fingers of women.
Now I will burn all these with a fiery blaze unto ashes,
Though it avail thee naught (since thou liest never upon them);
Yet good report shall obtain 'mongst the men and the women of Troia."

    Thus she spake, as she wept; and the women added their mourning.

ILIAD · XXIII · (Ψ)

Psi sings the rites of the decease
Ordained by great Aeacides.

THUS then all through the city the folk made moan; but th' Achaeans,
When they arrived once more at the Hellespont and the galleys,
Scattered all of the rest; each one went to his galley, excepting
Only the Myrmidons; these Achilles would not let be scattered;
Nay, but he spake out amid them, his comrades, lovers of warfare:

"Myrmidons, drivers of steeds fleet-footed, my trusty companions,
Not yet let us unhitch our whole-hoofed steeds from the chariots;
Rather, with horses and cars as they are, draw near and bemoan him,
Goodly Patroclus, for such is the meed of the dead and departed.
Then, when at last we have had our fill of grievous lamenting,
Let us unhitch our horses and all of us here have our supper."

Thus spake he; and together they moaned, and Achilles was leader.
Three times around the dead they drove their heavy-maned horses,
Weeping; and Thetis inspired desire of lamenting among them.
Teardrops wetted the sands, and the heroes' armor was wetted,
Seeing they grieved for a chief, so mighty a master of terror.
First of them Peleus' son began the loud lamentation,
Laying his man-slaying hands on the breast of his comrade belovèd:

"Hail, Patroclus, even though gone to the mansion of Hades,
Seeing that now I'm fulfilling all that I promised aforetime —
Hither to drag dead Hector and give him to dogs to be eaten
Raw, and twice six throats of youths at thy pyre to sever —
Glorious children of Trojans, because of my wrath for thy slaying."

Spake he; and treatment foul he devised for Hector, the godlike,
Stretching him prone in the dust by the bier of the son of Menoetius.
Meanwhile each of the others laid off his glittering war-gear,
Bronzen; the steeds they unhitched that neigh with their heads high up-
All now sat them down by the fleet-footed Aeacid's galley,   [lifted.

Numberless; ample insooth was the funeral feast that he spread them,
Many the sleek white oxen that gasped with the steel in their bodies,
Slaughtered, and many the sheep; and the bleating goats, too, were
Many a swine with gleaming tusks, rich-laden with fatness, [many,
Stretched full length to be singed above the flame of Hephaestus.
All round the corse of Patroclus the blood ran flowing, in cupfuls.

Then at length was the lord, the fleet-footed scion of Peleus,
Led by th' Achaean princes away to divine Agamemnon;
Hardly could they induce him, still wrathful at heart for his comrade.
When in their course they arrived at the barrack of king Agamemnon,
Straightway they gave command to the clear-voiced heralds and bade
Over the fire to set a great tripod, if haply they might thus [them
Tempt the Pelides to wash off the blood and gore from his body.
Natheless he firmly refused, and he swore an oath to attest it:

"Nay, not so, by Zeus, who is best and highest of godheads,
Sure it is noway right for *my* head to be wetted of water
Ere I've consigned Patroclus to flames and have builded his barrow,
Ere I have shorn these locks, since never again shall another
Such grief visit my heart while here I abide with the living.
Let us resign ourselves this once to a supper of sorrow.
But when the morning is come, O monarch of men, Agamemnon,
Hasten the people to bring us wood and to furnish whatever
Else seems meet for the dead as he enters the shadowy darkness,
So that the flame be sure, th' unwearying fire, to consume him
Speedily out of our sight, and the people return to their labors."

Thus spake he. They hearkened with diligence, heeding his counsel.
Each division in haste, then, making ready its supper,
Fell to feasting—no heart felt stint of a well-balanced banquet.
Now when desire for meat and for drink together was banished,
All other warriors went, each one, to lie down in his barrack;
Only Pelides alone by the sea-marge billow-resounding
Lay down amid the host of the Myrmidons heavily groaning,
Where in an open place the waves would plash on the shingle.
When now slumber, dispelling the cares of his soul, overcame him,
Softly enswathing him round—for his glorious limbs he had wearied
Sore as he set upon Hector in chase round Ilium windy—

Then it was came to him there the spirit of hapless Patroclus,
Allwise like to his living self in stature and visage
Beautiful, like him in voice, in the raiment worn on his body;
Over his head then it stood and spake a word to him, saying:
    "Lo! thou sleepest, Achilles, and now hast forgot me in slumber.
Not while I lived, only since I am dead, of me art thou careless.
Bury me now with all speed, that I enter the portals of Hades.
Far thence the spirits bar me, the phantoms of those who have labored,
Nor yet allow me to mingle among them, over the River.
Vainly I wander along the wide-gated palace of Hades.
Sadly now I entreat thee, O give me thy hand! I shall never
Come back from Hades, when ye have vouchsafed me a funeral fire.
Neither shall we in the land of the living, apart from our comrades
Dear, sit counseling counsel together; a fate that is hateful
Swallowed me up; this fate unto me at my birth was appointed.
Yea, unto thee is ordained a doom, thou godlike Achilles,
Under the wall of the Trojans, the high-born Trojans, to perish.
One word more will I tell thee and charge thee, if haply thou'lt heed me:
Lay not my bones away apart from thine, O Achilles,
Nay, but together — just as we twain grew up in your palace.
I was a little lad when my father Menoetius from Opus
Brought me to your fair land, on account of a murder most grievous,
That same day that I slew him, Amphidamas' son, in my blindness,
Childish — I did it unmeaning, in anger because of the jackstones!
Peleus, the knightly, received me then to dwell in his palace;
He it was carefully reared me and named me then as thy squire;
So then, one be the urn that our bones shall cover together,
Gold, two-handled, a gift unto thee from thy worshipful mother."
    Answered him then and addressed him in turn fleet-footed Achilles:
    "Why is it now thou hast come, O dear one of mine, O my brother,
Hither, to lay such charges on me? Why, I will accomplish
Verily all and obey thee in all things, e'en as thou biddest.
Come then, stand thou nearer; for one brief moment embracing,
Let us have our comfort in bitter lamenting together."   [brace him —
    Thus then he spake and stretched forth his dear hands both to em-
Vainly; he clasped him not; since gone was his soul, as a vapor,

Under the earth, with a gibber; Achilles sprang up in amazement,
Smote together his hands, and uttered a word of lamenting:
"Ah me, verily yet in the palace of Hades a something
Bideth, a soul and a semblance, though life-force none it possesseth.
All night long I beheld the soul of the hapless Patroclus;
There it had taken its place above me, weeping and wailing,
Giving me final instructions; the image was wondrously like him."
Thus he spake and inspired in all a desire of lamenting.
Still were they weeping and wailing about the piteous body,
When rosy-fingered dawn appeared; then lord Agamemnon,
Hurrying heroes and mules upon all sides, forth from the barracks
Sped them to forage for wood; and Meriones, valiant in warfare,
Squire of Idomeneus manly of soul, arose to o'ersee them.
They, as they went forth, bore keen axes fitted for felling,
Well-twisted cables besides, and the mules trudged onward before them;
Manyways, upward, downward and sideward, crossward they traveled.
When they had reached the foothills of many-fountainèd Ida,
Eager and lusty they set them to felling with long-edgèd bronzes
Oak-trees lofty of leafage — the tree-trunks crashing in thunder
Fell to the earth; and then the Achaeans split them asunder,
Bound them behind the mules. These then, as they strove for the valley,
Tore up the ground with their feet, through underwood breaking a path-
Laden with logs, the hewers of wood came back, for thus did   [way.
Manly Idomeneus' squire, Meriones, bid them. They threw them
Down in lines at the shore of the sea, in the place where Achilles
Purposed to build him a barrow, immense, for himself and Patroclus.
Thereby on all sides they cast the numberless logs, as commanded;
All then waited and seated themselves in a throng; but Achilles
Straightway issued command to the Myrmidons, lovers of warfare,
Bidding them gird on bronze, and he bade each harness his horses
Unto his car; and they rose and put their armor upon them,
Mounted the cars, both the charioteers and the fighters beside them.
First came warriors in cars, and a cloud came after of countless
Fighters on foot; in the midst his comrades were bearing Patroclus.
All of the corse they enclothed with shorn-off locks that they cast down
On it. Behind the bier, at his head, walked the godlike Achilles,

Grief-struck, seeing he speeded his faultless comrade to Hades.   [ders,
    When they arrived at the place where Achilles had given them or-
Straightly they lowered the corse, then piled up plentiful firewood.
One thing further bethought him fleet-footed Achilles, the godlike:
Standing apart from the pyre, he severed the golden and flowing
Locks he had let grow long for a gift to the river Spercheüs.
Heavy of heart then he spake, as he looked o'er the wine-dark waters:
    "Ah, far other, Spercheüs, the vow of Peleus, my father,
That on returning to thee, to the well-loved land of my fathers,
I should clip off this hair unto thee, and a hecatomb holy
Offer, and sacrifice rams e'en there to the number of fifty
Over thy springs, where thou hast a demesne and an altar of incense.
So did the old man vow, but his thought thou hast noway accomplished.
Since then I do not return to the well-loved land of my fathers,
Unto the hero Patroclus my locks may I give to take with him."
    Thus he spake; and he placed the locks in the hands of his comrade
Well-loved; therewith he inspired in all a desire of lamenting.
Now had the light of the sun gone down while they were lamenting,
Had not quickly Achilles addressed Agamemnon close by him:
    "Atreus' son (for to *thy* words most will the host of Achaeans
Render obedience), 'tis theirs e'en to sate themselves with lamenting.
Now then bid them disperse from the funeral pile and their supper
Straightly make ready. The rest of this service we will attend to—
We that were nearest the dead man. The princes let tarry beside us."
    So, when he heard this word, the monarch of men, Agamemnon,
Gave a command for the folk to be scattered among the trim galleys
Straight; his closest friends stayed there and piled up the firewood,
Raised up a pyre—four-square, and the feet on each side were an hun-
Laid the corse on the top, their hearts sore-smitten with anguish. [dred—
Many the lusty sheep and many the crook-horned, shambling
Kine they flayed at the pyre, there busied themselves; but Achilles,
Noble of heart, took the fat of them all and enveloped the body
Wholly from head unto feet, and he piled the flayed victims about it.
Jars two-handled he placed thereon, filled with oil and with honey,
Leaning them up on the bier; and the bodies of four strong horses
Swiftly he cast on the pyre, the while he was heavily groaning.

Nine were the dogs that the monarch had owned and fed at his table;
Two did Achilles butcher and fling them aloft on the pyre.
Twelve were the valiant youths, all sons of magnanimous Trojans,
Slaughtered with blade of bronze: grim deeds he devised in his spirit.
Fire, resistless as iron, he set then to pasture upon it.
Loudly then did he groan and call on his comrade belovèd:

"Hail, Patroclus, even though gone to the palace of Hades,
Seeing that now I'm fulfilling all that I promised aforetime.
Twelve are the valiant youths, all sons of magnanimous Trojans,
Whom now the fire consumeth with thee. But Priam's son Hector
Not to the fire—much rather to dogs—I'll give to devour him."

Thus spake he with a threat. But no dogs were busied with Hector,
But Aphrodite, the daughter of Zeus, kept the dogs from his body
Night and day alike and anointed it richly with rose-sweet
Oil ambrosial, lest in the dragging Achilles should tear it.
Phoebus Apollo had brought a dark cloud o'er the body from heaven,
Letting it down on the plain, and the whole place there he enveloped
Whereon the body lay, lest haply the might of the sunbeams
Too soon shrivel his flesh round about on his limbs and his sinews.

Natheless the pyre of Patroclus, the fallen, would not yet take fire.
One thing further bethought him fleet-footed Achilles, the godlike:
Standing aside from the pyre, to two winds he offered a prayer,
Zephyr and Boreas, promising each a sacrifice splendid;
Pouring libations from goblet of gold, he earnestly prayed them
Come, that the wood make haste to enkindle, and all of the bodies
There be speedily burned in a fiery blaze. And then Iris,
Hearing his prayer, went swiftly away to the winds with the message.
They at the home of the blustering Zephyr were gathered together,
Holding a frolicsome feast, when quick came Iris among them,
Stopped on the threshold of stone. When they with their eyes did behold
All sprang up, and each one called her to come sit beside him.   [her,
She in her turn refused to sit down and delivered her message:

"No seat for me; I am going back to the streams of the ocean,
Off to the Aethiops' land, for there they are hecatombs off'ring
Unto th' immortals, that I too may share in the feasts, in the victims.
Only, Achilles is praying to Boreas now and the boist'rous

486

Zephyrus that ye may come (and he promises offerings splendid) —
That ye enkindle a flame on the pyre where lieth his comrade,
Fallen Patroclus, for whom the Achaeans all are lamenting."

Thus she spake and departed; and both of the winds in a tempest
Rose with a marvelous roar and whirled the clouds on before them.
Swiftly they came on their way, blowing over the deep, and the billow
Rose up under their whistling blast; and they came to the deep-loamed
Troyland, fell on the pyre, and the flames roared mightily blazing.
All night long they kept lashing the flames of the pyre together,
Shrilly whistling the while. And all night long fleet Achilles,
Holding a two-handled goblet, was drawing wine from the golden
Bowl; and he poured it out on the earth and wetted its surface,
Calling again and again on the soul of the hapless Patroclus.
Even as waileth a father when burning the bones of his offspring,
Son new-wedded, a woe in his death to his parents unhappy:
So did Achilles wail, as he burned the bones of his comrade,
Dragging himself round the blazing pyre and heavily groaning.

But at the hour when the morning star the light comes to herald
Over the earth, and after it Dawn spreads her mantle of saffron
Over the sea, then the fire burned down and the flame had subsided.
Back went the winds, betaking themselves again to their homeland,
Over the Thracian deep, which roared in the rage of its swollen
Waters. Then did Pelides, turning away from the pyre,
Lay himself down, o'erwearied; and sweet sleep lighted upon him.
Atreus' son and his company with him were gath'ring together;
As they approached Achilles, their noise and confusion awoke him.
Raising himself, he sat and uttered a word and addressed them:

"Atreus' son and the rest, ye princes of all the Achaeans,
First with the sparkling wine extinguish the flames of the pyre —
All of it, far as the fury of fire hath extended — and after
Let us collect the bones of Patroclus, the son of Menoetius,
Clearly distinguishing all; for easy it is to discern them,
Since he lay in the midst of the pyre; apart were the others
Burned on the edge in a mass, both heroes and horses together.
Them will we place and preserve in an urn of gold, with a double
Layer of fat, till I myself shall be hidden in Hades.

Be not the tomb very large that I bid you rear for Patroclus,
Toiling, but fitting—no more; hereafter indeed let th' Achaeans
Broaden and build it aloft, whoever of you in the full-oared
Galleys yet may be left behind, when I have departed."

    Thus he spake; they obeyed the fleet-footed scion of Peleus;
First with the sparkling wine they extinguished the flames of the pyre
Far as the flames had extended—and deep lay fallen the ashes.
Then with tears the white bones of their gentle comrade they gathered
Into a golden urn, with fat laid double around them.
This then they placed in the barrack and covered it o'er with fine linen.
Next then they marked out the barrow's circle and laid the foundations
All round the pyre and piled up earth in a loose heap upon it.
When they had heaped up the mound, they were moving away. But Achil-
Held the folk there and made them sit down in extended assembly, [les
Then brought forth from his ships both cauldrons and tripods as prizes,
Horses and mules, and many a head of his sturdy cattle;
Fair-girdled women as well and hoary iron he brought forth.

    First for the fleet car-racers he set forth excellent prizes:
Even a woman to win, accomplished in handiwork faultless,
Also a tripod with handles, in content twenty-two measures—
These for the first. For the second a mare he offered, unbroken,
Six years old; and the mare with a mule-foal also was pregnant.
Then for the third one a cauldron untouched of the fire he presented,
Beautiful, bright as when first it was made, and holding four measures.
Talents—two talents of gold—he set up for the man fourth in order.
Last, for the fifth one an urn two-bowled, untainted of fire.
Upright he stood and uttered a word in the midst of the Argives:

    "Atreus' son and the rest, all ye well-greavèd Achaeans,
These are the prizes set up in the lists and awaiting the horsemen.
Now if the games were to honor another of us, the Achaeans,
I should indeed bear surely the first prize off to my galleys,
Seeing ye know how far my steeds excel all the others,
For immortal they are; Poseidon it was who once gave them
Unto Peleus, my sire; in his turn upon me he bestowed them.
Natheless I will stay here, both I and my whole-hoofed horses,
They that have lost the renown of a charioteer so glorious,

The Funeral Pile of Patroclus

One so kindly, who often would pour smooth oil of the olive
Over their manes, whenever in clear bright water he washed them.
Both stand mourning for him even now, and the manes of the horses
Trail on the ground as they stand, their hearts o'erburdened with sorrow.
Get ye, the rest, to your places, whoe'er in the host of th' Achaeans
Putteth his faith in his steeds and the firm-fitted joints of his chariot."
　　Thus spake Peleus' son, and the chariot-racers bestirred them.
First by far to stand forth was the monarch of men, king Eumelus,
Son of Admetus, a man who excelled in the handling of horses.
Tydeus' stalwart son, Diomedes, was next in arising;
Under the yoke he led forth the horses of Tros, which aforetime
He from Aeneas had taken — Apollo rescued their master.
Atreus' fair-haired son, Menelaüs, was next in arising;
Zeus-sprung prince, and he yoked swift horses anon to his chariot,
Aethe, a mare of his brother's, his own steed also, Podargus.
Her Echepolus, a son of Anchises, gave Agamemnon,
Gave her as gift, that he might not follow to Ilium windy,
But might stay and enjoy his home, for to him Zeus had given
Wealth in abundance; he dwelt in the wide-lawned regions of Sicyon.
Her he brought under the yoke; for the race she was eagerly yearning.
Fourthly, Antilochus fitted his sleek-coated steeds for the contest,
Glorious scion of Nestor, the high-souled monarch of Pylus,
Him that was Neleus' son. The fleet-footed steeds, engendered
Even in Pylus, speeded his car. And his father beside him
Counseled him for his profit — himself of good understanding:
　　"When thou wert yet but a youngster, Antilochus, Zeus and Poseidon
Loved thee and taught thee rare arts — all kinds — in the handling of
Therefore now to instruct thee is noway easy or needed.　　　[horses.
Thou well enough understandest to wheel round posts; but thy horses —
Slowest in running! Methinketh the prospect before thee is gloomy.
Swifter, of course, are the steeds of the rest; however, the drivers
Neither in knowledge nor cunning are able at all to excel thee.
Come then, call to thy mind all manner of cunning, belovèd,
Lest the first prize appointed in some way haply elude thee.
Cunning availeth a woodman indeed far more than his muscle;
Cunning it is of the pilot, too, that out on the wine-dark

Waters guideth his swift ship ſtraight, though winds buffet fiercely;
Cunning forsooth of the driver of one car wins from his rival.
Whoe'er, putting his truſt in his horses alone and his chariot,
Carelessly wheeleth, and wide, about one post and the other,
He it is loseth control, and his racers veer in the race-course.
He that is cunning of mind, though driving inferior horses,
Ever is eyeing the post, and he makes a close turn, and, observing
Inſtantly how he must pull them ſtraight with the reins made of oxhide,
Holds them firmly in hand, as he watches the racer before him.

"Now I will mention a mark quite plain—it will not escape thee:
Over the ground a fathom in height there riseth a dry ſtump,
Whether of oak or of pine, in the rainſtorms ſtill undecaying.
Two white ſtones on either side have been planted against it,
There at a junction of roads—the race-track is level around it—
Whether a tombſtone it be for a mortal that perished aforetime,
Whether a past generation ordained it a goal in their racing—
Now, too, divine fleet-footed Achilles set this as a limit.
Drive quite near and graze it, almost, with thy horses and chariot,
Leaning a bit thyself—in the car well-knitted together—
Off to the left of thy team, and goad on sharply the off horse,
Shouting to him aloud, and give him the reins with thy fingers.
But at the turn of the course let thy nigh horse hug close the goal-post,
So that the hub of thy well-wrought wheel may seem just to graze its
Outermost edge; but carefully guard that the hub of thy chariot
Touch not the ſtone, lest thou wound thy horses and smash up thy char-
That were a joy to the others, to thee thyself a discredit   [iot—
Afterward; but, my dear son, use thy good underſtanding and foresight,
Seeing that, if at the turn thou drive on speedily past them,
There is not one that will then with a spurt overtake or pass by thee—
Nay, not e'en if he drove from behind thee the goodly Arion,
Fleet-footed ſteed of Adreſtus, a ſtrain come down from th' immortals,
Nay, nor Laomedon's ſteeds, the best bred horses in this land."

Thus spake Nelean Neſtor, resuming his seat at his ſtation,
When he thus to his son had imparted the gist of each matter.

Fifth Meriones fitted his sleek-coated ſteeds for the contest.
Then they mounted the cars and cast their lots in a helmet;

This Achilles began to shake, and forth leaped the lot of
Neſtor's scion, Antilochus; after him lordly Eumelus
Won him a place; and next came Atreus' son, Menelaüs,
Famed for his spear; and next Meriones; last of the drivers
Tydeus' son, the best of them all, drew the lot for his ſtation.
Side by side they were ſtanding; Achilles showed them the turn-post
Far on the level plain and ſtationed beside it as umpire
Phoenix, a match for a god and the former squire of his father,
Bidding him note and report the truth in regard to the runnings.

　　All at the selfsame time then lifted the lash to the horses;
All smote down with the reins and with words called loudly upon them
Eagerly. Over the plain they soon were rushing on swiftly
Far away from the galleys. Beneath each breast in the running
Hung the dust that they raised, like a gathering cloud or a whirlwind,
While on the breath of the breeze the manes flowed waving above them.
Now were the chariots skimming the earth, the all-bountiful mother,
Now upbounding into the air; and the drivers the meanwhile
Stood erect in their boxes; their hearts beat quick in their bosoms,
Each one yearning for viĉt'ry; and loudly thcy called to the horses,
Each, as enveloped in dust along on the plain he was flying.　　　[ing

　　Now as the fleet-footed ſteeds the last lap of the course were fulfill-
Back toward the foam-flecked sea, then truly the powers of each one
Shone forth; the pace of the ſteeds was ſtrained to the utmost, and
Then shot forward the fleet-footed mares of the scion of Pheres; [quickly
After them forward shot the ſtallions of king Diomedes,
Steeds of the breed of Tros; they were not far behind but close to him.
Every moment it seemed they would mount the car that preceded; [lus,
Warm with their breath were the shoulders broad and the back of Eume-
Seeing they flew along with their heads bended downward upon him.
Now he had passed him by or had left the race undecided,
Had not Phoebus Apollo, in wrath with the scion of Tydeus,
Stricken the shining lash from his hands, to favor Eumelus.
Tears of vexation gushed forth in a ſtream from the eyes of Tydides,
When he saw that the mares sped on ſtill faſter than ever,
While for lack of a whip *his* ſteeds were thrown out of their running.
Nor was Apollo unmarked of the goddess Athena, outwitting

Tydeus' son, and she followed the shepherd of hosts in a moment,
Gave him his lash, and imparted besides fresh strength to his horses.
Then in a fury she went hard after the son of Admetus.
First the goddess shivered the yoke of his horses, and sideways
Veered both mares from the course, and the tongue to earthward was
Out from the car he was rolled; beside the wheel he was fallen; [twisted;
Stripped was the skin all around his mouth and his nose and his elbows;
Bruised right over his brows was his forehead; the eyes of the hero
Flooded quickly with tears, and his full-toned utterance halted.
Swerving his whole-hoofed horses aside, drove past him Tydides,
Far out-leaping the rest of the teams, inasmuch as Athena
Put strength into his steeds and shed a glory upon him.
Next after him was driving fair-haired Menelaüs Atrides.
Loudly Antilochus shouted and called on the steeds of his father:
    "Ye, too, go in and win, and quicken your pace to the limit!
Not that I bid you at all strive after those chargers a-leading,
After the steeds of Tydides, the wise, into which hath Athena
Now put the speed of a victor, on him bestowing a glory.
Nay, overhaul ye Atrides' steeds — don't let them outstrip you;
Catch up quick, lest a mare pour scorn on your racing; for Aethe,
Aethe is only a mare; then why lag behind her, my hearties?
This I will tell you insooth; it will surely find a fulfilment:
No more tendance for you there will be in the stables of Nestor,
Shepherd of peoples! Anon with the keen-edged bronze he will slay you,
If, by remissness of yours, we get but the worst of the prizes.
After them! Hotly pursue! Speed onward amain at the quickest!
Meanwhile I will consider a plan, I will deftly devise it,
Nor will I let it escape me — to slip past him in the narrows."
    Thus spake he; and the horses, in fear of the voice of their master,
Sped on faster a little while; and Antilochus quickly —
Sturdy in battle — beheld there a road-bed sunken and narrow,
Even a rift in the earth, where gathering waters of winter
Tore off part of the track and gullied the road-bed along it.
There, to avoid their running abreast, Menelaüs was slowing.
Swerving his whole-hoofed horses aside, Antilochus drove on,
Out of the course, and turned them to one side, only a little.

BOOK XXIII

Atreus' son was alarmed and aloud to Antilochus shouted:

"Reckless in driving art thou, Antilochus. Pull in thy horses
(Strait is the road, but soon thou'lt find a place wider for passing),
Lest with my car thou collide and bring us both to disaster."

Thus spake he, but Antilochus drove on fiercer than ever,
Pressing his steeds with the goad, as had he not heard Menelaüs.
Far as the cast of a disc flung forward, over the shoulder,
When it is hurled by a man, by a young man testing his vigor:
So far raced they along. It was then that the mares of Atrides
Gave back, seeing that he of his own will slackened in urging,
Fearing the whole-hoofed steeds in the track, if once they collided,
Might overturn both well-knitted cars, while both of the drivers
Headlong should fall in the dust in their too eager striving for vict'ry.
Thus with a sharp rebuke fair-haired Menelaüs addressed him:

"Nestorid, never was born more malicious a mortal than thou art!
Go thy mad way — we Achaeans spoke false when we said thou wert pru-
Natheless not even so shalt thou gain thee a prize unchallenged." [dent.

Thus he spake. To his horses he called out loud as he shouted:

"Do not relax now, I pray you, nor stand still, grieving in spirit!
Their feet sooner than yours, yea, *their* knees sooner will fail them,
Wearied; for both in the freshness of youthful vigor are lacking."

Thus spake he; and the horses, in fear of the voice of their master,
Quickened their pace, and they closed up fast on the runners before them.

Now were the Argives seated in concourse and watching the horses,
As, enveloped in dust, along the plain they were flying.
Then was the chief of the Cretans, Idomeneus, first to distinguish
Cars; for he sat outside of the concourse, up high in a clear space.
Also he heard, loud shouting, a far-off voice, and he knew it
Well, and distinguished one horse, conspicuous, leading the running —
Chestnut in color of coat all over and only its forehead
Marked with a circular star all-white as the moon in her fulness.
Upright he stood, and he uttered a word in the midst of the Argives:

"O my friends, ye princes and counseling chiefs of the Argives,
Do I alone distinguish the horses, or haply do ye too
Mark them? The team of horses now leading seems to be diff'rent,
Also the driver thereof now seemeth another. The fillies

Running ahead up to then must have met with an accident somewhere
There in the plain; for I saw them before coming round the far end-post.
Now nowhere can I see them, although my two eyes are peering
Everywhere, e'en as I gaze all over the plain of the Trojans.
Could the reins have slipped from the driver's hands? Was he able
Noway rightly to guide round the post? Did he fail in the turning?
There perchance he fell out, methinketh, and smashed up his chariot;
There have his mares got away from the track, unbridled of spirit.
Nevertheless do ye also ſtand up and look, for I cannot
Clearly, for my part, discern; but to me now the leading man seemeth
One of Aetolian birth to be, though a prince 'mongst the Argives,
Even the horse-taming Tydeus' son, Diomedes, the mighty."
    Then fleet Oïlean Ajax in ugly manner rebuked him:
    "Why dost thou prate prematurely, Idomeneus, seeing the horses,
High-ſtepping mares, away far over the plain are a-speeding?
Neither art thou among all the Argives *so* much the youngest,
Neither from out of thy head do *thine* eyes look ever the keenest;
Yet thou'rt always boaſting with words; it beseemeth thee noway
Thus to be prating; for others are here who are better than thou art.
Those are the same ones leading, the fillies that ſtarted as leaders,
Mares of Eumelus; he ſtandeth himself, and the reins he is holding."
    Thereat the Cretan leader was vexed and answered him, saying:
    "Ajax, perverted in judgment, a maſter of wrangling, in all else
Least of the Argives, because thy mind is forever unfriendly,
Come on then, let us wager a tripod or haply a cauldron,
Both agreeing on Atreus' son, Agamemnon, as umpire,
Which of the teams is leading — that thou mayest learn by thy paying."
    Thus spake he; and at once fleet Ajax, son of Oïleus,
Rose up in anger to answer in harsh words Creta's commander.
Then ſtill further the ſtrife had proceeded and waxen between them,
Had not Achilles himself ſtood up with a word of discretion:
    "Nay now! Be not exchanging your harsh words thus in contention,
Ajax, Idomeneus also, with ill speech; this is unseemly.
Were it another that did it, yourselves would be deeply indignant.
But do ye keep your seats in the concourse and watch ye with ſteadfast
Eyes on the horses; for soon, in their eager desire for viƈt'ry,

All will arrive right here; then both of you doubtless will know your
Argive horses, that come in first and those that come second."

　　Thus spake he. And Tydeus' son came driving close by them.
Ever he'd bring down the lash on the horses' shoulders. The horses
Lifted high their feet and quickly covered their distance.
Ever sprinkles of dust kept pelting and beating the driver,
Whileas the car, overlaid with gold and with tin in rich splendor,
Ran at the heels of the swift-footed horses; and slight were the traces
Left behind by the metal tires of the wheels of the chariot,
Marked in the thin-laid dust — the team so swiftly was flying!
Mid in the concourse he halted; and sweat gushed forth in abundance
Earthward, descending alike from the heads and the chests of the horses.
Down from the glittering car to the ground leaped out Diomedes,
Then on the yoke of the steeds up-tilted the lash. His attendant,
Stalwart Sthenelus, tarried no whit but at once on the guerdon
Laid hold and gave the dame to the care of his high-hearted comrades,
Also the tripod with ears. Then he loosed the steeds from the harness.

　　Next after him Nelean Antilochus drove in his horses,
Victor by cunning, for not by his speed he had passed Menelaüs.
Yet even so Menelaüs was driving his swift steeds anigh him.
Far as a horse is ahead of the wheel, when drawing his master,
Galloping on full speed and drawing the chariot behind him,
Whileas the tipmost hairs of his wide-blown tail on the wheel-tire
Touch — for it runneth behind him anigh, and the distance is little
'Twixt tire and horse, as over the plain afar he is speeding:
So far behind the faultless Antilochus ran Menelaüs
Now at the finish, at first by cast of a discus behind him;
Yet he was speedily gaining; the high-wrought mettle of Aethe
Constantly rose, the sleek-coated mare of king Agamemnon.
Had but the race been longer still for both of these heroes,
Then Menelaüs had passed and not left undecided the contest.
After them goodly Meriones, squire of Idomeneus, followed;
Left a whole spear-cast he was behind far-famed Menelaüs,
Seeing that slowest of all the teams were his sleek-coated horses;
He most incompetent was in driving a car in a contest.
Last came, trailing behind all others the son of Admetus,

Dragging his beautiful car and driving his horses before him.
When he saw thus his friend, the divine fleet-footed Achilles
Pitied him; rising, he spake wingèd words 'mid the Argives assembled:
 "Last, but the best man of all comes driving his whole-hoofed horses.
Natheless come, and let us award him a prize, as is seemly,
Even the second; the first shall take the scion of Tydeus."
 Thus spake he; and they all in approval applauded his order.
Now had he given Eumelus the mare — the Achaeans applauded —
Only Antilochus, son of the great-hearted Nestor of Pylus,
Rose with a claim of his rights and answered Achilles Pelides:
 "Sorely angered with thee shall I be, O Achilles, now if thou
Bringest this word to fulfilment: my prize thou art bent upon taking,
Thinking that he and his car and swift-footed steeds were disabled
Spite of his excellence! Natheless he ought to have prayed to th' im-
Then had he not come in the last of all in the running.   [mortals;
But if thou pity the wight, and he in thy heart is so cherished —
Lo! in thy barrack is gold, yea, also bronze in abundance;
Sheep, too, and handmaids thou hast, and there hast thou whole-hoofed
Take thou, give him of these, then, a prize hereafter, a nobler, [horses.
Or even straightway now, that th' Achaeans so may applaud thee.
But to surrender the mare I refuse. For her let make trial
Whatever man be willing to match my hands in a battle."
 Thus he spake; and smiled fleet-footed, godlike Achilles,
Pleased with Antilochus' spirit, for *he* was a comrade belovèd.
Answering him in his turn, he spake wingèd words and addressed him:
 "If thou, Antilochus, biddest me give aught else to Eumelus
Out of my store in addition, I haste to accomplish it also.
Yea, I will give him the corselet I stripped from Asteropaeus,
Bronzen, and on it a casting of tin bright-gleaming is moulded
Running around and about it. To him it will prove of much value."
 Thus he spake, then bade Automedon, comrade belovèd,
Bring from his barrack the corselet; he went and to him he brought it.
Then in the hand of Eumelus he placed it — who joyed to receive it.
 Therewith rose Menelaüs among them, aggrievèd in spirit,
Vehement, too, in his wrath with Antilochus; quickly a herald
Placed in his hand a sceptre, then shouted aloud to the Argives,

Calling for silence. And *he* then, a man like a god, spake among them:
   "What is this thou hast done, Antilochus, prudent aforetime?
Verily thou hast put shame on my skill, interfered with my horses,
Thrusting in front thine own, which were far worse truly than mine are.
Come now, ye that are leaders and counseling chiefs of the Argives,
Render decision between us two, with favor to neither,
Lest some day someone shall say of the bronze-clad Achaeans:
'Only through false pretense Menelaüs went off with the filly
(Overreaching Antilochus), seeing that worse were his horses
Far, but himself was higher in rank and in princely dominion.'
Nay, I will force it myself to an issue — no Danaans ever
Then shall reproach me, I ween; for the trial shall be even-handed.
Come then, nurseling of Zeus — as the ordinance saith — come hither,
Stand in the face of the steeds and the war-car, Antilochus; hold thou
Lifted in hand the flexible lash thou'st wielded in driving;
Touching the steeds, by the shaker of earth, earth's mighty enfolder,
Swear thou didst not foul my car with treachery wilful."
   Prudent Antilochus then in his turn addressed Menelaüs:
   "Bear with me now. I am younger by far, O king Menelaüs,
Younger than thou, far higher in station and older than I am.
Thyself knowest the way that a young man's trespass occurreth,
Seeing his mind is hastier far, and flighty his counsel.
So let thy heart endure. The mare of myself I surrender,
Even the filly I won. And if aught else, too, thou demandest,
Aught that is greater of mine, I would rather surrender it also
Straight unto thee, O nurseling of Zeus, than to fall thus forever
Out of a place in thy heart, in the eyes of immortals a sinner."
   Thus spake the son of the great-hearted Nestor and led up the filly,
Placed her forthwith in the hands of prince Menelaüs, whose heart was
Warmed, as when falleth the dew on the ears of corn of the rip'ning
Harvest, even the season when all the grainfields are bristling:
Even so warmed was the spirit in *thy* breast, O Menelaüs.
Then he lifted his voice, and with wingèd words he addressed him:
   "Lo! I will banish, myself, now all anger, Antilochus, from me,
Wroth as I was; for indeed thou never wert flighty aforetime,
Never before light-minded; this time youth conquered discretion.

Next time have thou a caution nor try overreaching thy betters.
Not so soon had another of all the Achaeans dissuaded
Me; but *thou* hast, for *thou* hast abundantly labored and suffered,
Thou and thy father, the goodly, and also thy brother, for my sake.
So will I yield to thy prayer and even give thee the filly,
Though she is mine, that also this folk may all understand it
Well, that ne'er overbearing my heart is and never unyielding."

    Spake he, and unto Noëmon, Antilochus' trusty companion,
Gave he the mare and took for himself the glittering cauldron.
Then did Meriones take up the two gold talents, the guerdon
Fourth—for he drave in that order—the fifth thus leaving unclaimèd.
Therewith Achilles gave it to Nestor, the two-bowled goblet,
Bearing it up through the concourse of Argives, and spake, standing by
    "Lo now, this be a guerdon for thee too, sire, a treasure!   [him:
Ay, a memento this of Patroclus' funeral. Never
Thou shalt behold him among the Achaeans again. And I give it
Unwon, since thou'lt strive not in boxing indeed nor in wrestling;
Nor for the javelin throw wilt thou enter, nor in the foot race
Run; for already the burden of grim old age weigheth on thee."

    Thus he spake; in his hand he placed it; with joy he received it,
Lifted his voice, and with wingèd words then Nestor addressed him:
    "Yea now, all these things, my child, thou hast fittingly spoken:
Neither my limbs nor my feet are now sound; and my fists no longer
Swing out light from my shoulders amain this side and the other.
Would I were young once more and my strength unshaken within me,
Even as when the Epeians were burying lord Amarynceus
There at Buprasium, whileas his sons held games for the monarch.
No one then could be found that was like unto me, of Epeians
Not one, neither of Pylians, nor yet of Aetolian great hearts.
Boxing, I first overcame Clytomedes, scion of Enops;
Wrestling, Ancaeus of Pleuron, a valiant who stood up against me.
Racing on foot with Iphiclus, fast as he was, I outran him;
Hurling the spear, I surpassed in that Polydorus and Phyleus;
Then in the chariot race alone did the two sons of Actor
Beat me, forcing ahead (the two of them), jealous for vict'ry;
Wherefore the principal prizes were left behind with those brothers.

These two were twins. The one would handle the reins with a firmness —
Handle with firmness — while one with the lash directed the horses.
Such I was *once!* Let the younger men now in *their* turn enter
Contests such as are these. I must yield to the suasion of grievous
Old age now; but of yore I made my mark 'mongst the heroes.
On then! Honor thy comrade with all these funeral contests!
Gladly I take this gift, and my heart is delighted in knowing
Thou dost remember me aye as a friend, unforgetting the honor
Wherewith 'tis meet that I among the Achaeans be honored.
Now unto thee may the gods grant bountiful grace in requital."

　　　Thus he spake; and Pelides was gone through the throng of Achae-
When he to all this tale of Neleus' scion had listened.　　　　　　[ans,
Then for the strenuous boxing match he set forth the prizes:
Leading a stanch mule forward, he tethered her there in the concourse —
Six years old, unbroken, the hardest of all to be broken.
But for the loser the hero appointed a twin-bowled goblet.
Upright he stood and uttered a word in the midst of the Argives:
　　"Atreus' son and the rest, all ye well-greavèd Achaeans,
These are the prizes for which two bravest heroes we summon:
Let them deliver their blows with their hands uplifted; to whomso
Granteth Apollo endurance, so all the Achaeans shall judge it,
He shall take the stanch mule and return with her to his barrack;
Who, however, is vanquished shall bear off the twin-bowled goblet."

　　　Thus spake he; and at once a man rose, goodly and stalwart,
Panopeus' scion Epeüs, a man accomplished in boxing.
He on the sturdy mule laid his hand and shouted amid them:
　　"Let him come hither, who's going to bear off the twin-bowled gob-
As for the mule, I say, no other Achaean shall take her,　　　　　[let!
Winning the contest of boxing; in this I claim to be champion.
Is it not haply enough that I'm wanting in war? It is never
Given to any one man to excel in all kinds of action.
This I will tell you in sooth; it will surely find a fulfilment:
All in a heap I will break his bones and bruise up his body;
So let his friends abide right here in a huddle, to bear him
Haply forth from the ring, whenso by my hands he is vanquished."

　　　Thus he spake. The others all mutely attended in silence.

Rose up against him only Euryalus, peer of a godhead,
Son of Meciſteus, him that was Talaüs' son and a sovereign.
He had come unto Thebes on a time for Oedipus fallen,
E'en for his burial. There he defeated all the Cadmeans.
Him Diomedes, famed for his lance, made ready for combat,
Cheering him on with his words, and he heartily wished him the viĉt'ry.
First he engirdled a belt all round and about him, and after
Handed him well-cut thongs from the hide of a bull of the paſture.
So were the boxers girt; to the midst of the ring they descended.
Thereupon both uplifted their ſtalwart hands for the ſtruggle,
Fell then each on the other, and clashed fiſts heavy in battle.
Terrible sounded the grinding of teeth, and a sweat was upon them
Pouring from all their limbs. But he sprang up, the goodly Epeüs,
Smiting Euryalus' cheek as he peered for an op'ning. No longer
Then could he ſtand, for right there his glorious limbs sank beneath him.
As when a fish is tossed on a sea-beach that tangle hath covered,
Under the north wind's ripple — and darkling a billow hath hid it:
Even so smitten he leaped; but the great-hearted viĉtor Epeüs
Caught him and lifted him up with his hands. Then his comrades belovèd
Stood round and led him off, with trailing feet, through the concourse,
Spitting thick clots of blood, and his head he was sidewise drooping;
Down he sank in a swoon, and his comrades set him amid them;
Then they went back themselves and fetched him the two-bowled gob-
  Next, for the third event Pelides appointed the prizes,   [let.
Offered the Danaans all for the ſtrenuous contest of wreſtling:
Unto the winner a tripod huge to ſtand over the fire,
Worth, at th' Achaeans' rating among them, a dozen of oxen.
Unto the loser he offered among them as guerdon a woman
Skilful in manifold work; four oxen they reckoned her value.
Upright he ſtood and uttered a word in the midst of the Argives:
  "Rise up, ye that in this event will also make trial."
  Thus he spake; then arose the great Telamonian Ajax;
Stood up the crafty-minded Odysseus of many devices.
So were the wreſtlers girt; to the midst of the ring they proceeded.
First they clasped in their arms with their ſtalwart hands one another;
Like unto rafters they seemed, that some famed builder together

Fitteth on high-built mansion, to baffle the might of a tempest.
Under the powerful hands of the wrestlers, firm in their grapple,
Both of their backbones creaked, and sweat poured down them abundant.
Thick were the weals that sprang up along on the ribs and the shoulders,
Weals dark-purpling with blood, while still those obstinate wrestlers
Struggled amain for the vict'ry and winning the rich-wrought tripod.
Nor was Odysseus able to trip and to bring him to earthward,
Neither was Ajax again, for Odysseus' prowess defied him.
Now as the twain were beginning to weary the well-greaved Achaeans,
Thus spake great Telamonian Ajax unto his rival:

"Zeus-born son of Laërtes, Odysseus of many devices,
Lift me, else I will lift thee; and Zeus shall care for the issue."

Thus he spake and heaved, but Odysseus forgot not the right trick:
Deftly he kicked him behind, where bendeth the knee, and he threw him
Backward, loosened of limb; and Odysseus followed him, falling
Down on his breast, while the folk all stared in utter amazement.
Next in his turn much-enduring, godlike Odysseus attempted　　[him,
Hoisting; he moved him a bit from the ground but could not quite lift
Hooked his knee in his rival's; and down on the ground both were fallen,
Close the one by the other, and both with the dust were defilèd.
Both upstarted again, and a third time now they had wrestled,
Had not Achilles himself stood up and wisely restrained them:

"Struggle no more with each other nor wear out your bodies with
Vict'ry belongeth to both of you. Equal prizes receiving,　　[bruises;
Go on your way, that other Achaeans may enter a contest."

Thus spake he. They hearkened with readiness, heeding his counsel,
Wiped the dust of the ring from their bodies, and put on their tunics.

Forthwith the scion of Peleus appointed the prizes for fleetness:
First was a bowl of silver for mixing, fair-wrought and containing
Measures six, in all of the earth far outstanding in beauty,
Seeing the cunningest craftsmen of Sidon had skilfully wrought it;
Men of Phoenicia over the wine-dark waters had brought it,
Landed it safe in the harbor, and giv'n it a gift unto Thoas.
Paying a ransom for Priam's son, Lycaon; Euneüs,
Scion of Jason, gave it in turn to the hero Patroclus.
This as a prize Achilles now offered, to honor his comrade,

Unto the man who should prove the fleetest of foot in the race-course.
Then for the second he offered an ox, huge and heavy with fatness.
Third and last of the prizes a gold half-talent he offered.
Upright he ſtood and uttered a word in the midst of the Argives:
  "Rise up, ye that in this event will also make trial."
    Thus he spake; and at once fleet Ajax, son of Oïleus,
Rose, and Odysseus of many devices; Antilochus followed,
Scion of Neſtor; all youths in his turn he outſtripped in his fleetness.
Side by side they were ſtanding; Achilles showed them the turn-poſts.
Forced from the scratch was the pace, and quickly the son of Oïleus
Shot to the lead; and after him sped the godlike Odysseus
Close as the weaver's rod is close to the breast of a woman
Beauteous-girdled, a woman that draweth it near, as she passeth
Deft in her fingers the shuttle along on the warp, and she holds it
Close to her breast: e'en so ran Odysseus nigh and behind him
Trod in his tracks or ever the ſtirred dust rose up around him.
Down on the head of Oïleus the breath of the godlike Odysseus
Poured, as he ran ever lightly; and all the Achaeans applauded
Loud, as he ſtrove for the viĉt'ry, and cheered his ſtrenuous labor.
But as they ran the last lap of the course, then inſtant Odysseus
Offered a prayer in his soul to the bright-eyed goddess Athena:
  "Hear me, goddess, and come, to *my* feet, I pray, a good helper."
    So spake he in petition; and, hearing, Pallas Athena
Lightened the hero's limbs, his legs and his arms up above them.
Just as they now were about to pounce on the prize set before them,
Ajax slipped as he ran (for Athena hampered his running),
Where had been poured out refuse of slain loud-bellowing cattle,
Kine that the fleet Achilles had slaughtered to honor Patroclus;
Ajax's noſtrils and mouth were filled with the refuse of cattle.
Then much-enduring, godlike Odysseus took up the mixer,
Seeing he came in first, famed Ajax winning the bullock.
Ajax ſtood with his hands on the horn of the ox of the paſture,
Sputt'ring refuse away, and he spake in the midst of the Argives:
  "Out on it! Surely the goddess hampered my feet, that of old time
Taketh her ſtand by Odysseus and helpeth him, like as a mother."
    Thus spake he; but they all in merriment laughed to behold him.
504

Lastly Antilochus lifted the last prize up, and he bore it,
Smiling, away, as he spake a word in the midst of the Argives:
    "All of you know, dear comrades, and yet I will tell you: th' im-
Vouchsafe e'en to this day unto elders tokens of honor.   [mortals
Ajax indeed is my senior in years, though only a little;
But of an earlier race, of a past generation, is this man.
Truly is he of a green old age (men say), and Achaeans
Hardly can rival his fleetness of foot, save only Achilles."
    Thus he spake and would honor the fleet-footed scion of Peleus.
Thereat Achilles made him an answer in words and addressed him:
    "Not unrewarded thy words of praise, Antilochus, shall be,
But I will render a gold half-talent to thee in addition."
    Thus he spake; in his hand he placed it; with joy he received it.
    Thereupon Peleus' son brought forward and laid in the concourse
'Mid them a spear, long-shadowed, along with a shield and a helmet,
Arms that were once Sarpedon's, from whom Patroclus had stripped
Upright he stood and uttered a word in the midst of the Argives: [them.
    "These are the prizes for which two bravest heroes we summon,
Clothed in armor to win them. With bronze flesh-cutting equip you,
Then make trial in sight of the war-host, each of the other.
Which of you two with his thrust first shall reach the fair flesh of the
Grazing a vital part—and draw dark blood through the armor, [other—
Him as a guerdon I'll give this sword—it is Thracian and goodly,
Studded with silver. I took it as spoil from Asteropaeus.
Then they may bear off the armor, the twain, and hold it in common.
Fair the feast we will set for the combatants here in my barracks."
    Thus he spake. Then arose the great Telamonian Ajax;
Tydeus' stalwart son, Diomedes, was next in arising.
Now the heroes, when armed on either side of the war-throng,
Met in the midway space of the two hosts, eager for combat,
Terribly glaring; and wonder confounded all the Achaeans.
Now as they came close up in the onrush 'gainst one another,
Thrice they assailed and thrice in a rush of an onset collided.
Thereupon Ajax, with lunge at the shield all evenly rounded,
Smote but reached no flesh, for a breastplate held off the javelin.
Over the rim of his shield, full ample, the scion of Tydeus

Aimed at his throat still aye with the point of his radiant javelin.
Smitten with terror for Ajax, the host of Achaeans commanded
Both to desist and to take up the prizes in equal division.
But to Tydides the hero the mighty sabre accorded,
Bringing him also the scabbard with well-cut baldric appended.

 Next the scion of Peleus brought forth a huge lump of metal,
Unwrought—aforetime often the might of Eëtion would hurl it.
When he had slain that ruler, fleet-footed, godlike Achilles
Brought it away in his galleys along with other possessions.
Upright he stood and uttered a word in the midst of the Argives:
 "Rise up, ye that in this event will also make trial.
E'en if the fields of the winner be far off, teeming with fatness,
Yet for a lustrum of years, in their circuit revolving, will always
This be enough for his use; nor ever, if needy of iron,
Shepherd or plowman shall fare to the city; but this will supply him."

 Thus spake he; and arose the steadfast in war, Polypoetes;
Rose up the valiant might of Leonteus, a match for immortals;
Ajax, Telamon's son, rose up, and the godlike Epeüs.
Lined up, they took their places; and godlike Epeüs then took it,
Whirled it and flung it; th' Achaeans, at seeing, all burst into laughter.
Second, away off hurled it Leonteus, a scion of Ares;
Third in the order of hurling was great Telamonian Ajax.
Out from his stalwart hand, and beyond all the others he flung it.
But when the steadfast in war, Polypoetes, took up the metal—
Far as a man that is herder of kine may hurtle his herdsman's
Staff, and along past the cows of the herd the staff flies a-whizzing—
So far beyond all the space of the concourse he hurled it. The people
Shouted aloud. The companions of Polypoetes, the mighty,
Rose up and carried away to the hollow galleys the king's prize.

 Next he appointed the archers a guerdon, dark-colored iron:
Axes he set in the midst—ten two-edged, ten of them one-edged.
Then he erected a mast of a dark-prowed galley afar off
There in the sands and a fluttering pigeon fastened upon it
Tight, with a fine cord tied by the foot, and bade them shoot arrows
At her: "Whoever shall hit the timid dove with his arrow,
All these two-edged axes shall *he* take and carry home with him.

Whoso misses the bird yet hits the cord with his arrow —
Seeing his shot is the worse — he shall win him the one-edged axes."
     Thus he spake. Thereupon rose up lord Teucer, the mighty;
After him goodly Meriones, squire of Idomeneus, followed.
Lots then they took and shook in a bronze-bound helmet; and Teucer
Drew the first place with his lot; and he ſtraightway sped him an arrow
Mightily then, but he made no vow to the lord that he'd offer
E'en an oblation of firſtling lambs, a hecatomb splendid.
So then he missed the bird, for Apollo grudged him to hit it.
Natheless he did hit the cord, where the foot of the pigeon was fettered;
Clean off was cut the ſtring by the bronze of the bitter arrow.
Skyward darted the pigeon; the cord from the maſthead dangled
Down toward the earth; and loud were the cheers of all the Achaeans.
Thereat Meriones haſted and caught from the fingers of Teucer
Quickly the bow — he'd been holding an arrow while Teucer was aiming.
Quickly he uttered a vow to offer far-darting Apollo
E'en an oblation of firſtling lambs, a hecatomb splendid.
High up under the clouds he beheld the timid dove flying.
There, as she circled about, right under a pinion he ſtruck her.
Clean through her passed the dart; and it fell to the earth and, alighting,
Faſtened itself in front of Meriones' foot. But the pigeon,
Lighting again on the mast of the dark-prowed galley beneath her,
Hung down from it her neck; there drooped thick-feathered her pinions.
Flitting, her soul left quickly the limbs of the pigeon; her body
Dropped down far from the mast, and the folk sat gazing aſtonied.
All ten two-edged axes Meriones lifted and bore them
Off; but the singles were borne to his hollow galleys by Teucer.
     Laſtly Pelides brought out a spear far-shadowed and set it
Down in the ring, and a kettle untainted of fire — a bullock's
Worth — and embossèd with flowers. Then rose up hurlers of javelins;
Rose up Atrides first, wide-ruling lord Agamemnon;
After him goodly Meriones, squire of Idomeneus, followed.
Spake then also amid them fleet-footed, godlike Achilles:
     "Atreus' son, forasmuch as we know how far thou excellest
All — how *thou* hast proved to be best in the power of thy caſting,
Therefore now, I pray, to thy hollow ships with this guerdon

Go thou; but unto the hero Meriones give we the javelin,
If thou consent in thy heart; for *my* part I would advise it."
　　Thus spake he; and the monarch of men, Agamemnon, assented.
So to Meriones gave he the javelin of bronze; and the hero
Unto the herald Talthybius delivered the beauteous guerdon.

ILIAD · XXIV · (Ω)

Omega sings the Exsequies
And Hector's redemptory prise.

So the assembly broke up; the folks were scattered: each troop
Went to its own swift ships. All others bethought them of supper,
Ay, and the sweetness of sleep, to joy in it; only Achilles
Ever would weep at rememb'ring his dear-loved comrade, and never
Sleep came upon him, all-conquering sleep; nay, this way and that he
Turned, as he longed for Patroclus, his manhood and excellent valor —
Yea, all the skeins of woe they had suffered and wound up together,
Facing the battles of men and cleaving the perilous billows —
While he remembered all this, he poured forth tears in profusion.
Tossing, he'd lay him down on one side, then on the other,
Now on his back or his face, and anon uprising would wander
Forth all frantic with grief by the salt-sea shore; and the morning
Never would find him asleep, as she rose o'er beaches and billows.
But whensoever he yoked his fleet-footed steeds to his chariot,
Hector's corse he would bind behind his car for to drag him;
Thrice he would hale him around the tomb of the fallen Menoetius'
Son and then in his barrack would rest again; and the body,
Stretched out prone in the dust, he permitted to lie. But Apollo
Guarded his flesh from disfigurement quite, for he pitied the hero
Even in death; and completely he covered him round with his golden
Aegis, lest, when he dragged him, Achilles should tear him.

Shamefully thus he entreated the godlike Hector in frenzy.
Now as the blessed gods beheld him, they pitied the hero,
Ay, they incited the keen-eyed slayer of Argus to steal him.
This was the pleasure of all of the others, but never of Hera
Nor of Athena, the bright-eyed maid, nor yet of Poseidon;
Nay, they persisted in hating the city of Ilium holy,
Priam, and all Troy-folk, as at first, for the blind Alexander's

509

Sin; he affronted those goddesses, when they came to his steading,
Whereas he praised the one who brought him lechery fatal.
But when the morning, the twelfth thereafter, had risen upon them,
Then it was Phoebus Apollo began to address the immortals:

"Hard of heart are ye gods and cruel! Hath Hector, pray, never
Burned thighs of spotless oxen and unblemished goats on your altars?
Now ye have not the courage to rescue even his body,
So that his wife may behold him again, and his child, and his mother,
Priam, his father, and also the people of Troy; they would promptly
Burn up his body with fire and give him due funeral honors.
Fain are ye gods, howe'er, to abet the cruel Achilles,
Nowise just in his passion, inflexibly fixed in the purpose
Held in his breast, of a temper as savage as lion's in fury,
Whenso with violent might and with haughty spirit that lion
Goeth to ravage the flocks of mortals and batten upon them.
So hath Achilles renounced all pity, and reverence even
Faileth him now, which a man both harmeth and profiteth amply.
Many a man, methinketh, shall lose one dearer than this one,
Whether a son, may be, or a brother, the son of his mother —
Yet he hath ceased, no doubt, from his weeping and sore lamentation,
Seeing the fates have implanted a heart of endurance in mortals.
This man, however, since taking the dear life of Hector, the godlike,
Binds him still to his car and drags him around his dear comrade's
Burial place. Not fairer nor better is that for Achilles!
Let him, good though he be, beware lest he waken our anger,
Seeing he foully entreats the insensate clay in his frenzy."

Then, with kindling wrath, the white-armed Hera addressed him:
"This proposition, O lord of the silver bow, might be valid,
If ye would mete like honor to Hector along with Achilles.
Hector was only a mortal and nursed at the breast of a woman;
Child of a goddess Achilles is; and I of mine own self
Nurtured her, reared her, bestowed her myself on a husband in wedlock,
Even on Peleus, him that proved dear to the heart of th' immortals.
All ye attended her bridal, ye gods, and among them with lyre
Thou, too, comrade of villains, faithless forever, wert feasting." [ing:

Thereupon Zeus, the compeller of storm-clouds, answered her say-

Hector's Body Dragged at the Car of Achilles

"Do not be utterly venting thy spleen on the deities, Hera.
Not unto both shall the honor be like; but even so Hector
Dearest was to the gods — of the mortals dwelling in Ilium —
Dearest at least unto me, for he failed not in gifts that were pleasing.
Never an altar of mine that wanted a well-balanced banquet,
Off'ring of drink or of meat, whatever in worship is due us.
Now, however, we'll talk no further of stealing the valiant
Hector; it could not be hid from Achilles, seeing his mother
Ever stays at his side, alike in the day and the night time.
Nay, but I wish that someone of the gods would call to my presence
Thetis, that I might speak a wise word unto her, that Achilles
Gifts may haply accept from Priam in ransom for Hector."

Spake he; and storm-footed Iris arose to bear her the message.
Midway between the rugged Imbros and Samothrace islands
Into the dark sea she leaped, and the mere closed roaring above her.
Down to the depths of the sea she plunged like a leaden sinker,
Which, on the horn of an ox of the field, as a gimp, firmly fastened,
Sinks in the sea, bringing death and doom to ravenous fishes.
Thetis she found in a hollow cave; close-gathered around her
Other goddesses sat, sea nymphs; in the midst of them Thetis
Wept for the doom of her faultless son; to her grief, he was destined
Far from the land of his fathers in deep-loamed Troyland to perish.
Close to her side came Iris, the fleet-footed, now and addressed her:

"Thetis, arise! for Zeus, of counsel immutable, calls thee."

Then unto her did Thetis, the silver-footed, make answer:

"Wherefore biddeth he me, that godhead mighty? I shame me
Now with immortals to mingle; unending the woes of my spirit.
Natheless I go, nor his word shall be vain, whatever he sayeth."

Thus she spake and enwrapped her, the goddess divine, in a dark-
Vesture — never was garment in color blacker than that one.   [hued
Forth went she then, and before her, shod with the wind, swift Iris
Led the way; all round them the deep sea sundered its billows.
Now, at the shore of the waters emerging, they flew up to heaven,
Found there Zeus of the far-borne voice. Around him together
Sat all the rest of the blessèd gods who live on forever.
Down at the side of Father Zeus sat Thetis; Athena

Yielded her place; and Hera put in her hand a fair golden
Goblet and cheered her with words. Then Thetis drank and returned it.
Then among them the father of men and of gods began speaking:
    "Goddess Thetis, in spite of thy grief thou art come to Olympus.
Grief unceasing thou hast in thy heart; I myself also know it.
Yet even so I will tell thee why I have summoned thee hither.
Nine days now hath been raging contention among the immortals
Touching Achilles, waster of cities, and Hector's dead body.
Some are inciting the keen-eyed slayer of Argus to steal him.
This, though, now is the glory I fain would accord to Achilles,
Keeping thy love and thy rev'rence for me for ages to follow:
Speed thee betimes to the army and bear thy son my commandment.
Tell him the gods are indignant with him, and of all the immortals
Me hath it angered most, that he holdeth in frantic distemper
Hector beside the curve-beaked galleys and hath not released him.
Haply he may fear me and give up the body of Hector.
Meanwhile I will send Iris down unto great-hearted Priam
Bidding him go to the ships of th' Achaeans his dear son to ransom,
Carrying gifts that may serve to gladden the heart of Achilles."
    Thus he spake; and, obedient, Thetis, the silvery-footed
Goddess, dropped like a flash from the pinnacle peaks of Olympus.
Into the barrack she came of her son, and there then she found him
Heavily groaning, the while his comrades beloved were about him
Eagerly busied, intent on serving the meal of the morning:
Shaggy and huge, already a sheep lay slain in the barrack.
Close by his side she seated herself, his worshipful mother,
Stroked him with gentle caress, then spake a word and addressed him:
    "How long, my child, with bitter lamenting and grievous affliction
Wilt thou ever devour thy heart, of food never mindful
Or of the couch. 'Tis a good thing in love to commingle with woman.
Thou, to my sorrow, not long shalt have life; but I tell thee, already
Death and the heavy hand of fate are standing close by thee.
Now then quickly give ear, for Zeus's messenger am I:
Saith he, the gods are indignant with thee, and of all the immortals
Him hath it angered most, that thou keepest in frantic distemper
Hector beside thy curve-beaked galleys and hast not released him.

514

The Judgment of Paris

Come then, deliver him up and accept for the body a ransom."

Then in answer in turn fleet-footed Achilles addressed her:

"So be it; he may return with the corse, who bringeth the ransom,
If in serious earnest th' Olympian himself so commandeth."   [mother,

Thus, at the gath'ring of galleys those twain, the son and his
Converse held, and they spake words wingèd and many together.
Meantime Cronides sped swift Iris to Ilium holy:

"Hie thee away, fleet Iris, and, leaving the seat of Olympus,
Bear unto great-hearted Priam in Ilium's city a message,
Bidding him go to the ships of th' Achaeans his dear son to ransom
(Carrying gifts that may serve to gladden the heart of Achilles),
All alone; let no other man of the Trojans go with him.
Only a herald may follow, an older man, one that shall rightly
Manage the mules and a well-wheeled wagon and back to the city
Carry the hero's corse, who was slain by the godlike Achilles.
Let no image of death now enter his mind nor of terror;
Such a one we will give him as guide, the slayer of Argus:
He shall lead him till, leading, he bring him unto Achilles.
When he hath led him, however, within the tent of Achilles,
Neither the hero shall slay him nor suffer another to harm him,
Seeing that neither unwitting nor heedless is he nor a sinner;
Nay, but a suppliant man he will spare with considerate kindness."

Thus spake he; and arose storm-footed, to bear him the message,
Iris, and, come unto Priam's, she found there weeping and wailing.
Sons were seated around their sire in the court of the palace,   [man,
Drenching their garments with tears; in the midst of his sons was the old
Close-wrapped all in his mantle, enveloped; and scattered upon him —
Even the old man's head and his neck — was dirt in abundance,
Dirt with his hands he had gathered, while prone on the ground he had
                                                                [groveled.

All in the palace were wailing — the wives of his sons and his daughters —
Ever at thought of the men so many and valiant, now fallen,
Men of theirs who had lost their lives at the hands of the Argives.
Came then the messenger Iris from Zeus unto Priam, beside him
Stood, and her whisper was low; but trembling seized on the king's limbs:

"Be of good cheer in thy heart, O Dardanid Priam, and fear not,

Seeing I come unto thee nowise with a boding of evil,
Rather with kindly intent; unto thee Zeus's messenger am I,
Who, though far off, careth for thee with exceeding compassion.
He, the Olympian, biddeth thee ransom Hector, the godlike,
Carrying gifts that may serve to gladden the heart of Achilles.
Go all alone; let no other man of the Trojans go with thee.
Only a herald may follow, an older man, one that shall rightly
Manage the mules and a well-wheeled wagon and back to the city
Carry the hero's corse, who was slain by the godlike Achilles.
Let no image of death now enter thy mind nor of terror;
Such an one will follow as guide, the slayer of Argus:
He shall lead thee till, leading, he bring thee unto Achilles.
When he hath led thee, however, within the tent of Achilles,
Neither the hero shall slay thee nor suffer another to harm thee,
Seeing that neither unwitting nor heedless is he nor a sinner;
Nay, but a suppliant man he will spare with considerate kindness."

Thus she spake and departed, the fleet-footed messenger Iris.
Priam then bade his sons make ready a well-wheeled wagon
Mules were accustomed to draw, and fasten a basket-box on it.
He, however, himself went down to his fragrant storeroom,
High-ceiled chamber of cedar, containing many a treasure.
Then he spake to his wife, to Hecabe, calling her to him:

"Good wife, from Zeus unto me hath come an Olympian envoy,
Bidding me go to the ships of th' Achaeans our dear son to ransom,
Carrying gifts that may serve to gladden the heart of Achilles.
Come then and tell me this, how seemeth the matter to *thy* mind,
Seeing my heart and my soul now urge me, mightily urge me
Thither to go, to the ships, to the wide-pitched camp of th' Achaeans."

Thus he spake; she uttered a wail and answered him saying:

"Ah me! whither departed the sense now, for which aforetime
Thou wert famed among strangers as well as those whom thou rulest?
Why thus eager to go all alone to the galleys Achaean,
There to encounter the eyes of a man that hath slain thy children,
Sons both many and brave? Thy heart is assuredly iron.
For, if he ever shall catch thee, and if with his eyes he behold thee,
Thirsty for blood as he is and faithless, he neither will pity

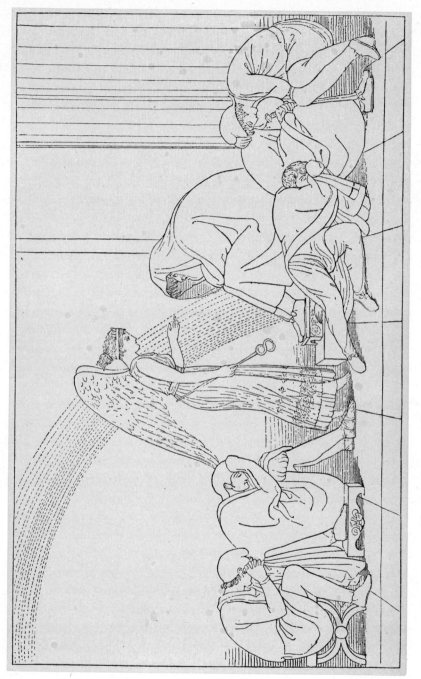

Iris Advises Priam to Obtain the Body of Hector

Nor yet revere thee at all. Nay, let us sit here in the palace,
Weeping for Hector from far; since so hath a fate overpow'ring
Spun with her thread at his birth, at the hour when I myself bore him
Destined to glut the swift-footed dogs, far away from his parents,
Held of a violent man—could only I feed on his liver,
Fasten and feed on its core; then only his deeds were requited,
Dread deeds wrought on my child, whom not as a coward he slaughtered,
Nay, but defending the men and the deep-bosomed daughters of Troia,
Holding his ground, not mindful of flight nor even of shelter."

    Then unto her in his turn made answer old Priam, the godlike:

   "Hinder me not! I am firmly resolved on the journey. And be not
Bird of ill omen thyself in these halls—thou shalt not persuade me.
Were it another, a mortal of earth, that commanded the going,
Seer, or a priest that divineth by means of sacrifice offered,   [rather.
Falsehood we should pronounce it, insooth, and would turn from it
Now, though, since *I* heard the voice and beheld the face of a goddess—
I myself—I am going (not idle this vow). If my fate is
There to lie dead at the ships of the bronze-clad sons of Achaia,
Ready am I. On the spot Achilles may butcher me, when I,
Folding my son in my arms, have sated my lust of lamenting."

    Thus he spake and threw open the fair-wrought lids of the coffers,
Whence he selected him robes, twelve goodliest robes for a woman,
Twelve single-folded cloaks, and of coverlets even as many,
Mantles as many and fair, and tunics as many besides them;
Twice five talents of gold full-measure he weighed, and he carried.
Forth brought he flame-bright tripods twain; he selected four cauldrons,
Also a goblet exceeding fair, which Thracian men gave him,
When on an embassy thither, a precious possession—not even
This would the old man grudge from his halls; for he above all things
Wished his dear son to ransom. He repulsed far from him the Trojans
All from the portico, chiding them sharply with words of upbraiding:

   "Off, ye scoundrels, reproaches! Have ye then, none of you, mourn-
Now in your homes, that ye have thus come hither to vex me?   [ing
Lightly esteemed ye the woes that Zeus, son of Cronus, hath sent me,
Loss of my best and my bravest? Indeed ye also shall feel it:
Easier far it shall be for th' Achaeans to slay you, methinketh,

Seeing that he, great Hector, is dead; but for my part truly
Ere mine eyes shall behold it — the city of Ilium pillaged,
Wasted, and razed to the ground — may I enter the mansion of Hades."

    Spake he and drove them off with his staff; and they made their
Quickly before the old man's haste. Then he called to his children [exit
Chiding them, Helenus first and Paris and Agathon godlike,
Pammon, Antiphonus too, and Polites, good at the war-cry,
Dius, the proud, and Deïphobus too, and Hippothoüs also;
These nine sons the old man called and gave them his orders:

    "Hasten, ill children of mine, ye disgraces! I would that together
All of you rather than Hector lay slain at the swift-faring galleys!
Woe is me, wholly unblest! The sons I begot were the bravest
Men in wide Troyland, of whom not one is (alas! I must say it!)
Left me — the godlike Mestor and Troïlus, chariot-warrior,
Yea, and Hector, who moved as a god among men, and he seemed not
Son of a man that is mortal to be, but a godhead's rather —
All those hath Ares destroyed, and all these caitiffs are left me,
Liars and light-heeled gentry, redoubtable knights of the ballroom,
Plunderers, ravagers all of the sheep and the kids of your own folk.
Would ye not, then, make ready for me with all speed a wagon,
Pile all these things upon it, that we may press forth on our journey?"

    Thus spake he; and his sons, in dread of the voice of their father,
Lifted a wagon forth, well-wheeled — for mules it was suited —
Beauteous, newly-built, and they fastened a basket-box on it.
Down from a peg that upheld it a mule-yoke also was lifted —   [fitted.
Boxwood, with knobs on the yoke, which with martingales also was
Forth then along with the yoke was a yoke-strap carried, of cubits
Nine, and they fitted it fast to the fair-wrought pole of the chariot,
Firm in the rest at the end — and a ring slipped over an upright
Pin — and with three turns lashed it from each side fast to the yoke-knob,
Binding it firm to a hook, and the tongue-straps twisting beneath it.
Forth then they brought from the chamber and heaped up high on the
Wagon the limitless treasures, to ransom the body of Hector. [polished
Lastly they yoked up the mules, strong-hoofed and working in harness,
Glorious gifts that the Mysians had given aforetime to Priam.
Under the yoke for Priam they led forth steeds that the old man

Kept for himself, and he fed them apart, at a well-polished manger.

　　Thus the twain let yoke up their teams in the lofty palace—
Priam along with his herald—and wisdom guided their counsels.
Then drew Hecabe near him; with sorrowing heart she approached him.
Honey-sweet wine in her right hand she bore in a golden goblet,
That they might pour a libation therewith before they departed.
Standing in front of the steeds, she spake a word and addressed him:

　　"Take this; pour a libation to Zeus, our Father; beseech him
Safe thou mayest come home from the foemen, seeing thy spirit
Urgeth thee on to the ships, against my wish and my counsel.
Offer a prayer then next to Cronion, lord of the storm-clouds,
Zeus Idaean, who watcheth o'er Troyland all down below him;
Pray him to send thee his messenger, swift of wing, as an omen
(Bird that is dearest to him of all birds, and its strength is the greatest)
Up on thy right, that with thine own eyes thou may'st see it and journey,
Trusting in it, to the ships of the fleet-horsed Danaan people.
But if Zeus of the far-borne voice his messenger grant not,
I, for my part, would bid thee with urgent entreaty in that case—
Seek not the Argive ships, albeit exceedingly eager."

　　Then in answer to her spake Priam, the godlike, saying:

　　"Wife, I will not disobey thee in this that thou hast commanded:
Good is the lifting of hands unto Zeus, if he will have mercy."

　　Thus he spake; and the old man bade a woman attendant
Pour on his outstretched hands pure water; the handmaid beside him
Came, and she held in her hands an ewer and basin for washing.
Then, upon washing his hands, he received the cup from his consort,
Stood in the midst of the courtyard, and poured out wine in libation;
Gazing the while into heaven, he lifted his voice in prayer, saying:

　　"Zeus, thou Father, that rulest from Ida, most glorious, greatest,
Vouchsafe welcome and mercy for me when I come to Achilles.
Send me thy messenger, swift of wings, I pray, as an omen
(Bird that is dearest to thee of all birds, and its strength is the greatest)
Up on our right, that with mine own eyes I may see it and journey,
Trusting in it, to the ships of the fleet-horsed Danaan people."

　　Thus he spake in prayer, and Counselor Zeus attended;
Straightway sent he an eagle, the surest of all wingèd omens,

Even the Hunter dark-winged—men call it the "black-spotted eagle."
Wide as the door of a high-roofed palace haply is fashioned,
Home of a man of wealth—a door well-locking, close-fitting—
Even so wide was the spread of either wing; and he speeded
Full into view on their right, clear over the city. Beholding,   ⌈dened.
All then joyed in their souls, and the hearts in their bosoms were glad-

    Thereat the old man mounted in haste to the seat of his chariot,
Then drave forth from the doorway and corridor echoing loudly.
Out in front the mules the four-wheeled wagon were drawing;
These wise-hearted Idaeus was driving; and, coming behind them,
Followed the steeds, with the old man plying the lash, as he drove them
Down through the city in haste, and his friends all followed with voices
Loud in lament, convinced that their king to his death was departing.
When they had come from the city down and arrived in the valley,
Back again all the rest to Ilium city departed,
Children and kinsmen. But when they came into view in the valley,
Not unmarked were the twain of Zeus of the far-borne voice: he
Looked on the old man and pitied, thus spake to his dear son Hermes:

    "Hermes, seeing the task unto thee is especially grateful
Both to attend on a man and to hear whomever it please thee,
Hie thee away and conduct to the hollow ships of th' Achaeans
Priam so that no one may behold him or any way mark him,
None of the Danaan host, till he come to the scion of Peleus."

    Thus spake he; and obeyed him the messenger, slayer of Argus.
Under his feet then quickly he bound his beautiful sandals,
Golden, immortal, alike o'er the sea and the measureless mainland
Wonted to bear him along as swift as the breath of the wind-blasts.
Thereon he took up his wand with which men's eyelids he lulleth,
Whoseso he will, while others, asleep, it awaketh from slumber.
Forth flew with this in his hands the mighty slayer of Argus.
Speedily then he arrived at the Hellespont and at Troyland,
Wended his way in disguise of a young man princely in bearing,
Blooming, with new-grown down on his lip—youth's comeliest season.

    When they had driven along past the massive barrow of Ilus,
There at the river they halted the mules and also the horses,
Letting them drink; for over the earth the darkness had fallen.

Then it was that the herald beheld hard by him and noticed
Hermes; he lifted his voice and spake unto Priam, saying:
  "Dardanus' son, be prudent; a moment is nigh us for prudence.
I see a man! Soon, I think, shall we be torn into pieces.
Come, let us flee in our car or, next best, let us entreat him,
Clasping his knees, if haply he will have mercy upon us."
        Thus spake he. The old man was confounded in mind and affrighted
Greatly; the hair stood up on his supple limbs and he stood there
Dazed. But the Helper came nigh himself, the bringer of blessings,
Clasped the old man's hand, and with these questions addressed him:
  "Whither, my father, art thou thus driving the mules and the horses
Through the ambrosial night, when all other mortals are sleeping?
Hadst thou at least no fear of the fury-breathing Achaeans,
Foemen of thine embittered, implacable, that now are nigh thee?
Should any one of them discover thee bearing such treasures [thine then?
Thus through the swift black night, what thought, peradventure, were
No youth art thou thyself, and an old man is he that attends thee,
Too weak to drive off a man, if the other were first to assail you.
I, though, will do thee no harm, nay even will ward off another
Seeking thy hurt; for I see in thee my dear father's own likeness."
        Then unto him in turn old Priam, the godlike, made answer:
  "No doubt true, dear child, all this, even so as thou sayest.
Yet e'en o'er *me* some one of the gods his hand hath extended,
Seeing that he hath sent such a wayfarer hither to meet me
Most opportunely; so wonderful art thou in form and in person;
Wise, too, art thou in spirit; and blessèd indeed are thy parents."
        Then in his turn the messenger, slayer of Argus, addressed him:
  "Yea now all these things, old man, thou hast fittingly spoken.
Come now and tell me this and tell it truly, I pray thee,
Whether thou carryest somewhere a great and glorious treasure
Unto the keeping of strangers, where these things may safely await
Whether in panic already the city of Ilium holy   [thee—
All of you now are forsaking; so far your bravest hath perished,
Even thy son; for in fight with Achaeans he never was wanting."
        Then unto him made answer the aged Priam, the godlike:
  "Who art thou, my very good sir? And who are thy parents?

525

Thou that so kindly hast mentioned the fate of my son, so ill-starrèd?"
Then in his turn the messenger, slayer of Argus, addressed him:
"Old man, thou wouldst try me and askest of Hector, the godlike.
Often indeed I have seen him with mine own eyes in the battle,
Bringing renown unto men, as when at the ships he was slaying
Argives, rending their flesh with the keen bronze, whom he had routed.
We all marveled the while, as idle we stood, for Achilles
Suffered us still not to fight, for with Atreus' son he was angered.
I am his squire; and one and the same sturdy ship brought us hither;
One of the Myrmidons I, and my father's name is Polyctor.
He is a prince in his wealth, an old man, even as thou art.
Six other sons hath he, and I myself am his seventh.
Casting lots with the others, it fell to *me* to come hither.
Now I am come from the ships to the plain; for at daybreak th' Achaeans,
Glancing-eyed, the battle will set in array round the city,
Seeing it chafeth them sore, sitting yonder inactive, and neither
Now can the kings of th' Achaeans restrain their yearning for warfare."
Then unto him made answer the aged Priam, the godlike:
"If thou art truly a squire of Achilles, scion of Peleus,
Come now, tell me the truth, the whole truth touching my Hector,
Whether my child still lieth beside those galleys, or whether,
Piecemeal hewn, he was served long since to the dogs by Achilles."
Then in his turn the messenger, slayer of Argus, addressed him:
"Old man, verily yet neither dogs nor birds have devoured him,
Nay, but he lies there still, outstretched by the ship of Achilles,
All unchanged, at the barracks; the twelfth morn now hath arisen
Over him there, and his flesh knows no corruption; the vermin
Prey on him not, whose wont is to feed on men slain in battle.
True, all around the tomb of his comrade belovèd he drags him,
Recking nought of his work, as oft as divine day dawneth.
Natheless he marreth him not; thyself wouldst marvel, on going
Thither, to see him, fresh as a dew-drop lying (the blood clots
All are washed off), undefiled; the wounds wherewith he was stricken
All of them closed; for many had plunged their bronze through his
So do the blessèd gods, I assure thee, care for thy scion,   [body.
Albeit only a corse, for deep in their hearts did they love him."

    Thus spake he; and the old man was glad and answered him, saying:

"Truly a good thing it is, my child, to give the immortals

Offerings due, since never my son — if mine he was ever —

Never forgot in our halls the gods who dwell in Olympus;

Hence they were mindful of him, though now unto death he's allotted.

Come then, prithee, receive at my hand this goblet so goodly

Unto thyself and protect, yea, guide with the favor of heaven

Me myself until I arrive at Peleus' son's barrack."

    Then once again the messenger, slayer of Argus, addressed him:

"Old man, thou wouldst try me, a youth — but thou shalt not per-

Bidding me take thy gifts behind the back of Achilles.   [suade me —

Him I would fear to defraud (my regard for him straitly forbiddeth),

Lest in the future some evil should come to pass, to my sorrow.

Yet, I would lead thee as guide, yea, even to far-famed Argos

Duly escorting thee either on foot or on swift-sailing galley.

None, then, lightly esteeming thy guide, would be like to attack thee."

    Thus spake the Helper and leaped up into the car with the horses,

Quickly caught up in his hands the whip and the reins, and new vigor

Breathed meanwhile into both the mules and the horses divinely.

But when they now were come to the towers and moat at the galleys,

There were the sentinels busied just then preparing their supper;

Soft sleep over them all the messenger, slayer of Argus,

Shed, then opened the gates, as he deftly thrust back the bolt-beams,

Then brought Priam within and the glorious gifts on the wagon.

They now, when they arrived at length at Peleus' son's lofty

Barrack, which for their king the Myrmidon warriors had builded,

Hewing the timber of pine; above they had thoroughly roofed it,

Thatching it o'er with downy reeds that they mowed in the meadows;

Round it for him, their king, a spacious court they constructed,

Girdled with thick palisades; one cross-bar only — of pine wood —

Fastened the gate; but it needed three Achaeans to drive it

Home, and for drawing it back, that powerful bolt of the doorway,

Three of the others — Achilles would drive it home, all unaided.

Hermes, the helper, now opened wide the gate for the old man,

Brought in the glorious gifts for the fleet-footed scion of Peleus,

Then from the car to the earth dismounted, and thus he addressed him:

"Old man, I that have come unto thee am a god, an immortal,
Hermes; for 'twas my father assigned me as guide to attend thee.
Now, however, will I go back; the eyes of Achilles
Will I *not* encounter; for just were the indignation
Thus for a god immortal to show open favor to mortals.
Thou, though, enter at once and clasp the knees of Pelides,
And for the sake of his sire, for the sake of his fair-haired mother,
And for his child, that thou mayest move the spirit within him."

Thus spake Hermes and hied him away to lofty Olympus
Forthwith. Thereupon Priam to earth leaped down from his chariot,
Leaving behind him Idaeus there in his place; he remained there,
Minding the horses and mules. The old man went straight to the dwell- [ing
Wherein Achilles, dear unto Zeus, to sit was accustomed.
There then he found him; his comrades were seated apart; two only,
Hero Automedon, namely, and Alcimus, scion of Ares,
Busied themselves in attendance; but late he had risen from supper,
Eating and drinking; the table was still there standing beside him.
Quite unobserved by them, the great Priam entered and, stopping [those
Close by him, clasped with his arms the knees of Achilles and kissed
Terrible, man-slaying hands that had slain of his children so many.

E'en as a grievous calamity comes on a man who has murdered
One in his native land and has come to the country of strangers,
Unto a rich man's court, and amazement seizes beholders:
So was Achilles amazed at beholding Priam, the godlike;
So were the others amazed and looked the one at the other.
Therewith Priam addressed him a word and began supplication:

"Thine own father remember, Achilles, match for immortals.
Old age holdeth him also, as me, at its sorrowful threshold.
Ay, even him now haply his neighbors, abiding about him,
Evil entreat, nor is any to ward off curse and destruction.
Nevertheless even he in his heart is rejoiced upon hearing
Thou art alive, and he hopeth day after day he may see thee,
Even his own dear son returning thither from Troyland.
Woe is me, wholly unblest! The sons I begot were the bravest
Men in wide Troyland—not one (alas! I must say it) is left me.
Fifty I had when there came to Troy the sons of th' Achaeans;

528

Nineteen were born unto me of one and the selfsame mother;
All of the others were children of women that dwelt in the palace.
Ares impetuous loosened the knees of most of my children;
One that was left me alone, who guarded the people and city,
Him of late thou hast slain as he fought in defense of his homeland,
Hector; for his sake now I am come to the galleys Achaean,
Seeking to win him from thee, and I bring a limitless ransom.
Yea, have awe of the gods and compassion on me, O Achilles,
Mindful of thine own father; and even more piteous I am;
Braved have I that which never on earth braved a mortal before me,
Lifting my hand to the lips of the man who hath slain my children."

    Thus he, and stirred in him a yearning to weep for his father.
Touching the old man's hand, he pressed him away from him gently.
Both of them then in remembrance, the one for man-slaying Hector
Bitterly wept as he groveled before the feet of Achilles,
Who was bewailing his father anon, and, anon again changing,
Wept for Patroclus; and moaning arose through all of the household.
But when godlike Achilles had sated himself with lamenting,
Also the lust therefor had forsaken his soul and his body,
Straight from his chair he arose, by the hand uplifted the old man,
Pitied his hoary head, and his hoary beard did he pity;
Then uplifting his voice he spake wingèd words and addressed him:

    "Ah, thou hapless! for many the ills thou hast felt in thy spirit!
How hast thou dared to come all alone to the galleys Achaean,
Here to encounter the eyes of the man that hath slain thy children,
Sons both many and brave? Thy heart is assuredly iron!
Come then, sit thee down on a chair, and, for all of our anguish,
Now let sorrow at rest lie deep in the heart, unawakened.
Verily profit is none in the voice of chill lamentation.
Such is the lot that the gods have spun for mortals unhappy —
That they should live in grief, while they themselves know no sorrow.
For on the floor of the palace of Zeus two great jars are standing,
Filled with the evil gifts that he gives, and a third one with blessings.
Whomso Zeus, the hurler of thunderbolts, giveth a mixture,
That man lighteth at times upon good and again upon evil;
Whom, however, he gives of the sorry gifts, he is an outcast,

Ay, and a ravening hunger the good earth over doth drive him
Wand'ring lone and regarded neither of gods nor of mortals.
Even so, glorious gifts the godheads gave unto Peleus,
E'en from his birth; for amongst all people he was outstanding
Both in his weal and his wealth and was king of the Myrmidon nation;
Also they gave him a goddess in wedlock, though he was but mortal.
Nevertheless God hath brought unto him, too, evil, for truly
Never was born in his palace a progeny princely of children;
One child alone he begat, untimely of doom; and I may not
Tend him as he grows old, for here afar from my country
Lo! I am set down in Troyland, for woe unto thee and thy children.
Yet thou also, we hear, old man, wast blessèd aforetime.
All that Lesbos, Macar's seat, on its north side boundeth,
All of inland Phrygia, too, and the Hellespont boundless —
All these folk, they say, in wealth and sons thou excellest.
Since, though, the Powers of Heaven have brought this calamity on
Ever seest thou battles and slaying of men round thy city.   [thee,
Bear up; do not lament unabatingly aye in thy spirit.
Verily naught it availeth bewailing thy son, though so goodly;
Thou wilt not raise him again, ere other evil thou suffer."
    Therewith Priam, the aged, the godlike, answered him, saying:
    "Nay, do not bid me yet, O nurseling of Zeus, to be seated,
So long as Hector is lying uncared for here at the barracks;
Give him with speed to be seen with my eyes and accept of the ransom
Manifold now that we bring thee, and thine be all its enjoyment,
Also a homeward return, since me from the first thou hast suffered
Even to live myself and to look on the light of the sun's rays."
    Scowlfully eyeing, addressed him in turn fleet-footed Achilles:
    "Vex me no further, old man. My own mind is to release thee
Hector, without being urged; for a messenger came from Cronion,
Even the mother that bore me, a child of the Ancient of Ocean.
Also I know full well in my soul, O Priam, it 'scapes me
Not, that a god led thee to the swift-faring ships of th' Achaeans.
Never a mortal had ventured, not e'en in the flush of his manhood,
Hither to come to the army, eluded the sentries, and found it
Easy to push back the bar of our doors, ay, e'en with a lever.

Therefore ſtir up my heart no more in the midst of my sorrows,
Lest, e'en though thou comest a suppliant, ſtill I may spare thee
Not in my barrack and thus transgress e'en Zeus's commandments."
    Thus spake he; and the old man quaked at his word and obeyed him.
Leaped forth like as a lion Achilles then from his dwelling,
Not unaccompanied: two of his squires were following after —
Hero Automedon, namely, and Alcimus, two that he honored
Most of all of his comrades, next after the fallen Patroclus.
These then loosed from under the yoke both the mules and the horses.
Into the barrack they led the old man's herald, his crier,
Gave him a seat on a chair, and off from the well-felloed wagon
Took down the countless ransom they brought for the body of Hector.
Two of the robes, however, they left and a well-woven tunic,
So that Achilles might shroud the corse therein, for returning.
Handmaids he summoned forth and bade them bathe and anoint him,
Taking him off to one side and out of the sight of old Priam,
Lest he reſtrain not his wrath in his sorrowing soul at beholding
Hector, his son, and Achilles' dear heart thereat be awakened,
So that he slay him there and transgress e'en Zeus's commandments.
After the handmaids, then, had washed and anointed the body,
Round it also had cast a beautiful robe and a tunic,
Lifting the body, Achilles himself on a litter disposed it;
Helping, his comrades raised it up on the well-polished wagon.
Loudly then did he groan and call on his comrade belovèd:
    "Be not, Patroclus, indignant, if e'en in the palace of Hades
Thou hear haply that I have surrendered Hector, the godlike,
Back to his father beloved, for the ransom he gave me is worthy;
Thee I shall deal off from it a portion, as much as is fitting."
    Thus he spake; and the godlike Achilles went back to his barrack,
Seated himself on a chair wrought cunningly, whence he had risen,
There by the opposite wall, then spake a word unto Priam:
    "Lo! thy son is released unto thee, old man, at thy bidding;
There on his bier he lieth; and thou, when the morning appeareth,
Bearing him hence, thyself shalt behold him. Now think we of supper,
Seeing that Niobe even, the beauteous-tressèd, bethought her
Also of meat, though her children twelve were slain in her palace,

Six fair daughters and six brave sons in the bloom of their manhood;
These did Apollo slay with his silver bow and his arrows,
Angered with Niobe — Artemis, rainer of arrows, the daughters —
All because Niobe matched herself against Leto, the fair-cheeked,
Saying that Leto had borne two only — herself, many children.
They then, though only the two, brought death to all of those others.
Nine days they lay in their blood, for no one was there to inter them,
Seeing the son of Cronus had turned into stone all the people.
Yet on the tenth day the gods, the sons of heaven, interred them.
Then she bethought her of food, when she with weeping was wearied.
Now somewhere 'mid the cliffs, in the deep solitude of the mountains,
Yonder in Sipylus, where — men say — are the goddesses' couches,
Even the nymphs, that whirl in the dance round the brook Acheloüs
Still she abideth, a stone, still broods o'er her god-ordained sorrows.
Come then, godlike old man, let *us* now also bethink us
Haply of food. And thy own dear son — anon thou mayst mourn him,
When thou hast borne him to Ilium. His portion of tears shall be ample."

    Thus fleet Achilles spake, sprang up, and a sheep of pure whiteness
Slaughtered. His comrades flayed it and fitly prepared it in order,
Cunningly carving the whole, with spits then piercing the pieces,
Roasted them carefully each, then drew off all of the slices.
Bread Automedon took and served it in beautiful baskets
Round on the table. Achilles in turn the sliced meats was serving.
They then reached forth their hands to the good cheer set out before
Now when desire for meat and for drink together was banished, [them.
Priam, Dardanus' son, looked on with amaze at Achilles,
How he was comely and tall: he was like to the gods in appearance;
Also Achilles beheld with amazement Dardanid Priam,
Looking upon his noble face and heeding his sayings.
When now sated with pleasure of gazing, each at the other,
First it was aged Priam, the godlike, spake to Achilles:

    "Presently strew me a bed, O nurseling of Zeus, that in slumber
Soft we may lay us down even now and fully enjoy it.
Truly I've closed my eyes not one time, under my eyelids,
Since at thy hands first my son lost his life in the battle,
But I unceasingly mourn, still brood over countless afflictions,

Groveling always amidst the filth in the close of the courtyard.
Now at last I have tasted of food and poured, too, the sparkling
Wine down my throat; till now I had tasted verily nothing."

    Thus spake he; and Achilles then bade his comrades and handmaids
Set up a bedstead under the portico, throwing upon it
Mattresses purple and fair, then strew all over them blankets,
Coverlets also of wool laid over the whole for a cov'ring.
Forth from the innermost hall came handmaids straightly with torches
Borne in their hands. Then quickly they hasted to spread the two couches.
Then with a bitter speech fleet-footed Achilles addressed him:

    "Sleep thou outside, my dear old man, for fear some Achaean
Hither come — some counselor — such as beside me are always
Sitting, devising counsels with me, as they have a right to.
Should anyone of them through the swift black night chance to see thee,
He at once would tell Agamemnon, shepherd of peoples;
Then a delay would arise in returning the body, it may be!
Come now and tell me this and tell it truly, I pray thee,
How many days thou wishest for burying Hector, the godlike,
So that myself may wait meantime and hold back the army."

    Therewith the aged Priam, the godlike, answered him, saying:

    "If thou consent that I finish the funeral rites for the godlike
Hector, in doing thus thou wouldst do us a favor, Achilles.
Well thou knowest that we in the city are hemmed, and from far off
Wood is to fetch from the mountain; and terror possesses the Trojans.
Nine days for him in our halls would we devote to lamenting;
Rites we would hold on the tenth, with festival spread for the people;
Over him we should like to erect a tomb on th' eleventh;
Then on the twelfth unto warfare address us again, if it need be."

    Him then answered in turn fleet-footed Achilles, the godlike:

    "This, old Priam, shall also be done for thee, as thou biddest:
Just so long as thou sayest the war I shall hold in abeyance."

    When he had uttered these words, he clasped the right hand of the
Close at the wrist, lest haply he feel some fear in his spirit.   [old man
So in the forepart there of the dwelling both sank into slumber,
Priam along with his herald — their thoughts were still of good counsel.
Deep in a corner, the while, of the well-joined barrack Achilles

Slept, and beside him there lay the fair-cheeked damsel Briseïs.

All others now, both gods and heroes, drivers of war-cars,
All night long lay sleeping, o'ercome in the arms of soft slumber.
But on Hermes, the helper, sleep took no hold: he was ever
Casting about in his mind the while how Priam, the monarch,
He might conduct from the ships unseen by the sentinels stalwart.
Over his head he came and stood and spake a word, saying:

"Surely with thee, old man, is no thought of ill, that thou sleepest
Still amid enemies thus, for that Achilles hath spared thee.
Now thou hast ransomed thy son beloved, and much hast thou given;
Threefold such ransom for thee yet alive, *they* haply would offer,
Even thy sons, who behind thee are left, if belike Agamemnon,
Atreus' son, be aware of thee here, and all the Achaeans."

Thus spake he; and in terror the old man awakened his herald.
Thereupon Hermes yoked the mules for them both and the horses,
Swiftly himself then drove through the camp, nor was any that knew it.
But when they now had come to the ford of the fair-flowing river,
Eddying Xanthus, that Zeus begot, the godhead immortal,
Forthwith Hermes hied him away to lofty Olympus.
All over earth was Dawn outspreading her mantle of saffron,
While 'mid weeping and wailing they drove to the city the horses
Onward; onward the mules went drawing the body; and no one
Knew of it earlier — whether of men or of fair-girdled women —
Till that Cassandra, a rival of Aphrodite, the golden,
Went up to Pergamus' height and was ware of her father belovèd
Standing up in his car and the public crier, his herald,
Also the one that lay in the mule-drawn cart, on a litter.
Loudly she shrieked; and she cried up and down through all of the city:

"Come, ye men and ye women of Troy, and look upon Hector,
If ye have ever rejoiced at his coming alive from a battle;
Hector was once the great joy of the city and all of our nation."

Thus she spake, nor was anyone left any more in the city,
Neither a man nor a woman — a grief overpowering seized them
All; and in front of the gate they met the king with the body.
First of them all in lament were his dear wife and worshipful mother,
Tearing their hair and throwing themselves on the well-wheeled wagon,

534

Laying their hands on his head, while the throng stood weeping around
So now all day long till the sun had gone to its setting　　　　[them.
They had lamented for Hector with tears in front of the gateways,
Had not the old man spoken from out of his car to the people:　　　[after

　　"Prithee make way for the mules to pass through; and ye may here-
Have your fill of lamenting, when unto his home I have brought him."

　　Thus he spake; and they stood apart and made way for the wagon.
When they now to his famous palace had brought him, thereafter
High on a bed of fret-work they laid him and seated beside him
Minstrels to lead in a dirge; and mournful the requiem sounded.
Dirges they sang, while women responsive added their mourning.
White-armed Andromache for them began the loud lamentation,
Clasping the while in her arms the head of man-slaying Hector:

　　"Husband, away from life thou art gone in thy youth; and a widow
Leavest thou me in our halls; thy son, too, is only an infant,
Child of unhappy parents, of thee and myself; and, methinketh,
Never will he reach manhood! Ere that the city will perish,
Utterly razed, for thou, its protector, hast perished, who kept it
Ever safe, with its noble women and innocent children.
Soon they now in the hollow ships away will go sailing,
I, too, among them; but thou, my child, shalt accompany cither
Me myself somewhither, to work at some labor ignoble,
Toiling before a merciless lord; or else some Achaean,
Seizing thy hand, from a tower shall hurl thee to awful destruction,
Filled with wrath because Hector some time may have slain his brother,
Father perchance, or son; for indeed full many Achaeans
Under the hands of Hector the dust with their teeth have bitten.
Gentle, indeed, he was not, thy father, in dolorous warfare.
Therefore also the folk all through the city bemoan him.
Ay, thou hast brought lamenting past words and grief to thy parents,
Hector, but chiefly is left unto me this grievous affliction,
Seeing that neither in death thy hands from thy bed were extended,
Neither a word of comfort thou spakest to me, to remember
Still, as I pour out my tears, daylong, nightlong, and forever."

　　Thus spake she as she wept, and the women added their mourning.
Hecabe then in the midst of the dames led the wild lamentation:

535

"Hector, to me in my heart far dearest of all of my children,
Verily, while thou wast living, beloved wast thou of the godheads;
Still, I see, did they care for thee, though death's doom was on thee.
Other children of mine, that fleet-footed Achilles would take as
Prisoners, o'er the unharvested sea he would sell into thralldom
Either to Samos or Imbros or Lemnos, the misty and smoky.
When with his keen-edged weapon of bronze of life he had reft thee,
Oft he would drag thy body around the tomb of his comrade,
Whom thou slewest, Patroclus; but not even so did he raise him.
Now, though, I see, in the palace, as fresh as the dew or as newly
Slain thou liest, like one whom Apollo, god of the silver
Bow, hath gently approached and slain with a merciful arrow."

Thus she spake in lament and awakened wailing unending.
Thirdly among them came Helen, who led in the loud lamentation:

"Hector, to me in my heart far dearest of all of thy brethren,
Truly a husband I have, even Alexander, the godlike,
He that to Troyland brought me — I would that ere that I had per-
This, I find, even now is the twentieth year that is passing   [ished! —
Since I came here from over yonder and left my own country.
Yet I have never from thee heard a word that was harsh or ungentle,
Never! But if in the palace's halls some other upbraided,
Brother or sister of thine or fair-robed wife of a brother,
Even thy mother — thy father was always kind as a father,
Thou with a word fair-spoken, thou would'st appease and restrain them
All with a gentleness thine, and with accents gently persuasive.
Therefore do I bewail thee in anguish of spirit, and with thee
Me ill-doomed, for another is not to be found in broad Troyland
Kindly or friendly to me; nay, all men hold me in horror."

Thus she spake as she wept, and a throng past telling mourned with
Then in the midst of the people old Priam spake a word, saying: [her.

"Bring ye wood to the city, ye Trojans; neither in spirit
Fear any hidden ambush of Argives, seeing Achilles
Made me this promise, as home from the black-hulled galleys he sent
No hostile move to make, till the twelfth day morn is arisen."   [me,

Thus he spake; and the folk to their wagons yoked up their mule-
Also their oxen and soon were gathered in front of the city.   [teams,

Nine days long they were hauling abundance of timber together;
But when the Dawn, the tenth, bringing light unto mortals, was risen,
Then, letting fall a tear, they bore forth Hector, the dauntless,
. Placed on the top of the pyre his corse, and kindled the fire.
Soon as the Dawn appeared, rosy-fingered daughter of morning,
Straightway gathered the folk round the pyre of illustrious Hector.
Soon as the people assembled, from all sides gathered together,
First with sparkling wine they extinguished the flames of the pyre—
All of it, far as the fury of fire had extended, and later
Brethren and comrades gathered together the white bones, lamenting;
All down over their cheeks the copious tear-drops were flowing.
Taking up Hector's bones, they laid them away in a golden
Casket, when they had shrouded them well in soft purple vestments.
Straightway the casket they laid in a hollow grave and above it
Piled up a cov'ring compact of huge stones set close together,
Speedily heaped up a cairn, then picketed watchers about it,
Fearing the well-greaved Achaeans before the time might attack them.
When they had heaped up the mound, they went back home and there-
Shortly assembled together and banqueted well at a splendid　　[after
Feast in the palace of Priam, the Zeus-fostered monarch of Troyland.
　　Thus did they hold the funeral rites of horse-taming Hector.

Index

References are to book and line.

A-ban′tes, Greeks from Euboea, II 536 ff.

Ab-ar-ba′re-a, a fountain nymph, VI 22.

A′bas, a Trojan, V 148 ff.

A′bi-i, Scythians, XIII 6.

A-ble′rus, a Trojan, VI 32.

A-by′dus, a city on the Hellespont, II 836.

Ac′a-mas, 1) Antenor's son, II 822 f.; slain by Meriones, XVI 342 ff.; 2) a Thracian, II 844; slain by Ajax, VI 7 f.

Ac-es-sam′e-nus, King in Thrace, XXI 142.

A-chae′an, Homeric word for Greek, I 2; 12; etc.

A-chai′a, Homeric name for Greece, I 254; etc.

Ach-e-lo′us, 1) the largest river of Greece, XXI 194; 2) a brook in Phrygia, XXIV 616.

A-chil′les, the hero of the Iliad, I 1; son of Peleus, I 1; fleet-footed, I 84; etc.; reared by Phoenix, IX 438 ff.; trained in music by Chiron, XI 832; leader of the Myrmidons, II 684; his armor, XVI 130 ff.; XVIII 82 ff.; 478–613; XIX 386 ff.; his beauty, II 673; XXIV 630; his character, XXIV 39 ff.; the mightiest warrior, II 769 f.; quarrels with Agamemnon, I 121 ff.; refuses his advances, IX 307–429; 678 ff.; chooses between long life of ease and short life of fame, IX 410 ff.; XVIII 98; his interview with Patroclus, XVI 6–100; mourns for Patroclus, XVIII 25 ff.; 316 ff.; XIX 315 ff.; XXIII 8 ff.; XXIV 3 ff.; dons

his new armor, XIX 15 ff.; 368 ff.; resigns his wrath, XIX 56 ff.; slaughters Trojans, XIX–XXII; combat with Aeneas, XX 158–339; slays Hector, XXII 35–404; drags his body, XXII 395 ff; XXIV 14 ff.; 416 ff.; buries Patroclus, XXIII; gives up Hector's body, XXIV 113 ff.; 134 ff.; 472–688. See under wrath.

A-cri′si-us, father of Danae, XIV 319.

Ac-tae′a, a Nereid, XVIII 41.

Ac′tor, 1) grandfather of Patroclus, XI 785; 2) grandfather of Eurytus, II 619 f.; XXIII 638; 3) grandfather of Ascalephus, II 513; 4) ancestor of Echecles, XVI 189 f.

Ac′tor-ids, grandsons of Actor, Eurytus and Cteatus, II 619 f.

Ad′a-mas, a Trojan, XII 140; XIII 560 ff.

Ad-me′tus, father of Eumelus, II 713–714; XXIII 288 f.

Ad-res-te′ia, city in Mysia, II 828.

A-dres′tus, 1) a king of Sicyon, II 572; V 412; 2) a Trojan ally, II 830; slain by Diomedes, XI 328 ff.; 3) a Trojan, captured by Menelaus and slain by Agamemnon, VI 37–65; 4) a Trojan, slain by Patroclus, XVI 694.

Ae-ac′i-des or Ae′a-cid, Aeacus' grandson, Achilles (q.v.), II 874; XI 805.

Ae′a-cus, grandfather of Achilles, II 860; XXI 189.

Ae-an′tes, same as Ajaxes, IV 273.

Ae′gae, city in Achaia, VIII 203; XIII 20.

Ae-gae′on, a giant of the sea, I 402 ff.

541

Ae-gi-a-lei′a, wife of Diomedes, V 412.

Ae-gi′a-lus, town in Paphlagonia, II 855.

Aeg′i-lips, a town of Odysseus, II 633.

Ae-gi′na, an island near Athens, II 562.

ae′gis, the terror-inspiring breast-plate of Zeus, XV 308 ff.; described, II 447 ff.; V 738 ff.; manipulated 1) by Zeus, IV 167; XVII 593 ff.; 2) by Athena, II 447; V 738; XVIII 204; XXI 400 f.; 3) by Apollo, XV 229; 308.

Ae′gi-um, harbor town of Achaia, II 574.

Ae-ne′as, son of Anchises and Aphrodite, II 820; V 247 f.; his pedigree, XX 230 ff.; greatest Trojan after Hector, V 467; XI 58; his interview with Pandarus, V 171–238; wounded by Diomedes, saved by Aphrodite and Apollo, V 297 ff.; 437 ff.; 512 ff.; fights with Achilles and is saved by Poseidon, XX 79–352.

Ae′ni-us, a Paeonian, XXI 210.

Ae′nus, a town in Thrace, IV 520.

Ae′o-lus, father of Sisyphus, VI 154.

Ae-pei′a, town in Messenia, IX 152; 294.

Ae′py, a town in Nestor's realm, II 592.

Aep′y-tus, his tomb in Arcadia, II 604.

Ae-se′pus, 1) river in Mysia, II 825; XII 21; 2) a Trojan, slain by Euryalus, VI 21.

Ae-sy-e′tes, 1) father of Antenor, II 793; 2) Alcathous' father, slain by Idomeneus, XIII 427.

Ae-sy′me, town in Thrace, VIII 804.

Ae-sym′nus, a Greek, slain by Hector, XI 303.

Ae′the, Agamemnon's mare, XXIII 295; 409; 524.

Ae-thi′ces, a Thessalian people, II 744.

Ae′thi-o-pe′ans or Ae-thi-o′pi-ans or Ae′thi-ops, dwellers by the ocean, I 423; XXIII 206.

Ae′thon, Hector's "sorrel" horse, VIII 185.

Ae′thra, Helen's handmaid, III 144.

Ae-to′lian, of Aetolia, a province of n.w. Greece, II 638; IV 399.

Ag′a-cles, a Myrmidon, XVI 571.

Ag-a-me′de, daughter of Augeas, XI 740.

Ag-a-mem′non (Atrides), son of Atreus, II 577; King of Mycenae, II 569 ff.; his appearance, II 477 ff.; III 166 ff.; mistreats Chryses and offends Apollo, I 8 ff.; quarrels with Achilles, I 121 ff.; takes Briseis, I 184 ff.; 335 ff.; would make amends, IX 119–170; IX 105 ff.; XIX 138 ff.; his army, II 569 ff.; reviews the army, IV 223–418; his interviews with Nestor, X 82–130; XIV 41 ff.; his deeds of valor, XI 15–283.

Ag-a-pe′nor, leader of Arcadians, II 609.

A-gas′the-nes, an Elean, II 624.

A-gas′tro-phus, a Trojan, XI 373.

Ag′a-thon, son of Priam, XXIV 249.

A-ga′ve, a Nereid, XVIII 42.

Ag-e-la′us, 1) a Trojan, slain by Diomedes, VIII 257 ff.; 2) a Greek, slain by Hector, XI 302.

A-ge′nor, son of Antenor, VI 298; XI 59; one of the bravest Trojans, IV 467; faces Achilles, XXI 545–598.

A-glai′a, mother of Nireus, q.v., II 672.

A′gri-us, a Calydonian, XIV 117.

A-i-do′neus, same as Hades (q.v.), V 190; XX 61.

A′jax, 1) son of Telamon, of Salamis, II 528; huge of stature, III 226 ff.; the mightiest, after Achilles, II 768; the handsomest, after Achilles, XVII 279 f.; duel with Hector, VII 182 ff.; fights for Patroclus' body, XVII 128 ff.; 237 ff.; wrestles with Odysseus, XXIII 708 ff.; 2) son of Oileus, leader of Locrians, swift of foot, II 527; XXIII 754; skilled spearman, II 530.

A-lal′co-me-ne′an, epithet of Athena, IV 8.

A-las′tor, 1) father of Tros, XX 463; 2) a Lycian, slain by Odysseus, V 677; 3) a Pylian, IV 295.

Al-can′der, a Lycian, V 678.

Al-cath′o-us, a Trojan chief, XII 93; slain by Idomeneus, XIII 428 ff.

Au'lis, rendezvous of the Greek fleet bound for Troy, II 303 ff.; 496.

Au-tol'y-cus, Odysseus' grandfather, X 266 ff.

Au-tom'e-don, Achilles' charioteer, IX 209; XVII 429 ff.

Au-ton'o-us, 1) a Greek, slain by Hector, XI 301; 2) a Trojan slain by Patroclus, XVI 694.

Au-toph'o-nus, a Theban, IV 395.

Ax'i-us, river in 1) Macedonia, II 849; XXI 141; 2) Paeonia, XVI 288.

Ax-y'lus, a Thracian, VI 12.

A'ze-id, Azeus' son, of Orchomenus, II 513.

Ba'li-us, one of Achilles' immortal horses, XVI 149; XIX 400 ff.; weeps, with his mate, for Patroclus, XVII 426 ff.

Bath'y-cles, a Myrmidon, XVI 593 ff.

Ba-ti-ei'a, a hill near Troy, II 813.

Bel-ler'o-phon, grandfather of Glaucus, VI 196 ff.; his adventures, VI 155–197.

Bes'sa, a city of Locris, II 532.

Bi'as, 1) a Pylian, IV 296; 2) an Athenian, XIII 691; 3) a Trojan, XX 460.

Bi-e'nor, a Trojan, XI 92.

Bo-a'gri-us, a stream in Locris, II 533.

Boe-be'ian Lake, near Boebe, II 711.

Boe'be, a city in Thessaly, II 712.

Boe-o'tian, from Boeotia, II 494; XIII 685.

Bo're-as, 1) the north-north-east wind, V 697; 2) personified, IX 5; ancestor of Aeneas' horses, XX 221 ff.

Bo'rus, 1) brother-in-law of Achilles, XVI 175 ff.; 2) father of Phaestus, V 43.

boxing-match, XXIII 634; 653–699.

Bri-a're-os, the hundred-handed, I 402 f.

Bri-se'ia, a town in Laconia, II 583.

Bri-se'is, daughter of Briseus, I 391; her beauty, XIX 282; loved captive of Achilles, I 184; IX 342 f.; taken by Agamemnon, I 184; 322 ff.; 335 ff.; restored to Achilles, XIX 246; laments for Patroclus, XIX 286 ff.

Bri'seus, Briseis' father, I 392; IX 273 f.

Bu-co'li-on, Laomedon's son, VI 22 ff.

Bu'co-lid, Bucolus' son, XV 338.

Bu-de'um, a town in Greece, XVI 572.

Bu-pra'sium, city in Elis, II 615; XXIII 631.

Ca-be'sus, a town in Thrace, XIII 363.

Cad-me'a, another name of Thebes, V 807.

Cad-me'ian, Theban, (see Cadmea), IV 385 ff.

Cad'mus, founder of Thebes, IV 385.

Cae'neus, a Lapith, I 264; father of Coronus, II 746.

Cal'chas, Greek seer, I 68–113; foretold the ten-year war, II 299–332.

Ca-le'sius, Axylus' charioteer, VI 18.

Ca-le'tor, 1) father of Aphareus, XIII 541; 2) kinsman of Priam, XV 419.

Cal'li-a-nas'sa, a Nereid, XVIII 46.

Cal'li-a-ni'ra, a Nereid, XVIII 44.

Cal-li'a-rus, town in Locris, II 531.

Cal'li-co-lo'ne, a hill near Troy, XX 53.

Ca-lyd'nae, II 677.

Cal'y-don, capital of Aetolia, II 640; war with the Curetes (q.v.), IX 531.

Ca-mi'rus, a city of Rhodes, II 656.

Cap'a-neus, father of Sthenelus, II 564; one of the "Seven against Thebes," IV 403 ff.; attends Diomedes, V 107 ff.

Ca'pys, Aeneas' grandfather, XX 239.

car, hamaxa, a four-wheeled wagon, VII 426; XXIV 324; Charles' Wain, XVIII 487; harma, war-car, II 384; etc.; horses and car, IV 306; XXIII 531; diphros, strictly the box of the car, V 160; the car itself, X 305; XVI 379; etc.; Hera's car, V 722–731.

Car-dam'y-le, city in Laconia, IX 150.

Ca-re'sus, river in the Troad, XII 20.

Ca'ri-a, a country in Asia Minor, IV 141.

Ca'ri-an, belonging to Caria, II 867.

Car'pa-thos, an island, II 676.

Ca-rys'tus, city in Euboea, II 539.

Ca'sos, island near Cos, II 676.

Cas-san'dra, Priam's daughter, wooed

✗ the battle-glow

En-y-a′li-us, an epithet of Ares, VII 166; etc.

E-ny′eus, king of Scyros, IX 668.

E-ny′o, a goddess of war, V 333; 592.

E′os, the dawn goddess, II 48; XI 1.

E-pal′tes, a Trojan, XVI 415.

E-pe′ia, home of the Epeians, XI 694.

Ep-ei′ans, a people of Elis, II 619.

Ep-e′us (builder of the wooden horse), winner of the boxing match, XXIII 664 ff.; loser of the discus throw, XXIII 838 ff.

Eph-i-al′tes, helps his brother imprison Ares, V 385 ff.

Eph′y-ra, name of 1) Corinth, VI 153; 2) home of Augeas in Elis, XV 531.

Eph′y-ri, a people of Thessaly, XIII 301.

E-pi′cles, a Lycian, XII 379.

Ep-i-dau′rus, a city of Argolis, II 561.

Ep-i′geus, a Myrmidon, XVI 571.

Ep-is′tor, a Trojan, XVI 695.

Ep-is′tro-phus, 1) leader of Phocians, II 517; 2) leader of Halizones, II 856; 3) brother of Mynes, slain by Achilles, II 692.

Ep′y-tus, Periphas' father, XVII 324.

Er′e-bus, the underworld of darkness, IX 572.

E-rech′theus, king of Athens, II 547.

E-re′tri-a, a city of Euboea, II 537.

Er-eu-tha′li-on, an Arcadian, IV 319.

Er-ich-tho′ni-us, Aeneas' ancestor, XX 219 ff.

E-rin′y-es, plural of Erinys (q.v.), XV 204.

E-ri′nys, goddess of vengeance, IX 571; XIX 87.

E-ri-o′pis, ſtep-mother of Ajax 2), XIII 697.

E′ris, ſtrife, V 518.

Er-y-la′us, a Trojan, XVI 411.

Er′y-mas, 1) a Trojan, slain by Idomeneus, XVI 345 f.; 2) a Lycian, slain by Patroclus, XVI 415.

Er-y-thi′ni, city in Paphlagonia, II 855.

Er-y′thrae, a town of Boeotia, II 499.

E-te′o-cles, son of Oedipus, IV 386.

E-te-o′nus, a town in Boeotia, II 497.

Eu-ae′mon, Eurypylus' father, II 736; V 76.

Eu-boe′a, large island east of Greece, II 536.

Eu-che′nor, Polyidus' son, XIII 663 ff.

Eu-do′rus, captain of Myrmidons, XVI 179 ff.

Eu-me′des, a Trojan herald, X 314.

Eu-me′lus, son of Admetus and Alceſtis, leader of Thessalians, II 713 f.; chariot racer, II 764 ff.; XXIII 288; 375–397; 460 ff.; 532–565.

Eu-ne′us, Jason's son, VII 468; XXIII 747.

Eu-phe′mus, a Trojan ally, II 846.

Eu-phe′tes, lord of Elean Ephyra, XV 532.

Eu-phor′bus, son of Panthous, wounds Patroclus, XVI 806 ff.; slain by Menelaus, XVII 9–81.

Eu-ro′pa, mother of Minos, XIV 321 f.

Eu′rus, the s.e. wind, II 145; XVI 765.

Eu-ry′a-lus, an Argive leader, II 565; VI 20; a boxer, XXIII 677.

Eu-ryb′a-tes, herald 1) of Agamemnon, I 320; 2) of Odysseus, II 183 f.

Eu-ryd′a-mas, dream-interpreter, V 149 ff.

Eu-rym′e-don, 1) charioteer of Agamemnon, IV 228; 2) servant of Neſtor, VIII 114.

Eu-ryn′o-me, an ocean nymph, XVIII 398 ff.

Eu-ryp′y-lus, 1) son of Euaemon, leader of Thessalians, II 736; wounded by Paris, XI 809 ff.; healed by Patroclus, XI 828–XII 2; XV 391 ff.; 2) king of Cos, II 677 ff.

Eu-rys′theus, grandson of Perseus, XIX 123; imposed the labors on Heracles, VIII 362 ff.

Eur′y-tus, 1) grandson of Aĉtor, II 620 f.; and brother of Cteatus; the brothers are called Moliones from their mother Molione, XI 709 f.; 2) son of Melaneus of Thessaly, II 596.

Eus-so′rus, father of Acamas, VI 8.

Eu-tre′sis, a town in Boeotia, II 502.

Ilus, q.v., II 37; XIII 717; XVI 831; sacked by Heracles, XIV 250 f.

I'lus, son of Tros and builder of Ilium, XX 232; his tomb, X 415.

Im'bra-sus, father of Pirous, IV 520.

Im'bri-us, of Pedasus, XIII 170 ff.

Im'bros, 1) an island in the n. Aegean, XIII 33; 2) a city on Imbros, XIV 281.

I-ol'cus, city in Magnesia, II 712.

I-o'ni-ans, dwellers in Attica, XIII 685.

I'pheus, a Lycian, XVI 417.

Iph'i-a-nas'sa, Agamemnon's daughter, XI 145.

Iph-i'clus, owner of famous flocks and herds, II 705; famous runner, XXIII 636.

I-phid'a-mas, Antenor's son, XI 221–250.

I-phin'o-us, a Greek, VII 14.

I'phis, Patroclus' concubine, IX 667.

Iph'i-tus, 1) father of Schedius, II 518; 2) father of Archeptolemus, VIII 128.

I-phi'tion, slain by Achilles, XX 382.

I'ris, messenger of the gods, shod with the wind, XV 168; to the Trojans, II 786 f.; to Hera and Athena, VIII 397–425; to Poseidon, XV 143–217; to Helen, III 122 ff.; to Hector, XI 185–210; to Achilles, XVIII 166–201; to the winds, XXIII 198 ff.; to Thetis, XXIV 77; to Priam, XXIV 143–188; conducts the wounded Aphrodite to Olympus, V 353 ff.

I-san'der, son of Bellerophon, VI 197; VI 203 f.

I'sus, son of Priam, XI 101–108.

Ith'a-ca, an Ionian island, home of Odysseus, II 632; III 201.

I-thaem'e-nes, a Lycian, XVI 586.

I-tho'me, a castle in Thessaly, II 729.

I'ton, city in Thessaly, II 696.

I-tym'o-neus, a Greek from Elis, XI 672 ff.

Ix-i'on, foster-father of Pirithous, X 317.

Jar'dan, a stream in Elis, VII 135.

Ja'son, leader of the Argonauts; father of Euneus, VII 468 f.

La'as, a town in Laconia, II 585.

Lac-e-dae'mon, another name of Laconia, II 581; III 239.

La-er'ces, a Myrmidon, father of Alcimedon, XVI 197.

La-er'tes, father of Odysseus, II 173; III 200.

Lam'pe-tus, father of Meges, XV 525 f.

Lam'pus, 1) Laomedon's son, XV 527; III 146; father of Dolops, XV 525 f.; 2) Hector's horse, VIII 185.

La-od'a-mas, a Trojan, XV 516.

La'o-da-mi'a, daughter of Bellerophon and mother of Sarpedon, VI 197 ff.; slain by Artemis, VI 205.

La-od'i-ce, 1) fairest of Priam's daughters, III 124; VI 252; wife of Helicaon, III 123 f.; 2) daughter of Agamemnon, IX 145.

La-od'o-cus, 1) the mighty son of Antenor, IV 87; 2) comrade of Antilochus, XVII 698 f.

La-og'o-nus, 1) a Trojan, slain by Meriones, XVI 603 f.; 2) a Trojan slain by Achilles, XX 460.

La-om'e-don, father of Priam, III 250; XX 237; owner of famous horses, V 640; defrauds Apollo and Poseidon, XXI 441 ff.

La-oth'o-e, a wife of Priam, XXI 85; XXII 46 ff.

Lap'i-thae, a warlike people of Thessaly, I 260 ff.; XII 127 ff.

La-ris'sa, a town in Aeolia, II 841.

Lec'tum, a promontory at the foot of Ida, XIV 284.

leech, doctor, II 732; see Machaon and Podalirius.

Le'i-tus, leader of Boeotians, II 494; slays Phylacus, VI 34 f.; wounded by Hector, XVII 602.

Lel'e-ges, a war-loving people of western Asia, X 429; XXI 86.

Lem'nos, large volcanic island (and city) in the n.e. Aegean, XIV 230; sacred to Hephaestus, I 593 f.; place of Philoctetes' banishment, II 721 ff.; source of food and drink for the Greek host, VII 467 ff.; VIII 230 ff.

Le-oc'ri-tus, a Greek, XVII 344.

war-cry," II 408; 586; etc.; his army, II 581 ff.; volunteers to fight Hector, VII 94–115; his duel with Paris, see Paris; fights for Patroclus' body, XVII 6 ff.

Me-nes'thes, a Greek, V 609.

Me-nes'theus, captain of Athenians, II 552; XIII 195 f.

Me-nes'thi-us, 1) lord of Arne, slain by Paris, VII 9; 2) captain of Myrmidons, XVI 173 ff.

Me-noe'tius, father of Patroclus, I 307; XXIII 85 ff.; etc.

Me'non, a Trojan, XIII 193.

Men'tes, captain of Cicones, XVII 73.

Men'tor, father of Imbrius, q.v., XIII 171.

Me'ri-on, same as Meriones, X 59.

Me-ri'o-nes, squire of Idomeneus, II 651; their interview, XIII 246 ff.; fleet of foot, XIII 249; "peer" of the war-god, VII 166; his helmet plated with boars' tusks, X 261 ff.; his interview with Idomeneus, XIII 246–329; gets the wood for Patroclus' pyre, XXIII 111 ff.; wins the archery contest, XXIII 860–883.

Mer'me-rus, a Mysian, XIV 513.

Me'rops, famous seer, XI 329 ff.; father of Adrestus, II 831.

Mes'se, harbor in Laconia, II 582.

Mes-se'is, a spring in Thessaly, VI 457.

Mes'thles, captain of Maeonians, II 864.

Mes'tor, Priam's son, XXIV 257.

Me-tho'ne, city in Thessaly, II 716.

Mi-dei'a, town in Boeotia, II 507.

Mi-le'tus, 1) famous city of Caria, II 868; 2) city of Crete, II 647.

Mi'nos, son of Zeus and Europa, XIV 321 f.; father of Deucalion, XIII 450 f.

Min'yae, people of Boeotian Orchomenus, II 511.

Min-ye'ius, a river in Elis, XI 722.

Mne'sus, a Paeonian, XXI 210.

Mo-li'on, a Trojan charioteer, XI 321 f.

Mo-li'o-nes, sons of Molione and Poseidon (reputed sons of Actor), XI 709–750.

Mo'lus, Meriones' father, X 269; XIII 249.

Mo'rys, a Mysian, XIII 792; XIV 514.

Mu'li-us, 1) son-in-law of Augeas, slain by Nestor, XI 738 ff.; 2) a Trojan, slain by Patroclus, XVI 696; 3) a Trojan, slain by Achilles, XX 472.

Muses, daughters of Zeus and inspirers of song, II 484 ff.; XI 218; entertain the gods with song, I 604; blind Thamyris, II 594 ff.

Myc'a-le, promontory in Ionia, II 869.

Myc-a-les'sus, town in Boeotia, II 498.

My-ce'nae, Agamemnon's capital, II 569; "golden," VII 180; especially loved by Hera, IV 52.

My-ce-nae'an, of Mycenae, XV 643.

My'don, 1) Pylaemenes' charioteer, slain by Antilochus, V 580; 2) a Paeonian, slain by Achilles, XXI 209.

Myg'don, king in Phrygia, III 186.

My'nes, king of Lyrnessus, and husband of Briseïs, II 692 ff.; XIX 295 ff.

My-ri'ne, wife of Dardanus; her tomb, II 811 ff.

Myr'mi-dons, Achilles' people, I 180; etc.

Mry'si-nus, a place in Elis, II 616.

Mys'ians, people of Mysia, II 858; etc.

Na'iad, fountain nymph, VI 21; XX 384.

Nas'tes, a Carian captain, II 867 ff.

Nau'bo-lus, father of Iphitus, II 518.

nec'tar, the drink of the gods, I 598; IV 3; used for embalming, XIX 38 f.

Ne-le'an or Ne-le'ian, 1) descended from Neleus, XXIII 349; 2) belonging to Neleus, XI 597.

Ne'leus, Nestor's father, XI 692; XXIII 652.

Ne-li'des, Neleus' son, Nestor, X 18.

Ne-mer'tes, a Nereid, XVIII 46.

Ne-op-tol'e-mus, Achilles' son, XIX 327.

Ne're-id, child of Nereus, q.v.

Ne'reus, father of the 50 (or 100) Nereids, XVIII 39 ff.; called "the

Ancient of Ocean," I 538; XVIII 141.

Ner'i-tum, a mountain of Ithaca, II 632.

Ne-sae'a, a Nereid, XVIII 40.

Nes'tor, Gerenian knight from Pylus, II 336; etc.; son of Neleus, II 20; father of 1) Antilochus, VI 32; etc.; 2) of Thrasymedes, XIV 9; the wisest of the heroes, II 370 ff.; VII 325; IX 94; ruling over the third generation, I 247 ff.; eloquent, I 248 f.; makes many long speeches, e.g., I 254 ff.; II 337 ff.; IV 318 ff.; VII 123 ff.; 327 ff.; IX 53 ff.; 96 ff.; XI 655 ff.; XXIII 306 ff.; 630 ff.; military leader, II 555; with Diomedes in battle, VIII 127 ff.

Nes'to-rid, Nestor's son, XXIII 439.

Ni'o-be, her pride and punishment, XXIV 602 ff.

Ni'reus, of Syme, II 671 ff.

Ni'sa, town in Boeotia, II 508.

Ni-sy'ros, an island near Cos, II 676.

No-e'mon, 1) a Lycian, slain by Odysseus, V 678; 2) Antilochus' comrade, XXIII 612.

No-mi'on, father of Nastes, II 870 f.

No'tus, the s. wind, II 145; brings moisture, III 10; clearing, XI 306.

Nymphs, minor deities of meadow, woodland, fountains, and streams, XX 8 f.

Ny'sa, a mountain in Thrace, VI 132 ff.

O-ca'le-a, a town in Boeotia, II 501.

Ocean, stream, VII 422; XVIII 607; personified, XX 7; parent of all things, XIV 201.

O-che'sius, father of Periphas, V 842 f.

O'di-us, 1) a Greek herald, IX 170; 2) captain of the Halizones, II 856; slain by Agamemnon, V 38 ff.

O-dys'seus, king of four Ionian islands and adjacent coast, II 631 ff.; Laertes' son, II 173; etc.; his appearance, III 193 ff.; "of many devices," II 173; etc.; his eloquence, III 216 ff.; pleads with Achilles, IX 223–306; wise counselor, II 169; 273; valiant warrior, II 273; IV 351 ff.; wrestler, XXIII 709–736; with Diomedes goes

as spy, X 220–298; they kill Dolon, X 370–459, and Rhesus, 477–497, and bring off his horses, 498 ff.; wins the footrace, XXIII 755 ff.

Oe-cha'li-a, capital of Eurytus, II 596.

Oed'i-pus, his funeral games, XXIII 679 f.

Oe'neus, of Calydon, II 641; father of Tydeus, V 813 f.; entertains Bellerophon, VI 216 ff.; offends Artemis, who sent the famous boar, IX 533 ff.

Oe-ni'des, Oeneus' son (erroneously for Oeneus), X 497.

Oe-nom'a-us, 1) an Aetolian, slain by Hector, V 706 ff.; 2) a Trojan, XII 140; slain by Idomeneus, XIII 506 ff.

Oe'nops, father of Helenus 2), V 707.

Oet'y-lus, a town in Laconia, II 585.

O-i'leus, 1) king of Locris and father of lesser Ajax, II 527 f., and of Medon, II 727 f.; 2) a Trojan, Bienor's charioteer, XI 93.

ointment, for 1) the living flesh, X 577; XIV 171; 2) the dead, XVIII 350.

O-le'ni-an Rock, a mountain peak in Elis, II 617.

Ol'e-nus, a town in Aetolia, II 639.

O-li'zon, city in Thessaly, II 717.

Ol-o-os'son, town in Thessaly, II 739.

O-lym'pus, 1) the heavenly mountain; abode of the gods, I 18; 221; 353; 566; V 404; 749 f.; VIII 12; 25; 2) the Thessalian mountain, XIV 225; epithets: starry, VI 108; many-ridged, I 499; many-enfolded, VIII 411; lofty, V 398; vasty, II 48; "pinnacled heights," IV 74; etc.; snowy, I 420; XVIII 186.

omens, birds' flight, XII 237 ff.; XIII 821 ff.; XXIV 292–321; eagle on the left with serpent, XII 200–229; cry, X 274 ff.; with fawn, VIII 247 ff.; serpent at Aulis, II 307 ff.; lightning, IX 236 f.; bloody dewdrops, XI 53 ff.

On-ches'tus, a town of Boeotia, II 506.

O-ne'tor, a Trojan, XVI 604.

O-phe-les'tes, 1) a Trojan, slain by Teucer, VIII 274; 2) a Paeonian, slain by Achilles, XXI 210.

O-phel'tius, 1) a Trojan, slain by

Euryalus, VI 20; 2) a Greek, slain by Hector, XI 302.

O-pi′tes, a Greek, XI 301.

O′pus, capital of Locris, II 531; home of Patroclus, XVIII 326; XXIII 85.

Or-chom′e-nus, 1) Minyan capital in Boeotia, II 511; IX 381; 2) a city in Arcadia, II 605.

O-res′bi-us, a Boeotian, V 707.

O-res′tes, 1) Agamemnon's son, IX 142; 2) a Greek, slain by Hector, V 705; 3) a Trojan, XII 139; slain by Leonteus, XII 193.

O-ri′on, the mighty hunter, XVIII 488; the constellation, XVIII 486; the "Dog of Orion," XXII 29.

O-ri-thy′ia, a Nereid, XVIII 48.

Or′me-nid, son of Ormenus, q.v., X 266.

Or-me′ni-um, town in Thessaly, II 734.

Or′me-nus, 1) father of Amyntor, q.v., X 266, and grandfather of Phoenix, IX 448; 2) a Trojan, slain by Teucer, VIII 274 f.; 3) a Trojan, slain by Polypoetes, XII 187.

Or-ne′iae, city in Argolis, II 571.

Or-sil′o-chus, 1) son of Alpheus, V 546; 2) son of Diocles, a Greek, slain by Aeneas, V 541–561; 3) a Trojan, slain by Teucer, VIII 274.

Or-thae′us, a Phrygian ally of Troy, XIII 791.

Or′the, a town in Thessaly, II 739.

O′rus, a Greek, XI 303.

O-thry′o-neus, a Trojan ally and suitor of Cassandra, XIII 363 ff.; slain by Idomeneus, XIII 361–384.

O′treus, king in Phrygia, III 186.

O-tryn′teus, Iphition's father, XX 382–393.

O′tus, 1) brother of Ephialtes (q.v.), V 385 ff.; 2) a Greek, slain by Pulydamas, XV 518.

Pae-e′on, the gods' physician; heals Ares, V 899 ff.; heals Hades, V 401 f.

Pae′on, Agastrophus' father, XI 338 f.

Pae-o′ni-a, a land n. of Thrace, XVII 350.

Pae-o′ni-an, coming from Paeonia, II 848.

Pae-on′i-des, Paeon's son, Agastrophus, XI 368.

Pae′sus, a town in Mysia (same as Apaesus, q.v.), V 612.

Pal′las, an epithet of Athena, I 200; etc.

Pal′mys, an ally of Troy, XIII 792.

Pam′mon, Priam's son, XXIV 250.

Pan′da-rus, Lycaon's son from Lycia, V 170 ff.; skill in archery, II 826 f.; V 171 ff.; wounds Diomedes, V 95 ff.; "peer of immortals," IV 88; V 168; treacherously wounds Menelaus, IV 86–219; slain by Diomedes, V 276–296.

Pan-di′on, Teucer's comrade, XII 372.

Pan′do-cus, a Trojan, XI 490.

Pan′o-pe, a Nereid, XVIII 45.

Pan′o-peus, 1) city in Boeotia, II 520; 2) father of Epeus, XXIII 665.

Pan′tho-us, a Trojan elder, III 147; father of Pulydamas, XIII 756, and Euphorbus, XVI 808.

Paph-la-go′ni-an, from Paphlagonia, a country on the Black Sea, II 851; etc.

Pa′ris, personal beauty, III 39; abducts Helen, III 443 f.; refuses her surrender, VII 357 ff.; lack of prowess, III 30 ff.; his duel with Menelaus, III 67–120; 136 ff.; 253 ff.; 314–382; saved by Aphrodite, III 373 ff.; his interviews with Hector, III 38–75; VI 326 ff.; reproached by Helen, III 427 ff.; VI 350 ff.; wounds Diomedes, XI 369 ff.; wounds Machaon, XI 505 f.; judgment of, XXIV 27 ff.; his palace, VI 313 ff.

Par-rha′sia, city in Arcadia, II 608.

Par-the′ni-us, a river of Paphlagonia, II 854.

Pa-sith′e-a, one of the Graces, XIV 269.

Pa-tro′clus, son of Menoetius, XVIII 325; native of Opus, XVIII 326; XXIII 85; murdered a playmate, XXIII 85 ff.; a refugee at the court of Peleus, XI 765 ff.; XXIII 85 ff.; intimate friend of Achilles, I 337; takes Achilles' arms, XI 798 ff.; XVIII 80 ff.; his last battle and

Phoe'bus, a surname of Apollo, I 43; V 343; etc.

Phoe-ni'cia, a country of Asia, XXIII 744 ff.

Phoe'nix, 1) Europa's father, XIV 321; 2) Achilles' foster-father, IX 485 ff.; 603; cursed by his father, Amyntor, IX 448 ff.; made ruler of Dolopians, IX 480 ff.; leads the embassy to Achilles, IX 168; pleads with Achilles, IX 434 ff.; umpires the chariot race, XXIII 359 ff.

Phor'bas, 1) king of Lesbos, IX 665; 2) Ilioneus' father, XIV 490.

Phor'cys, a Phrygian leader, II 862; XVII 312 ff.

Phrad'mon, Agelaus' father, VIII 257.

Phron'tis, wife of Panthous, XVII 40.

Phryg'i-a, a country of Asia, III 184 f.

Phryg'i-an, coming from Phrygia, II 863; X 431.

Phthi'a, 1) Peleus' capital, XIX 323; 2) Peleus' realm, I 155; IX 395.

Phthi'ans, people of Phthia, XIII 686.

Phthi'res, a mountain in Caria, II 868.

Phyl'a-ce, a city in Thessaly, II 695.

Phyl'a-cus, 1) Iphiclus' father, II 705; 2) a Trojan, slain by Leitus, VI 35 f.

Phy'las, king of Ephyra, XVI 191.

Phy'leus, 1) father of Meges, II 628; 2) famous spearman, XXIII 637.

Phy-li'des, Phyleus' son, II 626 f.; Epeian captain, XV 519; saved by his father's corselet, XV 528 ff.

physician, II 732; see Machaon and Podalirius.

Pi-dy'tes, a Percosian, VI 30.

Pi-e'ri-a, a district near Olympus, XIV 226.

Pi-rae'us, Eurymedon's grandfather, IV 228.

Pi'res, a Thracian chief, XX 484 (perhaps identical with Pirous, q.v.).

Pi-rith'o-us, a Lapith prince, I 263; husband of Hippodamia, II 741 f.

Pir'o-us, a Thracian captain, II 844; from Aenus, IV 520.

Pi-san'der, 1) a Trojan, slain by Agamemnon, XI 122 ff.; 2) a Myrmidon

captain, XVI 193; 3) a Trojan, slain by Menelaus, XIII 601 ff.

Pi-se'nor, a Trojan, father of Clitus, XV 445.

Pit'theus, Theseus' grandfather, III 144.

Pi-ty-e'ia, town in Mysia, II 829.

Pla'cus, mountain in Mysia, VI 396.

Pla-tae'a, city in Boeotia, II 504.

Ple'ia-des, the constellation, XVIII 486.

Pleu'ron, city of Aetolia, II 639; XIII 217.

Pod-a-lir'i-us, the physician, II 732.

Po-dar'ces, brother of Protesilaus and leader of Phthians, II 695–710.

Po-dar'ge, a Harpy, mother of Achilles' immortal steeds, XVI 150; XIX 400.

Po-dar'gus, 1) Hector's horse, VIII 185; 2) Menelaus' horse, XXIII 295.

Po'des, Hector's friend, XVII 575 ff.

Po-li'tes, Priam's son, II 791; XXIV 250.

Pol-y-ae'mon, Amopaon's father, VIII 276.

Pol'y-bus, Antenor's son, XI 59.

Po-lyc'tor, feigned father of Hermes, XXIV 397.

Pol-y-deu'ces, brother of Castor and Helen, III 237.

Pol-y-do'ra, Peleus' daughter, XVI 174 ff.

Pol-y-do'rus, 1) Priam's youngest son, slain by Achilles, XX 407 ff.; 2) a Greek spear-thrower, XXIII 637.

Pol-y-i'dus, 1) a famous seer from Corinth, XIII 663 ff.; 2) a Trojan, slain by Diomedes, V 148 ff.

Pol-y-me'le, the mother of Eudorus, XVI 179 ff.

Pol-y-me'lus, a Lycian, XVI 417.

Pol-y-ni'ces, Oedipus' son, one of the "Seven against Thebes," IV 377.

Pol-y-phe'mus, a Lapith, I 264.

Pol-y-phe'tes, a Mysian, XIII 791.

Pol-y-phon'tes, a Theban, IV 395.

Poly-poe'tes, son of Pirithous, II 738 ff.; defends the Greek ships, XII 127 ff.; winner of the shot-put, XXIII 826–849.

Pol-yx-i'nus, Epeian chieftain, II 623.

Trojan, slain by Patroclus, XVI 401.

The'tis, silver-footed Nereid, I 538; XVIII 369; etc.; unwilling bride of Peleus, XVIII 429 ff.; XXIV 54 ff.; mother of Achilles, I 351; comforts Achilles for loss of Briseis, I 357 ff.; pleads with Zeus for honor for her son, I 352 ff.; 419 ff.; 493 ff.; saves Dionysus from Lycurgus, VI 135 ff.; saves Hephaestus, XVIII 394 ff.; saves Zeus, I 396 ff.; visits Hephaestus, XVIII 369 ff.; talks with Achilles, XVIII 72–137; XXIV 122 ff.; brings new armor to Achilles, XIX 3 ff.

This'be, city in Boeotia, II 502.

Tho'as, 1) king in Aetolia, II 638; XV 281 f.; 2) king in Lemnos, XIV 230; XXIII 745; 3) a Trojan, slain by Menelaus, XVI 311.

Tho'e, a Nereid, XVIII 40.

Tho'on, 1) a Trojan, slain by Diomedes, V 152; 2) a Trojan, slain by Odysseus, XI 422; 3) a Trojan, XII 140; slain by Antilochus, XIII 545.

Tho-o'tes, Menestheus' herald, XII 342 f.

Thrace or Thra'cia, 1) the country north of Greece, IX 5; XXIII 230; 2) the island of Samothrace, XIII 13.

Thra'cian, 1) pertaining to Thrace, XXIII 230; 2) a native of Thrace, II 595; X 434.

Thra'sius, a Paeonian, XXI 210.

Thras-y-de'mus, Sarpedon's squire, XVI 463 ff.

Thras-y-me'des, Nestor's son, IX 81; XIV 9; lends Diomedes armor, X 255 ff.

Thro'ni-um, city in Locris, II 533.

Thry-o-es'sa, another name of Thryum, XI 711.

Thry'um, a city in Nestor's realm, II 592.

Thy-es'tes, brother of Atreus, II 107.

Thym'bra, a place near Troy, X 430.

Thym-brae'us, a Trojan, XI 320.

Thy-moe'tes, an elder of Troy, III 146.

Ti'ryns, palace-fortress with mighty walls, II 559.

Ti'tans, children of Uranus and Gaea, hurled into Tartarus, XIV 279.

Tit'a-nus, a town in Thessaly, II 735.

Tit-a-re'sius, a river of Thessaly, II 751.

Ti-tho'nus, Laomedon's faultless son, XX 237; wedded by Eos, XI 1.

Tle-pol'e-mus, 1) Heracles' son, II 653–670; slain by Sarpedon, V 628–670; 2) Damastor's son, slain by Patroclus, XVI 416.

Tmo'lus, a mountain in Lydia, II 866.

Tra'chis, town near Thermopylae, II 682.

Tre'chus, an Aetolian, V 706.

Tric'ca, a city in Thessaly, II 729.

Tri'to-born, an epithet of Athena, IV 515.

Troe'zen, a city in Argolis, II 561.

Troe-ze'nus, a Thracian leader, II 847.

Troi'a or Troy, 1) another name of Ilium (q.v.), I 129; XVIII 122; etc.; 2) the region of Troy-land, I 71.

Tro'i-lus, a son of Priam, XXIV 257.

Tro'jan, belonging to Troy, I 164; etc.

Tros, 1) the ancient king who gave his name to Troy and the Trojans, XX 230 ff.; his immortal horses, V 222 ff.; XXIII 376 ff.; 2) son of Alastor, XX 463.

Troy'land, the country about Troy, I 71; III 74.

Tych'i-us, a famous currier from Boeotia, II 220 f.

Ty'deus, son of Oeneus, V 813; sent as envoy to Thebes, IV 384; V 804; father of Diomedes, IV 365; XIV 380; etc.; in the war of the Seven, IV 372 ff.; VI 223; slain at Thebes, XIV 113 f.

Ty-di'des, Tydeus' son, Diomedes, V 26; etc.

Ty-pho'eus, a giant buried in Cilicia, II 782 f.

U-cal'e-gon, a Trojan elder, III 148.

U'ra-nus, the personified heaven, father of the Titans, V 898.

wagon, see car 1).